This book(S) — many others.
needs to be
rewritten
(updated) — from other eg. of perspective

OTHER BOOKS BY JAMES Q. WILSON

AS AUTHOR:

Negro Politics
The Amateur Democrat
City Politics
(with Edward C. Banfield)
Varieties of Police Behavior
Political Organization
Thinking About Crime
The Investigators: Managing F.B.I. and Narcotics Agents
American Government: Institution and Policies
Watching Fishes: Life and Behavior on Coral Reefs
(with Roberta Wilson)

AS EDITOR:

Urban Renewal: The Record and the Controversy
City Politics and Public Policy
The Metropolitan Enigma
The Politics of Regulation
Crime and Public Policy

BY RICHARD J. HERRNSTEIN

AS AUTHOR:

A Source Book in the History of Psychology
(with E. G. Boring)
Laboratory Experiments in Psychology
(with J. C. Stevens and G. S. Reynolds)
I.Q. in the Meritocracy
Psychology
(with R. Brown)

AS EDITOR:

Matching and Maximizing Accounts
Quantitative Analyses of Behavior, Vol. II
(with M. L. Commons and H. Rachlin)
Acquisition
Quantitative Analyses of Behavior, Vol. III
(with M. L. Commons and A. R. Wagner)
Discrimination Processes
Quantitative Analyses of Behavior, Vol. IV
(with M. L. Commons and A. R. Wagner)

CRIME

and

HUMAN

NATURE

James Q. Wilson and
Richard J. Herrnstein

A TOUCHSTONE BOOK
Published by Simon & Schuster, Inc.
NEW YORK

Copyright © 1985 by James Q. Wilson and Richard J. Herrnstein

First Touchstone Edition, 1986

Published by Simon & Schuster, Inc.

Simon & Schuster Building
Rockefeller Center
1230 Avenue of the Americas
New York, New York 10020

TOUCHSTONE and colophon are registered trademarks
of Simon & Schuster, Inc.

Designed by Eve Kirch

Manufactured in the United States of America

10 9 8 7 6 5 4 3 2
10 9 8 7 6 5 4 3 2 1 Pbk.

Library of Congress Cataloging in Publication Data
Wilson, James Q.
  Crime and human nature.
  Bibliography: p. 559
  Includes index.
  1. Criminal anthropology. 2. Criminal behavior,
Prediction of. 3. Crime and criminals. I. Herrnstein,
Richard J. II. Title.
HV6115.W54 1985   364.2   85-8371
ISBN: 0-671-54130-7
ISBN: 0-671-62810-0 Pbk.

ACKNOWLEDGMENTS

The funds used for the research and writing of this book came from several sources. We are most grateful for the support of the Alfred P. Sloan Foundation and the Lewis P. and Linda Geyser Fund at Harvard University. Arthur Singer at the Sloan Foundation has been a steady source of encouragement, and Lewis and Linda Geyser, generous benefactors.

This book grew out of a course we offered for several years in Harvard's Core Curriculum, an attempt to present to nonspecialists the "core" of academic disciplines as they apply to questions of general concern. We are greatly indebted to the hundreds of students whose attention and interest we sought constructively to engage, and to Harvard University for creating a framework for our collaboration.

Our principal research assistant was Dr. Mark Snyderman, who supplied us with invaluable aid and advice as well as with the unflagging faith that soon the Chicago Cubs would win. They almost did. We also appreciate the research help of Mara Chobanian, Michael Grossbard, Susan Herrnstein, Sharon Kantrowitz, Patricia Miranda, Rebecca Saikia-Wilson, and Ann R. Wilson.

Edward C. Banfield, David P. Farrington, and Travis Hirschi read virtually the entire manuscript. We were helped greatly by their penetrating comments and broad learning. Philip J. Cook, Emil M. Hartl, and Edward P. Monnelly gave us help with some technical matters on which they are expert. Individual chapters were read by Cook and by Dante Cicchetti, James

J. Collins, Gary D. Gottfredson, Harrison Gough, Monroe M. Lefkowitz, Rolf Loeber, John C. Loehlin, Glenn C. Loury, Robert M. Malina, Harvey C. Mansfield, Jr., Edwin Megargee, Mark H. Moore, David P. Phillips, Albert Reiss, Michael Rutter, Michael Sandel, Louise Shelley, Darrell Steffensmeier, Charles Wellford, Lee Willerman, Ann D. Witte, and Marvin Wolfgang. Of course, we bear full responsibility for what appears here.

Susan Herrnstein patiently typed—over and over again—much of the manuscript, and Robert Asahina, our editor at Simon and Schuster, greatly improved it. We thank them both for their labors.

Portions of Chapter 8 originally appeared in *The Atlantic Monthly* in September 1983 under the title "Raising Kids." An earlier version of parts of Chapter 16 appeared in *The Public Interest* in the Winter 1982 issue under the title "Crime and American Culture." These materials are reprinted by permission.

To Roberta and Susan

CONTENTS

Contents

V. History and Culture

VI. Crime, Human Nature, and Society

PREFACE

The reader may wonder, as we ourselves once wondered, why a political scientist and an experimental psychologist should be writing a book on the causes of crime. Our collaboration in this venture began in 1977 when our mutual curiosity about individual differences in criminality led us to teach at Harvard, together with Professor Mark H. Moore, a graduate seminar and then, the following year, an undergraduate course on crime and criminal justice. The three of us had come together to explore our belief that psychology, political economy, and political science each had something interesting to say about crime and what to do about it.

Over the many years during which the course evolved, our interest gradually shifted away from current issues in crime control and toward the causes of crime. Moore had by this time left our partnership because of other academic commitments, and we (Wilson and Herrnstein) began to wonder whether our growing familiarity with research findings on crime could be set forth and interpreted in the light of a single theoretical perspective. In so doing, we gradually became aware that we were, in effect, drawing together two ancient disciplines that had once been united but that, in recent decades, had drawn apart. Political science and psychology had arisen out of a common interest in understanding human nature and for centuries had sought to answer many of the same questions.

To a political scientist, the problem of social order is paramount: How can men and women live together in reasonable peace and security without subordinating themselves to the arbitrary demands of a tyrant? Every serious political philosopher has tried to justify his or her solution to the problem of order by reference to a theory of human nature; by reference, that is, to an implicit or explicit psychology. Many serious psychologists have tried to explain individual behavior by reference to the way in which individuals interact with one another, an interaction that is always patterned to some degree by the political and social institutions of which they are necessarily a part.

Crime is that behavior condemned by society; it occurs despite the rewards and punishments that have been devised to enforce that condemnation. If individual differences in criminality are to be explained, one must explain why some individuals, formed in part by their experiences within social institutions, nonetheless disobey many of the most important rules of those institutions and do so even when society has made it clear that it will try to punish that disobedience.

A political scientist begins with the law and the moral convictions and social understandings that sustain it. A psychologist begins with an individual whose characteristic way of behaving is formed out of a complex interaction between genetic materials and social experiences. If a political scientist is to explain the power and the limits of the law, he or she must understand why people sometimes obey it and sometimes do not. If a psychologist is to explain how those characteristic ways of behaving develop, he or she must understand individual differences in both the extent to which people internalize certain legal and moral commands and the degree to which they anticipate and act on the likely future consequences of their own actions.

When we first began teaching together, a change was occurring at the edges of criminology. Economists and political scientists were beginning to use the theory of rational choice to explain criminal activity just as that theory had been used to explain the actions of consumers, investors, and voters. Psychologists and sociologists were taking note of differences in intelligence and temperament, as well as differences in social circumstances, among persons who did or did not frequently break the law. It seemed to us that these new perspectives could help explain behavior that many traditional criminologists had explained almost entirely by reference to social circumstances. Bringing these newer perspectives to bear on the problem of crime was made easier by the fact that economics and behavioral psychology both had embraced theories of rational choice that seemed similar despite many differences in terminology.

As we have explored these matters, we have realized that the theoretical outlooks of political science, economics, and psychology do have much in common, but that their differences are not merely matters of terminology. Economists see individuals allocating scarce resources among competing alternatives in order to satisfy their preferences, but economists rarely have much to say about the source or content of those preferences. Psychologists have a great deal to say about how preferences are formed, but not much to say about how institutions frame the available alternatives and only a little to say about how an individual's sense of justice influences the way in which he or she evaluates those alternatives. Political scientists have a lot to say about how institutions maintain themselves and about the importance to that maintenance of their moral authority and capacity for equitable action, but little to say about why individuals act as they do within those institutions.

We hope to convince our colleagues, as we have convinced ourselves, that these academic perspectives can enrich one another. This book is the result of a truly interdisciplinary effort. That much-used and rarely accurate adjective applies in this case because each of us has worked hard to learn the language, methods, and findings of the other. The result is in every sense a joint and equal effort; the order of names on the title page was decided by a flip of a coin. Interdisciplinary work does not occur when two scholars from different fields contribute essays to a book or give lectures in each other's courses. It occurs only when each person begins to think like his colleague. An interdisciplinary effort is much like Aristotle's definition of friendship—two bodies with one soul. Indeed, we suspect that truly interdisciplinary work presupposes friendship in the deepest sense. We hope that our efforts will commend themselves to both our colleagues and the general reader. But we know that they have been one of our most rewarding intellectual experiences. We began as friends, we end as friends, but now wiser and, possibly, better.

J.Q.W.
R.J.H.

I

EXPLAINING CRIME

1

CRIME AND ITS EXPLANATION

Predatory street crimes are most commonly committed by young males. Violent crimes are more common in big cities than in small ones. High rates of criminality tend to run in families. The persons who frequently commit the most serious crimes typically begin their criminal careers at a quite young age. Persons who turn out to be criminals usually do not do very well in school. Young men who drive recklessly and have many accidents tend to be similar to those who commit crimes. Programs designed to rehabilitate high-rate offenders have not been shown to have much success, and those programs that do manage to reduce criminality among certain kinds of offenders often increase it among others.

These facts about crime—some well known, some not so well known—are not merely statements about traits that happen occasionally, or in some places but not others, to describe criminals. They are statements that, insofar as we can tell, are pretty much true everywhere. They are statements, in short, about human nature as much as about crime.

All serious political and moral philosophy, and thus any serious social inquiry, must begin with an understanding of human nature. Though society and its institutions shape man, man's nature sets limits on the kinds of societies we can have. Cicero said that the nature of law must be founded on the nature of man (*a natura hominis discenda est natura juris*). This book is an effort to set forth an understanding of human nature by examining one common, if regrettable, manifestation of that nature—criminality. We could have chosen to understand human nature by studying work, or sexuality, or po-

19

litical activity; we chose instead to approach it through the study of crime, in part out of curiosity and in part because crime, more dramatically than other forms of behavior, exposes the connection between individual dispositions and the social order.

The problem of social order is fundamental: How can mankind live together in reasonable order? Every society has, by definition, solved that problem to some degree, but not all have done so with equal success or without paying a high cost in other things—such as liberty—that we also value. If we believe that man is naturally good, we will expect that the problem of order can be rather easily managed; if we believe him to be naturally wicked, we will expect the provision of order to require extraordinary measures; if we believe his nature to be infinitely plastic, we will think the problem of order can be solved entirely by plan and that we may pick and choose freely among all possible plans. Since every known society has experienced crime, no society has ever entirely solved the problem of order. The fact that crime is universal may suggest that man's nature is not infinitely malleable, though some people never cease searching for an anvil and hammer sufficient to bend it to their will.

Some societies seem better able than others to sustain order without making unacceptable sacrifices in personal freedom, and in every society the level of order is greater at some times than at others. These systematic and oft-remarked differences in the level of crime across time and place suggest that there is something worth explaining. But to find that explanation, one cannot begin with the society as a whole or its historical context, for what needs explanation is not the behavior of "society" but the behavior of individuals making up a society. Our intention is to offer as comprehensive an explanation as we can manage of why some individuals are more likely than others to commit crimes.

The Problem of Explanation

That intention is not easily realized, for at least three reasons. First, crime is neither easily observed nor readily measured. As we shall see later in this chapter, there is no way of knowing the true crime rate of a society or even of a given individual. Any explanation of why individuals differ in their law-abidingness may well founder on measurement errors. If we show that Tom, who we think has committed a crime, differs in certain interesting ways from Dick, who we think has not, when in fact both Tom and Dick have committed a crime, then the "explanation" is meaningless.

Second, crime is very common, especially among males. Using interviews and questionnaires, scholars have discovered that the majority of all young males have broken the law at least once by a relatively early age. By examining the police records of boys of a given age living in one place, criminologists have learned that a surprisingly large fraction of all males will be arrested at least once in their lives for something more serious than a traffic infraction. Marvin Wolfgang found that 35 percent of all the males born in Philadelphia in 1945 and living there between the ages of ten and eighteen had been arrested at least once by their eighteenth birthday and 43 percent had been arrested before their thirtieth birthday.[1] Nor is this a peculiarly American phenomenon. Various surveys have found that the proportion of British males who had been convicted in court before their twenty-first birthdays ranged from 15 percent in the nation as a whole to 31 percent for a group of boys raised in London. David Farrington estimates that 44 percent of all the males in "law-abiding" Britain will be arrested sometime in their lives.[2] If committing a crime at least once is so commonplace, then it is quite likely that there will be few, if any, large differences between those who never break the law and those who break it at least once—even if we had certain knowledge of which was which. Chance events as much as or more than individual predispositions will determine who commits a crime.

Third, the word "crime" can be applied to such varied behavior that it is not clear that it is a meaningful category of analysis. Stealing a comic book, punching a friend, cheating on a tax return, murdering a wife, robbing a bank, bribing a politician, hijacking an airplane—these and countless other acts are all crimes. Crime is as broad a category as disease, and perhaps as useless. To explain why one person has ever committed a crime and another has not may be as pointless as explaining why one person has ever gotten sick and another has not. We are not convinced that "crime" is so broad a category as to be absolutely meaningless—surely it is not irrelevant that crime is that form of behavior that is against the law—but we do acknowledge that it is difficult to provide a true and interesting explanation for actions that differ so much in their legal and subjective meanings.

To deal with these three difficulties, we propose to confine ourselves, for the most part, to explaining why some persons commit serious crimes at a high rate and others do not. By looking mainly at serious crimes, we escape the problem of comparing persons who park by a fire hydrant to persons who rob banks. By focusing on high-rate offenders, we do not need to distinguish between those who never break the law and those who (for perhaps chance reasons) break it only once or twice. And if we assume (as we do) that our criminal statistics are usually good enough to identify persons who commit a lot of crimes even if these data are poor at identifying accurately those who commit only one or two, then we can be less concerned with measurement errors.

The Meaning of Crime

A crime is any act committed in violation of a law that prohibits it and authorizes punishment for its commission. If we propose to confine our attention chiefly to persons who commit serious crimes at high rates, then we must specify what we mean by "serious." The arguments we shall make and the evidence we shall cite in this book will chiefly refer to aggressive, violent, or larcenous behavior; they will be, for the most part, about persons who hit, rape, murder, steal, and threaten.

In part, this limited focus is an unfortunate accident: We report only what others have studied, and by and large they have studied the causes of what we call predatory street crime. We would like to draw on research into a wider variety of law-violating behavior—embezzlement, sexual deviance, bribery, extortion, fraud—but very little such research exists.

But there is an advantage to this emphasis on predatory crime. Such behavior, except when justified by particular, well-understood circumstances (such as war), is condemned, in all societies and in all historical periods, by ancient tradition, moral sentiments, and formal law. Graeme Newman, in a study we shall describe in greater detail in Chapter 17, interviewed people in six nations (India, Indonesia, Iran, Italy, the United States, and Yugoslavia) about their attitudes toward a variety of behaviors and concluded that there is a high—indeed, virtually universal—agreement that certain of these behaviors were wrong and should be prohibited by law.[3] Robbery, stealing, incest, and factory pollution were condemned by overwhelming majorities in every society; by contrast, abortion and homosexuality, among other acts, were thought to be crimes in some places but not in others. Interestingly, the characteristics of the individual respondents in these countries—their age, sex, education, social class—did not make much difference in what they thought should be treated as crimes. Newman's finding merely reinforces a fact long understood by anthropologists: Certain acts are regarded as wrong by every society, preliterate as well as literate; that among these "universal crimes" are murder, theft, robbery, and incest.[4]

Moreover, people in different societies rate the seriousness of offenses, especially the universal crimes, in about the same way. Thorsten Sellin and Marvin E. Wolfgang developed a scale to measure the relative gravity of

141 separate offenses. This scale has been found to be remarkably stable, producing similar rankings among both American citizens and prison inmates,[5] as well as among Canadians,[6] Puerto Ricans,[7] Taiwanese,[8] and Belgian Congolese.[9]

By drawing on empirical studies of behaviors that are universally regarded as wrong and similarly ranked as to gravity, we can be confident that we are in fact theorizing about *crime* and human nature and not about actions that people may or may not think are wrong. If the studies to which we refer were to include commercial price-fixing, political corruption, or industrial monopolization, we would have to deal with the fact that in many countries these actions are not regarded as criminal at all. If an American business executive were to bring all of the nation's chemical industries under his control, he would be indicted for having formed a monopoly; a British business executive who did the same thing might be elevated to the peerage for having created a valuable industrial empire. Similarly, by omitting studies of sexual deviance (except forcible rape), we avoid modifying our theory to take into account changing social standards as to the wrongness of these acts and the legal culpability of their perpetrators. In short, we seek in this book to explain why some persons are more likely than others to do things that all societies condemn and punish.

To state the same thing a bit differently, we will be concerned more with criminality than with crime. Travis Hirschi and Michael Gottfredson have explained this important distinction as follows. *Crimes* are short-term, circumscribed events that result from the (perhaps fortuitous) coming together of an individual having certain characteristics and an opportunity having certain (immediate and deferred) costs and benefits. Because the theory we offer in Chapter 2 takes into account both these individual characteristics and situational features, we think it helps to explain why an individual will commit even one crime, but for reasons already explained, we recognize that the capacity of that theory to discriminate in an interesting and well-supported way between persons who do and do not commit a single offense is weak. *Criminality* refers to "stable differences across individuals in the propensity to commit criminal (or equivalent) acts."[10] The "equivalent" acts will be those that satisfy, perhaps in entirely legal ways, the same traits and predispositions that lead, in other circumstances, to crime. For example, a male who is very impulsive and so cannot resist temptation may, depending on circumstances, take toys from his playmates, money from his mother, billfolds from strangers, stamps from the office, liquor in the morning, extra chocolate cake at dinner time, and a nap whenever he feels like it. Some of these actions break the law, some do not.

The Categories of Explanation

Because we state that we intend to emphasize individual differences in behavior or predisposition, some readers may feel that we are shaping the argument in an improper manner. These critics believe that one can explain crime only by beginning with the society in which it is found. Emile Durkheim wrote: "We must, then, seek the explanation of social life in the nature of society itself."[11] Or, put another way, the whole is more than the sum of its parts. We do not deny that social arrangements and institutions, and the ancient customs that result from living and working together, affect behavior, often profoundly. But no explanation of social life explains anything until it explains individual behavior. Whatever significance we attach to ethnicity, social class, national character, the opinions of peers, or the messages of the mass media, the only test of their explanatory power is their ability to account for differences in how individuals, or groups of individuals, behave.

Explaining individual differences is an enterprise much resisted by some scholars. To them, this activity implies reducing everything to psychology, often referred to as "mere psychology." David J. Bordua, a sociologist, has pointed out the bias that can result from an excessive preference for social explanations over psychological ones.[12] Many criminologists, he comments, will observe a boy who becomes delinquent after being humiliated by his teacher or fired by his employer, and will conclude that his delinquency is explained by his "social class." But if the boy becomes delinquent after having been humiliated by his father or spurned by his girl friend, these scholars will deny that these events are explanations because they are "psychological." Teachers and employers are agents of the class structure, fathers and girl friends are not; therefore, the behavior of teachers and employers must be more important.

We believe that one can supply an explanation of criminality—and more important, of law-abidingness—that begins with the individual in, or even before, infancy and that takes into account the impact on him of subsequent experiences in the family, the school, the neighborhood, the labor market, the criminal justice system, and society at large. Yet even readers who accept this plan of inquiry as reasonable may still doubt its importance. To some, explaining crime is unnecessary because they think the explanation is already known; to others, it is impossible, since they think it unknowable.

Having taught a course on the causes of crime, and having spoken to many friends about our research, we have become acutely aware that there is scarcely any topic—except, perhaps, what is wrong with the Boston Red

Sox or the Chicago Cubs—on which people have more confident opinions. Crime is caused, we are told, by the baby boom, permissive parents, brutal parents, incompetent schools, racial discrimination, lenient judges, the decline of organized religion, televised violence, drug addiction, ghetto unemployment, or the capitalist system. We note certain patterns in the proffered explanations. Our tough-minded friends blame crime on the failings of the criminal justice system; our tender-minded ones blame it on the failings of society.

We have no *a priori* quarrel with any of these explanations, but we wonder whether all can be true, or true to the same degree. The baby boom may help explain why crime rose in the 1960s and 1970s, but it cannot explain why some members of that boom became criminals and others did not. It is hard to imagine that both permissive and brutal parents produce the same kind of criminals, though it is conceivable that each may contribute to a different kind of criminality. Many children may attend bad schools, but only a small minority become serious criminals. And in any case, there is no agreement as to what constitutes an incompetent school. Is it an overly strict one that "labels" mischievous children as delinquents, or is it an overly lax one that allows normal mischief to degenerate into true delinquency? Does broadcast violence include a football or hockey game, or only a detective story in which somebody shoots somebody else? Economic conditions may affect crime, but since crime rates were lower in the Great Depression than during the prosperous years of the 1960s, the effect is, at best, not obvious or simple. The sentences given by judges may affect the crime rate, but we are struck by the fact that the most serious criminals begin offending at a very early age, long before they encounter, or probably even hear of, judges, whereas those who do not commit their first crime until they are adults (when, presumably, they have some knowledge of law and the courts) are the least likely to have a long or active criminal career. Racism and capitalism may contribute to crime, but the connection must be rather complicated, since crime has risen in the United States (and other nations) most rapidly during recent times, when we have surely become less racist and (given the growth of governmental controls on business) less capitalist. In any event, high crime rates can be found in socialist as well as capitalist nations, and some capitalist nations, such as Japan and Switzerland, have very little crime. In view of all this, some sorting out of these explanations might be useful.

But when we discuss our aims with scholars who study crime, we hear something quite different. There is no well-accepted theory of the causes of crime, we are told, and it is unlikely that one can be constructed. Many explanations have been advanced, but all have been criticized. What is most needed is more research, not better theories. Any theory specific enough to be testable will not explain very much, whereas any theory broad enough to explain a great deal will not be testable. It is only because they are friends that some of our colleagues refrain from muttering about fools rushing in where wise men, if not angels, fear to tread. This question of whether it is useful to think systematically about the causes of crime is so important that we devote a large part of the next chapter to a discussion of it.

But there is one version of the claim that explaining crime is impossible to which we wish to take immediate exception. That is the view, heard most frequently from those involved with criminals on a case-by-case basis (probation officers and therapists, for example), that the causes of crime are unique to the individual criminal. Thus, one cannot generalize about crime because each criminal is different. Now, in one sense that argument is true— no two offenders are exactly alike. But we are struck by the fact that there are certain obvious patterns to criminality, suggesting that something more than random individual differences is at work. We think these obvious patterns, if nothing else, can be explained.

Patterns in Criminality

Crime is an activity disproportionately carried out by young men living in large cities. There are old criminals, and female ones, and rural and small-town ones, but, to a much greater degree than would be expected by chance, criminals are young urban males. This is true, insofar as we can tell, in every society that keeps any reasonable criminal statistics.[13] These facts are obvious to all, but sometimes their significance is overlooked. Much time and effort may be expended in trying to discover whether children from broken homes are more likely to be criminals than those from intact ones, or whether children who watch television a lot are more likely to be aggressive than those who watch it less. These are interesting questions, and we shall have something to say about them, but even if they are answered satisfactorily, we will have explained rather little about the major differences in criminality. Most children raised in broken homes do not become serious offenders; roughly half of such children are girls, and as we shall see in Chapter 4, females are often only one-tenth as likely as males to commit crimes. Crime existed abundantly long before the advent of television and would continue long after any hint of violence was expunged from TV programs. Any worthwhile explanation of crime must account for the major, persistent differences in criminality.

The fact that these regularities exist suggests that it is not impossible, in principle, to provide a coherent explanation of crime. It is not like trying to explain why some people prefer vanilla ice cream and others chocolate. And as we shall see, especially in Part II of this book, there are other regularities in criminality beyond those associated with age, sex, and place. There is mounting evidence that, on the average, offenders differ from nonoffenders in physique, intelligence, and personality. Some of these differences may not themselves be a cause of crime but only a visible indicator of some other factor that does contribute to crime. In Chapter 3, for example, we shall suggest that a certain physique is related to criminality, not because it causes people to break the law, but because a particular body type is associated with temperamental traits that predispose people to offending. Other individual differences, such as in personality, may directly contribute to criminality.

There are two apparent patterns in criminality that we have yet to mention, though they are no doubt uppermost in the minds of many readers—class and race. To many people, it is obvious that differences in social class, however defined, are strongly associated with lawbreaking. The poor, the unemployed, or the "underclass" are more likely than the well-to-do, the employed, or the "respectable poor" to commit certain kinds of crimes. We are reluctant, however, at least at the outset, to use class as a major category of explanations of differences in criminality for two reasons.

First, scholars who readily agree on the importance of age, sex, and place as factors related to crime disagree vigorously as to whether social class, however defined, is associated with crime. Their dispute may strike readers who have worked hard to move out of slums and into middle-class suburbs as rather bizarre; can anyone seriously doubt that better-off neighborhoods are safer than poorer ones? As John Braithwaite has remarked, "It is hardly plausible that one can totally explain away the higher risks of being mugged and raped in lower class areas as a consequence of the activities of middle class people who come into the area to perpetrate such acts."[14]

We have much sympathy with his view, but we must recognize that there are arguments against it. When Charles R. Tittle, Wayne J. Villemez, and Douglas A. Smith reviewed thirty-five studies of the relationship between crime rates and social class, they found only a slight association between the two variables.[15] When crime was measured using official (e.g., police) reports, the connection with social class was stronger than when it was measured using self-reports (the crimes admitted to by individuals filling out a questionnaire or responding to an interview). This conclusion has been challenged by other scholars who find, on the basis of more extensive self-report data than any previously used, that crime, especially serious crime, is much more prevalent among lower-class youth.[16] Michael J. Hinde-lang, Travis Hirschi, and Joseph G. Weis have shown that self-report stud-ies tend to measure the prevalence of trivial offenses, including many things that would not be considered a crime at all (e.g., skipping school, defying parents, or having unmarried sex).[17] Even when true crimes are reported, they are often so minor (e.g., shoplifting a pack of gum) that it is a mis-take—but, alas, a frequently made mistake—to lump such behavior together with burglary and robbery as measures of criminality. We agree with Hinde-lang et al., as well as with many others,[18] who argue that when crime is prop-erly measured, the relationship between it and social class is strong—lower-class persons are much more likely to have committed a serious "street" crime than upper-status ones. But we recognize that this argument continues to be controversial, and so it seems inappropriate to begin an explanation of criminality by assuming that it is based on class.

Our second reason for not starting with class as a major social factor is, to us, more important. Unlike sex, age, and place, class is an ambiguous concept. A "lower-class" person can be one who has a low income, but that definition lumps together graduate students, old-age pensioners, welfare mothers, and unemployed steelworkers—individuals who would appear to have, as far as crime is concerned, little in common. Many self-report stud-ies of crime use class categories so broad as to obscure whatever connection may exist between class and criminality.[19] And studies of delinquency typi-cally describe a boy as belonging to the class of his father, even if the boy in his own right, in school or in the labor force, is doing much better or much worse than his father.[20] By lower class one could also mean having a low-prestige occupation, but it is not clear to us why the prestige ranking of one's occupation should have any influence on one's criminality.

Class may, of course, be defined in terms of wealth or income, but using the concept in this way to explain crime, without further clarification, is ambiguous as to cause and effect. One's wealth, income, status, or rela-tionship to the means of production could cause certain behavior (e.g., "poor people must steal to eat"), or they could themselves be caused by other factors (impulsive persons with low verbal skills tend to be poor and to steal). By contrast, one's criminality cannot be the cause of, say, one's age or sex. As we proceed through our analysis in the chapters that follow, we shall take up the various possible components of social class, such as schooling and labor-market experiences, to see what effect they may have on individual differences in criminality. But we shall not begin with the assump-tion that we know what class is and that it can be only the cause, and never the consequence, of criminality.

Race is also a controversial and ambiguous concept in criminological research. Every study of crime using official data shows that blacks are heavily overrepresented among persons arrested, convicted, and imprisoned.[21] Some people, however, suspect that official reports are contaminated by the racial bias of those who compile them. Self-report studies, by contrast, tend to show fewer racial differences in criminality, but these studies have the same defect with respect to race as they do with regard to class—they overcount trivial offenses, in which the races do not differ, and undercount the more serious offenses, in which they do differ.[22] Moreover, surveys of the victims of crimes reveal that of the offenders whose racial identity could be discerned by their victims, about half were black; for the most serious offenses, two-thirds were black.[23] Though there may well be some racial bias in arrests, prosecutions, and sentences, there is no evidence (see Chapter 18) that it is so great as to account for the disproportionate involvement of blacks in serious crime, as revealed by both police and victimization data and by interviews with prison inmates.[24]

Our reason for not regarding, at least at the outset, race as a source of individual differences in criminality is not that we doubt that blacks are overrepresented in crime. Rather, there are two other considerations. First, racial differences exist in some societies and not others, yet all societies have crime. Though racial factors may affect the crime rate, the fundamental explanation for individual differences in criminality ought to be based—indeed, must be based, if it is to be a general explanation—on factors that are common to all societies.

Second, we find the concept of race to be ambiguous, but in a different way from the ambiguity of class. There is no reason to believe that the genes determining one's skin pigmentation also affect criminality. At one time in this nation's history, persons of Irish descent were heavily overrepresented among those who had committed some crime, but it would have been foolish then to postulate a trait called "Irishness" as an explanation. If racial or ethnic identity affects the likelihood of committing a crime, it must be because that identity co-varies with other characteristics and experiences that affect criminality. The proper line of inquiry, then, is first to examine those other characteristics and experiences to see how and to what extent they predispose an individual toward crime, and then to consider what, if anything, is left unexplained in the observed connection between crime and racial identity. After examining constitutional, familial, educational, economic, neighborhood, and historical factors, there may or may not be anything left to say on the subject of race. What is left to say, we shall try to say in Chapter 18.

The Crime Rate

We measure the amount of criminal activity by the "crime rate," but that measure is more complex—and can be more misleading—than we sometimes realize. The rate is calculated by dividing the number of crimes committed in a given locality (city, state, nation) during a given period by the number of people living in that locality. That ratio combines two separate measures of crime: the number of criminals active in the locality and the number of crimes each active criminal commits.[25] The per capita crime rate equals the prevalence of crime times its incidence; in simple algebra,

$$\frac{\text{crimes}}{\text{population}} = \frac{\text{criminals}}{\text{population}} \times \frac{\text{crimes}}{\text{criminal}}.$$

The proportion of the population of a locality (or an age group) that consists of criminals is the *prevalence* of crime; the number of crimes committed (per year) by the average criminal is the *incidence* of crime. In most of this book, we shall be less concerned with the per capita crime rate (i.e., the number of crimes per capita per year in a given locality) and more concerned with the prevalence and incidence of crime. That is because we are not trying to explain why certain cities, states, or nations have more or less crime than others; we are instead trying to explain why, out of a given population, the number of criminals is large or small (prevalence) and why the frequency with which a given individual commits crimes is high or low (incidence). The reader might suppose that the crime rate of a given city would go up if crime became more prevalent, but that is not necessarily the case. The number of criminals may increase, but if the average number of crimes they each commit decreases, the city's crime rate may not change at all. By the same token, the crime rate of the city may rise even though the proportion of its residents who commit crimes has not changed, provided that the rate at which the average criminal commits crimes goes up.[26]

Because of our interest in individual differences in criminality—that is, in prevalence and incidence—only a small part of this book will be devoted to trying to explain why crime rates have gone up in this country, or why this country has more of certain kinds of crime than other countries. But since each of the variables that could explain such historical changes or cross-cultural differences is contained within our theory, there is no reason in principle why these trends and differences could not also be explained. In Chapters 16 and 17 we shall suggest what these explanations may be.

Measuring Crime Rates in the Aggregate

How many crimes an individual commits and the proportion of a locality's population that commits crimes can never be accurately known. Hence, we can never have a precise measure of the prevalence or incidence of crime. We can, at best, estimate those numbers by using one or more of six possible measures of crime. Each has some major limitations, but they are not exactly the same limitations. The safest statements we can make about crime rates are those supported by as many different measures as we can find. Fortunately, most of the more important generalizations about criminal behavior with which we are concerned are consistent with many different methods of measuring crime. Where they are not—where the generalization is true only if one particular measure is used—we shall indicate that fact. Nonetheless, it is important for the reader to know how these measures are derived and what their shortcomings and biases may be.

Three of these measures describe crime in the aggregate—how many crimes occur in a city, state, or nation in a given period of time. They provide different estimates of the overall crime rate but do not permit us to divide those estimates into separate measures of prevalence and incidence. These readily available aggregate sources are reports of crimes known to the police, crimes known to victims, and homicides known to coroners.

Police Reports of Crimes

By now, everyone must be aware that the police count of crimes is much smaller than the number of crimes that actually occur, and hence that the national compilation of those police counts—the Uniform Crime Reports (UCR), published by the Federal Bureau of Investigation—also understates the true amount of crime. Most of the discrepancy occurs because citizens fail to notify the police; it is estimated, based on the victim surveys discussed below, that at least half of all serious (i.e., Index) crimes go unreported. But if the only problem with police reports was that they undercounted crimes by some constant fraction, it would be a trivial problem; we could simply multiply the police count by the constant to get the true crime rate.

Unfortunately, that is not the case. Some police departments supply to the FBI a more reliable and consistent count of crimes than do others. A few departments, out of inefficiency or a desire to make their force look better, fail to report many crimes. When the FBI learns of these inaccuracies, it will sometimes suspend publication of that city's figures, but it does not always learn of them. During the 1960s, some large cities reported sharp increases in crime that, later analysis showed, were in part the result of improvements in reporting practices.[27] There is good reason to believe that local reporting systems have improved but no reason to suppose that they are perfect, even within the limitations imposed by the need to rely on information volunteered by citizens. And the citizens themselves may change their reporting habits. Their willingness to report rapes, for example, may be affected by changing social views as to the acceptability of making such admissions and by the extent to which the police encourage such reports.

Police and FBI reports tend to emphasize certain crimes more than others. Their greatest efforts are devoted to Index crimes. The Index crimes included (until 1978) seven major offenses: murder and nonnegligent manslaughter, forcible rape, robbery, aggravated assault, burglary, larceny, and motor vehicle theft. After 1978 an eighth offense, arson, was added to the Index. When one hears of the total crime rate, one is hearing of the total number of Index offenses divided by the (estimated) population. In interpreting this rate, it is important to bear in mind that it omits all non-Index offenses, including some, such as simple assault or selling drugs, that are often considered quite serious.

The UCR crime rate undercounts crime in another sense. If several crimes are committed during a single incident, only the most serious of them is counted. For example, if a man breaks into a home, rapes a woman, takes her money at gunpoint, and steals her car for his getaway, he has committed, at a minimum, rape, robbery, and auto theft. But only the most serious of these—in this case, the rape—will be counted in the national crime totals.[28]

Police reports provide almost the only source of information about long-term trends in the crime rate, but these reports were not available in many cities before the early 1930s. It is a mistake to attach too much significance to year-to-year changes or to small differences among cities in these police-based numbers, but they probably give a reasonably good measure of major trends in crime (sharply up during the 1960s and early 1970s) and large differences among cities (big cities have much more violent crime than small ones).

Victim Surveys

Since 1973, the Bureau of the Census has interviewed persons in a random sample of sixty thousand American households to find out whether they have been the victims of any one of several crimes during the preceding six months. The National Crime Survey (NCS), or more commonly, the victimization survey, gathers data on six major crimes: rape, robbery, assault, household burglary, larceny, and motor vehicle theft. It gathers no information on arson or on homicide; the latter is too rare an event to be reliably estimated by victim surveys (and in any case, the victim is dead and cannot be interviewed). In general, the UCR and the NCS define in the same way the crimes on which they report.

Though the definitions are the same, the different methods of measuring crime mean that the results of the UCR and the NCS are not directly comparable. The NCS counts only personal and household victimizations; the UCR counts crimes against businesses as well. The NCS counts only the victims living in a given city or state; the UCR counts all crimes reported to the police in that city or state, whether or not the victim lived there.*

Moreover, citizens are more likely to report some crimes to the police than to interviewers, and other crimes just the reverse. A woman who has been assaulted by her husband may notify the police (and thus generate a UCR statistic), but when the interviewer comes around several months later and asks about assaults, the woman may not feel inclined to mention her husband's attack, especially if he is sitting right next to her.[29] When residents of San Jose, California, who had reported to the police that they had been assaulted were later interviewed in a test of the NCS, only 48 percent said they had been assaulted; the percentage who admitted to being assaulted was lowest for those who had earlier told the police that their assailant was a relative.[30] Moreover, a minor theft may not be reported to the police because the victim knows the police can do nothing about it, but it may be reported to an interviewer who probes for any evidence of a theft, however small.

When crime rates are calculated, it is important to know when a crime occurred so that it can be assigned to the proper time period. Crimes are usually reported to the police soon after they happen, often the same day. Crimes reported to NCS interviewers are reported many months after they occur. As a result, victims may forget some crimes, especially minor ones, and they may mistakenly think they occurred in the last six months when in

---

* This can make a big difference in central cities with many commuters and visitors. The crime rate for such a city as calculated by the NCS would show the number of personal victimizations reported by residents of the city divided by the population of the city; the crime rate as calculated by the UCR would show the number of crimes reported to the police by residents, commuters, and visitors divided by the population of the city. Obviously, the UCR crime rate for that city is likely to be highly sensitive to how many commuters and visitors are in the city, which may change from year to year, as business conditions change, without any corresponding change in the size of the resident population.

fact they occurred eight or nine months ago. And since the NCS does not interview all sixty thousand households at the same time, but instead in waves (ten thousand households each month), the period over which the victimization data are totaled covers a year or more, with substantial opportunity for error. Thus, the crime rate for a given year will be calculated by the UCR on the basis of reports to the police made during that year, while the NCS crime rate will probably include some offenses that occurred the previous year.

The net effect of all these differences in method is this: The UCR crime rate tends to be more volatile than the NCS crime rate. From year to year, the UCR will, on the average, report a greater change in crime rates than the NCS.[31] There is little point in asking which measure is the true one, for the biases in each mean that neither is entirely correct.

Though the victimization rate produced by the NCS is an aggregate measure of crime occurring in American households, some inferences about the rates at which particular groups in the population commit offenses can be obtained from the answers victims give to certain questions. The NCS gathers a great deal of information not only about the circumstances of crime—where it occurred, whether it was reported to the police (and if not, why not), and the age, sex, and race of the victim—but also about the perceived characteristics of those offenders who were seen by their victims. These characteristics include the sex, apparent age, and perceived race of persons who commit rapes, assaults, and robberies. These estimates provide a way of verifying generalizations derived from other data about who is most likely to commit certain crimes.

Vital Statistics

Doctors, coroners, and medical examiners report through state agencies to the National Center for Health Statistics, a part of the Public Health Service, on homicides, suicides, and accidental deaths. These reports are not entirely accurate, since some coroners may mistakenly call a homicide an accident or a suicide, or vice versa. From this information, we have a way of measuring the homicide rate that is more or less independent of police reports. By this means we know that the homicide rate (homicides per 100,000 persons) doubled between 1961 and 1975, that males are twice as likely to be the victims of homicide as females, that males aged twenty-five to thirty-four are more likely to be such victims than those of any other age group, and that nonwhites are eight to fifteen times as likely as whites to be so victimized.[32] These findings are roughly consistent with what one learns from police reports.

We can also infer from these vital statistics something about the characteristics of those who commit homicides. We know that the great majority of deaths recognized as homicides are solved; the reason for this, in large part, is that most occur among persons known or related to each other (spouses, lovers, drinking companions, criminal accomplices), and so the police usually have a ready list of suspects and plausible motives whenever a homicide is reported to them. We also know that persons arrested for homicide tend to be of the same sex and race and, roughly, the same age as their victims.[33] Thus, if the public health statistics tell us that homicide victims are disproportionately young black males, we have good grounds for believing that those who commit homicides are disproportionately young black males.

Measuring Crime Rates of Individuals

In this book, we are principally concerned with individual differences in criminal behavior, and thus we wish to measure the frequency with which a given offender commits a crime (incidence*) and the proportion of persons who commit any crime (prevalence). Aggregate crime statistics give us only a few clues as to what these rates are. There are three measures of individual offense rates—arrest reports, self-reports, and direct observation.

Arrest Reports

Arrest reports are produced by the police. They provide information about the characteristics of known offenders, including the frequency with which they have come to the attention of the police—a measure of crime incidence. Arrest reports are probably subject to less error than police reports of crime, since few departments have any incentive to minimize reports of arrests. Nevertheless, those reports have important limitations. Not every police contact with a person who has committed a crime results in an arrest. Police may take drunk men or rowdy juveniles to the station house and then decide to release them without a formal arrest even though the individuals have admitted breaking the law (this is more common for minor than for major offenses[34]). Husbands who assault their wives even in the presence of an officer may not be arrested because the police are reluctant to interfere in what they regard as "family matters," especially if they believe that the wife will not press charges. Some police departments count each crime charged against a person as a separate "arrest," whereas others consider one offender to constitute one arrest.

* Some scholars refer to incidence with the Greek letter λ, or lambda.

Moreover, the police solve (technically, clear by an arrest) only a small fraction of all crimes—no more than about one in ten robberies, for example. One cannot assume that those that are solved by an arrest are a representative sample of all those committed. Thus, the average person arrested for a crime may differ in important but unknown ways from the typical person who commits such a crime. Some observers have even suggested that arrest reports are systematically biased by the tendency of the police to overarrest certain kinds of persons (e.g., poor blacks) and to underarrest others (e.g., affluent whites). This is a difficult issue to resolve, but in general there seems to be little evidence that bias in the decision to arrest accounts for most, or even very much, of the dissimilarity between arrested persons and the population at large. We have already noted research showing that the racial composition of all arrested persons is quite similar to the racial makeup of all persons who were seen by their victims.[35] Direct observations of police arrest practices in the field have suggested that race is not a major factor influencing the officers' decision to arrest, or to threaten with arrest, a suspect.[36]

We think that the more serious the crime, the less the likelihood that arrests will be affected by the class or race of the suspect and thus the greater the likelihood that the characteristics of arrested persons will be similar to those of all persons committing those crimes. This certainly seems the case for homicides, because most are cleared by an arrest. Besides, we believe that most high-rate offenders are eventually, and frequently, arrested; therefore, the pool of persons with a long arrest record is probably quite similar to the pool of persons who commit a lot of crimes.* The less serious the crime, the greater the opportunity for arrests to be unrepresentative of offenders, especially in the case of young offenders.

Self-reports

Since there are many crimes that do not result in an arrest and many offenders, especially low-rate ones, who are never arrested, scholars here and abroad have developed self-reports as a way of measuring what they call the "dark figure" of crime, or "hidden delinquency." Self-reports are obtained from a questionnaire or interview that solicits from a person, under the promise of confidentiality, a list of the offenses he or she has committed.

---

* At least one study claims that high-rate offenders often escape detection.[37] This finding, however, may well be in error, since it is based on only two years' worth of self-report and arrest data. The high-rate offenders in the sample may have been arrested after the self-report survey was conducted.

(This technique is not limited to criminological research nor was it pioneered by criminologists. For decades, psychologists and physicians have explored in this way many aspects of private behavior, including sexual conduct and drug use.) The most common finding of self-report studies of crime is that the great majority of persons, especially young males, have committed one or more crimes, and the majority of these persons have never been arrested.[38] Also, as we saw earlier, many self-report studies find a weaker association between delinquency and either class or race than is found from arrest reports.[39]

We have already noted one major defect of most self-report studies—the overrepresentation of minor offenses, including such things as skipping school, drinking beer, and defying authority, in the measures of delinquency.[40] Moreover, when respondents are asked about serious crimes (such as auto theft or burglary), they are often asked only whether they have "ever" committed such an act or, at best, whether they have committed it only once or twice or "more than three times." Such a truncated set of responses obscures differences between persons who break the law once or twice (many males have done that) and those who break it twenty, thirty, or fifty times per year.

There are also problems in the selection of persons to be questioned. One is the underrepresentation of those most likely to be serious offenders. The typical self-report study is of children in junior high or high school, which means that it omits youths who are truant or who have dropped out of school; it is precisely these youths—as we shall see in later chapters—who are much more likely than those in school to be offenders.[41] Even among those in school, the most delinquency-prone persons appear, in many studies, to be least likely to fill out the questionnaires.[42] In addition, persons of low verbal intelligence have difficulty with questionnaires and are likely to underreport delinquent acts; if there is a correlation between verbal intelligence and criminality, the inaccuracy caused by this bias could be quite large.[43]

Various methods have been used to check the validity of the responses to self-report questionnaires, including giving the subjects polygraph, or "lie detector," tests,[44] asking classmates to describe the behavior of the subjects,[45] and checking self-reports against police reports.[46] All these methods indicate that there is a significant amount of underreporting. But one should not assume that people only conceal crimes; they also may boast of offenses they never committed. Peer pressure may lead a boy to claim he did something that would provide status in the eyes of his friends when in fact he had not. In one study, over half the white boys who said on their questionnaire that they had been picked up by the police had, in fact, no police record.[47] A self-report study among male college students found a substantial number who falsely claimed to have started a fistfight;[48] perhaps these boys were eager to dispel the view that college students are less masculine than others.

All of these problems with self-reports have led, we believe, to the erroneous conclusion that the age, sex, class, and race differences among groups in the true prevalence of crime are much less than indicated by arrest reports. A properly conducted self-report study, of which a few have begun to appear, would ask a random sample of individuals about real criminal acts (and not merely about minor mischief), would attend carefully to the problem of estimating the frequency of offenses in a given time period, and would pay primary attention to differences at the extremes of the statistical distribution.*

Direct Observation

One can rarely observe people committing crimes; in fact, watching people is supposed to prevent crimes. There have been a few reports of direct observations, however. Walter B. Miller reports on the direct observation by social workers of 205 members of seven youthful street gangs with whom the workers were in close and continuous contact for (on the average) two years.[50] During this time, the workers recorded several hundred thefts and found that these crimes were more likely to be committed by males than by females, and by lower-status males than by (slightly) higher-status ones. There were no overall differences associated with race, though whites were more likely to steal from homes, businesses, and autos, and blacks more likely to steal from persons.

In summary: Each method of measuring crime has its defects, but taken together, all methods provide strong, consistent support for the view that individual differences in the incidence and prevalence of crime are associated with differences in age, sex, and place of residence, and they supply strong but inconsistent support for the view that the prevalence of crime

---

* The last point may require clarification. Since self-reports, like arrest reports, will provide a biased measure of the true offense rate of individuals, it is best to pay the most heed to the largest differences in self-reported individual offense rates, on the assumption that small differences may be an artifact of some quirk in the methodology. For example, the initial reports from the National Youth Survey suggested that there were very few differences by race or class, and much reduced differences by age and sex, in the self-reported frequency of delinquency among a national sample of 1,725 adolescents. But the reports also suggested that among youth who committed many delinquencies each year, there were clear differences associated with age, sex, class, and race.[49]

also varies with race and social class (somehow defined). Moreover, these methods also make it fairly clear that the incidence of crime is also higher for males than for females and for younger (say, under thirty) males than for older ones. These studies do not give us clear guidance as to whether the incidence of crime varies with race: Crime is more prevalent among blacks than among whites, but the average black offender does not appear to commit more crimes than the average white offender.[51]

Are There Types of Criminals?

We are concerned mainly with explaining criminality—why some people are more likely than others to commit, at a high rate, one or more of the universal crimes. But even if the behaviors with which we are concerned are alike in being universally regarded as serious crimes, are not the *motives* for these crimes so various that they cannot all be explained by one theory? Possibly. But this objection assumes that what we want to know are the motives of lawbreakers. It is by no means clear that the most interesting or useful way to look at crime is by trying to discover the motives of individual criminals—why some offenders like to steal cash, others like stolen cash plus a chance to beat up on its owner, and still others like violent sex—any more than it is obvious that the best way to understand the economy is by discovering why some persons keep their money in the bank, others use it to buy tickets to boxing matches, and still others use it to buy the favors of a prostitute. The motives of criminal (and of human) behavior are as varied as the behavior itself; we come to an understanding of the general processes shaping crime only when we abstract from particular motives and circumstances to examine the factors that lead people to run greater or lesser risks in choosing a course of action.

To us, offenders differ not so much in what kind of crimes they commit, but in the rate at which they commit them. In this sense, the one-time wife murderer is different from the persistent burglar or the organized drug trafficker—the first man breaks the law but once, the latter two do it every week or every day. As we shall see, the evidence suggests that persons who frequently break universal laws do not, in fact, specialize very much. A high-rate offender is likely to commit a burglary today and a robbery tomorrow, and sell drugs in between.

Explaining why some persons have a very high rate and others a low one is preferable, we think, to the major alternative to this approach: trying to sort offenders and offenses into certain categories or types. Creating—and arguing about—typologies is a major preoccupation of many students of crime because, having decided that motives are what count and having discovered that there are almost as many motives as there are people, the only way to bring any order to this variety is by reducing all the motives to a few categories, often described as personality types.

For example, a common distinction in criminology is between the "subcultural" offender and the "unsocialized" or "psychopathic" one. The first is a normal person who finds crime rewarding (perhaps because he has learned to commit crimes from friends he admires) and who discounts heavily the risks of being punished. The second is abnormal: He commits crimes because he has a weak conscience and cares little about the opinions of friends. Now, as even the authors of such distinctions acknowledge, these categories overlap (some subcultural thieves, for example, may also take pleasure in beating up on their victims), and not all offenders fit into either category. But to us, the chief difficulty with such typologies is that they direct attention away from individual differences and toward idealized—and abstract—categories.

Crime is correlated, as we have seen, with age, sex, and place of residence, and it is associated, as we shall soon see, with other stable characteristics of individuals. Understanding those associations is the first task of criminological theory. Our approach is not to ask which persons belong to what category of delinquents but rather to ask whether differences in the frequency with which persons break the law are associated with differences in the rewards of crime, the risks of being punished for a crime, the strength of internalized inhibitions against crime, and the willingness to defer gratifications, and then to ask what biological, developmental, situational, and adaptive processes give rise to these individual characteristics. In doing so, we are mindful of the argument of Niko Tinbergen, the ethologist who won a Nobel Prize, that there are four levels of analysis that must be brought together:[52] the developmental (how an individual grows up and is socialized by family and friends), the situational (how immediate circumstances, such as opportunities for crime, elicit behavior), the adaptive (how a person responds to the positive and negative rewards of alternative courses of action), and the biological (how evolution has equipped a person with certain attributes, such as intelligence and temperament[53]). The theory offered in the next chapter should be helpful in keeping all four levels in mind.

2

A THEORY OF CRIMINAL BEHAVIOR

Theories of crime abound. The lay reader will wonder whether any theory can be an improvement on common sense, and the scholarly one will groan at the prospect of yet another theory. But what may be irrelevant to the former and redundant to the latter is, to us, important, for theories, whatever else they may do, direct our attention to some features of the situation and away from others. Much of the confusion about the sources of individual differences in criminality arise, we believe, from bad theories—that is, from views about how the world works that are incomplete and thus lead us to attend to some things but not to others.

For example, the theory that unemployment or economic want causes crime can lead us to look for increases in criminality during economic recessions but to overlook the possibility that crime may also be caused by prosperity (if it loosens the social bonds), by the distribution of income (if it causes social envy), or by some underlying factor that happens to cause both criminality and unemployment. More generally, theories that call attention to the social setting in which crime occurs (such as the attitudes of parents and peers, the perceived costs and benefits of crime, the influence of drugs and television) direct our attention away from preexisting individual traits that make people more or less susceptible to such social factors; by the same token, theories that emphasize the preferences of individuals tend to de-emphasize the situational factors that determine how, or even whether, those preferences affect behavior. The quarrels among lay persons and scholars about what causes crime are basically quarrels about the relative importance of those factors that occupy a central place in competing theories. These arguments are made more intense by the fact that sometimes people do not choose theories at random; very often, they choose them in part because the central factors in the theories—individual morality, social setting, economic circumstances, or the prospects of punishment—are ones, which for political or ideological reasons, the defenders of the theories *want* to believe are central.

We suggest that most of the common theories purporting to explain criminal behavior are but special cases of some more general theory. Specifying that larger theory is useful because, to the extent it is correct and comprehensive, it will keep before our eyes the full range of factors that cause individual differences in criminality. This, in turn, will restrain our tendency to give partial explanations of crime or to make partial interpretations of the empirical findings of criminologists. Ideally, of course, a theory should do much more than this. In principle, a theory is a testable statement of the relationships among two or more variables, so that, knowing the theory, we can say with some confidence that if we observe X, we will also observe Y. For instance: If we observe a left-handed, red-haired male, then we are 70 percent certain that we are observing a burglar. Unfortunately, theories about crime, even ours, often do not permit us to make such statements, but for the reasons already given, they are important nonetheless. If, given this state of affairs, "theory" sounds too grand a term for the systematic speculations we and others have produced, consider what we offer as an organized perspective on the causes of crime.

Our theory—or perspective—is a statement about the forces that control individual behavior. To most people, that is not a very interesting assertion, but to many scholars, it is a most controversial one. Some students of crime are suspicious of the view that explanations of criminality should be based on an analysis of individual psychology. Such a view, they argue, is "psychological reductionism" that neglects the setting in which crime occurs and the broad social forces that determine levels of crime. These suspicions, while understandable, are ill-founded. Whatever factors contribute to crime—the state of the economy, the competence of the police, the nurturance of the family, the availability of drugs, the quality of the schools—they must all affect the behavior of *individuals* if they are to affect crime. If people differ in their tendency to commit crime, we must express those differences in terms of how some array of factors affects their individual decisions. If crime rates differ among nations, it must be because individuals in those nations differ or are exposed to different arrays of factors. If crime rates rise or fall, it must be that changes have occurred in the variables governing individual behavior.

Our theory is eclectic, drawing from different, sometimes opposing, schools of thought. We incorporate both genetic predispositions and social learning and consider the influence of both delayed and immediate factors. An individual act is sometimes best understood as a reaction to immediate circumstances and at other times as an expression of enduring behavioral dispositions; both sorts of explanations have a place in our theory. Though eclectic, the theory is built upon modern behavioral psychology.*

Crime as Choice: The Theory in Brief

In this section, we give a brief overview of our theoretical perspective. Many lay readers may wish, after reading the material under this heading, to skip to page 61. Scholars and others interested in the derivation of the theory will probably want to read all of the chapter, as well as the Appendix (pages 531–535) to it.

Our theory rests on the assumption that people, when faced with a choice, choose the preferred course of action. This assumption is quite weak; it says nothing more than that whatever people choose to do, they choose it because they prefer it. In fact, it is more than weak; without further clarification, it is a tautology. When we say people "choose," we do not necessarily mean that they consciously deliberate about what to do. All we mean is that their behavior is determined by its consequences. A person will do that thing the consequences of which are perceived by him or her to be preferable to the consequences of doing something else. What can save such a statement from being a tautology is how plausibly we describe the gains and losses associated with alternative courses of action and the standards by which a person evaluates those gains and losses.

These assumptions are commonplace in philosophy and social science. Philosophers speak of hedonism or utilitarianism, economists of value or utility, and psychologists of reinforcement or reward. We will use the language of psychology, but it should not be hard to translate our terminology into that of other disciplines. Though social scientists differ as to how much behavior can reasonably be described as the result of a choice, all agree that at least some behavior is guided, or even precisely controlled, by things vari-

* The specialist will recognize the debt we owe to, and the liberties we have taken with, the work of Edward L. Thorndike, Albert Bandura, B. F. Skinner, R. B. Cattell, H. J. Eysenck, I. P. Pavlov, and E. C. Tolman, among others.

ously termed pleasure, pain, happiness, sorrow, desirability, or the like. Our object is to show how this simple and widely used idea can be used to explain behavior.

At any given moment, a person can choose between committing a crime and not committing it (all these alternatives to crime we lump together as "noncrime"). The consequences of committing the crime consist of rewards (what psychologists call "reinforcers") and punishments; the consequences of not committing the crime (i.e., engaging in noncrime) also entail gains and losses. The larger the ratio of the net rewards of crime to the net rewards of noncrime, the greater the tendency to commit the crime. The net rewards of crime include, obviously, the likely material gains from the crime, but they also include intangible benefits, such as obtaining emotional or sexual gratification, receiving the approval of peers, satisfying an old score against an enemy, or enhancing one's sense of justice. One must deduct from these rewards of crime any losses that accrue immediately—that are, so to speak, contemporaneous with the crime. They include the pangs of conscience, the disapproval of onlookers, and the retaliation of the victim.

The value of noncrime lies all in the future. It includes the benefits to the individual of avoiding the risk of being caught and punished and, in addition, the benefits of avoiding penalties not controlled by the criminal justice system, such as the loss of reputation or the sense of shame afflicting a person later discovered to have broken the law and the possibility that, being known as a criminal, one cannot get or keep a job.

The value of any reward or punishment associated with either crime or noncrime is, to some degree, uncertain. A would-be burglar can rarely know exactly how much loot he will take away or what its cash value will prove to be. The assaulter or rapist may exaggerate the satisfaction he thinks will follow the assault or the rape. Many people do not know how sharp the bite of conscience will be until they have done something that makes them feel the bite. The anticipated approval of one's buddies may or may not be forthcoming. Similarly, the benefits of noncrime are uncertain. One cannot know with confidence whether one will be caught, convicted, and punished, or whether one's friends will learn about the crime and as a result withhold valued esteem, or whether one will be able to find or hold a job.

Compounding these uncertainties is time. The opportunity to commit a crime may be ready at hand (an open, unattended cash register in a store) or well in the future (a bank that, with planning and preparation, can be robbed). And the rewards associated with noncrime are almost invariably more distant than those connected with crime, perhaps many weeks or months distant. The strength of reinforcers tends to decay over time at rates that differ among individuals. As a result, the extent to which people take into account distant possibilities—a crime that can be committed only tomorrow, or punishment that will be inflicted only in a year—will affect whether they choose crime or noncrime. All of these factors—the strength of rewards, the problems of uncertainty and delay, and the way in which our sense of justice affects how we value the rewards—will be examined in the remainder of this chapter.

Reinforcers

All human behavior is shaped by two kinds of reinforcers: primary and secondary. A primary reinforcer derives its strength from an innate drive, such as hunger or sexual appetite; a secondary reinforcer derives its strength from learning. The line dividing reinforcers that are innate from those that are learned is hard to draw, and people argue, often passionately, over where it ought to be drawn. When we disagree over whether people are innately altruistic, men are innately more aggressive than women, or mankind is innately warlike or competitive, we are disagreeing over whether behavior responds to primary or to secondary reinforcers.

In fact, most reinforcers combine primary and secondary elements. Part of the benefit that comes from eating either bread or spaghetti must derive from the fact that their common ingredient, wheat, satisfies an innate drive—hunger. In this sense, both are primary reinforcers. But bread and spaghetti differ in texture, flavor, and appearance, and the preferences we have for these qualities are in part learned. These qualities constitute secondary reinforcers. The diversity of the world's cuisines shows, to some extent, how extraordinarily varied are the secondary aspects of even a highly biological reinforcer such as food.

The distinction between primary and secondary reinforcers is important in part because it draws attention to the link between innate drives and social conventions. For example, in every society men and women adorn themselves to enhance their sexual appeal. At the same time, styles in clothing and cosmetics vary greatly among societies and throughout history. As we are all immersed in the fashions of our place and time, we may suppose that fashion is purely arbitrary. But we are probably wrong, for these conventions of personal beauty are dependent on primary sexual reinforcers. But what constitutes acceptable adornment changes within broad limits. Once, for a woman to appear nude in a motion picture meant that she was wanton and the film was trash. Today, female nudity, though it is still offensive to some, is not construed by most viewers as an indication of the moral worth of the woman.

Not only do innate primary reinforcers become blended with learned secondary ones, the strength of even primary reinforcers (and of course of secondary reinforcers) will vary. Bread that we eat hungrily at seven o'clock in the morning may have no appeal to us at one o'clock in the afternoon, right after lunch. In fact, many forms of food may appeal to us before breakfast even though none may appeal after lunch. A class of reinforcers whose strengths vary together allows us to speak of a "drive"—in this case, the hunger drive.

Drives vary in strength. The various food drives can be depended on to assert themselves several times a day, but the sexual drive may be felt much less frequently and then in ways powerfully affected by circumstances. The aggressive drive (to be discussed later in this chapter) may occur very rarely in some of us and frequently in others, and it may appear suddenly, in response to events, and blow over almost as quickly. We repeat these commonplace observations because we wish to emphasize that though much behavior, including criminal behavior, is affected by innate drives, this does not mean that crime is committed by "born criminals" with uncontrollable, antisocial drives. We can, in short, include innate drives (and thus genetic factors) in our theory without embracing a view of the criminal as an atavistic savage or any other sort of biological anomaly.

Secondary reinforcers change in strength along with the primary reinforcers with which they are associated. Those secondary reinforcers that change the least in strength are those associated with the largest variety of primary reinforcers. Money is an especially powerful reward, not because it is intrinsically valuable (paper currency has almost no intrinsic worth), but because it is associated with so many primary reinforcers that satisfy innate drives. Money can buy food, shelter, relief from pain, and even sexual gratification. (It can also buy status and power, but we will not discuss here the interesting question of whether the desire for these things is innate.) The reinforcing power of money is relatively steady because the many primary rewards with which it is connected make it somewhat impervious to fluctuations in the value of any one drive.

Because of the constant and universal reinforcing power of money, people are inclined to think of crimes for money gain as more natural, and thus more the product of voluntary choice and rational thought, than crimes involving "senseless" violence or sexual deviance. Stealing is an understandable, if not pardonable, crime; bestiality, "unprovoked" murder, and drug addiction seem much less understandable, and therefore, perhaps, less voluntary or deliberate. People sometimes carry this line of thought even further: These "senseless" crimes are the result of overpowering compulsions or irrational beliefs. But this is a false distinction. Certain reinforcers may have a steadier, more predictable effect, but all behavior, even the bizarre, responds to reinforcement. It is sometimes useful to distinguish between crimes that arise out of long-lasting, hard-to-change reinforcers (such as money) from those that stem from short-acting, (possibly) changeable drives (such as sexual deviance), but we must always bear in mind that these are distinctions of degree, not of kind.

Conditioning

Thus far, we have spoken of the "association" between primary and secondary reinforcers. Now we must ask how that association arises. The answer is the process known as conditioning. The simplest form of conditioning is the well-known experiment involving Pavlov's dog. The dog repeatedly heard a buzzer a few moments before receiving some dried meat powder in its mouth. Soon, the dog salivated at the mere sound of the buzzer. Two different stimuli—meat and buzzers—were associated. The meat elicited an innate tendency to salivate; the buzzer came to elicit salivation through learning. Pavlov's successors extended his discovery to much more complex responses than salivation and to many other species, including man. These Pavlovian experiments involved what psychologists now call "classical conditioning," which typically involves the autonomic nervous system (that part of our neural structure controlling reflexive behavior, such as heartbeats, salivation, and perspiration, and internal emotional states, such as fear, anxiety, and relaxation) and in which the behavior of the subject (the dog or the man) does not affect the stimulus being administered.

Classical (or Pavlovian) conditioning can make an arbitrary stimulus reinforce behavior by associating the stimulus with either a primary (i.e., innate) reinforcer or some already-learned secondary behavior reinforcer. As we have seen, money is an arbitrary stimulus (a collection of scraps of paper and bits of metal) that has become one of the most universal and powerful secondary reinforcers. But there are many other examples. If a child is regularly praised for scrubbing his or her hands before dinner, then (provided that the praise is already felt to be rewarding), the child will in time scrub his hands without being told or praised. The satisfaction he feels in having scrubbed hands is now the internal feeling of reinforcement. In the same way, hand-scrubbing can be taught by scolding a child who does not wash up. If the scolding is already felt by the child to be punishing, in time the child will feel uncomfortable whenever he has dirty hands.

Classical conditioning does not produce only secretions or muscle twitches. These external responses may be accompanied by a complex array of internalized dispositions. The child who learns to scrub his hands, because of either parental praise or parental disapproval, will have learned things on which his mind and his subsequent experience will come to work in elaborate ways. In time, the satisfaction he feels from having clean hands may merge with other similar satisfactions and become a general sense of cleanliness, which he may eventually believe is next to godliness. He imputes virtue to cleanliness and regards filth with great distaste, even when he finds it in the world at large rather than simply on his own hands. Of course, all this presupposes growing up in a society in which neighbors, friends, and even the government regularly praise cleanliness and condemn slovenliness.

Although it does not do justice to the subtlety and generality of the process or the way in which its outcome is linked to social settings, H. J. Eysenck's remark that "conscience is a conditioned reflex" is not far off the mark.[1] And it calls attention to the intriguing possibility that individuals may differ in their susceptibility to classical conditioning. As we will show in Chapter 7, people are not alike in how readily they internalize rules, and thus they are not alike in the value they attach to the costs in conscience of a prospective crime. For some people, the benefits of a crime are not reduced as much by a "conscience decrement" as they are for persons who have been more successfully subjected to classical conditioning.

Many people have a conscience strong enough to prevent them from committing a crime some of the time but not all of the time. In ways that will become clearer later in the chapter, a reasonably strong conscience is probably sufficient to prevent a person from committing a crime that would have only a modest yield *and* that could not take place for, say, two days. This would be true even if the person was confident he would not be caught. But now suppose the opportunity for committing the offense is immediately at hand—say, your poker-playing friends have left the room after the hand was dealt and you have a chance to peek at their cards, or the jewelry salesman has left the store with a tray of diamond rings open on the counter. Now, if the bite of conscience is not sufficient by itself to prevent the offense, the would-be offender will calculate, however roughly or inarticulately, the chances of being caught. He will know that if the friends suddenly return or the jewelry salesman is watching, he will lose things—in the first instance, reputation, and in the second, his freedom. People differ in how they calculate these risks. Some worry about any chance, however slight, of being caught and would be appalled at any loss of esteem, however small or fleeting; others will peek at the cards or grab a ring if they think they have any chance at all of getting away with it.

When present actions are governed by their consequences, "instrumental" (or operant) conditioning is at work. Unlike classically conditioned responses, instrumental conditioning involves behavior that affects the stimulus (e.g., not peeking at the cards or not taking the ring avoids the costs of the offense). Instrumental behavior affects the stimuli we receive and this, in turn, affects subsequent behavior.

The distinction between classical and instrumental conditioning is by no means as clear as our simple definitions may make it appear. But if we bear in mind that behavior cannot be neatly explained by one or the other process, we can use the distinction to help us understand individual differences in criminality. Persons deficient in conscience may turn out to be persons who for various reasons resist classical conditioning—they do not internalize rules as easily as do others. Persons who, even with a strong conscience, commit crimes anyway may be persons who have difficulty imagining the future consequences of present action or who are so impulsive as to discount very heavily even those consequences they can foresee, and hence will resist the instrumental conditioning that might lead them to choose noncrime over crime.

Delay and Uncertainty

Our argument so far is that behavior is controlled by its consequences. Those consequences—the primary and secondary reinforcers and punishers—may be immediate or postponed, certain or uncertain. Because not everyone has a conscience sufficiently strong to prevent every illegal act, the influence of delay and uncertainty on individual differences in criminality is great. Consequences gradually lose their ability to control behavior in proportion to how delayed or improbable they are. We have just observed that instrumental conditioning works best with persons who can conceive of future consequences and who attach a high value to even distant consequences. It can easily be shown that for many people, improbable or distant effects have very little influence on their behavior. For example, millions of cigarette smokers ignore the (possibly) fatal consequences of smoking because they are distant and uncertain. If smoking one cigarette caused certain death tomorrow, we would anticipate a rather sharp reduction in tobacco consumption.

The theft of \$100 with eight chances in ten of getting away with it is worth more to a prospective thief than the theft of \$100 with a one-in-two chance of success. A convenient, though somewhat fictitious, way of expressing these differences is with the concept of "expected value," which equals the product of the value of the gain times the probability of obtaining it (\$100 × .8 = \$80; \$100 × .5 = \$50). In fact, people may evaluate alternative gambles somewhat differently from what is implied by these objective expected values, but those differences can be ignored here. Other things being equal, a crime more certain of success will be valued more than one less certain; a more certain punishment will be feared more than a less certain one.

The increase in criminality resulting from the decreased probability of punishment occurs as a result of two processes—one involving instrumental conditioning, and the other, classical conditioning. If the threat of being punished oneself is reduced, the rewards for noncrime (i.e., the punishment that is not received) are weakened, making noncrime seem less profitable: This is an example of applying the principles of instrumental conditioning. If the spectacle of others being punished becomes less frequent, the rewards of crime may be strengthened because it now seems less wrong. The tendency for the punishment of others to affect the extent to which we feel guilty when we contemplate committing the same crime is an example of the use of classical conditioning.

Delay affects crime because there is almost always a lapse between when the crime may be committed and when the legal or social consequences, if any, will be felt. Put another way, the rewards of crime usually precede the costs of crime (except for such contemporaneous costs as those of conscience). Because of this, time discounting becomes extremely important in explaining criminal behavior. Figure 1 illustrates the effect of time on crime.* In each of the three cases, the rewards associated with noncrime are greater than the rewards arising from crime. Were it not for the effects of delay, no crime would be committed in any of the three examples. But as we shall see, the three cases, which involve little, some, or much time discounting, portray increasing susceptibility to crime.

In each graph, the vertical axis represents, for a given criminal opportunity, the net value of the two alternatives: committing a crime, or not committing it. By "net value" we mean the sum of all the reinforcements, positive and negative, less the punishments, associated with either crime or noncrime, as expressed in the strengths of the competing behaviors. In the

* The curves are not invented but are based on laboratory studies of animal and human behavior.[2] The relevant equations are reported in the Appendix.

FIGURE 1

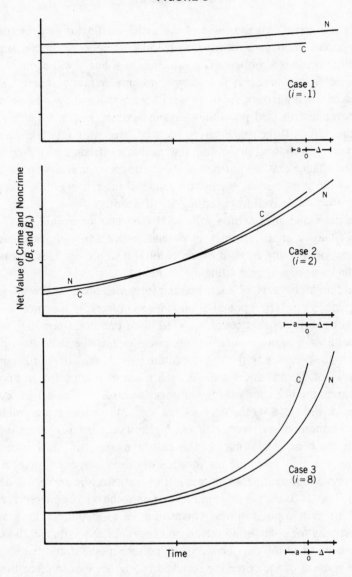

The value of crime (C) and noncrime (N) in relation to the time interval between each behavior and its reward. Noncrime is assumed to have a larger reward than crime, but the reward for noncrime is Δ time units more delayed than the reward for crime. The criminal act takes a time units to execute. In all three cases, Δ, a, and the rewards for noncrime and crime are the same. Only the time-discounting function varies from Case 1 to Case 3, as represented by the increasing value of i, the measure of impulsiveness. The more impulsive a person is, the more likely he or she is to find occasions when crime will seem to be more rewarding than noncrime, other things equal. In Case 2, the crossing curves imply that crime will seem more rewarding when a criminal opportunity is at hand, but not when it is remote. See Appendix for relevant equations.

case of crime, this means the value of the anticipated gains less the costs, if any, that occur contemporaneously with the crime. For example, suppose the potential crime is a robbery. The value of the robbery will equal the loot to be gained (a sum probably not known with any certainty) minus the risk of the victim's fighting back (perhaps with a weapon) and the cost of violating whatever internalized prohibition against crime (i.e., conscience) may exist in the robber. If the robbery is to be committed with a partner, the gain may also include winning or holding the partner's esteem, and the cost may include the chance that the partner will prove inept or untrustworthy. If the robbery victim is a personal enemy, the value of the crime will be increased by the satisfaction derived from settling an old score.

The net value of noncrime will equal the value of avoiding any legal penalties (fines or imprisonment) and social costs (family disgrace, lost social esteem, or inability to hold or get a job). The greater these costs, the greater the value of not committing the crime.

The horizontal axis of each graph represents time. The reader may think of time in terms of a potential offender's confronting a choice between a criminal opportunity that could be acted upon one hour, one day, or one week from now, and more distant consequences (i.e., the realization of the benefits of not committing the crime) coming sometime afterward, perhaps many weeks or months afterward. At each moment, the person in question will engage in the behavior with the stronger rewards. Which set of rewards is stronger is indicated by the curves. In Case 1, the curve representing the benefits of noncrime is at every moment higher (i.e., stronger) than the one measuring the benefits of crime. In this case, the crime will never occur. In Case 3, the curve representing the rewards of crime is at every point higher than the curve representing noncrime; in this instance, the crime will always occur. In Case 2—to us, the most interesting one—the curves intersect, crossing over at a certain point in time (measured, let us assume, in days before the opportunity for committing the crime exists). In this instance, the crime will not occur when the time between the present moment and the moment when the rewards of the crime are received is long enough to place the person on the left of the crossover point on the graph. But the crime will occur if the person is to the right of the crossover point—that is, if he is so close in time to the criminal opportunity that the rewards of crime seem stronger than the rewards of noncrime.

An example or two will make the significance of the crossover point easier to grasp. Consider a person on a diet. The benefits of not eating a rich dessert, such as chocolate cake, occur in the future and involve weight not gained and health hazards avoided. The benefits of the dessert—the marvelous taste of rich chocolate—are available immediately on eating the cake. Now, if the person on the diet thinks ahead to a meal he cannot eat for several hours or even a day, his thinking will be dominated by the (deferred) benefits of refusing the dessert. If asked, he will say, with absolute sincerity, that he will eat no dessert. But as the dinner hour approaches, his resolve may weaken. And when the cake is placed on the table, his resolve may collapse entirely as the benefits of eating it come to dominate the deferred benefits of refusing it. At some point, the dieter has passed through his crossover point. This example can readily be translated into a criminal opportunity. For many people, the benefits of noncrime exceed those of crime so long as the chance for committing the crime lies well in the future. These people would reject out of hand the suggestion that they might engage in shoplifting, because they are not now in a shop. But suppose later in the day they find themselves in a store with attractive merchandise casually displayed and no one watching. Now, some of these people will find the benefits of crime dominating the (deferred and uncertain) benefits of noncrime. They will grab something and stuff it under their coats.

The importance of the crossover point calls our attention to the importance of the shape of the curves that define it. These curves measure the rate at which individuals discount the future. All the curves in Figure 1 are hyperbolic for reasons well established in the scientific literature.[3] The steeper the curve, the more rapidly the individual discounts future rewards; the shallower the curve, the more the individual attaches value to future rewards.

In Figure 1, the horizontal axis, representing time, is marked off into two segments, *a* and Δ (delta). The period *a* is the time required to plan and execute a crime. Crimes that take a long time to devise and carry out—robbing the Brink's armored truck company, for example—will be engaged in only by persons either who expect gains that will substantially exceed the benefits of not committing the crime or who have a distant time horizon. We often refer to such persons as "professional" criminals, by which we mean that they attach little value to the benefits of noncrime, work to obtain a large amount of loot, or do not discount time very steeply, or some combination of all three. By contrast, crimes that can be committed on the spur of the moment—an unplanned assault, for example, or grabbing a woman's purse—appeal to persons to whom the prospect of even a small gain is appealing and for whom distant events are uninteresting. We call such persons "impulsive" or "opportunistic" offenders. For a given time-discounting curve, a crime that takes much planning must have a larger payoff than a crime that can be done on the spur of the moment. For a given payoff, a person with a steep time-discounting curve will be more likely to commit a crime than a person with a shallow discount curve. (The Appendix supplies the mathematics of these relationships.)

The period Δ represents the time between the crime and the delayed consequences of being caught for the crime (i.e., the value of noncrime). The length of this period depends on how swiftly a crime is detected and reported and on how quickly the perpetrator can be apprehended, convicted, and punished. The longer it takes for victims to report crimes and the criminal justice system to operate, the lower will be the rewards of noncrime as felt by a would-be criminal.

We can summarize the argument so far by noting that the three cases depicted in Figure 1 represent the effect of differing degrees of impulsiveness. In all three instances, the strength of the rewards of crime are the same, as are the rewards of noncrime. The time delays, a and Δ, are the same in all cases. All that changes is the steepness of the time-discounting curves. In Case 1, the value of noncrime exceeds the value of crime at all points in time because the absolute value of noncrime is greater than that of crime, and the person in question does not discount time very heavily. This person is not at all impulsive. In Case 3, the individual is very impulsive—that is, he discounts time very steeply. As a result, though the value of noncrime would be greater than the value of crime *if* they both occurred at the same moment, the delay in the criminal justice system (or in whatever other system, such as the marketplace, that rewards noncrime)—the magnitude of Δ—is sufficiently great so that the value of noncrime is discounted to a point below that of crime at all times shown. In Case 2, the individual is moderately impulsive, so that the value of noncrime exceeds the value of crime *provided* that the person is far enough in time from the chance to commit a crime—which is to say, he is to the left of the crossover point. But if the criminal opportunity is ready at hand (like the cake set before the weak-willed dieter), he will indulge.

Individuals differ in the degree to which they discount the future. These differences are often part of a personality trait that can be measured, and in Chapter 7 we will discuss efforts that have been made to measure it. They may also differ in their ability to conceive of the future or to plan for it. They may lack the imagination, experience, or intelligence to commit a crime that requires planning or to visualize what state of affairs may exist long in the future when the benefits of noncrime become available. This may help explain (as will be discussed in Chapter 6) why criminals tend to be less intelligent than noncriminals, though there are other possible explanations for this connection.

Individual differences in criminality may also exist because of the dif-

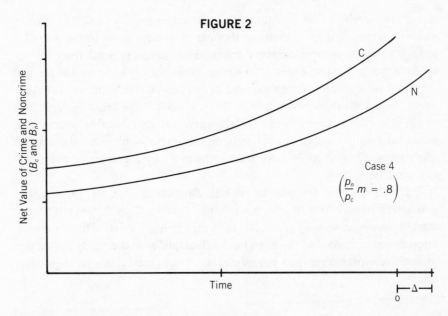

FIGURE 2

Same as Figure 1, except that the value of the reward for crime, adjusted for the probability of obtaining it, P_c, is here larger than that for noncrime, adjusted for the probability of obtaining it, P_n. Crime will seem more rewarding than noncrime at all delays of reward and for any degree of impulsiveness. See Appendix.

ferent values people assign to crime and noncrime. In Figure 2, we show a situation in which the perceived benefits of crime are greater than the perceived benefits of noncrime. At every point in time, rewards of crime are stronger than the rewards of noncrime. No matter how steeply the individual discounts the future, he will always find committing the crime preferable to not committing it. This is an illustration of a crime that from the offender's point of view is always rational though (paradoxically) society often supposes it is irrational. Circumstances that might create this situation are not hard to imagine. The value of the loot may be very large (millions are there for the taking) or the grievance against an individual may be very powerful (the victim is a political enemy or an unfaithful lover). The conscience of the offender may be especially weak and the support of peers participating in the crime especially strong. The value of noncrime may be low because the criminal justice system is ineffective, the perpetrator has no reputation to lose and no friends before whom to be disgraced, and there are no jobs or other sources of income worth what the crime will bring. The crime, in short, will be irresistible.

Persons who commit "irresistible" crimes, especially ones that involve violence or passion, are sometimes thought by society to be in the grip of a strange compulsion or a deranged mind. What seems rational from the offender's point of view appears irrational from society's. Some people will urge that such an offender be excused or his penalty mitigated because they cannot imagine themselves acting in this way. But if the crime is distinctive at all, it is only because the underlying drive for its reward is uncommon, or uncommonly intense. The crime is no more irresistible than cheating on one's income tax; it could have been suppressed by a greater or more certain penalty.

It is a mistake, for reasons we will develop in Chapter 19, to argue about whether a given offense is or is not "rational" or "irresistible," for there is no objective way to resolve such arguments. Crimes differ in the reinforcements attached to them, and individuals differ in the value they assign to such reinforcements and the degree to which they discount them over time.

Equity and Inequity

In assigning a value to the rewards of crime or noncrime, an individual often takes into account not only what he stands to gain but what others stand to gain from what he perceives as comparable efforts. The individual has some notion of what he is entitled to, and that notion is affected by what he sees other people getting.

This interaction between what one person thinks he deserves and what he sees other people getting is expressed by sociologists and social psychologists in terms of an "equity equation."[4] It is based on a much older notion of distributive justice, first elaborated by Aristotle in the *Nichomachean Ethics*. To Aristotle, an equitable allocation of goods or honors is one that gives to each person a share proportional to his or her merit.[5] In other words, the ratio of one person's share to another person's share will be the same as the ratio between one person's worth and the other's. The worth of the two parties will depend on their age, status, wealth, skill, effort, or virtue; which measure of worth is selected is influenced by the prior understandings of the parties or the nature of the political regime. For example, a sixteen-year-old boy lounging on a street corner may decide that what he and others ought to earn should be determined by how hard they work, their level of education, or by their racial or class status. The identity of the other person with whom one compares one's own merit will also vary. The sixteen-year-old boy may compare his income to that of other sixteen-year-old boys, to that of all males in the city, or to that of all persons in the nation as a whole. What standard of comparison he uses and with whom he makes the comparison will obviously determine whether he thinks he has less or more money than he is entitled to have. For a given standard and a given reference group, he will feel he has what he is entitled to if the ratio between his income and his worth is the same as the ratio of the relevant other fellow's income to worth.

The equity equation can be expressed formally in the following terms. Let G stand for the gains a person receives from some transaction and C for the contributions (of time, skill, effort, or moral worth) in return for which he obtains these gains. The subscripts s and o stand for "self" and "other." A transaction is equitable when the ratio of one's own gains to one's own contributions $(\frac{G_s}{C_s})$ is the same as the ratio of the other person's gains to his contributions $(\frac{G_o}{C_o})$, that is, $\frac{G_s}{C_s} = \frac{G_o}{C_o}$. When $\frac{G_s}{C_s} \neq \frac{G_o}{C_o}$, the person with the lower ratio feels a sense of inequity.

This equity equation is the general case. Egalitarianism and humanitarianism are special instances of it, the former arising when both parties are assumed to have contributed equally ($C_o = C_s$) and thus their shares must be equal ($G_o = G_s$), the latter when what one person needs (as opposed to what he has actually contributed) is considered to be part of his contribution. The familiar concept of "relative deprivation" is also a special, albeit somewhat misleading, case of social inequity. Relative deprivation is usually defined as a state of affairs in which somebody is less well off than another person to whom he compares himself. This concept is often advanced as an explanation for why riots and revolutions may occur not when people are in utter misery but when they are becoming better off. They upgrade their sense of worth faster than their material gains, and so they feel justified in rebelling. The reason why relative deprivation is an incomplete and thus misleading statement of the problem is that it fails to take into account how one person evaluates the contributions (the worth) of another person. Individuals do not simply compare their gains to the gains of others; they compare the *ratio* of gains and contributions.

During their lives, most people change the way they evaluate a distribution of goods or honors. As infants, they are selfish, wanting everything without regard to the worth or contributions of others. As children, they may feel they are entitled to the same share as everybody else because, though they recognize that others are entitled to something, they do not recognize that others may deserve more than they.[6] As adults, they make finer distinctions regarding whom they should compare themselves with and on what grounds; some may even come to endorse altruistic standards.[7] A similar progression also occurs as people enter into more intimate and enduring relationships with each other, from the selfishness that often governs the relations of strangers to the altruism sometimes tying together husband and wife or parents and children.[8] A distribution that would be intolerably inequitable between strangers or business associates might be quite acceptable among friends or within a family. Changes in the way in which equity is defined, in short, may result from natural mental and moral development, from social learning,[9] from situational factors, or from all three. Moreover, individuals may differ in what they define as equitable because of differences in their level of understanding and, perhaps, their general intelligence.[10]

While much remains to be clarified, there can be little doubt that equity considerations influence all human transactions, including criminal ones. Every society recognizes this influence by incorporating some conception of equity or fairness into its legal code, criminal as well as civil.[11] The universal recognition of the importance of equity arises, we think, from the fact that a concern for equity is naturally expressed in all personal relationships. Take something from another person without his permission and he will feel angry; let the other person obtain a larger salary than you without having displayed any recognized superiority of skill, effort, or merit, and you will feel angry. Fail to return a favor when asked, and the person who asks will be upset; do a favor for someone who cannot reciprocate and he will feel uncomfortable.

People differ in how they respond to a situation in which another person has received something without appearing to deserve it. Some people may blame the other party and direct anger at him or even try to take, by stealth or force, some part of what he has obtained. Other persons may blame themselves for not having worked hard enough to earn the larger share now going to the other party. The other party may flaunt his good fortune or attempt, by soothing words, self-deprecation, or exaggerated friendliness, to make it up to the aggrieved party. For example, suppose you and your co-worker in an office receive salaries that seem justly to reflect your relative contributions of time, skill, and effort. Suddenly the other person receives a key to the executive lounge, but you do not. The resulting inequity can be handled in a variety of ways. He may go out of his way to be nice to you so as to increase your rewards, while you may go out of your way to be nasty to him so as to decrease his. Or he may upgrade the amount or quality of his work to justify the extra prize, while you may reduce your efforts to compensate for the (comparatively) lessened rewards. One or both of you may make a show of belittling the value of the lounge or of having privileged access to it so as to minimize the deviation from equity.

Which equity-restoring tactic we adopt depends on the psychological costs of it and on our prior dispositions.[12] For most of us, certain ways of restoring equity—reducing our efforts, stealing the valued key, punching the holder of the key—would be too costly. Many of us keep the resentment or anger we feel to ourselves rather than express it overtly to the recipient of the unjustified benefit. But other persons may habitually express open anger at perceived inequities. Overtly aggressive reactions to inequity are more likely in an angry atmosphere, under the disinhibiting influence of drugs or alcohol, and among persons with a history of violence.[13]

Criminals and aggressive persons frequently defend their behavior by denigrating their victims.[14] They may not see themselves as modern-day Robin Hoods, but they are likely to think of their victims as somehow deserving their fate (they are "jerks," or "suckers," or "people who don't deserve what they have"). The injury and loss of property may, in the extreme case, be seen by the perpetrator as setting right, to some degree, inequitable social arrangements in general. To the extent that the criminal feels that his offense is justified by some perceived inequity, then the rewards of committing the crime, far from being reduced by the bite of conscience, are enhanced by the sense of restored equity.

Because of this, it is a mistake to explain crime (or its absence) on grounds of profit maximization narrowly defined.[15] Potential offenders do not, in many cases, simply evaluate the net tangible rewards of the crime and compare them to the time-discounted costs of the crime that may occur in the future; they also take into account the intangible rewards (a sense of rectified injustice) or penalties (a sense of guilt) that occur contemporaneously with the crime. A narrow economic explanation of crime is, to us, inadequate because it does not recognize that the value one person assigns to the outcome of a course of action depends in part on the outcomes of other persons' actions. At the other extreme, those who believe that crime is powerfully influenced by real or perceived injustice should bear in mind that individuals differ greatly in how they interpret and respond to a disproportionality between one's own ratio of gains to inputs and another person's ratio of gains to inputs. A sociological or political explanation of crime that is insensitive to individual differences is also inadequate.

The Context of Reinforcement

The effect of a reward or punishment is inversely proportional to the strength of all the reinforcements acting on a person at a given time. The

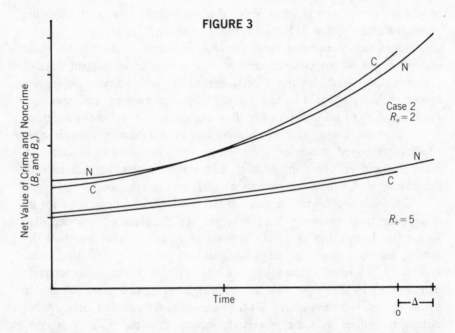

FIGURE 3

The upper pair of curves replots Case 2 from Figure 1. The lower pair of curves shows the same choice between crime and noncrime after an increase in the general context of reward, R_e. When the context increases, noncrime may rise above crime at all delays of reward. A crime that would have occurred, given the opportunity, is forestalled by a general improvement in the context of reinforcement. See Appendix.

more reinforcement a person is receiving, the less the value of any single reinforcement. The relativity of reinforcement has been demonstrated in the laboratory,[16] but it can be illustrated by everyday experience. Ten dollars received just after payday is less reinforcing than ten dollars received just before payday, when money is running low. The gentle pleasures of the elderly or the infirm, for whom rewards have become fewer, may be as reinforcing to them as the more boisterous pleasures of the young and vigorous.

When the amount of reinforcement acting on a person increases, the strength of a small reward decreases relatively more than that of a large one (see the Appendix). Since crime and noncrime usually have attached to them reinforcements of different magnitudes, changes in the context of reinforcement—that is, in the total amount of reinforcement operating—will affect the value of crime and noncrime differently. In Figure 3 we again show Case 2 (from Figure 1), but the context of reinforcement is expanded. The increase in the context of reinforcement reduces the rewards attached to both crime and noncrime, but the rewards attached to crime decrease more, with the result that now the person will not commit the crime. For example, a person who would commit a crime if the opportunity was sufficiently close in time and space (say, a boy who will grab a purse if he happens to come upon one being carried by a lone woman on the street) may not commit the crime if other reinforcers, having nothing to do with the value of crime or noncrime, start to operate (say, the boy has just fallen in love, is listening to some pleasant music on his portable stereo, and is enjoying a warm spring day).

There are other ways that a changed context of reinforcement might affect the probability of the commission of a crime. Suppose not only that our boy has fallen in love, but that his girl has agreed to marry him. Suddenly he has more to lose from crime—that is, the value of noncrime has increased because now it includes retaining the affection of the girl and the respect of her parents. In this and other ways, the richer the supply of reinforcements operating on a person, the less the chance he will commit a crime.

The Theory as a Whole

We began this chapter by asserting that the chief value of a comprehensive theory of crime is that it will bring to our attention all the factors that explain individual differences in criminality and thus prevent us from offering partial explanations or making incomplete interpretations of research findings.* The larger the ratio of the rewards (material and nonmaterial) of noncrime to the rewards (material and nonmaterial) of crime, the weaker the tendency to commit crimes. The bite of conscience, the approval of peers, and any sense of inequity will increase or decrease the total value of crime; the opinions of family, friends, and employers are important benefits of noncrime, as is the desire to avoid the penalties that can be imposed by the criminal justice system. The strength of any reward declines with time, but people differ in the rate at which they discount the future. The strength of a given reward is also affected by the total supply of reinforcers.

Some implications of the theory are obvious: Other things being equal, a reduction in the delay and uncertainty attached to the rewards of noncrime

* There is an advantage to stating the theory mathematically. We thereby make it easier in principle to deal simultaneously with the interaction of several variables, and thus we resist the tendency in thinking about crime to keep only two or three things in mind at one time and to treat those few things as either-or propositions. But the essence of the theory can be grasped without the mathematical notation, and so we have put that in the Appendix.

will reduce the probability of crime. But other implications are not so obvious. For instance, increasing the value of the rewards of noncrime (by increasing the severity of punishment) may not reduce a given individual's tendency to commit crime if he believes that these rewards are not commensurate with what he deserves. In this case, punishing him for preferring crime to noncrime may trigger hostility toward society in retaliation for the shortfall. The increased rewards for noncrime may be offset by an increased sense of inequity and hence an increased incentive for committing a crime. Or again: It may be easier to reduce crime by making penalties swifter or more certain, rather than more severe, if the persons committing crime are highly present-oriented (so that they discount even large rewards very sharply) or if they are likely to have their sense of inequity heightened by increases in the severity of punishment. Or yet again: An individual with an extroverted personality is more likely than one with an introverted one to externalize his feelings of inequity and act directly to correct them (see Chapter 7).

In laboratory settings involving both human and animal subjects, each element of the theory has received at least some confirmation and the major elements have been confirmed extensively.[17] Extrapolating these findings outside the laboratory, into real-world settings, is a matter on which opinions differ. In this book, we propose to bring together evidence from a variety of disciplines bearing on the connection between elements of the theory and the observed characteristics of crime and criminals.

The connection between crime and impulsiveness has been demonstrated (Chapter 7) as has the link between (low) intelligence and crime (Chapter 6). Those features of family life that produce stronger or weaker internalized inhibitions will be seen to have a connection to the presence or absence of aggressiveness and criminality (Chapters 8 and 9). Certain subcultures, such as street-corner gangs, appear to affect the value members attach to both crime and noncrime (Chapter 11). The mass media, and in particular television, may affect both aggressiveness directly and a viewer's sense of inequity that can affect crime indirectly (Chapter 13). Schooling may affect crime rates by bringing certain persons together into groups that reinforce either crime or noncrime and by determining the extent to which children believe that their skills will give them access to legitimate rewards (Chapter 10). The condition of the economy will have a complex effect on crime depending on whether the (possibly) restraint-weakening impact of affluence dominates the restraint-strengthening influence of employment opportunities (Chapter 12).

Though we will be using, for the most part, examples of rather common criminality to illustrate our argument, the theory is quite consistent with the more bizarre and unusual forms of crime. Psychopathic personalities lack to an unusual degree internalized inhibitions on crime (Chapter 7). Persons possessed by some obsessive interest—for example, pyromania—attach an inordinately high value to the rewards of certain crimes. If everyone loved fire too much, society would try hard to teach the moral evil of fire, as well as its practical danger. As it is, what society does teach is sufficient to overcome whatever slight tendency toward pyromania every average person may have, but it is insufficient to inhibit the rare pyromaniac. One reason society punishes arsonists is not only to make it more costly for persons to use fire for material gain but also to provide extra moral education to the occasional person who loves fire for its own sake.

In addition to pathological drives, there are ordinary ones that can, under certain conditions, become so strong as to lead to crime. History and literature abound with normal men and women in the grip of a too powerful reinforcement. Many people have broken the law for love, honor, family, and country, as well as for money, sex, vengeance, or delusion. Such criminals may be psychologically unremarkable; they transgressed because as they perceived the situation the reward for crime exceeded that for noncrime, and an opportunity presented itself. The legal system often tries to minimize the punishment inflicted on such people, raising issues that will be considered in Chapter 19.

Other Theories of Crime

Our approach to explaining individual differences in criminality is not meant to supplant but to encompass other theories. Following Travis Hirschi, we note that there are three main sociological perspectives on the causes of crime:

> According to *strain* or motivational theories, legitimate desires that conformity cannot satisfy force a person into deviance. According to *control* or bond theories, a person is free to commit delinquent acts because his ties to the conventional order have somehow been broken. According to *cultural deviance* theories, the deviant conforms to a set of standards not accepted by the larger or more powerful society.[18]

Strain theory assumes that people ordinarily obey society's rules but violate them when following those rules does not enable them to satisfy their legitimate aspirations. There is a strain between the goal they seek and the means at their disposal to reach that goal. Their opportunities are blocked; thus, strain theory is sometimes called the theory of differential opportunity.[19] In some versions of strain theory, persons who are frustrated in their efforts to achieve middle-class goals abandon them and embrace antisocial values.[20] In other versions, they persist in seeking wealth, property, and status, but use criminal means to do so.

Advocates of strain theory are calling attention to the importance of certain reinforcers associated with noncrime, in particular the value of jobs and other sources of wealth and status, and suggesting that as these decline in strength (because they are not available or are of little value) the reinforcers associated with crime come to dominate the choices confronting the individual. This is a useful but partial observation. It properly reminds us of the importance to the individual of whatever alternatives to crime are available to him, but it neglects other components of the rewards of crime and noncrime and pays little attention to individual differences in impulsiveness and internalized inhibitions.

The reinforcers associated with noncrime include avoiding the penalties of the criminal justice system as well as obtaining the benefits of jobs; thus, the reinforcement supplied by noncrime can decline because *either* jobs become less available *or* sanctions decline in certainty or severity, or both. The theory also neglects the fact that the value of committing a crime is the sum not only of the money-supplying or status-conferring components of the crime but also of the costs (if any) of violating some internal inhibition and the benefits (if any) of rectifying a sense of inequity. Finally, strain theory ignores individual differences in time discounting (or impulsiveness).

Because of these limitations, strain theory cannot account for all of the observed facts about crime. It can offer no explanation, for example, of middle-class crime. If crime is disproportionately committed by lower-class persons because they find their lack of schooling and job opportunities a barrier to realizing their legitimate aspirations, then persons with adequate schooling and reasonable job prospects should not commit crimes, yet they do. If the people most likely to commit crimes are those in great need of legitimate rewards who find their access to those rewards blocked, then crime should be most common among men with families and heavy financial responsibilities, but in fact crime rates are highest among unattached males in the adolescent and young adult years.

Control theory directs our attention to the importance of learned inhibitions against crime. Unlike strain theory, which assumes that people naturally want to do the right thing but are prevented from doing it by circumstances, control theory suggests that it is first necessary to explain why anyone should want to do the right thing. This is an important suggestion because it reminds us of the intangible components of the reinforcements associated with both crime (the bite, if any, of conscience) and noncrime (the value, if any, of the good opinion of decent folk). Control theory asks how the social bond is formed and maintained.[21] But important as this bonding may be, control theory does not explain all of the differences among individuals in criminality. In particular, it neglects differences in personality and orientation toward time: Some persons may commit crimes not because their attachment to legitimate norms is weak but because they are impulsive, unable to foresee the distant consequences of their actions, or confident that those consequences will not be costly. Moreover, control theory provides an incomplete account of the relationship between low intelligence and predatory criminality. The theory explains this connection largely by the claim that low-IQ individuals, frustrated by their inability to do well in their studies and jobs, fail to develop an attachment to school and work.[22] This may well occur, but it is also possible that cognitive deficits affect criminality more directly because they are associated with having a short time horizon.[23]

Cultural deviance theory also focuses on learning, but asserts that criminals have learned their values from deviant rather than law-abiding persons. Like control theory, this view directs our attention to the intangible reinforcers associated with crime and noncrime, suggesting that criminals are those who have learned that crime is worthwhile because it is reinforced by the good opinion of persons in whose company one commits the crime or who later learn of it. In some versions of this theory, deviant behavior is learned from other offenders by a process called "differential association";[24] in other versions, it is learned from a distinctive subculture composed of lower-class males who may not directly teach criminality but who value toughness, excitement, autonomy, and "street smarts," and who have a fatalistic attitude toward the future.[25] Useful as this perspective is, it cannot explain why some persons take their cues from street gangs while others take them from their families and other nondeviant individuals, nor is it consistent with the fact that high-rate delinquents seem to be boys who are *not* well integrated into gangs and who have few close or lasting friendships.[26] In short, cultural deviance theory provides no explanation for individual differences and thus cannot account for the fact that in a given neighborhood or social class some boys adopt deviant values and others adopt conventional ones. And the theory has no place for those tangible reinforcements associated with crime and noncrime that may lead persons with conventional values to commit crimes (because they are so profitable) or dissuade persons with deviant values from committing them (because they are so unprofitable).

The three kinds of theories discussed so far draw heavily or entirely on sociological thought; it is because of this that they have in common a disinterest in individual differences that arise out of psychological or biological predispositions. Other disciplines have sought to remedy this defect, but usually at the expense of any attention to the social setting in which crime occurs or to the complexity of internalized inhibitions. Criminals are more likely than noncriminals to have mesomorphic body types (Chapter 3), to have fathers who were criminals even in the case of adopted sons who could not have known their fathers (Chapter 3), to be of somewhat lower intelligence (Chapter 6), to be impulsive or extroverted (Chapter 7), and to have autonomic nervous systems that respond more slowly and less vigorously to stimuli (Chapter 7). These findings provide important clues to anyone seeking to explain individual differences, but taken alone they do not constitute a theory of crime, for they do not place the would-be offender in the full context of the reinforcements acting on his behavior. An impulsive person can be taught greater self-control, a low-IQ individual can engage in satisfying learning experiences, and extroverted mesomorphs with slow autonomic nervous system response rates may earn honest money in the National Football League instead of dishonest money robbing banks.

We believe that all of these views are implicit in our larger behavioral theory. The risk we run by attempting to state so general a theory is that a theory general enough to explain everything about crime will not provide many testable hypotheses explaining any one thing very precisely. At the least, however, our perspective allows us to put into some order the full array of particular findings about crime and human nature that one encounters in the literature. We turn to that task in the next chapter.

II

CONSTITUTIONAL FACTORS

3

CONSTITUTIONAL FACTORS IN CRIMINAL BEHAVIOR

Some individuals are more likely to become criminals than others. As we shall see in the next two chapters, males are more disposed than females to criminal behavior, and younger males are more likely than older ones to commit crimes at high rates. It is likely that the effect of maleness and youthfulness on the tendency to commit crime has both constitutional and social origins: That is, it has something to do both with the biological status of being a young male and with how that young man has been treated by family, friends, and society.

When we speak of constitutional factors, we are referring to factors, usually present at or soon after birth, whose behavioral consequences appear gradually during the child's development. Constitutional factors are not necessarily genetic, although they may be. A genetic factor, if not a mutation, is inherited from one or both parents. There is no "crime gene" and so there is no such thing as a "born criminal," but some traits that are to a degree heritable, such as intelligence and temperament, affect to some extent the likelihood that individuals will engage in criminal activities. The evidence on these matters will be reviewed in Chapters 6 and 7. Other constitutional factors are not hereditary. An individual may be born with a trait that is caused by a chromosomal abnormality—a defect in the arrangement of the genes—that is not acquired from either parent and is not passed on to any offspring. One such abnormality—the XYY chromosome—will be discussed later in this chapter. And some constitutional factors may be the result of prenatal or perinatal accidents. If, for example, the mother smokes heavily, takes drugs, is malnourished, or is exposed to environmental toxins while pregnant, this may affect the infant in ways that influence the chances of later displaying aggressive or criminal behavior. Similarly, if the infant experiences some trauma during birth—sustained oxygen deprivation, for instance—or is improperly fed and cared for immediately after birth, some organic damage may result that also may affect subsequent behavior, including criminal behavior. The evidence on the influence of such nongenetic constitutional factors is quite sketchy, but we shall review what little there is in Chapters 8, 9, and 14.

In this chapter, we wish only to establish the fact that individuals differ at birth in the degree to which they are at risk for criminality. The evidence of this is of two sorts. First, certain human features that are indisputably biological—an individual's anatomical configuration—are correlated with criminality. We do not argue that these anatomical features cause crime, only that they are correlated with criminal behavior. But the fact of their correlation indicates that there is *some* psychological trait, having a biological origin, that predisposes an individual to criminality. In Chapters 6 and 7, we consider various traits that are leading candidates for this role. Second, studies of the degree to which criminal behavior runs in families shed light on the extent to which some individuals are more prone to commit crime than others. These studies examine the prevalence of crime in twins and among the adopted children of criminal parents. The remainder of this chapter is devoted to the findings of these two lines of inquiry.

As should be clear from the theory we presented in Chapter 2, and as will become even clearer from the material presented in Parts III and IV of this book, we believe that criminal behavior, like all human behavior, results from a complex interaction of genetic and environmental factors. Our knowledge of this interaction is not yet good enough to permit anyone to say with confidence how much of the variation in the law-violating behavior of people can be attributed to genetic and how much to environmental factors. But we do know enough to be fairly confident that criminal behavior cannot be explained wholly by reference to the social circumstances in which an individual finds herself or himself. In short, the case for constitutional individual differences in criminality not only has a long pedigree, it also seems to have a future.

Anatomical Correlates of Crime

The belief in anatomical signs of criminality is far older than criminology itself, extending back to the very beginnings of speculation on human nature. It can be detected in Egyptian writings four thousand years old, in Homer's epics, in the Hippocratic and Galenic doctrines of ancient medicine, and in the Bible.[1] Socrates, in the fifth century B.C., was charged by a physiognomist (a reader of faces) with having a face that betrayed brutality. By then, physiognomy was an established profession, in which Socrates himself believed. A medieval law directed that "if two persons fell under suspicion of crime the uglier or more deformed was to be regarded as more probably guilty."[2] In Shakespeare's play, Caesar says:

> *Let me have men about me that are fat;*
> *Sleek-headed men, and such as sleep o' nights.*
> *Yond' Cassius has a lean and hungry look,*
> *He thinks too much: such men are dangerous.*
>   Julius Caesar, Act I, Scene II

It is possible that these enduring beliefs are based more on prejudice against the unusual, the unattractive, and the infirm than on science. But, from time to time, there have been earnest efforts to discover the facts, motivated in part by the desire to understand how deeply rooted in a person's nature his or her crimes are. It is still a question whether crimes are committed by special kinds of people or provoked by special kinds of situations. If it could be shown that criminals are constitutionally indistinguishable from noncriminals, then it would seem plausible to suppose that crime results from a criminal's economic, cultural, social, and political circumstances, rather than his constitution.

The other side of the coin should be obvious. Showing a constitutional correlate amounts to counterevidence against the purely environmental explanation of crime, or at least against the simple environmentalism implicit in most of the sociological theories of crime outlined in Chapter 2. Criminals cannot be equivalent except for their circumstances if they look a certain way or are built a certain way, as long as the appearance and the build are not themselves a result of the environment.

Prior to the rise of modern biology, the focus was on such external constitutional traits as faces, head shapes, and body build, often within the framework of long since discredited theories of human character, such as physiognomy or phrenology (the reading of skull shapes). The origin of the word "character" tells its own story, arising from a Greek word for any distinctive physical sign and coming to mean a set of behavioral predispositions. But even if the particular theories of anatomical signs deserve to be forgotten, an external correlate of character still bears on the nature-nurture question. If it turned out that most criminals were, say, redheaded and freckle-faced, we would be on the trail of genetic correlates of crime, just because redheadedness and freckles have a genetic basis.

We would be on the trail, but with quite a long way yet to go. Neither the physical facts nor the purely statistical evidence of genetic influence reviewed later in the chapter tells us what the constitutional criminal predisposition consists of, in psychological terms. Crime may run in families, along with freckles or red hair, but crime is ultimately behavior. The constitutional traits must, at some point in the analysis, be tied to behavioral variables, as subsequent chapters attempt to do.

Anthropometry

The effort to find physical correlates of crime is often dismissed by modern criminologists, for whom it is at best a historical stage in the development of their subject. According to the story told in most contemporary textbooks, the curtain fell on the constitutional stage around the turn of the twentieth century, with the discredited work of Cesare Lombroso, an Italian physician of the late nineteenth century. But the standard story is not quite right, for modern evidence argues strongly for physical and genetic correlates of crime, as this chapter will demonstrate. It therefore behooves us not only to survey the evidence but also to describe, briefly, the original Lombrosian work, and the reasons for its current low standing in criminology.

Lombroso advanced the first major theory of crime influenced by the Darwinian doctrine of continuity of man and beast, so it is not surprising that his name became eponymous for all biological theories of criminal behavior, even those which have little in common with it. There were serious defects in Lombroso's theory, and these too are often held, fairly or not, against modern "Lombrosian" theories. We will get to the defects after describing the theory.

In the course of examining many prisoners before and after their deaths, Lombroso became convinced that convicts often had distinctive physical features—that there was a "criminal man" (or woman) physically distinct from ordinary human beings. The idea of the "born criminal" was Lombroso's most controversial (if not most significant) contribution to criminology. In a speech given in 1906, Lombroso described the moment of discovery:

> In 1870 I was carrying on for several months researches in the prisons and asylums of Pavia upon cadavers and living persons in order to determine upon substantial differences between the insane and criminals, without succeeding very well. At last I found in the skull of a brigand a very long series

of atavistic anomalies, above all an enormous middle occipital fossa and a hypertrophy of the vermis analogous to those that are found in inferior vertebrates. At the sight of these strange anomalies the problem of the nature and of the origin of the criminal seemed to me resolved; the characteristics of primitive men and of inferior animals must be reproduced in our times.[3]

The key to the quotation is not just the anatomy but the date. By 1870, Darwin's theory of evolution (first published in 1859) was spreading well beyond biology, particularly into the social sciences. Lombroso's sudden realization was one among many such examples. If man did evolve from lower forms, as Darwin said, it was easy to suppose that the bestial behavior of some criminals had a physical basis, for animals clearly lacked human conscience and forbearance. This idea often cropped up in the fiction of the time, as in Robert Louis Stevenson's fantastic story of Dr. Jekyll and Mr. Hyde.[4] Respectable Dr. Jekyll drank a potion to transform himself into conscienceless Mr. Hyde, who, through the eyes of Stevenson's narrator, seemed "pale and dwarfish; . . . the man seems hardly human! Something troglodytic, should we say?" Mr. Hyde not only acted like a beast, he looked the part. Stevenson could have been fictionalizing Lombroso's "born criminal," though we have not found evidence that he was. It may have been enough that, in the post-Darwinian era, such ideas permeated the intellectual climate.

Lombroso believed that criminal behavior was associated with what he interpreted as physical atavism—sloping foreheads, long arms, primitive brains, and so on. Certain people, he suggested, were born primitive, throwbacks to an earlier biological epoch, not only morally but physically as well. The physical signs of criminality were at various times thought to include many features—for example, heads too small, too large, or of characteristic shape; distinctive hair, eyes, nose, ears, lips, palate, and jaw; short legs, sloping shoulders, and flat feet. Lombrosians thought that born criminals could be physically differentiated not only from ordinary people but also from each other according to the type of crime they were inclined toward; for example, sexual offenders supposedly had full lips; and murderers, very sloping foreheads.

Neither Lombroso nor his followers believed that all criminals, or even a majority of them, were born to transgress. Society, Lombroso eventually concluded, was responsible for more crime than evolutionary atavism. Between the born criminal and the essentially normal person impelled by circumstances to break the law, Lombroso thought he saw evidence for a continuum of "criminaloids," people who were less atavistic than Mr. Hyde but more so than Dr. Jekyll. Criminaloids, unlike born criminals, were not doomed to commit crime; they had a criminal tendency that might or might not be triggered by their experiences. The biological disposition to commit crime could, in other words, range from irresistible to nonexistent, according to Lombroso.

Whether crime was caused by biology or environment, Lombroso believed that crime was often *caused,* that it was not an expression of free and malicious intent, as it was and is depicted by many jurists and legal philosophers. The belief in causation was probably Lombroso's most lasting contribution. A causative theory of crime challenged the classical doctrine of *mens rea,* the free but "guilty mind" that usually must be established in court before a person can be punished for a crime. Whatever caused the crime, as long as it was caused rather than freely committed it would not deserve punishment, according to the traditional outlook. Accepting this principle, Lombroso and his school were therefore allied with the "reformatory" movement of nineteenth-century penology. They favored rehabilitation rather than retribution for prisoners, whom they saw as victims of bad biology or society. Indeterminate sentences, probation, and prisons with vocational and educational opportunities were appropriate for criminals whose offenses were caused by society, Lombroso believed. And to the extent that biology was the cause, punishment and inhumane treatment seemed to him futile and cruel. For the unfortunate throwbacks, nothing more was necessary than isolation from society.

The Lombrosian outlook, with its liberal, rehabilitative, and empirical orientation, outlasted the Lombrosian theory. Criminology itself, a branch of social science searching for crime's causes, is to some extent Lombroso's creation. Early in the subject's development, the great English physician Havelock Ellis wrote: "It is to Lombroso that the honour of founding the scientific study of the criminal must ever chiefly belong."[5] However, Lombroso's work was so flawed, as Ellis already suspected by 1914, that it failed to survive a generation, let alone to the present. The defects can be sorted into five types, which modern criminology can be seen as having developed in the effort to correct:

a) His measurement of physical characteristics was often casual, imprecise, and incompletely described.

b) His sampling methods were also casual, or worse. Criminals were compared to noncriminals without taking account of other differences between them, such as age, socioeconomic standing, and ethnic background. To show, for example, that criminals' head shapes, per se, are distinctive, it would have been necessary to compare them with noncriminals' matched for age, size, ethnic background, and perhaps also physique, all of which Lombroso apparently neglected to do.

c) Since criminology can only rarely and with difficulty use laboratory experiments to find out what is causing what, it must rely on statistics instead. The statistical methods available at the time were rudimentary.

d) Although inheritance is essential to Darwinian thinking, it took more than fifty years after 1859 for even the basic concept of genetics, the gene, to be widely grasped by biologists, let alone by nonspecialists like Lombroso. Without some clear notion of how traits pass from generation to generation, biological speculation was both hard to test and liable to be outlandish. Lombroso's was both.

e) Lombrosian psychology was as weak as Lombrosian biology. Corresponding to the physical atavism, there was supposed to be moral atavism as well. The born criminal was pictured as bestial inside and out. But there was no clear notion of what specific aspect or aspects of a criminal's psychology were deranged or undeveloped, nor how they got that way. Certain criminals were said to be criminal because of inborn inferiority, but they were apparently being called inferior mainly because they were criminal. Without a working theory of behavior, the notion of inferiority was circular, hence it explained little or nothing.

In summary, if criminology was to improve on Lombroso, its anthropometric measurements would have to become systematic and accurate, its studies more carefully designed, its data subjected to appropriate statistical analysis, and its concepts rooted in a more highly developed version of biology and psychology.

One of Lombroso's earliest and most penetrating critics took some of the first steps toward modern criminology. Charles Goring was an English prison physician who joined the Prison Service just after the inception, in 1901, of a national criminological project. By the time Goring published the first detailed account, over three thousand male inmates in prisons in and around London and various control groups of nonprisoners had been examined using the techniques of physical anthropology.[6] In addition, the study gathered data on occupational, familial, and ethnic backgrounds, age, educational levels, subjective judgments of intelligence, estimated frequencies of criminals in the convicts' families, and marriage rates, so as to see where and in what social settings crime flourished. Goring used correlational analysis—a then new statistical procedure for quantifying the degree of association between variables—which had been developed by his mentor, Karl Pearson (and which is known as the Pearson product-moment correlation coefficient). Goring's analysis of data was incomparably more sophisticated than Lombroso's, though still open to criticism, as we will see.

Looking back from our perspective, Goring's attempt to find the correlates of crime seems to be in the Lombrosian tradition, but he saw himself in conflict. He concluded that Lombroso's atavistic born criminal "has no existence in fact. The physical and mental constitution of both criminal and law-abiding persons, of the same age, stature, class, and intelligence, are identical. There is no such thing as an anthropological criminal type." But this did not mean that criminals were just like noncriminals, said Goring. Immediately following the sentences just quoted, he cautioned,

> But, despite this negation, and upon the evidence of our statistics, it appears to be an equally indisputable fact that there is a physical, mental, and moral type of normal person who tends to be convicted of crime: that is to say, our evidence conclusively shows that, on the average, the criminal of English prisons is markedly differentiated by defective physique—as measured by stature and body weight; by defective mental capacity—as measured by general intelligence, and by an increased possession of wilful antisocial proclivities—as measured, apart from intelligence, by length of sentence to imprisonment.[7]

A reader may have trouble discerning just what Goring was disputing in Lombroso. In fact, there were two substantive issues (and one not so substantive, which was simply Goring's unhappiness with Lombroso's careless methodology). First, Goring doubted the existence of a distinct criminal type, a separate sort of human being, throwback or otherwise. He could accept the continuum of criminaloids, but not the extreme. Second, he disputed many of the specific correlates of criminality claimed by Lombroso— the long arms, sloping foreheads, and so on. This second argument was usually inferential, not empirical. For example, consider the Lombrosian claim for head size as a sign of criminality. Goring, having showed criminals to be, on average, shorter than noncriminals, and head size to be correlated with stature, would then argue that the correlation between head size and criminality was explained away by the third variable, stature. He leveled similar arguments—not always based on stature, but on such other variables as social class, intelligence, and personality—against all the Lombrosian traits.

Of Goring's two criticisms of Lombroso, the first wore better than the second. The atavistic born criminal, if he or she exists at all, has yet to be found and would, at any rate, be so rare as to explain next to nothing about crime in general. Denying the criminal type, Goring acknowledged the existence of criminal tendencies that are probably present in all people, but to varying degrees. The antisocial tendency combined, he said, with low intelligence in many criminals. He concluded that criminal behavior ran in families more because of hereditary factors than environmental "contagion," his word for family environment. Using statistical procedures that were more ingenious than sound, he estimated that 60 percent of the variation in criminal behavior could be attributed to genetic, as contrasted with environmental, causes. Whether the estimate was right or wrong, it was a clear step forward to be looking for the subtle individual differences that predisposed essentially ordinary people to break the law, rather than for biological throwbacks.

But Goring may have gone too far in dismissing the rest of Lombrosian criminal anthropology. So, at any rate, thought E. A. Hooton, an American physical anthropologist who conducted a large-scale study on the characteristics of criminals in ten states.[8] Over ten thousand convicted male criminals were compared to about four thousand noncriminals on several dozen physical traits from head to toe, plus a few obvious sociological variables such as marital status, education, and occupation. Hooton said he had examined 10 to 12 percent of the male criminal population at the time. Not only was the sample large enough to uncover small but significant correlates of crime, its very size allowed meaningful comparisons within criminal categories for geographic and ethnic subsamples. It was therefore possible to compare, say, the characteristics of "nordic" or "alpine" or "Mediterranean" or "negroid" criminals and noncriminals, and to do so state by state, and criminal offense by criminal offense.

Even this most careful of all anthropological studies had its problems, as Hooton recognized. The sample of criminals was assembled with greater care than the smaller sample of noncriminals. Hooton tried to correct for the insufficient samples of noncriminals by indirect and not wholly convincing statistical adjustments. His conclusions, while better documented than Goring's, let alone Lombroso's, were not beyond question.

Hooton found physical differences between criminals and noncriminals, and between criminals convicted of different offenses. He found criminals in general to be smaller than noncriminals, as did Goring, but, in addition, he noted that the larger the criminal, the more serious his crimes were likely to be. A number of minor differentiating features also emerged in his data. First-degree murderers who were native American (having American-born ancestors for at least two generations) differed from native American criminals in general in having a narrower forehead relative to facial breadth, and narrower shoulders relative to stature, among other comparable differences.[9] Usually the native American criminals had straighter hair than native American noncriminals, as well as less beard and body hair, more mottled eye color, more folds of the upper eyelid, smaller head and chest circumference, shorter stature, shorter and broader noses, lower and more sloping foreheads, and flatter ears with a greater frequency of a bump known as Darwin's point. In summary, after a strenuous but not entirely successful effort to purge his study of the sampling flaws of earlier criminal anthropology, Hooton's data came closer to confirming Lombroso than Goring as regards physical correlates of crime.

How did Hooton interpret all this? Let's let him speak for himself, in two separate quotations:

> These facts lead to the important conclusion that native white criminals of native parentage are not only distinguished from each other by offense groups in sociological characteristics, but also in anthropometric and morphological features. Thus, it is suggested that crime is not an exclusively sociological phenomenon, but is also biological.[10]

> In every population there are hereditary inferiors in mind and body, as well as physical and mental deficients whose condition may be attributed to an unfortunate concatenation of environmental circumstances. Our information definitely proves that it is from the physically inferior element of the population that native born criminals of native parentage are mainly derived. My present hypothesis is that physical inferiority is of principally hereditary origin; that these hereditary inferiors naturally gravitate into unfavorable environmental conditions; and that the worst or weakest of them yield to social stresses which force them into criminal behavior.[11]

The second quotation strays further from the data than the first. As Hooton says in the first quotation, physical correlates implicate biology, assuming that they do not simply reflect the imperfect sampling in his study (and it is doubtful that they do). However, the mere fact of biological involvement fails to say what is going on to produce crime. The gap between breaking the law and having a narrow forehead is considerable, which the second quotation tries to bridge by asserting that the physical correlates of crime reflect biological inferiority. But here, as in Lombroso, the inferred inferiority is circular. Criminals may be constitutionally distinct in some small measure, but nothing in Hooton's data justified the hypothesis of inferiority, other than the very fact it was presumably explaining, namely the criminality itself.

Why did Hooton lapse into a Lombrosian circularity after so determined an effort to conduct an objective study of the traits of criminals? One possible answer is that he had no real alternative, since psychology had not yet developed to the point where it could trace the steps leading from static anatomical traits to dynamic events, like committing robbery or assault, particularly not in the objective terms Hooton would have wanted. Being a physical anthropologist, he would have been uncomfortable with the psychologizing he would have needed to put some behavioral flesh on the bare correlational bones in his data. The concept of inferiority may have seemed more legitimate and scientific to him, closer to Darwinian notions of survival and fitness.

Hooton's study suffered rough treatment by the criminological community, especially the sociologists who were bound to resent its skimpy treatment of sociological variables, and not mainly on the grounds of circularity in its use of inferiority. A reviewer in the *American Journal of Sociology* characterized one of Hooton's books (*Crime and the Man*) as "the funniest academic performance that has appeared since the invention of movable type."[12] That was quite a claim, hardly warranted by either Hooton's jokes or his mistakes. We must look beyond Hooton to explain the animosity not just of that reviewer but of most criminologists.

Hooton anticipated his critics (in tone and substance) in the opening sentence of *Crime and the Man:* "The anthropologist who obtrudes himself into the study of crime is an obvious ugly duckling and is likely to be greeted by the lords of the criminological dung-hill with cries of 'Quack! quack! quack!' " It may be worth quoting further from Hooton's view of the parlous state of his subject, for it has not entirely changed in the intervening years:

> The mere proposal to investigate seriously the racial anatomical characters which are the outward signs of inheritance, in their relation to psychological or sociological phenomena, is regarded as a sin against the Holy Ghost of Science. For this state of affairs we have to thank principally the Fascist prostitution of anthropology to political and economic oppression. Such a perversion of the science of race puts the anthropologist into a worse position than that of Caesar's wife. For he must be above suspicion of having anything to do even with Caesar. He is free to study environmental factors, but concern for his good repute makes him afraid to tackle heredity. He may work around the kitchen, but has to stay out of the bedroom. This enforced vestal virginity has sterilized human biology.[13]

The aversion to biological explanation prevailed, as Hooton expected. Partly the reason was the one he gave, the rise of Fascism and its vulgar and lethal perversion of the study of human biology. But other reasons also favored sociological explanations over biological ones. For one thing, people believe that it is easier to do something about a sociological cause of crime than about a biological one. The emerging themes in criminology[14] were poverty, social and economic inequity, and criminal contagion (in Goring's sense)—each, in principle, correctable. Not so for biological factors, which seem beyond the reach of legislation or politics. When expectations for public policy are high, such as in the recent past, sociological hypotheses are in tune with the times.

Moreover, many criminologists, most often trained as sociologists, are simply uneasy with biological and psychological concepts. It is only natural that people are reluctant to admit less than total expertise in their subject: Biologists or psychologists in a comparable situation would probably resist concepts from other disciplines just as much. Although interdisciplinary by its very nature, criminology became a sociological specialty by the 1940s, and this created a barrier to the flow of knowledge from physical anthropology, not to mention biology and psychology. The line of inquiry on constitutional factors, stretching from the unrecorded past to Hooton's enormous project, almost died out by 1940, despite positive findings.

A few minor studies pursued the physiognomic route, looking for facial correlates of crime. In 1939, Thornton showed photographs of 20 criminals convicted for a variety of offenses to 175 University of Nebraska students and asked them to identify the crime that each criminal had committed.[15] The criminals were selected at random from written records so as to avoid the experimenter's own stereotypes about appearance. Nevertheless, the students discriminated accurately at a level significantly better than chance. Thornton granted that his results were "of negligible practical importance," since the level of accuracy, though significant, was small, but they do provide a bit of evidence for an association between physical appearance and criminality in a study that appears to be free of the sampling biases in Hooton's or the earlier anthropological work. A similar conclusion was supported by Kozeny in a German study in which he divided 730 photographs of criminals into sixteen offense categories, then constructed a composite portrait of the typical offender in each category.[16] He found statistically significant differences in facial features across at least some of the categories.

In an English experiment by Bull and Green, a group of civilians and police officers was shown ten photographs of men and asked to say which of eleven listed crimes each man had committed.[17] Subjects were allowed to match more than one crime with each face. For arson, theft, rape, and burglary, no face was chosen significantly more frequently than any other. However, for each of the crimes of mugging, robbery with violence, company fraud, soliciting, auto theft, illegal possession of drugs, and gross indecency, a face was chosen more frequently than the others, different ones for different crimes. Civilians and policemen made essentially the same choices. What makes this study particularly interesting is that the photographs were actually of acquaintances of the experimenters, none of whom had been convicted of any crime. The experiment shows that people agree to some extent about the faces that go with certain crimes, and the few other studies in the literature suggest that they are often right. There are clearly stereotypes for criminal faces, which can at times mislead, but that would be expected for any weak correlate of crime, as facial configuration appears to be.

Somatotyping

Hooton had a hunch[18] that general physique, rather than the localized measurements of standard anthropometry, would provide the strongest anatomical correlates of crime, but he failed to pursue it vigorously, perhaps because he was not sufficiently familiar with a then new scheme for characterizing body build. The most highly developed system for classifying human physique was the creation of a physician, William H. Sheldon, who presented evidence suggesting that, if read correctly, body build correlates with behavioral tendencies, temperament, susceptibility to disease, and life expectancy.[19] We cannot here evaluate all of the claims made for Sheldon's system, but its clear relevance to criminality deserves recognition.

A person's "somatotype" is a characterization of his or her physique in terms of three components, called endomorphy, mesomorphy, and ectomorphy. The terms are adapted from embryology, where "endoderm" describes the inner layer of the embryo, origin of the digestive system and other viscera; "mesoderm," the middle layer, for muscle, bone, and connective tissue; and "ectoderm," for skin, brain, and sense organs. An endomorphic build tends toward roundness; a mesomorphic build, toward heavy-boned muscularity; an ectomorphic build, toward linearity. Mesomorphs tend to be shorter than average; ectomorphs, taller. It may be a help to think of more homely terms for the three components of physique, such as muffin, horse, and bird (terms learned by one of the authors from an undergraduate who had long used her own scheme of body-typing without knowing anything about Sheldon's), for endomorphy, mesomorphy, and ectomorphy, respectively.

According to Sheldon, every physique partakes of all three components to some degree, expressed on seven-point scales, with 1 as the lowest value, 7 as the highest. A variety of more or less equivalent techniques for applying the scales to a build have been standardized, some of which require no more than measurements from three nude photographs (see below) of a person, along with his height and weight. (In fact, although the system applies in principle to both men and women, it has not been fully standardized for women, apparently not because of any lack of interest but because of the difficulties in obtaining the required large sample of representative nude photographs.) Most people fall in the midrange of each scale. By one recent estimate[20] the median male has a somatotype of 4.0-4.0-3.5 (for components of endomorphy, mesomorphy, and ectomorphy, respectively, always listed in that order), while the median woman is something like 5.0-3.0-3.5, more endomorphic and less mesomorphic than men but equally ectomorphic.

Figure 1 presents the standard three-photograph sequence for a twenty-three-year-old with the median male physique, 4.0-4.0-3.5. By age forty, the median physique has typically added some weight, as shown in Figure 2 in photos of another man classified as 4.0-4.0-3.5. A skilled body-typer can take some account of such factors as age, nutrition, and health, which are reflected in a body's measurements without affecting the underlying physique as Sheldon conceives of it. Figure 3 is of a young man with a somatotype of 3.5-6.0-2.0. Since only about 3 percent of the population scores as high in mesomorphy as 6, and 80 percent scores more than 2 in ectomorphy, this is a mesomorph with an ectomorphic deficit. Not many men are as predominantly mesomorphic as this. Figure 4 shows a neighboring somatotype, a 4.0-6.0-1.5, an even rarer physique. In contrast to these mesomorphs is the young man in Figure 5, a 2.0-1.5-6.0, a true rarity, an extreme ectomorph severely deficient in both of the first two components. About 98 percent of the population scores above 1.5 in mesomorphy and only 1 percent scores as high as 6 in ectomorphy; together these unusual values define a physique estimated at a frequency of one case per five thousand.

In the population as a whole, the scale values are negatively correlated to some extent:[21] Men who have high ectomorphy scores tend to have low scores on the other two scales, and vice versa. Mesomorphy and endomorphy are also negatively correlated, but not as much as either is with ectomorphy. Nevertheless, the population of men spreads widely over the domain of combinations of the components, as Figure 6 illustrates. Shown here are approximate somatotypes of four thousand college men (each dot representing the average of twenty cases) on the diagram often used by Sheldon and his followers to portray a three-dimensional space on a two-dimensional surface. The corners of this spherical triangle represent the truly rare extremes of the dimensions; the center, the more typical midrange. The college population contains a slight scarcity of endomorphy and a slight excess of the other two dimensions, compared to the population as a whole.

A fuller explication of the system would touch on such secondary matters as the patterns of change with age or diet, and with the balance (or lack thereof) between body regions. However, for our purpose its seems enough,

FIGURE 1

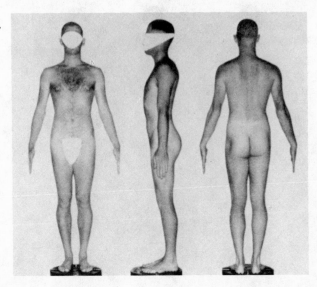

Standard somatotyping photographs of a twenty-three-year-old man with the average body build.

FIGURE 2

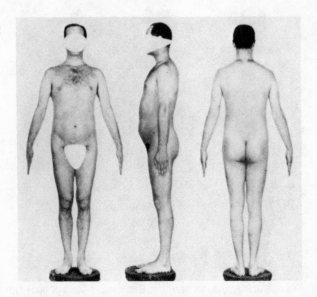

The average body build as it looks on a forty-year-old man.

Source: From W. H. Sheldon (with C. W. Dupertius and E. McDermott), *Atlas of Men: A Guide for Somatotyping the Adult Male at All Ages* (New York: Harper, 1954), pp. 220, 221.

FIGURE 3

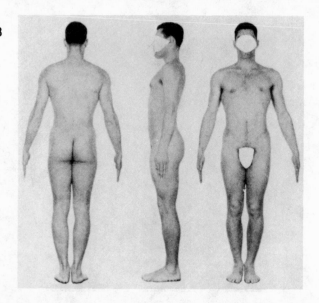

A young man with an unusually mesomorphic, nonectomorphic body build. This physique is disproportionately common in populations of offenders.

FIGURE 4

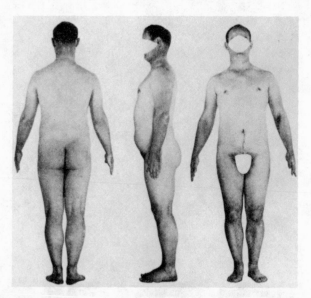

Similar to the physique in Figure 3, according to Sheldon's system of body typing. The two body builds are about equal in mesomorphy, but this one is less ectomorphic (and more endomorphic). It is even more characteristic of offender populations.

Source: From W. H. Sheldon (with E. M. Hartl and E. McDermott), *Varieties of Delinquent Youth* (New York: Harper, 1949), pp. 79, 81.

FIGURE 5

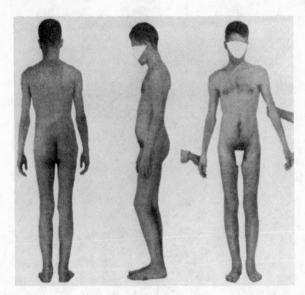

Extreme ectomorphy, deficient in both mesomorphy and endomorphy—far more common in mental hospitals than prisons, but a rarity overall. Its frequency in the general male population is estimated to be about one in five thousand.

Source: From W. H. Sheldon (with E. M. Hartl and E. McDermott), *Varieties of Delinquent Youth* (New York: Harper, 1949), p. 80.

having presented only the basic scheme, to show, in Figure 7, the somatotypes of the two hundred "delinquent" youths in Sheldon's application of his method to an institutionalized population. These young men were admitted to the Hayden Goodwill Inn over a period of several years around 1940 for antisocial or maladaptive activities, having been referred by social and legal agencies in and around Boston. As characterized by the investigators: "The youth who finds his way to a residential school like the Inn has generally been found so intolerable at home or in a foster home, at school, or in the community, that a court or social agency has intervened and placed him in a group home."[22] We might add that what seems "intolerable" at school or home or community depends not only on the youth's behavior but also on the capacity of others to put up with irritation and obstreperousness. The sample consisted primarily of recidivist delinquents, chronic runaways, and "unmanageable" school truants, mostly from socially disadvantaged backgrounds.

The most striking features of this population are, first, that they are mostly mesomorphs deficient in ectomorphy and, second, that they are elevated in a configuration called andromorphy, referring to such masculine traits as a broad chest flaring toward the shoulders, low waist, relatively large arms, prominent muscle relief, large bones and joints, fat distributed

FIGURE 6

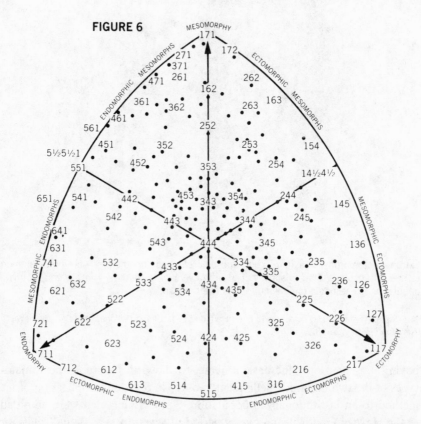

Source: From W. H. Sheldon (with E. M. Hartl and E. McDermott), *Varieties of Delinquent Youth* (New York: Harper, 1949), p. 728.

Somatotypes of about four thousand college men, with each dot representing the average of twenty cases. The groups of three numbers signify endomorphy, mesomorphy, and ectomorphy, respectively, on seven-point scales on which one is the lowest value, seven, the highest. Most men are clustered around the midvalues of each scale, but there are extreme cases along each of the three dimensions of physique.

throughout the body, etc. In a follow-up study of the sample conducted thirty years later, a subsample of fourteen cases was classified as "primary" criminals, which is to say that they had felony convictions as adults and no other significant distinguishing psychiatric or medical abnormalities. The somatotypes of these recidivists are in Figure 8, for an average of 3.5-5.0-2.3, compared to the whole sample, for which the somatotype was 3.8-4.5-2.9. The persistent criminals were relatively mesomorphic and non-ectomorphic, even compared to the others from the Inn. Likewise for

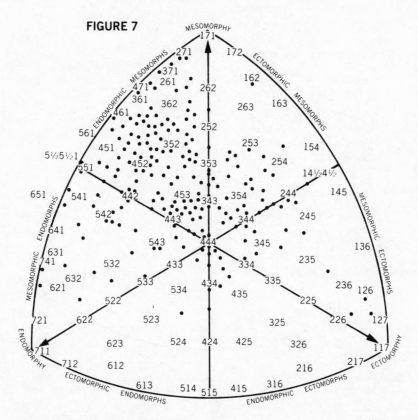

FIGURE 7

Source: From W. H. Sheldon (with E. M. Hartl and E. McDermott), *Varieties of Delinquent Youth* (New York: Harper, 1949), p. 729.

Somatotypes of two hundred male inmates of the Hayden Goodwill Inn for antisocial and maladaptive youths. This population is sharply skewed toward the mesomorphic, nonectomorphic part of the diagram (see Figures 3 and 4).

andromorphy—the primary criminals had a more masculine configuration than the sample as a whole.

A sample of two hundred is, of course, small, but the main conclusions have been confirmed wherever they have been tested, despite the initial skepticism of criminologists.[23] In 1952 Epps and Parnell compared the physiques of 177 female delinquents to those of 123 Oxford undergraduates and found the delinquents to be shorter and heavier in build, more muscular and fat; in other words, more mesomorphic and endomorphic.[24] In a larger study of male delinquency, Sheldon and Eleanor Glueck compared five hundred teen-age delinquents with five hundred nondelinquents matched for

FIGURE 8

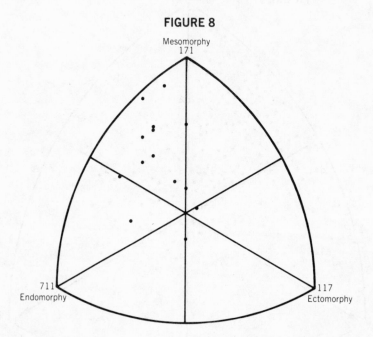

Source: From E. M. Hartl et al., *Physique and Delinquent Behavior: A Thirty-Year Follow-Up of William H. Sheldon's Varieties of Delinquent Youth* (New York: Academic Press, 1982), p. 499.

Of the two hundred cases in Figure 7, these fourteen were found, thirty years later, to be examples of "primary" criminals, that is to say, to be felonious recidivists not suffering from unusual medical or psychiatric abnormalities. The average body build in this group is even more mesomorphic and nonectomorphic than that in Figure 7.

age, IQ, race, ethnic background, and socioeconomic status (SES).[25] Delinquents were found to be significantly more mesomorphic and significantly less ectomorphic than nondelinquents. The body-typing was done from photographs by experts who did not know which boys were delinquent and which nondelinquent.

Similarly, Gibbens examined fifty-eight delinquent boys in London and found them to be significantly more mesomorphic (with a bias toward endomorphy) than a population of Oxford undergraduates.[26] Shasby and Kingsley compared fifty-one males, referred to the Kent State Youth Center for "persistent inappropriate behavior," to a control group drawn from junior and senior high schools.[27] Variables measured were body shape, percent body fat, and number of chin-ups. The behavior-disordered group was significantly more mesomorphic and had significantly less body fat than the control group (presumably signifying less endomorphy), but did fewer chin-ups. The authors attributed this last finding to lack of motivation rather than lack of strength.

Cortes and Gatti studied a group of delinquents who had been convicted of at least one crime.[28] Compared to a group of nondelinquents, the delinquents were more mesomorphic and somewhat less endomorphic and ectomorphic. Cortes and Gatti compared their results to those of Sheldon and the Gluecks, and found their own subjects to be more mesomorphic, relative to controls, than did the other two studies, perhaps because they used a more serious criterion for criminality or perhaps because they used a more strictly objective procedure for body-typing. A group of twenty adult felons was even more mesomorphic,[29] confirming the follow-up data from the original Goodwill Inn sample.

The general thrust of the evidence should be apparent. Wherever it has been examined, criminals on the average differ in physique from the population at large. They tend to be more mesomorphic (muscular) and less ectomorphic (linear), with the third component (endomorphy) not clearly deviating from normal. Where it has been assessed, the "masculine" configuration called andromorphy also characterizes the average criminal.

Physique does not cause crime, nor is it an inevitable correlate of it. In the Gluecks' study comparing five hundred delinquents with five hundred nondelinquents, many individuals differed from the averages. Mesomorphs could be found among the nondelinquents and ectomorphs among the delinquents. Sheldon himself noted that the mesomorphic, nonectomorphic physique often predominates, not just among criminals, but among other occupational groups, such as salesmen and politicians. In several studies the mesomorphic component has been associated with expressive, extroverted, domineering temperaments, given to high levels of activity.[30] In contrast, ectomorphy is often associated with introverted, inhibited, and restrained temperaments. The combination of mesomorphy and deficiency in ectomorphy therefore is likely to be found along with energetic behavior uninhibited by the internalized restraints of the ectomorph (with those traits perhaps exacerbated by an excess of masculinity—see Chapter 4). Sheldon called the resulting temperament "Dionysian," the spirit of unrestrained, impulsive self-gratification. While many criminals would hardly fit the Dionysian mold, and many Dionysians are law-abiding, Chapter 7 will confirm and elaborate further upon the statistical association between crime and personality traits given to impulsive, uninhibited self-gratification. Our purpose in this chapter is served simply by noting that the evidence leaves no doubt that constitutional traits correlate with criminal behavior.

Quantitative Genetics

In the search for constitutional correlates of crime, modern quantitative genetics deals not with arbitrary anatomical features (which may sometimes depend on pre- and postnatal environments, rather than genes) but with patterns of correlations among blood relatives and among people who, though unrelated by blood, share common environments. The logic of the method is to infer how much of the correlation across various degrees of relationship between people can be assigned to shared genes and how much to shared environments. If, for example, having a criminal natural brother is more predictive of crime for a person than having a criminal foster brother, then with certain reservations and qualifications, genes probably play some role in criminal behavior. We could not yet say *what* the genetic role is, for it would remain to be shown what inherited psychological characteristics are predisposing the individual to break the law, but, given enough data like this, we could estimate the size of the genetic contribution. Genetics tells us directly (though more abstractly) what anthropometry only implies obliquely. But saying that the analysis of intrafamilial correlations is direct is not to say it is simple. The statistical complexities of quantitative genetics often run deep; in this discussion, our hope is to stay afloat without superficiality. We will survey data from twins, from adopted children, and from men with a chromosomal abnormality.

Twin Studies

Twins provide the most comprehensible data for tracking down genetic influences on human variation, although not without complexities and ambiguities of their own.[31] Twins may be of two types, identical (MZ for monozygotic) or fraternal (DZ for dizygotic). Identical twins develop from a single fertilized egg that divided into two embryos, hence share all their genes. Fraternal twins develop from two eggs that were separately fertilized during the same act of conception, hence share only about half their genes, no more and no less than ordinary brothers and sisters. Fraternal twins may be of the same or different sexes; identical twins must be of the same sex.

Comparisons of identical and same-sex fraternal twins are a natural approximation to a controlled experiment for estimating the genetic involvement in a trait. Twins share a prenatal environment, then a common family environment at the same time in the life of a family, but they have either all (MZ twins) or only about half (DZ twins) of their genes in common. If their pre- and postnatal environments were literally identical, then greater similarity between MZ twins than between DZ twins would be prima facie evidence for a genetic factor, since the difference could be due to nothing else. Subjected to the statistical procedures of genetics, the difference in the degree of similarity between DZ and MZ twins yields a numerical estimate of the genetic contribution. An entirely heritable trait would be identical for identical twins and only as similar for fraternal twins as for ordinary siblings—that is, there would be a relatively large difference in the degree of similarity for MZ and DZ twins. An entirely nonheritable trait would be equally similar for the MZ and DZ twins. Essentially the same statistical procedures would be used whether the trait measures something physical (e.g., height), psychological (e.g., scores on a personality or intelligence test), or sociological (e.g., annual offense rate).

No empirical method is free of weaknesses; the twin method is no exception, and two of its weaknesses are peculiarly its own. The difference in MZ- and DZ-twin similarity tells us about genetic involvement only to the extent that the MZ-DZ difference is not due to environmental differences. But if the environment makes MZ twins more alike or DZ twins more different than they would otherwise be, the analysis overestimates the genetic contribution by including an environmental contaminant. This weakness can itself be calibrated for any given trait,[32] but typically has not been taken into account in the studies we will be summarizing. The other weakness pushes the other way, underestimating the genetic factor. To the extent that a study misclassifies twins as MZ or DZ, or otherwise suffers from unreliable measurements, the genetic contribution will seem smaller than it really is. For the most part, twin studies of criminal behavior are too flawed by measurement errors to provide a precise quantitative outcome, but a brief survey[33] reveals a clear trend.

The existence of two kinds of twins (MZ and DZ) was not widely accepted until the 1920s, not long before the first systematic twin study of criminality.[34] Johannes Lange, a German physician, located thirty pairs of same-sex twins of which at least one was a known criminal. Using the limited techniques of the time, Lange concluded that thirteen of the pairs were identical and seventeen fraternal. He then noted that in ten of the thirteen pairs of MZ twins, both were criminal, while in only two of the seventeen pairs of DZ twins were both criminal. So large a difference in "concordance" (i.e., both twins showing the same trait) between MZ and DZ twins is evidence for a genetic contribution to criminality. Although Lange took various precautions, such as having neutral experts check and, if necessary, correct his assignment of twins as MZ or DZ, the inherent limitations of the twin method dictate caution in interpreting the results of a single study.

Other studies rapidly followed Lange's, in Germany and elsewhere. His student Heinrich Kranz examined a sample of thirty-two MZ, forty-three same-sex DZ, and fifty different-sex DZ pairs of twins of which at least one twin had been imprisoned for a criminal offense.[35] The simple concordance rates were 66 percent for M, 54 percent for same-sex DZ, and 14 percent for different-sex DZ. A concordance difference of only 12 percent (66 percent to 54 percent) suggests only minor genetic involvement at most, but when Kranz refined his measurements by using indexes of the degree of similarity between twins for frequency of criminal offenses, severity of punishment, kind of crimes committed, and age at the beginning of a criminal career, the picture shifted somewhat. Basing concordances only on Kranz's estimate of a composite "strong similarity" between the twins' criminal histories, the result is 34 percent for MZ, 12 percent for same-sex DZ, and 0 percent for different-sex DZ, again suggesting a sizable genetic component to criminality.

Karl Christiansen reviewed nine studies of twins, all but one of which concluded that criminal behavior had a partial genetic basis mixed with environmental factors, though different workers localized the genetic ingredient at different points in the chain of events leading to the concrete criminal act. The one exception was a Norwegian study based on a sample of 139 MZ and DZ pairs of twins for which at least one member had a criminal record (including such minor offenses as traffic violations).[36] Using either all criminal offenses or only more serious offenses, concordance was as usual higher for MZ than for DZ twins, but not at the level of statistical significance. Dalgard and Kringlen presented evidence suggesting that concordance among DZ twins (though not among MZ twins) depended somewhat on how closely they felt identified with each other, perhaps indicating some influence of the emotional atmosphere of their upbringing. No clear reason for the discrepant Norwegian findings, if that is what they are and not just sampling error, has yet been established.

Table 1 reproduces Christiansen's survey of twin data (adding only the countries where the original work had been done). Needless to say, the studies vary significantly in definitions of criminality and concordance, as well as in the pains taken to determine whether the twins were fraternal or identical. Using blood typing or direct chromosomal assessment, modern studies can exceed 95 percent accuracy in determining twinship; accuracy was a good deal poorer in the past. Moreover, even if the studies were uniform in

TABLE 1

Summary of Twin-Criminality Studies

	MONOZYGOTIC		DIZYGOTIC	
	Number of Pairs	Pairwise Concordance Percent	Number of Pairs	Pairwise Concordance Percent
Lange (1929) (Germany)	13	76.9	17	11.8
Legras (1932) (Holland)	4	100.0	5	0.0
Rosanoff et al. (1941) (U.S.A.)				
Adult criminality	45	77.8	27	22.2
Juvenile delinquency	41	97.6	26	80.8
Stumpfl (1936)[a] (Germany)	18	64.5	19	36.8
Kranz (1936) (Germany)	32	65.6	43	53.5
Borgström (1939) (Finland)	4	75.0	5	40.0
Yoshimasu (1962)[b] (Japan)	28	60.6	18	11.1
Dalgard and Kringlen (1976)[c] (Norway)	31	25.8	54	14.9

[a] The same monozygotic concordant pair is found in both Stumpfl's and Kranz's samples.
[b] The figures from Yoshimasu (1962) stem from two investigations in 1941 and 1947.
[c] Crime in the strict sense.

Source: From K. O. Christiansen, A review of studies of criminality among twins. In S. A. Mednick and K. O. Christiansen (eds.), *Bisocial Bases of Criminal Behavior* (New York: Wiley, 1977), p. 72.

quality, we could not rule out the possibility that different countries might have different patterns of causation for criminal behavior, nor the chance that the patterns may have changed during the half century covered by the data. Nevertheless, we have pooled all the data (in effect weighting by sample size) to give a single, overall comparison of the MZ-DZ differences in concordance. Pooled concordance for MZ twins was .69; for same-sex DZ twins, it was .33, strongly indicative, within the limitations of the data and the twin method, of a substantial genetic component in criminal behavior.

In the earliest studies, sampling procedures probably overestimated concordance for both MZ and DZ twins. By searching for cases among prison or police records, the early studies had two chances to locate a concordant pair for every one chance to locate a discordant pair. Given any possibility at all of missing cases, errors of omission would probably have lost more discordant than concordant pairs. A sampling bias like this would inflate the MZ-DZ difference, hence would overestimate the genetic contribution to criminality. A sounder sampling technique is to start with a list of twins based on comprehensive birth records, then to check each individual's history for encounters with the law. It is important in such studies that the twins both survived into adulthood and that they were born long enough ago to have lived through the years when criminal behavior is most likely, namely young adulthood; otherwise there would be a tendency to overestimate discordance relative to concordance.

An approximation to the ideal twin study was reported by Christiansen,[37] based on a sample of 3,586 twin pairs from the Danish Twin Register, a full listing of twins born in Denmark between 1870 and 1920.[38] The subset used by Christiansen included almost all the twins born between 1881 and 1910 in a certain region of Denmark. Prison, police, and court records turned up entries (including minor offenses) for 926 people among the 7,172 twins, coming from 799 twin pairs. Pooling over males and females and for serious offenses only, the probability of finding a criminal twin when the other twin was a criminal was .50 for MZ twins and .21 for same-sex DZ twins. The concordances in this study were, as expected, lower than in the earlier work, but still significant and still indicative of a genetic contribution to criminal behavior.

A recent American study, conducted by David C. Rowe, relied on self-report surveys rather than official statistics.[39] Twins in the eighth to twelfth grades in almost all the school districts of Ohio (during the academic years starting in 1978 and 1980) received questionnaires by mail, along with a promise of a small remuneration for returning them filled out. The questions asked if and how often the twin had engaged in several categories of delinquent behavior, about the activities of their co-twins and friends, and about physical characteristics that are usually quite accurate in diagnosing whether twins are fraternal or identical (a few hard cases were also referred for blood tests). In all, completed questionnaires were obtained from 168 MZ and 97 same-sex DZ twin pairs, with more females than males responding. This was a return rate of only about 50 percent, but the sample was representative of a broad range of social-class backgrounds.

Concordances for self-reported delinquent behavior were greater for MZ than for DZ twins for both males and females, again implying some genetic involvement. Moreover, the twins who reported more activities shared with each other were no more similar to each other in delinquency than those who reported few shared activities. This lack of correlation suggests that neither the degree of concordance nor the difference in concordance between identical and fraternal twins could be explained by how much the twins had to do with each other. Rowe concluded from his analysis that the prime source of concordance was shared genes rather than shared environments.

The survey further showed a substantial correlation between how delinquent a twin was and how many of his or her friends were also delinquent.[40] This may seem to favor a "birds of a feather" theory of delinquency (see Chapter 11 for further details of this widely held theory), but Rowe and Osgood suggested otherwise. The pattern of within-twin differences in delinquency and delinquent associations, compared for MZ and DZ twins, indicated that the correlation between these two variables was also largely a result of shared genes. Rather than delinquent friends fostering delinquency, or vice versa, it appears that both are primarily expressing the same genetic factors. Inherited traits that made some twins susceptible to delinquency also predisposed them to friendships with other delinquents.

An alternative interpretation of the greater concordance for MZ twins is that they experience more similarity in their upbringing than DZ twins, which could explain all or part of their greater resemblance in criminality. Indirect evidence on this point tends not to support the hypothesis,[41] but if there were criminal statistics on twins raised in different homes, we could see how well the greater concordance rates among MZ twins persisted in the absence of shared environments. The few reported cases[42] of separated twins of which at least one has a criminal record are consistent with a genetic contribution, but there are too few to permit a decisive conclusion. But the logic of using data about people raised in foster homes, thereby separating their genetic and cultural heritage, applies not just to twins. It also applies to other kinds of family relations, as the next section shows.

Adoption Studies

In the ideal case for scientific purposes, a child would be separated at birth from his or her natural mother and father and placed at random in a foster home where parental behavior would in no way depend on the fact that the parent-child relationship was adoptive rather than biological. Then, the empirical question would be whether the child grows up resembling his or her natural relatives (e.g., parents and siblings) more or less than adoptive relatives, and by how much.

But the scientific ideal is not likely to be the humanitarian ideal, and, quite properly, the latter prevails. Children are put up for adoption at varying ages; couples who adopt children are not a random sample of all couples; adoption agencies often try to match children to their foster parents in various ways; the parent-child relationship may well be deeply conditioned by whether it is adoptive or biological. Thus, as a naturally occurring experiment for genetic influence, the adoptive-family method has inherent weaknesses and defects, just as twin studies do. However, the two methods

TABLE 2

"Cross Fostering" Analysis: Percent of Adoptive Sons
Who Have Been Convicted of Criminal Law Offenses

	Are Biological Parents Criminal?	
	Yes	No
Are Adoptive Parents Criminal?		
Yes	24.5% (of 143)[a]	14.7% (of 204)
No	20.0% (of 1,226)	13.5% (of 2,492)

[a] The numbers in parentheses are the numbers of cases in each cell, for a total sample of 4,065 adopted males.

Source: From S. A. Mednick et al., Genetic influences in criminal convictions: Evidence from an adoption cohort, *Science* (1984), 224.

do not suffer from quite the same liabilities, so that we can try to triangulate on the true facts of the matter by discounting some, but not all, of what we find in each kind of study.

The largest systematic adoption study of criminality is based on all non-familial adoptions in Denmark from 1924 to 1947.[43] The sample comprised 14,427 male and female adoptees and their biological and adoptive parents. Cases were excluded if criminal records or other kinds of demographic information were missing, which may or may not bias the results described below.[44] After all exclusions, the analysis was based on no fewer than ten thousand parents in the four parental categories (i.e., biological/adoptive, mother/father) and on over thirteen thousand adoptees. For just over four thousand of the male adoptees enough information was available to assess the contribution of parental criminality, as shown in Table 2.

If either mother or father had a criminal conviction then the parents are counted as criminal. The table shows that for boys who had neither adoptive nor biological criminal parents, 13.5 percent had at least one conviction. The percentage rises slightly, to 14.7, if adoptive (but not biological) parents are criminal; if biological (but not adoptive) parents are criminal, 20 percent of the boys have at least one conviction. The highest proportion, 24.5 percent, is for boys with both adoptive and biological criminal parents. The criminality of the biological parents is here more important than that of the adoptive parents, suggesting genetic transmission of some factor or factors associated with crime.

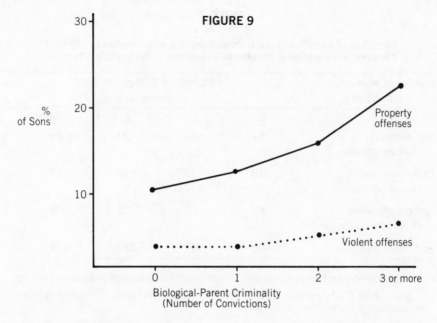

FIGURE 9

Based on criminal law convictions.
Adapted from S. A. Mednick et al., Genetic influences in criminal convictions: Evidence from an adoption cohort, *Science* (1984), 892.

The percent of adopted boys with convictions for property or violent crimes in relation to the number of such convictions of their biological parents. For this sample, none of the adopted parents had any convictions.

The recidivism of the biological parents is reflected in the adopted boys. Figure 9 shows what percentage of boys had at least one property or violent-crime conviction as a function of the number of convictions of their biological parents, using only noncriminal adoptive families. Whatever is being biologically transmitted appears to intensify with parental criminality, at least for property crimes. This is shown not just in the proportion of convicted adoptees plotted in Figure 9 but also in the adoptees' recidivism. Chronically criminal biological parents (three or more convictions) are three times more likely to produce a chronically criminal son than are biological parents with no convictions. The effects of biological-parent recidivism are summarized in Table 3 for adoptive families without any convictions. Only 4 percent of the male adoptees were chronic criminals, yet they were responsible for over 69 percent of all convictions of male adoptees. The 1 percent of the sample falling in the lower right-hand cell—the chronically

TABLE 3

Proportion of Chronic Offenders, Other Offenders, and Nonoffenders in Male Adoptees as a Function of Number of Convictions in the Biological Parents[a]

Number of Male Adoptee Convictions	Number of Biological-Parent Convictions			
	0	1	2	3 or more
Nonoffenders (No convictions)	.87	.84	.80	.75
Other offenders (1 or 2 convictions)	.10	.12	.15	.17
Chronic offenders (3 or more convictions)	.03	.04	.05	.09
Number of adoptees	2,492	547	233	419

[a] Table excludes cases in which adoptive parents have been convicted of criminal law violation.

Source: From S. A. Mednick et al., Genetic influences in criminal convictions: Evidence from an adoption cohort, *Science* (1984), 224. Table 2.

criminal adoptees with chronically criminal biological parents—accounted for 30 percent of the male adoptee convictions.

The sample included a number of full and half siblings raised in separate adoptive homes. Table 4 summarizes the concordances for unrelated males raised apart and raised together, and for half and full siblings raised apart. In the cases illustrated here, the concordance is at a peak for siblings (combining half and full siblings) who had a criminal biological father and were raised apart. For almost one-third of these cases, if one sibling was criminal, both of them were.

Adoptive-parent criminality has little apparent effect on the adoptees' tendency to break the law, in sharp contrast to biological-parent criminality. While strongly implicating genetic factors, this should not be taken as evidence against any influence of the adopting family. Adoptive parents are selected by the Danish adoption agencies only if they meet various social criteria, including no criminal convictions for at least five years prior to placement of the child. The adoptive parents were generally law-abiding, so that there may simply have been too little representation of the criminal environment in their homes to show up in these data. Nevertheless, both biological- and adoptive-parent socioeconomic status were correlated with criminality among the adopted males and females. Indeed, adoptive-parent SES was more correlated with crime by adopted sons than biological-parent

TABLE 4

**Concordance for Criminal Law Convictions in Male
Siblings Placed in Separate Adoptive Homes**

Degree of Genetic Relationship	Percent Pairwise Concordance
Unrelated raised apart	2.5
Half siblings raised apart	12.9
Full siblings raised apart	20.0
Half and full siblings raised apart; criminal father	30.8
Unrelated siblings raised together in adoptive home	8.5

Source: From S. A. Mednick et al., Genetic influences in criminal convictions: Evidence from an adoption cohort, *Science* (1984), 224.

SES was, and vice versa for adopted daughters.[45] The criminality of adoptees correlated with biological-parent SES, given any level of SES for the adoptive parents, and likewise for adoptive-parent SES, given any level of biological-parent SES.

A number of secondary but informative findings in this critical study should not be overlooked. We mention them briefly without dwelling on details. Adoptee crime was predicted by biological-parent crime no matter what the crime category, at least when the categorization was no finer than violent versus property. As far as this dichotomy is concerned, the genetic disposition is toward crime in general, not toward specific offenses. Over the period covered by the study (adoption from 1924 to 1947) no change in the major findings could be detected, despite the upheavals of a deep economic depression, a world war, and occupation by a foreign power, suggesting that the biological links in the chain of causation are strong. About a quarter of the adoptees were placed in adoptive homes immediately after birth, about another half by the end of the first year, and another 13 percent by the end of the second year. The age of placement exerted no effect on the relationship between biological-parent–male-adoptee criminality. Finally, the transmission of criminality from biological parents to their sons was unaffected by whether the biological parents committed their crimes before or after the children were placed in adoptive homes, or by whether the adoptive parents knew the biological parents' criminal records.

A large Swedish study has confirmed and extended much of these Danish findings.[46] Adopted males again followed their biological parents' tendency toward crime to a greater extent than anything in the adoptive family setting that could be identified. If the genetic disposition toward crime was combined with an apparently independent genetic disposition toward alcoholism, the crime tended to be more violent than otherwise (see Chapter 14). Besides the 862 adopted males, the Swedish study also examined the origins of crime for 913 adopted females. Essentially the same genetic predispositions make women criminal, but for women, the genetic predisposition has to be even stronger than it is for men (see Chapters 4 and 7 for more evidence of the greater deviance of female offenders).

An American study of the adopted children of a group of convicted mothers supports the Danish and Swedish findings as regards the importance of genetic factors in crime.[47] The forty-one mothers had been convicted for a variety of offenses, mostly felonies, including bad-check passing, prostitution, larceny, etc. Their children were put up for adoption in early infancy, and at the time of this study, fifty-two of the adoptees had reached fifteen years or older, averaging about twenty-six years. The adopted sample was at the age of risk for offenses, but, because of its youth, probably had not yet left its full imprint on the criminal records. The sample was nevertheless compared with a control group of fifty-two adoptees matched for age, sex, race (all white), age of separation from mother (about 3.9 months), and socioeconomic and marital status of adopting families. The two groups clearly differed in criminal histories. Three of the sample, but none of the controls, had records of felonies. None of the control group had ever been incarcerated; six of the sample had been. Four of the sample, but none of the controls, had multiple arrests. Seven of the sample, but only one of the controls, had been hospitalized for psychiatric reasons. Antisocial behavior (short of criminal) was more common among the sample than the controls, and was more serious when it occurred. All told, this small sample, like the much larger Danish and Swedish ones, suggests a strong biological resemblance between a parent and a child given up for adoption in some trait or traits that predispose people toward trouble with the law. This does not preclude environmental influences. Indeed, further analysis of this and other samples of American adoptees suggests that the genetic predispositions in combination with an adverse adoptive home environment result in more antisocial behavior by an adopted child than either the genes or the environments would by themselves.[48]

Cytogenetic Studies

In 1965, a brief scientific report raised the possibility of a specific genetic correlate of criminality, namely the XYY chromosome configuration.[49] Subsequent data have not confirmed the more lurid, almost Lombrosian, accounts of fiendish "supermales" found in many popular articles on the subject, but they do teach us something significant about the link between genes and criminal behavior. A "cytogenetic" abnormality, like the XYY configuration, is potentially revealing because it is genetic without being hereditary. That is to say, it arises in a person's germ plasm without having passed down from parents, hence its effects are not confounded with the family environment.[50]

Jacobs and her co-workers found a disproportionately high frequency of men with an extra Y chromosome among the inmates of a maximum-security state hospital in Scotland. In human beings, gender is determined by one of the twenty-three pairs of chromosomes inherited. For the sex-determining pair, a female receives an X chromosome from each parent; a male receives an X from his mother and a Y from his father. However, infrequently, defects in the production of egg or sperm result in genetic anomalies, of which one type is the XYY male, who receives not one but two Y chromosomes from his father. The resulting abnormalities are caused by having the extra Y chromosome.

From studies by Jacobs and her associates[51] and other population surveys[52] in places other than Scotland, we can estimate that the frequency of XYY males in the general population is about one per one thousand. In penal institutions of various types, the frequency of XYY is ten to twenty times larger, about 1 to 2 percent of the institutionalized male population. From the raw statistical data, it is plain that the extra Y chromosome increases the risk of incarceration.

What form does the risk take in an XYY male's psychology? Before we consider an answer, we must note that the risk is only relative. By far, most of the men in prisons are cytogenetically normal, with just the usual XY chromosomes, and most XYY men, perhaps as many as 98 percent of them, are not institutionalized at any given time. The XYY configuration contributes little to the totality of crime in an absolute sense. Its main significance is that it can tell us something about a particular genetic predisposition to crime, which may or may not generalize to the population at large.

The most revealing study of the XYY population to date was again conducted in Denmark because of the availability of comprehensive records.[53] From the total Danish population of men born between 1944 and 1947, the study selected only the tallest 15 percent. Since it is well established that XYY males are a good deal taller than average, virtually all of them would be concentrated in this sample. Sex-chromosome determinations on over 90 percent of the tall men comprised 4,139 cases. Cytogenetic techniques turned up twelve XYY men among them, of whom five had a criminal record of one or more offenses, a prevalence rate of over 40 percent. Among XY men, the prevalence rate was only 9.3 percent, which is significantly lower. Though they were more often criminal, XYY men did not appear to be more violent or aggressive than the XY men with criminal records, contradicting the occasional reports in the press of the special cruelty of XYY crimes. In fact, most of the 149 recorded offenses committed by the five XYY criminals were minor property offenses.

The study looked at the correlation between criminality in the sample of 4,139 men and four variables besides chromosome pattern: parental SES, score on an intelligence test, educational achievement, and height. Except for height (the range of which was restricted in the sample), all the variables were associated with crime among the XY men: lower SES, tested intelligence, and educational achievement each contributed independently to the probability of acquiring a criminal record. Moreover, it was found that XYY men, though not differing in parental SES, had, on the average, lower tested intelligence and educational achievement. Like many other chromosomal abnormalities, the extra Y takes a toll on intellectual development. The question now was whether the intellectual and educational deficits of the XYY men fully accounted for their excess criminal prevalence. The answer was that the deficits apparently accounted for not quite half of the excess. The intellectual and educational deficits by themselves would have raised criminal prevalence for the XYYs from the population value of 9.3 percent to 17.2 percent, but the actual value was 41.7 percent. Possibly, more sensitive measures of intelligence or educational achievement would have closed some of the remaining gap, though not likely all of it. It is more likely that the extra Y chromosome produces not only a deficit in intelligence but also some unmeasured nonintellectual correlates of criminal behavior, such as personality traits.

In summary, this careful Danish study tells us that XYY men are at risk for crime partly because they suffer from depressed intelligence and performance in school and partly because of other, as yet unidentified, effects of the extra chromosome. Generalizing the result, the study implies that the genetic ingredient in criminal behavior is partly, but not entirely, accounted for by intellectual and educational variables.

Conclusions

We can answer unequivocally the question posed near the beginning of the chapter. The average offender tends to be constitutionally distinctive, though not extremely or abnormally so. The biological factors whose traces we see in faces, physiques, and correlations with the behavior of parents and siblings are predispositions toward crime that are expressed as psychological traits and activated by circumstances. It is likely that the psychological traits involve intelligence and personality, and that the activating events include certain experiences within the family, in school, and in the community at large, all large topics in their own right and dealt with in chapters of their own.

The existence of biological predispositions means that circumstances that activate criminal behavior in one person will not do so in another, that social forces cannot deter criminal behavior in 100 percent of a population, and that the distributions of crime within and across societies may, to some extent, reflect underlying distributions of constitutional factors. Perhaps the simplest thing to say at this point is that crime cannot be understood without taking into account individual predispositions and their biological roots.

4

GENDER

The Belgian statistician Lambert Adolphe Jacques Quetelet observed early in the nineteenth century that females accounted for less than 25 percent of all arrests.[1] Why the sexes differed in criminality may have been uncertain, as Quetelet acknowledged, but the sheer fact itself proved robust enough to cross the boundaries of place and time. Table 1 shows the percentage of female arrests in twenty-five countries surveyed by the International Police Organization, averaged over the years 1963, 1968, 1970, and 1972.* The range, from a low of 2.02 percent in Brunei to a high of 20.90 percent in the West Indies, no doubt reflects local variations in laws, in their enforcement, in the accuracy of records, and perhaps also in actual rates of male and female crime, but a clear tendency is evident. Males are five to fifty times as likely to be arrested as are females.

Whether the true world figure is 2 percent, 20 percent, or even higher, gender demands attention in the search for the origins of crime. From official arrest records and other data, we hope to learn, first, about differences in how much and what kind of crime men and women commit, and, second, whether the differences are changing in ways that shed light on criminal behavior generally. Perhaps because crime has been predominantly male behavior, the criminological literature has largely concentrated on the criminal man.[2] The prototypical criminal is a young male, and it is his behavior that

* The percentages are obtained by dividing the arrests for females by the total arrests for males and females (and multiplying by 100 to convert into percent).

104

TABLE 1

Female Arrestees as Percentage of Total Arrests, by Nation
(1963, 1968, 1970, and 1972)

Brunei	2.02	Israel	11.71
Fiji	2.67	Tunisia	13.06
Hong Kong	2.76	England and	13.61
Malawi	4.27	Wales	
Cyprus	6.38	United States	13.66
Finland	6.66	Austria	13.75
Tanzania	6.85	France	14.25
Monaco	7.00	Jamaica	15.46
Japan	9.69	Luxembourg	16.38
Canada	9.77	West Germany	16.66
Netherlands	10.25	Thailand	17.38
Korea	10.51	New Zealand	20.56
Scotland	11.53	West Indies	20.90

Adapted from R. J. Simon and N. Sharma, Women and crime: Does the American experience generalize? In F. Adler and R. J. Simon (eds.), *Criminology of Deviant Women* (Boston: Houghton Mifflin, 1979), p. 394.

most theories have tried to explain. As a result, when we address the quantity and significance of sex differences in crime, we must start by examining the often neglected criminal woman.

Female Crime and Its Incidence

Arrest Statistics

For contemporary America, the largest source of data on crime is the FBI's Uniform Crime Reports (UCR). Ideally, we would like to know the breakdown of the sexes for crimes committed, or at least reported to the police, but the UCR records on reported crime have no separation by sex. For many reported crimes, little is known about the offender, including his or her sex. A survey of female crime must therefore start, not with reported crime, but with the UCR data on arrests, reserving for later the question of possible inaccuracies surrounding arrest records.

Figure 1 traces arrests for Index crimes (i.e., murder and nonnegligent manslaughter, aggravated assault, forcible rape, robbery, burglary, larceny theft, motor vehicle theft) and non-Index crimes (i.e., everything else) for the years 1960–1980, for males and females. Each graph summarizes male

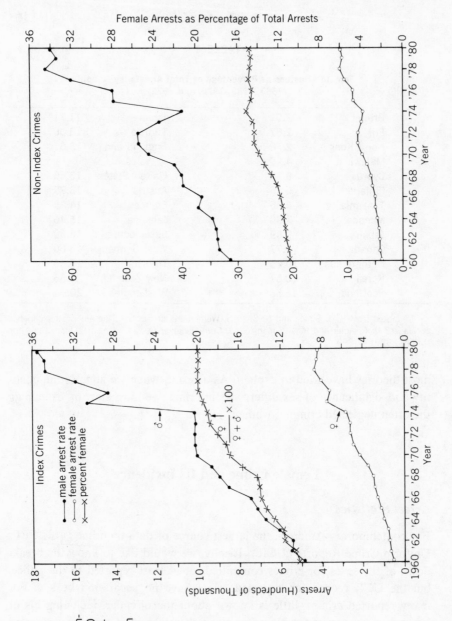

FIGURE 1

Arrests of men and women for Index and non-Index crimes, from 1960 to 1980, and the proportion of all arrests that were of women, based on the FBI Uniform Crime Report data on arrests.

arrests, female arrests, and female arrests as a percentage of total arrests, year by year. The sex differential here (as in Table 1) is based on numbers of arrests, rather than on numbers of different offenders, which are much harder to come by. Since males commit crimes at a higher rate than females,[3] numbers of offenders show a smaller sex differential than arrests.

Variations among jurisdictions included in the FBI's tally—in legal categories and in the accuracy of reporting procedures—bar too close a reading of the statistics in Figure 1, but the trends are nevertheless clear. Crime rose sharply during the period. Index crime arrests rose by over 300 percent from 1960 to 1980; non-Index crime arrests, by over 100 percent. Our concern here, however, is not the general increase, but gender and any change in its role in crime. It is obvious from Figure 1 that male arrests rose in absolute numbers much more rapidly than female arrests. Nevertheless, female arrests have become a larger fraction of total arrests, especially for Index crimes, for which it nearly doubled from about 10 percent to just under 20 percent. For non-Index crimes, the female percentage rose less dramatically, from about 11 percent to not quite 15 percent. The increase in the percentage of female arrests was essentially over by 1974 for non-Index crimes, and by 1976 for Index crimes. From 1973 to 1980, the total number of arrests rose by almost 50 percent, but the distribution between the sexes varied by less than 1 percent.

The increase in the proportion of female arrests in the 1960s and early 1970s clearly warrants further examination. Figure 2, separating Index crimes into the two broad categories of violent and property crimes, suggests that the increase in female Index crimes was due mostly, if not entirely, to an increase in property offenses. For violent crimes, the proportion of females remained nearly constant, at about 10 percent of total arrests from 1960 to 1980, while the proportion for property offenses rose from about 10 percent to about 22 percent. Whether the relative rise in female arrests for property crime looks large or small depends to some extent on how we choose to express it. Property Index crime arrests for females rose from 43,424 in 1960 to 368,354 in 1980, a change of almost 750 percent, while male arrests in that category were rising by a "mere" 250 percent. However, because females started at such a low level, their 750 percent increase was diluted by the large and growing number of total arrests, so that, as a percentage of total arrests, the change was only about eleven percentage points.

The twenty-one years from 1960 to 1980 may seem too short to reveal long-term changing patterns for the sexes. Consequently, an analysis of urban arrests from 1934 to 1979 (UCR data are continuous only for urban

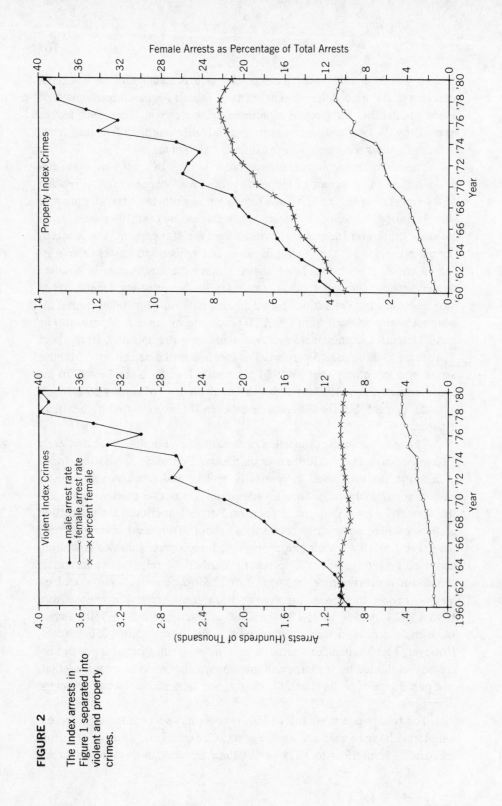

FIGURE 2

The Index arrests in Figure 1 separated into violent and property crimes.

arrests over this period) has special value.[4] Table 2 summarizes the forty-six-year period broken into seven intervals dictated by changes in methods of tallying arrest frequencies and by significant historical events, such as the world war. "Percent of arrests" is the female arrest rate divided by the sum of female and male arrest rates, thereby taking into account the size of female and male populations.

Disregarding the transient changes of the war years of 1942–1945, female arrest proportions increased only slightly, except in the few cases where they increased substantially and steadily. Female larceny, for example, increased from 7.8 percent of total larceny arrests in 1934–1941 to 31.4 percent in 1973–1979, with most of the increase again occurring in the 1960s and early 1970s. Fraud and forgery, which are often classified along with larceny as "petty property" crimes, also rose steeply. In contrast, serious (excluding larceny) and violent crimes, such as criminal homicide, robbery, burglary, and auto theft, rose by less than 6 percentage points. Without "petty property offenses," the percent of female crime as a whole increased by 3.7 percentage points over the four and a half decades, from 7.7 percent to 11.4 percent. And even this increase may be an overestimation. Growing equality in the application of the law, better data gathering (early UCR data mislabeled many women as men), and the movement of blacks into the urban areas surveyed in the UCR (the sex differential is smaller for blacks) no doubt account for at least some of the shrinking sex differential.

The long-term consistency of the sex differential in most arrest categories in Table 2 suggests that most crimes have been predominately masculine to more or less the same extent, even as American crime rates have risen over recent decades. But how to interpret consistency over so long a period may seem problematic, for, even if nothing else was changing, legal categories, arrest practices, reporting procedures, and the attitudes of the criminal justice system toward women doubtless were changing, with largely uncertain effects on the sex differential. The benefits, noted above, of looking at sex differentials over a long stretch of time may be partly offset by the difficulty of maintaining comparability in the statistics. It would therefore be helpful to examine a set of data less likely to be perturbed by extraneous variables. Steffensmeier's analysis of adult (i.e., eighteen to fifty-nine years) male and female arrest rates (adjusted for the population sex ratios and excluding forcible rape because it is so underrepresented in arrest statistics) in 1965 and 1977, bracketing a dozen years when crime rates were rising steeply, is one such set.[5]

Table 3 extracts, for 1965 and 1977, the seven crimes for which males predominated most (besides rape); the seven for which they predominated

TABLE 2

% Female Arrests for Twenty Offense Categories and for Total Indices, by Grouped Years

Offense Categories	1934–41	1942–45[a]	1946–51	1952–57	1958–66	1967–72	1973–79
Criminal homicide[b]	9.6	8.8	11.8	13.4	15.6	14.7	13.8
Robbery	4.3	2.3	4.3	3.9	4.8	5.8	6.8
Burglary	1.2	2.2	2.4	2.1	3.2	4.3	5.5
Larceny theft	7.8	12.2	11.5	12.5	19.4	27.1	31.4
Auto theft	1.7	1.4	2.2	2.4	3.7	5.0	7.2
Assaults[c]	8.4	8.9	9.6	12.3	11.2	12.6	13.4
Fraud[d]	4.9	11.1	8.9	14.7	17.5	26.2	34.3
Forgery	6.2	12.2	11.7	14.2	17.5	22.9	29.2
Stolen property	7.5	7.3	8.2	9.2	8.3	8.7	10.4
Weapons violations	3.6	4.4	4.3	5.4	6.0	6.6	7.8
Gambling	5.4	7.1	8.2	9.1	8.0	7.8	8.4
Prostitution	72.4	65.4	60.0	68.6	73.9	76.7	70.1
Disorderly conduct	11.6	24.2	13.0	15.4	13.2	13.9	17.0
Vagrancy	7.7	30.4	15.8	10.7	8.2	16.0	23.9
Suspicion	8.4	14.3	10.3	9.6	11.2	15.8	13.6
Drunkenness	5.5	10.9	8.4	7.3	7.4	6.7	6.9
Driving while intoxicated	2.4	4.8	4.0	4.1	6.1	6.6	8.1
Liquor law violations	14.0	12.9	14.8	17.5	12.8	12.4	14.1
Narcotics	24.8	7.4	11.6	15.5	13.7	15.0	13.5
Offenses against family	2.7	7.0	5.3	8.9	10.3	11.0	15.3
Total	7.6	13.8	9.6	9.8	10.1	12.6	15.1

[a] Sex differentials for this period adjust for changes in sex-age structure of the prewar and wartime population (Steffensmeier et al., 1980).

[b] From 1952, criminal homicide combines murder and nonnegligent manslaughter with manslaughter by negligence.

[c] From 1952, assaults combine aggravated assaults with other assaults.

[d] From 1953, fraud and embezzlement combine the sep-arate category of fraud with that of embezzlement. Since for any given year, more than 90 percent of the fraud/embezzlement arrests are for fraud, the latter is the designation used to define this offense category.

Source: From D. J. Steffensmeier and M. J. Cobb, Sex differences in urban arrest patterns, 1934–79,, *Social Problems* (1981), 29:41.

least; and the single crime, prostitution, for which females predominated. (Strictly speaking, female prostitution is no more a crime of females than of the males who patronize them, but in arrest rates, females certainly predominate.) As far as male preponderance is concerned, much the same crimes turn up in 1965 and 1977. Among the seven most "masculine" adult crimes in both years (as reflected in arrest rates), six turned up both times—auto theft, burglary, robbery, driving under the influence, drunkenness, and weapons offenses. For the seven least sex-differentiated crimes, five turned up in both years—larceny theft, fraud, murder, forgery, and embezzlement. Vagrancy and disorderly conduct joined the list in 1977 as the overall arrest rates in these categories declined precipitously, but relatively more for males than females, perhaps as much because of a change in arresting practices as in behavior more generally. The pattern of highly, and not so highly, sex-differentiated crimes did not change much between 1965 and 1977, even though the gap narrowed at least slightly across the board. In 1965, arrests for the most sex-differentiated crime (auto theft) were 3.8 percent female; in 1977, for the most sex-differentiated crime (burglary), they were 5.9 percent female, and so on down the list in Table 3. At every level of male (or

TABLE 3

Adult Arrest Rates for 1965 and 1977
(With Female Arrest Rates as Percentage of Total Arrest Rates, by Category)

	1965	1977
Males Predominate Most	Auto theft (3.8%)	Burglary (5.9%)
	Burglary (3.9)	Drunkenness (6.6)
	Robbery (5.3)	Auto theft (6.8)
	Driving under influence (6.1)	Robbery (7.3)
	Drunkenness (7.2)	Driving under influence (8.0)
	Weapons (7.3)	Weapons (8.1)
	Gambling (7.6)	Sex offenses (8.5)
Males Predominate Least	Larceny theft (25.2)	Vagrancy (36.5)
	Fraud (19.8)	Fraud (36.2)
	Murder (18.4)	Larceny theft (33.7)
	Forgery (17.9)	Forgery (28.8)
	Embezzlement (16.9)	Embezzlement (22.6)
	Arson (16.4)	Disorderly conduct (16.4)
	Aggravated assault (13.8)	Murder (14.9)
Females Predominate	Prostitution (76.9)	Prostitution (70.0)

Adapted from D. J. Steffensmeier, Sex differences in patterns of adult crime, 1965–1977: A review and assessment, *Social Forces* (1980), 58:1088–89.

female) preponderance, from "extremely" male through only moderately male, to the one preponderately female arrest category, the difference between the sexes shrank at least a percentage point or two. The gender gap has narrowed least in the crimes in which males have historically predominated most, and has narrowed most in the crimes in which males have predominated least. Whatever may be the social forces or police practices that are pushing male and female arrests toward each other, their effects are most evident where the gender gap has been the smallest.

It is, indeed, easy to lose sight of the similarities in male and female crime while trying to make sense of the differences. The changes of the recent period have been played out against a background of substantial uniformity between the sexes in the relative position of various crimes. Drunkenness, disorderly conduct, and driving under the influence are common arrest categories for men and women alike. Even though males account for over 90 percent of arrests for drunkenness and driving under the influence (see Table 3), these are large categories for women as well as men. Similarly, murder, negligent manslaughter, and arson are relatively rare among arrests of men as well as women, even though at least 80 percent of the arrests in those categories are of men. In between are the arrest categories that occupy about the same middling ranks for both sexes, such as liquor law violations and assaults. The rank-order correlations between arrest rates for men and women were moderately large (about .8) in 1965 and 1977, and did not seem to be rising or falling.

The few crimes that occupy substantially different ranks within the sexes are therefore conspicuously related to gender as such. Prostitution, of course, is a higher-ranking crime for women than for men, but, in recent years especially, so are fraud, forgery, and larceny. A change in larceny, in particular, because it is such a high-volume crime, has a clear and detectable impact on aggregate crime statistics for men and women. In contrast, burglary, auto theft, and weapons offenses are chronically higher-ranking male than female crimes, and the recent rise in both male and female robbery has pushed it higher in the list of male arrest categories than female, but robbery, as a much smaller crime category than larceny, has a smaller impact on arrest statistics as a whole.

Other Evidence

Can arrest statistics be trusted to tell us about sex differences in crime rates? It has been argued that conventions of male chivalry or paternalism toward women[6] reduce the number of female arrests so that the true sex difference in crime may be much smaller than arrest records imply. For a variety of reasons, it is conceivable that police officers may think of a female offender as less dangerous than a male, even for an offense of a given severity, so that arrest statistics (let alone data from subsequent stages in the justice system, such as bail, trial, sentencing, etc.) would be tainted by a bias exaggerating the gender gap.

Victimization surveys, based on interviews with samples of households and businesses, provide one way of checking on biases in arrest data because the victim is asked about the sex of his or her assailant. National Crime Survey (NCS) victimization data from 1976 were compared with UCR arrest reports for the same year to see how well they agreed.[7] For rape, robbery, assault, burglary, face-to-face larceny (e.g., purse snatching), and auto theft, female crime as a proportion of total crime rarely differed by more than a few percentage points in victimization and arrest data. What small differences there were violated the chivalry hypothesis, since, in this comparison at least, arrests contained slightly *higher* proportions of females than victimization reports. Gender is at least as significant a variable in victimization as in arrest data. Other studies find some support for the notion of gentler treatment of women by the criminal justice system, but at later stages than arrests, such as in the sentences after conviction.[8]

When respondents were asked if they reported crimes to the police, half of those victimized by males, but only one-third of those victimized by females, said yes. The discrepancy, however, seems to have had more to do with the seriousness of the crime than the sex of the criminal. Male victims of serious personal crimes were more likely to report a female than a male assailant, while female victims had the reverse bias. On balance, reporting to the police showed no clear sex difference, once seriousness was taken into account.

Besides victimization surveys and UCR records, self-report studies, typically conducted on juveniles, provide anonymous self-descriptions that bypass some of the biases in arrest or police records, but (as we noted in Chapter 1) they introduce biases of their own. Not everyone is equally willing to be candid about breaches of conduct, and the range of candor extends from understatement to overstatement. High-frequency offenses are usually underestimated, so sex differences for them will typically be underestimated by self-reports, because males, who are generally the more frequent offenders, will be more affected by the tendency to underestimate a high-frequency offense.[9] Many minor crimes show up in self-reports but not in official statistics, and these often have smaller sex differences than serious crimes. Despite their biases, self-reports often contain information about noncriminal antisocial behavior, as well as about crime, which can reveal patterns missed by official statistics.

Since most self-report studies are about juveniles, the comparisons with juvenile arrest data contain several instructive discrepancies. Female juvenile arrests include relatively more runaways and sexual misconduct cases, as compared to male juvenile arrests. Female juveniles appear more likely to be arrested for sexual offenses, running away, and curfew violations than their male counterparts, and less likely to be arrested for other offenses (unless the girl is black). A given offense is more likely to be labeled as sexual in nature if a girl is arrested than if a boy, as in cases of vagrancy, for example. But, compared to these gender differences in arrests, in self-report studies[10] male and female patterns of juvenile delinquency are typically quite similar, except that females engage in crime at a lower rate than males. The sex difference in overall levels of crime is greater in official statistics than in self-reports, partly because of differential treatment of juveniles by the criminal justice system as well as because of the biases in self-reports already mentioned.[11]

Women convicted of violent crimes in California and Minnesota during the mid- and late sixties were the subjects in one of the few self-report studies of adult female offenders.[12] Relatively few of the women had been arrested for serious crimes, or for unassisted robberies of healthy, adult males. If involved in such a robbery, they generally played a supporting role to male confederates. The victims of violent attacks by women were most often relatives or personal acquaintances; rarely did women commit violence in the course of some other felony like robbery. When the victim was an adult male, the woman usually used a weapon or waited until the man was drunk or asleep. The male and female style of offending was so different even within crime categories that Ward et al. concluded "that female criminality is a separate and distinct order of criminal behavior."

An overview of sex differences has been provided by pooling the results of forty-four studies of crime and related forms of deviant behavior by males and females.[13] The analysis included every relevant and statistically suitable study using official statistics and self-reports from 1940 to 1975. Many of the trends seen in individual studies and summarized here were substantiated. In addition, so large an aggregation of data uncovers factors that affect the size of the sex differential itself. Sex differences are larger in official data than in self-reports. They are greater for adults than for juveniles, for property offenses than for personal offenses, for more serious crimes than for less serious ones, and for whites than for nonwhites. For property crimes, self-reports suggest that the larger the take, the bigger the sex differential.[14]

Whether offenders are urban or rural, or from intact or broken families, makes no independent contribution to the sex differential, though such factors may contribute to overall levels of offense rates.[15]

In summary, the historical gender gap in crime has survived to the present, despite the rising tide of crime in general and the changes in sex roles in recent decades. But it has been changing. Across the board, the gender gap has narrowed at least slightly, and for petty property crimes it has narrowed considerably. Where it has narrowed a lot, more than just police behavior is involved. Sex differences appear to be diminishing more for minor and for juvenile offenses than for serious and for adult offenses, which may be another reason they look smaller in self-report studies, with their youthful subjects admitting generally minor infractions. The narrowing gender gap in self-reports could be either a by-product of rapidly growing rates of minor crimes by females or the leading edge of a significant trend in female crime of all sorts, including serious and soon-to-be adult female crime. Only time will tell if females are significantly catching up with males in categories besides the minor offenses that have already shown the larger changes.

Explaining Gender and Crime

Characteristics of Female Offenders

No less than for males, any attempt to characterize female offenders must be hedged by disclaimers. No single description can capture all the susceptibilities, traits, or sheer random influences that impel people to break the law. The descriptions found in the empirical literature are based on a rough aggregation, dominated by common configurations of traits and circumstances. Compounding the problems of aggregation are any distorting effects of biases in the criminal justice system as it deals with female crime. These same reservations will be expressed in our later (Chapters 6 and 7) discussion of intelligence and personality, but they may have even more bearing on the female offender, because the data are thinner and because the changing status of women in society and before the law may be reflected in a shifting set of predisposing traits. Given all the potential sources of error and distortion, the convergence on a particular set of distinguishing characteristics is all the more remarkable.

Although long out of date, one of the richest studies of female offenders is *Five Hundred Delinquent Women* by Sheldon and Eleanor Glueck.[16] Five hundred women ending a parole period at a Massachusetts reformatory were selected at random between 1921 and 1925, their life histories were scrutinized, and they were followed after release. The factors that evidently predisposed these women to crime were generally the same as those for men (as reported in the Gluecks' *Five Hundred Criminal Careers*[17]): poor family background, poor childhood behavior (including many contacts with the criminal justice system), low intelligence, and emotional instability. Expressing themselves more vividly than has become the custom in criminology, the Gluecks said, *"The women are themselves on the whole a sorry lot.* Burdened with feeblemindedness, psychopathic personality, and marked emotional instability, a large proportion of them found it difficult to survive by legitimate means"* (italics in original).[18] Of the marriages prior to detention, three-fourths were dissolved by desertion, separation, or divorce. Three-fourths of the husbands were judged irresponsible. Half of the women had had illegitimate pregnancies, and over half had been prostitutes. Most had hostile attitudes toward their children, which the Gluecks took as a warning that the factors that had produced criminal behavior in these women may be passed on to their children. During the five years after parole, 38 percent of the women were rearrested, but as many as 75 percent engaged in some form of legally punishable activity. The Gluecks considered this an improvement over behavior before confinement, though still substantial recidivism.

Recent studies confirm the Gluecks' major findings.[19] Extensive interviewing and case histories of hundreds of delinquent girls in and out of various institutions throughout the U.S. and the U.K. paint a picture reminiscent not just of the Gluecks' sample but of comparable samples of males. Female crime is often found accompanying economic hardship, poor family life, poor school record, and lower intelligence, combined with loneliness, hostility toward school and family, and, according to Konopka, a low self-image, an incapacity for friendship, and a turbulent onset of puberty. Psychiatric interviews of convicted female felons revealed marked parental deprivation, psychopathological disturbance, and severe adjustment problems in all areas of life.[20] Poor school performance and job records, running away from home, sexual maladjustment, and marital discord were common.

On the Minnesota Multiphasic Personality Inventory (MMPI), a personality test that is described in Chapter 7, delinquent girls and adult female offenders have the elevated Psychopathic deviate score also typical of male offenders.[21] Such people usually show deficiencies in, and perhaps also hostility toward, internalized social standards of conduct. Female offenders often have higher Paranoia scores than male offenders, expressing a more intense feeling of being misunderstood and of being different. According to the MMPI, female offenders are more introverted than male offenders. On the Eysenck Personality Inventory (EPI), women offenders appear to have disturbances of thought and tendencies toward excitability and impulsiveness, as do male offenders.[22] If there is a sex difference according to this test, it is that female offenders often have even stronger psychotic tendencies than male offenders. Both have, on the average, lower than average standardized intelligence scores (see Chapter 6). Some evidence[23] suggests that the typical female offender has an even lower IQ than the typical male offender, but it cannot be taken as proved.[24]

Whence the Gender Gap?

Are female offenders even more deviant psychologically or from even more deprived backgrounds than males,[25] as if a higher hurdle had to be cleared before a woman would break the law? Fragmentary bits of evidence suggest yes, but in a sense, the answer is yes by definition, for the female offender is a greater rarity by a factor of about ten than the male, hence more deviant in the sense of more atypical, especially for serious crimes. But it is much harder to identify the form taken by this greater female deviance. We should not expect the forms to be simple, for just as criminal behavior itself depends on multiple factors, as Chapter 2 suggested, so also may the role of gender.

Accounts of the sex difference in crime have often focused on differences in aggression, for two reasons: First, aggressiveness correlates with male criminality[26] (see Chapter 7) and, second, the sexes may differ in aggressiveness for reasons that are not entirely cultural. If aggression or its antisocial expression is stronger in the average male than the average female, then females would be less likely to pass over the threshold into criminal behavior and, when they did, they would be more atypical, or deviant, among women than male offenders are among men. The evidence for a sex difference in aggressiveness has been reviewed by Eleanor Maccoby and Carol Jacklin, who concluded by saying:

> It is time to consider whether the sex difference in aggression has a biological foundation. We contend that it does. This is not to say that aggression is unlearned. . . . There is clear evidence that aggression is learned. But the learning process calls for a form of reactivity that is not well understood, and with respect to which the sexes may have different degrees of preparedness. Let us outline the reasons why biological sex differences appear to be involved in aggression: (1) Males are more aggressive than females in all human societies for which evidence is available. (2) The sex differences are found too early in life, at a time when there is no evidence that differential socialization pressures have been brought to bear by adults to "shape" ag-

gression differentially in the two sexes . . . (3) Similar sex differences are found in man and subhuman primates. (4) Aggression is related to levels of sex hormones and can be changed by experimental administration of these hormones.[27]

The main thrust of this conclusion is not that human aggression is immutable or that every male is more aggressive than every female, but that, in given environments, typical males are more aggressive than typical females. Maccoby and Jacklin cite the results of some ninety-four studies to support their conclusions.

Each of the four reasons given by Maccoby and Jacklin can, with varying plausibility, be challenged.[28] Let us consider the common objections and try to assess their plausibility. First, while in most, perhaps all,[29] societies, males are more aggressive and occupy more of the aggressive roles (e.g., as warriors) than females, it seems to be true that some cross-cultural variation is related to child-rearing practices.[30] Thus, it has been suggested, cross-cultural data show the impact of cultural practices as much as, if not more than, biological predispositions. But it is widely agreed that the expression of aggression is molded by experience and by prevailing contingencies of reinforcement. An aggressive drive may provoke a brawl in a barroom or a quietly nasty exchange during a restrained dinner-table conversation, depending on the other factors controlling the behavior of the participants. Consequently, the universality of predominant male aggression argues strongly for a biological basis, though not for inflexibility in how it is expressed (see Chapter 2 on primary and secondary reinforcers).

Second, although psychological and physical differences between baby boys and girls are indisputable, it is hard to prove that the differences bear on aggression. Baby boys are, on average, larger, more muscular, more active, and usually play more roughly, but it can be argued that none of these characteristics unambiguously points toward adult aggression, let alone criminal behavior. Moreover, even if infant males are not directly conditioned to behave aggressively, as apparently they are not,[31] it can still be the case that parents, in subtle ways, probably do react differently, on the average, to their male and female offspring, possibly conditioning aggression in boys inadvertently. And their differing reactions probably affect, in the long run, how adult males and females behave.

But parents' reactions are not just to the child's gender as such; they are reactions to how the child behaves, and the evidence[32] indicates that among young children, boys greatly outnumber girls in frequency of peer-directed aggression, even though they are neither differentially reinforced nor punished for behaving aggressively. Youthful male aggression does not appear to be the same as male hyperactivity. Sex roles emerge from a process of mutual interaction between behavior and environment. By how he or she acts, the developing child elicits stimulation from the world around him or her, which in turn elicits subsequent behavior, and so on. Young males and young females, on the average, start off on slightly different paths, and the biological and cultural forces that guide them thereafter produce the divergences we recognize as sex roles. The universality of a gender difference in early childhood behavior points toward an inborn sex difference.

In contrast, Maccoby and Jacklin's third line of argument, drawing evidence from cross-species generalizations, seems inherently shaky. Who can say, for example, which is a more accurate model for human beings—the gibbons with their minimal sex differences in aggression, or the baboons with their extreme sex differences?[33] The extent and character of psychological sex differences among apes and monkeys seem to be associated with, for example, whether the animals live mostly in trees or on the ground, in open savannas or sheltered woodlands, or with whether they form lasting sexual relationships or are in frequent competition for mates. While most data confirm the preponderance of male aggression among primate (and other mammalian) species, there is enough variation that extrapolations to human aggression can be questioned.[34] Only in the context of the other kinds of evidence for biological differences in how or how much males and females are aggressive does the evidence from other primates lend any support to the general thesis, and then only circumstantially.

The fourth kind of evidence is based on sex hormones, and this too has been challenged on various grounds.[35] For example, estrogens (female hormones), not just androgens (male hormones), can trigger aggression in chimpanzees and monkeys.[36] Much of the clearest evidence of hormonal control of aggression is from animals,[37] with all of the attendant ambiguities of cross-species generalizations. Male hormones have been more positively tied to high activity levels in humans than to aggression per se; only pathologically high or atypical hormone levels have been involved in at least some of the studies offered in evidence for a role in ordinary sex differences, raising doubts about their relevance.

Knowledge has not yet advanced to the point where it can be said positively that human sex differences in aggression have been directly traced to differences in hormones.[38] Yet the evidence for some sort of connection is stronger than the foregoing list of objections may suggest. In a study of college wrestlers, for example, Elias measured various hormones circulating in the bloodstream just before, just after, and a half hour after a wrestling match.[39] The level of testosterone (an androgen) rose significantly during the course of the match, then subsided soon thereafter. A comparable rise also showed up in other hormones (adrenocortical steroids) believed to be associated with stressful situations. Perhaps the most interesting outcome of the study was that the surge in hormone levels was significantly larger for winners than losers. Athletes who take steroid supplements prior to a match or contest often describe the effect in terms of an increase in aggression or competitive intensity.

A genetic enzyme deficiency unusually common in several villages in the Dominican Republic provided a natural experiment on the role of biological maleness, as well as that of early environment, in shaping at least certain sex roles.[40] Genetic males, often with normal testosterone levels in utero and neonatally, were born with what appear to be female genitalia (pseudohermaphroditism). Until scientists discovered the condition and could alert parents to the true biological sex of babies suffering from it, the pseudohermaphroditic males were often reared as females. Then, at puberty, with a rising level of androgens and perhaps other physiological changes, more or less total physical virilization would occur, and the ostensible females would develop male genitalia, deep voices, male musculature, and other masculine features.

Eighteen cases of such biological males raised as females have been located and studied for sex-role differentiation. Seventeen of them shifted their subjective self-identification from female to male during or just after puberty, and sixteen shifted in almost all respects, including sexual behavior, dress, occupation, and, most relevant for our purposes here, aggressiveness. Even though child rearing in these villages distinguishes sharply between young girls and boys, with girls kept close to their mothers and housework, and with boys playing more freely away from home, almost all the pseudohermaphroditic males, though raised as females, eventually assumed adult male roles. In at least this instance, biological endowment was far more important than early experience in defining a person's sexual identity and behavior.

A few studies of hormones and aggression bear more directly on criminal behavior. Young males in prison for violent crimes were tested for levels of testosterone over a two-week period.[41] While their hormone level did not differ from that of a control group of prison guards, it was correlated with the violence of their past histories. Another study found prisoners labeled aggressive or socially dominant to be higher in testosterone level than nonaggressive and nondominant prisoners.[42] Testosterone did not discriminate between aggressive and socially dominant prisoners. In two clinical studies, injections of long-acting estrogens (female hormones) eliminated aggressive behavior in violent male sex offenders, presumably by weakening the sexual reinforcers for their crimes.[43]

The tendency of women to commit crime appears to be exacerbated by the so-called "premenstrual syndrome," further suggesting hormonal influence.[44] For many women, the monthly cycle touches an emotional bottom just before and during the early portion of menstruation, when feelings turn negative, often involving depression, anxiety, and hostility.[45] Despite questions about the quality of some of the supporting evidence and about the precise character of the emotional state,[46] it seems clear that there is at least a statistical association between the menstrual cycle and female crime. Pollak observed the relationship, but presented generally anecdotal support.[47] More recent studies make a stronger case. Among a sample of volunteers at Westfield State Farm in New York, 62 percent of unpremeditated crimes of violence were reportedly committed in the premenstrual week and another 17 percent during menstruation.[48] Among inmates of a British women's prison, almost half of the women committed their crimes during menstruation and premenstruation; 63 percent of those suffering from premenstrual tension committed their crimes at the time of their symptoms.[49] In a controlled study the behavior of forty-five inmates of the North Carolina Correctional Center for Women was observed for three complete menstrual cycles.[50] Aggressive behavior increased just before and during early portions of menstruation. Girls at an English boarding school committed more offenses at about the same point in their cycles.[51]

While aggression is often situationally controlled and the forms it takes are shaped by learning, the durability, universality, and generality of the relative aggressiveness of males cannot plausibly be blamed entirely on arbitrary sex roles. At the same time, male and female behavior, as well as differences between them, are social behavior, controlled to some extent by the full range of primary and secondary reinforcers. Neither criminal behavior nor any other kind in society is entirely under the control of a single drive, such as aggression. The model outlined in Chapter 2 shows how broadly influenced criminal behavior is; comparable theories of other sorts of human social behavior would similarly need to consider many interacting factors. The reason for focusing so sharply on aggression here is not that crime is purely, or even largely, aggressive, but that only for aggression or its expression is there evidence for constitutional sex differences of a magnitude sufficient even to approach accounting for the universality of the gender gap in crime.

Nature and Nurture in Theories of the Role of Gender

As is so often the case in social science, biological explanations vie with the sociological. Although antiquated, the prototype of the biological approach to gender and crime was Lombroso and Ferrero's search for constitutional factors.[52] They believed they had evidence of an inborn female passivity, as contrasted with inborn male vigor. Crime, they believed, required a level of energy that was more characteristic of males than females, just as it was of the sperm more than the ovum. Women were also ill-suited for crime unless they lacked the innate maternal feelings of compassion for others. In addition, Lombroso and Ferrero believed that women were less advanced evolutionarily than men, therefore less differentiated biologically. The very height of the male's evolutionary development was precarious, they believed, making him more vulnerable to the "atavism" (see Chapter 3) that they believed made certain men innately criminal. Having climbed so low on the evolutionary tree, women faced a smaller risk of plunging into criminogenic atavism. With all these biological forces distinguishing males and females, it was small wonder to Lombroso and Ferrero that there were fewer female criminals than male.

No one subscribes to Lombrosian biology anymore, but it provides a dramatic contrast to contemporary theories centered on male and female sex roles. Lombroso and Ferrero also noted the different sex roles, but considered them yet another result, along with different crime rates, of constitutional sex differences. Modern theorists, in contrast, often take close to the diametrically opposite position on the nature-nurture continuum—sex roles are said to be arbitrary, entirely a result of convention, so that changes in female sex roles should go hand in glove with changes in patterns and levels of female crime. Freda Adler's book *Sisters in Crime*[53] not only exemplifies a feminist perspective on sex differences in crime but was its dominant expression for a time. The benefits of socioeconomic equality between the sexes, said Adler, are obvious, but

> . . . there is a darker side . . . to this movement toward equality. Just as women are clamoring for and attaining opportunities in the legitimate fields, some among them are prying their way into the arena of major crime by succeeding at illegitimate endeavors which traditionally have been "for men only." When we consider that the barriers which once protected male prerogatives are breaking down and socially defined gender roles are looking increasingly alike, it should come as no surprise that once women are armed with male opportunities they would endeavor to gain status, criminal as well as civil. The fact that woman is advancing so aptly into male positions strongly suggests that the old order rested much more on male cultural domination than on female genetic destiny.[54]

Different as they are, both theories require female offenders to be masculine in some sense. For Lombroso and Ferrero, the supposed masculinity was an accident of biology; for Adler, it is the "darker side" of women's liberation. But while masculinity may apply to some female offenders,[55] it seems not to typify female offenders in general. The study by Ward et al. of violent female offenders, summarized earlier, suggested that female crimes of violence differed characteristically from male crimes of violence, and that, within the criminal social setting itself, females often take a womanly, supportive role.[56] More direct investigations of the masculinity of female offenders lead to the same conclusion. Among a group of women awaiting trial in Massachusetts, self-characterizations provided no evidence of increased masculinity, compared to nonoffenders.[57] Questionnaires administered to junior and senior high school students from a large southeastern city indicated that masculinity, defined as leadership, aggressiveness, competitiveness, ambitiousness, and successfulness, had no relation to female delinquency.[58] For males, masculinity correlated with status offenses, but not property or aggressive offenses. The absence of a correlation between masculinity and crime within each sex can be reconciled with gender's central role in crime if the differences *between* the sexes are much greater than the variations *within* each sex. The factors that make one man or woman commit a crime and another not seem to have little to do with the factors that make men in general more criminally disposed than women in general.

According to Adler's theory, the presumed narrowing gap in sex roles is creating a new, fundamentally masculinized woman, which should increase crime rates across the board and masculinize the distribution of offenders. The data provide little support for any part of the theory. The proportional rise in female crime occurred during a few years in the 1960s and early 1970s. Nothing in the theory explains why it should have been transient, as it seems to have been, given the data we so far have. The rise has mostly been in property offenses, particularly larceny, fraud, and the like. If, as the theory says, men and women are converging in their social roles, all crimes, not just property, should be converging. The distribution of offenses has long been moderately similar for men and women—even though the style of offending has been different—and, for serious offenses aside from larceny, it has not yet grown significantly more similar with the rise of the women's movement.

Another modern theorist[59] deals with the rise in property crimes by emphasizing the changing opportunities for women, rather than a changing female self-image. "The more parsimonious explanation is that as women increase their participation in the labor force their opportunity to commit certain types of crimes also increases. . . . Their propensities to commit crimes do not differ, but, in the past, their opportunities have been much more limited."[60]

But even this attenuated version of sex-role theory does not stand up to the most recent data, perhaps because women have not enjoyed a sufficient rise in opportunities.[61] The narrowing gap between male and female crime includes plenty of, for example, shoplifting.[62] While a property crime, it is hardly associated with rising status in a job market. On the contrary, shoplifting and at least some of the other increasing categories of female crime are offenses associated with low status and poverty.[63] Single-parent households, disproportionately often headed by women, are, according to recent estimates, below the poverty line in about 40 percent of the cases—a corollary of what has been called the "feminization of poverty."

If the women's movement has accelerated the rise of single-parent families, then its contribution to increased female offending is not as pictured by many contemporary theorists: "Rising rates of larceny, fraud, and forgery by women may be an indication of the increasing struggle for survival, in ways traditionally engaged in by females, of marginal women living on fixed incomes who have limited job opportunities."[64]

Other studies confirm that the typical female offender is poor, undereducated, disproportionately a member of a minority group, and dependent on her limited resources for her own support and often the support of her children.[65] Rather than a modern woman rising in a previously male-dominated economy, the typical female offender has little sympathy for the women's movement,[66] and her social and economic situation is not getting better. It may be getting relatively worse. The defective family bonds associated with male crime are also associated with female crime.[67] The Gluecks' conclusion that women and men are both led into crime by essentially the same social forces and individual dispositions seems no less correct today than it was fifty years ago, despite the increasing rates of female offending and the changes fostered by the women's movement.

Conclusions

If most women commit crimes for essentially the same reasons as most men, as the evidence suggests they do, why do they commit fewer of them? At present, our best guess centers on the difference in aggression and perhaps other primary drives that flow into the definition of sex roles. As the next chapter shows, males and females first diverge sharply in antisocial and criminal behavior in the years of early adolescence, just as the primary and secondary reinforcers of adulthood emerge and begin to shape the full range of differences in sex roles. Just as the gender gap in crime has survived the changes of recent decades, so also have the major sex roles, and most probably for similar reasons. The underpinnings of the sexual divisions of labor in human society, from the family to commerce and industry to government, may not be rigidly fixed in the genes, but their roots go so deep into the biological substratum that beyond certain limits they are hard to change. At least until now, the gender gap in serious criminal behavior has fallen outside the limits of change in the sexual divisions of labor. If it is possible at all, a world in which males and females committed serious crime at the same rate would probably be next to unrecognizable in countless other activities besides crime, from the innermost structure of family life to business, play, and government.

5

AGE

Criminal behavior depends as much or more on age than on any other demographic characteristic—sex, social status, race, family configuration, etc.—yet examined by criminologists. And it depends on age both in rate and in type of offense, as we will see. Public policy cannot do much about age, any more than it can about gender. (It would not help, for example, to pass a law banning teen-age males.) But because it is a major criminogenic trait, knowing how and why age affects crime should at least enrich our understanding. Influences that are localized at certain stages of life, such as parental care, schooling, and particular peer groups and labor markets, are separable from the influence of age itself, and are dealt with elsewhere (Chapters 8–12). This chapter reviews the major contemporary facts about crime in relation to age as such. Then it attempts, if not quite to explain them, at least to provide some theoretical context.

Life Cycle of Criminal Behavior

The Uniform Crime Reports (UCR) arrest data for 1980 are our point of departure. Of the total American population of over 226 million, the arrest statistics illustrated in Figure 1 summarize what happened in 1980 for the arresting agencies responsible for 208 million of them (about 92 percent). The curves trace the two major Index categories—property crimes

126

FIGURE 1

UCR Arrests for 1980

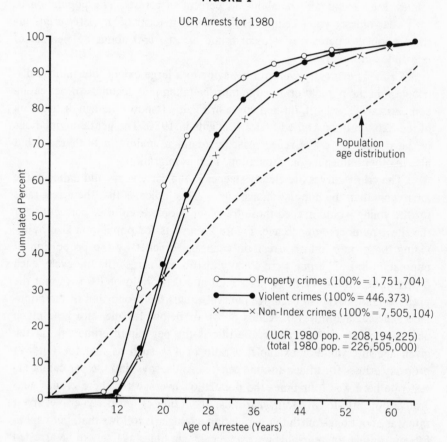

For UCR arrest data in 1980, the percent arrested that were at or below the ages indicated, for property and violent Index crime and non-Index crime. The dashed line shows the percentage of the population at large that fell into the corresponding age categories.

(i.e., burglary, larceny theft, motor vehicle theft, and arson) and violent crimes (i.e., murder and nonnegligent homicide, forcible rape, robbery, and aggravated assault)—and all non-Index crimes as a single third category containing about 77 percent of all arrests for the year. Each point on a curve shows what percentage of the total number of arrests in a crime category was of people at a given age or younger. The figure shows, for example, that almost 60 percent of (Index) property crime arrests were for twenty-year-olds or younger. For (Index) violent crimes, twenty-year-olds or younger accounted for about 37 percent of arrests, while for non-Index crimes, they accounted for about 33 percent of arrests. The population of forty-year-olds or younger included about 93 percent of property crime arrests, about 90 percent of violent crime arrests, and about 85 percent of non-Index crime arrests.

Crime is evidently youthful behavior to a large extent, but the age distribution in the population at large must be taken into account for per capita comparisons. The light, dashed curve in Figure 1 shows the age distribution of the 226.5 million United States residents in 1980. The gentle undulations in the population curve reflect past fluctuations, mainly in birth rates, but also in other influences on population, such as migration.

The crime curves are clearly steeper in the early years and flatter in the later years than the population age curve. This indicates that the arrest rates for the young would exceed those for older people even after correcting for the sheer numbers at each age. Figure 2 corrects for population size by dividing the proportion of arrests in each age bracket by the proportion of population in it. If crime were equally distributed across the life cycle, each of the three curves would be horizontal at 1.0. A ratio of 1.0 says that the proportion of arrests in each age interval equals the proportion of the population in that age interval. Ratios above or below 1.0 measure how much above or below the average crime rate is the per capita crime rate in the given age interval. For example, a ratio of 4.0, such as that for (Index) property crimes for fifteen-to-nineteen-year-olds, says that the per capita arrest rate here was four times the population average for these crimes generally. For fifty-to-fifty-four-year-olds, the (Index) property crime arrest rate was about one-fourth the population average. It follows that, per capita, fifteen-to-nineteen-year-olds were about sixteen times as likely to be arrested for these crimes as fifty-to-fifty-four-year-olds. (The ratios are plotted on a logarithmic scale so as to make distances above and below 1.0 directly comparable.)

Disregarding children below age fifteen, the arrest rate corrected by population falls throughout life in the population as a whole. Index property crimes peak most sharply and drop most rapidly; Index violent crimes are next, and non-Index crimes are the least shifted toward youthful offending. Yet, even non-Index crimes are radically skewed toward the young, as the declining ratios make obvious. By the age of forty, the population-adjusted arrest rates for all three categories of crime have fallen below their average rates in the population as a whole; and by age sixty-five, far below. Whatever they may say about criminal behavior or about the arrest patterns of the criminal justice system, the data for 1980 (which are, in general outline,

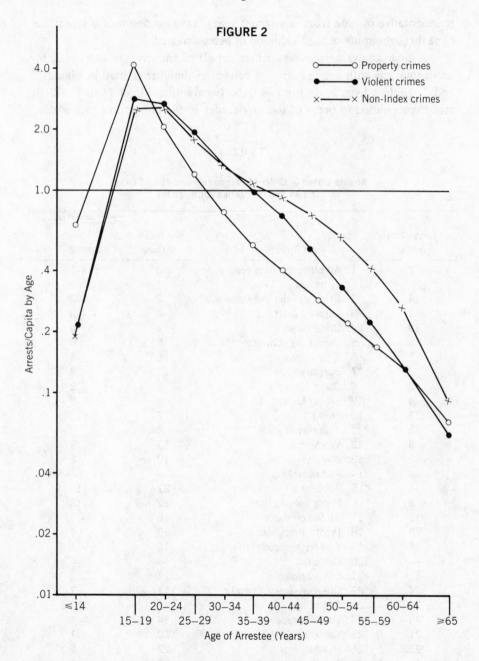

FIGURE 2

Proportion of arrests (in 1980) per proportion of the population at large in each age category for property and violent Index crime and non-Index crime, plotted on a logarithmic axis. If arrests were equally spread over the life cycle, the curves would be horizontal at a value of 1.0.

representative of data from any recent year) leave no doubt of a steady decline throughout life of the likelihood of being arrested.

A finer analysis uncovers further details of the average life cycle, for crime interacts with age in narrower categories than are plotted in Figures 1 and 2. Table 1 lists, again for 1980, the twenty-nine crimes from the UCR arrest compilation in order of their frequency in the population as a whole.[1]

TABLE 1

Arrests Listed in Order of Frequency, and Their Ranks
for Two Age Categories (UCR, 1980)

Less Than 18 Years	All Arrests	40 Years or Over	Column 1 Ranks Minus Column 3 Ranks
2	1. All other offenses (except traffic)	3	−1
14	2. Driving under the influence	2	12
1	*3. Larceny theft	4	−3
10	4. Drunkenness	1	9
5	5. Disorderly conduct	5	0
7	6. Drug abuse	11	−4
3	*7. Burglary	13	−10
8	8. Other assaults	6	2
4	9. Liquor laws	9	−5
19	10. Fraud	7	12
12	*11. Aggravated assault	8	4
6	12. Vandalism	15	−9
15	13. Weapons	10	5
—	(14. Runaways)	—	—
11	*15. Robbery	21	−10
9	*16. Motor vehicle theft	22	−13
13	17. Stolen property	16	−3
23	18. Prostitution, etc.	19	4
17	19. Forgery and counterfeiting	18	−1
—	(20. Curfew)	—	—
16	21. Sex offenses	14	2
24	22. Offenses against family	17	7
25.5	23. Gambling	12	13.5
20	*24. Forcible rape	24	−4
21	25. Vagrancy	20	1
25.5	*26. Murder, etc.	23	2.5
22	27. Suspicion	26	−4
18	*28. Arson	25	−7
27	29. Embezzlement	27	0

* Index crimes.

Index crimes are asterisked. The most common arrest category was the residual catch-all, all other offenses; the second most common was driving under the influence; the third was larceny theft, an Index crime; the least common was embezzlement. In the first column are the frequency rankings for
the population under eighteen years of age, omitting runaways and curfew
violations because they are inherently age-related. For youthful offenders,
larceny theft was the most common arrest category; all other offenses was
second; burglary was third; and embezzlement was again last. In the third
column are the rankings for the population aged forty or older. Drunkenness was the most common arrest charge; driving under the influence was
second; embezzlement, last.

From Figures 1 and 2, we know that arrests generally decline with age,
but the three lists of ranks in Table 1 show that some categories become relatively less common; some, relatively more common; and some maintain
about the same relative position among crimes. Using *ranks* of arrest rates,
rather than the arrest rates themselves, focuses attention on the pattern of
offending within age categories, independent of the general age-related decline in arrest frequencies. The fourth column, which lists the results of sub-
tracting the forty or older rank (column three) from the under eighteen
rank (column one), shows how the patterns of offending depend on age.
Any large negative number, such as the −10 for burglary, signifies a crime
that is decidedly youthful, for it indicates a large age-related drop in the
rank of a category, above and beyond the changes in sheer frequencies. Positive numbers are for crimes of later adulthood, such as gambling. Between
the teens and the forties and beyond, burglary subsides from the third-
ranking to the thirteenth-ranking arrest category. Over the same interval,
driving under the influence rises from the fourteenth-ranking category to the
second-ranking category and drunkenness rises from tenth to first. Fraud becomes relatively more common while vandalism becomes less so. Of the
eight Index crimes, all but murder and its close relation, aggravated assault,
grow relatively less common with age, especially burglary, robbery, and motor vehicle theft. Alcohol-related crimes become more common with age
while physically active or demanding crimes become less so. Several crimes
do not shift much in rank—such as disorderly conduct, vagrancy, embezzlement, forgery, and the residual category—although they may change in character. The vagrancy or disorderly conduct of a teen-ager probably differs
from that of a fifty-five-year-old. These changes in the life cycle generally fit
with intuitions about how behavior changes with aging. At the end of the
chapter, we try to tie the data, and our intuitions about them, to the model
of criminal behavior described in Chapter 2.

Considering the excess of juvenile and youthful arrests, for whatever reason, it is not surprising that crimes at the other end of the life cycle earn only negligible attention from researchers. Even so, a few broad generalizations seem possible. A substantial portion of the arrests of the elderly (for these purposes, persons over forty) are for relatively passive offenses committed by hard-core, lifelong criminals engaging in such crimes as fraud, receiving stolen property, and illegal gambling, which typically require little physical activity but some contact with a criminal network.[2] There are, of course, first-time older offenders, and their crimes tend to be more violent than those of the recidivists. They commit most of the murders, assaults, rapes, and other sex crimes of the elderly, often in association with drunkenness and other forms of substance abuse.[3] Pollak attributes this group of crimes to the psychopathologies of aging—senility, excessive fear, delusions, etc.—but even so, violent crime, almost as much as other crimes,[4] declines with age. It is possible that the violence one sees in all age groups becomes more conspicuous in older offenders because there are so few Index property offenses (see Figure 2) late in life.

While young people unquestionably account for a disproportionate share of arrests, official statistics are open to question because of the possibility of biases that may interact with age. Only a relatively small proportion of crimes are cleared by arrest, and the proportion may depend on age if there are significant age differences in the styles of offending, in the selection of crimes to commit, or in the tendencies of law enforcement agencies to be more or less lenient toward particular age groups. Consequently, it is appropriate to look at some other sorts of data besides arrest statistics in even a brief review of the role of age in crime.

Using National Crime Survey (NCS) victimization data from twenty-six major American cities for the years 1973–1977, Hindelang and McDermott examined reports of crimes such as rape, robbery, assault, and some burglaries and other thefts in which the assailant is seen by the victim.[5] Despite the uncertainty in victims' estimates of the age of an offender, the victimization survey data matched the UCR arrest statistics in general outline, although, as usual, offenses far outnumbered arrests. For the "personal" crimes (rape, robbery, and assault), Figure 3 shows the annual rates of offending per 100,000 potential offenders in three age categories. The highest rates of offending were by eighteen-to-twenty-year-old males, with twelve-to-seventeen-year-old males the second most frequent offenders. Among female offenders, twelve-to-seventeen-year-olds generally committed crimes at a higher rate than eighteen-to-twenty-year-olds. In each sex, the lowest offense rates were by twenty-one-year-olds or older. The extraordinarily high figures (particularly for young males) are, it should be noted, for crime *incidents,* not criminals, since victimization data cannot readily be used to identify particular offenders. (They do not show that out of 100,000 males between eighteen and twenty, 25,800 are criminals, but that for every 100,000 men of that age, 25,800 personal offenses were committed annually in the five years from 1973–1977.)

The exceptionally large excess of male to female crime in Figure 3 reflects the crime categories, which include the more predominately male offenses of rape, robbery, and assault, rather than the less predominately male offenses, such as larceny theft (see Table 3, Chapter 4). From arrest statistics, we would expect the violent offenses represented in Figure 3 to show relatively less age decline than the still larger categories of property crimes, but it is nevertheless clear that from the victim's standpoint, no less than from the arresting agency's, crime rates peak in the teens.

Though more active criminally, juveniles (below eighteen years) committed fewer serious crimes than adults, according to victimization surveys, as measured by weapons use, by completion of theft, and by the size of financial loss. Juvenile felons injured their victims more often than adult felons, probably because, with fewer weapons, they resorted to physical force more often. Juveniles committed more of their crimes in groups (thereby inflating juvenile arrest statistics). Their crimes were apparently less well planned, and, even for crimes classified under "property," were more often motivated, judging from the small gains, by other than financial considerations, such as peer pressure or sheer adventurousness. Except for the many senior citizens victimized by juveniles looking for easier targets (perhaps again a by-product of fewer weapons), the age of the victim correlated with age of the offender.

Yet another approach to the age-crime relationship is to ask people directly about their criminal inclinations or histories and see how the answers vary with their ages. In just such a study, Rowe and Tittle analyzed the responses of almost two thousand people living in New Jersey, Iowa, and Oregon, chosen to represent the adult populations in the three states.[6] In a one-hour interview (in 1972), subjects were asked about their own propensities and past behavior concerning four crimes: (1) a theft worth about $50; (2) illegal gambling; (3) deliberately harming somebody; and (4) cheating on income taxes. If their responses are extrapolated to the population at large, the respondents acknowledged seventy to two hundred times as many assaults and two to thirteen times as many felonious thefts as were reported in FBI records, but the age-crime relationship was nevertheless clearly in evidence.

Figure 4 shows the percentages for successively older groups of respondents, from fifteen-to-twenty-four-year-olds to sixty-five-to-ninety-three-year-olds, in four broad age categories. The filled circles give the percentages of

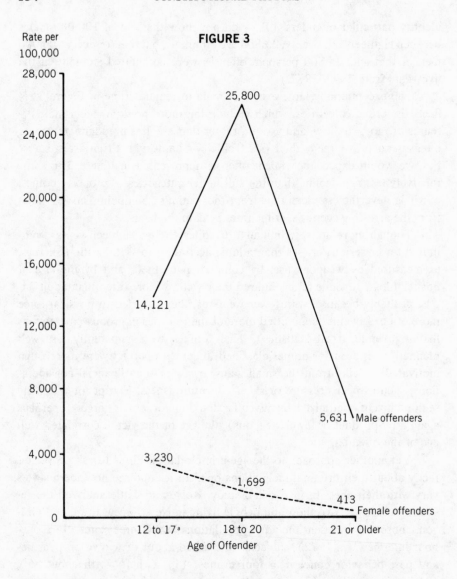

FIGURE 3

[a] The numerator of the rates of offending for 12-to-17-year-olds includes incidents (about 1 percent of the total) in which the offender was perceived by the victim to be under 12 years of age. The denominator of the rate is the number of 12-to-17-year-olds in the general population.

Source: From M. J. Hindelang and M. J. McDermott, *Juvenile Criminal Behavior: An Analysis of Rates and Victim Characteristics* (Washington, D.C.: Government Printing Office, 1981), p. 45.

Male and female annual rates of offending (personal offenses only) per 100,000 potential offenders in each of three age categories, as estimated from National Crime Survey victimization data for 1973–1977.

FIGURE 4

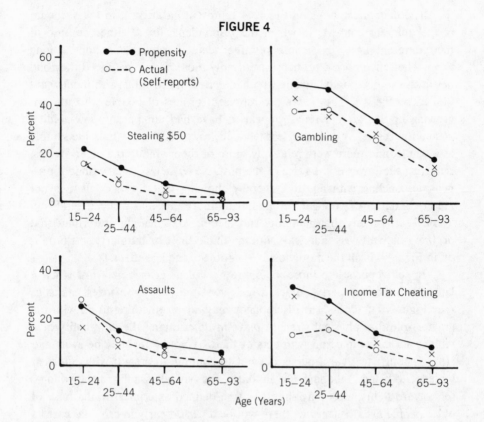

Adapted from A. R. Rowe and C. R. Tittle, Life cycle changes and criminal propensity, *The Sociological Quarterly* (1977), 18:228.

Respondents in the indicated age brackets were asked if they had, within the preceding five years, committed any of the four offenses (actual) or if they thought they were capable of doing so in the future (propensities). The Xs are propensities for respondents who said they have never personally known anyone in trouble with the law. Plotted are the percentages of respondents answering in the affirmative.

those who admitted any chance whatever of committing the crime in question "tomorrow," given a strong desire or need to do so; the open circles, the percentages of those who acknowledged having engaged in the crime sometime during the preceding five years. The two measures are nearly parallel, with self-reported propensities yielding higher estimates than self-reported past behavior in almost all cases (assaults being the single exception), and both unambiguously confirm the decline of criminality with age.

The unconnected Xs on Figure 4 represent an attempt to take account of the different contexts in which the respondents lived, either because of their different ages or because of other demographic distinctions among them. The self-reported propensities of only those people who said they had never known personally anyone who had gotten into trouble with the law are plotted by the Xs. They therefore represent groups of people who, though growing up at different times, appear to have had comparably law-abiding acquaintances. They admitted less tendency to break the law than the sample as a whole, and there were relatively more of them among the older groups, reflecting the lower crime rates of the past. Nevertheless, their criminal propensities decline with age too, thereby showing that the age effect is not merely a matter of younger people having more criminal associates. (From Table 1, it is likely that gambling and income tax cheating are crimes that decline relatively less than, say, motor vehicle theft or burglary, so the fall-off in Figure 4 is all the more positive support of the age effect.)

In self-reports like those in Figure 4, violent crimes may not reach a later peak than property crimes, which is at variance with arrest statistics (see Figures 1 and 2). The discrepancy may have something to do with the greater role that physical strength plays in determining the criminality of a violent act in comparison with acts of theft. A youngster may be swift and strong enough to steal a purse, but not to commit an assault with sufficient violence to bring in the law. Or, similarly, the typical assaults of the young—schoolyard fights, etc.—may simply not be defined as crimes, while those of older people are. Either way, there will be a period early in criminal careers when a general propensity to commit crime will show up differentially in property and violent *arrests,* but not in self-reports gathered the way Rowe and Tittle's were.[7]

Rowe and Tittle concluded from their survey that there is a genuine life cycle for criminal behavior, above and beyond the effects of any artifact of official statistics or intergenerational changes in the overall crime rate, and attempted to evaluate some possible causes of it. Their evaluation, along with other perspectives on age, will be discussed later. But first we need to examine more deeply this criminal life cycle that emerges in official arrest statistics, victimization surveys, and self-reported tendencies and past behavior.

More Than One Kind of Life Cycle

Neither juvenile nor adult criminals are homogeneous groups. Within each age category are individuals who commit only one or a few crimes during their lifetimes, and other individuals, fortunately less common, who commit a disproportionately large share of crimes, particularly the more violent and serious offenses. These different patterns may be running their course in any unselected cohort, each one obscuring somewhat the characteristics of the others in average statistics. The contrast is illustrated in a longitudinal analysis of police and court records of three birth cohorts (born in 1942, 1949, and 1955) of 6,127 males and females in Racine, Wisconsin, spanning a period from 1948 to 1976.[8] The most common individual pattern of delinquent behavior was a decrease in seriousness and an eventual cessation of offending after the teen-age years. Over 90 percent of the males and about 65 percent of the females by their own report engaged in at least some illegal activity in childhood or adolescence, but most of them stopped as they grew up, without any direct contact with the law. In contrast, of the 12 percent of the sample judged to be habitually delinquent, about 50 percent went on to adult criminal careers characterized by even more serious offenses of various sorts, at least during early adulthood and perhaps thereafter. In that small fraction of the population committing many offenses, youthful crime was highly predictive of adult offending.

The large Philadelphia cohort study agrees in several respects with the Racine study, as far as age trends are concerned.[9] A representative sample of about one thousand males born in Philadelphia in 1945 and still resident there at least between the ages of ten and eighteen have been followed into their thirties through various school, police, and Selective Service files, and, where possible, have been directly interviewed to ascertain their personal histories and psychological attributes. By the age of twenty-six, 43 percent had some sort of police record; by thirty, 47 percent had a record. The likelihood of being an adult offender (by the age of twenty-six) was more than three times as great for former juvenile offenders as for former juvenile non-offenders. For those with just a single police contact, almost twice as many had it prior to the age of eighteen as had it between eighteen and thirty. Of those who had five or more police contacts by the age of thirty (i.e., chronic offenders), 87 percent already had five or more by the age of eighteen. Put another way, almost nine out of ten chronic offenders could have been identified as such by the age of eighteen. For offenders generally, about three out of four had police records by the age of eighteen. The Philadelphia and Racine studies, as well as others,[10] leave no doubt that crime is not only disproportionately packed into the teens and early twenties, but that active offenders are usually active early.

The offenses committed by the Philadelphia sample grew more serious as the cohort grew older. This fact is open to several interpretations. It could, for example, mean that as the typical juvenile offender gets older, he commits graver crimes. But it turns out that the criminal population at different ages is made up of different sorts of offenders, with more dangerous people more heavily represented in older offender populations, who, in fact, get more dangerous as they get older, at least for some period of their careers. Similarly, in and of itself, the much-documented decline in crime rates with age is also equivocal. Is it that the typical juvenile offender commits fewer crimes as he or she grows up, or that a shrinking population of offenders is committing crimes at a steady, or even an increasing, rate beyond the teens? The Racine and Philadelphia cohorts suggest the latter alternative for a subset of chronic offenders, but we should scrutinize this important question further.

In an attempt to separate variations in individual arrest rates from variations in the composition of the offender population, arrest histories were analyzed for 5,338 adult offenders arrested (over thirty-two thousand arrests) for homicide, rape, robbery, aggravated assault, burglary, or auto theft in Washington, D.C., during 1973.[11] The Washington population differs from the national population in racial makeup and perhaps in other ways as well, and the arrest records were unavailable for offenders younger than eighteen. In addition to excluding juveniles, the selection procedure made it highly likely that the sample was biased toward high-frequency, serious offenders. Even so, beyond the age of eighteen, the sample approximated the national pattern of declining arrest rate with age, though its decline to the age of forty was not as sharp as in the country as a whole.

In order to disentangle some of the reasons for the decline in arrests with age, four separate age cohorts were isolated within the sample, defined by whether the offender had turned eighteen in 1963, 1964, 1965, or 1966. Only those who had at least one arrest between eighteen and twenty-one were included, and their records were searched for arrests between the year when members of each of the cohorts reached the age of twenty-one and 1972 (i.e., 1966–1972, 1967–1972, 1968–1972, 1969–1972 for the four cohorts). In this way, arrestees from different cohorts, whose criminal careers began "recently enough to provide reasonable numbers of cases and distant enough to provide several years of observation," could be compared.[12] When the oldest cohort was twenty-one, for example, it had .19 arrests per year for any single type of crime, but for the youngest cohort, though only about three years younger, the corresponding arrest rate was .32 at the age of twenty-one, an increase of almost 70 percent in just three years. Each successively later cohort had a higher average arrest rate at a given age than the earlier cohorts at that age. Within each cohort, over the limited age intervals observed (i.e., twenty-one to twenty-seven for the oldest cohort, twenty-one to twenty-four for the youngest), there was no sign of a declining arrest rate with age. The apparent age decline in the Washington sample as a whole was at least partly due to the rising arrest rates in more recent cohorts.

Carrying the analysis still further, individual arrest rates were estimated within each of the four cohorts for specific crimes. Rather than declining with age during the third decade of life, individual arrest rates increased with age for burglary, narcotics, and the residual "all others"; arrest rates for robbery, larceny, and auto theft were independent of age; for aggravated assault and weapons offenses, arrest rates increased with age in one cohort but not for the others. No other crime categories were examined.

From the evidence of longitudinal data, it seems that the early peak in per capita arrests in national statistics probably reflects a large number of teen-age offenders whose criminal careers end quickly, and also a rising crime rate, so that the young offenders at any given time come from criminally more active cohorts. The method of selection for the Washington sample excluded many of the short-term youthful offenders and yielded a preponderance of adult chronic offenders, whose individual rates did not decline during their twenties. Over the relatively short segment of their careers analyzed, the rate of offending depended more on criminal specialization and cohort than on age. In these respects, the Washington sample resembled the chronic, serious offenders isolated in the Racine, the Philadelphia, and other longitudinal studies.

Let us summarize these studies by constructing from them a somewhat simplified picture of the life cycles of criminal behavior during the past two decades. In aggregate, cross-sectional statistics, crime rates decline with age beyond the late teens. The decline partly reflects the increasing level of crime: Younger people at any time belong to criminally more active cohorts. In addition, the decline with age occurs because people who will commit only one or a few offenses during their lifetimes tend to do so early. Consequently, the offenders at older ages will tend to commit more, and, as it turns out, more serious, crimes. The life cycle of criminal behavior for these hard-core offenders no doubt also declines with age, but the decline is postponed by at least a decade and perhaps by more in many instances.

Interactions with Age

Crime Rate

Whether the age decline in crime is due to declining individual crime rates or to a contracting core of offenders among older populations, or both, a change in the age composition of the population must affect the total crime rate. Shifts toward a more youthful population, such as during the "baby boom" years after World War II, would be expected to produce increasing crime rates as the babies grew into adolescence in the 1960s. As the war babies passed out of the peak crime years of the late teens, not being suc-ceeded by as large a population of new teen-agers, the aggregate crime rates should have fallen, if only these simple population factors mattered. To the extent that the simple demographics do not fully account for changes in crime rates, other explanations need to be found.

Various estimates place the contribution of the changing age distribu-tion to the rising crime rates of the 1960s at between 10 to 50 percent, de-pending on specific details of the methods of estimation.[13] Between 1958 and 1969, for example,[14] the rate of actual Index crimes per capita (esti-mated from UCR arrest statistics, clearance rates, and census data) rose by about 175 percent; taking the age distribution into account reduces the in-crease in the total offense rate (per person of a given age) to 97 percent. The rate of offending within age intervals thus still rose, but by 45 percent less than the rate for the population as a whole, according to this estimate and for these years. The demographic changes by themselves would have ex-plained almost half of the observed increase in Index property crimes, but only about 10 percent of that in Index violent crimes, for which the rate among teen-agers of given ages rose dramatically during the period, particu-larly for robbery and aggravated assault. Fifteen-year-olds born in 1953 or 1954 committed Index violent crimes at four times the rate of those born in 1943 or 1944; sixteen-year-olds born in 1952 or 1953 committed them at 3.6 times the rate of those born in 1942 or 1943; and so on.

Since 1960, crime has risen more rapidly than population, even within age brackets. The pattern of offending has also been changing, as Table 2 shows for arrest data. The percentages give the increases in arrests within the time periods indicated for the population as a whole, and for those under eighteen and those eighteen and over, all corrected for population size within the relevant age categories. From 1960 to 1968, both violent and property Index crime arrests of juveniles (less than eighteen years old) in-creased disproportionately, that is to say, more than arrests for the popula-tion as a whole. The juvenile disproportion was much greater for violent than property crime. Then in the late sixties and early seventies the increase in youthful crime began to level off to about that for the whole population. (Gold and Reimer report a virtual decrease in their self-report data, but their sample was somewhat unrepresentative.[15]) Since the mid-seventies, there have been disproportionately small, or nonexistent, increases in the

TABLE 2

Total Arrest Trends of Index Crimes (Excluding Arson)a

Years	Type of Crime	Total All Ages	Under Age 18	Age 18 and Over
1977–1981	Violent	11.8	5.6	12.3
	Property	4.2	−9.6	19.5
1973–1977	Violent	6.6	10.9	4.1
	Property	19.9	17.9	25.9
1968–1973	Violent	37.4	57.6	28.6
	Property	14.7	14.6	22.7
1960–1968	Violent	42.8	109.7	30.0
	Property	46.5	59.1	33.5

a Expressed as percent increase during specified periods net of changes in population.

rate of arrests of juveniles, especially for property offending, which actually decreased from 1977 to 1981. Overall, during the past two decades, arrests of adults (eighteen or over) for Index crimes have risen more for property offenses, while for juveniles (younger than eighteen) arrests for violent crimes have risen more sharply.

Other demographic variables, such as degree of urbanization, socio-economic status, educational level, etc., would need to be considered in an analysis of historical trends, as distinguished from age effects.[16] For our purposes here, it can be concluded that only a fraction of the post–World War II rising crime rates can be explained by changing age distributions as such. Crime rates have risen more than the age distribution would have implied, and they have risen most for juvenile violent crimes.

Gender

In every age bracket, males commit more crimes, or are more often arrested, than females, but the degree of difference has its own life cycle. Figure 3 presented victimization survey data for 1973–1977, separated by gender. Corrected for population differences, males accounted for 81 percent of the personal (i.e., rape, robbery, and assault) crime incidents committed by twelve-to-seventeen-year-olds, 94 percent of those committed by eighteen-to-twenty-year-olds, and 93 percent of those committed by those twenty-one years or older.

The pattern of a rising proportion of male offending in the teens, then leveling off in early adulthood is characteristic of arrest data, as well as victimization surveys. Figure 5 presents the percentage of male arrests in the 1981 UCR data, corrected by the population sex ratios, in successive age brackets. Total arrests (plotted as squares) rise from 76 percent male in the below-age-fifteen category to 85 percent in the eighteen-to-twenty-one category, and remain almost level before rising to 87 percent in the forty-to-sixty-four category and to just over 90 percent for those over sixty-five. Most of this later increase is due to rising alcohol-related crimes, which are predominately male. Property Index crimes (open circles) are similar up to twenty-one, then the male percentage declines as female larceny theft rises in middle and later adulthood, but at no point does the male percentage fall below 65 percent. The male percentage for violent Index crimes (filled circles) runs nearly parallel to that for total crimes throughout life. We may assume that the rising percentage of male violence in later life also arises in part from the effects of alcohol abuse.

Males in general accounted for 85 percent of all arrests (see Chapter 4), Index and non-Index, but in certain categories at certain ages, the male percentage was much higher. For sex offenses and rape at sixty-five or older, for example, there were 1,345 males arrested and 7 females, for a percentage of 99.6. For twenty-two-year-olds, the male percentage in these categories was 90.4 percent, still a clear preponderance but not virtually a male crime, as it becomes in old age. The occasional bits of evidence for a "second peak"[17] in female crime, comprising first-time offenders in the menopausal period of the late forties and early fifties, are not supported by national arrest statistics, but that could be because such a "peak" is washed out by overriding age trends in most criminal categories.

The most pervasive interaction between crime, age, and gender is the rise in the male proportion as soon as the statistics begin, in the range of ten to sixteen years. If anything, the true male proportion of crime, as distinguished from arrests, rises even more steeply (as the victimization data, in fact, do), for, judging from self-reports[18] at the very early ages, boys are more likely to be arrested than girls for a given offense. Since, for older offenders, this particular sex bias gets smaller or disappears, the curve in Figure 5 would be expected to decline during the teens if just police behavior were involved. Instead, the curve rises in virtually every crime category. The most probable explanation is that the years of puberty and early adolescence are when much of the sex difference in crime (see Chapter 4) is established. Prior to this period of life, the precursors of criminal behavior may differ for males and females, but not as much as after the changes of adolescence. And after this period, other forces further shape the

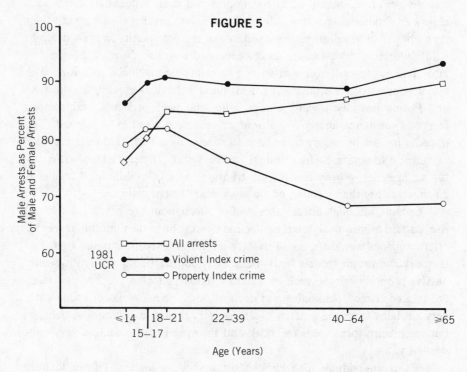

FIGURE 5

For the age and crime categories indicated, the percent of all arrests in 1981 that were of men.

sex ratios, such as the emergence in the middle years of female larceny theft or, in the later years, of male public drunkenness.

Conclusion: What the Age Effect Means

In general, the tendency to break the law declines throughout life. Only a few qualifications are needed to square this broad generalization with the facts as we know them.

First, crime declines only after an initial rise in childhood and the early teens. Although this may seem too obvious to warrant attention, the low crime rates of the first dozen years of life deserve explanation as much as the higher crime rates of the adolescent years do. Children are typically closely watched by adults who have the power, physically and by arranging contingencies of reinforcement, to control their behavior, and their major needs and desires are attended to. The strongest and most influential people in a child's environment—parents, adult relatives, and teachers—usually consider it an obligation to reinforce the standards of the community in their dealings with children. Only later, in adolescence and beyond, do most people run into "bad influences" able and willing to reinforce antisocial activities. The major sources of reinforcement for criminal behavior—money, sex, intense and lasting hostility toward others, antisocial peer pressure, and various forms of substance abuse—are absent or relatively weak in childhood. The appetite for sex or money takes time to reach full power, as do the cravings of various addictions. The criminal justice system, from its laws to its arresting agencies, mostly ignores the transgressions of childhood, but this is an effect, rather than a cause, of the low crime rates of children.

Second, although crime rates decline throughout life beyond the initial rise, certain crimes peak later, or decline slower, or both, than the aggregate crime statistics would suggest. Property crimes of a vigorous nature—such as burglary and motor vehicle theft—peak early and decline quickly. Physically passive property crimes, such as fraud or receiving stolen property, or alcohol-related crimes, peak later and decline slowly. No significant crime category deviates from the pattern of an early peak and a subsequent decline, but the precise location of the peak and the speed of the decline vary substantially.

Third, individuals also vary. Most juvenile offenders (if we include those who acknowledge offenses in self-reports but have never been arrested for them) do not become adult offenders. Almost all chronic adult offenders were also juvenile offenders; most of them were, in fact, chronic juvenile offenders. The most active offenders can be expected to have the longest criminal careers—typically starting early, not reaching a peak until perhaps as late as the mid-twenties, and then declining more slowly than the population average. To these chronic offenders, society owes not only a disproportionate share of offenses (as many as 75 percent of them by some estimates[19]) but also a disproportionately serious brand of crime.[20] Less prolific criminal careers typically start later, though still usually in the teens, peak sooner, then decline more rapidly. To be sure, any sort of offender, from one-time to chronic, may turn up at any age, but the odds are strongly weighted toward the teen-age years.

Why does age affect crime? It is not hard to find or to invent explanations by the dozen.[21] Youth is the adventurous time of life; old age, the settled time. This leads not only to more youthful crime, according to this line of thought, but also to more detectable youthful crime. Older people often occupy positions of trust, in which they can commit surreptitious crimes.

Young people are less skilled in their work than older people, hence more likely to be caught when they break the law. Youth is a time of intense and unfulfilled passions, leading to crimes for goods and pleasures that older people either crave less or can enjoy legally. Young people suffer more unemployment, hence have not only the need but the time for illegal gains. Young people experience more inequity than older people, and tend to express their feelings more overtly. Older people have learned that crime does not pay. Youthful criminals live fast and dangerously, and therefore tend to die young, leaving a more law-abiding population to grow old. The criminal justice system is lenient toward the very young and old, producing an apparent peak in offending in between. Young people are more exposed to the disinhibiting influences of the mass media; old people are more interested in religion, with its moral injunctions. And so on.

While such explanations are more or less plausible, and may, indeed, be more or less correct, none of them has gained much empirical support. In their self-report study, for example, Rowe and Tittle controlled for the possible explanatory power of a host of demographic factors, such as education, occupation, family size, home life, and so on. The age effect survived them all. They questioned their subjects on their degree of integration into social life, on their moral commitments, on their concern about legal sanctions, and on the extent of their need for the fruits of various crimes. Virtually all of the predictive power of age was left after controlling for any one of these variables; combining the variables explained some, but far from all, of the effects of age. That is to say, an older person is likely to have a lower propensity for crime than a younger person, even after they have been matched in demographic variables such as education, occupation, need, moral commitments, fear of sanctions, and social integration as measured by survey methods.

Age, like gender, resists explanation because it is so robust a variable.[22] None of the correlates of age, such as employment, peers, or family circumstances, explains crime as well as age itself. It may be plausible, for example, that the economic deprivations of early adulthood or late adolescence contribute to youthful crime, but economic circumstances predict crime (see Chapter 12) less than age and therefore can hardly be the explanation of the age effect. Also, not much has come of efforts to show that marriage and family obligations, rather than age, account for the declining criminal activity.[23] Although each correlate of age, such as income, marriage, family, and energy level, may contribute something to criminal behavior, age itself as a variable combines enough of them to be the prime predictor.

Age is robust not only across contemporary conditions but across time and geography, again like gender. Hirschi and Gottfredson have reviewed data from England, Wales, France, and the United States over the past 150 years and have found a high degree of invariance in the age distributions, in spite of the large differences in overall rates of offending. Indirect evidence suggests a similar picture in the Soviet Union. The early peak and subsequent decline of crime have been virtually ubiquitous, although, as the overall crime rate increases, the peak may occur at a younger age. Even in the homogeneous environment of prison, the per capita rate of infractions rises to a peak in the early twenties and declines thereafter.[24]

The historical and geographical generality of the age effect argues against theories that rely on highly specific features of contemporary life, such as the coincidence between the end of compulsory schooling and the peak of criminal activity.[25] It is apparently true that crime rates rise during the final compulsory school year, but the growing propensity toward delinquency may influence where society sets the school-leaving age no less than the reverse. School may exacerbate criminal tendencies in certain adolescents, but it does not entirely explain them (see Chapter 10). Theories that focus on the post–World War II "youth culture" or the "counterculture" of the 1960s or the contemporary "drug culture" shed light on certain youthful crimes, but not on the basic shape of the age distribution, which has prevailed through all these sociological changes, plus many others. To understand age in relation to crime, we need to consider more lasting features of the life cycle.

Let us consider how the model outlined in Chapter 2 may be applied hypothetically to the age distribution in offending. The rise in crime in childhood and early puberty accompanies the awakening of major sources of reinforcement for delinquent behavior—money, sex, and peers who value independence of, or even defiance of, conventional morality. At the same time, the growing child is becoming literally, as well as psychologically, independent of powerful adults (parents, etc.) who might enforce conventional standards. Given energy, strength, potent new sources of drive but few legitimate means of consummation, a lack of economic and social skills, and peers who are similarly vigorous and frustrated, the adolescent years are destined to foster a rise in delinquency. Self-report studies confirm that almost all teen-agers, 90 percent or more in some populations, commit at least one criminal offense.

It is hard to picture a modern society in which youngsters would not pass through a period of nonconformity, and, indeed, the data do not call on us to picture any such, given the apparent ubiquity of the early peak. However, depending on other factors, the juvenile rise may be steep or shallow, early or late.[26] Societies that maintain strong parental or adult control should have a later peak. Industrialization and the accompanying rise of youth cultures (see Chapter 17) foster juvenile crime. If money and sex are for any reason less reinforcing, because of their availability or of strong negative conditioning against them, there may be less adolescent crime; likewise if there are simply fewer teen-agers providing peer support for unconventional or antisocial behavior. The model provides an account of why crime rises in the transition to adulthood, but leaves room for considerable variation in when and how much.

In adulthood one would expect crime to subside. The small gains from petty crimes will lose their power to reinforce most adults who now have legitimate sources of money, sex, alcohol, or status. At the same time, the reinforcers for noncrime grow, as ties to the adult community develop, perhaps along with a family. The opinions of adult peers will, in most cases, further diminish the attractions of crime by inculcating internalized prohibitions against it. For that reason, as well as for purely developmental changes in how people view right and wrong, the typical person passing into adulthood shifts from the egocentric and hedonistic focus of childhood to more abstract and principled guidelines to action.[27] Meanwhile, time horizons extend further into the future; the average adult delays gratification more readily than the average child or adolescent. If for no other reason, with stronger internal constraints against wrongdoing and a greater weight on delayed consequences of behavior, the average adult should more often choose noncrime than those less "mature" in these respects.

Of course, at each age, people vary along all of the criminogenic variables, as subsequent chapters describe. Those few individuals who fail to find legitimate means of success, who get especially adept at benefiting from crime, who do not form ties to the community (or who actively scorn it), who do not internalize prohibitions, or who are afflicted with extreme impulsiveness or intense, antisocial drives that overwhelm the ordinary contingencies of reinforcement, may well continue active criminal careers beyond the usual term. But they too slow down eventually, perhaps as the drives cool off, or the prohibitions or community ties finally sink in, or the time horizons finally stretch out, or the increasingly severe penalties of the criminal justice system for recidivists finally make crime insufficiently rewarding. Or, failing all that, simply the diminishing capacities of later life make crime too dangerous or unlikely to succeed, especially where there are younger and stronger criminal competitors, or victims who will not be cowed.

6

INTELLIGENCE

To many people, it would seem absurd to imagine that low intelligence could have an important effect on individual differences in criminality. To these skeptics, crime is caused by abusive families, or blocked opportunities, or wanton selfishness, or moral bankruptcy. We can all think of dull people who struggle along honestly and decently, and smart people who cheat and connive. Even if we grant—as, in view of the evidence presented in the last two chapters, we must—that gender and age are powerful contributors to criminality, intelligence seems a different sort of factor. Whereas maleness may make some people more aggressive, and youth may make them more reckless, dullness would seem to make people no more or no less likely to commit crimes than smartness. If anything, being dull might make one more passive.

In fact, there appears to be a clear and consistent link between criminality and low intelligence. That is, taking all offenders as a group, and ignoring differences among kinds of crime, criminals seem, on the average, to be a bit less bright and to have a different set of intellectual strengths and weaknesses than do noncriminals as a group. Before we can understand why intelligence, or its lack, may contribute to crime, we must first understand what is meant by intelligence and how it is measured.

With extraordinary speed, the idea of objective intelligence testing grew in a few decades around the turn of the twentieth century from a theoretical possibility to psychology's major practical contribution to society, for good or ill. In the 1880s and 1890s, a few academics in Europe and the United States were describing in learned works the results from unstandardized and unsubstantiated tests administered to a few dozen volunteers or schoolchildren; by the end of World War I in 1918, almost two million American soldiers had taken Army intelligence tests based on at least a degree of standardization and validation for the American population. Since then, the uses and varieties of standardized testing have continued to multiply; by now, billions of tests of intellectual aptitude have been administered all over the world for all sorts of purposes.[1]

Intelligence testing evidently suited the times. The expansion of public education in industrial countries called for the creation of school curricula appropriate to the broad range of abilities and cultural backgrounds of the children entering the school system, often from families with little or no history of formal schooling. Matching a child to an appropriate curriculum became, and remains, one of the jobs for which tests are used. The growing mobility of people within and across national boundaries similarly encouraged a search for ways to gauge learning ability as much as possible without regard to a child's past exposure to schooling. Conscription into increasingly mechanized armies and navies also raised the problem of assessing learning capacity. Industrialization itself, with its complex machines, tools, and services, created a growing use for tests that could measure vocational aptitude and on-the-job teachability. The decline of simple manual labor was accompanied by the growth of specialized occupations for which greater intellectual potential or higher levels of education were a prerequisite.

Besides the practical pressures that promoted testing, its implicit democratic assumption was also in tune with the changing times. The same societies that were willing to invest in free public education were likely to be receptive to tests that presupposed no bounds of social class, race, or nationality on intellectual capacity, at least in principle. Why tests now seem to many to have failed to live up to this democratic ideal is a story of its own, beside our point here, which is simply that tests reflected the growing egalitarian spirit. Testing did, in fact, uncover a wide range of intellectual capacities in all social classes, races, and nationalities. Theories of racial or national superiority cannot rationally survive in the face of evidence of the overlapping distributions of ability for broad and diverse populations. But the corollary of the comparability (if not precise equality) of all large social and national populations was, as we will see, that the range of variation in individual intelligence within a society could have deep social significance.

People obviously vary in intelligence, and, to most observers, it is apparent that the variations are somewhat inherited. Great or lesser talents, as well as major or minor intellectual disabilities, seem to run in families, much the same way as height or physique or hair color or the shape of the family chin. What had been missing was the ability to quantify these intuitions about the variation and inheritance of intelligence. The attempts in the 1860s, 1870s, and 1880s by Francis Galton, Charles Darwin's younger cousin, to find an objective index of human intelligence were largely unsuccessful, but the underlying conception was convincing enough that others rapidly joined the search, either as followers of Galton or independently inspired by the same evolutionary thinking.[2]

Galton's tests did not gain acceptance, but those of Alfred Binet, a French psychologist whose efforts started in the 1890s, did. Binet's approach to testing differed from Galton's in two crucial respects. First, whereas Galton's tests concentrated on sensory acuity and sensory-motor reactions, Binet's involved self-evidently intellectual skills directly, such as reasoning, using language, comparing situations, making judgments, and so on.[3] It was quickly apparent that Binet's approach was more promising than Galton's, for, among other reasons, the latter's sensory-motor tests did not find much reliable individual variation, while Binet's did, given the measuring instruments of the time. Moreover, the variation on Binet's tests evidently had something to do with the subjective impressions people had of each other's intelligence. More often than not, people who earned high scores on Binet's tests also seemed intelligent to those who knew them, and conversely for those who earned low scores. The items on Binet's tests seemed self-evidently pertinent to intelligence, but not so on Galton's.

Another difference was that Binet's tests, unlike Galton's, were age-graded.[4] Binet was trying to find tests to measure intelligence among young children; Galton, among adults. Tests that can discriminate among three-year-olds are bound to differ from tests that discriminate among ten-year-olds. As Binet accumulated a battery of age-graded test items, he discovered that at each age any sample of children would span a range of "mental ages," as measured by the performances on his tests. A six-year-old who could, for example, pass items up to the eight-year-old level plus, say, half of the nine-year-level items had a mental age of eight and a half years, two and a half years ahead of his or her chronological age. Such a precocious child almost invariably seemed brighter in many respects than a six-year-old who passed only the items up to the four-year level, and whose mental age was consequently retarded by two years.

Because intelligence does, in fact, develop chronologically, and because youngsters who are advanced, average, or retarded at an early age tend to stay that way, Binet's search for age-graded, self-evidently relevant test items eventually paid off, but the search was neither brief nor easy. Finding test items that were relatively insensitive to different histories of education, yet still diagnostic of intelligence, proved a substantial challenge. Even for the earliest tests, scores were based on performance relative to one's peers, not simply on the number of right and wrong answers, but it was hard to establish suitable standards for the comparisons. Because scores on intelligence tests typically use relative rank in some population, it was some time before reliable and representative norms were established. Many of the necessary statistical procedures were unknown or undeveloped at the time that Galton, Binet, or their immediate successors launched their studies. In fact, the requirements of sampling and test construction became a major source of innovation in the evolution of the theory and technique of statistics itself.

While the chronological approach to testing was one of Binet's strengths, it also created distortions in tests for adults. Most aspects of mental development level off in adolescence or early adulthood; mental age reaches a limit while age in years marches on. Knowledge and wisdom may continue to grow, but, for the most part, sheer intellectual capacity does not. If the average person reaches full mental capacity by, say, the age of eighteen, a simple comparison of mental and chronological age would absurdly imply deepening mental retardation with every year thereafter. The point is obvious, but it took a while before testers devised adequate ways to deal with it. Until they did, Binet's tests applied beyond childhood tended to overestimate retardation.[5] The relevance to crime of these early difficulties in testing should soon be apparent.

We do not mean to imply that all the difficulties in intelligence testing are behind us. Psychometrics, the branch of psychology that deals with mental measurement, continues to evolve and to grow more complex. Nevertheless, by the 1930s and 1940s, tests without major invalidating defects or biases (such as the Otis Tests of Mental Ability, the Wechsler-Bellevue, and the 1937 revision of the Stanford-Binet) were available for the usual purposes of predicting educability in a wide variety of settings, from school to industry to the military.

In summary, an intelligence test is simply a controlled sample of a person's behavior with a known relationship to his or her behavior in other settings. Intelligence-test items are to intelligence as samplings of blood pressure, body temperature, or blood chemistry are to general physiological performance. As in medicine, the goal is to find tests that are convenient, that are reliable, and that capture the attributes one hopes to capture. Test items that probe a person's grasp of vocabulary, that require inferring relationships among words, numbers, or pictures, that pose problems to solve or rules to interpret, are among an enormous variety of materials discovered, mostly by trial and error, to be particularly diagnostic of intelligent behavior generally. Test items of all sorts yield scores that usually correlate with one another to some degree. Or, to put it another way, a relatively small number of underlying mental aptitudes, fewer than a dozen, account for large portions of all the variation among people on the full range of items that anyone has thought to include in tests of intelligence. Precisely because of this underlying parsimony, the score on an intelligence test lasting an hour or so predicts a person's performance in many different settings at many other times.

Crime and Test Scores

Among the earliest applications of intelligence tests was to use them on populations of institutionalized offenders. H. H. Goddard, American translator and popularizer of Binet's early intelligence tests, author of the famous study of the Kallikak family,[6] concluded in 1914, from the rudimentary data then available, that "25% to 50% of the people in our prisons are mentally defective and incapable of managing their affairs with ordinary prudence."[7] By itself, an intellectual defect did not cause crime, said Goddard, but in certain unwholesome environments and combined with "psychopathic" personality traits, it contributed to a criminal predisposition.[8] Goddard believed that his conclusions argued against the morality of punishing criminals retributively. Only if punishment had some rehabilitative value, Goddard believed, would it be right to inflict it on people whose crimes flowed from their disabilities.

For a few years, Goddard's conclusions seemed to be enjoying at least some confirmation,[9] but by 1926, when the Clark University psychologist Carl Murchison published his book *Criminal Intelligence,* the intellectual deficits of criminals no longer seemed so large or so certain. Murchison presented evidence that the scores earned by samples of enlisted men during World War I were lower than those earned by prisoners in the federal penitentiary at Fort Leavenworth. Other comparisons around the country convinced him that criminals are no less intelligent than the population at large, especially after allowing for biases that might make prisoners a sample of the less intelligent sector of the criminal population. More intelligent criminals are more likely to escape detection, he noted; moreover, if detected, they would be more able to manipulate the system to their advantage. They were also likely to be more able to afford sharp lawyers. He therefore disagreed with Goddard about the facts and also about the implications. Instead of rehabilitation, Murchison advocated severe penalties, including elimination of probation, parole, and release on bail, and a mandatory death penalty for the third felony conviction. He justified his hard line mainly with what he thought was conclusive evidence that criminals suffered no particular intellectual disadvantage and thus deserved no special "maternalism" (as he called it) from the state.

Whatever the merits of the philosophical positions, Murchison's sampling and testing procedures were not much stronger than Goddard's, as later workers pointed out.[10] We can, in fact, divide most of the early history of opinion on the relation between intelligence and crime into two antithetical and extreme positions, neither of them well supported by modern evidence. At the beginning of testing, exemplified by Goddard's work, it seemed that many, perhaps most, criminals were seriously deficient intellectually. But later on, it was argued that they had no intellectual deficits at all. For example, Edwin Sutherland, the leading criminologist of his generation, concluded (as had Murchison) that the deficiencies were not in the criminals but in the studies purporting to find them, particularly in the inadequate sampling procedures and in the questionable standardization and validation of intelligence tests.[11] Sutherland correctly observed that as the methods of testing improved, the apparent intellectual deficits of offenders shrank. However, he then jumped to the unsupported conclusion that any apparent intellectual deficiencies remaining in the most advanced findings of his time resulted from the lingering flaws in the research or the tests themselves. He implied that before long it would be obvious to all honest scholars that offenders and nonoffenders did not differ in intelligence.

Sutherland's conclusion, though more than a half-century old, continues to dominate criminology. Contemporary textbooks often say nothing at all about intelligence, or simply deny its relevance to crime. Haskell and Yablonsky's 1978 textbook tells its introductory criminology students: "Over the years . . . criminologists have alleged that there was a high correlation between low intelligence and crime. This belief has almost disappeared in recent years as a consequence of more cogent research findings."[12] Reid's 1979 introductory textbook says: "The finding of insignificant differences [in intelligence] between prisoners and the rest of the population has led to the practical abandonment of the theory of feeblemindedness as a cause of crime."[13] But that comes from Reid's second edition; in the third edition (1982), consideration of intelligence vanished altogether. A few textbooks deviate from the standard view. As Bartol warns his beginning students: "Criminologists (and many psychologists) have been all too eager to label invalid and spurious the relationship between intelligence and delinquency."[14] He then proceeds to summarize the conclusions of Travis Hirschi and Michael Hindelang, from whose review of the data we too will draw material.[15]

Soon after Murchison and Sutherland had concluded that intelligence and crime were uncorrelated, new tests, improved statistical methods, and greater caution about sampling procedures resulted in a nearly stabilized estimate of the average offender IQ, which has not changed appreciably since the early 1940s. For example, in 1947, Maud Merrill reported that on the new revision of the Stanford-Binet test, the average IQ was 92.5 for five hundred consecutive referrals to the juvenile court in a north California county. She compared this average not to the national average of 100 but to 101.8, which was the average for American-born whites in the standardization sample of the 1937 revision, because that more accurately reflected the population in the county she was examining.

Reviews of the literature since the 1940s repeatedly place the average offender IQ at about 91–93, when the offender population is broadly representative of the full range of offenders, and the level of seriousness of the offense is approximately consistent with the typical case involving court referral.[16] The tested intelligence of noninstitutionalized delinquent gang members or of predelinquent misbehavior cases also appears to be below the general population average.[17]

On modern intelligence tests, the general population average is fixed at an IQ of 100, but that value reflects all groups, including offenders. Offenders therefore differ from nonoffenders not by eight or nine points but by something more, depending on what we guess the true percentage of criminals in the general population to be. (As the true percentage of offenders rises, the nonoffender average IQ must be higher to produce the general population average of 100.) Conservatively estimating the male offender population to be 10 to 20 percent of the total male population, we estimate a ten-point gap between offenders and nonoffenders, which probably sets something close to a lower limit on the true value.

A small amount of evidence, as well as common sense, suggests that, despite the lower average IQ, the offender population contains relatively few very low IQs.[18] In a search of police records for a California county, Hirschi and Hindelang, for example, found a higher frequency of delinquency (defined as two or more officially recorded incidents) among white males in the next-to-the-bottom quintile of IQ scores (scores for the 20th to the 39th percentile) than in the bottom quintile. At each successively higher quintile above the next to the bottom, the delinquency level declined.[19] Below some

degree of intellectual deficiency, even the requirements of the most unplanned crime will be too great. The population of nonoffenders therefore
extends farther down into the range of subnormal scores than that of offenders, yet still averages ten points higher, if not more. The relationship between intelligence and crime is thus curvilinear, with most offenders falling
in the low normal or borderline subnormal range, approximately from IQ
60 to 100; their relative frequencies decline on either side of this range.

Alternative Interpretations

Despite over forty years of confirmation, the correlation between intelligence
and crime has yet to penetrate most of the textbooks or the conventional
wisdom of criminology. It is natural to wonder why criminology has rejected
"what might appear to be a first class relationship between delinquency and
intelligence," to quote one conscientious scholar who himself rejects it.[20]
There appear to be several reasons.

Nathan Caplan summarizes the data as follows: "Most recent evidence,
based on a variety of intelligence tests, consistently reveals a difference of
about 8 points between the mean IQ's of delinquent and the general population samples [i.e., $100 - 8 = 92$]."[21] Nevertheless, later in his assessment of
the relationship, he concludes, "Once proper care is taken to consider the
various sources of bias, there is either no difference or . . . the difference
in favor of the control groups [i.e., nondelinquents] is so small as to be of
theoretical interest only."[22] The main source of bias invoked by Caplan, as
well as by other criminologists, is socioeconomic bias. We will consider SES
bias first, then proceed to the other kinds of arguments frequently leveled
against the suggestion of a true association between crime and intelligence.

As Caplan correctly points out, the average offender is drawn from a
lower SES than the average unselected individual in standardization samples
for intelligence tests. It is well established that SES and IQ are themselves
correlated in the population at large, so that any criterion, such as criminality, that sorts people according to SES is likely, willy-nilly, to sort them according to IQ as well, and vice versa. Perhaps, this line of reasoning proceeds, the essential difference between offenders and nonoffenders is SES,
with the IQ difference incidental, of no causal significance in its own right.

It is customary in criminology to test this line of argument by examining IQ differences between offenders and nonoffenders who have been
matched for SES. An even stronger test is to compare the IQs of siblings,
one of whom is an offender and the other not.[23] Within a family, the SES
(and cultural) level is likely to be even more uniform than for the cruder

indexes used for matching nonoffenders and offenders in SES. Later we will comment on the logic of this approach to SES bias, but first we summarize the data.

In general, attempts to equalize the SES, cultural, or family backgrounds of offenders and nonoffenders reduce, but do not eliminate, the IQ separation between them. In a study of juvenile court records for over nine thousand white offenders in Tennessee, Reiss and Rhodes found IQ to be a stronger correlate of offense rate than parental occupational status (i.e., SES).[24] For the whites in Hirschi's sample of California schoolchildren, IQ was more strongly correlated than father's education with the number of individuals committing two or more officially recorded delinquent acts.[25] Almost nine thousand males had their IQs measured in the Philadelphia cohort study;[26] within social classes, chronic offenders had consistently lower intelligence-test scores than those without police records. A similar result was obtained in a longitudinal study of just over four hundred London boys.[27]

Despite this evidence, it remains true, as Caplan and other criminologists have noted, that matching offenders and nonoffenders for status or other measures of cultural advantage often results in a diminished difference in IQ.[28] But it is as fallacious to conclude that the SES difference is essential and the IQ incidental as it would be to conclude the reverse, that IQ is essential and SES incidental. Since IQ and SES are correlated, matching for one automatically matches for the other, *unless* the association with crime depends on whatever IQ and SES do *not* have in common, an eventuality for which it would be hard even to imagine a plausible reason.

In Sheldon and Eleanor Glueck's classic study,[29] five hundred institutionalized delinquent boys were compared to five hundred nondelinquent boys of the same approximate age, IQ, and SES. Here, four major correlates of criminality (sex, age, IQ, and SES) were controlled for, so other correlates emerged with more vividness than they would in less well matched comparisons. Body type, personality, attitude toward authority, family adjustment, and a history of alcoholism and mental disease were among the correlates of crime that the Gluecks uncovered with their matched samples. But this does not imply that sex, age, IQ, and SES are irrelevant to criminal behavior. To survive the matching procedure, a variable must have a degree of independence from the variables used for matching. The greater the independence, the more important the variable will seem, given that it has any effect on crime at all. But when the effects of one variable are weakened as a result of matching between groups for a correlated variable, we learn only that other influences on criminal behavior are accounting for more of the difference between these two groups than is the case between offenders and nonoffenders drawn at random. It is a curious, and common, lapse in the logic of criminology to assume that merely controlling for a variable, such as SES, endows it with explanatory power. More to the point, the evidence suggests that in direct comparisons of IQ and social class, IQ is generally more predictive of offending than social class or cultural backgrounds, as in the studies cited above.

Another reason criminologists have been reluctant to accept the evidence about tested intelligence is a commonly held opinion that intelligence tests are biased against the very groups that are disproportionately represented in offender populations, primarily the poor and certain racial and ethnic minorities (see Chapters 12 and 18). This is a topic more often discussed with passion than understanding, but we will try to resist any such impulse. The general notion of "test bias" has various concrete meanings, none of them the mere fact that one group earns lower or higher scores than another.[30] By itself the existence of an average difference separating the IQs of middle-class and lower-class children no more proves test bias than the average difference in height between Swedes and Japanese proves bias in yardsticks. Human populations differ in innumerable ways, mostly of small significance, and their measurements are not necessarily biased simply for having measured them.

Something more is necessary to show bias. In the case of intelligence tests, the most persuasive evidence of bias would be that the same score earned by different groups predicted different intellectual performances for the different groups. For example, if a given IQ was consistently associated with better schoolwork for one group than for a second, the test could be accused of bias against the first group. People in the first group, noting that the test underpredicted their school performance compared to the second group, would have reasonable grounds for protesting the use of the test without some sort of adjustment for its bias against them. But a comprehensive survey of intelligence testing commissioned by the National Academy of Sciences concluded that "tests predict about as well for one group as for another."[31] Whether for school grades or job success, test scores appear to have approximately the same predictive power for members of varying ethnic, racial, and socioeconomic groups.[32] Whatever test scores mean, most experts agree that they appear to mean the same thing to the various groups whose differences in offending have been shown to be associated with differences in test scores.

There are other interpretations of test bias, but the upshot is the same.[33] Whether the test items involve specific cultural information, learned verbal connections, or abstract, nonverbal reasoning, analysis almost always fails to substantiate the existence of bias; in no case is there compelling evidence of bias one way or the other. It may be too strong to say that intelligence

tests have been proved bias-free, but not to say that strenuous efforts to uncover test bias against native English-speaking socioeconomic or ethnic
groups have failed to find it. Despite the frequent charge of bias by criminologists, tests appear to measure the same thing in the major sociological categories of the population.

What do tests measure? The answer is often the basis of yet another
line of resistance to the evidence on intelligence and crime. Many criminologists do not believe that the tests measure intelligence, arguing instead that
"anybody can learn anything," or that they measure "only socioeconomic
status of the respondent," or that they are an "index of the ability of the
child to meet middle-class expectations."[34] There is a certain amount of
purely semantic quibbling here—for example, if we rename intelligence "middle-class expectations," then we can insist that that is what tests measure.

But the objections to tests are not purely semantic or definitional; sometimes the objections have empirical implications, and the criminological ob-
jectors often seem unfamiliar with the relevant data. Test scores at each
SES level or in any well-populated ethnic group in the United States cover
the full range. Of the total variance in test scores, one estimate suggests that
more than three-quarters resides among individuals within SES levels or
racial (i.e., black and white) groups, the remainder in group average differences.[35] In other words, if, by some sociological magic, we could eliminate
all the ethnic and socioeconomic correlates of test scores, the total variance
would still be about 75 percent of what it is now. Variance among siblings
within families accounts for more of the total variance than that between
families, even though siblings share not only SES but also a variety of other
cultural and intellectual influences, while families as a whole may differ
along any of the social dimensions. Given the way scores vary, and, more
simply, given the number of people from the lower classes who outscore
those from the middle classes, it cannot plausibly be argued that tests measure only middle-class values, expectations, or knowledge.

Can a single number, an IQ score, really represent so complex an attribute as "intelligence"? The answer is clearly no. People with the same IQ
are likely to differ intellectually: One of them may be better with numbers
rather than words; another, vice versa; and so on through all the modalities
of cognition. Insofar as the resistance to IQ is based on this intuition about
the complexity of intelligence, it is not unreasonable. If offenders and nonoffenders differ intellectually, it should be possible to describe the difference
more illuminatingly than as ten points of IQ. As it turns out, and as the next
section shows, a number of studies have addressed the qualitative aspects of
the typical offender's cognitive deficit.

One final objection to test data is the possibility that arrested offenders in most studies are not representative of offenders in general. It is easy to suppose that the criminals who fail to show up in police or court records, or in prison, have higher IQ scores than those who do. Perhaps they fail to show up because they pick lower-risk crimes or are more successful at eluding the law, or because, being wealthier on the average, they buy better legal representation, or, finally, because the stages of the criminal justice system, from police to parole boards, are in effect biased in favor of people who earn high scores.

Parts of this objection appear to be right; other parts, wrong; and for some parts, we simply do not know. It has been reported, for example, that less intelligent children suffer a greater risk of institutionalization for delinquency than more intelligent children.[36] On the other hand, studies of non-institutionalized delinquents find intellectual deficits comparable to those of official delinquents.[37] In self-reports there is less correlation between IQ and criminal behavior than in official records, but this, like most findings, is open to multiple interpretations, as we will show later in the chapter. Some crimes are more consistently associated with lower intelligence than others, and these often happen also to be the ones most likely to result in arrest. The way people behave, including how they behave as criminals, correlates with their tested intelligence. The criminal justice system need not be directly biased against offenders with low IQs for them to be disproportionately arrested, tried, convicted, and imprisoned. But, by the same token, we cannot rule out a direct bias.

In summary, IQ scores, though admittedly a blunt instrument for measuring human intelligence, cannot be discounted as purely a measure of social class or cultural advantage. For four decades, large bodies of evidence have consistently shown about a ten-point gap between the average offender and nonoffender in Great Britain and in the United States. Most of the data are for official offenders, at the level of arrest or beyond. There is a small amount of confirming data for comparably serious offenders who have not been caught, but not enough to allow us to say that their deficits are just as large. In any event, criminology acted rashly when, in the 1930s, it virtually ceased considering IQ a significant correlate of criminal behavior, for it was just at that moment in the evolution of mental testing that the tests were beginning to yield solid data on the cognitive predispositions toward offending.

Qualitative Signs of Criminality

Among the major new intelligence tests of the 1930s, the Wechsler-Bellevue scale (and its modern descendants) lent itself especially to discovering the cognitive characteristics of offenders. David Wechsler's tests yielded not

only an IQ score (a score which, incidentally, did not have the age complications noted above for the Binet tests) but also "subtest" scores for as
many as a dozen component abilities. In different versions, the subtests vary
somewhat, but typically they include a comprehension test, posing hypothetical problems and asking for a solution; an information test, drawing on
formal knowledge ranging from commonplace (e.g., how many months in a
year?) to esoteric (e.g., what is the Koran?); a vocabulary test; a similarities test involving word analogies; a digit span test to see how many digits a
person can repeat after one hearing; an arithmetical reasoning test; a block
design test in which colored blocks are arranged to match a pictured design;
a picture arrangement test that involves ordering comic-strip-like drawings
in a logically feasible sequence; a picture completion test in which drawings
have missing elements that are to be spotted; an object assembly test, which
is like a jigsaw puzzle; and a digit symbol test for which the person has to
learn as quickly as possible the association between digits and a set of arbitrary symbols. Each subtest results in a score that has been standardized for
the population as a whole. About half of the scores can be combined to give
a "verbal" IQ (information, comprehension, digit span, arithmetic, similarities, and vocabulary), and the other subtest scores combine into a "performance" IQ (picture arrangement, picture completion, block design, object
assembly, and digit symbol). Combining all the subtest scores yields the full-
scale IQ.

In the population as a whole, the verbal and performance IQs are standardized so as to be equal, and to give a full-scale IQ of 100. Wechsler himself noted early that a sample of "psychopathic" adolescents had a distinctive pattern of subtest scores when compared to the typical adolescent.[38]
The particular pattern that has been most widely pursued and confirmed by
subsequent research is the tendency for performance IQ to exceed verbal IQ.

If the psychopathic adolescents in Wechsler's observation are taken as
a high-risk population for offending (as they should be; see Chapter 7),
then the relative deficiency of verbal skills among delinquents had already
been noted before Wechsler and had given impetus to the use of vocational
training for delinquents and adult offenders, on the grounds that developing
their nonverbal abilities could help in rehabilitation.[39] The availability of
standardized testing put this old belief on a much firmer basis and has led
to still unfolding insights into the nature of the predisposition toward crime.

In the Glueck study of five hundred seriously delinquent and five hundred nondelinquent boys, the two samples were closely matched for full-
scale IQ, with the delinquents averaging 92 (a typical value for such groups)
and their nondelinquent controls, 94.[40] Both groups were below average, but

the delinquents were significantly below the nondelinquents in verbal IQ. On performance IQ, the groups were within a point of each other, both slightly below the general population average.

A more general review of the data confirms this result. Prentice and Kelly collected Wechsler scores for samples of randomly selected male and female delinquents committed to the Massachusetts Youth Service Board in 1958–1959 and found an average verbal deficit of 7.1 points for boys and 6.0 for girls.[41] They also assembled data from other sources, which we have now pooled. In twenty-one different studies, involving over two thousand white, male and female, youthful and adult offenders, the average verbal deficit was 7.9 (in units in which the typical performance or verbal IQ would equal 100 and weighting for sample sizes). In other words, for the average offender, performance IQ was almost eight points higher than verbal IQ. For female offenders alone, performance IQ was 7.4 points higher. In every study but one, the performance IQ was higher than the verbal IQ, the one exception being a sample of thirty-five federal prisoners characterized as "successful readers," for whom the verbal IQ was 0.9 points higher than the performance IQ.[42] Overall, the offenders in these studies had an average full-scale IQ of 92.8, further substantiating our earlier conclusion about the offender population in general. But now we can add that the general IQ deficiency usually comprises a small, perhaps negligible, performance deficit and a larger verbal deficit. A few samples, not included above, involved nonwhites (i.e., Maoris in New Zealand, American blacks), who also showed higher performance than verbal scores, though the data are too sparse to allow us to compare the size of the difference across races.

In the national standardization sample for the Wechsler scale for children, large differences between verbal and performance scores among children with high full-scale IQs typically involve higher verbal than performance scores, and vice versa among children with low full-scale IQs. Similarly, the large discrepancies in professional and "technical" families are typically higher verbal than performance scores while those in minor white-collar, blue-collar, farm, and laborer families are typically the reverse.[43] Such findings may seem to suggest that the relative verbal deficit is just a by-product of lower full-scale IQ or low SES among offenders, but other data suggest otherwise.

In the Glueck sample, for example, the verbal deficit showed up across groups at least approximately matched for both IQ and SES. It also showed up quite strongly in a sample of serious adult male offenders assigned to Patuxent Institution in Maryland for "persistent aggravated antisocial or criminal behavior."[44] Full-scale Wechsler IQ for the group ranged from 45 to 139 and averaged 90.5. The average excess of performance over verbal scores was 9.4 points, which is larger than that for unselected offender populations. If the verbal deficit were just an artifact of low IQ among offenders, then it should show up disproportionately in low-IQ offenders. Among the Patuxent inmates, who are admittedly somewhat atypical because of their intense antisocial tendencies, the reverse was the case. The relative verbal deficit disproportionately characterized inmates with the higher IQs. Taking full-scale IQ of 90.5 as the cutting line, 85.6 percent of those above the group average showed the deficit, while for those below the full-scale average, it was 75.4 percent. Among the twenty-three inmates with full-scale IQ below 68, performance IQ was as often below verbal IQ as above.

Although the verbal deficit is not just an artifact of low IQ or SES, neither is it invariably found as a concomitant of criminal behavior. Occasional studies that fail to find it in offenders often involve atypical populations, such as those who suffer from a serious mental disease or mental retardation, or who have had a superior education.[45] It is important to recall here that many factors cause crime, with no single characteristic either necessary or sufficient to account for it. Of the many correlates of crime, the relative verbal deficit is common enough to be worth considering a bit further.

The Patuxent sample and other data are consistent with a familiar hypothesis that deficits of verbal IQ in particular predispose people to offending. People with high IQs would therefore need a large verbal deficit to be offenders, while those with low full scale would not, before their low verbal IQs would become a predisposing factor toward crime. Verbal IQ has been shown to be inversely associated with a variety of individual traits that could plausibly predispose a person to offending.

Low ratings on a measure of interpersonal maturity, for example,[46] have been shown to be associated with delinquency, with low verbal IQ, with performance scores higher than verbal, and inversely with age.[47] It is not known to what extent those three correlates of interpersonal maturity and delinquency are measuring essentially the same or different traits, but it is clear that some sort of deficiency in verbal development is involved. The interpersonal maturity scale is not unlike other scales of moral development, which typically classify people at levels ranging from rampant egotism and hedonism at the lowest end up through various stages of more abstract and principled rule following, often with an increasing capacity for delay of gratification. Sheer youth, low verbal IQ, and a substantial gap between performance and verbal scores all converge more or less together on a low level of moral development or interpersonal maturity and a tendency to break the law.

The "adolescent problem inventory"[48] presents hypothetical problem situations (e.g., "Your father gives you an ultimatum about getting your hair cut") and rates the answers for social competence (as determined by a set of presumably impartial judges classifying answers independently). In one study,[49] three groups of teen-age boys were selected: a group of institution-alized delinquents, a group of nondelinquent boys characterized as "good citizens" by their high school counselors, and a group of boys characterized as "leaders" (school newspaper editors, class presidents, star athletes, etc.). On the problem-inventory scale, the leaders outscored the good citizens, who outscored the delinquents. (Leaders came from a higher SES back-ground than the other two groups, which did not differ significantly from each other in SES.) The sizes of the differences are revealing. Each of the forty-four problems on the scale earned a mean rating that was characterized as competent or incompetent. For the leaders, no problem had an average response in the incompetent region; for the good citizens, one problem earned an incompetent mean rating; for the delinquents, thirty-six problems out of the forty-four were incompetently disposed of.

Leaders had a higher and less variable IQ than the good citizens, but the difference fell short of statistical significance. Both of these groups had significantly higher IQs than the delinquents, who scored 93 on a nonverbal test and 87 on a verbal test of intelligence, displaying the usual relative ver-bal deficit. For the boys in the three groups as a whole, verbal IQ was the strongest correlate of the social competence score. Even so, when a subse-quent study deliberately matched delinquents and nondelinquents for IQ (delinquents' verbal score matched to nondelinquents' full-scale score), the social competence score still differed.[50]

In other studies,[51] a deficiency of "internal speech," or the ability to use language constructively in problem solving, has been a predisposing fac-tor for aggressive behavior in elementary-school children, even after verbal or performance IQ as such is held constant. Such findings make a point worth noting: Measures of intellectual capacity inevitably are associated with other traits that seem more closely tied to personality or temperament, such as the strength of one's internal monologue.[52] Whether such traits as the tendency toward verbal or nonverbal thinking, or toward impulsiveness or impulse control in behavior, are classified as cognitive or temperamental is somewhat arbitrary; they are noted here and will be more fully discussed in Chapter 7.

Conversely, the distinction between verbal and performance IQ also has to be qualified, for the two measures are themselves closely associated with each other. For example, people who do well on vocabulary or comprehen-sion or similarities tests usually do well on block design or object assembly tests (or vice versa). Some of the same mental skills appear to be involved in both verbal and performance items on intelligence tests. It is as if a verbal exercise, for example, tests a range of mental competences, extending from the narrow verbal skill involved (such as knowledge of vocabulary in a vocabulary test) to more general cognitive skills that it shares with, say, the solution of a jigsaw puzzle. Consequently, scores on a vocabulary test correlate to some extent with those on an object assembly test. This underlying integrity of some significant part of mental capacity has no doubt been one of the most surprising, most important, and, at times, most controversial outcomes of intelligence testing.[53] For some theorists, it justifies the concept of "general intelligence," while for others, who doubt the existence of general intelligence, it may seem to arise mostly from a fortuitous association of large numbers of unrelated mental skills. In any event, the intellectual deficit of the average offender is primarily verbal, but no sharp line can be drawn between verbal and nonverbal intelligence.

Differences Among Offenders

We hasten to add, as we often do in this book, that generalizations based on aggregate statistics are dominated by the most common categories of offenders. In the case of intelligence, considerable evidence shows that no single generalization can cover its contribution to crime. For example, self-reported delinquency has a considerably weaker association with tested intelligence than official records of delinquency have.[54] This may suggest that the association between the variables in official records is due to biases in the criminal justice system tilting in favor of offenders with high scores, but, as Hirschi and Hindelang point out, other factors may be more pertinent.

An earlier study by Hirschi showed that good students of English without police records were more than twice as likely to cooperate with his self-report survey than poor students of English with police records.[55] Nonrespondents were disproportionately low-ability juveniles with police records, precisely the kind of bias that would weaken the association between crime and intelligence in self-report surveys. Respondents with low IQs probably give less valid answers than those with higher IQs. In addition, self-reports generally uncover a population of less serious offenders than official statistics. As a result, many of the correlates of crime, such as sex and age, are attenuated in their apparent effect (see Chapters 4 and 5). The effects of race and socioeconomic status are also weakened, perhaps even washed out,[56] in self-reports of relatively minor offenses. Although the correlation between offending and IQ diminishes in self-reports, it apparently diminishes less than does the correlation between offending and race or class.[57]

At the other extreme from the generally mild offenders identified by self-reports are populations of recidivists. We noted earlier that the seriously chronic offenders in the Patuxent study[58] had somewhat lower IQs than offenders in general. Similarly, West's sample of London boys[59] and Wolfgang et al.'s Philadelphia cohort[60] both suggest lower IQs among recidivists than among nonrepeating offenders. Low verbal IQ scores characterized recidivists, as compared to nonrecidivists, in a sample of male and female delinquents.[61] Other studies[62] likewise have found recidivists to test lower than nonrepeating offenders, but there are exceptions. For example, in Merrill's study of young adult offenders, no significant difference in IQ distinguished recidivists from single offenders.[63] It may be relevant that this particular offender sample as a whole had a somewhat higher IQ (98.4) than offenders generally, and therefore lacked some portion of the low-IQ offender population. Hartman found *higher* IQs among recidivists than among first offenders for certain criminal categories (robbery and larceny) and the reverse for sex offenders.[64] Not surprisingly, a number of workers[65] have concluded that the evidence simply does not support the claim that low IQ favors recidivism. Part of the confusion in the picture may reflect interactions between the criminal justice system and individual characteristics, so that offenders released on parole, hence free to be reconvicted or not, are somewhat unrepresentative of the offender population as a whole. In general, the few prospective studies that bear on the issue suggest that low scores do, in fact, correlate with frequency of offending.

The nature of the crime committed has a clear relationship to IQ (which even Sutherland granted in his general condemnation of the relevance of testing to criminology[66]). It has been found[67] that such crimes as forgery, bribery, securities violations, and embezzlement are associated with higher IQs than is the average for the offender population in general, whereas assaults, homicide, rape, and sex offenses in females are associated with lower IQs. In the center of the IQ distribution for offenders are found, not surprisingly, the high-frequency property offenders, such as the burglars and auto thieves, and the drug and alcohol offenders. Because these are high-frequency offenses, they naturally weigh heavily in determining the average offender's characteristics, such as IQ. In Fox's assessment of over five thousand prisoners, property offenders averaged 92.8, five points higher than his entire sample, but right where we estimate the prison population as a whole to lie.[68] In Merrill's study of a sample of delinquents, those convicted of "stealing" averaged 92.4 on the 1937 Stanford-Binet.[69] Automobile thieves in Caplan and Gligor's study averaged 93.6.[70]

To the extent that the prison system itself segregates offenders by the character of the crime committed, we should expect a range of average IQs at different institutions. The Patuxent sample, for example, had a lower IQ than the offender population as a whole because it housed more violent than average inmates. By contrast, in Megargee and Bohn's study of prisoners in a federal prison,[71] a sample of almost one thousand inmates averaged a nonverbal IQ of 101, which, even allowing for the relative verbal deficit, is considerably higher than the average performance IQ of 95 in the studies assembled by Prentice and Kelly.[72] The prisoners in a federal institution of this type are, on the average, atypically nonviolent, compared to offenders generally. Their offenses were disproportionately drawn from the higher end of the IQ distribution, such as fraud, misrepresentation, counterfeiting, illegal interstate transportation (the largest offense category in this sample), possession of contraband, and violations of federal alcohol and drug laws and of the Selective Service Act. Even the relatively rare crimes of violence tended to be somewhat atypical, such as the destruction of federal property and kidnapping.

Just as the prison system inadvertently segregates by intelligence, it is likely that the success rate of the police does too. From the FBI Uniform Crime Reports, it is evident that violent crimes, such as murder, aggravated assault, and forcible rape, have a much higher likelihood of arrest than burglary, larceny theft, and auto theft. In all likelihood, perpetrators of risky crimes, from the point of view of arrest probabilities, consequently have lower test scores than perpetrators of "safer" crimes. Even if the criminal justice system is not directly biased against low-IQ offenders, the offenders' own choices of offenses would lead to their disproportionate representation in official records and in prison.

How Intelligence Affects Crime

In his critical review of mental deficiency and crime, Sutherland said his most significant conclusion was that the relation between them "cannot be determined by dealing with it in isolation from other factors."[73] With that, at least, we agree. The question for us is how the various empirical connections between intelligence and criminal behavior may be integrated into the model described in Chapter 2. Several plausible alternative connections can be imagined.

Consider, for example, the finding just presented—the inverse association between intelligence and clearance rates. It makes intuitive sense that more intelligent criminals would be more guided by the risk of arrest and prosecution and so, as compared to less intelligent criminals, would be drawn disproportionately to crimes with low clearance rates. The contribution of intelligence to this particular fact would be explained simply by the supposition that people with higher scores are generally more attuned to the actual contingencies and risks of various sorts of offending.

But that is at best only a partial reason for the relationship. The typical crimes of less intelligent offenders are often crimes with an immediate pay-off—crimes of violence in which the reward is the damage inflicted on one's antagonist of the moment, or sexual crimes that yield immediate gratification, or minor property crimes occasioned by a target of opportunity, such as a nighttime encounter with a solitary stranger on a quiet city street. In contrast, the characteristic crimes of more intelligent offenders involve preparation, planning, occasionally even negotiation with confederates, and a pay-off that may be long deferred. In short, insofar as the rate of time discounting is itself a correlate of intelligence, low intelligence will favor impulsive crimes with immediate rewards, and high intelligence, the inverse. Perhaps not coincidentally, clearance rates are lower for crimes that take longer to plan, to carry out, and to deliver the goods. What evidence there is suggests that low test scores are in fact associated with impulsive crimes.[74]

Finally, tested intelligence may, to some extent, be an indirect representation of a potential criminal's opportunities for crime. To be an embezzler or a counterfeiter or an organizer of illegal interstate transactions requires a variety of skills or social contacts not often found in association with an IQ below 90 or 95. But it should not be supposed that high test scores are a guarantee of careful and profitable crime. On the contrary, in a direct comparison of fifty bright young delinquents (average IQ 126) with fifty delinquents matched for age and ethnic background, and with an IQ typical (i.e., IQ 96) of those being remanded to a particular London institution, the brighter delinquents gained about half as much from their property crimes as did the typical delinquents.[75] The differentiation in choice of crime by virtue of IQ had not yet emerged in these twelve-to-seventeen-year-old delinquents. In this sample, what differentiated the bright delinquents was a higher level of psychiatric disturbance. As in other studies, the brighter delinquents received more lenient treatment, but one can think of so many reasons for this it would be rash to try to pinpoint one. For the sample at hand, however, one common hypothesis is not borne out, since the bright and typical delinquents did not differ in SES. In other samples, IQ does, as noted earlier, correlate with SES, and for those, IQ translates into criminal opportunities of various sorts that may, in turn, lead to differing risks of arrest.

If there are several plausible explanations of the correlation between IQ and type of crime, it is hardly surprising that there are also several explanations of the primary relationship between IQ and crime. In their review of the literature, Hirschi and Hindelang conclude that the link between intelligence and crime is a person's experience in school.[76] They point out that in studies that provide measures of both tested ability and school performance,[77] the latter accounts for criminal behavior no less than the former, if not more so. If "troublesomeness" in school in the primary grades replaces IQ in analysis, then most, if not all, of the correlation between IQ and later delinquency is accounted for, at least statistically.[78]

Noting the "hundreds of studies" that have shown an association between academic competence and criminal behavior, Hirschi says, "its assumed lack of relation to delinquency must be considered one of the wonders of social science."[79] Hirschi refers to intelligence-test scores as "academic competence" not just because they do, in fact, predict success in school but because he has concluded that between scores and crime, the crucial connection is mediated by the school experience. It is in school that a youngster lacking intellectual skills is most likely to encounter for the first time the frustrations and failures that his or her deficits are heir to, given the nature of contemporary society in which intellectual skills play a major role. Combined with other predisposing individual factors and with a family and cultural setting that, for one reason or another, fails to teach strong internal prohibitions against crime, the academic penalties of low intelligence provide an emotional impetus to asocial behavior, in Hirschi's view.

While the school experience is often crucial (see Chapter 10), there may be other connections between intelligence and crime, which are usually masked by school's strategic position in contemporary life. In Hirschi's own revealing study of several thousand junior and senior high school students in the San Francisco–Oakland metropolitan area, self-report surveys were buttressed with police and school records, intelligence-test scores, and data on family status.[80] Among many other findings, Hirschi showed that the tendency to break the law was associated with a set of attitudes that could be characterized as unconventional, antisocial, irresponsible, and present-oriented. In criminological theory, such attitudes have traditionally been attributed to social class, but Hirschi's data show that present-orientation is more a matter of intelligence than of class.

Figures 1 and 2 summarize the data. Figure 1 shows, as functions of family occupational status or verbal aptitude score, what percentage of this sample of over eleven hundred male teen-agers rejected such present-oriented fatalistic statements as: "A person should live for today and let tomorrow take care of itself" or "What is going to happen will happen, no matter what I do." The rejection rate—that is, the rejection of present-orientation—rose more gradually with a boy's family's occupational status than with his own verbal aptitude score.

Family occupational status is, of course, correlated with individual test scores, so Figure 2 attempts to disentangle them graphically. The sample has been subdivided into the four grades of occupational status, from semiskilled to professional, within each of which is shown the relation between rejection of present-orientation and individual verbal aptitude. In each occupational class, the higher the aptitude, the greater the rejection. (No point is plotted at the highest aptitude for the semiskilled subsample because it contained too few boys with such high scores.) If status were a major contributor to present-orientation, the lines in Figure 2 would be clearly displaced from one another, which they are not.

Some small and possibly complex contribution of status may be suggested by the vertical ordering of data points within aptitude categories, but not enough to substantiate the typical claims made for the role of status in determining attitudes toward the consequences of one's actions. These data indicate that test scores may have other ties to crime than simply their association with school performance. A tendency to see oneself as helplessly tied to the present, with little control over one's long-term prospects, may affect both school performance and conformity to the law, since both kinds of behavior depend on the range of one's time horizons, what we called "impulsiveness" in Chapter 2. School failure may well be a motivating factor for antisocial behavior, but even in a society with no schooling, we would expect short time horizons to be a predisposing factor toward crime, assuming that the rewards of crime in this hypothetical society arrive well before any punishment for it.

Yet another link between intelligence and crime is suggested by the finding, noted earlier, that a person's level of moral reasoning is correlated with intelligence, particularly verbal intelligence. If we think of moral reasoning as just another form of reasoning, it should not be surprising that a variable, such as IQ, that predicts abstract reasoning ability also predicts that particular form of abstract reasoning entailed in decisions about right and wrong. As Robert Gordon says in his discussion of the correlation between intelligence and crime: "Perhaps it is no coincidence that those with the ability to erect large, anonymous hierarchical communities based on abstract relations between strangers, also have the ability to live amicably within them."[81]

Gordon summarizes the way boys in delinquent gangs evaluate, on rat-

FIGURE 1

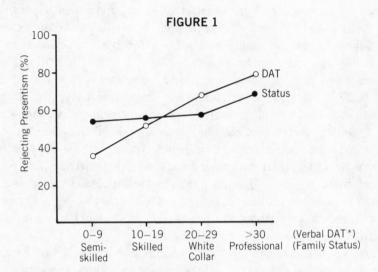

* Differential Aptitude Test—a battery of scores of which the verbal score is correlated with verbal IQ.

Graph based on tabular data from T. Hirschi, *Causes of Delinquency* (Berkeley, Calif.: University of California Press, 1969).

Percent of a sample of male teen-agers who rejected fatalistic and present-oriented attitudes, in relation to their family's occupational status and their own verbal aptitudes.

ing scales like good-bad or fair-unfair, people characterized by over a dozen descriptions ranging from "someone who works for good grades in school" to "someone who makes easy money by pimping and other illegal hustles." The delinquents' responses were compared with nondelinquents', matched for race and SES. All groups rated essentially the same descriptions as good and bad, but the depth of disapprobation for the "bad" activities was much shallower for the delinquents. They may say they disapprove of, for example, fighting and illegal hustling, but they do not express as much disapproval as the matched, presumably nondelinquent, boys do. Across the various groups of boys, varying not only in delinquency but also in race and SES, the average IQ was consistently associated with the expressed level of disapprobation.

As far as the underlying psychological mechanisms are concerned, the connections between crime and intelligence may not be quite as diverse as this discussion may seem to imply. Depth of disapprobation for socially disapproved conduct may, for example, not be entirely independent of time horizons, and neither may be entirely independent of success or failure in

FIGURE 2

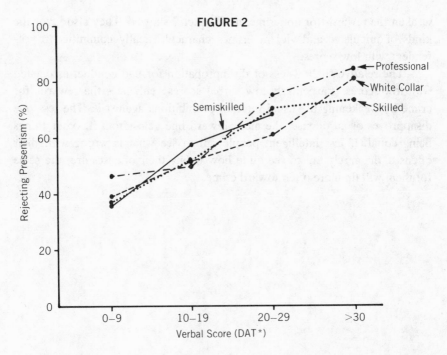

* Differential Aptitude Test—a battery of scores of which the verbal score is correlated with verbal IQ.

Graph based on tabular data from T. Hirschi, *Causes of Delinquency* (Berkeley, Calif.: University of California Press, 1969).

The same data as in Figure 1, segregated by family occupational status. This shows how the tendency to reject fatalistic and present-oriented attitudes relates to verbal aptitude at each occupational level.

school. Even so, we can distinguish among these influences on crime using the model described in Chapter 2. When we do so, it is plain why the association between intelligence and crime is as robust and significant as the data show it to be.

A child who chronically loses standing in the competition of the classroom may feel justified in settling the score outside, by violence, theft, and other forms of defiant illegality. School failure enhances the rewards for crime by engendering feelings of unfairness. In addition, failure in school predicts, to a substantial degree, failure in the marketplace.[82] For someone who stands to gain little from legitimate work, the rewards of noncrime are relatively weak. Failure in school therefore not only enhances the rewards for crime, but it predicts weak rewards for noncrime.

Short time horizons, another correlate of low intelligence, further weaken the rewards for noncrime, as Chapter 2 showed. They also favor the kinds of impulsive and violent crimes characteristically committed by offenders with low scores.

The relative shallowness of disapprobation for bad conduct associated with low scores (particularly low verbal scores) enhances the rewards for crime by weakening the usual internal prohibitions against it. The less one disapproves of an offense, the more reward one gains from it, other things being equal. If less intelligent people fail to see what is wrong with their offenses, or merely fail to see quite how wrong their offenses are, the scale for them will tip more often toward crime.

7

PERSONALITY AND PSYCHOPATHOLOGY

People who break the law are often psychologically atypical. This is not to say that they are necessarily sick (although some are), or that atypicality of any sort characterizes every single lawbreaker. Rather, the evidence says that populations of offenders differ statistically in various respects from populations of nonoffenders. The preceding chapters have already illustrated some of the differences: Offenders are, for example, disproportionately young, male, mesomorphic and nonectomorphic, and from the low normal or borderline region of the distribution of intelligence-test scores. Offenders are also atypical in personality.

The Porteus Maze Tests were developed by S. D. Porteus to supplement conventional intelligence tests, particularly for cross-cultural comparisons.[1] The tests use a series of paper-and-pencil mazes graded in difficulty; the mental-ability score depends on how far through the series a person can successfully advance and on how many attempts are necessary to solve each maze. The maze test has proved its value as a measure of nonverbal reasoning, but that is not why we introduce it here. Since Porteus believed that his test would measure, among other things, planning ability, judgment, and impulsiveness, he anticipated that it might also be capable of predicting delinquency, job stability, and other signs of social adjustment.

The usual measure of reasoning drawn from maze performance is only moderately correlated with standard IQ scores, as would be expected of such a nonverbal test. Given the special relevance of *verbal* intelligence to criminal behavior (see Chapter 6), it is not surprising that the nonverbal maze ability score has at best a shaky association with offending, contrary to Porteus' hunch.[2] However, since the 1940s,[3] a second measure of performance on the mazes, called the Q score (for "qualitative"), has been found to be strongly associated with criminal and other sorts of antisocial or maladaptive behavior.[4] The Q score records the quality of performance by counting the times the subject breaks the rules by lifting his or her pencil from the paper, by cutting corners, or by allowing the pencil to drift out of the maze channels. The poorer the quality of performance, the higher the Q score.

In at least a dozen studies, juvenile delinquents, adult criminals, recidivists, and institutional behavior problem cases have earned higher Q scores than matched control groups. After reviewing the data from the continental United States, Hawaii, the Philippines, Sweden, and Great Britain, in a variety of correctional institutions, ordinary schools, and places of employment, Roberts and Riddle concluded that "within any group, those with more delinquent characteristics will obtain higher Q scores than will those with fewer delinquent characteristics."[5] In tests of impulsiveness, defined as the inability to forgo a small, immediate reinforcer instead of waiting for a more valuable one to come later, more impulsive people earned higher Q scores than less impulsive ones. Averaging over studies comparing groups of delinquents and nondelinquents, a single cutoff Q score identified over 70 percent of delinquents (score above the cutoff) and over 70 percent of the nondelinquents (score below the cutoff).[6] It takes a higher cutoff to distinguish female, as compared to male, delinquents from nondelinquents, in keeping with the suggestion (in Chapter 4) that female offenders tend to be more deviant than male.

Besides their obvious bearing on our subject, the maze-test data make a more general point. They illustrate that people behave with enough consistency so that behavior in one setting may generalize to other times and places. Actions in different settings need not literally resemble each other; as long as such actions correlate, it may be possible to invent diagnostic instruments for predicting behavior. A reluctance or inability to follow the rules for a paper-and-pencil maze thus predicts antisocial conduct generally.

To be sure, the diagnostic power of any particular test is less than perfect, often far less. There is ample room for many competing approaches to the study of the enduring behavioral tendencies that fall under the heading of "personality,"[7] and even for skepticism about the very idea of a distinct and enduring personality, apart from the behavioral consistencies attributable to the consistent environments in which most people live.[8] But, properly administered and interpreted, many modern tests reveal reasonably stable behavioral tendencies,[9] and as far as criminogenic tendencies are concerned, this chapter should resolve any doubts about their existence.

There are many definitions of personality,[10] but, for our purposes, a dictionary definition seems a good place to begin: "The organization of the individual's distinguishing character traits, attitudes, or habits."[11] It is not the reasoning component of maze behavior that correlates much with crime and delinquency, but something closer to a behavioral style—of interacting with a particular environment—that generalizes to other environments. Porteus' discovery supports the claim that personality affects criminal behavior; more generally, by showing an underlying connection among different activities, it supports the very idea of personality itself, just as the predictive power of intelligence tests supports the very idea of intelligence. Both intelligence and personality have to do with a person's psychological distinctiveness, though in different respects. Intelligence reveals something about mental structure; personality, about motivational profile. No sharp line divides intelligence from personality, but common sense insists on distinguishing between a person's cognitive and temperamental makeup, as by the two scores extracted from maze-test performance. In this chapter, we review the noncognitive traits that predispose people to breaking the law.

The Continuity of Misconduct

Because there have been more longitudinal studies—in which a population is followed over time—bearing on crime than we can summarize here,[12] we shall discuss only representative ones that also illuminate key issues. Sheldon and Eleanor Glueck conducted what was, and has remained, one of the most detailed and comprehensive longitudinal and cross-sectional studies of male delinquency.[13] We have already encountered some data on physique (Chapter 3) and intelligence (Chapter 6) from their study; here we consider it more fully. Starting in the late 1930s, the Gluecks gathered data on a sample of five hundred white boys, averaging fourteen and a half years of age, incarcerated in correctional schools for serious delinquent behavior ranging from recurrent juvenile offenses to felonious homicide. Almost all the boys came from homes in Boston. As a basis of comparison, the Gluecks matched them with a sample of five hundred nondelinquent Boston boys of about the same age, ethnic background, and IQ, from neighborhoods equivalent in general quality and delinquency rates. Then they surveyed a large number of variables describing the boys themselves, as well as their homes, parents, and grandparents.

As we noted in Chapter 6, any variable used for matching delinquent and nondelinquent samples is thereby ruled out of consideration as a correlate of delinquency. For example, both groups came mostly from English, Italian, and Irish family backgrounds, and from slum neighborhoods. The lack of an ethnic or neighborhood difference between the samples only reflects the way the study was designed, not an absence of ethnic or neighborhood correlates of delinquency in the population at large. Similarly, the delinquents had an average IQ of 92; the nondelinquents, 94, an insignificant difference showing that the matching procedure for IQ had succeeded in excluding IQ as a variable that might be correlated with delinquency in this study.

For numerous other variables, the two groups differed significantly. Although both groups lived in comparably poor neighborhoods, with matching delinquency rates, and although their families paid about the same rental per room, the delinquents' homes were more crowded, less clean, and less well provided with sanitary facilities. Similarly, although both groups were drawn from about the same, generally low occupational levels, the delinquents' families had lower average earnings, both in per capita income and in number of breadwinners. In short, the two groups differed in general social and economic conditions, even after the effort to match them. This was further reflected in the educational backgrounds of the two samples, which were less good for the delinquents' parents and grandparents. The delinquents' parents came from poorer homes than the nondelinquents' parents, and their families had a history of more public welfare support. They also had a family history of more serious physical illness, mental retardation, emotional disturbance, alcoholism, marital discord between parents, and crime.

These differences suggest that even within a relatively narrow and underprivileged sector of society, still finer gradations, at the level of the individual home, further predispose certain individuals toward crime. But beyond even those finer gradations, the Gluecks found differences between the groups of boys in personal characteristics. They were about the same height and weight and were judged to be approximately equally healthy, but they had different physiques, as summarized in Chapter 3. Many of the delinquents were nonectomorphic mesomorphs, while the nondelinquents showed a greater variation in body build. Also, despite the approximate equality in overall IQ, the pattern of abilities differed, with the delinquents relatively weak, compared to the nondelinquents, in verbal ability, even though the nondelinquents were verbally weak compared to the population as a whole, an example of the relative verbal deficit of typical offenders reviewed in Chapter 6.

The delinquents did worse in school than the nondelinquents by any measure—academic, attitudinal, or motivational. When nondelinquents were asked to give reasons for disliking school, they often blamed feelings of inadequacy as students. In contrast, the delinquents were likely to resent the school routine or to be bored. Delinquents' vocational hopes included more adventurous occupations, like aviation and going to sea, than nondelinquents'. The delinquents misbehaved in school earlier, more often, and more seriously than the nondelinquents. Almost 90 percent of the delinquents had misbehaved prior to the age of eleven, several years before the typical adolescent male delinquent gangs form.

Using the Rorschach inkblot test, an effort was made to characterize the boys' personalities. The boys were shown the ten standard inkblots and asked to report what, if anything, they saw in them.[14] The theory behind a "projective" technique like this is that, because the inkblots are ambiguous and unstructured, the subject reveals something about his own personality when he imposes enough structure to see recognizable objects. The Rorschach no longer enjoys the popularity it had in the 1940s, having been largely supplanted by more objective, or at least more easily scored, psychological inventories (see below), but it distinguished between these two samples. The written Rorschach responses were interpreted "blind," that is to say, by experts who had no information about the boys other than their responses to the inkblots. Table 1 presents the breakdown of traits, paraphrasing only slightly and for convenience the experts' own characterizations. The first two columns list descriptions that were significantly more often applied to delinquents and nondelinquents, respectively. In the third column are descriptions that did not differ significantly for the two groups.

Table 1 reveals two distinct personalities for the two groups. The delinquents were assertive, unafraid, aggressive, unconventional, extroverted, and poorly socialized. The nondelinquents were self-controlled, concerned about their relations with others, willing to be guided by social standards, and rich in internal feelings like insecurity, helplessness, love (or its lack), and anxiety. Psychiatric interviews conducted independently confirmed the major distinctions between the two samples.

The Gluecks were able to follow most of the two samples into adulthood and later published a second account of them.[15] The differences in academic and socioeconomic success and in personality endured into young adulthood, and so did the differences in criminal behavior. Of the 442 nondelinquents who were located in adulthood, 62 were convicted for crimes by the age of thirty-one. The crimes were, on the whole, minor, involving mostly drunkenness, violations of license laws, and offenses within the fam-

TABLE 1

Personality Traits in the Glueck Sample

Delinquents Exceed Nondelinquents	Nondelinquents Exceed Delinquents	No Significant Difference
Self-assertive	Submissiveness	Feeling not being taken
Social assertion	General anxiety	care of
Defiance	Enhanced insecurity	Feeling not being taken
Ambivalence toward	Feeling unloved	seriously
authority	Feeling helpless	Resignation
Feeling unappreciated	Fear of failure	Depression
Feeling resentment	Adequate contact with	Kindliness
Difficulty in contact	others	Competitiveness
with others	Cooperativeness	Isolation
Hostility	Dependence on others	Suggestibility
Suspicion	Concerns about others'	Spontaneity
Destructiveness	expectations	Feeling able to cope
Narcissism	Conventionality	Introversion
Feeling others will	Masochism	
take care of one	Self-control	
Sadism	Compulsiveness	
Impulsiveness		
Extroversion		
Mental pathology		

Source: From R. J. Herrnstein, Some criminogenic traits of offenders. In J. Q. Wilson (ed.), *Crime and Public Policy* (San Francisco: ICS Press, 1983), p. 36, adapted from S. Glueck and E. T. Glueck, *Unraveling Juvenile Delinquency* (Cambridge, Mass.: Harvard University Press, 1950).

ily, plus a few serious crimes—an armed robbery, an assault with a dangerous weapon, an abuse of a child, and the like. In contrast, the delinquent group proved prolifically criminal. By the age of thirty-one, they had committed fifteen homicides, hundreds of burglaries, hundreds of larcenies (greater than petty), hundreds of arrests for drunkenness, over 150 robberies, dozens of sex offenses, and so on. Four hundred and thirty-eight of the original 500 in the delinquent sample were located, of whom 354 were arrested between the ages of seventeen to twenty-five. From twenty-five to thirty-one, only 263 were arrested, perhaps showing the characteristic decline of crime with age, or perhaps only the shrinking numbers not in prison. One hundred and forty-seven men from the delinquent sample spent five or more years in jails or prisons during the eight years from seventeen to twenty-five, and 45 did so during the six years from twenty-five to thirty-one. Despite the hundreds of man-years spent in correctional institutions, the delinquents had ample time outside for scores of arrests.

Although the Glueck study was internationally cited, American sociologists criticized it intensely.[16] Modern criminological texts usually give it short shrift, as if the criticisms had found their mark. Some of them did, but most, if not all, of the distinguishing traits of the Gluecks' delinquent boys have been repeatedly confirmed in other samples. The methodological criticisms of this aspect of the study were, in hindsight, less decisive than they seemed to a criminological community whose sociological theories had little room for the individualistic variables considered by the Gluecks, such as personality traits and physique. (Sheldon Glueck's rejoinder to his critics was published in 1960.)

Another longitudinal study of male delinquency was conducted by Conger and Miller, using all the boys entering the tenth grade in Denver, Colorado, public schools in 1956, provided the school records were reasonably complete.[17] Among the 2,300 boys, 271 were delinquent (or became so by the age of eighteen) by the criterion of having been charged with an offense in juvenile court. Conger and Miller attempted to match the delinquents, case by case, with nondelinquents of approximately the same IQ, age, socioeconomic status, ethnic background, and school environment. They succeeded for only 184 delinquents, so their study was based on 368 cases, half of whom were delinquent and half nondelinquent.

The school records contained not only the usual sorts of academic histories but also teacher evaluations, from the early grades on, of the boys' personalities, general behavior, and social adjustment. In addition, when the boys entered the study, at the age of about fifteen, they took a battery of tests of personality and value structure. At fifteen, delinquents could be differentiated from nondelinquents either by the standard personality tests or by teacher evaluations. On the average, they were characterized as emotionally unstable, impulsive, suspicious, hostile, given to "petty expressions of pique," egocentric, and generally more unhappy, worried, and dissatisfied than their nondelinquent matches. These traits were already present to a considerable extent in the teacher evaluations at the third-grade level, six years before the study began and presumably before the emergence of serious delinquency.

Summarizing their analysis of third-grade school records, Conger and Miller concluded:

> By the end of the third grade, future delinquents were already seen by their teachers as more poorly adapted than their classmates. They appeared to have less regard for the rights and feelings of their peers; less awareness of

the need to accept responsibility for their obligations, both as individuals and as members of a group; and poorer attitudes toward authority, including failure to understand the need for rules and regulations in any well-ordered social group and the need for abiding by them. They both resented and rejected authority in the school situation. Their over-all social behavior was simply less acceptable, not simply with teachers, but with peers; they had more difficulty in getting along with peers, both in individual one-to-one contacts and in group situations, and were less willing or able to treat others courteously and tactfully, and less able to be fair in dealing with them. In return, they were less well-liked and accepted by their peers. They were significantly less likely than their nondelinquent matches to be viewed as dependable, friendly, pleasant, considerate, and fair.[18]

Mostly, these traits echo Table 1, from the Gluecks' study, but one difference between the two is that the Denver delinquents seemed more worried, anxious, and even hypochondriacal. As we will see later, although some of the difference may be attributable to the difference in evaluation techniques, it is more likely to be a reflection of the more serious criterion of delinquency used by the Gluecks, which was institutionalization, as compared to court referral. In the Denver sample, when the delinquents were further subdivided into recidivists versus nonrecidivists, the recidivists were more unstable, less sociable, and less capable of following rules than the nonrecidivists. They were apparently no more anxious, but also no less, as far as the measures could tell.

A different sort of longitudinal study was reported by Terence Taylor and David Watt.[19] Instead of starting with a group of identified offenders and searching retrospectively for correlates of delinquency, Taylor and Watt started with data on a sample of young schoolchildren in a district in England (Buckinghamshire) and then, seven years later, returned to see what best predicted later troubles of various kinds. Prospective studies like this are generally superior methodologically to retrospective studies because they are less subject to distorting reconstructions of the past. They are also not so rigidly tied to a particular stage in the criminal justice system as is a retrospective study that starts with a sample of, say, court cases or convictions. But they are harder and more expensive to do, for they must start with large samples in order to find enough delinquency or crime for the predictors to be statistically reliable.

Taylor and Watt examined six thousand children whose parents answered questionnaires concerning "symptoms . . . commonly regarded as indicative of emotional disorder,"[20] and for whom there were family background data and teacher reports. A child was characterized as deviant if he or she had more than three deviant symptoms; this comprised about one child in ten. A symptom was defined as deviant if it turned up in fewer than 10 percent of the cases, such as "crying once a week." The task was to see how well and in what ways childhood deviance predicted appearance in juvenile court or in guidance clinics seven years later.

Since almost all of the court cases were for boys, the girls were dropped from further analysis. Of the 3,415 boys in the sample, almost 300 were referred to court or clinic within seven years. Court referrals outnumbered clinic referrals by a ratio of about 3.5 to 1. Boys who were "deviant" seven years before had about twice the risk of showing up in court as those who were not, and almost six times the risk of showing up in a guidance clinic.

Combining court and clinic referrals, Figure 1 shows a direct and continuous relationship between symptoms in childhood and trouble later. The broader the range of symptoms, the greater the risk of delinquency or need for guidance. Moreover, the symptoms that foretold delinquency differed from those that foretold need for help in a clinic. Court cases were likely to have been described by their parents seven years earlier as very restless, as having stolen, and as crying a lot by the age of ten. In contrast, clinical cases were described, at the age of ten or younger, as moody, highly strung, disliking school, given to temper tantrums, and *less* restless than typical. The clinic-bound boys had a variety of physical complaints—stomach cramps, headaches, etc.; the court-bound boys were about average in this respect. The only symptom that the court- and clinic-bound boys shared was trouble in learning to read.

Reports by teachers generally confirmed the parents' questionnaires. Seven years before, the teachers had described boys headed for court as assertive and disruptive, and less shy, worried, and timid than the average boy. Boys headed for the clinic had been described as uncooperative or uninterested in school as compared to the average. Both court and clinic cases had academic problems.

The court-bound boys generally came from poorer backgrounds than the clinic-bound (whose backgrounds were about par for the sample as a whole), and from larger families with more parental absence from home. Indirect evidence (drawn from a different, but presumably comparable, sample of boys) suggested that the parents of court-bound boys expressed less concern about their sons' behavior than parents of clinic-bound boys. But the difference in parental concern was not the result of a difference in socioeconomic status nor the cause of the boys' deviance. It may, rather, have been a manifestation of family characteristics often found alongside delinquency, as discussed in Chapters 8 and 9.

The continuity between childhood symptomatology and adult behavior also emerged in Lee Robins' thirty-year follow-up of 526 white childhood patients in a St. Louis, Missouri, guidance clinic in the 1920s.[21] Robins re-

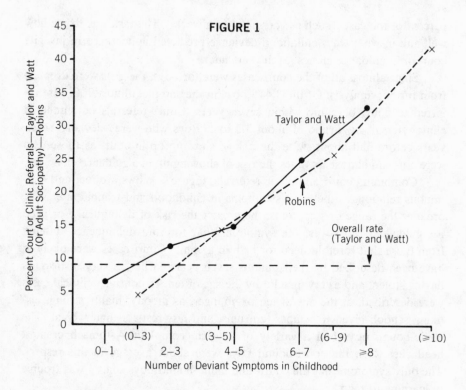

FIGURE 1

In two studies (Taylor and Watt's and Robins'), the number of symptoms of deviance in childhood predicted the percent of a population that experienced personality disorders or trouble with the law later in life. The horizontal dashed line is the average rate of later difficulty in Taylor and Watt's sample.

constructed the life histories of her subjects from clinic, school, and police records, and interviews at follow-up, when the subjects were in their forties. Robins was looking for the precursors not specifically of crime but of adult "antisocial personality," or "sociopathy," which includes offending as one of its major manifestations. Later, we will consider sociopathy (also called psychopathy) more fully, but here we use Robins' own characterization:

> We refer to someone who fails to maintain close personal relationships with anyone else, performs poorly on the job, who is involved in illegal behaviors (whether or not apprehended), who fails to support himself and his dependents without outside aid, and who is given to sudden changes of plan and loss of temper in response to what appear to others as minor frustrations. These characteristics must be chronic and more or less typical of the whole life history up to the point of diagnosis.[22]

What sort of child grows up into this sort of adult? Robins' answer, if she excluded cases involving organic brain damage, frank schizophrenia, mental retardation, or symptoms appearing only after heavy drug or alcohol use, was that the adult sociopath is invariably an antisocial child grown up. Indeed, she found *no* case of adult sociopathy without antisocial behavior prior to the age of eighteen; in boys, the symptoms often began well before adolescence. Over 50 percent of the sociopathic males showed an onset of symptoms prior to the age of eight. A second study, using only black school-boys, confirmed the total absence of adult sociopathy without symptoms in childhood.[23]

No single symptom characterized all cases of childhood antisocial personality, but among the more common ones (shown by at least two-thirds of the antisocial cases) were theft, sexual activity (in girls), "incorrigibility," running away, poor school performance, and truancy. About a third of the adult sociopaths had been described in childhood as reckless, slovenly, impulsive, and lacking guilt. The more of these symptoms a child had, the greater was the risk later on, as in Taylor and Watt's English sample. Although the two studies used somewhat different childhood symptoms and outcome measures, the results were quite similar. We have added Robins' data[24] to Figure 1 as *X*s, showing the percentage of adults diagnosed as sociopathic, given various numbers of antisocial symptoms in childhood. The greater the range of deviance in childhood, the poorer the prognosis in adulthood.

A great deal of detailed information about another English sample has been reported in a series of publications by West and Farrington, drawn from a prospective study of 411 boys growing up in a working-class district in London.[25] All the boys at the fourth-grade level (i.e., eight to nine years old) in six neighborhood schools in 1961–1962 have since been studied by means of self-report questionnaires, school and family records, and self-reports and official records of offenses, enabling the authors to examine "the extent to which young adult delinquents differ from their social peers in personal circumstances, attitudes, and behavior."[26] The latest comprehensive report uses interviews of the sample at the age of eighteen to nineteen, but the official records carry them to the age of twenty-five or thereabouts. New findings about the sample continue to appear at the time of this writing.

About 30 percent of the sample had some sort of official record of delinquency by the age of twenty-one. Although about twice the national average, 30 percent was close to the figure for comparable urban districts in England at that time. But from the 22 percent of the sample that had been rated prior to the age of eleven as "troublesome" by teachers and peers came about 60 percent of the recidivists by the age of eighteen. Teachers' ratings of classroom aggressiveness of the boys as early as the age of eight predicted later juvenile and adult crime, violent and otherwise.

West and Farrington devised a scale to measure "antisocial" tendencies, based on measures of attitude and such activities as smoking, loitering, getting tattooed, heavy drinking and gambling, involvement in rowdy or nonconventional groups, and promiscuous sex. Of the 110 young men who scored the highest (i.e., most antisocial), over 60 percent were delinquents; of the 72 who scored lowest, 4 percent were delinquents. Commented the authors, "One could hardly imagine a clearer demonstration of the close connection between officially recorded delinquency and particular attributes of character and life style—the delinquent way of life."[27] In this study, in which institutionalization could not have fostered traits or behavioral tendencies that surfaced well before a boy might run into the law, offenders were at least as distinctive as in the Gluecks' or other samples of prisoners.

Personality Inventories

Patterns of deviant or antisocial behavior at one time of life are correlated with patterns of deviant or antisocial behavior at other times. That is the single most inclusive way of characterizing the results of longitudinal research on crime and delinquency, such as those just reviewed, as well as in Chapters 8 and 9 on the family, and in the literature as a whole.[28] In cross-sectional, as contrasted with longitudinal, research, it is not usually possible to interrelate behaviors at different times of life. Rather than lives in progress, cross-sectional studies look at a slice of time, a snapshot rather than a motion picture.

In fact, many studies are neither purely cross-sectional nor longitudinal; they contain elements of both. In the Gluecks' study, for example, two groups of boys were compared at a particular time, while their life histories were retrospectively reconstructed, reaching as far back as grandparents for facts on education, police contacts, and the like. Similarly, many primarily cross-sectional studies also collect life-history data or follow their subjects for a time. But the blurred distinction between cross-sectional and longitudinal studies is no problem here, for our purpose in directing attention to it is conceptual, not procedural.

Rather than relying on naturally occurring behavior in its life setting, a cross-sectional study may use a contrived sample of behavior—a test, such as telling stories about inkblots or pictures, tracing a maze, affirming or denying statements on a self-report inventory, or answering questions in an interview. (Peer ratings are also just descriptions of behavior, as seen through the eyes of friends, parents, etc.) As a substitute for the missing information about how a person behaved in the past, or, for that matter, how he or she might have behaved in situations never encountered, a test can, in principle, predict future behavior even better than life-history data, and do so more efficiently. A predictive test substantiates not only the test but the concept of personality with its enduring traits. Personality traits ultimately represent a person's characteristic values for the variables that govern behavior. But for criminal behavior, it has not always been accepted that personality traits matter.

A 1950 survey of the empirical literature relating crime and personality as measured by tests of various kinds found it "impossible to conclude from these data that criminality and personality elements are associated."[29] The skeptical outlook (which was shared by many criminologists) seemed justified by the data at the time. Of the more than 110 studies reviewed, only about 40 percent reported personality differences between criminals and noncriminals. To the authors of the study, Schuessler and Cressey, and others, the cup looked more than half empty rather than almost half full. The many studies using prisoners as subjects raised the possibility that institutionalization itself was causing the atypical personality traits of some samples of criminals. Criminals and noncriminals often differed in socioeconomic status, intelligence, and cultural background, any of which may have contaminated the results of personality tests. In 1950, and even more recently, there has been a worry about unmatched samples. As Passingham put it: "Before it can be concluded that there is a relation between criminality and personality, it is necessary to show that delinquents and criminals differ on personality variables, even when all the other relevant variables have been controlled."[30] (Rather than restate what is wrong with this logic, we refer readers to Chapter 6.)

As it turned out, matching criminals and noncriminals for background variables like age, sex, IQ, or social status eventually *strengthened* the evidence for personality correlates of crime. In a review of the empirical literature that appeared between 1950 and 1965, and included only matched comparisons, over 80 percent of the studies showed significant personality differences between groups of criminals and noncriminals.[31] Subsequently, in a further updating of the literature from 1966 to 1975, also including only matched groups, offenders again differed in personality from nonoffenders in about 80 percent of the comparisons.[32] The improving case for a difference was partly due to improved sampling procedures, but more so to the standardization and increasing use of two broad-gauged personality tests not widely available before 1950, the Minnesota Multiphasic Personality Inventory (MMPI) and the California Psychological Inventory (CPI). Since both tests have discriminated between samples of criminals and noncriminals over 90 percent of the time, they deserve specific attention.[33] Other tests (such as Porteus' Maze Tests) may discriminate as well or better, but they have not enjoyed the popularity of either the MMPI or the CPI.

Minnesota Multiphasic Personality Inventory

The MMPI asks a subject to respond true or false (or cannot say) to a series of 566 statements. The statements are self-descriptive, ranging from such items as "Everything tastes the same" to "I have never been in trouble with the law." The items were selected not on theoretical grounds but for their proved ability to discriminate the responses of average, presumably normal, people from people suffering from certain psychopathological problems, such as hypochondria or schizophrenia.[34] In addition, some of the items are included to probe attitudes toward the test itself and to detect any tendency toward misrepresentation. From these checks on internal validity, it is supposed to be possible to decide whether or not a respondent's answers are so distorted as to be meaningless.

Ten clinical populations were used to establish the ten clinical scales of the MMPI. The clinical scales are identified with the populations used to construct them, and numbered and labeled as follows:

1. Hypochondriasis (Hs)—abnormal preoccupation with physical complaints.
2. Depression (D)—hopelessness and self-deprecation.
3. Hysteria (Hy)—stress avoidance by conversion into physical or mental symptoms.
4. Psychopathic deviate (Pd)—conflict with authority and shallow personal attachments.
5. Masculinity-femininity (Mf)—high scores represent opposite-sex attitudes and behaviors.
6. Paranoia (Pa)—undue defensiveness, suspiciousness, and sensitivity.
7. Psychoasthenia (Pt)—plagued by anxiety, indecision, fearfulness, and guilt.
8. Schizophrenia (Sc)—bizarre thought and affect, and withdrawal from personal contact.
9. Hypomania (Ma)—unproductive hyperactivity.
0. Social introversion (Si)—social insecurity and shyness.

What is known about these scales is that people diagnosed as having the named clinical conditions answer certain items of the inventory with a given pattern of trues and falses. For example, the Schizophrenia scale involves 78 of the 566 items, which schizophrenics typically answer in a characteristic way. If someone's answers on those items approximate the pattern for schizophrenics, he or she may or may not be schizophrenic, but a high score on scale 8 has been shown to correlate with a variety of schizophrenic symptoms, such as peculiarities of thought and emotion, that may occur in the absence of the full-blown psychosis. Answers to test items can also be partitioned into any number of scales besides the ten original clinical scales. Many dozens of these new "experimental" scales have been shown to have greater or lesser predictive power for various psychological characteristics. A number of specialized scales, for example, are intended to discriminate among various categories of offenders, occasionally with some success.[35]

From the beginning, high scores on the Pd scale (Psychopathic deviate) were expected to go with criminal behavior, for the initial clinical population included convicted offenders, as well as psychiatric patients diagnosed as psychopathic. Some, but not all, of the items for this scale are, in fact, simply questions about a respondent's past criminal behavior. Countless studies have by now confirmed the correlation between the Psychopathic deviate score and crime; we will review one study to illustrate the MMPI's power to predict antisocial behavior.

Starke Hathaway, the author of the MMPI at the University of Minnesota, and Elio Monachesi, a sociologist specializing in research on delinquency, examined the test's capacity to detect criminal tendencies in advance of encounters with the law.[36] Most of the children entering ninth grade in the Minneapolis public schools in 1947 were given the MMPI—a sample of almost four thousand boys and girls. At two two-year intervals thereafter, Monachesi and Hathaway searched police, court, and social-agency records in the area for the names of the children they tested, looking for those with more than a single criminal offense. Since they found mostly boys meeting their criterion, the analysis focused on boys only.

Delinquents (especially the serious delinquents) predominated among the boys whose highest scores had been on scales 4, 8, and 9—the Psychopathic deviate, Schizophrenia, and Hypomania scales. Delinquents were relatively scarce among boys with highest scores on scales 2, 5, and 0—Depression, Masculinity-femininity, and Social introversion. The delinquents also distinguished themselves by a high level of questionnaire invalidity, due to dishonest or biased responding. A larger statewide sample of Minnesota's ninth-grade population later confirmed the major results, and also showed that girls had similar patterns of scores. The high scores on scales 4, 8, and

9 among offenders, and, usually, the lack of criminal tendencies among those whose highest scores are on scales 2, 5, and 0 are by now commonplace in the empirical literature on crime.

It would be unlikely in the extreme if so broad a category as criminal behavior reduced to a single personality type. The more interesting, and potentially useful, applications of the MMPI (and other tests) involve attempts to isolate narrower categories of offenders. For example, Megargee and his associates have proposed a new system of classification validated, in part, on MMPI responses for over twelve hundred young males incarcerated in a federal prison over a two-year period.[37] (All federal, and many state and local, correctional institutions routinely administer the MMPI when a prisoner is admitted.[38]) Using just the ten clinical scales, Megargee and his colleagues could sort over 95 percent of the prisoners into one of ten characteristic MMPI profiles, about two-thirds of them by computer and the remainder with the help of a trained clinician.

Figure 2 shows the overall profile of prisoners (filled circles), the most deviant of the profiles (Xs; 13.3 percent of classified prisoners), and the least deviant of the profiles (open circles; 19.3 percent of classified prisoners). On each clinical scale, almost 70 percent of the general population lies between 40 and 60, and averages 50. The prisoners have elevated values for Psychopathic deviate (No. 4), Schizophrenia (No. 8), and Hypomania (No. 9), just as Monachesi and Hathaway's predelinquent ninth graders did. In this sample, as in many others, the average offender lies at about the 98th percentile of the general population's Psychopathic deviate value, and at lesser, though still abnormally high, scores on the Schizophrenia and Hypomania scales. The scale values as a whole are somewhat high, with the most nearly normal scale for Social introversion (No. 0). Differences among the ten profiles could be related to differences in offenses, in institutional behavior and adjustment, in recidivism, and in other demographic characteristics.

The group of prisoners with the most deviant profile had the highest probability of reincarceration after release and the highest fraction in trouble during imprisonment. Their work in prison earned the lowest performance ratings; their siblings were most likely to be deviant; and they had relatively severe problems of adjustment outside of prison, in school and on the job, as well as inside. In contrast, the prisoners with the least deviant profile, that is, scores closest to 50 on the ten clinical scales, had good prison adjustment, and a history of relatively minor crimes, such as draft offenses and drug and liquor law violations, in addition to a variety of property offenses. They had relatively few problems in school and high ratings

FIGURE 2

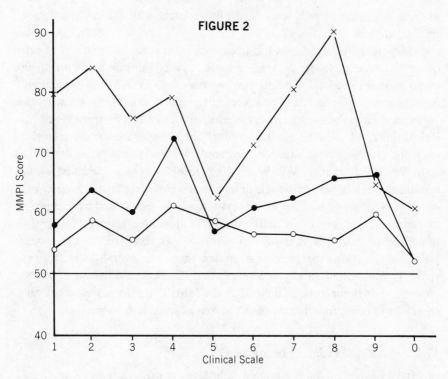

Source: From R. J. Herrnstein, Some criminogenic traits of offenders. In J. Q. Wilson (ed.), *Crime and Public Policy* (San Francisco: ICS Press, 1983), p. 41, adapted from E. I. Megargee and M. J. Bohn, Jr. (with J. Meyer, Jr., and F. Sink), *Classifying Criminal Offenders* (Beverly Hills, Calif.; Sage, 1979).

MMPI profiles of prisoners in a federal prison. Filled circles are for the prisoners as a whole; open circles, for the group of prisoners with the least deviant profile, and *X*s, for that with the most deviant. The general population scores 50 on each scale.

for dependability at prison jobs. By any measure examined, they had the second-lowest rate of recidivism, with the lowest rate earned by another group of prisoners with a low level of personality deviance.

Although prisoners with different MMPI profiles differed somewhat, certain generalizations follow. As a whole, prisoners deviated from the population at large in the typical way—in those traits associated with high values on the Psychopathy, Schizophrenia, and Hypomania scales of the MMPI, namely, deficient attachments to others and to social norms, bizarre thinking and alienation, and unproductive hyperactivity. The more deviant prisoners usually had more serious behavioral problems, more serious crimes in their past, poorer prognosis for future contact with the law, and more trouble while in prison.

Megargee's classification has been applied to other populations of prisoners[39]—female prisoners as well as male; county jail and state prison inmates as well as federal. The proportions may shift in different populations, but upwards of 90 percent of prisoners fall in one or another of the ten categories, and have the life histories, offenses, and prospects for recidivism typical of those with similar MMPI profiles. They also make the characteristically good or bad impressions on the people who interview them, depending on their MMPI profiles. Within the 10 percent or so not classified by the system, there may be additional, though much rarer, types of criminal personality. Whether or not Megargee's system will have practical uses in prison management and inmate rehabilitation,[40] it illustrates vividly that institutionalized offenders have atypical personalities as compared to the general population; it shows that, among offenders, there are several distinctive personality profiles; and, finally, it confirms that Psychopathic deviance, Schizophrenia, and Hypomania, as defined by the MMPI, are the major personality correlates of crime for adult criminals as well as juvenile delinquents.

California Psychological Inventory

There are many ways to subdivide personality. Just the 566 items of the MMPI, for example, have provided hundreds of experimental scales and special profiles, and the MMPI is just one test among many. The complexity of personality allows endless schemes to represent it. What may seem distinct in one system of analysis may coalesce into a single trait in another. Multiply this intrinsic diversity by the variety of different vocabularies—psychoanalytic, sociological, biological, behavioristic, statistical, etc.—and it should be obvious why criminology's picture of criminal personality has developed slowly. Nevertheless, the outlines of a set of predisposing characteristics should become clear beneath the diversity as we take up the findings from various systems.

Closely related to the MMPI is the California Psychological Inventory (CPI), developed by Harrison Gough and his colleagues at the University of California (Berkeley). Though born in Berkeley, the CPI was conceived in Minneapolis (to borrow a phrase from Megargee[41]), where, at the University of Minnesota, Gough took his undergraduate and graduate degrees, having studied and worked with the team that developed the MMPI. Like the MMPI, the CPI is a self-descriptive inventory of true-false items (480 of them), but it is broken into eighteen, rather than ten, basic scales. Approximately one-third of the CPI items are, in fact, also on the MMPI, but the two tests differ nevertheless. The CPI's standard scales are supposed to describe characteristics of normal populations, in contrast to the psychopathological populations used for establishing MMPI items. The CPI is justified theoretically rather than empirically, then checked against the responses of various reference groups and by other procedures, such as peer ratings and objective indexes of performance.[42] That is to say, the CPI attempts to measure adjustments in everyday life, what Gough called "folk concepts,"[43] such as "social presence" or "self-control," to mention two of its eighteen scales. Despite the differences, the CPI and MMPI yield correlated profiles[44] and, more pertinent here, they describe offenders similarly.

The "socialization" scale of the CPI embodies Gough's view of psychopathy as a deficiency in role playing. The psychopath, said Gough, has difficulty seeing himself or herself as others do, or in projecting himself or herself into the reactions of others. The result is behavior characterized as antisocial, psychopathic, or sociopathic, which Gough described as:

> overevaluation of immediate goals as opposed to remote or deferred ones, unconcern over the rights and privileges of others when recognizing them would interfere with personal satisfaction in any way; impulsive behavior, or apparent incongruity between the strength of the stimulus and the magnitude of the behavioral response; inability to form deep or persistent attachments to other persons or to identify in interpersonal relationships; poor judgment and planning in attaining defined goals; apparent lack of anxiety and distress over social maladjustment and unwillingness or inability to consider maladjustment qua maladjustment; a tendency to project blame onto others and to take no responsibility for failures; meaningless prevarication, often about trivial matters in situations where detection is inevitable; almost complete lack of dependability of and willingness to assume responsibility; and, finally, emotional poverty.[45]

The CPI socialization scale has proved to be a powerful discriminator between populations of offenders and nonoffenders. In a tour de force, Gough reported the results of applying the socialization scale in eight languages (Afrikaans, English, French, German, Hindi, Italian, Punjabi, and Spanish) to samples of male and female juvenile and adult offenders in ten countries (Austria, Costa Rica, France, Germany, India, Italy, Puerto Rico, South Africa, Switzerland, and the United States) in eighteen independent comparisons involving over twenty-six thousand people.[46] Not only did the scale discriminate between offenders and nonoffenders in every comparison, but the average scores for offenders fell within a narrow range, as did those for nonoffenders, despite the different cultures and languages. No sample of

TABLE 2

CPI So Scores of Male and Female Groups Differing in Socialization

Male Samples:	[Number of Cases] N	[Averages] M	[Standard Deviations] SD
1. High school "best citizens"	90	39.44	4.95
2. Medical school applicants	70	39.27	4.82
3. Bank officers	71	39.06	4.61
4. City school superintendents	200	37.58	4.19
5. Business executives	116	37.47	4.72
6. College students	1,745	37.41	5.28
7. Electronic technicians	55	36.93	5.66
8. Correctional officers	620	36.72	5.47
9. Skilled and semiskilled workers	108	36.62	5.17
10. High school students	4,474	36.46	5.56
11. Social work graduate students	182	36.40	4.62
12. Military officers	495	36.38	4.74
13. Machine operators	105	35.99	4.98
14. Psychology graduate students	89	34.24	4.23
15. Selective service inductees	139	32.83	6.71
16. High school "disciplinary problems"	91	31.25	5.40
17. County jail inmates	177	29.27	6.44
18. Young delinquents, California	206	28.66	5.86
19. Prison inmates, New York	94	28.28	5.80
20. Prison inmates, California	177	27.76	6.03
21. Training school inmates, New York	100	26.53	4.89
Total, samples 1–15 [nonoffenders]	8,559	36.70	5.65
Total, samples 16–21 [offenders]	845	28.58	5.98

diff. = 8.12 [between nonoffenders and offenders]
C.R. = 10.55 [critical ratio]
$p < .01$ [level of statistical significance]

Female Samples:	[Number of Cases] N	[Averages] M	[Standard Deviations] SD
1. High school "best citizens"	90	41.51	4.55
2. High school students	5,295	39.69	5.57
3. College students	3,452	39.37	5.05
4. Factory workers	291	38.99	4.76
5. Nurses	142	38.24	4.89
6. Airline hostesses	60	38.07	4.51
7. Social work graduate students	320	37.99	4.38
8. Psychology graduate students	37	36.65	3.59
9. High school "disciplinary problems"	87	34.79	7.00

TABLE 2 (Continued)

Female Samples:	[Number of Cases] N	[Averages] M	[Standard Deviations]
10. Unmarried mothers	213	32.92	6.24
11. County jail inmates	51	29.61	5.86
12. Prison inmates, Indiana	127	28.37	6.24
13. Prison inmates, California	135	28.36	5.68
14. Prison inmates, Wisconsin	76	26.83	7.04
15. Youth authority cases, California	47	25.79	5.30
Total, samples 1–8 [nonoffenders]	9,687	39.48	5.33
Total, samples 9–15 [offenders]	736	30.21	6.92

diff. = 9.27 [between nonoffenders and offenders]
C.R. = 11.24 [critical ratio]
p < .01 [level of statistical significance]

Source: From E. I. Megargee, *The California Psychological Inventory Handbook* (San Francisco: Jossey-Bass, 1972), p. 63, from H. G. Gough, Cross-cultural validation of a measure of social behavior, *Psychological Reports* (1965), 17:22.

offenders earned as high an average score as even the lowest-scoring sample of nonoffenders (high scores represent higher levels of socialization). The socialization scale, said Gough, discriminates between offenders and nonoffenders independently of any correlation with intelligence, age, or socioeconomic status.

Besides simply discriminating between groups of offenders and nonoffenders, socialization scores appear to reflect a continuum from highly social to antisocial attitudes. Table 2 reproduces Gough's survey of socialization scores for American samples of males and females in various settings. High school boys and girls rated as "good citizens" are at the top; prisoners and inmates of correctional institutions, at the bottom. (We will not say which of the present authors is more surprised by the low scores of psychology graduate students.) The discriminating power of the socialization scale of the CPI, either among groups of offenders or among nonoffenders, is well documented.[47] For example, frequent marijuana users (by self-reports) had lower (i.e., worse) scores than occasional users or nonusers.[48] College students who habitually cheated on tests had lower scores than noncheaters.[49] Young unwed mothers had lower scores than girls who had had no pregnancies, even after controlling for their own home backgrounds.[50]

Among the CPI scales, socialization has been most extensively related to criminal behavior, but it is not the only one. Of the eighteen scales, at least two others besides socialization appear to tap criminal tendencies: Low scores on the "responsibility" scale and the "self-control" scale characterize both male and female offenders.[51] The responsibility scale is often said to measure the understanding of social controls; the socialization scale, the tendency to behave with "rectitude and probity";[52] and the self-control scale, the approval of social goals. However, since socialization, responsibility, and self-control scores are themselves intercorrelated, it would be a mistake to try to distinguish them too sharply. As a group, the three scales figure prominently in a characteristic described as "conformity," "value orientation," or "social adjustment," the lack of which is apparently part of the typical criminogenic personality.

Some Finer Distinctions

Using the offender categories provided by the criminal justice system itself, corresponding personality differences are usually hard to find.[53] Offenders are generalists in crime more often than specialists;[54] on that ground alone (not to mention plea bargaining and other sources of ambiguity in the criminal justice system) we should not expect prisoners to be neatly sorted into personality configurations corresponding to the offense categories for which they happen to be serving time on a particular occasion.

Panton, for example, administered the MMPI to over thirteen hundred men just entering a state prison in North Carolina and segregated their response profiles into six criminal categories: white collar, aggravated assault, robbery-burglary, larceny–auto theft and other property crimes, aggravated sex, and sex perversions.[55] All the groups showed the characteristic elevation of the Psychopathic deviate scale; all of them had the Schizophrenia score among their top three readings; and all of them also showed the general elevation of scores suggesting psychopathology. Perhaps because they were just starting their terms, their Hypomania scores lacked the extreme elevation seen in some samples of offenders, and they had unusually high Depression scores. This was, in short, a typical, if somewhat subdued, sample of prisoners. But, on the average, the six categories did not differ from one another in MMPI profile, with only a few notable exceptions. The sexual-perversion group had atypically elevated Masculinity-femininity scores, indicating unusually feminine attitudes (they were also the most atypical group in overall MMPI profile); the white-collar criminals had less elevation on the Schizophrenia scale and more elevation on the Hysteria scale than the other groups. On the average, only one scale out of the ten differed significantly between any pair of groups, or between any one group and the thirteen hundred inmates as a whole. Panton concluded that the "mean personality type" of the prisoners was "irresponsible, impulsive, undependable, tactless, egocentric, deficient in ability to calculate own stimulus value, incapacity to evaluate the consequences of their behavior, and a marked facility in rationalization. . . . However, there appears to be no marked difference between the profiles of six major crime classification groups."[56]

If criminals are placed in better-defined categories than those used by the legal system, their personalities may be more distinctive. For example, Gough, Wenk, and Rozynko compared groups of male parole violators and parole successes (i.e., men who did not violate parole over a three-year period).[57] Parole success was predicted by higher scores on the CPI socialization and self-control scales, and, to a lesser extent, on the "communality" scale, which measures the typicality of the responses and is often taken as an additional measure of socialization, or merely of cooperation with the test itself. Parole success was *inversely* related to high scores on the "social presence" scale, a measure of poise. "Poise" may have something to do with a person's ability to manipulate a social situation like a parole hearing. Another measure of poise, the "social acceptance" scale, also had a marginally inverse relationship with parole success. Some social skills may get a prisoner past a parole board, but not do much good afterward in keeping him out of trouble.

As Gough and his associates pointed out, the CPI did not predict parole violation as well as did past history, with young property offenders with long criminal records having the worst prognosis. However, supplementing the past record with test data improved prediction. The tests also permitted a further analysis that would otherwise have been impossible. A sample of one hundred men with no known criminal records took the CPI and also allowed themselves to be observed and interviewed over a six-day period by a panel of observers. The observers then individually characterized the men by using an adjective check list.[58] The question was which adjectives were most often applied to men who, if they had been prisoners, would have been most likely to be parole successes on the basis of CPI scores, and which men would have been most likely to be parole violators. Table 3 attests to the saliency of personality by listing the ten adjectives most correlated with good and poor CPI prognosis for parole success. Even among noncriminals, the CPI detects the personal styles of behavior, evident to interviewers, that distinguish CPI-predicted recidivists from CPI-predicted nonrecidivists.

Gough and others have concluded that the standard scales of the MMPI, with the possible exception of the Hypomania scale, were less useful than the various CPI scales in predicting parole violators.[59] However,

TABLE 3

Adjectives Used to Describe Noncriminal Men Who Would Have Had Good or Poor
Prognosis for Parole Success, Measured by the CPI

Good Prognosis	Poor Prognosis
Conscientious	Adventurous
Conservative	Egotistical
Conventional	Mischievous
Mild	Opinionated
Moderate	Outspoken
Modest	Pleasure-seeking
Painstaking	Quick
Patient	Shrewd
Quiet	Touchy
Unassuming	Witty

Source: Adaptation from H. G. Gough et al., Parole outcome as predicted from the CPI, the
MMPI, and a base expectancy table, *Journal of Abnormal Psychology* (1965), 70: 439.

new MMPI scales have served the purpose to some extent—for example, a
"Parole Violator" scale, a "Recidivism-Rehabilitation" scale, and others.
Still other new MMPI scales have identified prison escapees, general prison
adjustment, and the like well enough to confirm the presence of differentiating traits, if not well enough to be useful in practice.

Inasmuch as one of our recurrent themes in these test data is the lack
of internalized constraints, we should mention what are apparently clear
counter instances. Personality assessment has uncovered a kind of *extremely*
violent criminal who may have more, rather than fewer, internalized prohibitions than those engaging in moderate or nonviolent crimes.[60] In one study
by Megargee, the most violent criminals among a sample of male juvenile
offenders were rated as more cooperative and controlled, and less overtly
aggressive, than less violent offenders.[61] The most violent offenders included
the largest proportion of first offenders. Other workers[62] have confirmed the
existence of a type of criminal who seems to be less overtly hostile and more
introverted, self-controlled, and conformist than criminals in general, and
who commits perhaps just one crime, but an exceedingly violent one. Not all
extremely violent criminals fall into this category, but enough of them do to
turn up in most samples.

Megargee and his associates have derived a new MMPI scale, the *O-H*
scale, to identify this type of *"O*ver-controlled *H*ostility."[63] Although the
scale has discriminated between extremely violent offenders (e.g., those com-

mitting murder, assault with a deadly weapon, mayhem) and other offenders, it is not a measure of a tendency toward violent offending in general. Criminals falling into the *O-H* category give "false" responses to such items as "Often I can't understand why I have been so cross and grouchy," or "My hardest battles are with myself," or "At times I feel like swearing." They give "true" responses to such items as "I feel sure that there is only one true religion" or "I do not mind being made fun of."[64] Conforming to this pattern does not suggest a tendency toward the uninhibited aggression of the typical psychopath. Indeed, the *O-H* scale does not discriminate between moderately violent and nonviolent criminals, only between the extremely violent ones and all others. Megargee's view of the high *O-H* offender is someone whose hostile impulses have been in conflict with unusually strong internal controls. On the rare occasions when hostility bursts forth, according to his theory, it is uncommonly violent. The quiet neighbor who, without obvious warning, brutally exterminates his family may be an example.

A different theoretical view of what may be close to the same phenomenon has been outlined by Hogan and his associates.[65] They use the CPI (rather than the MMPI) to define a trait referred to as "ego control," an excess of which predicts caution, obsessiveness, and a tendency to perseverate, and a deficit of which predicts impulsiveness, stimulation-seeking, and fluctuations in attention. In one comparison of small samples of heroin addicts and murderers, the murderers had more ego control than the drug addicts. The two groups did not differ on the standard CPI scales; they were both deficient in socialization, responsibility, and self-control, as are most criminal samples. Combined with the typical criminal predispositions, high ego control means a criminal for whom all but the most assaultive crimes are inhibited, according to this analysis.

Yet one more type of violent but passive offender was noted by several teams of workers.[66] On the MMPI, these men often had elevated Hysteria (No. 3) scores, in addition to the usual high Psychopathic deviate scores (No. 4). The "4-3" profile seems to go with unpredictable outbursts of assaultive behavior and a relative imperviousness to treatment. Whether these are the same men identified by the *O-H* scale or the ego-control configuration, we cannot say, but at least some overlap can be safely inferred.

The many dimensions of individual variation intersect the many dimensions of criminal law at many points. Given the complexities in both personality assessment and the criminal justice system, it is the homogeneity of personality in criminal populations that surprises us, not the heterogeneity. Among convicted offenders or precriminal juveniles, by any measure of personality or behavioral tendencies, some concept like psychopathy, sociopathy, or antisocial personality looms above all others as the major predisposing trait, either alone or in combination with other traits, as in the 4-3 profile just described. Psychopathy is by all odds the prime criminogenic personality trait. For that reason, it has been extensively studied, as the next section reviews.

Psychopathy

The modern notion of psychopathy traces back to older conceptions of "moral insanity" or "moral defect," recognized and described well before the advent of personality tests. The British Mental Deficiency Act of 1913, for example, defined "moral imbecility" as a condition of "persons who, from an early age, display some moral defect, coupled with strong vicious or criminal propensities on which punishment has had little or no deterrent effect."[67] This describes a more extreme point on a continuum between normal and abnormal than is occupied by the average modern offender, but it is nevertheless the continuum approximated by, for example, the MMPI's Psychopathic deviate scale or the CPI's socialization scale. If the average offender is at about the 98th percentile on the continuum of psychopathy, we assume that the British law had a still more extreme exemplar in mind in a statute that defined categories to be exempt from legal punishment.

Similarly, the modern medical category of psychopathy, or psychopathic personality, typically refers to a condition so unusual and debilitating that it may be considered a disease. We have encountered no psychiatric account of psychopathy more vivid than that of Harvey Cleckley, whose book *The Mask of Sanity* was in part an appeal to psychiatrists to acknowledge that psychopathy could be a serious illness, not just a neurosis, despite its "mask of sanity." The severe psychopath, says Cleckley, may seem to be enjoying "robust mental health. Yet he has a disorder that often manifests itself in conduct far more seriously abnormal than that of the schizophrenic."[68] The essence of the disease, according to Cleckley, is an inner emptiness: "We are dealing here not with a complete man at all but with something that suggests a subtly constructed reflex machine."[69]

The inner emptiness expresses itself, among other ways, as an insensitivity to remote consequences of action. It is likely to lead to trouble, as Cleckley observed:

Apparently blocked from fulfillment at deep levels, the sociopath is not unnaturally pushed toward some sort of divertissement. Even weak impulses, petty and fleeting gratifications, are sufficient to produce in him injudicious, distasteful, and even outlandish misbehavior. Major positive attractions are not present to compete successfully with whims, and the major negative deterrents (hot, persistent shame, profound regret, etc.) do not loom ahead to influence him.[70]

Cleckley's extreme psychopath may be more common in hospitals than prisons, but a less exaggerated version of the syndrome should by now be familiar.

Psychopathy only overlaps with criminality; it is not identical with it. If for no other reason than the vagaries of personality description and of the criminal justice system, there would be many nonpsychopathic offenders and many psychopathic nonoffenders. Nevertheless, to understand psychopathy better is to understand more about the individual traits that foster criminal behavior in the typical offender. The following discussion considers four topics bearing on psychopathy as it may relate to criminal behavior: arousal level, susceptibility to learning and conditioning, impulsiveness, and anxiety.

Arousal Level

Theories of emotion and motivation for well over a century have, in various ways, suggested that people (and members of other species) seek intermediate levels of stimulation, avoiding inner or outer stimuli that are either too intense or too feeble. Survival seems to be promoted by levels of alertness and stimulation that shun extremes. Psychopathic recklessness would fit the picture if it could be shown that the condition involves a low level of internal stimulation or arousal. The psychopath might then be engaged in a restless search for external stimulation to compensate for the lack of stimulation inside.[71] On questionnaires designed to evaluate "sensation seeking" tendencies,[72] psychopaths (as well as, say, recreational skydivers and spelunkers) score unusually high.[73] Such findings strengthen the idea that, in an ordinary environment, psychopaths suffer from stimulation hunger, perhaps because their nervous systems are set at too low a level, providing too little internal stimulation.

Many problems plague the hunt for relevant data. It is not obvious, for example, which physiological systems should be measured to gauge a person's subjective state. Where in the nervous system should the electrodes go, or what neurochemicals need assaying? Besides, even if we knew in principle *where* inside to look, we may not know *how,* for the techniques available for monitoring the physiological processes of intact human beings are rudimentary. And how shall the psychopathic subjects in these investigations be chosen—by the MMPI or CPI, by clinical evaluation, or by a history of psychopathic activities? Since there are no sure answers, the many investigators have used many different techniques for examining psychopaths selected according to many different criteria. If we set our expectations for these data at a realistically low level, we should not be disappointed with the findings.

One standard measure of psychological alertness or arousal is the electrical conductance of the skin. Small changes in the stimuli acting on a person, or just in his train of thought or emotion, may produce transient rises in skin conductivity, owing to activity in peripheral nerves of the autonomic nervous system. Breaking into a sweat may be a familiar example of the autonomic nervous system at work. Perspiration is one reason (though probably not the only one) electrical conductivity rises during a wave of emotion or increased alertness. It is this connection to otherwise hidden emotional states that explains the use of skin conductance in "lie detection" tests.

In some but by no means all studies, psychopaths have had diminished resting levels of skin conductance, or diminished spontaneous fluctuations in skin conductance, or diminished reactivity or habituation to stimuli.[74] There seems to be much more, though still not complete, agreement in the data that psychopaths' skin conductance responds especially weakly to aversive stimuli, such as electric shocks or injection by hypodermic needle, whether they themselves are, or anticipate, being stimulated, or they are witnessing someone else pretending to be aversively stimulated.[75] Experts have yet to agree on precisely how to characterize the psychopath's atypical performance, but despite a mixed set of findings, the overall evidence suggests diminished autonomic functioning as expressed in skin conductivity. Lie-detection tests are, it seems, least effective with the very people we may most want to catch lying.[76] A psychopath's lies may come easily for roughly the same reasons that they are not readily detected by measures of autonomic arousal.

Skin conductance taps the autonomic nervous system at the periphery, but the electroencephalogram (EEG) supposedly monitors arousal or alertness at a higher level of the nervous system, measuring as it does the electrical traces on the skull of the activity of the brain below. For the EEG too the evidence of a correlation with psychopathy is mixed but suggestive. Brain-wave abnormalities of one sort or another are often observed in about half the psychopathic population, as compared to about 15 percent of a "normal" population.[77] The specific abnormalities of psychopaths vary, but they include EEG patterns associated with drowsiness or unalertness, or patterns normally seen only during sleep that are present in psychopaths when awake. Some common abnormalities are of a type associated with epilepsy or other convulsive disorders. A few studies have failed to find anything distinctive about the brain waves of psychopathic populations, or, more accurately, they find abnormalities at about the same rate in psychopathic and normal populations. Nevertheless, to quote an expert, "It seems clear that a subset of subjects labelled sociopaths do show an excessive incidence of EEG abnormalities."[78] We may add that the abnormalities are often consistent with a view of the psychopath as being less alarmed than a nonpsychopath by the numerous electrodes dangling from his skull to record the EEG. During EEG testing sessions, psychopaths are more likely than nonpsychopaths to fall asleep altogether.[79] The depressed brain arousal of psychopaths may be, in part, another example of the unreactivity to aversive stimulation noted above.

If EEG abnormality is characteristic of psychopaths, then, given the role of psychopathy in criminality, it might be possible to find brain-wave abnormalities in predelinquent populations. That, at any rate, was the hypothesis examined in a sample of almost six hundred youngsters in Gothenburg, Sweden.[80] To be included in the sample, a child had to have had an "uneventful" birth; to be free of any psychosis or brain disease or symptomatology, or of any other disease that might have affected the brain secondarily; to come from a family free of convulsive disorders (such as epilepsy); to have had no severe headaches, tics, stuttering, or excessive nail-biting; and to have no record of delinquency. The boys and girls were given both waking and sleeping EEG examinations prior to the age of fifteen. Twelve years later, the records of the Swedish National Police Register and various social agencies identified 54 (of the original 571) as having committed at least one crime. The analysis of the EEG obtained twelve years before focused on 20 of the offenders who had at least one theft in their records, in comparison with the 517 who had no recorded offenses of any type.

The average offender had had distinctive EEGs at the original testing, even though, on the average, six and three-quarters years separated the EEG test and the first recorded crime. Offenders had more atypically slow brain-wave rhythms of a type associated with low arousal, abnormal patterns in sleep, and immature patterns, especially if the crimes began early.[81] A second study, of 129 Danish males given EEG tests in 1972 and examined for criminal records in 1978, confirmed the correlation between theft and an atypical pattern signifying low arousal.[82]

The syndrome known as "hyperactivity" appears to be another childhood precursor of adult psychopathy. Between 5 to 15 percent of children (and about five to ten times as many boys as girls) suffer from the condition, characterized by excessive movement, distractibility, impulsivity, and, perhaps as a result of those symptoms, academic troubles in school and behavioral troubles generally. Hyperactive children are at an elevated risk for adult criminality, alcoholism, and, for females, hysteria.[83] A variety of "minor physical anomalies," as they are called, may foreshadow hyperactivity.[84] Hyperactivity is also associated with the atypical EEG patterns and diminished skin conductance that may signify low levels of internal arousal. The abnormal need for stimulation that impels a child toward hyperactivity may later express itself in a tendency toward psychopathy and its consequences, such as criminal behavior.

Conditionability

Common among descriptions of psychopathy is some sort of deficiency in learning. Cleckley's list of the sixteen traits of severe psychopathy includes "poor judgment and failure to learn by experience."[85] Ziskind's list includes an "inability to profit from past experience or punishment."[86] Cleckley and Ziskind and the latter's associates point out that the learning deficiency may be independent of any generalized lack of intelligence; in pure psychopathy, the deficiency is specifically related to the learned prohibitions against antisocial behavior. The problem has been to identify the form that the learning deficiency takes.

Using Cleckley's description of psychopathy, Robert Hare and Michael Quinn asked the professional staff of a Canadian prison to identify clearly psychopathic, marginally psychopathic, and clearly nonpsychopathic inmates.[87] The men were then subjected to a Pavlovian conditioning procedure (see Chapter 2) in a single, highly controlled session lasting about ninety minutes, but only if they would do so voluntarily. (Of the nine men who refused out of sixty-three initially classified, seven had been classified as clearly psychopathic.)

Seated in a padded chair and wearing a variety of devices to measure skin conductance, heart rate, blood-vessel constriction in a finger and on the forehead, and breathing, the subject looked at a blank screen and listened for tones of three different frequencies piped into a headset at varying intervals averaging fifty seconds. Once on, a tone lasted for ten seconds; what happened afterward depended on the frequency of the tone. For each subject, one tone frequency signaled a brief, painful but tolerable electric shock of an arm; another tone frequency signaled a two-second look at the projection of a slide containing a nude female. The sixteen slides used during the session were selected to progress toward greater sexiness, to offset the rapid loss of interest experienced by a panel of viewers in preliminary research. The third tone frequency signaled nothing at all. The tones were presented sixteen times each, in random order, which is usually enough to track the course of conditioning in a highly controlled setting like this.

By the end of the session, both the electric shock and, to a lesser extent, the pictures produced conditioning of heart rate and blood-vessel constriction in the finger. During the tones leading up to either the shock or the pictures, pulse rate slowed and blood vessels constricted for all three groups of inmates. However, for skin conductance, which is often considered a more sensitive measure of emotional state or alertness, the two psychopathic groups failed to display any conditioning at all. Their skin conductances rose briefly when a shock or a picture actually arrived, but nothing changed during the ten seconds of tone preceding it. For the nonpsychopathic offenders, skin conductance conditioned strongly for electric shock and weakly for the pictures.

Other studies have confirmed the general outline of this experiment,[88] but it takes some care to trace the outline properly. Psychopaths are not impervious to conditioning, but the autonomic nervous system that mediates emotional responses, quite sensitive in nonpsychopaths, is insensitive in them, especially (but not exclusively) when the conditioning involves anticipating a punishing stimulus like an electric shock or, by extrapolation, such social punishment as the loss of positive reinforcement accompanying disapproval and the like.[89] The psychopath may know that punishment is coming, and some of his responses may be conditioned normally, but the skin conductance response, presumably tied to emotions, is peculiarly dormant until the punishment actually arrives (and, even then, is often muted).

The mass of not always consistent data on conditioning in relation to personality can be summarized in many reasonably accurate ways, though each does at least some violence to one discrepant finding or another. Science has not yet taken account of all the complex sources that may produce individual differences in performance in conditioning procedures. Nevertheless, we believe it is correct to conclude that psychopaths are poor Pavlovian conditioners for emotional responses, particularly when the motivating stimulus is aversive, or when the conditioning calls for a sensitivity to delayed stimuli, or both. Add to this the general lack of arousal or alertness in at least some settings, and most of the poor conditionability of psychopaths can be explained.

The conditionability of autonomic emotional responses may affect social behavior in general, not just in regard to crime.[90] Autonomic conditionability is correlated, for example, with success in school, independent of the contribution of general intelligence as measured by IQ scores.[91] In some laboratory tests, psychopaths did not show much enthusiasm for tasks that earned social reinforcement, such as verbal approval.[92] Boys with low socialization scores on the CPI were less reinforced by the experimenter's approval in a laboratory conditioning study than boys with high scores.[93] Social motivators (the desire for praise, approval, etc.) typically depend on a sensitivity to disapproval, blame, etc., and they require enough temporal integration in a person's feelings so that a reprimand at one moment draws some part of its power to punish from the threat that positive reinforcers will not be forthcoming in the future. A psychopath may not work to gain social approval because he or she places a low value on it, or because the tangible benefits of social approval are much delayed, or both.

The psychopath's lack of internal motivation, whether to do well in school and elsewhere or to obey the law, seems to have a fundamental connection to the conditionability of emotional states. The habitual criminal's deficient sense of guilt flows from the same source as his lack of interest in society's conventions and approval. These internal conditioned responses weave a normal person's emotional life into something approaching coherence; without conditioning, the emotions drift apart into unconnected fragments. For that reason, we find on Cleckley's list of psychopathic traits not just a "failure to learn by experience" but a "failure to follow any life plan."

Impulsiveness

Since descriptions of psychopathy always include impulsiveness or some close analogue, it would not be much of a discovery to find impulsiveness in the data on psychopaths. The demonstration, for example, that criminals judged to be highly psychopathic get worse Q scores on the Porteus Maze Tests than those judged less psychopathic[94] was worthwhile, but its value was to validate the criteria used for psychopathy and of the Q score as a measure of such psychopathic traits as impulsiveness, not to show that psychopaths are impulsive. Psychopathy implies impulsiveness simply by definition, but impulsiveness may explain many things about criminal behavior.

Impulsiveness can be thought of as either the cause or the effect of the poor conditionability of psychopaths. Either way, in their emotional lives psychopaths discount future events more steeply than nonpsychopaths, particularly if the event is aversive. The relevance of this peculiarity to criminal behavior can hardly be overestimated (see Chapter 2 for the specific connections), for crime often pits a quick gain against avoiding a remote punishment. Because of impulsiveness, the psychopath is driven toward the wrong end of the choice. To the extent that success at the competing lawful pursuits depends on an ability to work for deferred benefits, so much the worse for those who discount time quickly, such as psychopaths.

Many of the correlates of offending may relate to impulsiveness, besides full-blown psychopathy. Young people, who are especially susceptible to crime, tend to discount remote events more than older people.[95] At a given age, or under otherwise comparable circumstances, the steeper time discounters have the greater criminal tendencies.[96] Tests of impulsive performance on simple psychomotor tasks by seventh graders in several Texas towns successfully discriminated between those who, five years later, have dropped out of school or become delinquent and those who did neither.[97]

The key role of verbal intelligence for crime (see Chapter 6) may depend on the importance of language in connecting an act with its delayed consequences. Language is the medium par excellence for keeping in mind which act goes with which outcome. Children who tend not to verbalize their own behavior appear to be prey to uncontrolled aggressiveness and other sorts of impulsive outbursts,[98] even after taking account of general intelligence. Without the internal monologue, time horizons shrink; behavior becomes more tied to its immediate consequences.

Alcohol and other brain depressants, neurological damage or disease, and so on may favor impulsiveness by steepening the time-discounting curve, perhaps by disrupting verbal mediation of remote consequences (among other reasons). Impulsive, violent behavior has been shown to be associated with subtle brain disturbances, as well as the more dramatic ravages of drunkenness, brain tumors, rabies, and blows to the head.[99]

Even left-handedness may be correlated with impulsiveness, albeit slightly. Of the 9 percent of the total population that is left-handed, a large proportion has less than average dominance of the left hemisphere of the brain, where the language centers mainly are.[100] People without a strongly dominant hemisphere, including the affected left-handers, seem to be more impulsive, less analytic, and less guided by verbally articulated codes of behavior than average.[101] The implication, confirmed by a few small samples of criminals,[102] is that populations of offenders should contain an elevated frequency of left-handers. The elevation is slight, and is probably at least compensated for by the greater creativity or spontaneity of left-handers, but, if confirmed in larger samples, it nevertheless lends support to the present theoretical framework. This is not to say that left-handers are psychopathic, for while psychopathy implies impulsiveness, the reverse is not necessarily true. Impulsiveness in and of itself predisposes a person toward offending, even without the other characteristics of psychopathy. In a sample of prison inmates, the prisoners judged to be psychopathic did not include more left-handers than those judged to be nonpsychopathic, but there was a suggestion in the data that more prisoners in general were left-handed than in the population at large.[103]

Anxiety

The prototypical extreme psychopath should be relatively free of anxiety. Fleeting, even if intense, resentments, irritations, or urges should take the place of the more lasting worries or goals of the nonpsychopath. The pure psychopath's emotional life should comprise pangs rather than aches. And, indeed, when David Lykken instructed prison staff members of several Minnesota correctional institutions on how to identify inmates most reminiscent of Cleckley's description, they chose prisoners who had not only elevated Psychopathic deviate scores on the MMPI but also low scores on various questionnaire tests of anxiety level and neurosis, and below par reactivity and conditionability of the skin conductance response.[104] Their learning of a shock avoidance task was also below par, as compared to a control group of nonoffenders.

Inmates in a second group denied that they met the stated criteria for psychopathy after having been picked according to the instructions just described. This second group was just as high on the Psychopathic deviate scale as the first, but its members were more anxious; in fact, they were at least as anxious as normal controls and perhaps even more neurotic. Their skin conductance conditioning and shock avoidance learning were better than the first group's, but poorer than the normal controls'.

Despite the small samples in his study, Lykken's distinction between nonanxious and anxious (or neurotic) psychopathy has found echoes in the empirical literature for decades in one form or another. Even before Lykken's experiment, Benjamin Karpman had distinguished between two types of psychopaths, the "idiopathic" and the "symptomatic," or simply the "primary" and the "secondary."[105] In Karpman's view, primary (or idiopathic) psychopaths behave antisocially because they are more or less impervious to fear, anxiety, and guilt. Secondary (symptomatic) psychopaths behave antisocially as a result of some other emotional disturbance. They may seem psychopathic (and, in a purely behavioral sense, are psychopathic), but they may be experiencing intense conflict, fear, and anxiety. They may be neurotic or psychotic, in addition to symptomatically psychopathic. In Karpman's estimation, most people by far who seem psychopathic are secondary, not primary, psychopaths.

Other workers have other ways to deal with the diversity of patterns. Spielberger and his associates suggest that the criminogenic tendencies of psychopathy are to some extent independent of anxiety and neurosis, so the symptoms can occur with or without each other among samples of prisoners. However, anxious psychopaths may be more susceptible to conditioning, hence to certain kinds of psychological rehabilitation for their antisocial activities.[106] Anxious offenders have been shown to be less prone to recidivism.[107]

In Eysenck's system of personality description,[108] the various components of psychopathy—the impulsiveness, shallowness of emotions, unconventionality, and so on—can to some extent vary separately. In fact, Cleckley's idea of psychopathy as such does not emerge as a unified entity in Eysenck's analysis, for its features are scattered along three dimensions identified as "extroversion," "neuroticism," and "psychoticism."[109] Extroverts in the system, for example, tend to be both sociable and impulsive, but it is the impulsiveness, not the sociability, that is part of psychopathy and that predisposes them to criminal behavior.[110] Karpman's primary psychopath may be unusually high on Eysenck's dimension of psychoticism but low on neuroticism, and vice versa for his secondary psychopath. But rather than following these diverging lines of analysis, it is time to tie them together as well as we can.

Dimensions of Personality

Instead of a sharply defined entity, psychopathy is made up of deviations along some of the common dimensions of personality. In a medical metaphor, it is more like anemia than like a broken bone. Everyone has a red blood count; the anemic's is just too low. Likewise, everyone has a rate of discounting future events; the psychopath's is relatively high. Everyone has some level of internal arousal or emotionality and a susceptibility to the conditioning of internalized prohibitions; the psychopath's are relatively weak. Everyone has his or her own habitual level of internal speech; the psychopath's level tends to be minimal. People who deviate toward psychopathy, but not as much as the full-blown psychopath, will suffer a smaller risk of asocial behavior, but still more than average. People who deviate in the other direction—toward more gradual time discounting, greater verbal mediation, a richer inner life, and a more deeply ingrained set of standards for behavior—should be less susceptible to the temptations of ordinary crime.

The symptoms of psychopathy affect two elements in our theory (see Chapter 2), specifically the rewards for noncrime and the internalized decrements ("conscience") in the rewards for crime. Legal punishment deters psychopaths less than it does others because it is delayed and aversive, and aversive stimuli are especially ineffective for psychopaths if they are delayed. At the same time, crime is more attractive for psychopaths because it is not so much weakened by internalized prohibitions. However, the choice between crime and noncrime may vary with individual differences along dimensions besides those of psychopathy. There are other atypicalities that increase the relative strength of crime.

If criminals are, for example, unusually aggressive,[111] it could be because, as psychopaths, they express anger overtly rather than internalizing it as self-blame or high blood pressure, or because they do not fear retaliation. But criminals may be aggressive not because of deficient internalization or fear; they may instead simply be predisposed toward excessive anger or sadism or delusions of persecution or other characteristics that foster unfounded aggression. Their aggression may even be well founded, but what that means is that it arises from provocative circumstances rather than deviant traits. Our theory implies that crimes may be committed by people with other sorts of deviance than psychopathy, or by utterly average people, if the circumstances push the rewards for it high enough.

If some people hear voices telling them to steal or to commit murder, and if they identify the voices with supernatural agents who are best obeyed, then their schizophrenic hallucinations may tip the balance toward crime. Other forms of deranged thought may likewise foster crime. For someone addicted to drugs, the rewards of more drugs may swamp the rewards for noncrime, especially if the drug also weakens internalized inhibitions against antisocial behavior, as alcohol does. Uncommonly strong or bizarre sexual urges may cause sex crimes by people who are otherwise normal. When their sex drives abate, they may deeply regret what they have done, but that will not help at the next opportunity if the urge has again pushed the reward for crime high enough.

The "criminal types" of early criminology dissolve into individual variation along the dimensions that govern social behavior, namely the drives, the time-discounting rates, the histories of reinforcement and conditioning, and the moment-by-moment environments incorporated into the theory of criminal behavior (Chapter 2). The practical (as distinguished from the ethical) difference between someone who breaks the law because of provocative circumstances and someone who does so because of deviance is not in the behavior itself, but in its predictive implications. The latter offender will repeat more often than the former in the ordinary course of events, for the crucial variables are personal, not situational.

But this just restates, somewhat more broadly, what we said earlier about personality traits. Traits are what consistencies in behavior over time look like in snapshots. To say that someone has a criminogenically deviant characteristic is to say that in settings in which more ordinary people would not offend, he or she would. A dark city street may strike one person as tempting and another as frightening. The difference may depend on many variables, some already considered and others to be taken up in the next section. Age, sex, physique, a history of academic or socioeconomic success or failure, impulsiveness, fearfulness, cruelty, momentary need, and long-standing habits and values are among the factors that may distinguish the potential offender from his victim. The offender offends not just because of immediate needs and circumstances but also because of enduring personal characteristics, some of whose traces can be found in his behavior from early childhood on, as this chapter, and succeeding ones, show.

Consistencies in behavior can arise either from inherited predispositions or from consistencies in the environment, or both. As an approximate guideline, this part of the book has leaned toward the inherited sources and the next part leans toward the environmental. But the guideline cannot avoid being approximate, for many of the ordinary variables of behavioral analysis combine the effects of both genes and environment.

Personality, intelligence, and psychopathologies of various sorts each involve some genetic inheritance. This may seem controversial to some readers, but it is the clear consensus of those most intimately acquainted with the data.[112] The details of inheritance are complex and incompletely understood, but it would be hard to find a serious contemporary student of these topics who denies a genetic contribution, and, in many cases, a substantial one. Current estimates place the heritability of intelligence between 50 and 80 percent, and the heritability of most common dimensions of personality perhaps 20 percent lower, on the average. If the predictors of criminal behavior are genetic to some degree, it follows that crime should be too.

The cognitive and personality correlates of criminal behavior summarized in this and the preceding chapter thus explain the constitutional and genetic data reviewed in Chapter 3. Criminal behavior runs in families because variation along its controlling dimensions have both genetic and environmental origins. The genes may express their influence at any point in the model of criminal behavior, just as the environment may. The strengths of various reinforcers, the time-discounting rates, the opportunity costs of legal punishment, the likelihood of success in crime or noncrime, the social consequences of a certain physique or face—all of these potentially criminogenic variables are rooted in individual characteristics shaped by both inheritance and experience.

III

DEVELOPMENTAL FACTORS

8

FAMILIES

The role of the family in producing criminal behavior seems to be a greater mystery to social scientists than to parents. If asked why some persons are more likely than others to commit crimes, the average parent would very likely attribute these individual differences to family experiences. And if asked then why children from the same family should differ in their criminal tendencies, the parent would probably say that because children have different temperaments they will react differently to the same treatment or be treated differently by their parents, or both.

At one time, criminologists supported, with little dissent, the view that some combination of constitutional traits and family experiences accounted for criminal behavior. When Sheldon and Eleanor Glueck published in 1950 the results of their ten-year study of delinquent boys in the Boston area, they concluded that if one held constant age, race, neighborhood, and (roughly) intelligence, then delinquency appeared to be the result of an interaction between certain constitutional factors (body type and temperament) and a family environment in which one or both parents were indifferent or hostile to the child and followed lax or erratic disciplinary practices.[1]

There were criticisms of the Gluecks' research. Some scholars suggested that the observations of the boys and their circumstances were not independent, and thus may have been colored by the observer's knowledge of whether or not the boy was delinquent. For example, the boys' families were evaluated by investigators who knew whether the home they visited was that of a delinquent. Some psychological interviews and tests were conducted by clinicians who knew which boys were delinquent; indeed, at the time of the test or interview, the delinquents were confined in correctional facilities. Judgments about family background, conclusions from interviews, and the interpretation of some tests are inevitably somewhat subjective; thus, the ascription of traits to the boys and their families may have been influenced by prior knowledge of their delinquent status.

Moreover, some of the factors thought to be most important in producing delinquency, such as the degree of affection and the disciplinary practices of the parents, were not observed directly but were inferred from statements by the boys and their parents. (Some of these statements were supported by the records of social-work agencies, but it is not clear how often or how consistently.)

But if the only problems with the Gluecks' findings were these and similar methodological difficulties, one would have expected better studies to be mounted that would test their conclusions more rigorously. By and large, that did not happen. The reason, we suspect, is that the beliefs of social scientists as to what constituted the appropriate objects of research changed. Owing in part to an apparent rise in gang violence in the 1950s and in part to the advent of a newer group of criminologists, the importance of the family as an explanation for criminality declined and that of constitutional factors almost vanished. By the mid-1950s, the newer perspectives focused attention on forces outside the family.

One of these was the theory of differential association propounded by Edwin Sutherland: "A person becomes delinquent because of an excess of definitions favorable to violations of the law over definitions unfavorable to violations of the law."[2] Though the family is one source of these "definitions," peers, schoolmates, neighborhoods, and gangs are other, more numerous ones. The family has no special role, its injunctions no special force except, perhaps, as its class position influences what values its members accept. Lower-class boys may come to disparage the conventional ethic of success and embrace instead the values of toughness and immediate gratification.[3] In these views, individuals do not differ in their receptivity to various definitions or values; they are blank slates on which "society" writes at will.

Another perspective was strain theory, based on the view, first formalized by Robert K. Merton, that man is governed by the relationship between his aspirations and the means available to achieve them.[4] Families may lead boys to want a good car or social respect, but if society denies to the boys legitimate means for obtaining these things, the boys will react by stealing to get the car and with violence to earn the respect. Richard A. Cloward and Lloyd E. Ohlin applied this view to delinquency by asserting that economically disadvantaged adolescents turn to crime as a way of both achieving material goods and avoiding the shame that accompanies economic failure.[5]

Other writers claimed that delinquency was less the result of having learned from peers to commit crimes or of being driven to crime out of frustrated expectations than of being arbitrarily labeled a criminal by society and its institutions.[6] Young persons who violate some social convention are called criminals; once treated as criminal, they become criminal.

As we remarked in Chapter 2, each of these perspectives may have some value, though none constitutes a complete theory of criminality. What is important here is not their value or their defects, however, but the minor role they assigned to the family and the large role they assigned to peers, neighborhoods, social class, economic opportunities, and the operation of the criminal justice system. All of these newer perspectives were the product of sociological thought that tends to draw attention away from individual differences and toward social categories. As we suggested in Chapter 1, sociologists are trained to be suspicious of psychological explanations of human behavior; they prefer, as did Emile Durkheim, to find "social" explanations for social facts such as crime.

These perspectives embodied not just sociological thought, but a particular variety of such thought. With the exception of Sutherland's theory of differential association, which suggested, among other possibilities, that delinquency might result when innocent boys associated with wicked companions, most sociological theories sought to explain crime, as Travis Hirschi has observed,[7] not by reference to manifestly wicked influences but by reference to supposedly good ones. Whereas an older generation of criminologists, of which the Gluecks were very much a part, thought that evil causes evil (for example, bad families produce bad children), many members of the newer generation were attracted to the idea that "good" often causes evil (for example, that the desire for achievement, or the decisions of police and judges, will cause people to break the law). This view was most clearly suggested by Merton: "a cardinal American virtue, 'ambition,' promotes a cardinal American vice, 'deviant behavior'."[8]

The critical stance of many criminologists was reinforced by reformist impulses that led them, implicitly or explicitly, to explain social problems by reference to those factors that are, or appear to be, susceptible to planned change. The 1950s were a period of worry about gang violence; the 1960s, of attention to civil rights and economic opportunity. It was natural to assume that if one wishes to deal with these problems, one must first make such problems the central categories of one's analysis. Gangs, race prejudice, social class, and criminal justice were concepts that seemed close to the problem and amenable to change. By contrast, the family as a concept suffered from two defects: It was not on the public agenda and it was not clear how its practices might be altered.

There would be no point in speculating on the reasons for this change in focus if the evidence had supported the change by showing the relative unimportance of the family compared to other factors. But little such evidence was adduced.

The study of the family did not stop, of course, but it did begin to sever its connection with criminological matters. Research on child development, for example, was a vigorous enterprise but one not much concerned with crime. And understandably so. The best such research is based on observing the child and his parents directly, at home or in the laboratory. This is much easier to do with infants than with adolescents, and so the best data on child rearing are about children who are still many years away from committing a crime. Possibly one can infer the connection between early childhood experiences and later criminality, but that requires first making a number of assumptions about the continuity of human behavior that, until recently, were hard to defend. Moreover, since the best developmental studies are based on direct observation, there are limits to how many children can be studied, and the resulting small (and often unrepresentative) samples make it difficult to produce reliable statistical interpretations of the relationships among child-rearing variables. It is hard to imagine more careful direct-observation research than that carried out by Diana Baumrind and her co-workers at the University of California at Berkeley, but the children she studied were hardly typical. One group[9] involved only 32 white children of above average intelligence from well-educated, middle-class parents, and another[10] involved 134 equally bright children of equally advantaged parents. She found that different child-rearing practices had interesting behavioral consequences, but it is hard to imagine that many of these children will ever become seriously involved in crime, or that in this group the full range of individual differences was confronted by the full range of parental styles.

Of late, matters have improved. Some criminologists have resumed the study of how children grow up, and some developmental psychologists have increased the attention given to the childhood antecedents and adolescent expression of aggressive behavior. Still, no truly comprehensive direct-observation study of the consequences of child rearing exists, and so we must piece together an account of the role of families out of many different kinds of partial inquiries.

An Overview of Development

Though there is no such thing as a "criminal personality," we concluded in Chapter 7 that persons who are markedly more likely than others to commit predatory crimes tend to rank high on two dimensions of personality. Compared to nonoffenders or occasional offenders, they are more impulsive (they cannot or will not defer gratifications) and they are less socialized (they display little regard for the feelings of others). To the extent temperamental traits affect criminality, it is largely, we think, by their influence on these two dimensions.

The family can moderate or magnify any natural predispositions. The interaction between parent and child may make the latter more or less impulsive, more or less willing to take the feelings of others into account. That interaction involves three processes. The first is the development of *attachment,* by which we mean the inculcation in a child of a desire to win and hold the approval of others and the belief that, given certain conditions, he can count on having that approval.* The second is the development of a *time horizon,* by which we mean the shaping of a child's ability and inclination to take into account the more distant consequences of present actions. The third is the development of *conscience,* by which we mean an internalized constraint against certain actions, the violation of which causes feelings of anxiety.[11]

Before proceeding, we should take up the objection some scholars (but rarely any lay persons) have to using the term "conscience." For some, it is at best a murky mental state and at worst an invention of "mushy-headed" psychoanalysts (who call it the superego); in neither case is it thought to have much effect, if any, on behavior. Behavior, in this view, is the result of external reinforcements; if people confronting a criminal opportunity display anxiety, it is only because they fear the objective consequences (loss of esteem or freedom) the crime may entail. We disagree, taking instead the view of H. J. Eysenck[12] and others who note that conscience differs from calculation and is a powerful force in its own right. To be sure, conscience is learned, and is thus a product of conditioning and of the reinforcers used in conditioning. But what is learned is not simply how best to calculate one's own advantage but also the capacity for self-reward. Eysenck's example of

---

* As will shortly become evident, we here use the word "attachment" somewhat differently and more broadly than do developmental psychologists, for whom the term means, roughly, a nurturant proximity between a child and his principal care giver (usually the mother). We will argue that attachment in this developmental sense is essential to attachment in the larger sense.

self-reward (or self-punishment) in operation is that of a polygraph, or "lie detector." The working of such a machine does not depend on our becoming anxious about being caught out in a lie (there is no way for the machine to know what is true or false in our statements) but on the anxiety most of us spontaneously feel about merely uttering a lie. It is this automatic change in pulse rate, breathing, and skin conductance that the machine detects. If we were calculators pure and simple, we would realize that we can say with impunity anything we wanted while hooked up to the polygraph. A few people are capable of acting this way, but we think them rather odd, as indeed they are: The ability to lie without emotion is a mark of the psychopath.

Others err not in ignoring conscience but in ascribing too much power to it. Persons whose anxiety is easily aroused may nonetheless break the law, and not just in extreme situations. The evidence on this score from the experiments of Stanley Milgram is quite compelling.[13] Ordinary folk were willing, when instructed by an apparently authoritative scientist, to administer what they believed were very high, probably dangerous shocks to innocent "victims" even when the latters' cries could be clearly heard. The subjects' willingness to do this was not significantly affected by their intelligence, social class, national origin, or educational attainment. But they did display considerable anxiety during the experiment, indicating that the pangs of conscience were present though not in control. Here, even apparently weak reinforcers—the instructions of an authoritative figure—were sufficient to overcome an internalized prohibition against inflicting pain.

Attachment

Acquiring a desire for the approval of others and the confidence that, under reasonable and well-understood circumstances, approval will be forthcoming is a process that begins at birth, or shortly thereafter. That it occurs at all is in part the result of the fact that the infant is innately a social creature. Far from being an organism all of whose behaviors either must be learned or are innately selfish, the newborn child is biologically endowed with a predisposition to initiate contact with others by sucking, smiling, crying, vocalizing, or rooting about. Moreover, the vigor with which he or she displays these behaviors and the reactions he or she has to the responses of others will be affected by temperamental qualities that are, to a degree, constitutional and thus precede parental socialization.

This understanding of the infant is today generally accepted by most pediatricians and developmental psychologists, but it is quite at odds with earlier understandings. Once, the child was thought to be as John Locke described him, a blank slate, a *tabula rasa,* on which his parents and society could write whatever they wished. And even though we now know that the infant enters the family equipped with important predispositions, some persons still think of him and, worse, do research on how he is raised by his family based on the implicit assumption that whatever happens to him is wholly the result of parents acting on the child and not at all of the child acting on the parents. Accordingly, many otherwise sophisticated studies of child rearing pay little or no attention to the temperament, intelligence, adaptability, and activity level of the child even though there is by now an impressive body of evidence that these traits have a substantial constitutional, and possibly genetic, basis.

Few parents need to be told this. Every mother can, within a few days after giving birth, describe her baby as cuddly or fussy, active or passive, a good eater or a colicky one, wakeful or a sleeper-through-the-night. If the development of an attachment and the beginning of socialization depend on the nature of the interaction between parents and child, then knowing what the infant brings to this interaction is as important as knowing what the parents bring to it.

That infants differ systematically has been shown by scholars who have carefully observed them starting in the first few days or weeks of life and extending, in some cases, for over a decade. Alexander Thomas, Stella Chess, and H. G. Birch were able to classify babies shortly after birth into three types—"easy children" (adaptable, cheerful, regular in body functions and sleep habits), "difficult children" (withdrawn, intense, irregular in habits, and given to crying), and "slow to warm up children" (relatively inactive, slow to adapt, but not especially prone to tantrums).[14] These qualities were independent of how the parents handled the infants, and tended to persist in most children for several years. The easy children readily adapted to almost any child-rearing style; the difficult children, by contrast, required exceptional patience and skill. About 70 percent of the difficult babies later developed behavioral problems calling for psychiatric attention; only 18 percent of the easy ones had such problems.

Evidence that such temperamental differences are partly constitutional in origin comes from a study by Daniel G. Freedman of twenty pairs of newborn twins of the same sex.[15] Some were identical (MZ) and others fraternal (DZ) twins, but until their observations were complete, the investigators did not know which was which (and neither, at the time, did the parents). The infants were scored for certain behavioral tendencies, such as being responsive to others, displaying fear of a new situation, and having a long attention span. Overwhelmingly, the identical twins were more similar in behavior than the fraternal twins, especially with regard to fearfulness, social awareness, and the tendency to smile and vocalize. Comparable results were obtained in a study of how MZ and DZ twins at the age of about two years dealt with strange situations.[16]

These temperamental differences may not be randomly distributed in the population. Freedman also examined twenty-four newborn Chinese-American babies and twenty-four newborn Caucasians who were similar in weight, physical vitality, mothers' age, length of labor, and use of drugs during labor.[17] Though there was a substantial overlap between the two groups, in general the Chinese-American babies, within (on the average) thirty-three hours of being born, were less perturbable, more placid, and more easily consoled than the Caucasian ones.

Similar findings have been reported by Jerome Kagan and his co-workers.[18] Six-month-old Chinese-American babies were more inhibited, less extroverted, more wary, and less gregarious than Caucasian babies of the same age. And from a very early age, the Chinese children displayed a more stable pulse rate, implying, according to the authors, "an inborn disposition that contributes to the wariness and inhibition" displayed in the laboratory.[19]

Not all these differences need be genetic in origin. Some may result from prenatal (intrauterine) or perinatal (during birth) experiences. There is evidence, for example, that oxygen deprivation (anoxia) in the fetus and premature birth have a harmful effect on early measures of intelligence and possibly on temperament.[20] Early IQ scores are not highly predictive of adult intelligence, [21] and other consequences of pre- or perinatal experiences have (so far) a largely unknown effect on adult behavior.[22] But these experiences may have an effect on the infant-parent interaction which in turn may influence (along with other factors) the development of a strong attachment. As we will note in the next chapter, premature and low-birth-weight babies are inordinately at risk as the objects of child abuse, possibly because such infants are less likely than those who have lived their full term in the womb and been of normal weight to be intelligent and responsive to stimuli, and thus to reinforce parental care.

The infant's predisposition to attractive as opposed to unattractive behaviors need not determine the extent of attachment, but it can influence, at the margin, how readily an attachment will form. Anneliese F. Korner has shown through a careful study of babies only a few days old that there are persistent differences in their tendency to cry, to be wakeful, and to make eye contact with the mother, and that many of these differences are sex linked.[23] The newborn female infants are, compared to newborn males, more receptive to certain stimuli (especially touching and talking), more likely to smile, more likely to cling to their mothers,[24] more sensitive to contact with a piece of cloth or a jet of air,[25] and equipped with less upper-body strength.[26]

Parents, of course, treat baby girls differently from baby boys. How infants are socialized contributes importantly to how they later behave, including whether or not they break the law. But there is no reason to assume that these differences in treatment are wholly arbitrary or entirely independent of the infant's characteristics. The evidence suggests that male and female infants differ from birth in the way they interact with parents; it is likely that these differences in temperament influence (though they do not wholly determine) differences in child rearing. For example, when adults were asked to play with very small infants who were dressed so as to conceal their gender and randomly assigned masculine and feminine names, the adults played in ways that were affected both by the actual actions of the children as well as by their perceived sexual identity. We need not decide the knotty, controversial, and perhaps insoluble question of how much nature and nurture contribute to sex-linked differences in behavior to acknowledge that both play some role.[27]

The kind of attachment, or bond, that forms between infant and parent will be influenced to some degree by the kinds of demands the infant makes and how he or she responds to the attentions of others. Infants who smile frequently, have sensitive skin, and cling to their mothers may be more likely to be smiled at, tickled, and soothed than are infants with the opposite traits. The parent also brings something to this relationship. Mothers and fathers who are eager for a child, who understand that an infant makes many and often inconvenient demands, and who find the sights and sounds of an infant rewarding will be more responsive to the infant's demands than will those who find these demands exasperating or incomprehensible.

The significance of the bond between infant and mother was placed squarely at the center of developmental research by John Bowlby, who for over three decades presented arguments and evidence designed to show that "maternal deprivation" causes great harm.[28] He defined this deprivation as the absence of a warm, intimate, and continuous relationship between infant and mother and attributed to it all manner of later physiological and behavioral problems, including depression and delinquency.

So strong a set of assertions was not likely to go unchallenged. Critics pointed to methodological difficulties in Bowlby's studies, especially those purporting to show a connection between maternal deprivation and delinquency.[29] They noted that deprivation was an ambiguous term that did not distinguish clearly among physical separation, the absence of a loving relationship, and the failure to supply verbal stimulation. Moreover, psychologists disagreed over whether the bond must be to the mother or whether it could as easily be to the father, another adult, or even a group of adults.[30]

We need not resolve all these issues. Attachment is now defined as the "affectional bond or tie that an infant forms between himself and his mother figure—a bond that tends to be enduring and independent of specific situations."[31] We have come to understand that this attachment develops in clear stages, from the undifferentiated responsiveness of the newborn infant to any figure, through specific attachment to an identifiable person, and on to a development in the child of a sympathetic understanding of the parent's point of view. We also now believe that adults other than the biological mother may serve as suitable objects of this attachment. What is important is that the emergence of an affectional bond between child and parent is not inevitable and that its absence has important psychological and behavioral consequences.

The evidence seems to suggest that there is little chance of this bond's forming at all if the infant is deprived of a mother figure during the first three or three and a half years of life, and a much reduced chance of its forming if the process is delayed by as much as eighteen months.[32] Within this critical period, attachment is fostered by mothers (or possibly other adults) who respond promptly to the baby's cries, who initiate interaction with the infant,[33] and who soothe, hold, and talk to the child.[34] Contrary to what one might suppose, devoted attention to the infant's needs at this stage does not seem to produce a spoiled child. During the first year of life, the infant cries to signal distress—hunger, discomfort, loneliness—and not, so far as we know, to control the behavior of others in any sophisticated fashion. Responding to these signals reassures the infant and facilitates attachment; ignoring them impedes attachment and makes the infant even more demanding. Later on, during the postattachment period of socialization, when the child needs to be taught the consequences of his actions, quite different responses are in order.

The effects of maternal (or parental) deprivation appear to depend on the reason for the deprivation. Michael Rutter, in his summary of the evidence on this matter, distinguishes between children who never form an affectional bond and those whose bond, though formed, is disrupted by parental discord or separation.[35] When established bonds are disrupted, the child experiences distress, but perhaps not distress with major long-term significance. For example, infants may be hospitalized for long periods, but if an affectional bond has already formed, the ensuing distress may be short-lived and unrelated to later deviance.

But if the bond never forms, the consequences can be very severe. Rutter suggests that the absence of attachment may lead to "affectionless psychopathy," which he describes as beginning with "an initial phase of clinging, dependent behaviour, followed by attention-seeking, uninhibited, indiscriminate friendliness and finally a personality characterized by the lack of guilt, an inability to keep rules and an inability to form lasting relationships."[36] Ainsworth agrees, arguing that the most important long-term result of the failure to form an affectional bond is the "inability to establish and to maintain deep and significant interpersonal relations."[37]

Much of the research on which these conclusions were based was done retrospectively on infants raised in orphanages, where the opportunity for parental attachment is obviously low (though, of course, some surrogate parenting is possible). Pringle and Bossio, in trying to explain why some institutionalized children were stable and others maladjusted, found that the stable ones had in almost every case lived with their biological mother for the first year of life and thus had formed some attachment prior to institutionalization.[38] Goldfarb discovered that children who were placed with foster parents after being in an orphanage for less than the first three years of life were much more likely to form a bond to their new parents than were those who were in an institution for a longer period. The latter tended to lack a sense of guilt, to crave affection, and to be unable to observe rules or form lasting relationships.[39]

Recently, some prospective studies have been done that shed more light on the significance of attachment. Scholars at the University of Minnesota have been closely observing a group of children and their mothers almost since birth and have shown that infants securely attached to their mothers at age six months or earlier were more likely at age two years to seek their mothers' help in performing difficult tasks,[40] and at age five years to be more resourceful in adapting to changing circumstances and more persistent in coping with tasks; by contrast, toddlers who lacked such attachment, as measured by their tendency to avoid their mothers, would fall apart when confronted with a difficult task, becoming angry, distressed, and contrary. In one of their many important studies, the Minnesota psychologists observed for many weeks the behavior of four-year-old children whose attachment to their mothers had been assessed at infancy. The securely attached children displayed stronger egos, more self-esteem, less dependency, and better deportment than those who, as a consequence of weak attachments, were either impulsive or aggressive. Weak attachment did not lead to a single form of misconduct. One child, for example, was "wild-eyed"—he was extremely impulsive, could not cope with even the slightest frustration, and found it impossible to cooperate with other children, and so they avoided him. But his teachers liked him because he so obviously craved affection. Another boy, by contrast, was devious, hostile, and manipulative and took pleasure at the discomfort he caused in others; he infuriated his teachers, but some children, noting his skill at controlling others, were drawn to him. It is not hard to imagine what kind of adults such children may become. What is striking is that these behavioral patterns were so clear before the children had even entered school.[41]

These conclusions are supported by research on animals in experimental settings. The best-known of these are those by Harlow and Harlow on the effects on young rhesus monkeys of being raised in isolation.[42] When placed in contact with other creatures, these maternally deprived animals displayed abnormal fear; if the isolation lasted much beyond the first six months of life, the social and sexual behavior of the animals was significantly impaired.

It is not clear that the effects of deprivation are irreversible. There are accounts of war orphans from Greece, Korea, and Lebanon suffering from acute signs of maternal deprivation but managing, when placed in foster homes in this country, to make good progress toward normality in intelligence and social functioning.[43] Even some of the monkeys studied by the Harlows showed some improvement if, after prolonged isolation, they were placed with normal animals.[44] But these findings offer little grounds for optimism about ordinary instances of deprivation. People are not monkeys. Most of the war orphans were adopted while still young enough to develop attachments; moreover, the change in their environment was complete and permanent. Their successful adaptation says little about the possibility that a brief, partial, or easily managed treatment will have any effect on severe cases of deprivation.[45]

Of late, the term "attachment" has been applied not to the affectional ties and physical proximity of infant and parent but to the attitudes of school-age children toward their parents. In the influential formulation of Travis Hirschi, delinquent behavior becomes more likely as an individual's bond to society becomes weaker; among the important components of that bond is the degree of attachment a person has to his parents.[46] By attachment Hirschi means caring about the opinions and expectations of others. Hirschi's view, called social-control theory, is that most if not all of us would commit crimes if we were not under the control of certain social forces and that one of those forces is the extent to which we care about retaining the good opinion of our parents. His own data, based on self-reports of delinquency taken from several thousand West Coast schoolchildren, are consistent with this view, as are data gathered among pupils at a rural New York school by Hindelang[47] and among a national sample of high school students.[48]

In these studies, attachment was variously measured by asking people questions about how close they felt to their mother and father, how much time they spent with their parents, and how closely the parents supervised them. A person who felt himself attached in any of these senses could also have been attached in the sense of having formed as an infant a strong affectional bond with his mother or father, but it is also possible that the attachment felt by a teen-age child might arise independently of whether the early affectional bond existed. Thus, the fact that there is a strong association between attachment in Hirschi's sense and delinquency is not proof that there will be a causal relationship between attachment in Bowlby's sense and delinquency.

We think that "attachment" is not the best term to describe Hirschi's measure of parent-child relations in the adolescent years. What he is actually measuring, in our view, are two fairly different things: first, the extent to which a person takes into account the approval of others (in this case, parents) in assigning a value to noncrime and, second, the extent to which some other persons (in this case, parents) will in fact reward or punish his behavior. Logically, a person might assign so high a value to parental approval that he would commit no act that might earn their disapproval, however remote and unlikely the discovery of the act might be. On the other hand, he might attach very little value to parental approval but believe that his parents monitor his behavior closely and will swiftly and certainly punish (perhaps by withdrawing privileges rather than approval) any deviant act he might commit.

Seen in these terms, Hirschi's theory can be assimilated to the general behavioral model we outlined in Chapter 2, a possibility that has already been raised by Conger.[49] Parents can influence both the strength of the rewards of noncrime and the probability of those reinforcements' being delivered. For reasons to be adduced in the next part of this chapter, we think that most parents affect the behavior of their offspring by doing both things simultaneously—instilling a desire for their approval and making that approval contingent on proper behavior. But as we shall also see in the next section, some parents, however much they may want their children to value their approval, lack the inclination or the ability to make their rewards contingent on the child's displaying the behavior necessary to win that approval.

Attachment, in the sense of an early affectional bond between infant and parent, is certainly a desirable and probably a necessary precondition for the development in the child of a confident belief that parental approval will be forthcoming under reasonable and understandable conditions. There is strong evidence, at least among young children, that the absence of this bond has harmful effects. But even if it is a necessary condition for training children, it is not a sufficient one. What remains is the task of socialization.

Socialization

As the child leaves the first year or two of his life, he enters a period in which he is able to differentiate among other persons in his environment, he can use words that permit symbolic interaction with them, and he has acquired a distinct sense of self. These and other changes lead the child to make more complex demands than simply expressing needs and moods that enable him to manipulate others to his advantage. It is at this point that developmental psychologists look for signs of socialization, defined as the process whereby a child acquires, or fails to acquire, those behaviors, beliefs, and motives valued by the family and the culture of which he is a part.[50] Here begins the conventional study of child rearing.

We have seen, however, that a great deal has already happened before socialization begins. Constitutional predispositions and the presence or absence of a strong affectional bond can make socialization relatively easy or immensely difficult. If it is difficult, then it demands more patience, skill, and effort from the parents. But to the extent it is difficult because of the child's genetic predispositions, then it is somewhat more likely that one or both of the parents will themselves have that predisposition, and thus be less well-equipped than other parents to supply that extra measure of patience, skill, or effort. In short, it is possible that for some proportion of families, the child encounters a double deficit: predisposing factors that make socialization difficult and parents who cannot easily manage difficulties. This does not mean that a bad outcome is inevitable, only that it is more likely. We shall return to this possibility when, later in the chapter, we consider some traits of the parents of delinquent children.

Psychologists disagree over how best to describe and explain the socialization process. Freudians emphasize the workings of latent sexual energy and the way in which the child manages these drives by identifying (or failing to identify) with one or the other parent. "Stage" theorists such as Lawrence Kohlberg stress the growth of moral reasoning by age-related stages, beginning with a simple desire to avoid punishment and advancing to higher levels, with a few reaching the highest stage of choosing for oneself universal ethical principles. Social psychologists often rely on the concept of observational learning or modeling whereby the child learns what is acceptable or useful behavior by watching how others, especially his parents, behave. Behavioral theorists argue that a child learns what he ought or ought not to do by having approved behaviors rewarded and disapproved ones punished. A useful summary of these perspectives can be found in Gardner.[51]

Our own view and most of the evidence we shall cite are drawn from behavior theory. Though we might give a number of reasons for this preference, only one is important: We believe that this theory accounts better for the facts. Neither Freudian theory nor the cognitive development work of Kohlberg has produced much systematic evidence that explains individual differences in behavior. Freudians tend to interpret the subjective states of isolated individuals who are undergoing treatment rather than to supply systematic data about the behavior of large numbers of persons representative of the population at large and observed in a reasonably scientific manner. Kohlberg and his followers have produced a great deal of information about how people reason when faced with hypothetical moral dilemmas, but relatively little evidence about how people behave when faced with a real choice or about whether their moral reasoning influences their behavior.[52] Recall the Milgram experiments: People *said* they had high moral standards, but in the experimental setting, they did things, under orders, they believed might hurt others.

We do not deny that children are affected by observational learning, but we shall argue later in this chapter that, in our view, more of their behavior can be explained by conditioning than by modeling. We recognize, however, that this is an important issue among psychologists and we wish to give the modeling theorists their due. They have gathered a great deal of information[53] showing the impact on children of the behavior they observe; in Chapter 13, we shall take up in detail one particularly interesting impact, that of the mass media, especially television.

One conclusion of some exponents of observational learning is so important, however, that a discussion of it cannot be postponed. There is a body of research that seems to suggest that punishment may not affect the behavior of children or, worse, may affect it adversely by making misconduct more rather than less likely.[54] In one famous study, the parents' use (as reported by the mothers) of punishment was positively correlated with the children's misbehavior: "the more severe the punishment, the more aggression the child showed."[55] Barclay Martin noted that the evidence about how young (two- to five-year-old) children go about seeking attention from their mothers seemed to suggest that punishing attention-seeking behavior increased rather than decreased the frequency of such behavior.[56] The implication of such findings was either that the use of punishment is as likely to teach children, by observational learning, to be aggressive as it is to teach them, by conditioning, to be pacific, or that being punished elicits a desire for retaliation, perhaps against another person.

But, as both Berkowitz and Martin point out, there are some reasons to be skeptical of such conclusions. First, most are based on the mother's report of the child's behavior and the parent's discipline; both may be seriously in error. A mother trying to raise a difficult child may exaggerate how often punishment is used, while a mother raising an easy one may understate how often it is used; these reporting errors would create a false positive correlation between punishment and aggression. Second, most such studies neglect the way the child is predisposed to behave. An active, restless, fussy child may be punished more frequently than a placid, easygoing one. The greater punishment of the former may in fact reduce the rate of such misconduct, but because that rate, for temperamental reasons, is already very high, it appears to the observer that more frequent punishment "causes" more frequent aggression. Third, measuring the amount of one reinforcer (e.g., physical punishment) without taking into account the other reinforcers at work (what we called in Chapter 2 the context of reinforcement) can easily lead to erroneous conclusions. Consider two children who are physically punished for hitting someone. The first is often told that it is important to be tough, encouraged to retaliate against other children who tease him, frequently exposed to the sight of his parents fighting, and treated in a cold or indifferent manner when he does something right. The second is punished for unjustifiably hitting anyone, told that it is more important to be fair than to be tough, exposed to parents who settle their differences by discussion, and treated in a warm and supportive manner when he does something right. One does not have to be a social scientist to guess which child will react to physical punishment by increasing his own aggressiveness ("observational learning") and which will react by decreasing it.

These criticisms raise hypothetical, though we think quite real, possibilities. And there is evidence, though not yet as complete as one would like, that the relationship between punishment and behavior is more complex than some social-learning theorists suggest. That relationship can best be understood by recognizing that the effect of any consequence of behavior, whether a penalty or a reward, will depend not simply on whether it is delivered but also on whether it is delivered in a consistent and contingent manner.

A contingent reinforcement or punishment is one delivered only after the occurrence of a certain behavior that one wishes to strengthen or reduce; if it is always so delivered, we say it is consistent. Suppose a child who nags his mother for attention often gets her attention, but on occasion is slapped instead. The child will come to believe that he can usually get his mother's attention by nagging, even though he is sometimes slapped. Sometimes he wins, sometimes he loses, but if he values her attention enough or if he gets his way more often than he gets slapped, he will redouble his nagging.[57] (Technically, what we see at work are rewards and punishments delivered on a variable ratio schedule. Such schedules can make behavior extraordinarily persistent. To see why, imagine how often a child would return to a coin telephone if occasionally he found a coin in it, even if most of the time he found none.) If nagging works often enough, the amount of nagging can be very great, and thus the number of times he gets slapped can be very large as well. This can cause the unwary observer to conclude that slapping has "caused" the nagging.

Or the parent may slap the child without regard to whether he has broken a rule, because the parent is grouchy, or irritated by behavior that ordinarily is permitted, or acting under the erroneous belief that a rule has been broken. Such punishment, not being clearly contingent on behavior defined by some rule, is not likely to produce observance of any rule; on the contrary, to the extent it is (from the child's view) random or erratic, it may lead him, just as social-learning theorists argue, to believe that violence is a normal and acceptable method of expressing one's feelings.

These last two possibilities—discipline that is inconsistent or not contingent—can help us understand why parental aggression can cause aggression in children even after one allows for the children's temperamental predispositions and has cut through the ambiguities of self-reports by directly observing the behavior in question. This is what Gerald R. Patterson and his colleagues at the Oregon Social Learning Center have done.

For years they have been trying to reduce the antisocial behavior, mostly aggressiveness and theft, of young (preadolescent) children referred to the Center by various agencies in and around Eugene, Oregon. By meticulously observing during many hours in the family home the actual behavior of parents and children as they dealt with each other, they were able to measure the probability that a certain action by the child (pushing, crying, whining, smart talk) would be followed by a certain other action by the parent (a slap, a reproach, nothing), and to compare these probabilities and those characteristic of similar (in size, age, and socioeconomic status) families with normal children.

Their central conclusion was that the families of problem children differed from those of normal children not so much in whether they punished too much or too little, but in that the former did not know *how* to punish. The parents of antisocial children did not make their use of penalties contingent on the child's behavior.[58] More precisely, these parents were less likely than others to state clear rules, monitor compliance with those rules, and punish violations of those rules. Instead, they "nattered" at the child, occasionally and unpredictably interrupting the nattering with a slap or a loss of privileges.[59] Patterson and his colleagues suggested that nattering instead of effective discipline occurred in part because the parents were less attached to their children, in part because they did not know how to control behavior effectively, and in part because they felt personally overwhelmed by a succession of minor problems that, cumulatively, amounted to a crisis.[60] The irritable parent who does not use discipline effectively tends to produce aggressive children; the indifferent and ineffective parent tends to produce larcenous ones.[61] In the first case, the child discovers he can bully his parents; in the second, that he can evade them.

The notion that there is a defect in parental *skill,* as opposed to personality, mental health, or economic resources, that accounts for failures to socialize young children may not be a surprise to many normal parents, but it is a revolutionary conclusion in the field of family psychology. As Patterson observes, some psychologists, confronted by a young person who becomes violent or criminal, have sought explanations "at least as dramatic as the phenomena they purport to explain," and so we are treated to accounts of a primal instinct for aggression, a lurking Oedipal complex, or a shattering divorce. "Rather than cataclysmic episodes, flood tides of rage, or crumbling defense structures," what in fact is happening is the mismanagement of "coercive family processes," something that is comprised of events "that are inherently banal."[62]

Among these banal events are the routine interactions of parents and children as they convey, by word, tone, gesture, and expression, their approval or disapproval of the behavior of others. Though the literature on family socialization is heavy with discussions of the merits of "love" versus "punishment," most of the socialization process is carried out by the (often reflexive) display of attention or irritation, interest or disinterest, approval or disapproval. This is not to deny the impact of some extraordinary events; a large fraction of the children in this study had been physically abused or had come from broken homes, and in the next chapter we will consider those factors.

The failure of parents to use reasonable reinforcements contingent on steadily monitored behavior places the child in a situation in which he comes to understand that he cannot control by his own actions what happens to him. When one receives penalties unconnected to one's own behavior, one experiences a kind of stress that Seligman has called "learned helplessness," just as when one receives rewards that are unearned one develops "learned laziness."[63]

If it is the mismanagement rather than the excessive use of discipline (or of rewards) that accounts for the young child's behavior, then we can better understand the role of observational learning or modeling. One can "learn" violence (i.e., come to grasp its nature and uses) by observation. Patterson concludes that within the first few years of life the typical child—normal as well as deviant—has learned all he needs to know about the routine forms of violence—yelling, grabbing, shoving, hitting. The crucial question is not what differentiates persons in what they have *learned,* in the sense of comprehending, but what differentiates persons in their willingness to *behave* in accordance with what they have learned.[64] The object is to explain individual differences in the use of violence (or the rate of theft, or whatever). A child who is the object of an inconsistent, noncontingent set of parental reinforcers will feel freer to use violence as a routine means of self-expression, and not as a rare and special means to attain certain ends. This is not the end of the story, of course, for there are other agents of socialization in our society besides parents; three of them, gangs, schools, and television, will be discussed later.

The conclusions of other direct-observation research on child rearing are similar to those of Patterson. Diana Baumrind and her colleagues have watched children at play in both nursery schools and laboratories. Since the children were bright (the average IQ was about 125) and the parents were well-educated, middle-class whites, the results of this research cannot be generalized to all families. However, despite the similarity in the children's backgrounds, there were significant differences in their behavior—some were happy, curious, and self-reliant, others were discontent, withdrawn, and uncooperative. These differences in behavior were strongly associated with differences in parental practices. The child-rearing method that was "particularly effective" in the control of undesirable behavior, including aggression, was called by Baumrind[65] the "authoritative" style, by which she meant a combination of a high degree of control (involving setting clear standards and directing the children to conform to those standards) coupled with a high degree of nurturance, support, and encouragement.[66] If the parents exercised close control but were cold and detached (the "authoritarian" mode), the children tended to be withdrawn; if the parents were nurturant but failed to control behavior (the "permissive" mode), the children tended to lack self-control. Summarizing her findings from three studies, Baumrind suggests that the authoritative mode, because it makes parental approval systematically contingent on the child's behavior, induces more self-control.[67]

That two of the best observational studies—one of deviant children, the other of normal ones—should come to such similar conclusions greatly strengthens our confidence in the impact of consistent, contingent reinforcement on youthful behavior. But we still want to know whether that influence operates only on the young child in the family setting or whether it continues to operate among adolescents on the street. Our knowledge of these matters comes chiefly from longitudinal studies of boys growing up. The best-known and longest-running such study began in 1937 in the Cambridge-Somerville area of Massachusetts; data from it are still being published. From these industrial communities, 650 boys were selected to participate in a program designed to prevent delinquency. Half were chosen because teachers or social workers thought they were likely to bcome delinquent, the other half because these adults thought they were normal boys. They entered the program at (on the average) age eleven, well before most had committed any delinquent acts. The object was to test the efficacy of a counseling program in preventing delinquency, and to that end the boys were randomly assigned to treatment and control groups. There is little evidence that counseling worked, but that is not what interests us here. Rather, the study is valuable because of the relationship it found between family background (as reported by counselors, teachers, social workers, and doctors) and behavior.

In 1955, eighteen years after the program began, William and Joan McCord analyzed the voluminous records of these boys "blind"—that is, without knowing in advance which boys had been convicted of crimes and which had not.[68] Thus, whatever biases may have existed in the Gluecks' research owing to their prior knowledge of who was delinquent could not have affected the McCords' investigation. The latter found that the delinquent boys were about twice as likely as the nondelinquent ones to come from homes where parental disciplinary practices had been rated as erratic or lax. Delinquents were also much more likely to come from homes with a quarrelsome rather than affectionate or cohesive atmosphere. The combined effect of these two factors—warmth (or its absence) and consistent discipline (or its absence)—was powerful: *All* the boys from quarrelsome families with erratic discipline, but only one-fourth of those from cohesive families with consistent discipline, were convicted of a crime.[69] Interestingly, the McCords found that it was the mothers' behavior that made the greatest difference in the boys' criminality.

Lest someone suppose that these findings were biased by the possibility that the courts were more likely to convict boys from unhappy than from happy homes, the McCords analyzed separately the backgrounds of those boys who were described by counselors or others as aggressive but who had not yet been officially labeled delinquent. They found that these aggressive boys had essentially the same family backgrounds as the convicted delinquents.[70]

It is possible that these differences in family background reflect how the boys were originally selected for inclusion in the study; children chosen because they appeared especially good or especially bad might differ more in family circumstances than a random sample of boys. Indeed, it is possible that some of the boys were chosen because of what the teachers or others already knew about their families. There is not much evidence in the Cambridge-Somerville project that this was the case, but it cannot be ruled out entirely. Fortunately, another longitudinal study, this one in England, was carried out in ways that eliminate this potential source of bias. In Chapter 7, we described how West and Farrington followed the careers of 411 boys chosen at random from a working-class section of London, starting at age eight and continuing for seventeen years. The boys were given batteries of tests and interviews and their parents were interviewed about once a year. West and Farrington gathered information about self-reported, as well as officially recorded, delinquency. By the time they reached the age of twenty-five, a third of the boys had acquired a criminal record. About thirty of the boys became persistent, repeat offenders; in fact, these thirty accounted for over half of all the convictions recorded by the entire group.[71]

The delinquent boys were more likely than the nondelinquent ones to have lower IQs and to have parents who were cruel, neglectful, or passive.[72] Boys described as aggressive by teachers or by themselves had the same background as the officially reported delinquents.[73] Parental behavior could not explain all of the observed delinquency, however. If the father had a criminal record, this materially increased the chance that the son would be delinquent independently of family income and parental behavior.[74] In all, five factors seemed to play the largest role in predicting which boys would become delinquent—low intelligence (as measured by both verbal and nonverbal tests), large family size, parental criminality, low family income, and poor child-rearing practices.[75] Unfortunately, the number of cases was too small to permit a statistical estimate of the amount of variation in delinquency which each factor independently explained.

It is worth noting, however, that some of these factors interacted with others. For example, large family size contributed to delinquency only at the lower income levels; if the income was higher, family size made little difference.[76] There may be many reasons for this connection. It could result from the fact that a poor large family cannot afford to live in housing or in a neighborhood as nice as can a poor small one, or that the struggle to feed many mouths produces more stress than the effort to feed a few. But there is no reason to assume that family size and income are independent conditions. Large families and low incomes may both arise from a common underlying cause: for example, a profligate, uncaring father. Similarly, the fathers with criminal records may have been more likely than law-abiding fathers to have low incomes; indeed, there was evidence that criminal fathers were over-represented among those who became dependent on public welfare programs.[77] Given the small number of cases, West and Farrington could not explore these and other connections.

What is indisputable in the London study is the impact of adverse child-rearing practices:

> A particularly noticeable characteristic of the parents of many of the delinquents in the study was carelessness or laxness in matters of supervision. They were less concerned than other parents to watch over or to know about their children's doings, whereabouts and companions, and they failed to enforce or to formulate fixed rules about such things as punctuality, manners, bedtime, television viewing or tidying up.[78]

This conclusion duplicates almost precisely the observation by Patterson that parents of antisocial children do not seem able or inclined to make rules, monitor behavior, or make rewards and penalties contingent on that behavior.[79]

Though less useful than a longitudinal study, the cross-sectional study by Hirschi of several thousand junior and senior high school children in northern California came to conclusions that were broadly consistent with those of the Gluecks, the McCords, and West and Farrington.[80] Hirschi asked the children to describe their own delinquent behavior, if any, and the feelings and beliefs they had about their parents, schools, and friends. The self-reported delinquents were more likely than the nondelinquents to say that their mothers did not supervise them closely, that they did not share their thoughts and feelings with their parents, that their parents were unlikely to explain rules to them, and that they would not like to be the kind of person their father was.[81] Hirschi summarizes these relationships by saying that delinquents have a weaker attachment to their parents than nondelinquents, but we think it better to separate these findings into two categories—those that bear on the attachment, narrowly defined, of the child (his affection toward his parents and his desire for their approval) and those that involve the degree of parental monitoring of behavior and the reinforcements such monitoring supplies. The data suggest that both aspects of attachment—an affectional bond and an awareness of supervision—are associated with self-reported delinquency.[82] The two measures of attachment are, not surprisingly, correlated, but not strongly ($r = .25$), indicating that, as we have argued, two rather distinct aspects of socialization are at work.

To see how these two processes work, Rand D. Conger has taken a closer look at Hirschi's data.[83] Conger argues that a child may not act so as to retain parental approval if he does not value it (the affectional-bond aspect of socialization) *and* that he will not take into account his parents' attitudes if they do not act in ways that will reinforce his conduct. He is able to show that it is not just a boy's communicating with his parents that reduces delinquency, it is communication that is met with a positive parental response (such as explaining the rules or helping the child understand something). The power of this reinforcement is affected by how strong the affectional bond is. Conger is able to show that when parents respond to their children's communications and the affectional bond is strong, the reduction in delinquency is much greater than when only one of those factors is present.

So far, we have assumed that parents try to teach their children law-abiding behavior but differ, with important results for the children, in their ability or willingness to use effective methods. But one can imagine the opposite—namely, parents rewarding criminality, and thereby producing more crime the more effective are their child-rearing techniques. The behavior of Dickens' character Fagin is the prototype of this process. And since we know that delinquent children tend to have criminal fathers, it might seem obvious that what accounts for the intergenerational transfer of criminality is the skill criminal parents have in reinforcing delinquency in their offspring.

Plausible as this may seem, the evidence is almost all against it. Some parents, especially lower-class ones, may reward toughness, masculinity, and fighting ability in their sons,[84] but they do not favor, and apparently do not reward, actual criminality. Hirschi found that a boy strongly attached to a father who was an unskilled laborer was no more likely to report being delinquent than a boy strongly attached to a father in the professions.[85] West and Farrington[86] report that even fathers who are criminal disapprove of their sons' criminality; "parental attitudes toward delinquency were almost always censorious, regardless of the parents' own delinquent history."[87]

It seems more likely that a parent with a criminal record rarely wishes his child to be a criminal also, but rather passes on to the child some genetic predispositions (lower intelligence, impulsiveness, extroversion, or perhaps other, as yet unidentified factors) and subjects the child to certain child-rearing practices (weak affectional bonds, inconsistent and noncontingent reinforcement) that increase the chances of the offspring's becoming an offender. We have evidence, for example, that the parents of delinquent boys are more likely than the parents of socially similar nondelinquents to have distinctive personality profiles, as measured by the Minnesota Multiphasic Personality Inventory (MMPI), including higher scores on the Pd (Psychopathic deviate) scale.[88] Patterson[89] found, as did Goodstein and Rowley,[90] that the mothers (but not the fathers) of antisocial children had elevated MMPI scores, especially on the Psychopathic deviate scale. The parents, particularly the mothers, of delinquents tend to be irritable, easily angered, and often depressed. Some of those feelings may have resulted from their attempting to cope with an especially difficult child ("insanity is hereditary, you get it from your children"), but we think that for the most part they predate the arrival of the child.

That individual differences in criminality are profoundly affected by the interaction between individual predispositions and family experiences is perhaps the best-documented (though, of late, least-repeated) generalization in all of criminology. Loeber and Dishion have recently reviewed a large number of the efforts (including all the important ones) that have been made to predict who will become delinquent. These efforts were evaluated by comparing the predicted with the actual delinquency by means of a formula that allows one to measure relative improvement over chance achieved by introducing into the equation any given measure of the child's status.[91] They concluded that a composite measure of child-rearing techniques provided the best predictors of delinquency. (The socioeconomic status of the family turned out to be a rather poor one.) This review, however, did not include measures of cognitive and temperamental predispositions.

In study after study, the child-rearing factors associated with aggression and delinquency are described in similar, if not identical, language. The Gluecks,[92] Baumrind,[93] Hirschi,[94] West and Farrington,[95] and Patterson[96] all find much the same thing. Nor are these patterns found only in America or England. In Finland, Pulkkinen followed a cohort of children beginning at age eight and found that the children who later became most aggressive lived in homes with indifferent, selfish parents.[97] In Sweden, Olweus found that aggression among young boys was the joint product of the boy's temperament (calm or hot-tempered while an infant) and the extent to which the mother was "negative" (hostile, rejecting, cold, indifferent) and "permissive" (lax in monitoring and controlling behavior).[98]

Dimensions of Parental Care

So consistent have been these findings that some psychologists have reduced the many terms used to describe parental behavior to two (occasionally three) simple factors that, taken in combination, predict much of a child's behavior. Earl S. Schaefer examined the correlations that had been reported among thirty-two aspects of maternal behavior and found that these could be reduced to two main, independent dimensions that he called "autonomy versus control" and "love versus hostility."[99] He was able to reproduce these dimensions by applying the same methods to observations made by others. Subsequently, other scholars suggested that one or possibly two additional dimensions could also be extracted from accounts of parental behavior. One of these has been termed "anxiety versus calm detachment";[100] the other, "harsh versus mild punishment."[101] Since these additional dimensions have not acquired general acceptance, and since we wish to keep our exposition simple, we shall discuss only the two original dimensions proposed by Schaefer. To make clearer their meaning, as well as to strip them of some of their misleading connotations,* we shall relabel these dimensions as "permissive versus restrictive" and "warm versus cold."

A restrictive parental style is one in which the mother or father states clear rules, monitors behavior to insure that it conforms to those rules, and reinforces compliance by the consistent and contingent use of reinforcers. Permissive parents fail to do these things, though they may imagine that they do them because they know they are always yelling at the child, but inconsistent and ineffectual nattering is not, as we have seen, a form of control that alters behavior in accordance with parental intentions. A warm parent is approving and supportive of the child, frequently employs praise as a reinforcement for good behavior, and explains the reasons for rules. A cold parent acts in the opposite manner, frequently displaying irritability, passiveness, or indifference and relying more on negative than on positive reinforcements.[102]

There are at least two defects in these labels. First, though the concepts can be extracted from empirical research on child rearing, many accounts employing these terms assign somewhat different meanings to them (e.g.,

* For example, Schaefer called one of his dimensions "love versus hostility." This confuses the generalized feeling parents have toward their children ("we love them" or "we hate them") with the behavior they display in specific circumstances. Parents may love their children in the abstract or when calm but frequently act toward them in a cold or irritable manner. Moreover, we suspect that very few parents lack any love for their children.

some writers speak of "warm" parents as those who both support the child and minimize rule enforcement even though these two behaviors are both empirically and logically quite different). Second, using these concepts implies that child rearing can best be understood by looking at "types" of parents, whereas in fact these concepts ought to be thought of as variables which measure, in varying (but hard to calculate) degrees, parental behavior. We remind the reader that actual behavior is much more complicated than what is implied by reference to these types.

Robert Hogan and his colleagues have utilized these two dimensions to make predictions about the outcomes of differing child-rearing styles. Ignoring for the moment the constitutional differences among children, they suggest that each of the four possible combinations of the extreme positions on the parental dimensions will produce distinctive behavioral patterns:[103]

(1) *Warm-restrictive parents:* Their children will value adult approval, readily internalize rules, and be rule-abiding.

(2) *Warm-permissive parents:* Their children will be self-confident and socially outgoing, but will frequently ignore or bend the rules; in everyday language, they will be affable but spoiled.

(3) *Cold-restrictive parents:* Their children will be anxious and sullen, but compliant; their anger may turned inward on themselves.

(4) *Cold-permissive parents:* Their children will be hostile and rule-defying, with a high probability of delinquency.

A similar typology had been suggested fourteen years earlier by Wesley C. Becker,[104] with one important difference—whereas Hogan et al. thought that the warm-restrictive parents were best able to socialize children (to achieve what they called "rule attunement"), Becker clearly preferred the warm-permissive style because it fostered gregariousness and individuality. Hogan and Becker did not disagree over the facts so much as over the value they attached to the outcomes—what Becker liked as gregarious, Hogan disliked as self-centered.

It is not hard to see how these styles might affect the three aspects of child rearing described earlier in this chapter. Parental warmth facilitates attachment, thereby leading the child to value parental approval and to attach a high cost to its possible withdrawal. If in addition the parents are restrictive, then rules will be clearly stated and behavior governed by those rules consistently reinforced. This will assist the development in the child of a long time horizon as he learns that approved behavior has predictable consequences. Promises made today will be kept tomorrow and the next day;

thus, action taken today is more likely to be governed by distant as well as immediate consequences. Moreover, if rules are consistently enforced by parents whose approval the child values, then the experience of conforming to the rules will itself become pleasurable and the prospect of breaking them will be a source of anxiety. In this way, the impact of conscience is enhanced.

The child of warm but permissive parents will certainly value parental approval, which is readily forthcoming, but he will not learn that this approval is contingent on behaving in certain ways. This may weaken the extent to which a long time horizon develops and reduce the growth of conscience.* Cold and restrictive parents will develop in the child a long time horizon, but without the affectional warmth that makes the child assign a high value to the approval of others. (In terms of our theory, coldness implies a shortage of secondary reinforcers supporting conformity; restrictiveness means an excess of punishments for transgressions.) The child's conformity to rules may be rigid and his expectation that others conform to them high, but that conformity and these expectations may be governed more by external consequences than by internal prohibitions. Cold and permissive parents will not encourage the bonds of attachment, will leave the child with a foreshortened time horizon that makes him intensely present-oriented, and will generate little or no capacity for feeling guilt.

One must use caution in assigning families to one of the categories because the personality of the parents can lead to the child's being treated differently at different stages of his life. Arthur Hippler has given us a vivid account of how children were raised a decade ago in Hunter's Point, a lower-income black ghetto in San Francisco composed disproportionately of female-headed families.[106] Babies were greatly valued and much loved, even though the mother often had no husband. The infants were fondled and played with to the evident satisfaction of both child and mother. "This comparatively nurturant childhood pattern, however, tends to give way to a rather severe rejection about the time the infant shows sufficient individuality to try to explore and manipulate his environment by walking and making verbal demands." Often this rejection occurred simultaneously with, and was heightened by, the arrival of a new infant who now became the object of the mother's attention. The older child was increasingly told, " 'Get out of here—you bother me.' " Some children reacted against this sudden lessening of affection by becoming sullen or rebellious, behavior that often provoked

---

* Richard H. Blum studied middle- and working-class white, black, and Hispanic families in the San Francisco Bay area and concluded that those in which there was a high risk of drug use by the children were more likely than those with a low risk to be permissive and self-centered and to value self-expression over self-control.[105]

the mother to send the child out of doors to get him " 'out of her hair.' "[107]
Hippler did not observe any family in the newer public housing project that
did not lock the child out of the house at least occasionally by the time the
child was about two years old. (The better-off families in the older projects
were less likely to do this.) Punishment typically involved not only exclusion but also beatings or a denial of food, much of it meted out more in
response to the mother's mood than to the child's behavior. The mothers
professed to love their children but were obviously irritated by the demands
the latter made on them. The result was to produce, in Hippler's view, children who were emotionally dependent but physically independent, whose
behavior (being so often outside) was neither closely monitored nor consistently reinforced. Early warmth was replaced by later coldness, and a
promising beginning to effective socialization was interrupted by a failure to
clarify rules or make rewards dependent on their observance.

What is lacking in these inquiries are the results of research that carefully integrate the effect of constitutional predispositions with the effect of
child-rearing practices on later behavior. We have good reason to believe
(see Chapters 3–7) that these predispositions are important; though students
of deviance increasingly accept this view in principle, in practice it is rare to
find research that shows the joint effect of predisposition and child rearing
on behavior. And these predispositions may affect the parents equally with
the child. For example, there is substantial evidence that children are more
likely to obey rules that have been clearly explained to them than rules that
are little more than abrupt commands.[108] Parents deficient in verbal skills
may have difficulty in communicating rules just as children of low intelligence may have difficulty in comprehending them. Similarly, if children who
are temperamentally impulsive have impulsive parents, the mutual interaction of these sudden urges can lead to the mismanagement of many of life's
daily problems, resulting in an upward escalation of irritability and aggressiveness.

Continuity in Behavior

For some scholars, the major problem in interpreting the effect of either
individual predispositions or child-rearing experiences is the necessary assumption that these factors importantly affect adult behavior. An infant may
be irritable, a parent may be uncaring, a childhood may be tempestuous, but
all may count for little if the person's adult behavior is shaped more by later
contingencies, such as his experiences in school, with peers, or in the labor

market. At one time it was widely assumed that the child is father to the man—that there were great continuities in attitude and behavior from infancy on. Then, as we have seen, childhood was subordinated to gangs and social structure. Even some psychologists who have retained a belief in the importance of the family have begun to question the assumption of continuity, arguing instead that individuals are more plastic and adaptable than once supposed and that "personality" in particular is a poor concept if it implies that a person's nature, more than the situation in which he finds himself, shapes his behavior. A recent review of the literature brings this issue into sharp focus.[109]

We need not decide whether early experiences shape personality in ways that determine later behavior in general in order to address the particular question of whether early signs of aggressiveness are reliable predictors of later misconduct and crime. We have already described research that strongly supports the view that misbehavior among young children is powerfully predictive of misbehavior among older ones. The London cohort study, for example, concluded that boys who were aggressive at age eight or ten were likely to be aggressive at age sixteen or eighteen.[110] Of the boys officially determined to be delinquents while young, 61 percent were later convicted of crimes as adults; by contrast, only 13 percent of the boys not officially delinquent acquired adult records. Another English longitudinal study, this one of boys growing up in Buckinghamshire, also concluded that parental descriptions of the boys' behavior at an early age were predictive of later criminality.[111] And similar findings come from the study of a Finnish cohort.[112]

Recall the study by Lee Robins, described in Chapter 7, in which she retraced the personal histories of a group of adults who, while young, had been referred to a child-guidance clinic.[113] She was able to classify the reason for these referrals as involving either antisocial behavior (truancy, delinquency, aggressiveness) or "other" (learning problems, temper tantrums, anxiety, or neuroticism). Thirty years later, half the persons who had initially been referred for delinquency had acquired serious police records compared to one-sixth of those referred for neuroticism or learning problems. The delinquent referrals also displayed as adults more marital discord, higher rates of alcoholism, more unemployment, and poorer military records. This is quite consistent with what the Gluecks found with the five hundred delinquent boys in Boston.[114] First studied when they were, on the average, age fourteen, by the time they had become twenty-five they had been arrested for 7 homicides, 100 robberies, 172 burglaries, 225 larcenies, and countless other lesser offenses.

But all of these studies, a critic might argue, start when the youths are between the ages of eight and fourteen, already in school and exposed to neighborhood and peer influences. Is there any reason to suppose that very young children, still wholly under the influence of their constitutions and their parents, will display any comparable constancy in behavior?

It seems there are good reasons for such suppositions even though many individual personality traits of the very young are only weakly predictive of later behavior. Jerome Kagan and Howard A. Moss followed eighty-nine children who at birth had entered a longitudinal study (starting between 1929 and 1939) and who had been periodically (usually, every year) observed and tested.[115] Aggression toward peers was one of the personality traits that, at least among males, was quite stable from childhood to adulthood.

Two recent reviews of all the research[116] concluded that, at least for youths who are highly antisocial at an early age, there is a great deal of consistency in behavior; indeed, the early onset of misconduct is one of the best predictors of a child's becoming a chronic and persistent delinquent. Olweus's review is of special interest because it attempts to calculate quantitatively the stability of aggression in males.[117] He estimated that measures of aggression are almost as stable over time as measures of intelligence. Marked individual differences in aggressiveness appear very early in life, certainly by the age of three years. Moreover, the persistence of aggressiveness is apparent regardless of whether it is directly observed by the researcher or reported by a teacher. What makes this persistence all the more remarkable is that aggressiveness is a behavior that is often punished (though as we have seen, not always very efficaciously). We might expect that behavior that is naturally rewarded—being outgoing and friendly, for example—would persist because it is frequently rewarded, and that behavior that makes persons dislike and avoid you, such as aggression, would slowly be extinguished. Obviously, this is not the case, perhaps because aggressive persons in fact find that its pays (timid people give in to you), perhaps because it was reinforced so well at an early age as to have become a habitual mode of acting, or perhaps because it is indicative of a constitutional predisposition that society can only partially moderate.

Conclusions

There are strong reasons for believing that the interaction between constitutional and familial factors has a powerful effect on later misconduct, especially physical aggression. We have suggested that most of this effect can be explained in behavioral terms—that is, as the result of patterns of reinforcement. To say this, however, is not to say that only external consequences (or material ones) control behavior, for what is learned by the early association between activities and responses is not merely how best to achieve rewards controlled by others but also the extent to which one rewards oneself (by the averted pang of conscience) and how far in the future it is reasonable to value consequences. Moreover, people not only learn what behavior will affect the approval of others but also how valuable (i.e., how reinforcing) that approval is.

Neither the studies that observe childhood aggression directly nor those that follow it, using official data or self-reports, over time provide us with direct measures of the growth of either conscience or a distant time horizon. But everything they do tell us is consistent with the findings of research that describe the subjective states of offenders. For example, offenders are much more likely than nonoffenders to prefer an immediate small reward to a delayed larger one.[118] And among offenders, recidivists are more likely to be impulsive than nonrecidivists.[119] Moreover, impulsiveness is strongly associated with other kinds of behavior—aggressiveness, hyperactivity, and having problems in school—that are, in turn, often precursors of criminality.[120]

Most children who have conduct disorders are also hyperactive, and vice versa. Among delinquents, the hyperactive ones tend to be the most antisocial. Though there is some disagreement about how distinctive hyperkinesis is, Michael Rutter and Henri Giller, in their review of the evidence, conclude that it is a recognizable disorder consisting of inattentiveness and extreme impulsiveness that appears before the age of three.[121]

Being impulsive is to some degree a characteristic of all young children, but especially of less bright ones; in a sense, the child who remains impulsive as he grows older suffers from a kind of arrested development, such that he approaches the larger world with a temperament more appropriate to the nursery school. As Mischel puts it in his summary of research on this subject, "It is difficult to conceive of socialization (or, indeed, of civilization) without such self-imposed delays."[122] A predisposition to impulsiveness, arising out of factors described in Chapters 3, 5, 6, and 7, when combined with a family setting in which rewards and penalties are not systematically made contingent on behavior, leads to inadequate socialization and a strain on civilization.

After taking these factors into account, it is not entirely clear how much of the individual differences in criminality remains to be explained. Some offenders are late bloomers who have no record of youthful misconduct, and many delinquents are casual offenders who stop breaking the law before they reach adulthood. It is easier to explain why misconduct stops in these later years than why it should begin then. As we noted in Chapter 5 on age, as a person grows older he becomes subject to a larger and more various array of reinforcers, and this is sufficient, for most casual offenders, to induce them to alter their behavior in approved ways. Behavior that was useful in winning a schoolyard fight or stealing a neighbor's bicycle becomes much less useful—indeed, downright disadvantageous—when one wants to find a wife, get a regular job, or enlarge one's circle of friends. The explanation for late bloomers is harder to devise, but probably has much to do with later experiences—in school, the neighborhood, or the world at large—that reinforce responses that had not previously been rewarded.

But these late bloomers are only a small minority of adult criminals.[123] Most important, they are rarely the serious, repeat offenders. The chronic recidivists begin their misdeeds at a very early age.[124] This means that constitutional and familial factors are most important in explaining the behavior of the most serious offenders. Later experiences, especially among peers and in schools, will have some effect on the behavior of this group, but probably a second-order effect. Before we consider those effects, however, we will pause for a closer look, in the next chapter, at certain extreme aspects of family life that are often thought to play an especially important role in socialization, or its absence.

9

BROKEN AND ABUSIVE FAMILIES

Given what was said in the preceding chapter about the importance of family experiences in accounting for individual differences in criminality, one might suppose that the families most likely to produce delinquent children are those that are either broken or abusive or both. A broken home presumably supplies less opportunity for creating a strong attachment between child and parents and thus reduces the ability of the parents to condition the child so that he will internalize conventional rules. An abusive home presumably uses inconsistent and violent disciplinary practices that both weaken the child's capacity to learn what consequences follow from what acts and instruct the child, through observational learning, in the value—or at least the acceptability—of relying on violence to settle quarrels.

So plausible are these assumptions that it is with a small shock that one discovers how uncertain is the evidence bearing on them. With respect to broken homes the evidence is inconsistent and with respect to abusive ones it is incomplete. This is not to say that the assumptions are false, only that their truth—or more accurately, the circumstances under which they are true—is unclear.

Broken Homes

For many years, no one seriously questioned the view that a home from which one parent, usually the father, was absent would be more likely than an intact family to produce a delinquent child. Sir Cyril Burt in 1925 found broken homes to be more common among delinquent than nondelinquent boys in England, and a quarter of a century later Sheldon and Eleanor Glueck found the same thing among boys in Boston.[1] An analysis of children referred to the Philadelphia Municipal Court between 1949 and 1954 seemed to show that the recidivists—that is, those who were making at least their second appearance in court—were more likely than first offenders to come from broken homes.[2] A major longitudinal study of over five thousand children born in the United Kingdom during the first week of March 1946 and followed for three decades suggested that children raised in families broken by divorce or desertion were more likely than those living in intact families to become delinquent.[3] A study of all juveniles born in Franklin County (Columbus), Ohio, between 1956 and 1960 who had at least one arrest for a violent offense found that they were less likely than the average juvenile in the area to live in two-parent homes, though among blacks there was no significant difference between the proportion of single-parent homes of arrested youth and nonarrested ones.[4]

Other studies have found a connection between broken homes and self-reported offenses among Arizona high school children,[5] police reports of delinquency among Mexican, black, and Anglo boys in the Southwest,[6] and observed aggressiveness in the family.[7] The National Youth Survey of 1,725 adolescents found that self-reported delinquency was more prevalent among youth living with only one biological parent than among those living with both; moreover, the incidence (i.e., delinquency rate per youth) was higher in the former than the latter group.[8]

Evidence has even been adduced indicating that the crime rates of entire cultures may differ for reasons of family structure. Scholars at Yale compared the family patterns and rates of personal crime found among forty-eight preliterate societies and learned that crime, particularly theft, was especially high in cultures with "polygynous mother-child families"— that is, families in which a husband has several wives, each of whom lives with her children in a separate domicile apart from the husband.[9]

But other scholars have come to quite different conclusions. The Cambridge-Somerville boys followed by William and Joan McCord for many decades were no more likely to commit crimes if they came from broken homes than if they came from intact ones.[10] Lee N. Robins looked at the family backgrounds of over five hundred adults in St. Louis who many years earlier had been referred to a child-guidance center and discovered that those who were "sociopaths" (almost all of whom had criminal records) were no more likely to come from broken homes than from intact ones.[11]

There seemed to be no connection between family structure and aggressiveness in play situations among preadolescent inner-city males, though there was some connection when race was controlled; father-absent white boys were more aggressive and father-absent blacks less aggressive than their ethnic counterparts who were living with both parents.[12] Belson could find no association between family structure and self-reported delinquency among over fourteen hundred London boys,[13] Sterne could find none between broken homes and officially recorded delinquencies among white boys in Trenton, New Jersey,[14] and Tennyson could find none between growing up in a female-headed or female-dominant home and membership in a gang or self-reports of being picked up by the police among black youth in Chicago.[15] A survey of students in the San Francisco Bay area by Travis Hirschi uncovered no connection between self-reported delinquency and living in a home from which the father was absent (though there was a slight tendency for boys living with stepfathers to be more delinquent).[16] Other self-report studies have found some relationship between self-reported delinquency and coming from a broken home, but it has been a weak one, far overshadowed by other, more powerful correlates of crime.[17]

A review of eighteen studies of female-headed families carried out between 1950 and 1970 concluded that seven found more delinquency in father-absent homes, four found less, and seven produced mixed results.[18] Several things may explain why the evidence is so contradictory. First, studies that use official reports of delinquency[19] as the measure of criminality are probably biased because the agencies that compile such reports—the police, probation officers, and judges—will frequently and understandably take the family status of a youth into consideration when deciding whether or not to institute formal proceedings. A juvenile from an intact home who has committed a routine offense is more likely to be turned over to his parents without court action than one from a broken home.[20] This may produce a spurious correlation between delinquency and single-parent families.

When self-report measures are used, they are often not used the same way in all studies. As we noted in Chapter 1, general scales of self-reported delinquency often lump together trivial offenses with serious ones and sometimes exclude very serious offenses altogether. If broken homes have a major impact only on serious offenders, self-report data may understate this effect and thus suggest, wrongly, that there is no correlation between delinquency and single-parent families.

Moreover, the effect of a broken home may differ depending on the context. There are many more children living in single-parent families in New York than in London; it is possible that where such families are rare, their effect is less, though to the best of our knowledge, no one has examined this possibility. It is also conceivable that living in a broken home affects the child's delinquency only when other factors are also present. For example, coming from a broken home may intensify the rate or seriousness of crime among children already disposed to criminality but have little or no effect on those not so disposed; in this case, broken homes would affect the incidence or the severity more than the prevalence of crime. Wadsworth, who followed over five thousand British babies from birth to age twenty-six, discovered that boys from homes that were broken by separation or divorce before the age of four had slower pulse rates than did boys from homes that were intact or broken at a later age.[21] While having a slow pulse was not by itself associated with later delinquency, *if* the boy was delinquent, then having a slow pulse was associated with committing sexual and violent crimes.

But perhaps the most important reason for the equivocal findings is that there is not much agreement about what we mean and how we measure a "broken home." Some studies[22] mean by that phrase only that one parent is absent from the home. But surely it makes a difference whether the absence is the result of accident (one parent dies) or conflict (there is a divorce) and, if conflict, whether it is protracted and bitter or short-lived and civil. A father who deserts his wife and young child at the climax of a long history of drunken rages will probably affect his family differently than if he is divorced by his wife because she suddenly discovers a carefully concealed pattern of infidelity.

Even if we do suppose that all desertions and divorces involve a serious rupture of familial relationships, we must recall that these ruptures may be no more significant than their causes. Couples that are tense, angry, disaffected, or violent may or may not terminate their relationship; what affects the child, if anything does, may be the tension, anger, disaffection, and violence more than the separation to which these things may or may not give rise. "Intact" families may display as many of these unhappy traits as broken ones; indeed, an intact family may be more quarrelsome than a broken one because its members continue to live together. If, as the evidence of Chapter 8 suggests, a family racked by hostility is less likely to establish bonds of affection and constructive methods of socialization, then any family with these traits—broken or intact—will produce more than its share of delinquency. Even if we grant, as seems reasonable, that homes broken by desertion or divorce are often those with the most extreme history of discord, we still must bear in mind that we are now speaking of differences in degree, not kind, and thus we should expect to find statistical associations with criminality that are partial, easily obscured by other factors, and heavily dependent on the nature of the sample and the measures of criminality.

That it is discord, or the parental traits that produce discord (such as a tendency toward alcoholism, impulsiveness, or frequent rages), that is the principal source of inadequate socialization seems to be supported by such evidence as we have, though the matter cannot be regarded as settled. The Cambridge-Somerville data suggest that intact families that are quarrelsome and neglectful produced over twice as high a percentage of boys convicted of delinquency than did broken families.[23] The same differences appeared when other measures of deviance—such as being involved in a delinquent gang— were employed.[24] F. Ivan Nye found that there was some relationship between self-reported delinquency and broken homes among high-school-age boys, but that unhappy intact homes produced, in general, more such delinquency than broken ones.[25] The St. Louis study indicated that "sociopaths" came from discordant families, whether intact or broken, much more frequently than from harmonious ones, whether intact or broken.[26] Hirschi found that the strength of the parent-child attachment was much more predictive of self-reported delinquency than the marital status of the parents.[27] Among the London boys followed by West and Farrington, it was the youngsters who had lost a parent from desertion or divorce, not those who had lost one from death or hospitalization, who were more likely to become delinquent.[28]

Apparently, mothers can make up for whatever loss in child-rearing capacity is caused by the absence of the father, especially if prior to the break the child developed a strong and warm attachment to at least one parent and if the break was not associated with continuous and painful discord. But if the mother must try harder, we should expect some to fail; stated another way, if one parent must do the work of two, then, at the margin, less of that work will get done.* And if it was the mother herself who was the principal cause of the discord that led to the father's desertion, then she is not likely to shoulder very effectively the extra burden of raising a child in a single-parent family. Thus, we should expect to find more delinquency among some kinds of broken homes.

Some evidence as to what kinds of parents are most at risk in this regard comes from a study of one thousand families, mostly female-headed, living on welfare who were compared with another thousand nonwelfare

---

* It is because of the greater costs of being a single parent, among other reasons, that the mother-father-child triad is the universal family unit. Winch finds little evidence, among preindustrial or industrial societies, of mother-child families being common except when unusual economic or other difficulties prevent the formation of the normal triad. "The evidence seems to indicate that one woman cannot serve simultaneously as tender of small children, household maintainer, and provider. It appears that women who are thrust into [this situation] generally extricate themselves from it through forming a new liaison and/or seeking help from relatives, friends, or agencies."[29]

families from the same lower-income area of New York City. Estimates of delinquency as well as characteristics of family life were obtained from parental interviews. The prevalance of delinquency among both welfare and nonwelfare families was best explained by a factor the authors called "parental coldness." But this coldness was most strongly associated with delinquency among the welfare families because, the authors speculated, the "welfare child is in double jeopardy"—either he has a cold father or no father at all, and living on welfare without a father makes maternal coldness all the more serious.[30]

The speculation that female-headed families, especially those living on welfare, are a breeding ground for delinquency is most commonly advanced with respect to black families, 40 percent of which have no father present. In Chapter 18 we take up this matter in detail and find that, for the most part, the scholarly literature is as equivocal with respect to black single-parent homes as it is regarding such families generally. There is, however, an important potential exception to this confused state of affairs—important because it, almost alone of all inquiries into this matter, involves actually following children as they grow up in various kinds of families. It is still only a potential exception because the study is not yet complete.

A research team directed by Sheppard G. Kellam has been following for over ten years more than one thousand children growing up in the predominately black Woodlawn section of Chicago.[31] The families of these children represented every conceivable combination of adults (mothers, fathers, stepparents, aunts, uncles, grandparents, and so on). About one-third, however, involved only the mother living with one or more children (another third had both the mother and father present, while the remainder chiefly involved the mother living with various other adults). The children were classified by their teachers as either "adapting" or "maladapting"; a maladapting child was further classified as either aggressive or not.

By the time the children entered the third grade, it was clear that those coming from mother-only families were the most likely to be maladapted; every other kind of family, but especially the mother-father families, had children with fewer problems. This connection between behavior and family structure remained after controlling for family income, the number of children in the family, and the sex of the child. Moreover, the children's problems became worse between the first and third grades.

By 1982, when Kellam and his colleagues had followed the children for ten years, mother-only families accounted for nearly half of all the families. The researchers then gathered self-report data on the delinquencies of those teen-agers who could still be located (about 75 percent). The boys who, when they were six or seven years old, lived in mother-only families were more likely than other boys to report committing delinquent acts when they were sixteen or seventeen. Interestingly, whether the boy lived in a mother-only family as a teen-ager seemed to make little difference; it was the *early* experience that counted.

Family structure interacted with the aggressiveness of the boys in an instructive way. If the boy lived in a family with both his mother and another adult, preferably the father, and he had an aggressive temperament, he might become delinquent, but if he had a nonaggressive temperament, he was much less likely to break the law. These "low-risk" families, as Kellam called them, seemed better able to socialize their offspring so as at least to prevent unaggressive boys from becoming delinquent. But if the boy at an early age lived in a "high-risk" family (primarily, one with a mother only), he was more likely to become aggressive; moreover, even unaggressive boys in such circumstances would later become delinquent.[32] Family income seemed to make no difference.

At least in Woodlawn, boys who were, for whatever reason, aggressive at an early age were likely to become delinquent regardless of the kind of family they lived in. But boys who were not aggressive early on benefited significantly from living while young in a low-risk family—one in which the mother lived with the boy's father (or in some cases, with his aunt or grandmother). The data from this study have not yet been fully analyzed and we do not know whether other longitudinal studies will confirm this finding, but these preliminary reports suggest that, as we argued in Chapter 8, family conditions alone may be less important than the interaction of those conditions with temperamental characteristics.

If mother-only families reduce the extent to which some boys are adequately socialized, we still wish to know what is going on (or not going on) that accounts for this failure. There are several possibilities: Mother-only families may give less attention to children because there is only one parent to provide that attention; in terms of our theory, the available reinforcements may be too few or inconsistently given. Children in such families may experience more stress and discord, and hence less attachment; perhaps a young woman coping alone with a small child may be more likely to display the changeable moods and erratic demands described by Gerald Patterson in his studies of families with aggressive children.[33] Perhaps children in single-parent families are understimulated and suffer from a lessened development of verbal skills. Perhaps they lack a masculine role model. We do not know enough to choose among these explanations, even if we are certain that there is something to explain.

There are several studies that find that children raised in female-headed families tend to have lower verbal and full-scale intelligence scores, holding social class constant, than those of similar children raised in two-parent, stable families. A recent review by Marybeth Shinn of fifty-four studies of this relationship concluded that it existed, though more clearly for whites than for blacks.[34] Perhaps the most impressive of these, because it involved over twenty-six thousand children followed from before birth to age four, found that children had somewhat higher early IQ scores if their father was present rather than absent, even after holding constant race and socioeconomic status.[35]

One study suggests that boys in female-headed households are more likely to develop neuroses and to lack achievement motivation than boys in intact homes.[36] Whether boys who grow up in female-headed homes are more or less likely to develop a masculine (or an excessively masculine) identity is an unsettled matter: Biller[37] and Anderson[38] find the absence of a father impedes normal development of a masculine identity, especially when the boys approach adolescence, but Hartnagel[39] and Nobers[40] find that the effect of absent fathers differs by race; black mothers are more effective than white ones when the father is absent.

Anthropological studies that find more male aggressiveness in societies in which the father is aloof or distant (often sleeping apart from the wife) have been interpreted as implying that aggression is partly the result of boys having failed to resolve conflicts over their sexual identity,[41] but this interpretation could as easily be reversed. Perhaps those societies which for other reasons (such as economic or biological ones) have warlike customs deliberately separate the men from the women, as do the Masai, in order to create and maintain fraternal support for the warrior tradition.

Some Norwegian boys were studied whose fathers, being sailors, were absent from home for periods as long as two years. Various tests suggested that the boys were immature and dependent and displayed "compensatory masculinity," but an effort to duplicate the study in Genoa, Italy, failed to produce comparable results.[42] In Trinidad and Grenada, youngsters were asked whether they preferred to have a two-cent candy bar today or a ten-cent one next week. In both places, the children whose fathers were absent preferred the more immediate reward—that is, were more impulsive.[43]

Tantalizing as these clues may be, they offer no basis for any strong conclusions. A survey of studies of masculine identity concluded that nothing could be concluded.[44] Indeed, the role of the father in raising children has been the subject of so little systematic inquiry that we have little more than guesswork to rely on in interpreting any findings of the effect, if any, of a father's absence on later behavior.[45]

Among the many reasons for the unsatisfactory nature of our knowledge of these matters is the fact, apparent in our treatment of family socialization in the preceding chapter, that much of the writing on this topic—especially by sociologists and anthropologists—ignores individual differences among children that precede and may well influence parental behavior. Just as family discord may arise because parents are faced with the task of dealing with a difficult child, so too may families break up because of their inability to agree on how such a child should be treated. Russell found that the parents of babies who were more demanding (they cried a lot or had feeding problems) were more likely to experience crises and discord than did parents with quiet infants.[46] When Gath compared families having infants afflicted with Down's syndrome (i.e., mongolism) with a matched group of parents having normal children, he noted that the former group experienced a greater number of broken or discordant marriages than the latter.[47] This does not mean that problem children will always wreck marriages; indeed, there is evidence that some marriages—those that are strong to begin with—become even stronger when faced with the need to manage children with birth defects.[48] But we do mean that the child can be as much the cause as the consequence of family patterns, including broken homes and even abusive ones.

Abusive Homes

It is hard to imagine a child who is seriously abused by his parents not suffering some ill effects from the experience. When we note, then, that the consequences of child abuse are poorly understood, it is not from a desire to cast doubt on a commonsense understanding of family life but from a wish to achieve greater clarity about the effects of such abuse on one particular form of behavior, criminality. And when we observe, as have others, that the child is sometimes both a cause and a victim of parental abuse, it is not out of any desire to blame the victim for his suffering (willfully injuring a child is an inexcusable and usually criminal act) but out of a wish to grasp the complex interactions that generate abusive conduct.

The scholarly studies of the causes and consequences of child abuse are large in number but uneven in quality. There is no settled definition of abuse: Some studies limit themselves to cases of willful physical injury,[49] others include any form of physical punishment whether or not it causes an injury,[50] and still others include mental, sexual, and psychological abuse.[51] Most studies are of small groups of children who have been, by some definition, abused, with no effort to select the group so that it is representative of some larger population or to compare it with a control group of similar but nonabused children. Information about the family backgrounds of abused children are typically gathered retrospectively from parental interviews, with all the attendant problems of errors, distortions, and misrepresentation; when the families are observed directly, it is rarely done blindly—that is, by an observer unaware of whether the family is abusive or normal.

Perhaps the best studies are of very young children who, having been identified as physically maltreated, are then followed for a number of years by observers who actually watch the children at play or with their mothers. The chief limitation of these infant studies is that they tell us nothing about adolescent or adult criminality; however, if one accepts the conclusion, defended in the preceding chapter, that there is a high degree of continuity between infant and adolescent aggression, at least for males, some strong inferences can be drawn.

The central conclusions of these inquiries are that physical maltreatment (as well as some forms of psychological deprivation) impedes or even prevents the formation of a strong and confident attachment between infant and parent (usually, the mother) and that maltreated children tend to display more aggression in both psychological tests and play situations. George and Main compared ten toddlers who had been physically abused with ten nonabused children similar in age, sex, parental background, and social status.[52] The abused children were less likely to approach adults and more likely to harass or assault other infants and adults. Comparable results have been obtained from a comparison of twenty physically abused and twenty-two matched nonabused children in Chicago. The former were more likely than the latter to exhibit aggression on a Thematic Apperception Test (TAT) and during a brief play period and to be rated by their teachers as aggressive.[53] Aggressive responses to psychological tests were also found by Kinard to be more common among abused than matched nonabused children.[54]

But when Elmer followed abused and similar nonabused children, all from lower-income families, over an eight-year period, she was unable to detect any differences between the two groups in aggressiveness, intellectual development, or self-concept.[55] These contradictory findings are probably inevitable when researchers pick children known to be abused and then "match" them with others. The matching is usually limited to the readily observable features of family life, such as race, age, income, or neighborhood. There is no reason to assume that children and parents similar in these sociological categories are similar in those psychological variables, such as intelligence and temperament, that we know to be associated with aggressive or delinquent behavior, or to assume that the nonabusive parents do not maltreat or neglect their children in all ways save officially reported physical injury.

To resolve these issues, it is necessary to conduct a prospective, longitudinal, observational study of children picked more or less at random without any prior knowledge of whether they were abused. Just such a study has been under way for a number of years at the Minnesota Mother-Child Project, where two hundred children, all drawn from lower-income urban families with mothers who were mostly young, unwed, and relatively uneducated, were followed from just before birth for (so far) two years. Though these families might be especially at risk, there was no effort to choose families in which abuse had occurred. Such abuse or neglect as developed was detected after the observations began. Based on interviews and observations in the home, the mothers were divided into five groups—physically abusive, verbally abusive, neglectful or uncaring, psychologically "unavailable" (i.e., withdrawn, unemotional, or unresponsive), and normal. There were, of course, some overlaps among the first four groups. By age twelve months, the physically abused infants were less than half as likely as the normal ones to be securely attached, emotionally, to their mothers and three times as likely to be "anxious/avoidant"; the same pattern persisted at age eighteen months.[56] The abused children were also much more likely to express anger and frustration. Interestingly enough, the children of the psychologically unavailable mothers formed even weaker attachments than did those of the abusive ones: By age eighteen months, *none* of the infants with unresponsive mothers had developed an attachment (by comparison, nearly three-fourths of the children with normal mothers had). Similar findings have been reported by others.[57] Abusive or unavailable mothers also lower the performance of their children on certain measures of infant intellectual and verbal development,[58] though the relationship between this and adult intelligence or language skills is unclear.

These studies provide strong evidence that abuse and neglect make an important difference in a child's behavior. Some of that difference may rise from the beatings themselves (children who are often but unpredictably assaulted will, quite naturally, be a bit apprehensive about approaching their assaulters), but it is also possible that it is other aspects of the child-rearing practices of abusive families that most affect the children's behavior. Burgess and Conger have taken a close look at just how parents known to be abusive treat their children in routine situations.[59] For a total of six hours on four separate days, observers watched parents and children at play in their homes. The observers were not told which of the families were known to be abusive or normal, and when asked later, the observers could not guess which was which. The parents, but especially the mothers, of the abused children were much less likely than those of the normal children to initiate verbal or physical contact with their offspring. This suggests that it is not simply physical maltreatment that affects the child, but the reduction in reciprocally rewarding stimulation. A child in such a family will not only be somewhat fearful of his parents and learn through observation that aggression is an acceptable way of managing conflict, but will also find fewer rewards in daily interaction with his parents and thus be less likely to have his ordinary behavior reinforced by parental responses.

There are, in short, good reasons to think that abuse and, perhaps just as important, those child-rearing practices that may be associated with abuse contribute to a weakening of the infant-parent attachment and to the socialization process that ensues.

As the child grows to adulthood, it becomes progressively more difficult to link early experiences with later conduct. Longitudinal, observational studies cease (no one has tried to watch the same children for twenty years or more) and greater reliance must be placed on what people say happened to them when they were young and what they say they do as adults. Most of the research at this stage in the life cycle has been devoted to two questions. Do persons who were abused as children abuse their own children? Do persons who were abused as children commit crimes other than child abuse?

On the first question, the consensus of scholars is that abused children grow up to be child abusers. Spinetta and Rigler begin their review of the literature this way: "One basic factor in the etiology of child abuse draws unanimity: Abusing parents were themselves abused or neglected, physically or emotionally, as children."[60] Allan's review reaches a similar conclusion, quoting one author who refers to the intergenerational transfer of abusiveness as "the hostile pedigree."[61] But of course this formulation of the matter begs the question because it defines "abuse" to include neglect and defines "neglect" to include psychological as well as physical deprivation. Given what we learned in the preceding chapter, we are not surprised to learn that childhood experiences affect adult behavior; the question here is whether physical abuse, above and beyond levels of attachment and socialization practices, later causes a greater resort to physical abuse among adults. Put another way, does abuse cancel out the effects of an otherwise caring family, or does its absence add anything to an otherwise uncaring one? As Allan notes, very few studies on which the apparent scholarly consensus rests are free of sample bias, utilize control groups, or adequately cope with distortions and errors in recall.[62] Studies have shown that mothers are often unreliable sources of information about their parenting methods,[63] and thus there may be good reason for questioning parental reports of their own up-bringing. As Belsky observes, a consensus is not the same as an established fact.[64]

But even allowing for the methodological problems, it would be foolish to disregard the consensus, especially since it comports with common sense. Perhaps the fullest statement of the "hostile pedigree" thesis derives from the large national survey carried out by Murray A. Straus, Richard J. Gelles, and Suzanne K. Steinmetz.[65] They interviewed a random sample of over two thousand intact American families (a defect of the study, pointed out by the authors themselves, is that it excludes broken homes and that one-third of the families in the original sample refused to cooperate). They claimed to find strong evidence for the "social heredity" of violence. Family members who reported that their parents frequently hit them and each other were much more likely to say that they had used physical force on their own spouses and their own children. This connection seemed to persist after ex-cluding from the definition of force such things as pushing, grabbing, or slapping, and looking only at the potentially more serious forms of violence, such as hitting with a fist, object, or weapon. Unfortunately, their data were so poorly presented as to make it unclear what exactly the relationship was between the kind of force a person experienced and the kind he inflicted, and they had no information at all on whether the force produced an in-jury. It certainly seems clear that parents who were frequently subjected to physical punishment themselves inflicted physical punishment, but whether any of this constituted abuse of the sort found in the observational studies to which we earlier referred, we cannot say.

A parent who willfully and without justification injures a child has committed a crime, and so if being abused as a child leads one to abuse one's own child, we can conclude that child abuse contributes to subsequent criminality. Serious as this form of criminality may be, however, we still wish to know whether an abusive home will produce children who, other things being equal, are later more likely to commit crimes outside their families.

Here again, there is a strong scholarly consensus, and here again it is suspect. There are many studies of offenders, especially violent ones, that reveal them to have been exposed to highly abusive parents, but many if not most of these studies are clinical reports of five or six persons charged with murder or attempted murder who happened to come to the attention of a court physician or psychologist.[66] The subjects were not compared to any control group nor was any effort made to disentangle abuse from other predisposing factors; furthermore, in at least one study[67] most of the youthful offenders committed no further offenses against property or person during the ten years after discharge.

One of the few efforts to compare violent persons with nonviolent ones similar in age, sex, and race involved interviewing persons admitted to the Boston City Hospital because they had been engaging in violent behavior. The forty violent patients were more likely than the (roughly) matched nonviolent control group to say they had been severely beaten as children.[68] These conclusions are suggestive but are weakened by the possibility of a severely biased sample—many persons approached in the hospital refused to cooperate with the study.

One of the few large-scale studies of the criminal careers of abused or neglected children was done in eight counties in New York State by tracing, through official records, several thousand children referred to the Family Court. There was a tendency for children with an abusive or neglectful family background to be overrepresented among the more violent offenders, but it is hard to know what significance to attach to this in view of the absence of any control group.[69]

All this may well leave the reader baffled, recalling to his mind the cynical view that if all the scholars in the world were laid end to end, they still wouldn't reach a conclusion. Though the confusion and irritation are understandable, the reasons for them are inherent in the subject being studied. Child abuse can rarely be observed directly; it must be inferred from other, less reliable indicators. And such abuse probably does not occur in isolation from other factors—neglect, coldness, illness, poverty, immature parents, broken homes, social isolation, and various individual traits—that may also influence subsequent criminality. It would be remarkable if we could be certain that abuse and injury had an independent effect on criminality, or that their effect was the same for all children.

As we stressed in the preceding chapter, children are not merely the objects of parental behavior; they themselves contribute to it by virtue of their constitutional differences, sometimes eliciting support, other times producing hostility. Children and parents are embedded in a complex pattern of reciprocal stimulation and reinforcement. The differences among parents and children make the assumption that abuse will have a single major and readily observable consequence untenable on its face.

There have been efforts, for example, to distinguish among different kinds of abusive parents. Merrill[70] described four types. First, there are parents who are continually and pervasively hostile and aggressive. Their rage is general, sometimes focused on the world at large and at other times on a particular individual in response to seemingly trivial incidents of everyday life. Second, there are parents who are rigid, compulsive, and cold. They may be obsessed with cleanliness and continuously distressed by the normal messiness and high spirits of children. Third, there are parents who are passive, dependent, and indifferent; their moodiness reflects emotional immaturity. Finally, there are young, intelligent fathers who suddenly find themselves disabled and unemployed, forced to assume household duties while their wives work. The reader will see in these categories distinctions similar to those alluded to in Chapter 7 about personality factors that influence criminality more generally. In particular, one may recall how the aggression of "undercontrolled" personalities differs from that of "overcontrolled" ones.[71] In view of these differing kinds of potentially abusive parents, it would be a mistake to look for a single or major cause of abuse.

Children differ in the extent to which they elicit abusive behavior and in the ways they respond to it. Though most studies find, as we have seen, that abused children become more aggressive, some studies find them becoming more passive and withdrawn. When Rolston compared twenty abused foster children with twenty matched controls, he found that the former displayed *less* overt and fantasy aggression.[72] Indeed, the list of adjectives that have been applied to abused children in the available studies makes one wonder whether the investigators are all talking about the same thing. The children have been variously described as whiny, fussy, passive, compliant, fearful, listless, unsmiling, smiling, excessively vigilant, inhibited, withdrawn, aggressive, indiscriminately friendly, and totally unresponsive.[73] It is possible that these studies are of different kinds of abused children, or of children who, owing to constitutional factors, respond differently to similar treatment, or of children whose responses depend on situation and context, or all three.

Several constitutional differences affect a child's chances of being abused. Premature babies are more likely than those who go to term to be abused.[74] Both hyperactive[75] and excessively passive babies[76] may stimulate hostile mothering, perhaps because neither kind of child adequately reinforces a mother's friendly overtures. Closely spaced children in large families are more at risk;[77] so are stepchildren.[78] This has been interpreted to mean that the parents' capacity and inclination for nurturance are reduced when their attention must be spread over many children with similar demands or children who are not of their own blood.

Only in the last ten years or so have serious efforts been made to understand abusive behavior in the context of the reciprocal relationship between child and parent, and the results, though suggestive, remain unclear.

Far more research has been done on whether child abuse is more common among lower-class families. In part this focus reflects the assumption that membership in a social category, such as class, can explain behavior. But without some understanding of the psychological sources and consequences of class membership, that assumption is dubious, for reasons we shall set forth in Chapter 12. To some degree, though, this concern about the association between class and child abuse is an integral part of the argument about the extent to which abuse causes crime.

There has been a spirited debate on this question. Those who argue that child abuse is common to all social classes point out, correctly, that official reports of child abuse are inaccurate and incomplete. They also claim that upper-status persons are more disposed or better able to conceal child abuse from official notice; if this hidden abuse were added to that officially known, we would discover that it is a classless phenomenon.

On this matter, at least, we can speak with some confidence. Virtually all empirical studies, including those relying on self-reports rather than official reports, conclude that while abused children can be found in all social strata, they are disproportionately found among lower-status families. This was the conclusion of the surveys by Elmer,[79] Gil,[80] and Straus and colleagues.[81] A review of the available evidence led Pelton to conclude that both the prevalence and the severity of child abuse and neglect are strongly related to poverty.[82] Even among lower-income families, abuse is more common and more serious among the poorest of the poor.

What remains unclear is why this association should exist. One possibility, of course, is that poor families suffer from disadvantages that lead to heightened stress and this stress, in turn, finds expression in violent behavior of which the child is the innocent victim. This theory is a version of the view that frustration leads to aggression, a view which may be partially correct (no doubt some frustration does lead to aggression) but which we must not assume is wholly correct. The theory presented in Chapter 2 makes clear that there are many ways of responding to perceived inequity, of which aggression is but one; a full account of the matter must specify the circumstances in which people who find themselves receiving fewer rewards than what they expect will attack others, blame themselves, or alter their expectations.

Another possibility is that both child abuse and family deprivation have common causes. Parents who are impulsive and violent may find it as difficult to hold a job as they find it easy to abuse a child, especially if the parental personality conforms more to what Merrill called the pervasively hostile than to the rigid or passive.[83] Indeed, if there is any truth to the view that abusive parents were themselves abused and that abusiveness is part of a general pattern of family discord and neglect, then we would expect to find that disorganization as well as abuse are transmitted from one generation to the next.

Conclusions: Boys at Risk

Broken homes and abusive parents are the most dramatic indicators of an unsatisfactory family life and as such have become the focus of research, popular concern, and public policy. This is quite understandable: Single-parent homes are often unhappy ones, abusive parents are frequently criminal ones, and both kinds usually come to the attention of society. But because we are impressed by the gravity of these problems we should not assume that they are discrete events that can be described and explained in isolation from the entire pattern of family life and personal circumstance. There is strong evidence that abusive homes produce more aggressive children, and there are good reasons for supposing that early aggressiveness in the family is associated with later aggressiveness outside the family. But when we look for evidence of a direct connection between broken or abusive homes and subsequent criminality, we find that it is less clear-cut than we had supposed. The reason for this, we suggest, is that a broken or abusive home is only an imperfect indicator of the existence of a complex array of factors that contribute to criminality.

Some but not all broken homes will also be characterized by a weak parent-child attachment and inconsistent discipline, and children in these families will be less likely than those in affectionate and consistent families to internalize rules and temper their actions to the consequences. Some abusive parents will teach their children to express their frustrations by resorting to violent action, but the object of the child's later violence can vary greatly depending on other aspects of the family experience and on the situation in which he finds himself. Abused children may become tough soldiers instead of violent criminals, and of the latter, some will confine their violence to intimate settings and others will attack strangers.

Whether broken or intact, abusive or not, stressful and discordant families seem to have a greater adverse effect on boys than girls. Exactly why boys should be more vulnerable than girls to marital discord is not clear, but the fact seems well established. In their review of the relevant studies, Rutter and Giller show that, however measured, parental hostility and quarrelsomeness tend to be associated with conduct disorders among sons but much less so, if at all, among daughters.[84] There are several possible explanations. Hostile parents may quarrel more frequently in front of their sons than their daughters,[85] the constitutional traits inclining boys to greater aggressiveness than girls may unleash antisocial behavior whenever the socializing capacity of the home has been weakened,[86] or boys may be more dependent than girls on having a stable adult role model.[87]

There is, to the best of our knowledge, no careful, prospective longitudinal study that assesses the independent contribution of broken homes and abusive parents to later criminal behavior, holding constant individual predispositions, parent-child attachment, and family socialization. Were there such a study, we doubt very much that it would suggest that broken homes or abusive parents are beneficial to the child. Both would probably turn out to be factors that further impede adequate socialization. But for now, the safest conclusion is that the central features of family life—a fortunate biological endowment, secure attachments, and consistent discipline—are more important than whether it is a two-parent family, one with a working mother, or one in which corporal punishment is frequently employed.

Some idea of how these factors interact can be gleaned from asking a different question—not what kinds of families produce delinquent or miserable children, but what circumstances enable children to survive personal and familial circumstances that ordinarily lead to mental illness or criminality. One study that has tried to account for these remarkably resilient children has been done on the island of Kauai in Hawaii, where Emmy E. Werner and Ruth S. Smith followed all the children born there in 1955 for over two decades and subjected them to an elaborate battery of tests, home visits, and interviews.[88] Most of the six hundred or so children were Asian or Polynesian and lived in low-income families. Many of the children experienced a variety of stressful events in addition to poverty, including birth defects, perinatal complications, serious parental discord, absent or unemployed fathers, mentally ill parents, siblings with conduct or school problems, and unhappy relationships with either parent. The majority of children who, by the age of two, had experienced four or more of these stressful events developed serious learning or behavioral problems, including delinquency, by the time they were eighteen. But some did not. These resilient children were specially studied to find out what explained their ability to become normal adolescents despite familial backgrounds that ordinarily spell trouble. Among the boys who were resilient despite poverty and family crises—who, in the words of the authors, were "vulnerable but invincible"—the factors that seemed to make them able to cope with adversity were these: being the first-born, being perceived by the mother as a cuddly, active, and affectionate infant, having few early health problems, growing up in a family with four or fewer children, forming an especially close bond to the mother in the first year or two of life, and having a high IQ. In short, the fortunate children were those who combined certain constitutional traits, the luck of being first-born, and a responsive mother.

10

SCHOOLS

When a child enters school, he or she becomes part of one of the few state-supervised institutions in our society that attempt to alter, by plan, individual differences in behavior. As a result, the schools become for many of us the locus of our fondest dreams and greatest disappointments. We hope that within their walls dull children will become brighter and gifted ones brighter yet, unruly children will settle down and quiet ones will assert themselves. Sometimes this happens, but just as often whatever differences existed among children upon entering school seem to become, if anything, greater by the time they leave.

Both as parents and scholars, we are aware that children begin school with differing intellectual abilities; though we expect all children to benefit from their experiences there, we are not surprised when children who seemed brightest in the early grades turn out to be among the brightest in the later grades and when the slower children remain slower than the others during all of the grades. We naturally become distressed when bright children do less well than expected and not-so-bright children seem to fall farther behind; in these cases, we often speak to the teachers or complain to the school authorities. But when a child's experiences in school seem to conform to the child's natural aptitudes, we are usually contented, or at worst resigned.

We often have much different expectations, however, about the child's conduct in school. As parents, we want all children to comport themselves well in the classrooms. If a child begins the first grade displaying restless and impulsive behavior, we expect him to "settle down"; if a child starts off by being shy and withdrawn, we hope he will "open up." If the restless child becomes unruly and even violent, we often believe that it is because the teachers do not understand him, or even "pick on" him; if the withdrawn child never blossoms, we are inclined to think that it is because the teachers are "insensitive" to him. Sometimes we are right, but sometimes we are entertaining exaggerated expectations about the ability of schools to alter behavior. That exaggeration is often much greater among scholars than parents. Many students of child behavior and juvenile delinquency suppose that, though children may enter school with important constitutional differences in intellectual abilities, the only differences in behavior among children have been socially learned and hence can be socially unlearned. Children come equipped with a set of values and attitudes and labeled with a socioeconomic status; the attitudes and values can be modified and the socioeconomic status can be ignored, discounted, or (possibly) changed.

To the extent that one assumes that behavior is primarily determined by some continuing interaction between attitudes and social setting, the schools must bear a heavy responsibility for whatever behavior is displayed. There are at least two views about how schools ought to deal with a child who, on entering school, seems surly, rude, or impulsive. Persons who think the schools are "too soft" believe that teachers fail to discipline unruly children and thereby fail to inculcate proper standards of conduct in them. Whatever the child may have learned in the home, the school can, within broad limits, produce proper behavior in the classroom, and this in turn will help produce proper behavior later on in the child's life.

People who find the schools too harsh or restrictive, on the other hand, believe that teachers who confront an unruly or indifferent child will label him a "troublemaker" in ways that reinforce his tendency to make trouble. If the child seems uninterested in his studies or prefers some studies, such as manual arts, to others, the school's failure to adapt to these predispositions may frustrate his capacity to attain legitimate goals. If the child falls in with a group of disorderly youth during recess, he may well learn values that are at odds with what the school professes, and thus the school should worry about these peer relations.

Because schools exist chiefly to teach things that can be learned from books, because such teaching requires orderly classrooms and motivated pupils, and because the school system is embedded in the value system of the larger society, it would seem obvious that the schools are likely to satisfy neither kind of critics. In the view of both, the role of the schools in accounting for misconduct is likely to be a negative one—to the extent they make a difference at all, schools will tend to make matters worse. They will either fail to obtain the necessary level of conformity or require too much conformity, and thus they will harm difficult students by either rewarding their misconduct or stigmatizing, frustrating, or alienating their personalities.

That would, indeed, appear to be the lesson one could infer from the great majority of studies of the relationship between schooling and crime. Virtually every inquiry has concluded that young persons who have difficulty in school—low achievement levels, poor behavior—are much more likely than other children to be delinquents and become criminals. "A long series of studies—from 1936 to the present—have found negative associations between school performance (grades, educational tests, or liking for school) and delinquency."[1] Moreover, students who misbehave in school (by skipping classes, hitting teachers, or damaging school property) are much more likely than other students to drop out of school and to be delinquent.[2]

These findings, however, are consistent with several inconsistent theories. One is that children predisposed, by familial or constitutional factors, to misbehave will misbehave during and after school without regard to what happens there. Another is that predisposing factors are exacerbated by schooling so that individual differences in criminal tendencies existing independently of schooling are increased by school experiences. A third is that there are few, if any, important predisposing factors; rather, schools by means of either inadequate or excessive efforts to induce conformity produce delinquent behaviors in some children. In short, both the direction and the mechanism of the causal link between schooling and crime are unclear.

Alternative Explanations

Whatever else may be wrong with schools, they cannot be the sole cause of individual differences in criminality. For much of our early history, children did not go to school at all, yet some became criminals. Today, when most children are in school, some become involved in crime and others do not. Obviously, there must be some predisposing factors that, perhaps by interacting with school processes, determine which children are more likely to become delinquent. We already have a clue as to who the offenders are likely to be. Even after allowing for the defects of both official police statistics and self-report studies, it is clear that delinquent children are disproportionately males drawn from lower socioeconomic groups.[3]

The two most important theories of the school-crime linkage are the "common cause" and the "intervening variable" models. The first suggests that both difficulty in school and delinquency are the result of preexisting personal traits (the "common cause"); the second suggests that schooling is an important intervening variable that converts some preexisting (and possibly quite benign) personal traits into a disposition to commit crimes. If the first model is correct, schooling has little effect on criminality; if the second is correct, it has a great (though not exclusive) effect.

Common Causes

There are at least three sets of personal traits that might lead to both difficulty in school and to committing delinquent acts. First, children of low intelligence, especially the verbal component of intelligence, will have difficulty with schoolwork, particularly in those aspects that emphasize verbal skills. And if they do poorly at schoolwork, it stands to reason that they might express a dislike for it and drop out of school at the first opportunity. As we have seen, persons of low intelligence are also more likely than others to commit common predatory crimes. This may be because they do not understand the likely consequences of their actions, especially consequences deferred into the future, or because they find it difficult to manage their relations with other people by verbal communication, or for some other reason. Second, children who are temperamentally impulsive, extroverted, and aggressive are likely to find school—which demands sitting still, being attentive, and acting cooperatively—boring, confining, and unrewarding. They will not do as well as others in their schoolwork and will find it more exciting to skip classes, act up, and drop out. Though impulsive, aggressive personalities may not differ in intelligence from more passive individuals; the former are overrepresented among delinquents and criminals (see Chapter 7). Third, children who have been conditioned by their parents to ignore or discount the connection between actions and consequences (by, for example, being subject to inconsistent disciplinary practices) or who have been denied the opportunity to form a strong and affectionate bond with one or both parents may, whether they are constitutionally aggressive or not, find little connection between schoolwork and personal gratification, distrust or feel cold toward any source of adult authority, and not take seriously any claimed relationship between rules and conduct. Such persons will be troublesome in and out of school. Obviously, all of these factors may operate together in varying degrees.

One implication of the common-cause model is that the best predictor of current behavior will be past behavior. Persons delinquent in the twelfth grade will be the same as those delinquent in the eighth grade or even earlier. Another is that, holding constant the traits of entering students, delinquency rates will not vary among schools. One thing that is *not* implied by this model is that the delinquency rates of schoolchildren from the same family will be the same. Even traits that have a genetic origin will differ among siblings (unless they are identical twins), and of course siblings may well be raised differently by the same parents.

Schools as Intervening Variables

The same personal traits that in the common-cause model create both school problems and delinquency are among those attributes that may lead the school to create or heighten delinquent activity. In this view, a boy (or, occasionally, a girl) with below-average intelligence, an impulsive or restless temperament, or a hostile or suspicious attitude toward schooling and adults may become delinquent as a consequence of being victimized by one or both of two processes. First, he may suffer from being labeled (or "stigmatized") by the school as a misfit, so that he engages in misconduct he would not otherwise commit, as a result of a loss of self-esteem, receiving poor instruction from teachers who have decided in advance that he is a "failure," or being thrown into the company of similarly labeled youth who become unruly after being rejected by their teachers. Indeed, some proponents of this view doubt that there are any significant individual differences that determine school success—what appears to be a low IQ may in fact be the result of being tested unfairly, what seems to be low academic achievement may be the result of a "self-fulfilling prophecy" that leads teachers to give low marks to pupils they wrongly believe are dull, and what seems to be an unruly temperament may simply be the biased perception of teachers who judge all conduct by inappropriate "middle-class" standards.

Second, individual differences in aptitude and temperament may be real enough and teachers may avoid stigmatizing or rejecting such youth, but the school may offer a curriculum that the below-average or impulsive youth cannot master and finds irrelevant to his ambitions and life prospects. Misconduct and delinquency arise in this case out of frustration: Unable to do well in schoolwork that emphasizes verbal skills, some students will rely more heavily on their physical skills (including skills at fighting); unable to see any payoff from attending classes in history or mathematics, some students will act up in these classes or skip them entirely; convinced that students who do well in their schoolwork are no more deserving of the honors and opportunities that come their way than are students with less inclination to please the teacher, some of the latter will set right their own equity equations by taking things they want or by making life miserable for the "good" students.

Attentive readers will have noted that many of these explanations of how schools contribute to delinquency are merely special cases of the several sociological theories of crime presented in Chapter 2. The views that schools create crime by causing a loss of self-esteem or by causing excluded persons to seek out each other's company in order jointly to express their defiance are variants of labeling theory. The view that schools frustrate the attainment by some youth of legitimate goals is an example of strain theory. The view that schools provide an arena within which certain young persons can find friends who share their rejection of the values of middle-class society is an instance of subcultural learning.

The intervening-variable model of how schooling affects crime implies that rates of misconduct among children who are at risk should increase during their school careers as the effects of labeling, subcultural learning, or frustration become more acute. It also suggests that, holding constant individual differences on entry, rates of misconduct should vary among schools and among classrooms within schools, if there are variations in teacher practices or student populations. This model is unclear as to the long-term effects of schooling on crime. If the school effect is only the result of labeling, then crime caused by this process may end or be sharply reduced once schooling and its stigmatizing processes are ended. If schools frustrate the desires of certain boys to learn things that are relevant to their realistic job prospects, then presumably any crime or aggressive act that results from this frustration will end once the boy has managed to enter the labor market but may continue for boys who find such entry difficult. If schools affect crime by involving boys in deviant subcultures, then these effects may be long-lasting, unless the boy later (perhaps as a consequence of marriage) learns new values.

Evaluating the Models

It is not possible to evaluate conclusively these competing explanations of the connection between having problems in school and committing crimes. The necessary research—carefully measuring individual differences among children in early life and then closely observing their experiences and misconduct during and after school—has never been done. And some of the research that has been done is woefully inadequate. For example, one study sought to show the adverse effects on children of "tracking" (i.e., assigning pupils to classes based on the child's ability) without controlling statistically for individual differences in aptitude.[4] Even otherwise highly sophisticated analyses of delinquency often fail to take into account intelligence and temperament.[5] We can, however, narrow the area of disagreement by referring to studies that test, using a variety of methods, some implications of the models.

There is a substantial body of data suggesting that whatever effects schooling has on delinquency, they cannot be great. Sheldon and Eleanor Glueck followed the school careers of five hundred delinquent and five hundred nondelinquent white boys, selected from among similar neighborhoods and matched for age, ethnic origin, and (roughly) intelligence.[6] As we have already seen (Chapter 6), though the average full-scale IQ of the two sets of boys was about the same (92 for the delinquents, 94 for the nondelinquents), the nondelinquents tested significantly higher than the delinquents on the verbal tests and the delinquents tested slightly higher than the nondelinquents on the performance tests. Moreover, the delinquent boys changed schools more often than the nondelinquent ones, in part because they were in and out of reformatories. The Gluecks concluded that "despite the essential similarity of the two groups of boys in age and intelligence quotient, and taking into account the greater irregularity in school attendance of the delinquents, their [i.e., the delinquents'] school achievements were far below those of the non-delinquents."[7] For our purposes, what is most interesting about the findings is how early in their school career the delinquents began breaking the law and how long after their schooling ended they continued to do so. About 30 percent of the delinquents displayed their first "marked school misbehavior" before the age of eight; the average age at which the delinquent boys began misbehaving was nine and a half. Nearly half the delinquent boys had become troublesome before entering the fourth grade, three-fourths before beginning the sixth grade.[8] If school has a large effect, it must appear early in grammar school, long before tracking occurs or the curriculum begins to emphasize college-preparatory subjects.

The Gluecks followed these boys to age thirty-one. The criminal careers of the delinquents were long and serious and by no means came to an end once the presumed frustrations of compulsory schooling had ended (see Chapter 7). Only 2 percent of the delinquents graduated from high school (22 percent of the nondelinquents graduated); nearly two-thirds of the delinquents had left school by the time they were sixteen.[9]

Because the nondelinquents were selected from the same neighborhoods as the delinquents, they were of roughly the same socioeconomic status—about a third of each group had fathers who were unskilled laborers, another 40 percent or so had fathers who were truck drivers, teamsters, or in the semiskilled or skilled trades. Very few of either group's fathers held white-collar jobs.[10] Despite their comparable economic status, whatever labeling or class discrimination may have existed in the schools was not enough to convert the nondelinquent boys into delinquents. The two groups of boys did differ sharply, however, in their attitudes toward school—62 percent of the delinquents but only 10 percent of the nondelinquents disliked school. Moreover, the reasons given for disliking school were quite different. Of the delinquent boys who did not like school, nearly half (46 percent) said it was because they resented the restrictions and routine of school or simply had no interest in schooling; of the nondelinquent boys who did not like school, half said it was because they were "unable to learn" and scarcely any said it was because they resented restrictions or lacked interest.[11] In short, the delinquents did not like school and blamed their dislike on the school itself; the nondelinquents liked school, and when they did not, they blamed it on themselves.

Comparable results were obtained from another study of (primarily) working-class youth in Cambridge and Somerville (Massachusetts). About five hundred boys, selected (unlike in the Glueck study) before any had had a chance to become seriously delinquent, were followed throughout school and for decades thereafter. On examination, it turned out that the most delinquent boys were significantly less intelligent than the least delinquent ones and were more likely to be described by their teachers as troublemakers, show-offs, impatient, aggressive, talkative, uninterested in schoolwork, easily distracted, and impulsive.[12] Of course, it is possible that the boys became delinquent because the school failed them (by, for example, not trying to help those who displayed these temperamental problems), but in this case, we know that a special effort was made to help some of them. The boys were divided at the outset into treatment and control groups by matching pairs of boys for intelligence and fathers' occupation; a program was then provided for the treatment group (home visits by counselors). Over a long follow-up period, there was no difference in the delinquency rates between the two groups, and the relationship between delinquency and school problems was unaffected by the treatment.

The delinquent behavior of the four hundred or so working-class boys followed as they grew up in London also seemed largely unaffected by the kind of school they attended. Boys rated as troublesome by their primary-school teachers became delinquent in secondary schools at rates that were largely independent of the level of delinquency at the school they attended.[13]

All three of these studies had shortcomings. By picking known serious delinquents for their study, the Gluecks increased the chances that they would find that the boys had been getting in trouble from a very early age, almost regardless of their school experiences. By matching these boys with boys known not to be delinquent, they increased the chances that the two groups would differ sharply in other ways as well. Neither the Gluecks, the authors of the Cambridge-Somerville study, nor the researchers in London examined the nature of the boys' educational experiences in any detail. And the schooling these boys underwent was the kind that was available (in America) in public schools in the 1930s and 1940s or (in all three cases) in essentially working-class neighborhoods; perhaps more recent educational practices or those in different kinds of neighborhoods have a greater effect, for better or worse, on crime. Still, these studies so clearly show a pattern of delinquency beginning early and continuing unaffected by school that one must, at a minimum, be skeptical of any claims that school experiences will explain a great deal of the variance in delinquency, even when (as in all these studies) the youth involved are drawn from the less advantaged segment of society.

With this in mind, we can turn to a closer examination of the mechanisms by which schools may have some effect on individual differences in criminality. The first of these is, loosely, the process of stigmatization. The argument has been made by several authors; perhaps the best-known are Kenneth Polk and Walter E. Schafer, who have written two major accounts criticizing the schools for creating delinquency,[14] the first of which was published as part of the report of a United States government task force on juvenile delinquency. Though they claim that schools cause delinquency in many ways, an important part of their argument—and almost the only part for which they supply original data—has to do with the schools' tendency to label some children as lacking in ability or interest and thereby instilling in the students a lowered self-esteem and in the teachers an indifference (or even hostility) to the stigmatized pupils' educational needs.

The principal study by Polk and Schafer that provides support for the stigmatization argument was based on school data they gathered during the 1960s on nearly thirteen hundred students three years after they had entered one of two Midwestern high schools and, thus, at about the time they were either seniors or had dropped out.[15] The authors were especially interested in the effect on students of tracking, and so they examined separately the academic achievement, dropout rate, and extent of school misconduct and officially recorded delinquency of pupils in the college-preparatory and the noncollege tracks. The authors concluded that the rates of school misconduct and officially recorded delinquency were higher for students in the noncollege tracks than for the students in the college-preparatory tracks, and explained this by a combination of the mechanisms already described— the stigmatizing effect of being labeled "noncollege," poor teaching, arbitrary grading policies, exposure to an antischool student subculture, and the apparent lack of any connection between schooling and future employment prospects. The difficulty with drawing any of these conclusions is that the statistical tables apparently showing a relationship betwen tracking and misconduct do not control for those factors—intelligence and socioeconomic status—that are also associated with crime and that may explain all the relationship without reference to tracking. The way in which Polk and Schafer analyzed their data was so primitive as to render almost any conclusions for or against the stigmatizing theory (or any other theory) unwarranted.

A more careful effort to discover what relationship, if any, may exist between tracking and delinquency grew out of one of the most comprehensive surveys of high school males ever done. In 1966 over two thousand white and black males, randomly selected, were interviewed as they entered the tenth grade. They were then reinterviewed two years later as they neared the end of the eleventh grade, again a year later as they were about to graduate, and yet again a year after graduation. The surveys, part of the Youth in Transition study carried out by scholars at the University of Michigan led by Jerald G. Bachman, provided information on academic ability and achievement, family characteristics, personal values and self-concepts, occupational plans, and self-reports of delinquent behavior.[16] The students had been placed in various educational tracks; as one would expect, placement in tracks was strongly affected by academic ability, school grades, and social class. The authors were able to estimate the independent contribution that tracking (and every other measured variable) had on self-reported delinquency three and four years after the students' high school career began. They found that, holding constant personal attributes, tracking had no effect on either the frequency or the seriousness of the reported delinquency. The most powerful predictor of delinquency in the later high school years was the level of delinquency at the beginning of the high school years. Holding constant everything else, prior involvement in delinquent acts explained nearly half the variation in criminality among the students three or four years later. Strengthening the conclusion that tracking had no effect on delinquency was the fact that the track in which a student was placed had very little effect on whether he liked school; indeed, 87 percent of the students said, at the end of their junior year, that they were satisfied with the track (whatever it was) in which they had been placed and the curriculum which they were given.

The Youth in Transition data are broadly consistent with the earlier findings of the Gluecks—that delinquency begins early and that delinquents do not like school and perform poorly in it. It is, of course, possible that school experiences preceding high school have an important effect on delinquency. Neither the Youth in Transition study nor any other contemporary study of which we are aware can say much about this. But tracking does not ordinarily occur in the grammar schools or even in the first year or so of junior high school. If teacher attitudes cause delinquency by stigmatizing some youth, it must occur very early and in an informal way—if the Gluecks are to be believed, well before the fourth grade. It seems unlikely that elementary-school teachers can have so much and so long-lasting an effect on the delinquency rates of their pupils, but we cannot conclusively disprove this possibility.

There is another possibility that we can examine, however. We have noted throughout this chapter, and in greater detail in Chapter 6, the connection between intelligence and crime. But suppose that the intelligence tests used in this and other analyses are unreliable. Suppose that the tests, on the basis of which children are often tracked, are not valid predictors of academic achievement and that children placed in the noncollege track would do better, scholastically and behaviorally, if placed in the college track. We have already reviewed some of the criticisms of such tests (see Chapter 6); here we wish to consider the possibility, explicitly raised by Polk and Schafer, that the tests reflect teacher expectations about pupil performance and as a result cannot explain delinquency (or school achievement) by reference to any innate abilities. If delinquency is associated with measured intelligence, it may only mean that delinquency is associated with—even caused by—low teacher expectations of how the child will perform.

On the basis of a well-known study by Rosenthal and Jacobson entitled *Pygmalion in the Classroom*,[17] Polk and Schafer suggest that the expectations teachers have about pupil performance affect that performance so much that an IQ test may be nothing more than a self-fulfilling prophecy. What Rosenthal and Jacobson did was to have teachers in an elementary school located in a lower-income San Francisco neighborhood administer an intelligence test to their pupils after being told that the test would predict which students were most likely to show academic progress in the year ahead. The teachers were then given a list of those pupils who had allegedly done the best on the test and thus were most likely to spurt ahead. Actually, the students' names had been selected randomly. Then the pupils were tested again, several months later, again a year later, and yet again two years later. Compared to children in a control group who had not been described to their teachers as "bloomers" or "spurters," the children tested and taught by teachers who had formed favorable (though erroneous) expectations about them showed significantly greater gains in measured intelligence. This gain was greatest for children who had been placed in the middle track. In the early grades, some children gained twenty or more points in IQ.

The "Pygmalion effect" is used by Polk and Schafer, and by many others as well, to discount or dismiss claims that intelligence is a stable trait and, in particular, claims that intelligence and delinquency are connected. The difficulty with the argument is that it rests on a seriously flawed study, one that has been severely criticized[18] and never fully replicated. By Rosenthal and Jacobson's own data, many teachers did not, in fact, alter their expectations of their pupils' likely achievement and such gains in IQ as may have occurred apparently were limited to a few children in the very early grades.[19] And even these gains have proved hard to verify. By 1971, nine efforts had been made to duplicate in other settings the Pygmalion effect on IQ; none had succeeded in finding more than a very small one.[20] One careful effort to test the Pygmalion effect was done in twenty-two schools and involved over a thousand pupils.[21] There was some effect of teacher expectancy on the scores of some students from middle-income families but no significant effect on pupils from lower-income families. Moreover, interviews with the teachers revealed that they were often aware of the deception in the research: They knew that some of the IQ scores they had been given after the first test had been inflated. In several studies of teacher expectations, little evidence was found that these expectations were correlated with the social class of the students.[22] A recent review, by authors sympathetic to the Pygmalion concept, concluded that, though teacher expectations may affect grades, the efforts at replicating the Rosenthal-Jacobson claim of an effect on intelligence has led to "largely negative findings" and the criticisms of the original study "appear to be justified."[23] In sum, the connection between intelligence and delinquency in school cannot be dismissed on the grounds that measures of intelligence are nothing more than a proxy for teacher expectations.

We are not here asserting that individual differences in intelligence explain all or even most individual differences in crime among schoolchildren, only that the alleged spuriousness of IQ tests cannot be used to remedy the defects in those studies that claim to show how tracking (which is done in part on the basis of measures of student ability) causes delinquency by means of its stigmatizing effect.

But students may be disadvantaged by schools in other ways. Teachers may ignore, deprecate, or unjustly punish restless, slow, or impulsive students other than by assigning them to tracks. The association between poor school achievement and delinquency may involve a process of informal, hard-to-detect stigmatization. Since it is hard to detect, it is not surprising that cross-section or longitudinal studies of students in school fail to detect it. But perhaps it could be detected if schools were to make a special effort to help students who, because of ability or temperament, are most at risk. We have already seen how one helping program—in the Cambridge-Somerville youth project—did not have any effect, but that involved home visits by counselors, not the systematic provision of a special educational program.

At least two evaluated programs have made special efforts to overcome whatever disadvantages delinquency-prone youth have in school, including their vulnerability to being stigmatized or ignored. The first took place during the 1960s in Columbus, Ohio, where schoolteachers were asked to classify the boys in their sixth-grade classes as either likely or unlikely to get into trouble. Not surprisingly, the potential "bad boys," compared to the "good boys," were more likely to be from broken homes, to have a lower IQ, to be doing poorly in school, and to have come into contact with the police. The bad boys were then randomly assigned to either a treatment or a control group. Those in the control group were left in their regular classes in junior high school (as were all of the good boys); those in the experimental group were assigned to special all-boy classes in which the pupils were given programs in remedial reading, there was an emphasis on respecting the rights of others, and much of the curriculum was devoted to discussing positive role models, how one enters the work force, the nature of family life, and the like. One might suppose that being singled out for a special and remedial program might itself be stigmatizing. On the contrary: When interviewed, the boys in the experimental classes were overwhelmingly favorable to the program, thought all boys should be enrolled in it, and were convinced that their friends would benefit from it. Over seventeen hundred boys were followed over a four-year period. At the end, it was clear that the experimental program had failed—there were no significant differences in the frequency of seriousness of officially recorded delinquent acts between the bad boys in the experimental and the control groups.[24]

The other program took place in Kansas City, Missouri, also during the early 1960s. Four hundred inner-city boys, thought by teachers and peers alike to be seriously maladjusted and having below-average school records, were assigned, randomly, to either an experimental or a control group. The experimental group was given a special work-study program designed to orient its members to the world of work and to provide them with part-time paid employment during the school year and full-time employment thereafter. The amount of time the boys had to spend in regular classes was reduced. The students were followed for six years. There was no apparent effect of the program on delinquency—two-thirds of the boys came into contact with the police, and of these, two-thirds committed a serious crime.[25]

These experiments and others like them[26] do not prove that nothing can be done to help troubled youth (though they certainly cast doubt on any easy optimism one might have in this regard); perhaps other, better programs might have succeeded. But they are inconsistent with the view that the schools create delinquency as a result of neglecting, stigmatizing, or underteaching vulnerable boys.

The second mechanism by which schools might affect crime rates is the frustration hypothesis. Even if schooling does not stigmatize some boys in ways that lead them into crime, it may frustrate their ability to gain some legitimate goal. It may do this if pupils with poor verbal aptitude find themselves increasingly unable to master class material that requires verbal skills and, as a consequence, come to dislike school and rebel against it and its rules. Schooling may even produce this frustration-bred aggression, despite sincere efforts by teachers to help vulnerable students, if the students believe that none of the rewards of adult life to which they can reasonably aspire are contingent on doing well in schoolwork. Arthur Stinchcombe argued, on the basis of his study of students in a logging town in California, that boys from working-class families became rebellious (though not necessarily delinquent) as they realized that the schooling they were receiving had no payoff for them—they would end up with unskilled or semiskilled jobs regardless of what they did in school.[27]

The most complete and careful statement of this hypothesis is that supplied by Travis Hirschi.[28] His important research, alluded to in many other parts of this book (see, for example, Chapter 8), was based on questionnaires completed by over five thousand students attending public junior and senior high schools in Contra Costa County (near San Francisco), California. He analyzed the relationship between delinquency, both self-reported and officially reported, and a wide variety of familial and school factors. Here and elsewhere[29] he finds that delinquents have lower intelligence than nondelinquents, though in this study his measure of intellectual ability is not an IQ test but the Differential Aptitude Test (DAT) verbal scores, which are highly correlated with the verbal components of IQ.

Hirschi explicitly rejects the possibility that intelligence affects delinquency directly—for example, by reducing the ability of a person to foresee the consequences of his actions or to underestimate the risk of detection. Rather, the link between intelligence and delinquency is mediated by school experiences that have weakened his commitment to the conventional order.

In terms of our model presented in Chapter 2, the value attached to not committing crime (a good reputation, a quiet conscience) has been reduced for the less gifted person who has been frustrated by his inability to do well at schoolwork. A difficulty with this explanation, acknowledged by Hirschi, is that the correlation between aptitude scores and statements about whether the students like or dislike school, though in the predicted direction, is quite small: +.11.[30] If students who have difficulty with school turn to delinquency because of the dislike of schooling engendered by that difficulty, one would expect the correlation to be higher. On the other hand, Hirschi's multivariate analysis of the data suggests that, when the effects of aptitude, grades, and attitudes toward school are simultaneously taken into account, each makes some independent contribution toward explaining the number of self-reported delinquent acts.[31]

Consistent with Hirschi's findings are studies suggesting that the number of crimes committed by young persons, especially those from lower-income families, may decline after they drop out of school and certainly gets no worse. For decades, well-meaning reformers have tried to devise ways of keeping youth in school as long as possible, at a minimum through high school, partly in hopes that the more schooling a boy has, the better citizen he will be. If Hirschi and others are correct, the opposite is more likely to be the case, at least for boys with little verbal aptitude and a dislike of school. The longitudinal study of high school boys mentioned earlier—the Youth in Transition project—discovered that boys who reported having committed delinquent acts were much more likely than others to drop out of school before graduating, but that after they dropped out, their self-reported delinquency rates did not change.[32] Another study, this one involving boys from several California schools, found that the delinquency rates of lower-status boys (but not higher-status ones) decreased after they dropped out of school.* [33]

But there are some important difficulties with the theory that low aptitude leads to poor schoolwork, which in turn causes frustration, a dislike of school, a rejection of its authority and, thus, delinquency. One is that, at least in the few studies that have been done on this topic, the association between low IQ and antisocial behavior is found in children well before they are of school age.[35] Of course, later on schools may intensify misconduct because of the frustration low-IQ pupils experience there, but so far as we can tell children with low IQs are more likely to have behavior problems even when they are four or five years old.

Another difficulty with the frustration theory arises from the fact, sug-

---

* Some scholars[34] have claimed that crime rates always peak just before the school-leaving age, but for reasons discussed in Chapter 5, we are not convinced of this.

gested by some studies, that students may do poorly in school for reasons having nothing to do with low intelligence, without becoming delinquent. Chief among these other reasons are specific learning disabilities, such as dyslexia (an impaired ability to understand written words) and aphasia (a reduced ability to understand spoken words). These perceptual or motor handicaps are not correlated with intelligence—a dyslexic child, for example, is just as likely to be bright as a nondyslexic one. One review of all the studies of the presumed link between such learning disabilities and delinquency that had appeared through 1975 failed to disclose any reliable evidence of such a connection.[36] A 1981 study involving over sixteen hundred boys, ages twelve through fifteen, found no evidence that learning-disabled boys were more delinquent than normal ones, though it seems that when a boy committed a delinquent act, he was more likely to be *convicted* if he was learning disabled than if he was not.[37] If children who do poorly in school because of low intelligence become delinquent, then why not children who do poorly because of other handicaps?

There are two possibilities—that low intelligence leads *directly* to higher crime rates (because, for example, low IQ makes it more difficult for persons to adapt their actions to the consequences of those acts) or that there are other factors, found in association with low IQ but not with learning disabilities, that cause crime. Or both.

Almost every study we have of delinquent schoolboys finds that they are temperamentally as well as intellectually different, on the average, from other children. In Hirschi's study, the delinquent boys were "fatalistic"— that is, they felt that they had little control over the future, could not anticipate it, and hence should live for the day and let tomorrow take care of itself.[38] The Youth in Transition survey found that dropouts were more likely than those who stayed in school to be impulsive, aggressive, irritable, anxious, resentful, and to have a variety of "somatic symptoms," such as trouble sleeping and difficulty getting up in the morning.[39] We have already seen (Chapter 7) that criminals do poorly on the Porteus Maze Tests and on other measures of impulsiveness even when these scores are not strongly related to intelligence.[40] The poor school achievement of delinquents probably is the result of some combination of intelligence and temperament, and this combination may, in turn, help explain their delinquency.

Changing Delinquency by Changing Schools

Perhaps the best way to find out whether schools contribute to crime independently of the personal attributes of their pupils is to see whether different kinds of schools lead to different rates of delinquency, controlling for the characteristics of the students. It is remarkable and a bit dismaying, given the great attention devoted to schools as influences on delinquency, that so little effort has been made to find out if different kinds of schools lead to different behavioral outcomes. On second thought, perhaps it is not so astonishing; after all, scholars often assumed that schools made a large difference in learning until research, such as the so-called Coleman report in the 1960s, cast doubt on whether any obvious or measurable features of schools—buildings, expenditures, pupil-teacher ratios, and so forth—had any effect at all, at least within the existing range of variation in such factors, on what children learned, independent of the family background of the students.[41]

Whatever the failures of social scientists, parents believe that schools make a difference, and they act, often at considerable expense, on that belief. Parents sometimes decide where to live on the basis of the presumed ability of the local schools to teach and control their children; at other times parents will spend money they can ill afford to send their children to private schools where the "atmosphere" is better. Of course, just because parents act on these beliefs does not make them correct. And even if schools do affect how children behave while in school (as they almost surely do), it does not follow that schools will have any lasting effect on the criminality (or law-abidingness) of young persons after they leave school.

One of the few systematic efforts—and without much doubt, the best of these efforts—to see what difference schools make was undertaken by Michael Rutter, a British professor of child psychiatry, on the effect of secondary schools in London on the children who entered them.[42] The research began in 1970 with a survey of all the ten-year-old children living in one part of London. It found that the behavioral problems of these children were strongly linked with "family adversity"—discord, mental disorder, parental criminality, and low occupational status. The children were then followed through 1974, after they had turned fourteen and been in secondary school for about three years. The schools served an inner-city, largely working-class area with a substantial immigrant population; over a quarter of the fathers of the children had been convicted of some offense, and 8 percent had been in prison. On tests of mental aptitude, the children were, on the average, well below the national norm. The twelve schools that were studied had many things in common (e.g., all required their pupils to wear some kind of uniform and all maintained a rather formal relationship between teachers and students). But there were also important differences: Some schools were all-boy, some all-girl, and some coeducational; some were small and some quite large; some were entirely financed by the government and some were dependent on church organizations.

Police records were combed for information on all delinquent acts committed by the students through age seventeen. As one would expect based on other research, the lower the verbal intelligence score of the youth and the lower the occupational status of the parents, the higher the probability of being delinquent.[43] These individual differences accounted for most of the differences in delinquency rates among schools, but not all. Comparing boys (girls had too few delinquencies to be included in the analysis) of similar verbal intelligence and socioeconomic status revealed that which school they attended made a significant difference in the probability of being a delinquent. For example, for similar boys, the proportion delinquent was three times greater at the "worst" school than at the "best" school.[44] (Unfortunately, the authors tabulated only the proportion of boys who were ever delinquent, and not the *rate* at which boys committed offenses. For reasons explained in Chapter 15, this may be misleading.) Within a given school, the relationship between intelligence and social class on the one hand and delinquency on the other was more or less stable. Schools, in short, did not eliminate the effect of these individual differences on crime, but they did seem to alter the magnitude of that effect.

On the whole, the schools that did the best job of reducing the expected level of delinquency were also the ones that did the best job of improving educational achievement, maintaining good attendance, and reducing misbehavior in school. This finding is interesting enough, but the great contribution of the Rutter study is that it also sheds light on why some schools do a better job than others. The physical and administrative arrangements of the schools made no difference: Size, floor space per pupil, age of buildings, pupil-teacher ratios, the source of financial support, and the socioeconomic makeup of the student body were unimportant. What was important was the "intellectual balance" of the student body and the "ethos" of the school organization. The schools that did the best job in reducing delinquency were those with the highest proportion of the most able students; the schools that did the poorest were those that had the highest proportion of low-IQ students.[45] Bear in mind that none of the schools had a large proportion of gifted children, who had mostly gone to highly selective British schools. But given the students they had, the schools that did the best—not only in reducing delinquency but also in improving attendance and enhancing educational attainment—were those with a "reasonable balance" of academically gifted children who, the authors speculate, found school rewarding, identified with its aims and rules, and set the tone for the rest of the students. When the proportion of low-IQ students became too high, they then set the tone for the school as a whole, a tone expressive of frustration and restlessness.[46] Whether the student body was balanced in socioeconomic terms was not important.

By "ethos" Rutter and his colleagues refer to the social organization of the school and the classroom. A desirable ethos—one that contributes to lessened delinquency and higher achievement—involves a teaching style that emphasizes the value of schoolwork, rewards good performance, and utilizes fair but firm disciplinary procedures. Good teachers are free with their praise while insistent on their rules. The attentive reader will note the striking similarity between Rutter's account of a good school ethos and our account in Chapter 8 of a constructive family environment: Both are "warm and restrictive."

These two variables—intellectual balance and school ethos—contributed independently to reducing the expected level of delinquency, with the former being the more important.[47] We cannot say, of course, whether the decline in delinquency persisted after leaving school, whether Rutter's finding would hold true for American schools, whether he would have obtained different results if he had used delinquency rates (crimes per year per boy) rather than the percentage of boys ever delinquent, or whether any results would have changed if he had used self-reported rather than officially reported delinquency.[48] But as it now stands, this is the best research we have that shows how intelligence contributes both directly and indirectly, through school processes, to delinquency.

There is growing agreement among scholars as to the characteristics of those schools that seem able to enhance learning and maintain order. One recent review of several studies led to conclusions remarkably similar to those drawn by Rutter and his colleagues. Effective schools have an ethos based on clear goals, high expectations, and fair but firm discipline, and this ethos, in turn, seems chiefly to require parental involvement, strong leadership by the principal, and a stable and well-motivated staff that collaborates in planning a clear program.[49] For example, a large American survey sponsored by the National Institute of Education found that schools with low levels of crime were (not surprisingly) located in low-crime communities. But after allowing for that, the schools with little crime on campus were described by their students as having teachers who enforced the rules and who did so without displaying hostile or authoritarian attitudes.

A careful analysis of these data—drawn from over six hundred public schools and involving more than thirty thousand students—concluded that "when students report that rule enforcement is firm and clear, their schools experience less disruption." There was little evidence that "student partici-pation in the generation of these rules is a necessary ingredient." What was essential was the "firm, clear, persistent, and even-handed application of rules."[50] Beginning in 1980, efforts have been under way in several schools across the country to implement this lesson, and a preliminary evaluation suggests that some may have been successful in reducing criminal victimiza-tion within schools and among specific groups of individuals within those schools.[51]

If deliberately altering the ethos of a school helps reduce delinquency, this will only confirm what many parents have long believed—namely, that the "warm but restrictive" environment of private and parochial (i.e., Cath-olic) high schools creates more orderly classrooms than can be found in public schools, even after controlling for differences (in family background and the like) among the entering students. James Coleman and his col-leagues support this view with data gathered on nearly sixty thousand stu-dents attending over a thousand public, private, and parochial high schools in the United States during 1980.[52] They show that private and Catholic high schools are much less likely than public high schools to have a serious problem of fighting, vandalism, truancy, drug abuse, alcoholism, or verbal abuse of teachers, and that these differences persist, albeit at a lower level, after taking into account the measurable skills and traits of the students. (We do not, of course, know whether the students differed importantly in unmeasured ways. No one can prove conclusively that different kinds of schools produce different effects except by randomly assigning students to them—a procedure that is rarely possible.)

Moreover, the ability of private and parochial schools to induce better behavior among their students and to maintain a stricter disciplinary en-vironment seems to benefit the educational process—student achievement scores, notably in reading and mathematics, are higher in these schools than in public ones *because* of the more orderly atmosphere of the classroom.[53] We do not know, however, whether the apparent ability of certain schools to produce order has any lasting effect on the delinquency of their students. The order produced may be short-lived or may have no effect, not even a short-lived one, on student behavior out of school.

Efforts to use schools to produce more law-abidingness among children often focus on junior or senior high schools. This emphasis is understand-able, given the fact that it is in these schools that the greatest problems of disorder and delinquency are likely to occur. But since we know that the high-rate, serious offender is likely to begin his career at an early age, we must wonder whether it might not be better to devise school programs to reduce the onset of delinquent inclinations among very young children than to organize such programs to cope with delinquent behavior among teen-age children.

There is some evidence that certain programs for preschool children may affect the prevalence of delinquency a decade later among the graduates of those programs. The Perry Preschool Program was begun in Ypsilanti, Michigan, in 1962 for three- and four-year-old children drawn from one of the poorest neighborhoods in the city. Most of the children came from families on welfare; nearly half lived with only one parent, usually the mother. All the children selected had IQs between 70 and 85 (average = 79). The 123 children were randomly assigned to experimental and control groups. Those in the first group attended a special preschool program for about twelve hours a week for one or two years; those in the second were in no program. The two groups were repeatedly tested, and when they reached the age of fifteen, those youth who could be located (80 percent of the original participants) were interviewed and self-report data on their delinquent acts were gathered. Their parents and teachers were also interviewed.

The teen-agers who had been in the experimental program were much less likely than those in the control group to have been arrested or to report having committed more than one crime. Over half the members of the control group, but only one-third of those in the experimental group, reported having committed five or more offenses.[54] Those who had been in the preschool program also were rated by their elementary-school teachers as better behaved. There is some evidence of a temporary gain in IQ scores, though by age eight these had pretty much disappeared. Whether these achievements of the Perry program can be verified and duplicated remains to be seen, but they suggest the possibility of an early intervention that might produce more beneficial effects than do the dismal findings from experimental efforts in junior and senior high schools.

Conclusions

The full story of the effects, if any, of schooling on crime cannot be told; the studies we have, informative as they are, leave many questions unanswered. But the evidence from the best of these studies is consistent with the view that individual differences affect crime rates both directly (the common-cause model) and indirectly (the intervening-variable model), the latter occurring as personal attributes interact with school processes. Boys with below-normal verbal intelligence will commit more crimes, on the average, than boys with higher verbal skills, whether or not they attend a good school, but if they attend a good one, their probability of committing a crime—and the probability of their brighter friends committing a crime—will drop. Perhaps the same relationship between schools and behavior exists with respect to other personal traits, such as temperament and attitudes. A "good school" seems to be one that, regardless of its socioeconomic composition, is not swamped with low-aptitude students and provides a firm but nurturant social environment in its classrooms. In the United States, such an environment appears to be more readily attained in private and Catholic schools than in public ones.

Boys who attend a poor or mediocre school are likely to find that the personal deficits with which they begin their schooling are unaffected or made worse. Success in schools comes to students with good verbal skills; boys without those skills are likely to seek other rewards, such as those that accrue to physical prowess. The benefits of schooling lie in the future; boys who are impulsive are likely to discount those future rewards heavily and allow their actions to be governed by more immediate consequences. Teachers expect their students to conform to rules and to defer to their authority; boys from cold families with inconsistent disciplinary practices are likely to attach little value to such teacher expectations and, if the teacher attempts to enforce those expectations in the same cold and inconsistent manner as the parents, the boys may well rebel even more. In this way, deficits that had a constitutional or familial origin accumulate and, possibly, worsen.

The accumulation of deficits can be moderated or reversed, but only with difficulty and then chiefly for the less serious offenders. The chronic, major offenders, as we have seen in study after study, begin their delinquent careers very early in life, well before schools make any very difficult demands. Special programs designed for the most troublesome youth, such as those in Columbus and Kansas City, are not likely to have much effect, even though the boys themselves like them. There is some evidence—but as yet not much—that preschool programs aimed at preventing the emergence of high-rate offending may have some value.

Schools may also affect criminality in ways that are largely independent of what teachers do. A school, after all, brings together a large number of young persons. If the school is in a high-crime neighborhood, boys attending it will be more likely to meet high-rate offenders than if the school were in a low-crime area. Thus, the school may contribute to criminality because of the peer groups that form there. These peer and community influences are the subject of the next chapter.

IV

SOCIAL CONTEXT

11

COMMUNITY

Since the early nineteenth century, criminologists have been struck by the fact that some places consistently have more crime than others. In 1835, Quetelet mapped the distribution of crime in France; a century later, two sociologists, Clifford Shaw and Henry McKay, were mapping the distribution of delinquency in Chicago.[1] For decades this approach to the study of crime—now called the ecological or areal approach—dominated much of criminological thought, drawing its influence not only from scholarly findings of an apparent connection between crime and area but also from the common experience of citizens who understood that in every city there were bad neighborhoods that one avoided.

Since some areas persistently displayed higher crime rates than others, it was only natural for scholars to suspect that this connection between geography and crime was not accidental but the result of profound, territorially based social forces, and so a search was launched to identify and, where possible, correct those forces. The most influential effort was that of Shaw and McKay, who discovered not only that certain Chicago neighborhoods had high delinquency rates but also that they had them despite large and often rapid population turnovers. A community populated by members of one ethnic or racial group would retain, after a period of instability, its distinctive delinquency rate, even after having been invaded and settled by members of a quite different group. This finding suggested that there was something about the neighborhood itself that was more important in determining the crime rate than the people who happened to live there.

What this something was could be learned by seeing neighborhoods as the result of a process of urban growth in which land uses were determined by the social and economic needs of citizens. The central area of every city, because of its centrality, would be devoted to commercial uses; surrounding it would be undesirable residential areas in which homes were mixed with industrial properties. As people could afford nicer neighborhoods, they would move away from the central and interstitial areas and be replaced there by less affluent newcomers. Each neighborhood would acquire a distinctive character that reflected its mixture of land uses and institutions (stores, churches, schools, entertainment facilities), a character that would be transmitted from one generation (or one ethnic group) to the next. Inner-city areas, unable to sustain normal family and social life, would be characterized by social disorganization that would persist over time, producing high rates of delinquency (and of truancy, adult crime, infant mortality, and mental illness) among whatever group happened to live there.[2] When the delinquency rates of neighborhoods were displayed on a map, they would follow a distinctive pattern—high rates in or near the central city, steadily declining rates as one moved away from the center.

Shaw and McKay had few, if any, direct measures of "community culture" or of the processes by which it was passed from one generation to the next. But theirs was, at the time, an intuitively satisfying account of crime patterns, for it accorded with everyday experience, it was consistent with the sociological view that impersonal social forces and not individual traits were the principal cause of high crime rates, and it suggested a strategy for action—physically improving slum neighborhoods and socially enhancing slum institutions. Urban renewal and community development, such as the Chicago Area Project, were direct outgrowths of this perspective.

Subsequently, various scholars attempted to find more and better measures of neighborhood characteristics that could be used, statistically, to explain crime rates.[3] These attempts have produced few results that command much support. One important reason is that any effort to explain the behavior of individuals by means of the characteristics of the areas in which they live is likely to involve the ecological fallacy—that is, falsely imputing to an individual the properties of a group to which he belongs. For example, a high-crime neighborhood may have few churches, many factories, and a large proportion of female-headed families, while a low-crime area may have many churches, few factories, and no female-headed families. But without data about individuals, we cannot say whether those who commit crimes are influenced by churches or factories or are members of female-headed families.

Another reason is that the ecological theory leaves the question of causality unsettled. A neighborhood may have much crime because conditions there cause it or because certain kinds of neighborhoods attract persons predisposed to criminality.[4] A test of the possibility that people shape neighborhoods more than neighborhoods shape people was made possible in Great Britain by the fact that the government there has devoted great energy and large sums to relocating persons from decaying inner-city areas to new public housing in outlying areas, so much so that in many large English cities today as much as half the housing is publicly managed. Yet relocating families to new and better public housing has not reduced levels of delinquency, which have continued to rise.[5]

Moreover, the stability once displayed by Chicago neighborhoods in the face of ethnic succession seems to have disappeared. A careful study of delinquency rates from 1940 through 1970 suggests that the stability found by Shaw and McKay held true only through 1950; since then, the officially recorded delinquency of the neighborhoods has changed sharply with changes in their social—especially their racial—composition.[6]

The possibility that neighborhoods have only a modest effect on criminality should not be surprising to readers familiar with the longitudinal studies of criminal careers that we have reviewed in the preceding chapters. Once we take into account the influence of constitutional factors, family socialization, and school experiences, there is not much left to explain, at least insofar as serious offenders are concerned. The great majority of persons who commit crimes at high rates begin their criminal careers at quite early ages;[7] there are relatively few "late bloomers." In studies of schoolboys, the best predictor of delinquency in the higher grades is delinquency in the lower grades (see Chapter 10).

However, we cannot leave matters at that. Though children are shaped by families (and possibly school) experiences, families and schools may be shaped by community conditions. Some of those conditions—labor markets and the availability of drugs and alcohol—will be discussed in later chapters. Here we wish to look more closely at three aspects of the social setting of neighborhood life that might affect the recruitment of young persons into crime or the rate at which they commit crimes once recruited: peers and gangs, the social boundaries of the neighborhood, and the density of criminal targets and social surveillance. Unlike the traditional ecological studies of crime, we first take into account individual differences and then ask how, if at all, the behavioral effect of these differences is amplified or constrained by the social setting in which they are found. Though this setting may have many effects, we shall examine in particular those most obviously related to the behavioral theory sketched in Chapter 2. Peers may affect the value a person assigns to the rewards of crime, the social boundaries of the community may affect the value he attaches to the rewards of not committing a crime, the density of targets may affect the time delay between a given moment and the opportunity for committing a crime, and the intensity of informal community surveillance may affect the probability of being caught and punished.

Peers and Gangs

There are two views of the influence of peers on a young person's criminality. One, popularized by such accounts of gang life as *West Side Story* and given academic expression by Edwin Sutherland's theory of differential association, is that gangs—and more generally, peer groups—cause crime by altering the values or changing the rewards of an individual. Bad boys produce badness in other boys: Rotten apples spoil the barrel. The other view, having few popular versions but many academic ones, is that young persons are criminals before they join gangs; instead of being led into a life of crime by the influence of peers, they merely seek out those peers who share their interest in delinquency: Birds of a feather flock together.

The strongest evidence for the influence of peers on a young person's criminality is the fact that most juvenile crime, unlike most adult crime, is committed by persons in groups. Using official police or court data, Shaw and McKay,[8] Eynon,[9] and the Vera Institute[10] found that the proportion of arrested juveniles who had committed their offenses in groups was never less than 50 percent and for most property offenses was well over 70 percent. Using self-report studies, Erickson,[11] Erickson and Jensen,[12] and Hindelang[13] all found that crimes to which juveniles admit are usually committed in groups, though the extent of group involvement based on these self-reports is less than what appears in official statistics. A Rand survey of prisoners in California found that offenders aged eighteen to twenty were much more likely to have been arrested in a group than those aged twenty-one and over.[14] Finally, analyses of victimization surveys, in which victims report, where possible, on whether their assailants acted alone or as part of a group, show that younger offenders are more likely to act in groups than older ones, though the surveys (which generally have data only on those offenders committing crimes of violence) suggest lower group involvement rates than either official or self-report studies.[15] (Some self-report studies suggest that most delinquent acts are committed alone rather than in groups.[16]) In sum, most youthful property crimes, at least of those that come to the attention of the police, and a small but significant proportion of youthful personal crimes are committed by young persons in groups.

This fact, combined with the reasonable supposition that young persons are influenced—perhaps profoundly—by the expectations of their peers, has led scholars to offer a variety of theories purporting to explain how youth groups cause or increase crime and delinquency. Peers supply a young person with values conducive to crime,[17] reinforce the core values of lower-class culture,[18] satisfy the need of males to prove their manhood,[19] provide, in the case of violent gangs, a stimulus for unstable, sociopathic personalities,[20] teach criminal ways of achieving middle-class goals whose attainment by legitimate means is blocked by the larger society,[21] or inculcate opposition to the goals of middle-class society as a way of coping with "status frustration."[22] These theories differ in their account of how, and for what reason, peers and gangs contribute to crime, but they are in agreement that the contribution is a large one.

Unfortunately, scarcely any of these theories is supported by adequate empirical data. While group involvement is consistent with the theory of peer influence, it does not prove it. Youth crimes may be committed in groups because young criminals like to associate together, not because the group has had any effect on its members. And offenders who act alone may be responding to rewards (in prestige or protection) conferred by peers not present at the time. Indeed, many of the theorists offered no data at all.[23] When others have attempted to test the extent of peer influence, the results have been, at best, inconclusive. For example, Short[24] showed that there was a strong correlation between being delinquent and saying that one had delinquent friends, but that does not prove that one's peers caused one to become delinquent. Similarly, Erickson and Empey[25] found that having delinquent associates was more strongly associated with becoming delinquent than was social class, but this conclusion is as consistent with the view that birds of a feather flock together as it is with the view that rotten apples are spoiling the barrel. Any study claiming that having delinquent peers causes delinquency is suspect if it does not first take into account the fact that much juvenile crime occurs in a group setting for reasons that may or may not have anything to do with the influence of peers on one another.

One major study provides evidence that peers have, at best, only a weak influence on self-reported delinquency. Hirschi administered questionnaires to junior and senior high school children in the San Francisco Bay area; the answers of the boys, over two thousand in all, formed the basis of the analysis.[26] Hirschi found, as have others, that over three-fourths of the

boys who reported having committed two or more delinquent acts had at
least one close friend who had been picked up by the police, while only a
third of the boys reporting no delinquency had a close friend with a police
record.[27] But Hirschi looked closely at this connection in light of other
things he knew about the boys and concluded that both being delinquent
and having delinquent friends were the result of the breakdown (or the absence) of those social controls, chiefly deriving from being strongly attached
to parents and schools, that ordinarily inhibit crime. When Hirschi held constant the number of delinquent friends the boys had, he found that the boys
who committed crimes were those who had a low stake in conformity; when
he held constant the stake in conformity, the association between delinquent
companions and delinquent acts dropped significantly.[28]

Moreover, contrary to the assumptions of many gang theorists, Hirschi
found that the more delinquent the boy, the *less* value he attached to the
opinions of his friends.[29] Gangs (or criminally inclined peer groups), far
from attracting the loyalty of their members, seem to be the refuge of boys
with little respect for the opinions of friends; by the same token, boys who
do value the opinions of their friends, even friends who are delinquent, are
least likely to break the law. This conclusion is comparable with one reached
earlier by Short[30] and by Short and Strodtbeck[31] and with the even earlier
findings of Sheldon and Eleanor Glueck,[32] who, in their study of five hundred delinquent boys, found that the onset of delinquency preceded participation in juvenile gangs.

After Hirschi's book appeared, its main conclusions regarding the weak
influence of peers on delinquency were supported by other studies. In one, it
was learned that the greater the cohesion among the members of Chicago
youth gangs, the less the rate of property crime committed by their members;[33] in another, delinquents awaiting trial in Illinois were found by an
interviewer to have no real commitments to anyone, peer or otherwise,[34]
and tended to drift in and out of both crime and peer groups in a way previously predicted by David Matza.[35] Comparable results have been obtained
by Hepburn[36] and Gould.[37]

If a boy does not greatly value the opinions of his peers, then his peers
are not likely to be an important source of reinforcement for his actions,
delinquent or otherwise. And delinquent boys seem to suffer from a general
social disability that makes it difficult for them to form strong attachments. For example, Short and Strodtbeck found that gang boys in Chicago
had a significantly lower intelligence, even when measured by "culture-free"
tests, than did nongang boys of the same race and social class.[38]

But it would defy common sense to think that peers have *no* influence on youth otherwise disposed to delinquency. However weak the attachment to friends may be, those who join together with their peers must assign *some* value to their company, else they would not join with them at all. And if peers can supply any rewards at all to one another, then to that extent they can reinforce some behavior at the expense of other behavior. Hirschi readily concedes as much: Even though having a stake in conformity and being attached to family and school strongly influence a boy's choice of friends and sharply reduce the capacity of delinquent friends to influence him, a boy with a low stake in conformity is susceptible, though perhaps not as much as earlier scholars and "countless mothers" once thought, to prodelinquent influences in his environment, including the rewards (not great, but not trivial either) supplied by delinquent friends.[39]

There is not much agreement among scholars as to how large is the effect of peers on criminality. Johnson analyzed the responses of 734 Seattle high school students to a questionnaire asking about their delinquent acts, family background, and personal friends, and found that having delinquent associates made a much larger difference in the number of self-reported offenses than did parental behavior or the socioeconomic status of the family (a major defect of this study was its failure to measure the temperament or intelligence of the students or to take into account that many young persons commit crimes while in groups without necessarily being influenced by the group).[40] Other studies suggest that both parents and peers have an effect,[41] including one[42] that reanalyzed Hirschi's data.

Correlations extracted from questionnaire data may offer clues, but only close observation of group processes can supply answers. Muzafer Sherif provided experimental evidence of how compelling those processes can be in his "Robbers Cave" project.[43] Twelve-year-old boys in a summer camp were arbitrarily divided into two groups, each of which was given its own clubhouse and told it could win prizes by competing with the other group. Quickly each group assumed a distinctive identity and soon antagonisms between them emerged, leading to food fights, vandalism, and hostile chants. Of course, this antagonism may have been especially strong because these boys, unlike many chronic delinquents, greatly valued the good opinion of their colleagues in the gangs, and the expression of this antagonism may have been rather mild because, again unlike delinquents, preexisting inhibitions (conscience) as well as a fear of retribution constrained the amount of violence the campers were willing to perpetrate. In any case, it is impossible to conceive of a face-to-face group forming that does not have some effect on the behavior of its members.[44]

The circumstances under which that effect will be great or small will depend on both the kind of behavior and the kind of group. Studies of self-reported crime among high school students and incarcerated delinquents found that the offenses most often committed in a group setting were drinking, using drugs, breaking and entering, and damaging property; those most often committed alone included stealing small sums, selling drugs, and robbery.[45] Though these studies do not prove that groups cause certain behaviors, they do suggest that, to the extent group effects exist, they influence certain behaviors more than others. Drinking and drug use, especially the latter, are preeminently acts that are learned from peers (see also Chapter 14).[46] The reinforcements associated with drinking and drugs are group-based for all but the confirmed alcoholic or addict, so that, absent a group setting, they are much less likely to occur. Damaging property is not usually individually rewarding; unlike theft, it confers no material advantages on the perpetrator, though it may confer some psychic ones (such as a sense of vengeance wreaked and thus equity restored). Property is damaged maliciously by persons who are rewarded by the approval of friends who have joined in the activity. Stealing, by contrast, confers individual rewards.

There is evidence that peer influence may be greatest for the casual, low-rate offender and least for the continuing, high-rate criminal. The casual offender, especially the younger one, may find the daring challenges and mischievous expectations of his friends adequate reward for an occasional theft, assault, or rowdy display, but the serious, high-rate offender is more likely to find the crime itself rewarding and thus, when he acts with a group, it is with a set of chosen accomplices rather than a spontaneously formed clique. This conclusion is consistent with the finding that peer influence may be greatest on youths from upper-middle-class backgrounds for whom the "fun" of breaking the law is more valuable than the proceeds, if any, of the crime.[47]

Of course, peers can influence individual behavior by the way they help shape the individual's moral development (the standards he internalizes) as well as by the immediate reinforcement of deviant (or law-abiding) actions. Strangely—and sadly—we have little systematic information regarding the effects, if any, of peers on the moral development of adolescents.[48]

If group influences may differ with the kind of behavior involved, they probably also differ with the kind of group involved. We—and most other scholars—have used until now such terms as "peers" and "groups" rather loosely, as if any combination of associates has the same stock of rewards and the same capacity for reinforcing behavior. Obviously this is not the case. An organized gang with a distinctive name and emblem, ritualized initiation ceremonies, and a specific "turf" that it defends controls a much larger and probably more valuable set of incentives for its members than does a casual group of friends with whom one occasionally drinks a beer or plays basketball.

Walter B. Miller has devoted a lifetime to the study of organized gangs in large American cities and is convinced that these gangs account for a significant fraction of all violent crime, a fraction that increased during the 1970s owing to their greater access to firearms.[49] Many police officers and prosecutors agree. The more powerful gangs may have the ability, through intimidation, to affect the behavior of nonmembers as well as members, and thus the scope of their influence may be larger than their membership. In a detailed study of the attributes of inner-city boys in Philadelphia, about half of whom were gang members, Friedman, Mann, and Friedman found that the single most powerful predictor of gang membership was the boy's own history of self-reported violence.[50] The study sheds no light on the direction of causality but does suggest that, whether by influence or selective recruitment, inner-city gangs consist of violence-prone youth. This high level of violence, often practiced without regard to its value in securing material gain, is for Yablonsky[51] the aspect of modern gangs that most clearly distinguishes them from the street-corner groups of the 1920s and 1930s as described by Frederic M. Thrasher[52] and William F. Whyte.[53] After controlling for violence, the variable that had the strongest association with gang membership was parental defiance, a self-reported measure of rebelliousness that included the boys' admission that they had struck one or both parents. The significance of defiance suggests that gangs may be most appealing to boys with weak parental attachments (as Hirschi has claimed), though earlier research indicates that, at least among lower-income black youth, gangs are less an alternative to family life than an extension of it.[54]

Since gangs differ greatly among cities and ethnic groups and since there is very little scholarly research on modern gangs, it would be a serious mistake to generalize about their influence on the criminality of their members. Joan W. Moore has given us an account of the Chicano gangs of Los Angeles in which she notes ways in which the rewards they offer to their members may differ, in degree if not in kind, from those supplied by, say, black gangs in New York or Chinese gangs in San Francisco.[55] Chicano gangs have especially deep and lasting territorial roots; as a consequence, they probably recruit (and thus influence) a larger fraction of the neighborhood boys, and for a longer period in their lives, than do other gangs. Second, these gangs are deeply involved in the use and marketing of drugs; she estimates that roughly half of the gang members are heroin addicts. Third, the gangs organize the prison as well as the street life of Chicano men and provide a degree of continuity missing among smaller, more ephemeral peer groups.

Many gangs have become a powerful force in the informal management of prisons. James B. Jacobs has provided a graphic account of how three black gangs, the Blackstone Rangers (later renamed the Black P Stone Nation), the Devil's Disciples, and the Conservative Vice Lords, and a Chicano gang, the Latin Kings, all based in Chicago neighborhoods, came to organize about half the inmates in Stateville, the huge Illinois prison near Joliet.[56] Prisoners who were not members of a gang were often terrorized, and so they had a powerful incentive to join a gang while in prison (if they had not already become members while growing up in the city). The rise of such quasi-political gangs that can determine the safety of young men both on the streets and in prison will probably affect the criminal activity of those boys (and grown men) who elect, out of fear, greed, or whatever, to join.

The values and circumstances of the neighborhood influence the kind of peer or gang activity that emerges. Irving Spergel has compared the distinctive youth subcultures of three lower-income neighborhoods in a large eastern city in the late 1950s.[57] In one, a largely Italian area that he called Racketville, the young delinquents saw their chance to participate in the adult-controlled rackets (gambling and loan-sharking) as a major source of career rewards. The delinquent boys living there were much more likely than those living in the other two neighborhoods to endorse various illegal activities and to express approval for adult racketeers. There is no evidence that this disposition led the boys to commit more crimes; rather, it seemed to influence the kinds of crimes they committed. The youth felt that it was possible to get ahead by emulating the tough, disciplined behavior of the racketeers, and so they chiefly valued crimes that permitted them to display these qualities. Another neighborhood, called Slumtown, was primarily a Puerto Rican and black area in which organized rackets were weak and legitimate opportunities for work few; because of this, Spergel argued, the delinquent boys organized themselves into fighting gangs in which the principal rewards were safety and "reputation." And in Haulburg, a lower-class area of northern and eastern European immigrants, there were few major rackets or fighting gangs and many examples of residents who had made good in legitimate work; as a result, the delinquents tended to be free-lance, unorganized or semiorganized thieves engaged in burglary, auto theft, and shoplifting. These neighborhood characteristics may well have changed in the two decades since Spergel did his research—in particular, the spread of drug use in the 1960s may have altered the connections he observed between neighborhood culture and criminal reinforcements. But it is surely the case that the kinds of gangs that will form, and thus the kinds if not the numbers of offenses boys commit, will be influenced by the circumstances of neighborhood life.

In sum, the weight of the research suggests that conventional opinion and much research, especially that done in the 1950s and early 1960s, exaggerated the influence peers had on explaining individual differences in criminality. Boys (scarcely any research has been done on girls) who become chronic delinquents are strongly disposed to such behavior long before acquiring adolescent peers, as a result of cognitive and personality traits that reflect constitutional predispositions, family socialization, and early school experiences. Boys weakly attached to parents and lacking any strong stake in conformity associate with similarly inclined peers, but their general social disability makes it hard for them to form strong loyalties to, or to value the opinion of, even those boys most like themselves. Nonetheless, to the extent they do acquire delinquent peers, the weakly attached boys will commit more offenses than they otherwise would, especially those (such as drinking, fighting, drug use, and vandalism) that are chiefly reinforced by group-based rewards. Organized inner-city gangs may well have a much stronger effect on individual crime rates; certainly, they have many violence-prone and defiant members, though whether as a result of gang influence or selective recruitment, we cannot say. Under some circumstances, as with the Chicano gangs of Los Angeles, the Italian gangs of Racketville, and the other big-city gangs that have organized so much of prison life, the gang becomes an enduring, highly organized, territorially based social unit that shapes the behavior of its members over a long period of time and provides the organizational structure necessary to commit certain kinds of crime, such as drug dealing (among Chicanos) or gambling and loan-sharking (among Italians).

Social Boundaries

Neighborhoods are not merely areas where families live and friends associate; they are also complex societies in which interactions shape attitudes, boundaries set limits to what is seen or imagined, and physical circumstances supply opportunities and constraints. An older tradition of social science produced inquiries into such communities seen whole; one recalls the account of the Jewish ghetto by Louis Wirth,[58] of the Chicago Gold Coast and its adjacent slum by Harvey W. Zorbaugh,[59] and of Italian boys on the street corners of Boston's North End by William F. Whyte.[60] Perhaps because such studies do not lend themselves to quantitative measurement and thus to the complex analysis made possible by modern statistical methods, perhaps for other reasons, they have fallen into disfavor, with the result that much of modern sociology operates at two very different, weakly linked, and inadequately conceived levels of analysis—individuals, defined by their attitudes, class, and ethnicity; and society, defined as a structure that rewards and penalizes those individuals. Missing are not only the full array of individual differences but also the complex web of interactions in neighborhood and community settings that may shape attitudes, give meaning to such abstractions as "class" and "ethnicity," and bring a person into—or keep him apart from—the larger society.

The various concepts of a "criminal subculture" have in common a belief that the connection between neighborhood and individual criminality is to be found in the transmission of attitudes conducive to crime from one generation to the next as a consequence of each generation growing up in an area of restricted opportunities[61] or lower-class values.[62] We have seen that there is not much systematic evidence that this transmission is by peers who cause otherwise law-abiding youth to become criminal, but there remains the possibility that neighborhood effects are more pervasive and subtle than is implied by the "rotten apple" (or differential association) theory.

The cultural-transmission view implies that neighborhood effects are not simply a proxy for economic effects. A Marxist would dismiss this view, and thus most sociological writing about the link between crime and neighborhood. Instead, he would argue that crime has little to do with values or attitudes that are learned by some persons and not others; on the contrary, crime is caused by economic want and capitalist oppression, which are more acute in some neighborhoods than others. In Chapter 12 we shall take a closer look at this claim; for now, it is enough to note that though high-crime areas are often low-income areas, low-income areas themselves differ so greatly in their crime rates as to suggest that some factor in addition to (or other than) economic want is at work.

In their effort to show that there is a "subculture of violence" that leads persons raised in it to resort to assault and murder more frequently than do persons raised in a different subculture, Wolfgang and Ferracuti note that homicide is more common in certain regions of Sardinia and Colombia than in other places no different in economic development or structure.[63] The abnormally high rates of homicide in the American South persist among southern migrants to northern cities, often long after the migration occurred.[64] In Kampala, Uganda, slum areas matched in physical and economic conditions differed greatly in their crime rates, with the low-crime slum having a higher level of community integration and less tribal diversity.[65] In Guyana, crime rates differed not only between urban and rural areas and between lower-income and higher-income ones but also between areas populated by East Indians and those inhabited by Africans.[66]

Michael Rutter and his colleagues in England have spent over ten years in a painstaking comparison of working-class families living on the Isle of Wight with comparable families living in an inner part of London.[67] The researchers gathered information on the individual families living in the two places, and especially on the children, from detailed interviews with parents and schoolteachers, including reports of deviance and mental illness. No matter how they measured the behavioral problems, they were at least twice as common among ten-year-old children living in London as among those living on the Isle of Wight, even though the economic circumstances of the two sets of families were virtually the same. The key factor seemed to be this: Working-class families in London experienced much higher levels of stress, experienced as severe marital discord and broken homes, than did those on the Isle of Wight. "For some reason," Rutter writes, "the stresses of inner city life impinge particularly strongly on working-class women" and not simply for reasons of social class.[68]

Why these differences among cultures should exist is beyond the scope of this chapter, though we shall return to the question in Chapter 17. For now it is enough to know that social science evidence confirms common experience—while poor neighborhoods are often more dangerous places than affluent ones, there are very large differences among poor neighborhoods. Some of these differences may well reflect variations in the degree of social control exercised by different ethnic and religious groups. But within a single ethnic group, neighborhood differences in criminality may reflect the mix of families in a given area. In their study of self-reported delinquency among white boys in Nashville, Tennessee, Reiss and Rhodes found that both the crime rates of the neighborhood as well as the social class of a boy living there affected his chances of becoming delinquent.[69] In any kind of neighborhood, the low-status boy was much more likely than the middle- or upper-status one to break the law, but a boy living in a high-crime area was much more likely to break the law than a similar boy in a low-crime neighborhood. The neighborhood effect was greatest for the poorest boys.

We can only speculate on how these neighborhood effects operate. We suggest that a neighborhood is, among other things, a set of boundaries constraining physical movement and social communication in ways that alter the value a person living there will assign to various reinforcers. Persons of high social status are (virtually by definition) least constrained by these boundaries. Having (ordinarily) high incomes, much schooling, and great mobility, they regularly come into contact with a variety of sources of reinforcement—university campuses, complex business markets, professional colleagues, governmental agencies, and specialized communications media. Indeed, their orientation to the larger world may be so great as to lead them to make special arrangements to reduce the extent to which they come into contact with and are thus influenced by the neighborhood at all; they may, for example, live some distance from relatives, dwell in guarded, high-rise buildings, travel in closed, air-conditioned cars, and socialize in other parts of the city with friends acquired in occupational settings. Robert K. Merton called such persons "cosmopolitans," as distinct from "locals."[70]

Persons with low incomes, little schooling (and perhaps little aptitude for schooling), and not much mobility are sharply constrained by neighborhood boundaries. Doc, the leader of the Norton Street gang, remarks to Whyte that "fellows around here don't know what to do except within a radius of about three hundred yards."[71] As a result, they assign a higher value to reinforcements and punishments found near where they live than they do to those that exist—or are reputed to exist—in some other place or some other setting. Of course, some idea of what these other rewards look like will come to them, albeit in distorted form, via magazines and television, and they may wish very much to have the fine cars and fancy homes they see there, but they do not attach a very high probability to actually getting such things. By the same token, the good opinion and well-being of persons living outside the neighborhood are not an important consideration in evaluating the locals' own course of action; since they have so little contact with outsiders, they are not likely to worry much about what outsiders think of their behavior. In the extreme case, outsiders are the enemy, the cause of their being (as they see it) confined in a small and undesirable neighborhood, and if their behavior harms such outsiders, so much the better.

Gerald D. Suttles has given us a careful, sensitive portrayal of what he calls the "social order of the slum" that emphasizes the boundary-setting aspects of neighborhood. He concludes his account of the Addams area on the near west side of Chicago by remarking that its "most general characteristic" is its "provincialism."[72] Since individuals who are more likely to commit street crimes are overrepresented in slum areas, the problem of personal safety is more acute for the residents of such places than it is for people living in affluent neighborhoods. Personal safety cannot be taken for granted because it is not produced by reciprocal self-restraint or enforced by police agencies. The provincialism of the slum is in part a response to this problem and leads its residents to be preoccupied with those differences among people—chiefly, age, sex, ethnicity, territoriality, and reputation—that are useful in discerning who, in their eyes, are more or less likely to be threats to their safety. The distinctions that are important to persons outside the slum—occupation, educational attainment—are less significant to those inside it. In the slum, young men carry weapons and join gangs, not simply to prove their manhood or gain a reputation, but also to cope with the problem of safety; much of the life of the gang, according to Suttles, can be explained as ways of coping with fear and the needs of self-defense. That being in a gang gives its members an incentive to act as if they are fearless should not obscure the fact that the original incentive for membership involves an element of fear.

This description of the social order of the slum can easily be translated into the theoretical concepts we have used to explain criminal behavior. Provincialism, arising naturally from the fact of slum life, means that the value of rewards—jobs, status, careers—available from sources outside the slum is lowered; such reinforcements are not thought to be as valuable or as available as are those arising out of the interactions of daily life. Slum residents may dream of good jobs, nice homes, and fancy cars, but they have little if any reliable information about how to get them and probably do not think that they have a realistic chance of getting them. Arthur E. Hippler has observed this among the black residents of Hunter's Point, a ghetto neighborhood in San Francisco that he studied much as Suttles studied the Addams area of Chicago, which contains not only blacks but Italians, Mexicans, and Puerto Ricans.[73] In Hunter's Point, people are "mildly pessimistic and resigned," skeptical of their chances of advancement and thus skeptical of the value of advancement as a reward that might shape their behavior; to this general slum provincialism blacks add the view that their chances of advancement are not only remote but deliberately kept low by the larger white society.[74] Whether they are correct about this or not, they in fact underparticipate in the larger job market that is managed by classified advertisements and employment agencies, relying more on word of mouth about locally available jobs. This contributes to what some economists have called the "dual" or "segmented" labor market (see Chapter 12). The neighborhood becomes the only relevant job market and "street hustles" become an important source of income.

Distant, low-probability reinforcements have a weaker effect on behavior than do immediate, high-probability ones. The conduct of persons living outside the slum is influenced by cosmopolitan as well as local rewards—their reputation in the community at large, their chances for career advancement, the stories that may be written about them in the newspapers—and so, other things being equal, their probability of committing a crime, at least of the sort that might easily be detected, is lower than it is for persons exposed to fewer, less consequential, or more improbable reinforcements. The short time horizon of lower-status persons may be the result not only of the cognitive predispositions described in Chapter 6 but also of the community setting in which they happen to live.

In the slum, some persons may attach not simply a low value to reinforcers available from outside their neighborhood but a negative value. "Straight jobs" are for "suckers," outsiders who are robbed or assaulted "deserve what they get," and having an arrest record is a badge of honor and a measure of one's toughness. Some blacks may value, at least verbally, anything that "permits them feelings of power over whites and allows for fantasized aggression against whites."[75] How common such views are, we cannot say, but it is plausible to assume that the provincialism of slum life, when intensified by racial or ethnic cleavages, will lead some residents to invert the value normally assigned to the well-being of others.

If this view is correct, the effect on crime rates of living in a low-status neighborhood does not arise because slum families, unlike others, approve of crime or have "antisocial" values; virtually every account of such neighborhoods emphasizes how conventional are the values shared by most such families. Rather, the effect depends on the existence in the area of young persons already disposed to crime whose behavior creates the problems for others (and for themselves) of assuring their safety, problems that must be resolved within a setting in which many reinforcements that might otherwise constrain threatening behavior seem remote and improbable; thus one must fall back on one's own resources. These resources include mutual suspicion (strangers are dangerous until they prove themselves otherwise), ties of kinship and ethnicity ("our own kind" are safer than people who are different), knowledge about character ("street gossip"), and clues as to probable behavior (husky, ill-dressed young men are more threatening than slender, neatly dressed ones). Though all people everywhere attend to such distinctions, slum life requires that they be attended to with special care. Suttles summarizes his account thus:

> The subcultural commonalities of the Addams area consist primarily of a selective search for private information rather than the invention of normative ideals. The residents express admiration for unrelenting respectability, complete frankness, and a general restraint from force. In the real world they live in, however, the residents are willing to settle for a friend of doubtful repute, guarded personal disclosures, and the threat of force to meet force.[76]

What they settle for may help them manage their individual problems of security, but it has the unintended effect of intensifying the problem for the neighborhood as a whole. Settling for friends of doubtful repute weakens the strength of the reinforcements associated with high repute; settling for guarded personal disclosures and relying on ties of ethnicity and kinship lessens the chances that universal rather than particular standards will reinforce behavior; and meeting force with force increases the value attached to physical prowess and pugnacity at the expense of those rewards that might come from cooperative action and official law enforcement. A divided and parochial neighborhood becomes more divided and parochial, especially if it is ethnically diverse.

What this theory leaves out is an explanation of why street life has apparently become so much more threatening than it once was. In reading older accounts of low-income neighborhoods, one is struck by the fact that the neighborhood social order had a certain stability. There was crime, but not gratuitous street violence. Criminals were either in the rackets, were professional thieves, or were "bums"; street gangs broke the law, but not routinely, and with fists not guns. Then, organized politics was pervasive and attachment to the community was strong;[77] today, fewer organized economic or political systems crossing neighborhood boundaries operate and attachment to the community is weak.[78] Some of the change may have technological or pharmaceutical causes—the greater availability of guns (in the pursuit of self-defense, there has been an urban arms race) and the spread of drug addiction (and thus the creation of opportunities for large financial gains for those who could dominate street life). Some may have organizational causes—the decline of citywide political systems and the movement of large-scale employment to the periphery of the city. And some may have occurred because the social structure of inner-city neighborhoods has been altered by the movement out of stable families and law-abiding workers, thereby not only diluting the level of social control exercised by such groups and weakening even further the rewards of noncrime available to young persons otherwise disposed to such behavior, but also increasing the concentration of persons predisposed to crime. We can only speculate, for we have no accounts that trace the evolution of a single slum community over several decades.

Targets and Surveillance

The rise in urban crime rates during the 1960s and 1970s led some observers to resurrect the views of Shaw and McKay that it was in the defective social organization of urban neighborhoods that the causes of high crime were to be found. To some, controlling crime meant creating stronger social structures, and to that end a number of public and private programs were begun. But to others, viable social systems that would effectively control the behavior of their members could not be created by plan. They either arose naturally, out of the subcultural traits of some ethnic groups (the cohesive Italian neighborhoods of Boston's North End or New York's Greenwich Village were hailed by Jane Jacobs as vanishing examples of how a community could insure its own safety[79]), or indirectly, as a consequence of physical arrangements that made it easy for law-abiding citizens to keep the unruly under surveillance.[80]

All of these views were in keeping with a long-standing theory of urban life that its essential feature, and what made it both more appealing to those who valued liberty and more threatening to those who valued order, was its anonymity.[81] As anyone who has read this book will surmise, we do not find anonymity to be of central importance in explaining crime, for it ignores individual differences that exist prior to communal life and overstates the extent to which urban life is, or need be, anonymous. (Urban neighborhoods can draw people together as easily as they can drive them apart; everything depends on the kind of people who live there and on the way in which they manage their relations with others.) There is something distinctive about urban life apart from the characteristics of the population, but such terms as "anonymity" do not quite capture it. Urban life changes the scale of human interaction by reducing the distances that separate (and possibly protect) people, increases the number of criminal opportunities in a given area (if people rob banks because that's where the money is, then cities have more bank robberies because they have more banks), and shapes the interactions of persons by the physical arrangement of streets, buildings, and windows. These consequences of living in an urban (that is, thickly settled) area as opposed to a rural or small-town one can be summarized by saying that residing in the former increases the density of certain kinds of reinforcements.

If a boy values the opinion of his peers, cities bring more boys into more frequent contact with one another than do small towns, and hence the strength of whatever reinforcement a boy derives from peer opinion will be greater. And since there are more boys in an urban area, any given boy has greater choice: He can select, within limits, to associate with nice guys or tough guys, students or athletes. Thus, a boy will encounter not only stronger reinforcements but also more consistent ones. (In social science language, there will be fewer "cross-cutting pressures.") If the boy is impulsive, in cities he will encounter more frequent opportunities to exercise that impulsiveness, whether by buying things from stores or stealing them, running off to watch a fire or setting one, flirting with a girl or assaulting one. The time delay between the present moment and opportunity for committing a crime will be less in densely settled areas than in a sparsely settled one; thus, if the strength of the rewards attached to crime decline steeply (see Chapter 2), they still may dominate the rewards of not committing a crime if a chance to commit the crime is only a moment away.

The data we have on the characteristics of neighborhoods with high rates of crime are consistent with this interpretation. Using victimization surveys from 1973 to 1978, Sampson, Castellano, and Laub calculated the rate at which persons were victimized in different kinds of neighborhoods and found that the higher the density of dwelling units in a neighborhood, the greater the rate of victimization.[82] Other studies find that the more people per square mile, the more likely they are to be victimized by robbers.[83] Similar conclusions have been reached on the basis of police reports of crime.[84]

The data are also consistent with the view that the social structure of the neighborhood can affect crime rates. The more rapid the population turnover in an area, the higher the victimization rate, even after controlling for the racial and age composition of the neighborhoods.[85] High residential mobility reduces the opportunity (or possibly the inclination) for individuals to form close personal attachments to neighbors, and this in turn reduces the strength of some of the rewards ("neighborhood opinion") that reinforce noncrime.

Just how the physical and social structure of a neighborhood affects the crime rate and what, if anything, might be done to reduce crime by improving those effects is a matter much in dispute among scholars. Oscar Newman has supplied the best-known theory of these effects.[86] In essence, he argued that, apart from the economic circumstances of an area and the characteristics of the individuals living there, low-crime neighborhoods have certain features that make them more "defensible." These include a stronger sense of territory, greater natural surveillance of public spaces, and a better image.[87]

By territoriality, Newman meant that when people feel attached to a physical location (neighborhood, street, home), they are more inclined to defend it against intruders. By natural surveillance, he meant that it is easier in some neighborhoods than in others for residents to keep watch over places where crime might occur; knowing they are likely to be spotted, potential offenders go elsewhere. By image, he meant that neighborhoods that appear run-down or vandalized are more inviting targets for further depredations than those that have a kept-up appearance.

These concepts can readily be assimilated into a behavioral theory of crime. A strong sense of territory and a greater ease of surveillance increase the probability that sanctions (both formal and informal) will be imposed on offenders. A well-kept image deters the marginal offender by making a neighborhood appear to be the province of people who care and thus who are likely to respond to any vandalism by imposing sanctions, while a run-down area suggests to the offender that no one cares and thus sanctions will be less likely or less severe or both.[88]

That such concepts are theoretically intelligible does not necessarily make them useful, however. We do not have clear evidence that a strong sense of territory or a neighborhood structure that facilitates natural surveillance will reduce crime.[89] There is some evidence that crime is more likely to occur on streets with either very little pedestrian traffic, perhaps because there are too few eyes on the street to produce natural surveillance, or a great deal of such traffic, perhaps because then there are so many people about that no one person feels responsible for taking action in the event of a crime; the safest community is presumably the one that has the "right amount" of traffic.[90] Public housing projects have been improved by fixing up their appearance, installing play areas and better lighting, setting up barriers to through traffic, and organizing the tenants; there was evidence of a reduction in some crimes but of an increase in others.[91] Even a change that most people assume would reduce crime by improving natural surveillance—better street lighting—has had disappointing results. A review of several dozen street-lighting experiments found some short-lived crime reductions but no lasting ones.[92]

In Hartford, Connecticut, the Newman theory was put to its most comprehensive and carefully evaluated test. Major changes were made in a racially mixed working-class neighborhood so as to improve territoriality, surveillance, and image. Community organizations were formed or enhanced and the police presence in the area was strengthened. In one part, through streets were closed and the neighborhood was more clearly marked off from the surrounding city by various structural and landscaping changes. Over the ensuing three years, residents reported that they walked in the neighborhood, including in the park and at night, more frequently than they once had; that they found it easier to recognize strangers; that they more regularly made arrangements with neighbors to watch each others' houses; and that they were more likely to intervene in a suspicious situation in the area. One year after the project began, the burglary rate had dropped significantly in the area that had experienced the physical changes. But two years later it had gone back up to what it had been before the project started and to what it was expected to be, based on citywide trends.[93] The increase in crime, despite what appeared to be a greater level of natural surveillance and a stronger sense of territory, coincided with a reduction in police activity in the area. Given all these facts, it cannot be said that natural surveillance or territoriality reduced crime, at least without the support provided by more intensive police work.

In sum, there are physical changes that may reduce the rates of some kinds of crime, but the role played in this reduction by such factors as territoriality, natural surveillance, and neighborhood image remains unclear. Though the theory that such social factors can make a difference remains plausible, it also remains unproved.[94] If we recast the theory of "defensible space" into the behavioral model of criminal choice given in Chapter 2, we might understand why the results of even the best efforts to test the defensible-space concept are so equivocal. In essence, people who have a stronger sense of territory are presumably more willing to intervene to prevent or punish improper action by scolding, chasing, restraining, or informing on wrongdoers; if the design of the community facilitates natural surveillance, then there is a higher probability that they can act on these territorial instincts on any given occasion. Of course, for these processes actually to affect criminal behavior, the would-be offenders must believe that citizens will act this way. Improving the image and milieu of a neighborhood, by contrast, acts directly on the offender by suggesting to him how much disorder, incivility, or vandalism an area will tolerate.

The extent to which these processes will affect a potential offender's behavior will depend on many other factors: how greatly he values the rewards of crime, how much he fears the scolding, chasing, or restraining actions of others, how likely he thinks it is that a citizen report will bring about a police response, and the extent to which he assigns any value to an unmarked wall or an unbroken window as a sign of property that is, and ought to be, left intact. Persons who assign a low value to the rewards of crime and a higher value to the rewards of noncrime will take these informal social processes heavily into account. But if the value of crime is high, if the scorn of conventional opinion means little, if the individual is impulsive, these processes may not count for much, and thus the space that is being defended by law-abiding persons will not prove very defensible.

Sally Engle Merry has described the views that offenders and residents have of one another in a small, racially mixed housing project in a large eastern city.[95] The older Chinese-Americans, who are the majority group in the area, worry about crime and are especially fearful of the blacks who live near them and with whom they have virtually no contact. Older blacks, in turn, are equally critical of the Chinese, whom they believe live wantonly in filthy, overcrowded apartments and whose hostility to blacks they resent. The respectable black families are also worried about crime, but blame it on a few young persons and some outside troublemakers whom the families are at pains to avoid. White families are equally suspicious of the Chinese and the blacks. Few of the black street youth, however, think of the neighborhood as particularly dangerous, and in any event no one would think of bothering them. To the youth, the real troublemakers are the older persons who are "nosy" and who fail to "mind their own business."[96] They are especially critical of persons who frequently call the police; some feel that the persons who are robbed or burgled the most often had "big mouths" and deserved what they got. Indeed, Merry—who in general was quite sympathetic to the young people's perspective—estimated that about 40 percent of the robberies and burglaries of black families were retaliatory acts.[97]

In a neighborhood beset with such deep cleavages and mutual animosities, it is hard to imagine how a shared sense of territory could develop or how natural surveillance might be effective. In her interviews with the young men who actually committed the crimes, Merry was struck by their sophisticated, pragmatic orientation. What mattered was not who could place whom under surveillance or who did or did not have a sense of territory, but who had things worth stealing and who was likely to call the police. Chinese adults were ideal victims because they were afraid and because, not speaking English, they had difficulty calling the police or testifying in court. Moreover, stealing from the Chinese was especially rewarding because it addressed the sense of inequity arising from the belief that they had amassed undeserved wealth.[98] If anyone attempted to interfere, the predators were inclined to assault them, not run away. What mattered to the criminals were not the symbols of territory, surveillance, and image but real risks of real punishment.[99] This conclusion was supported by a study comparing high- and low-crime-rate neighborhoods in Atlanta.[100] Physical circumstances, in particular the existence of easy routes by which to approach and flee from attractive targets, made a difference in crime rates; the existence of informal social control mechanisms made little difference.

None of this means that informal social control is of no importance in explaining crime, only that its explanatory power is probably limited to certain conditions. Territoriality, surveillance, and image are likely to make the greatest difference when the subjective rewards of crime are low, the value assigned to neighborhood opinion is high, and the background reinforcements are substantial. And those areas are likely to be ones where crime rates are already low and social cohesion already high.

Conclusions

Aspects of community life—friends on the street corner, the boundaries of the neighborhood, the density of opportunities, the informal processes of social control—affect individual crime rates to some degree, but the magnitude of that effect is hard to estimate. Moreover, we do not know whether community factors chiefly affect the prevalence of crime (i.e., what proportion of a group of young persons ever commits a crime) or the incidence of offending (i.e., the number of crimes a given offender commits per year). In our view, most of the variation among individuals in criminality can be accounted for by personal traits, family socialization, and (perhaps) school experiences, and this is especially true for variations in incidence. The evidence of previous chapters strongly suggests that high-rate offenders begin offending very early in their lives, well before communal factors—whether peers who are "rotten apples" or neighborhood social processes that set boundaries, supply targets, or provide surveillance—could play much of a role. We speculate that neighborhood conditions affect prevalence more than incidence, especially to the extent that those conditions create threats to personal safety that are met by reciprocal violence or provide dense criminal opportunities. There is some evidence from self-report studies of young persons in an upper-middle-class suburb that peer effects may be greatest on delinquency rates among affluent children for whom offending is more a form of "play," and thus more likely to require shared experiences to be enjoyable, than a quest for material gains.[101] And even among lower-status youth, peer effects may be greater for those offenses, such as drug use and vandalism, that derive their reinforcement from the group setting than for rapes and robberies that supply individual rewards.

The search for the mechanism by which aspects of community life affect criminality has involved the use of some rather vague, hard-to-grasp concepts—anonymity, mobility, territoriality—that might better be stated as sources of reinforcement and punishment. Peers and gangs can affect the value a person assigns to the rewards of crime (by adding the approval of colleagues to the perceived value of the loot or the direct gratification of the act); the social boundaries of the neighborhood can affect the value he assigns to the rewards of noncrime (by narrowing the range of persons whose good opinion is valued and widening the range of persons who are thought to be undeserving of consideration); the density of human settlement can affect the frequency with which one encounters opportunities for crime (by presenting a chance to steal a purse or a car when one is to the right of his "crossover point"—that is, when the rewards of crime appear stronger than the delayed rewards of not committing the crime); and the extent of natural surveillance of the streets, provided it is carried out by persons willing to act on the basis of what they see, may affect the probability of being caught and punished.

12

LABOR MARKETS

In paradise, there would be no crime; amidst mass starvation, there might be a great deal. Because it is easy for us to imagine how the extremes in the human condition might affect crime rates, it is easy for us to assume that at each intermediate step—for example, with each change in the level of wealth or employment—there will be a corresponding change in the crime rate. And there is some evidence consistent with the supposition that such a continuous, readily observable connection between crime and unemployment exists. Neighborhoods with high rates of street crime are often neighborhoods with high rates of joblessness.[1] Studies of burglars and robbers regularly show them to have poor employment records.[2] The increase in the crime rate during the 1960s and 1970s occurred at the same time as an increase in the unemployment rate of young males; it would appear at first glance that there was a connection between the two trends.

In view of all this, it may come as a surprise that the scholars who have looked most closely at the presumed connection between crime and employment disagree as to what that connection is, or even whether it exists at all. Robert W. Gillespie reviewed the efforts made between 1959 and 1975 to measure the relationship between crime and unemployment by methods that were either cross-sectional (i.e., comparing cities or states) or longitudinal (i.e., studying changes over time in the nation as a whole). Of these studies, three found such a connection, seven did not, and four gave equivocal results.*[3] Thomas Orsagh and Ann Dryden Witte reviewed the studies that appeared between 1975 and 1981 and concluded that they supplied very little strong, consistent support for the claim that unemployment and crime are connected. In their words, "Research using aggregate data [i.e., data pertaining to geographic areas, such as cities or states] provides only weak support for the simple proposition that unemployment causes crime."[5] When the Vera Institute in New York City undertook its own evaluation of the literature, the strongest statement it could make was that "studies based on aggregate statistics present mixed results" and that "social experiments have not fully demonstrated the impact of employment programs on crime."[6] In 1983 Richard B. Freeman went over this now well-plowed terrain one more time and, though clearly sympathetic to the view that crime and unemployment were related, concluded by saying that this relationship is "not an open-and-shut case."[7]

One reason the empirical research is so inconclusive is that it is enmeshed in some formidable methodological problems. Obviously, the analyst must control for the effect of other factors that might affect the crime rate, such as the changes in the age composition of the population and differences among states in the probability of being punished for committing a crime. Yet several of the studies analyzed in the reviews mentioned above failed to do this. Moreover, both the unemployment rate and the crime rate are measured inaccurately; if these inaccuracies vary from place to place, the conclusions of the study may be seriously in error. And the results may differ depending on whether "unemployment" is defined as meaning all persons out of work, or only those persons out of work who say they are looking for work, or only those persons in certain critical age and sex groups (such as males between the ages of sixteen and twenty-four) who are both out of school and out of work. The results may also differ according to the crime involved—theft, rape, assault, or murder.

But the most important reason for the unsatisfactory nature of most studies is that they are based on an incomplete and thus misleading view of the possible relationship between unemployment and crime. Some are based on no theory at all except for a hunch that unemployment causes crime. Others are based on a quite explicit theory, but one that overlooks the many different ways crime and participation in the labor market may be connected. Economists who have done the most sophisticated studies of the crime-employment connection usually assume that an individual chooses between

* Curiously, Gillespie himself interpreted this result as providing "general, if not uniform, support for a positive correlation" between unemployment and crime.[4] This conclusion seems at odds with his own review of the literature.

crime and some alternative to crime (either a legitimate job or more leisure). He makes this choice on the basis of the net value of the alternatives
confronting him—that is, on the basis of the present value of the costs and
benefits of committing a crime, getting a job, or doing nothing. The choice is
an exclusive one (he either chooses crime or noncrime), is made without regard to the preferences of others, and reflects the operation of his (unexplained) tastes.

The model we presented in Chapter 2 has some things in common with
this theory, but it also differs in important ways. We do not assume that a
person chooses between crime and noncrime; he may choose both, depending on the way in which opportunities present themselves (while riding
home in the subway, an employed delivery boy may grab a woman's purse
if he thinks he can get away with it, and a skilled burglar may take a day-
time job as a taxi driver if it doesn't interfere with his criminal business).
Moreover, the value a person attaches to crime and to employment depends
in part—perhaps in great part—on the value his friends and family attach to
these pursuits. Finally, we are especially interested in how a person's "tastes"
are formed. More precisely, we want to know what individual characteristics
lead one person to attach a low value to even a lucrative crime and a high
value to even a menial job, whereas another person has just the opposite
preferences; by the same token, we want to know why one person cannot resist the rewards of an immediately available opportunity (so that he snatches
a purse if it is ready at hand and no one is looking) whereas another returns
purses to their owners, waits long hours in line at the employment office, and
saves his money for a rainy day.

We do not claim that our model is for all purposes superior to that of
the economists. They make a number of simplifying assumptions (in particular, that individuals have similar tastes and that the value one person attaches to crime does not depend on how much another person—say, a wife
or buddy—values it) because they are trying not to explain human behavior
but to predict what changes will occur, at the margin, in human behavior if
the costs and benefits of alternative courses of action change. We, on the
other hand, want to explain why different individuals behave differently.
Should it be the case, for example, that crime rates fall whenever (other
things being equal) unemployment rates fall, then this would not only be an
interesting prediction, it would be a useful one, as it would suggest to governments that they ought to reduce unemployment in order to reduce crime.
But when it is the case that changes in unemployment are not accompanied
by any readily observable changes in crime, then we should either try harder
to observe the changes (that has been done, and with few results that com-

mand general assent) or revise our prediction in order to take into account the many different ways that labor markets might be related to criminal behavior.

Causes and Effects

There are at least four ways in which employment and crime might be related. First, the labor market might cause crime because the expected value of available jobs is so low (jobs are scarce or very low paying) that the net benefits of crime (the expected yield, less the expected risk of being caught and punished) are higher. We will call this the "need effect." This relationship is implied by some economic models of crime.[8] Men respond to incentives by trying to maximize their welfare. In some sense, that assumption is surely correct. To believe otherwise would be tantamount to arguing that crime is wholly or largely the result of pathological or irrational behavior, and nothing we have learned so far would support that claim. So long as a significant number of persons act *as if* they were responding to material incentives by changing (at the margin) their conduct as incentives change, then it is a useful theory. But when people do not act in this way, one has to ask whether there is a fault in the theory.

One possible fault may be that crime and unemployment are not causally related at all; rather, each is the expression of some underlying common cause. This possibility, which we shall call the "no effect" theory, might be true of people who are intensely present-oriented and thus find looking for a job unattractive but stealing a purse irresistible.[9] Those of low intelligence may find it hard both to get a job and to internalize rules of conduct (because they have trouble recalling the consequences of past misconduct or anticipating the likely consequences of future misconduct). Or having a low IQ may lead to difficulty in school, which in turn reduces their employability and, because of their frustration with schoolwork, increases their involvement in more satisfying delinquent activities. There are other possibilities. Theories about the "culture of poverty"[10] suggest that some people are inducted, by family and neighborhood experience, into a world in which they acquire wasteful consumption patterns, self-defeating attitudes, and an inability to obtain a legitimate job. Theories about "lower-class culture"[11] suggest that young men in such milieus value trouble, toughness, excitement, fate, autonomy, and "street smarts" over a "respectable" job and life-style. The effect of all of these factors would be to lead the young men to discount heavily both delayed benefits (jobs for which one must search and train) and delayed penalties (the risk of being caught), to lower the value of holding a job (the esteem of conventional people), and to increase the benefits of committing a crime (the esteem of unconventional people). For one or more of these reasons, some individuals would be both unemployed and criminal, without the former having caused the latter.

A third possibility is that crime may cause unemployment. Suppose some people find that crime is more profitable than working, even though jobs at decent wages are available. They would tell government agencies they are "unemployed" when in fact they are working at crime. This could easily be the case for persons involved in selling illicit drugs or running gambling operations. But it might also be true of those who find that holding up liquor stores or burgling homes produce gains that, even after being discounted for the risk of apprehension and punishment, exceed the gains of legitimate employment (after these have been discounted for the burdens of having to work from nine to five, five days a week). Crime rates could go up simply because there is more loot to steal (a productive economy has stocked store shelves and living rooms with lots of things worth having), because it is easier to take things worth having (stores are more poorly guarded or guns are more available to criminals), because social and geographical mobility has brought more offenders into contact with more targets, because prosperity has weakened familial controls that instill conscience and character, or because the burdens of unemployment have been reduced (by family support or more generous welfare payments). These factors draw more persons into crime and out of jobs, thereby causing the unemployment rate to go up (more accurately, the labor force participation rate to go down). We call this the "affluence effect."

The final possibility we call the "envy effect." Strictly speaking, it does not involve unemployment so much as the distribution of wealth and the perceived relationship between wealth and work. But to the extent it exists, the envy effect will produce more criminality and less employment. Recall our discussion of equity in Chapter 2. A person may believe that the ratio of his efforts to his rewards is greater than the ratio of another person's efforts to rewards. The first person does not get a return on his investment of time and labor that is proportional to what the second person gets, even though, in the eyes of the first person, both individuals are equally deserving. There are several ways in which the first person may respond to this: He may blame himself (and thus judge his efforts to be less deserving of rewards than he had first supposed), he may increase his efforts so as to increase his rewards (by, perhaps, getting more training or finding a better job), or he may decide that the other fellow's rewards are undeserved and take some of them (or the rewards that have accrued to similarly situated persons) by stealth or force. In this last instance, a person reduces his legitimate employment and increases his criminality out of a sense of inequity. This might occur even if the aggrieved person has, over the years, become better off as a result of earning higher wages, provided only that other persons seem to have become still better off *and* people have changed the standards by which they judge the equity of social outcomes.

Obviously, these four possible relationships between employment and crime, though analytically distinct, may be difficult or impossible to separate in reality. But by bearing them in mind, we may be better prepared to understand why, even allowing for the methodological difficulties, it has been so hard to establish empirically that unemployment causes crime and why, to the extent one or another relationship exists, efforts to reduce crime by reducing unemployment may have unexpected or even perverse effects. If the need effect operates, a rise in unemployment will cause a rise in crime, and programs that reduce unemployment will also reduce crime. If crime and unemployment have common causes, then an increase in the proportion of persons in society affected by these causes (say, impulsive young males of limited intelligence) can cause crime and unemployment to rise simultaneously, but programs aimed at reducing the unemployment of young males will have little effect on either unemployment or crime. If the affluence effect operates, a decrease in unemployment that is part of a general growth of prosperity may cause an increase in crime; should society want to cut crime, it may be well advised to produce an economic recession. And if the envy effect operates, an increase in the inequality of incomes may produce both crime and unemployment even if those persons with lower incomes have become better off in absolute terms. Efforts to reduce crime by reducing unemployment will have little effect; efforts to reduce it by redistributing incomes may have some effect, no effect, or a perverse effect depending on whether relative income shares change *and* on how persons evaluate the relationship between effort and outcome. (If my income rises relative to yours but I now decide that my effort deserves an even greater reward, I may feel myself to be the victim of injustice even though I am both absolutely and relatively better off than before. Or if my income falls relative to yours, you may now feel that justice is served but I may feel that a just ratio has been replaced by an unjust one, and so the decrease in your crime rate will be offset by the increase in mine.)

If all these relationships may exist (and none can be ruled out in advance), then estimating empirically the causal connection between crime and labor markets will be quite difficult, as will shortly become abundantly clear.

Measuring the Effects

The Need Effect

Jean Valjean, the central figure in Victor Hugo's *Les Misérables,* stole to feed his hungry family. No doubt many others, before and since, have stolen out of economic compulsion. But others steal while employed—tellers pilfer bank funds, workers take factory tools, business persons embezzle corporate accounts, and police officers help themselves to loot taken from criminals or even to goods in stores the officers are instructed to protect. And what kind of economic need explains the behavior of the rapist or the wife murderer?

But let us set aside pilferage, white-collar crime, official misconduct, and violent offenses without material gain. Let us even abandon the idea of "need" as a motive for crime, and think instead of persons turning to property crime because, though in little danger of starvation, they find crime the only alternative to idleness or unemployment. Does it not make sense that as unemployment rises, more persons will turn to crime, even if most do not?

Perhaps. But to put matters in perspective, we should begin by recalling certain facts that, at a minimum, set the outer limits for the operation of economic factors. First, the general upward trend in crime rates that has occurred in this and most other industrialized nations since the late 1950s or early 1960s has been more or less steady, with little apparent regard for short-term fluctuations in the unemployment rate.[12] Second, there were in 1970 (a typical year) more unemployed males in the age group forty-five to sixty-four than there were in the age group sixteen to nineteen. Yet the crime rate for the older group is very low while for the younger one it is quite high. (The age-specific arrest rate for the younger group is about four times higher than for the older one.) Third, even among unemployed young males, a large fraction are looking for jobs while in school. In 1975, for example, 277,000 of the 382,000 unemployed males ages sixteen and seventeen were in school.[13] Though a schoolboy may want a job or even, in some sense, need one, his need can hardly have the same meaning as that of an adult male who is out of school with a family to support.

Even if we acknowledge that other facts must explain why some persons are more likely to commit crimes than others, there is still plenty of room for the influence of labor-market conditions, at least on young males who are out of school and looking for work. The most common way of trying to discover that influence has been to examine the effect of changes in unemployment rates on crime rates, holding certain other factors constant. We have already noted earlier in this chapter that the results of many of these efforts were inconclusive. This is especially true of the cross-sectional studies that compare cities, metropolitan areas, or states. Freeman considered fifteen of these and found only four that showed a clear (statistically significant) relationship in the predicted direction (i.e., that higher unemployment is associated with more crime).[14]

Stronger results have been obtained from longitudinal studies that estimate the effect of changes in employment or business conditions on changes in crime rates for the country as a whole. But even here, the apparent effects of economic conditions on crime are quite modest. Freeman calculates that if unemployment could be cut in half, there would at the most be a 5 percent reduction in the crime rate,[15] much too small a change to explain the sharp increase in crime rates during the 1960s and 1970s. For example, no aggregate change in unemployment rates can explain why in 1961 the Index crime rate was 1.9 per hundred thousand persons and the unemployment rate was 6.6 percent, but in 1969 the Index crime rate had nearly doubled (to 3.7 per hundred thousand) despite the fact that the unemployment rate had been cut nearly in half (3.4 percent). Similarly, business recessions may sometimes be associated with increases in robbery and burglary, but the effect is quite modest.[16]

The connection over time between crime and employment may become a bit stronger if we focus our attention on the labor-market experiences of the persons most at risk, namely, young males. During the 1950s the unemployment rate of white eighteen- and nineteen-year-old males rose from 7 percent in 1952 to over 16 percent in 1958, while that of nonwhite males of the same age rose from 10 to 27 percent; these high rates persisted throughout most of the 1960s and 1970s.[17] Even this figure understates the extent to which young males were not employed, for the "unemployment rate" is the number of persons out of work but looking for it divided by the number in the "labor force"; the latter is the sum of those either employed or actively looking for work. Persons who are not looking for work are not counted as being either unemployed or in the labor force. During the 1950s and 1960s, the proportion of males aged eighteen and nineteen who were in the labor force declined. Some of these, of course, had decided to enter school (the proportion of young males enrolled in school rose steadily during this period), but some were out of work, out of school, and not looking for either work or schooling. They may be thought of as the chronic dropouts from conventional society. Some research suggests that the increase in the number of these dropouts helps explain the increase in the rate of property crimes,[18] but other research finds no effect of either unemployment or labor-force participation.[19]

Perhaps the best-known studies claiming to show that unemployment increases certain kinds of crime are those of Harvey Brenner,[20] whose work was commissioned and given considerable currency by the Joint Economic Committee of the United States Congress. Brenner estimated the effect of changes in the unemployment rate on the homicide rate and the prison admission rate for the periods 1940–1973 and 1950–1980. Unlike economists who assume that people prefer crime to employment when the net benefits of the former exceed those of the latter, Brenner assumes that unemployment (and other forms of economic instability) creates personal stress, which in turn leads to a number of social pathologies—not only crime, but also poor health, mental illness, and suicide. Though he is careful to state that his finding of a correlation between unemployment and these pathologies does not prove that the former causes the latter, his conclusions have been presented and interpreted by the Joint Economic Committee and the media as constituting just such a proof. For example, Brenner calculated in his first study that a 1.4 percent increase in unemployment during the 1970s was associated with 1,740 additional homicides and 7,660 more admissions to state prisons. In his preface, the (then) chairman of the committee, Senator Hubert H. Humphrey, stated that the increase in unemployment was "directly responsible" for these unhappy changes.[21]

One part of this conclusion can probably be rejected out of hand. There is no good reason to suppose that the number of admissions to state prisons is a reliable measure of the rate of serious crime. States and judges within states differ greatly in their willingness to impose prison terms on convicted offenders. In Texas, for example, a higher proportion of robbers and burglars go to prison than in California or Michigan,[22] and judges in one state differ widely in severity among themselves[23] and over time.[24] And during the 1960s, when the rate of serious crime was rising sharply, the number of offenders in state prisons was declining.[25] Moreover, whether or not a person is unemployed may affect whether he goes to prison. A convicted burglar, for example, may receive probation if he has a steady job and a prison term if he does not. In this case, changes in the unemployment rate could affect the number of persons sent to prison without affecting the number of crimes committed. (A similar argument with respect to Brenner's conclusions regarding the effects of unemployment on mental health is made by Catalano and Dooley.)[26]

The conclusions with respect to homicide are more complicated matters. In his first study, Brenner found that, after holding constant (sometimes) the changing proportion of young males in the population, an increase in unemployment, inflation, and (in several variants of the equation) per capita income are associated with increases in the homicide rate.[27] It is not quite clear what one should make of this. If economic stress leads to more homicides, apparently such stress can be caused not only by unemployment but also by prosperity (as measured by increases in per capita income). It is hard to imagine how the government could reduce homicides by reducing the rate of increase of both unemployment and income. Moreover, one variable that might well affect the homicide rate—the certainty or severity of sanctions for murder—is not included in Brenner's analysis; this omission causes his estimate of the effect of unemployment on crime to be biased. In any event, an effort to see whether Brenner's findings could be replicated or whether his theory could account for changes in the homicide rate after 1973 was unsuccessful, leading the authors to conclude that there was something seriously wrong with the theory.[28]

Brenner returned to these matters in his study of the period 1950–1980. Here he found that homicide rates go up not with increases in the general unemployment rate, or even with the unemployment rate of young persons, but with increases in the *ratio* of the youthful (ages sixteen to twenty-four) unemployment rate to the total unemployment rate, though in some places in his report he says that unemployment does affect homicide among middle-aged women and elderly persons.[29] But the asserted correlation between the "unemployment ratio" and homicides is quite misleading. The "unemployment ratio" is *not* just another way of measuring unemployment; in fact, the former is negatively correlated with the latter. This means that the unemployment *ratio* goes up when the unemployment *rate* goes down. Thus, whereas Brenner appears to be saying that homicides increase when the economy turns sour, in fact he is saying that homicides increase when the economy is improving. In fact, he may be saying neither, because other scholars—in particular, Philip J. Cook and Gary A. Zarkin at Duke University—have been unable to duplicate Brenner's findings using the data he claims to have used.[30]

The inconclusive or unsatisfactory state of studies using aggregate data leads us to turn our attention to systematic inquiries into individuals confronting a choice between crime and work (or searching for work). Unfortunately, very few have been done. Ann Witte followed the careers of 641 men released from prison in North Carolina. Most were rearrested, but the availability of jobs did not seem to make a difference.[31] However, another study of individual offenders (released from federal prison or the Maryland state penitentiary) came to the opposite conclusion—sanctions made no difference and economic prospects a considerable difference in the likelihood of recidivism.[32] Philip Cook tracked 325 men released from Massachusetts prisons and discovered that those who found a "satisfactory" job (not just any job) were less likely to have their parole revoked for having committed a new crime during an eighteen-month follow-up period, and this was true even after controlling for the race, intelligence, education, marital status, and prior occupation of the parolee.[33]

A careful study of the experiences of persons released from prisons in Georgia and Texas showed that those who got jobs were somewhat less likely than those who remained unemployed to commit property crimes: Ex-offenders who managed to hold a job for a year after release committed between one and one and a half fewer property crimes, even after controlling for differences in age and family status, than did those who were unemployed.[34] But these ex-convicts, on the whole, did not look very hard for jobs. As part of an experiment called TARP (Transitional Aid Research Project), they were randomly assigned either to a group that received unemployment compensation payments of between $63 and $75 per week (provided they registered at a local employment office and stated that they were ready and able to accept a job) or to a group that was offered help in finding a job but no weekly unemployment checks. Though the unemployment checks were quite small, those who received them took much longer to find a job, were much less likely to get a job at all, and when employed worked for many fewer weeks and earned less money than did those who received no checks. Of course, most of the released prisoners had serious employment problems; they were, after all, rather poor risks for most employers. Even so, most did not seem highly motivated to find and hold a job, as one would have predicted if one believed they had turned to crime chiefly for lack of employment. As the authors of the study concluded:

> Clearly, work per se did not mean much to them since they were so easily swayed from working by the small TARP payments. This negative appraisal of working may be the outcome of years of bad experiences, a function of the types of jobs available to them, or some combination of the two. Whatever the causes, it appeared that ex-prisoners do not find the employment opportunities available to them as attractive as reduced income and no work.[35]

The TARP project offered money payments and job assistance to ex-convicts, but it left them pretty much on their own when it came to getting, mastering, and keeping a job. Perhaps these persons were so lacking in skills and so unsuccessful in previous efforts to hold a job that they lacked the confidence and the experience necessary to succeed. Knowing this, they might have accepted a pittance so long as it enabled them to avoid a job search. Being thus unemployed, but not in dire need, they drifted back into their criminal habits.

An important test of this possibility was made by the Manpower Demonstration Research Corporation (MDRC). In various cities around the country, MDRC organized "supported work" programs that provided special assistance before and during the job to, among others, ex-convicts and young school dropouts (most of whom had a police record). The supported-work concept providing training and work experience for these hard-to-employ persons is based on three ideas: The participants should have peer support (by being allowed to work in crews composed of similarly situated persons), close supervision (through training and guidance supplied by a sympathetic instructor, himself often an ex-offender), and graduated stress (resulting from steadily increasing demands on the workers). Some participants worked at renovating old houses, others at building furniture, and still others at supervising a public park or operating a messenger service. A vivid account of life in the training and work programs has been provided by Ken Auletta.[36] Happily for scholars, the participants were randomly assigned either to a work and training group or to a control group so that the effects, if any, of the experience could be measured during the three years the participants were observed (one year in training, two years on their own). On their entry into the program, the ex-convicts had been incarcerated at least once during the previous six-month period and had been arrested, on the average, nine times. Most were black; only a quarter had graduated from high school. The school dropouts were between the ages of seventeen and twenty and had been arrested, on the average, two times.

The evaluation was almost entirely discouraging. Though some other persons in the program (women on welfare and ex-addicts) seem to have benefited, the ex-convicts and the delinquent dropouts did not. There was no lasting, significant effect on their employment record, earnings, or level of criminal activity.[37] Older persons with families did seem to benefit somewhat. (This is exactly what one would expect given what we know about the association between age and crime.) There was some evidence that persons who were unemployed were a bit more likely to be arrested than those who had jobs, but the difference did not last much beyond the early months of the program and could not be attributed to any program effects.

In sum, the studies using aggregate data find, at best, only equivocal support for the proposition that changes in crime rates and in unemployment rates are associated. And it is not clear that if such an association exists it should be interpreted as proving that unemployment (or withdrawal from the labor force) causes crime; the association is also, in most studies, consistent with the theory that increases in crime cause unemployment.[38] (An exception is the study by Phillips et al. that measures the effect of labor-force participation rates in one year on crime rates in subsequent years.) While studies of individual offenders find a connection between unemployment and crime, these data are as consistent with the theory that crime and unemployment have common causes as they are with the view that unemployment causes crime. The former interpretation gains credence from the carefully evaluated efforts to improve the employment opportunities of ex-convicts and delinquents: The difficulties encountered suggest that much more than mere job shortages is responsible for their poor employment records or their criminal activities. It is possible, of course, that the individuals in these studies are past the age at which they could be affected by the training and employment opportunities. This in itself is a significant conclusion, for it calls into question the common supposition that the labor-market experiences of adults have an effect on crime rates. But it does require us to look more closely at the relationship between crime and employment among young persons.

No Effect: Common Causes

To discover whether crime and unemployment have common causes and whether these causes are sufficient to explain most or all of the observed association between crime and unemployment, one would ideally want to follow closely a large group of persons from shortly after birth until they are well into their twenties or thirties. Though such prospective longitudinal studies have been done, they are typically on so small a scale, of such short duration, or so lacking in data on criminality as to tell us very little. There are, of course, retrospective longitudinal studies (studies in which the past activities of persons are recovered from memories or official records), but these cannot easily decide questions of causality. Neither memories nor records are likely to be accurate on the all-important issue of developmental sequence: Did behavior or attitudes predisposing one to delinquency occur before or after the appearance of traits making employment difficult, and if before, did the appearance of the former determine the emergence of the latter?

At least two important prospective studies shed some light on the matter. The first is the Youth in Transition (YIT) survey that began in 1966 by interviewing about two thousand boys, randomly chosen from among all boys entering American high schools that year, and following those boys for eight years as they went through high school (or dropped out), found a job or joined the ranks of the unemployed, entered the military, or committed crimes.[39] Three-fourths of the boys first interviewed were still being interviewed eight years later. By 1974, their average age was twenty-four, half were married, and about 70 percent were working (17 percent were continuing their education, 6 percent were in the military, and 5 percent were unemployed). About 90 percent were white, 9 percent black. Roughly a fifth lived in a big (over 500,000 population) city or its suburbs; an equal proportion lived in a rural area. While this group of young men is representative of all young men of that age, it is not representative of the young men born and raised in the inner parts of our large cities, where we find the highest rates of serious crime.

Delinquency and crime were measured by means of self-reports. As we observed in Chapter 1, such reports are not wholly reliable. In this case, the reliability of the measure was unusually low because, among other reasons, the wording of the questions changed somewhat from one interview to the next.[40] As a result, the correlation between the offenses reported in two different surveys is somewhat lower than one would wish. However, as will become clear, this does not invalidate the principal conclusions of the study.

Those conclusions can best be summarized by the authors' own paraphrase of Wordsworth: "The child is the father of the man."[41] The differences among these young men five years after their high school class graduated were very similar to the differences among them in the tenth grade. Educational attainment, occupational status, and self-reported misconduct could be predicted from factors measured in the first year of high school.

Boys who dropped out of high school were twice as likely to be unemployed (after controlling for intelligence and the socioeconomic status of their families) as were boys who got their high school diploma, and were much more likely to be self-reported delinquents, at least during their teenage years, than were boys who graduated. As we would expect, the delinquency scores of all the boys declined with the passage of time, with the decline greatest (as we noted in Chapter 10) for the dropouts, so much so that by the eighth year, there was only a small difference in delinquency rates between dropouts and high school graduates (though still a big difference between these two groups and those who went on to college).

Unemployed young men reported more misconduct than employed ones—twice as much interpersonal aggression and 60 percent more theft and vandalism. But these differences between those who, in the eighth year, were employed and those who were unemployed were pretty much the same as the differences between the two groups when they were still in school.[42] Controlling for delinquent behavior in school reduced the association between unemployment and misconduct, though it did not eliminate it. However, because the measures of delinquency were somewhat unreliable, the apparent correlation between early and later levels of delinquency was smaller than the true correlation. Because of this, the YIT findings overstated (as the authors admit) any effect on delinquency of such factors as unemployment. To put the matter differently, some of the effect on later delinquency rates attributed to unemployment is in fact the effect of the (underreported) earlier delinquency levels.[43]

Taking all this into account, the authors conclude that "the delinquency differences linked to educational and occupational circumstances at Time 5 [i.e, eight years after the first survey] are largely a reflection of long-standing patterns which preceded the specific post-high school experiences we have been examining."[44]

Roughly the same conclusion is reached by West and Farrington in their longitudinal study of about four hundred boys growing up in a working-class area of London.[45] The boys who by their early twenties were either official or self-reported delinquents were much more likely to hold low-status (though often high-paying!) jobs and to have an unstable job record with frequent changes and periods of unemployment. For example, of those with an unstable employment history, half were known to the police as delinquents and four-fifths reported themselves to be highly aggressive.[46] Their criminality did not cause their poor employment history; it turns out that scarcely any of the boys lost their jobs as a result of being convicted for an offense. Did their unstable employment record cause their criminality? As we reported in Chapters 7 and 8, most of the boys' behavioral problems had become apparent very early in their lives, long before they entered the labor market. West and Farrington did not attempt to measure how much of the boys' criminality might be attributed to their employment experiences, holding constant other traits which had familial origins. But they did conclude that the delinquents not only had done poorly in school, they also "lacked motivation, often adopting a casual, haphazard, and indifferent attitude to work" and were more likely to "display an aggressive, anti-authority attitude toward situations arising at work," to drink and smoke immoderately, and, though they earned more than nondelinquents, to save little and to get into debt.[47]

These longitudinal studies do not disprove the view that unemployment can cause crime, but they do indicate, at a minimum, that for many persons individual differences of long standing are associated with both criminality and employment difficulties so that, at least for these samples, the effect of unemployment alone on the criminality of young men is not likely to be great. Moreover, these findings are broadly consistent with studies that show that intelligence, personality factors, family background, and educational attainment, separately and in interaction with one another, explain much of the relative success or failure of persons in labor markets.[48] On the other hand, neither of these studies examines the special circumstances confronting young men seeking income in the inner parts of large American cities. This is a matter to which we alluded in Chapter 11 and to which we shall return later in this chapter.

The Affluence Effect

Prosperity, accompanied by declining unemployment, might increase crime rates if that prosperity changes the value some persons attach to crime and noncrime, including work. This possibility may seem so implausible to some that they will reject it out of hand. We confess that we know of rather little systematic data that shed light on it. But it is not at all implausible. Affluence may affect crime by making the opportunities for crime more abundant: More homes and garages are stocked with consumer goods worth having, and more stores stress "self-service" (which to some persons may mean, "Take what you want because nobody is watching"). Affluence may also increase the value of crime by changing the secondary reinforcers attached to it, in particular by lessening the extent to which the bite of conscience reduces the worth of loot or the pleasure of an assault. This might happen if, as a consequence of greater prosperity, the ability of families to induce their children to internalize anticrime values is weakened. In Chapter 16 we shall offer some reasons for believing that, over the long term, changes in American society have indeed reduced the extent to which families and other intimate groups have the capacity and the inclination to inculcate norms of self-control.

Affluence may also lower the value attached to not committing a crime if prosperity provides a safety net that mitigates the consequences of not working. For example, when jobs are abundant, it may be easy for even a criminal to get part-time work that gives him the opportunity to steal or buy drugs without having to worry about becoming destitute. The largess of families and friends may lead some persons to think that the material value of a job, or at least of the relatively low-paying jobs available to young men in cities, is not much better than doing nothing and waiting for interesting (and often criminal) opportunities for quick gain. And affluence may also affect the nonmaterial value of a job to the extent it reduces the belief that being unemployed is shameful.

Rising levels of employment need not have this effect on anyone and certainly will not have this effect on everyone. Had we good data, we might well learn that during many periods of our history, the only effect of reduced unemployment was reduced want, so that as unemployment fell, crime fell. Perhaps swings in the business cycle were then not associated with important changes in how families raised their children, how consumer goods were distributed, what resources were available to the unemployed, and what value was assigned to work, reputation, and idleness. If these latter changes have occurred in recent history, it is difficult if not impossible to find any quantitative measure of them. All we might know is that a connection between unemployment and crime that might once have been observed is no longer observed.

Whatever may have been true in the past (we shall offer some speculations in Chapter 16), we are struck by the difficulty in recent decades of finding a clear correlation between changing rates of unemployment and crime. We also note some studies that find that changes in crime rates and in per capita income are positively associated: That is, as incomes rise, so does crime. Wolpin, using longitudinal data from England, found that the robbery rate went up with increases in the real wage rate.[49] Ehrlich, using cross-sectional data for 1940, 1950, and 1960 and controlling for other socioeconomic factors and for the probability of punishment, discovered that increases in median family incomes were associated with increasing rates of property crime.[50] Fox, using longitudinal data and controlling for the age structure of the population, found that crime rose with increases in the consumer price index.[51] Each of these studies has been criticized,[52] but one cannot dismiss out of hand similar findings from different authors using different methods. Or more accurately, there is at least as much reason to accept the conclusion that rising levels of wealth affect crime as there is to accept the view that rising levels of unemployment affect it.

It is not clear, however, how this affluence effect may operate. There are at least two possibilities: that increasing wealth is simply a measure of increasing opportunities for crime, or that increasing wealth is a measure of changing values and socialization practices. The first possibility has been investigated by Leroy Gould and others. They find that changes over time in the rate of auto theft are highly correlated with changes in the number of available automobiles in this country[53] and in Norway.* [54] Using a more complete set

* The correlation has an interesting form: Auto theft rates in both countries rose with increases in per capita car ownership until there were about two hundred cars registered per 100,000 population, then the theft rate declined until there were about three hundred cars registered per 100,000 persons, and thereafter the theft rate rose steadily. The authors explain this by arguing that when few people own cars, auto theft is dominated by professionals who steal cars for resale to persons wanting them; when the market reaches a certain level of saturation, the returns to professional auto thieves

of variables (in particular, controlling for the age structure of the population and the unemployment rate), Cohen, Felson, and Land did not find that auto thefts can be explained by changes in the numbers of registered cars, but did find that the burglary rate increased with increases in expenditures on durable consumer goods (such as television sets) two years earlier.[55] Even short-run increases in available property caused crime rates to rise. Interestingly, increases in unemployment were associated with decreases in crime in this model.

Beyond this, not much can be said. There is consistent evidence that increases in affluence, variously measured, are associated, at least since the 1940s, with increases in property crime, but whether this reflects only a growth in the density of criminal opportunities or a shift in the values shaping the decision making of offenders, we cannot judge.

The Envy Effect

The perceived equity of social arrangements may change if what John gets in return for his efforts (or worth) declines relative to what Paul gets for his, provided that John judges his efforts (or worth) to be the same as Paul's. What John once thought was equitable he now thinks is inequitable. But even if neither effort nor reward changes, John may come to believe that an inequity exists if he changes the standard by which he measures his efforts and Paul's. If John once believed that Paul's efforts were more deserving of rewards than his, but John now thinks Paul's efforts are no better than his, then differences in rewards John once accepted without resentment he may now find intolerable.

For example, if John builds automobiles in a factory owned by Paul, John probably expects to get less compensation than Paul. But if Paul's earnings go up or John's go down, and nothing else in the situation changes, John may think of himself as the victim of an injustice. By the same token, if the compensation of both remains relatively the same, but John has come to believe that "property is theft" and that people who own factories should earn no more than people who work in them, he will believe he is being treated unjustly.

---

decline and they accordingly steal less; and when cars become very abundant, amateurs, seeking cars for their own immediate use, dominate the stealing at a high and growing rate. Other explanations for this curve are possible, however, including the changes in values suggested above. The decline in auto theft rates (and in other crimes as well) occurred during the 1930s and early 1940s, when, possibly, the effects of the Depression and World War II were to draw tighter the social bonds and strengthen the internalization of anticrime values. We return to this issue in Chapter 16.

There have been a few efforts to test empirically whether a sense of inequity affects crime rates. Unfortunately, all the efforts of which we are aware are conceptually flawed in that they do not state the equity equation fully. Some ask whether crime rates vary with differences in income, on the assumption that where these differences are large there will be more crime. But inequalities in income are by themselves not a source of perceived inequity. What matters is whether people believe that these inequalities are justified, that the efforts (or worth) of the wealthier entitle them to that wealth. Many observers, notably Alexis de Tocqueville, have pointed out that disorder and political protest are greatest not in those societies where the least advantaged part of society is destitute and makes the slowest progress but in those where change has occurred and the least advantaged have made gains—but not enough to satisfy their heightened expectations.[56]

Others have asked whether changes in crime rates are associated with changes in the distribution of income. This is closer to the mark. Many public opinion surveys have shown that in any given nation, wealthier people are happier than poorer ones and that most people say that their economic circumstances are the chief source of their happiness or unhappiness. But increases in wealth in a given nation do not lead to increases in happiness, and wealthy nations are not, as a whole, happier than poorer ones.[57] The reason is that people compare themselves not to people in other nations but to people in their own, and as they make economic progress their standard of evaluation changes. Philip Brickman and Donald T. Campbell say that such people are on a "hedonic treadmill."[58]

Sheldon Danziger and David Wheeler estimated the impact on crime rates in the United States of both absolute differences in income (the dollar gap between the average income of individuals above the national mean and the average income of those below the national mean) and relative income shares (the ratio of the income of the better off to the income of the less well off).[59] They tested these income variables over time (1949–1970) for the country as a whole and across metropolitan areas in 1960, holding constant age structure, unemployment, the probability of punishment, and other factors. They found that, over time, either a widening of the absolute income gap or an increase in the ratio of higher to lower incomes was associated with an increase in crime, other things being equal. (Unemployment seemed to have no effect, but the probability of punishment did.) Across metropolitan areas, absolute differences in income did not affect crime rates, but the shape of income distribution did. (Comparable results for the cross-sectional data were obtained by Eberts and Schwirian.)[60]

These are suggestive but not conclusive findings. Since a general rise in incomes will automatically produce a wider absolute gap in incomes (provided the income distribution remains constant), the effect of a growing absolute income gap on crime could be interpreted as an affluence, not an inequity, effect. Crime may rise because of the consequences, in opportunities and weakened social controls, of prosperity. Nor is it clear that the income distribution is accurately measured. Per capita income levels cannot be judged simply from dollar incomes reported to the Census Bureau, since many individuals with low cash incomes have substantial in-kind incomes (from welfare, Social Security, food stamps, Medicare, public housing), and the amount of these in-kind payments has risen sharply over the last twenty years and varies greatly among regions of the country. Failing to take all this into account may lead to an overestimate of the effect of relative income on crime. Moreover, many persons with low incomes are retired; as they grow in number, or increasingly live apart from their children, they will produce an apparent increase in income inequality. But it is hard to imagine that crime increases because of the increasing number of envious old folks.

The most recent effort to show the connection between crime and economic inequality was made by Judith and Peter Blau.[61] They found that there was a strong association between inequality in family income and rates of violent crime in 125 U.S. metropolitan areas in 1970, an association that persisted after controlling for race, region, city size, and the level of poverty. This means, it should be noted, that income inequalities *within* each race, and not simply those between races, are associated with high rates of violent crime.

It is not clear that this finding can be interpreted as meaning that people act violently because they believe that the distribution of income in their community is unjust. Before accepting that interpretation, one would first have to rule out alternative explanations, including the operation of unmeasured individual attributes that might account for both differences in income and high rates of crime. (One such factor, the youthfulness of the population, was not included in the Blaus' analysis.) In addition, it is a bit puzzling that income inequality is associated with violence but not theft. And even among violent crimes, inequalities are related to homicide and assault but not robbery. If some people feel unjustly treated by a society that gives (in their view) undeservedly high incomes to other people, why wouldn't the aggrieved persons respond by stealing rather than assaulting, especially since most of the victims of such assaults are acquaintances and family members?

In sum, a sense of inequity or social envy may contribute to crime rates, but the data we have do not permit us to say more than that this possibility exists. If it does have an effect, it could arise as much from changing standards regarding what constitutes an equitable distribution of wealth (changes that might be influenced, for example, by the mass media, as we suggest in Chapter 13) as from changes in the actual distribution. Whatever effects a sense of inequality may have, they tend to contribute, for reasons we do not understand, more to violent than to property crimes, a matter to which we shall refer again when we compare, in Chapter 17, crime rates in various nations and when we discuss, in Chapter 18, crime rates among blacks.

Economy and Community

Thus far we have reviewed studies that assume, for the most part, that marginal changes in the rate of unemployment, the level of affluence, or the distribution of incomes may cause changes in the crime rate, other things being equal. This is a reasonable assumption under most circumstances, but not, perhaps, under all. Suppose that some young men live in areas of pervasive unemployment or underemployment. Suppose they lack the educational achievement and personal temperament that would make them attractive to employers. Suppose further that very few firms providing jobs with long-term prospects for advancement choose to locate in these areas because of high crime rates, a shortage of skilled workers, or other environmental or economic handicaps. Under these circumstances, marginal changes in the national (or even state or city) unemployment rates or income levels would have little or no effect on crime rates, for one or both of two reasons.

First, these young persons may grow up believing, from all the evidence around them, that the value of jobs is low and will always be so. Very few persons they know work steadily and for high wages. Some of those who do work at the available jobs have personalities that make them—and by association, the jobs they hold—undesirable; they were the unpopular conformists in school and are now the "jerks" willing to work as delivery boys, car washers, or shipping clerks. Work in such "dead-end" jobs is thought to be demeaning, whereas crime, and even being arrested, are not thought to be shameful and may even be a source of pride. This attitude may also reflect a degree of self-deprecation. If the young men have been taught to believe that education is the key to success and if they have done poorly in school, then they may think of themselves as unqualified for a decent job, and the rejections they are likely to encounter in their first job hunts will only confirm this. A self-fulfilling prophecy comes into play, the adverse consequences of which are rationalized by regarding jobs as unworthy, employers unreasonable, and crimes acceptable.

Second, the available work may in fact consist mostly of "dead-end" jobs that produce low returns, high turnover, and no prospects. This view has been developed by theorists of the dual (or segmented) labor market. In this view, the labor market has two components—a primary market, consisting of the better jobs that supply on-the-job training and offer prospects for advancement, and a secondary one, providing low-paying jobs that involve little training and no advancement. Unemployment in the primary market tends to be involuntary (people are laid off in bad times) but infrequent; unemployment in the secondary market tends to be voluntary (people often move from one low-paying job to another) and frequent.[62] Some dual-labor-market theorists suggest that the secondary labor market is one of several similar economic sectors in the inner parts of large cities, the others being property crime, illegal or quasi-legal "work" (street hustles), welfare payments, and government-subsidized training programs. Individuals move among these sectors frequently and casually, with each sector sharing many characteristics—low per capita incomes, high turnover, little advancement. Few persons in the secondary market break out into the primary one.[63] Based on interviews conducted with over two thousand young black males in Boston, Chicago, and Philadelphia, Kip Viscusi concluded that about one-fourth of all the income for the men in the sample came from criminal activity, with most of the serious crime concentrated among a small number of high-rate offenders.[64]

Both these sets of arguments are designed to explain why changes in economic variables, such as unemployment rates, have little or no effect on the behavior of persons in certain communities. The first set emphasizes the subjective state of (especially) young men growing up in these communities, the second the objective conditions of the labor market and its alternatives. The first implies that if one could change the subjective state of the young men (by raising their educational attainment, altering their expectations, heightening their ambitions, lengthening their time horizons, and improving their presentability), they would participate in whatever labor market exists. The second implies that larger investments in education and character formation will have little effect and that only by altering the structure of the labor market itself (by, for example, inducing large employers providing primary-segment jobs to locate in communities now dominated by secondary-segment employers) will employment rise. Both views criticize the conventional economic theory of the relationship between unemployment and crime. The first agrees that the value of a job may affect the attractiveness of crime, but argues that this value is assigned by a communal, not an individual, process. (In technical language, utilities are interdependent because the value one person gives to working depends in part on the value a friend gives to it.) The second agrees that the value of work may affect the crime rate, but argues that the structure of the labor market can prevent general economic conditions from altering the value of work. Both draw attention to the influence of community (and communal institutions) on the economy.

There is evidence that inner-city economies are different from the economy at large. Labor-force participation rates are lower in such areas, especially among blacks, partly because the better jobs are increasingly located on the periphery of the city, where some persons (again, especially blacks) find it difficult to move.[65] And there is evidence that young men whose first efforts to find jobs are unrewarding are much more likely to experience unemployment later in life.[66]

But how much of the higher unemployment rates in inner-city areas can be attributed to the existence of a dual labor market is still unclear. A leading labor-market text concluded that the theory was still "in its formative stage,"[67] and a recent effort to test the claim that a segmented market caused unemployment (by offering only unappealing jobs to discouraged workers) led to inconclusive results.[68] Several economists have noted that advertisements of low-skill, modestly paid jobs attract large numbers of applicants in the big cities, consistent with the view that it is the shortage of jobs, not the social characteristics of a neighborhood, that causes high unemployment rates.[69] Even among young men with relatively little schooling, most find jobs. They begin looking, often while still in school, in the secondary labor market. During these early years (according to one longitudinal study of boys aged sixteen to nineteen followed for seven years), black and white males start out with hourly pay and annual earnings that are about the same; the gap that opens in later years is strongly correlated with whether the men get married and acquire additional schooling or training.[70]

The fact that these studies find only modest evidence for a community effect on employment histories may only mean that such an effect cannot readily be detected with conventional economic data that do not measure social structure or personal expectations and are not drawn from small, inner-city areas. Close observation by various authors of street-corner life in the inner city provides a portrait of communal effects on employment and crime that, though not quantitative, is nonetheless hard to dismiss. Some of those studies were reviewed in Chapter 11; others can be added here. Bernard Rosenberg and Harry Silverstein described the attitudes toward work encountered among one of the three groups they studied, young blacks living on one street in Washington, D.C.[71] Every boy interviewed had been employed at one time, but the turnover was very high. When asked why they left a job, they typically answered that they found it monotonous or low paying. Petty theft was well-nigh universal and more serious crime hardly unusual, much of it done, as we have already seen, in small groups. The value these young people attached to crime and to noncrime (including work) was heavily influenced by the expectations they had of each other and by the conduct they saw everywhere about them. The shape of these values, in turn, was influenced by the ethnic subculture of which the young persons were a part—the southern-born blacks in Washington differed from the Appalachian whites in Chicago and the Puerto Ricans in East Harlem. Cultural (i.e., learned) factors affected how labor-market conditions were interpreted; there was no single "culture of poverty."

These cultural influences may be so important in areas with very high crime rates that changes in city-wide or state-wide economic conditions will not lead to changes in crime rates. Since there is in even the poorest neighborhoods a variety of social structures, no one should assume that communal and cultural forces in a given area have the same effect on everyone. Within a block or two, one can encounter people who value work and people who do not; thieves who steal regularly and systematically and thieves who steal occasionally and casually, even while employed.[72] But for reasons having to do with some combination of cultural factors and objective conditions, it seems clear that a significant fraction of young men in many inner-city areas assign a low, perhaps even negative, value to success achieved through legitimate employment. In the Hunter's Point area of San Francisco, Hippler finds that being able to " 'make it' while avoiding the 'work game' is a strong, pervasive, and consistent goal."[73] Though scholars disagree profoundly over whether such views are shaped by familial, cultural, or economic factors, there is little reason to believe that persons holding such views will have their work habits or crime rates affected by moderate variations in economic conditions.[74] Moreover, the fact that so many job-training programs aimed at young persons with especially poor employment records (such as the supported work projects of MDRC, reviewed earlier in this chapter) have little or no effect on either employment or crime suggests that long-term personal and social factors are more important than the immediate availability of jobs or training in explaining the crime rates of persons who are likely to be high-rate offenders.

Conclusions

The connection between crime and unemployment (or economic conditions generally) is likely to be quite complex, as becomes evident once one sets forth a full theory of criminal behavior. The inconsistent and often counterintuitive results of so many studies of the crime-economy link arise in large measure, we think, from relying on an overly simple model of choice, one in which a person chooses between crime and work on the basis of stable preferences and without regard to the preferences of others. These simple models compare crime and noncrime almost entirely in terms of their money values, neglecting the nonmaterial components of these values, which can make so large a difference among individuals as to lead some to prefer crime to noncrime even when the discounted money value of the latter exceeds the money value of the former. Moreover, these models neglect the extent to which changing economic conditions can cause (or at least be associated with) changes in the social processes that determine the value of reputation, the bite of conscience, and the perception of inequity.

Our assessment of the evidence leads us to conclude that common causes—the "no effect" theory—explain most of the observed connection between unemployment and crime, with some influences (how much, we cannot say) from the need effect, the affluence effect, and the envy effect. These latter effects probably operate over the entire life history of a person and thus can be observed only dimly (if at all) at the moment when that person is choosing between crime and noncrime.

13

TELEVISION AND THE MASS MEDIA

When, in the eighteenth century, Goethe published *The Sorrows of Young Werther,* the authorities in several nations worried that readers captivated by this popular novel would commit suicide in imitation of the book's tragic hero. Though no such wave of suicides was ever established, the book itself was banned in several places.[1]

Today, television and newspapers have become so pervasive a part of our lives that it seems only reasonable to suppose that their combined effect on our tendency to resort to violence must be many times greater than that of a single novel. Moreover, if so many commercial and political interests invest so much money in media advertising, it would seem absurd to believe that the media have no effect on our behavior, including, perhaps, our criminal behavior. Otherwise, billions of dollars are being wasted by advertisers. And if the media changed only the noncriminal aspects of our behavior, that would be only slightly less remarkable.

The media, and especially television, might alter our tendency to commit crimes in several ways. Viewing programs (or watching films, or reading newspapers or magazines) might increase the material value we attach to crime by calling to our attention things we did not realize we wanted until we saw them attractively portrayed, or by suggesting to us that things we always knew we wanted are more accessible than we had imagined. We might in this way discover the lure of fancy sports cars or, if we had long wanted one, learn that, contrary to what we had supposed, they are frequently left

337

unlocked and unguarded. The media might also increase the intangible rewards of crime by making us envious of young persons who own sports cars without, apparently, having had to work hard or wait long to get them. In this way our personal equity equation might be altered as a result of thinking that our efforts are the same as those of persons we see on television or in films enjoying things we do not have. One way to correct that sense of inequity is to take what another person has. Television and motion pictures can also increase the nonmaterial rewards of crime by convincingly portraying to us the excitement one may feel from successfully stealing a car or the satisfaction we will get from beating up a person who has a car we covet.

But the media could also alter the rewards attached to *not* committing a crime. Since most TV crime programs show the criminal being caught, we might come to believe that the risks of crime are much greater than we once supposed and than in fact they are. Television might also change our perceptions of the benefits of legitimate work. If television depicts hardworking people ending up with good jobs and nice lives, it may make work more attractive because of its consequences. And if television shows persons having fun on the job, it might make work intrinsically more appealing regardless of its consequences.

Viewing television may also increase the extent to which we are impulsive—that is, unwilling to defer gratifying our desires. Even if television were to have no effect on the value we assign to the rewards that come from owning a fancy car or punching somebody in the nose, it may play so large a role in our lives and be a source of such instant gratification that addiction to it will make us restless and impatient. We "can't wait" to enjoy the car or the punch. If we become very impulsive we may commit a crime regardless of what we have also learned about the (possibly great) costs of crime. Those costs will be delayed beyond the point when they can affect our behavior once we are on the street and encounter the fancy car or the punchable nose. And if this heightened impulsiveness is combined with a sharpened sense of inequity, we might become much more likely to commit crimes whatever the cost or however attractive legitimate careers may appear to be.

Given the many ways in which the media might affect individual differences in criminality, it is something of a surprise to learn that almost all the research seeking to establish a relationship between television and crime has focused on the extent to which television causes us to commit acts of violence, and has done so by exploring the possibility that viewing television either enhances or replaces the satisfaction we get from acting violently. This enhancement may occur because the restraining influence of our conscience is weakened ("disinhibition") or because we find the portrayal of violence to be exciting or stimulating ("modeling"). Conversely, viewing televised violence may lead us to reduce our own level of aggression by allowing us to enjoy, vicariously, the aggression of others ("catharsis"). All of these processes have in common the fact that they are part of the immediate rewards or penalties associated with the criminal act.

One of the advantages of the model of criminal behavior we presented in Chapter 2, by contrast, is that it forces us to consider all of the circumstances that might influence behavior, and not just those present at the moment the opportunity for crime presents itself. The model directs our attention to the extent to which a person is temperamentally impulsive and to the delayed costs and benefits of crime, as well as to the immediate costs and benefits of the act itself. Moreover, the model requires us to consider crime for material gain as well as crime for psychic satisfaction. Given this larger view, we must be dissatisfied with research on television and crime that looks only at whether portrayals of violence change the immediate satisfaction we may get from becoming violent, with little thought to whether television (or again, the media generally) has a larger, more complex effect on our behavior by changing our willingness to delay gratification, our equity equation, or our perceptions of the delayed penalties that might (or might not) be associated with crime.

One of the reasons so much of the research is aimed at identifying the direct effect of pictorial violence on human aggression is popular concern, reinforced by the ideological predispositions of certain scholars. Social scientists tend to abhor violence and dislike much of popular culture; it is only natural, therefore, that when the public worries about what television may be doing to their children, especially when there is a rising level of violence in society, scholars would concentrate their efforts on showing how televised violence, by means of disinhibition or modeling, increases the violence of television viewers, especially children.

But it is not public concern or scholarly predilection alone that explains this focus. The larger effects of the media on criminality are very difficult to identify by any feasible social science methodology. As we shall see, it is hard enough to study the extent to which viewing violence leads immediately to increases in violent acts. But it is much harder—in practice, it may be impossible—to study whether a society raised on television and movies has a shorter time horizon than one raised without them, or whether filmed portrayals of affluence make us act on the belief that society "owes us a living," or whether televised portrayals of crime and detection lead us to increase or decrease our own estimates of the chances of making crime pay.

Methods of Studying Media Effects

There are three principal means by which scholars have attempted to measure the effect, if any, of television on crime—the observation of natural variation, laboratory experiments, and real-world (or field) experiments. When we observe natural variations, we ask whether the amount or the kind of television viewing found among some group (say, third-grade children) is correlated with the amount of aggression they display verbally or physically. When we conduct a laboratory experiment, we expose some persons in a laboratory (and thus artificial) setting to films or pictures of aggressive and nonaggressive acts to see if those who watch them are more likely than others to behave aggressively in the laboratory. And when we carry out a real-world (or field) experiment, we observe how people in natural settings (living at home or in a summer camp) respond to some change made in the television programs they see. Some of these changes may occur naturally (as when a town that never had any television suddenly acquires a broadcast station) and some may occur artificially (as when boys living in a boarding school are shown, in some cottages, violent programs, and in other cottages, nonviolent programs, all under the control of a researcher). The first kind of real-world experiment is called a natural field experiment (or quasi experiment) and the second kind a planned field experiment.

Each mode of inquiry has both its advantages and disadvantages. Studying natural variation is the easiest (nobody has to be manipulated), but it cannot readily answer questions of causality. If aggression and television viewing are correlated, does that mean that watching television causes aggression or that aggressive persons happen to enjoy television, especially television featuring violent programs? Moreover, even when causality can be established (as by seeing which comes first, aggression or television watching), we are still dependent on what people are willing to tell us about their behavior and habits, and these reports may be seriously in error. Finally, even when the data are accurate and causality has been established, we cannot be certain we have gathered enough information to show that any apparent connection between behavior and television is not in fact the result of some unmeasured third factor (such as intelligence, temperament, or peer pressure).

Laboratory experiments avoid some of these problems. Causality is easier to establish because one can directly observe how people behave before they see the films and how they behave afterward in comparison with others who differ only in not having watched the films. Also, the distorting effect of unmeasured personality factors can be controlled by randomly assigning persons to the experimental and control groups. But these advantages are purchased at a price, perhaps a heavy one. A laboratory setting cannot possibly duplicate the conditions under which people behave in the real world. Indeed, if the laboratory did duplicate the real world, it would no longer be a laboratory. Behavior, especially criminal behavior, occurs in settings in which people are stimulated by friends or antagonized by enemies; moreover, in the real world the chance of being punished by a victim who retaliates is often high, but the risk of being punished by the criminal justice system is low. In a laboratory, even one in which friends are present and policemen absent, the subjects are not likely to encounter the kinds of situations that might provoke them to commit serious acts of violence or the kinds of restraints that might prevent them from committing trivial ones. Moreover, a person who sees a violent film in a laboratory may well assume that the experimenter approves of the film and thus condones expressing some minor forms of violence. Finally, a laboratory experiment cannot last very long—perhaps an hour or two a day for, at most, a few days. Such short exposure to stimuli (such as violent films or programs) may have no effect or, if it has an effect, it might be quite short-lived.

Real-world or field experiments offer the best opportunities for learning how the media affect behavior, but they also have limitations. Though the exposure to the programs may occur in natural settings and for prolonged periods, the behavior of those who viewed the programs may be hard to observe because it occurs in the real world and not in laboratories on the other side of one-way mirrors. And the persons exposed to the natural experiments may differ in important but undetected ways from those not exposed to them. The people of a city that suddenly gets its first television station may, during the period of the study, change through in-migration and out-migration or because of other contemporaneous forces, such as an economic downturn, a political controversy, or a rise in crime. Persons exposed to planned real-world experiments may change their behavior because they know they are the subjects of an experiment, and not because of the kinds of programs they are viewing.

That there are difficulties with each method of inquiry does not mean that nothing can be learned about the effect of television on crime. It does mean, however, that one should be cautious about drawing any conclusions about that effect. The strongest conclusions are those supported by findings from many different kinds of studies. It is unlikely that a causal connection between the media and crime is spurious if all three kinds of studies produce evidence supporting it. On the other hand, if no study finds an effect, that does not mean no effects exist. Some effects, for reasons discussed earlier in this chapter, are likely to be so subtle, pervasive, and slow to develop that no research will uncover them. This is especially the case for effects *other* than short-term aggression, such as the effects of weakened impulse control on theft. In what follows in this chapter, we shall review the major findings of the studies that have been done and summarize the relationship, if any, found in several different kinds of inquiries.

Studies of Natural Variation

The most dramatic evidence that the mass media can have effects that lead to violent behavior comes from studies of newspaper and television accounts of actual violence. In a series of articles, David P. Phillips of the University of California at San Diego has shown that the authorities who banned *Werther* may have had cause for concern. The number of suicides in Britain and the United States goes up significantly after a well-publicized suicide. The more newspaper space given to the suicide, the more suicides occur in the area exposed to the news stories. Moreover, a well-publicized suicide is also followed by a sharp increase in the number of automobile fatalities, especially single-car accidents of the kind that frequently represent the suicide of the driver.[2] Phillips calculated that within two months after the suicide of Marilyn Monroe in 1962, there were three hundred more suicides in this country than would have occurred in the absence of her death.*[3]

Phillips also discovered that just after the appearance of newspaper and television accounts of a heavyweight prizefight the number of reported homicides increased by about one-eighth. The increase peaked three days after the fight, was greatest for the most highly publicized fights, and tended to involve as victims persons who were similar in race to the loser of the prizefight.[4] He suggested that these additional homicides were not committed by persons frustrated by having lost a bet on the outcome of the fight, because championship football games—the Super Bowls—on which even more money is bet were not followed by any noticeable increase in homicides. In an earlier study, Leonard Berkowitz and Jacqueline Macaulay found that highly publicized murders, such as the assassination of President John F. Kennedy

---

* The technique used by Phillips in this and other studies summarized here involved, essentially, predicting the number of suicides or homicides one would expect on a given day from the historical records for that day of the week and that season of the year and comparing the predicted number with the actual number for the days following a publicized suicide, homicide, prizefight, or execution.

in 1963 and the multiple murders committed by Richard Speck and Charles Whitman in 1966, were also followed by an increase in the number of violent crimes in a sample of forty American cities.[5]

If some kinds of publicized violence can lead to additional violence, then it is possible that some kinds of publicized penalties for violence might lead to its reduction. By examining changes in the number of homicides over sixty-three years (1858–1921) in London, Phillips was able to find evidence of a decline of one-third in the number of homicides immediately following a publicized execution. The greater the publicity, the greater the decline. The decline lasted about two weeks, followed by an increase during the next three. The deterrent effect of the publicized executions, thus, was temporary. A similar short-term decline seems to occur in American homicides during the period immediately after the publication of stories about murderers being punished by life sentences or executions.[6]

Since we know nothing about the persons responsible for the upsurge in suicides and homicides following certain kinds of newspaper accounts, we do not know why the increase occurs. The best guess is that these people are emulating the behavior of others; that is, "observational learning" or "modeling" has occurred. Moreover, we cannot be certain whether the media accounts are affecting the prevalence of violence (by increasing, for example, the proportion of persons who assault others), altering its incidence (by making already violent persons increase the rate at which they use violence), or increasing its severity (by stimulating a person who was going to hit somebody anyway to use a lead pipe instead of his fist).

What chiefly concerns critics of media violence, however, is not the occasional imitative suicide or the (possibly) homicide-generating power of a prizefight, but the possibility that long-term exposure to accounts of violence—especially on television—will strongly affect the prevalence or incidence of violence over the lifetimes of many people.

There have been many crude efforts to study the relationship between watching television and violence by correlating the answers children give to questions about their habits and beliefs. For example, some researchers have sought to discover whether children who say they watch a lot of television also say they approve of or engage in violence.[7] Obviously such studies can tell us little. What constitutes "violence," in either TV programs or personal behavior, is not clear; it could include everything from shouting, shoving, or trying to trip someone to attacking a person with a knife. In fact, it is not even clear whether the children actually behave the way they say they do. Moreover, it is hard to tell what causes what; children predisposed to violent behavior for reasons already discussed in this book might spend more time watching television and take more pleasure in programs that feature violence.

An effort both to measure behavior and to untangle the pattern of causality was begun in 1960 by Leonard D. Eron, L. Rowell Huesmann, Monroe M. Lefkowitz, and Leopold O. Walder.[8] Known as the Rip Van Winkle Study, it involved examining the television viewing habits and behavior of all the third-grade children (875 subjects) in a semirural county in upstate New York. Aggression was measured by asking each child's peers who he or she knew who did any one of ten things, such as starting a fight over nothing. Each child was assigned an aggressiveness score based on these peer nominations. The researchers also obtained an IQ score for each child as well as an estimate (based on interviewing the parents) of how discordant the child's home was. Television viewing habits were determined by asking each mother to name her child's three favorite programs; the contents of these programs were then classified as either violent or nonviolent.

Ten years later, when the children had entered high school, their aggressiveness and viewing habits were again measured in much the same way as before. In addition, the youths were given the MMPI (i.e., a personality test), they were questioned about self-reported acts of aggression, and state police records were checked to see whether they had been arrested. Of course, not all the original subjects could be located or persuaded to cooperate; in fact, less than half were re-examined. After another ten years the authors again contacted their subjects (about half could still be located).[9] By now they were around thirty years old. They were interviewed (as were most of their spouses and their children), and again their criminal records were checked.

Three things that were discovered will come as no surprise, for they have been found in almost every other study of this subject. First, early signs of aggression, especially in males, were highly predictive of later signs of aggression. Second, the children who were the most aggressive watched the most television. Third, persons with a lower IQ were also more likely to be aggressive.

The central issue, of course, was whether television viewing habits caused aggressiveness. The authors of the Rip Van Winkle Study concluded that television at an early age was not simply correlated with later aggressiveness, it actually helped cause it, and did so independently of intelligence, father's occupation, parental discipline, and even the amount of television watched. Low-IQ boys were more likely to be aggressive, because of both the direct effects of intelligence on behavior and the indirect effects (low-IQ boys spent more time than others getting lost in the world of television). TV viewing habits seemed to have no connection with aggressiveness in girls.[10]

The Rip Van Winkle Study quickly became one of the most widely cited pieces of evidence supporting the proposition that prolonged viewing of violent programs would, independently of other individual characteristics, contribute to later aggressiveness. The staff of the Surgeon General's Scientific Advisory Committee on Television and Social Behavior made it the centerpiece of one of their reports. In his preface to that report, Steven H. Chaffee summarized the nine studies it contained, including the New York longitudinal study, by saying that "a significant positive correlation has been found much more often than not, and there is no negative correlational evidence."[11]

But there were some serious limitations to the New York study, some clearly stated by the authors at the outset and others that became evident only after other scholars had re-examined the data. One problem was that the study did not discover how much the children were exposed to televised violence; all we know is what programs their mothers said they preferred. Thus, we cannot be certain exactly what was watched and for how long. Moreover, the statistical method used in that study (and in others like it[12]) to determine causality was faulty for technical reasons too complex to discuss here. David Rogosa[13] was able to show that the method—"cross-lagged correlation"—was likely to produce spurious results.

A fresh start was made. Two new sets of longitudinal studies were launched by different scholars at about the same time and using essentially the same methods. Some of the authors of the Rip Van Winkle Study, led by L. Rowell Huesmann, followed for three years several hundred elementary school students in a suburb of Chicago; at the same time, similar studies were being mounted abroad, in Australia, Finland, Israel, the Netherlands, and Poland. A different research team, headed by J. Ronald Milavsky, began following, also for three years, several hundred youngsters in two midwestern cities. Both teams made efforts to measure the amount as well as the kind of television viewing and to employ more acceptable statistical methods for determining causal connections.

Both sets of studies found, once again, that the aggressive children watched a lot of violent television. Both found that there was a small correlation between watching television at an early age and being aggressive three years later. But beyond that, the studies diverged. The Huesmann group argued that the correlations they found among the Chicago children between early viewing and later aggressiveness were statistically significant and showed a causal effect; the Milavsky group, on the other hand, said that in their

study these correlations were not statistically significant (in fact, they disappeared once one controlled for the social class of the child) and hence there
was no causal effect.[14] One possible way to explain the differing conclusions
is that the Chicago study found the greatest link between TV viewing and
aggression was among those boys who identified with violent fictional characters.

Something like the following may be at work: Aggressive children, because they are not very popular, and low-IQ children, because they have
trouble with schoolwork, spend more time watching television than other
children. These children identify with the television characters and may
come to accept the apparently easy and sometimes violent solutions these
characters have for the problems that confront them. To the extent they emu-
late this violence or further neglect their schoolwork, their reliance on television may increase. Television, in short, provides for such children reinforcements that are not supplied by peers or schoolwork.

But even if this interpretation is correct, the amount of violence that
can be explained by these studies is quite small. There is no doubt that aggressive boys, including those who grow up to acquire significant criminal
records, spend a lot more time than other boys in front of the television
screen, but we are not much closer to being able to say that these viewing
habits cause much of the violence than we were twenty years ago. The best
studies come to contradictory conclusions and, even when all doubts are resolved in favor of a causal effect, they account for only "trivial proportions"
of individual differences in aggression.[15]

Laboratory Experiments

In principle, a laboratory experiment provides us with a better chance
of resolving the knotty problems of measuring influences and determining
causality that plague studies of natural variation. After all, in an experimental setting, we observe behavior directly, not through self-reports or peer
ratings, and by randomly assigning persons to the experimental and control
groups we control for the confounding effect of any unmeasured personality
factors. But it has proved to be exceptionally difficult to devise a satisfactory
experiment. For one thing, the experimenter cannot in good conscience allow
his subjects to engage in real aggression—that is, to inflict injury on another
person. So he must devise some substitute, such as permitting the subject to
attack an inanimate object (e.g., a doll), or he must limit the "aggression"
to verbal insults, or he must try to deceive the subject into thinking that he is

inflicting injury when in fact he is not (e.g., letting the subject believe he is administering painful electric shocks to another person).

Obviously, however, children who can be induced to punch a doll may differ in important ways from those who can be induced to punch a real person. For one thing, dolls don't punch back. At best, individual differences in doll punching can tell us only what factors may reduce the internalized inhibitions against playing roughly with a toy. By the same token, the effort to deceive a person into thinking he is administering a shock to another person may or may not be successful. The early experiments using fake shocks, conducted by persons such as Stanley Milgram (see Chapter 8), have been rather widely publicized, especially in college psychology courses, and many of the subjects recruited for studies of aggression using this method are college undergraduates. Naturally, experimenters attempt to guard against these problems by, for example, interviewing subjects before and after the experiment to see if they were in fact deceived, but no one can be certain that the interview reports are entirely accurate. If psychologists try to fool undergraduates, it stands to reason that some undergraduates will try to fool psychologists.

With these qualifications in mind, we can summarize the laboratory experiments by saying that, with some exceptions, their results are consistent with the view that watching filmed violence increases the frequency with which persons display, shortly thereafter, behavior that the experimenter has chosen to call aggressive. The stimuli include cartoons displaying violence, special films of persons attacking dolls, and regular motion pictures; the responses include punching large dolls, playing roughly with toys, administering fake shocks, and (in a few cases) attacking an adult dressed up in a clown suit.[16] Though interpreting these studies as proving that the media cause violence is fraught with difficulties, at a minimum one can say that they supply little or no support for the catharsis theory—the view that watching pictorial violence will lead to less personal violence because any violent emotions have been safely discharged by vicariously enjoying the display of violence by others.

Some of the experiments are of more interest than others. We are not impressed by elaborate efforts to show that if you expose four-year-old children to scenes of persons happily beating up on dolls, the children will beat up on dolls themselves, or that children who just watched a violent cartoon are more likely to want to burst a toy balloon than those who had watched a nonviolent cartoon. At most, such experiments show that children will (at least in the short run) imitate the behavior of others, especially when no one tells them not to, and that they will lose some of their inhibitions against displaying violent feelings if they have just been excited by the sight of Woody Woodpecker losing his inhibitions, especially when the excitement occurs in a group of similarly excited children.

We take more seriously the discovery in the early 1960s, before the use of fake electric shocks in experiments had become widely known, that ordinary working-class men would administer longer and more severe "shocks" to subjects after seeing a knife-fighting scene from the James Dean movie *Rebel Without a Cause* than would similar men who had just seen a nonviolent film.[17] When the same experiment was done a few years later using middle-class college students as subjects, it turned out that the subjects who administered the most "shocks" were the ones who had watched a violent fight from the Kirk Douglas movie *Champion* and who had previously been angered by the experimenter.[18] Perhaps some persons are more suggestible than others, or some persons display violence when they are in an excited state while others do so only when, in addition, they have been frustrated.

One might dismiss these findings if the effect of pictorial violence were short-lived. All of us have had the experience of feeling hostile, angry, or excited after seeing a motion picture or television program that portrayed either violence or some obvious injustice that seemed to require violent retribution. But few of us are then immediately confronted with a chance to punch a doll, administer a "shock," or start a fight. Instead, we are usually confronted with the need to wash the dishes, catch a bus, or do our homework. By the time we have a chance to act violently, the excitement is gone, the anger subdued, and our time horizon lengthened. Conscience and prudence have returned to govern our actions in their customary ways.

But for some of us, an opportunity for violence occurs almost immediately or the suppression of our conscience (or of our inclination to calculate consequences) is long-lasting. We know from the newspaper headlines what then may occur. A crowd of teen-agers at a violent movie spills out onto the streets and starts a riot; a football fan punches a fan of the other team; the grisly details of a fictional murder are copied by a real murderer. The studies by Phillips provide some evidence for these effects. Laboratory experiments cannot explain exactly why these things occur, but they can test whether the disposition to imitate pictorial violence persists much beyond the end of the experiment. There have been some efforts to measure the extent to which children retain for a week, a month, or even several months any tendency they may have formed to imitate filmed violence, but the results are not conclusive.[19] To the extent that these studies show the effect of pictorial violence enduring at all, it is largely the result of imitation (copying an observed method of inflicting harm) rather than disinhibition (a weakening of internalized restraints).

Real-World Experiments

Ideally, we would answer questions about the effect of the mass media on crime in the same way we would answer questions about the effect of family discipline or school organization on crime—by changing the conditions operating in the real world, randomly assigning persons to these changed conditions, and observing the result. Obviously, we can rarely make such changes or observe, in any reliable fashion, the result of whatever changes do occur. Occasionally, however, something approximating this method of inquiry is possible, and the results of these studies are the most interesting of all.

One of the first such opportunities occurred in England in the 1950s when a new television transmitter was installed in Norwich, thereby enabling the residents of this city to watch television for the first time on a regular basis at home. Hilde T. Himmelweit and her colleagues administered a questionnaire to virtually all the children ages ten to eleven and thirteen to fourteen in the Norwich schools when scarcely any families had a television set at home and again a year later when many did; the attitudes of children before and after being exposed to television for the first time could then be analyzed.[20]

Not only were questionnaires completed, the children were asked to keep diaries in which they recorded all their daily activities, and teachers were asked to assess the children's behavior. The authors concluded: "We did not find that the viewers were any more aggressive or maladjusted than the controls; television is unlikely to cause aggressive behaviour, although it could precipitate it in those few children who are emotionally disturbed."[21] Attenuating the force of this conclusion is the failure of the authors to present any systematic, quantitative data to support it, and the weakness of their measure of aggression (teachers were simply asked whether the child was an "aggressive type" or a "submissive type").[22] Moreover, there was little attention to the kind of programs being watched during the year—children who watched violent ones and children who watched nonviolent ones were apparently lumped together in the analysis.

These difficulties in drawing conclusions from naturally occurring field experiments have led a number of scholars to make planned changes in the viewing habits of children in various real-world settings, such as schools and camps. One of the first of these involved showing violent programs (such as *The Untouchables*) to boys living in certain dormitories, and nonviolent programs (such as *Lassie*) to boys living in other dormitories, over a period of six weeks. During this time, the aggressive behavior, if any, of the boys was recorded every day by teachers and others who could observe them as they went about their daily routines. Not only were the boys who watched violent programs no more aggressive than those who watched non-violent ones, there was some evidence that watching violent shows was associated with being *less* violent.[23] There was at least one major difficulty with this study, however. It seems that some of the boys condemned to watching *Lassie* or its equivalent got bored and demanded something more exciting, such as *Batman,* and got it. As with many real-world experiments, the demands of reality became more important than the requirements of experimentation. Others have speculated that the higher levels of violence associated with the *Lassie* watchers was the result of their being bored with their tame fare and envious of the boys who got something better.[24]

A more careful effort to make a planned change in the viewing habits of children was carried out among about one hundred boys and girls, ages three to five, who were attending a summer nursery school in Pennsylvania. After their play habits had been observed, the children were randomly assigned to groups that watched (for four weeks) violent shows (such as *Batman*), neutral ones, or "pro-social" ones (such as *Mister Rogers' Neighborhood*). The children were observed at play during this period and for two weeks thereafter. There was some increase in the amount of aggressive behavior among the children who had already shown themselves to be rather aggressive and who now watched the violent programs; there was no increase in aggression among the children who showed themselves to be relatively unaggressive before watching the programs. Boys and girls responded in about the same way.[25]

Even more interesting than the modest and sharply qualified support this study gave to the connection between the visual media and aggression is the light it shed on how that connection operated. Children shown *Batman* and the like displayed a decline in their ability to tolerate delay, whereas those who watched Mister Rogers and the like revealed an increase in their tolerance for delay. And this increase in tolerance was greatest for the high-IQ children. Filmed violence, in short, seemed to increase the impulsivity of children who were already more aggressive than the average; filmed "pro-social" behavior seemed to decrease the impulsivity of children who were above average in intelligence.

To find out whether these relationships might exist among older children, a series of comparable field experiments was conducted in the United States and Belgium. In each case, the study was done in an institution to which delinquent or troublesome boys had been sent, and thus each study was of persons more disposed to aggression than the normal population. In the United States, the boys were ages fourteen to eighteen, mainly white (though with a sizable black minority), all living in cottages to which they had been randomly assigned. For five nights, boys in one cottage were shown violent films and boys in another nonviolent ones. Their behavior was observed during the movies and for three weeks thereafter.* In the first experiment, the boys who saw the violent films were more likely to display physical aggression than those who saw the neutral ones; in the second experiment, the boys who saw the violent films became verbally but not physically more aggressive.[26] In the Belgian study, the boys who watched the violent movies displayed more physical aggression than those who watched the neutral films.[27] Prior levels of aggression did not seem to affect the results.

Perhaps the most ingenious field experiment was carried out by Stanley Milgram and R. Lance Shotland.[28] The researchers recruited adults to watch in a New York studio a preview of an episode scheduled for a popular television program, *Medical Center*. The episode involved a young man who, having lost his job, stole money from charity boxes located in hospitals. There were two showings of the program; unbeknownst to the audiences, each had a different ending. In one, the man was punished; in the other, he was not. After watching the program, the members of the audience were given, as a reward, a gift certificate that could be redeemed at a certain store for a free transistor radio. When they arrived at the store, they found a charity box containing some bills and coins. Near the box was a sign saying that the store was closed, or, sometimes, that it had run out of radios. Obviously, the persons coming to the store were disappointed and probably rather irritated to discover that they could not get their reward. A few customers broke into the charity box or committed other antisocial acts in the store, but whether they had seen the version of the program showing the man punished or the one showing him getting away with the theft made no difference. However, the more frustrated the customers were by the signs at the store (some learned that the radios were all gone, some merely learned that they had to go to another place to get their radios), the more likely they were to vandalize the charity box. In short, this study gives evidence that some people will take matters into their own hands when their equity equation is violated, but little evidence that whether they do it depends on the kind of television program they have just seen.

---

* The observations, however, were made by persons who knew which boys were seeing violent or nonviolent programs, and this knowledge may have affected how the boys' behavior was rated.

The Media and Violence in Perspective

How one assesses these studies depends in part on where one thinks the burden of proof lies, how strongly one wants to believe or not believe that media violence is a serious problem, and what one thinks constitutes solid scientific evidence. The bitter controversy that surrounded the report of the Surgeon General's Scientific Advisory Committee on Television and Social Behavior provides ample opportunity to see scholarly claims and counter-claims swirl about studies and experiments that, because they were trying to measure very short-term effects (i.e., watching certain programs for a week or two) on behavior that is hard to observe (aggression) and the product of lifelong forces and temperamental predispositions, are inevitably going to produce modest findings surrounded by many qualifications. The Committee concluded that many studies "document" that "children are capable of imitating filmed aggression" and many other studies "have been widely interpreted as indicating" that viewing filmed violence "increases the likelihood of aggressive behavior."[29] Many scholars and editorial writers attacked this phraseology as excessively cautious, ignoring the "strong evidence" of a causal connection; other scholars and editorial writers attacked the report, and in particular the claims made in and on behalf of its studies, as going well beyond what the evidence warranted.[30]

Since that report, other summaries of the evidence—including evidence not available in 1972—led to equally opposed conclusions. Andison reviewed sixty-seven research studies and found that television "probably does stimulate a higher amount of aggression in individuals,"[31] but Kaplan and Singer, after reviewing that same year many of the same studies, concluded that "this research has failed to demonstrate that TV appreciably affects aggression in our daily lives."[32] The following year, Edgar concluded after her review of the literature that "we have no clear-cut answers on the effects of television violence on behaviour,"[33] but one year later Eysenck and Nias ended their review with the remarkably strong statement that there is "ample evidence that media violence increases viewer aggression."[34]

In 1982, the National Institute of Mental Health issued a report that was written to bring up to date the 1972 report of the Surgeon General's Committee. The new survey concluded that "to many researchers, the evidence accumulated in the 1970s seems overwhelming that televised violence and aggression are positively correlated in children."[35] Of course the phrase "positively correlated" begs the question of causality entirely, and nowhere in the report is there any serious discussion of the criticisms made of studies that purport to find even a correlation, much less a causal connection. The question-begging phraseology and the absence of any careful scientific discussion were lost on the print media. *Time* magazine misstated the report, claiming that the "overwhelming" evidence proves that television violence "causes" aggression in children; *Newsweek* said that this "overwhelming" evidence shows that televised violence "spills over" into the playground and the streets, where, the story implied, it causes violence.[36] When the National Research Council assembled a panel of experts to review the NIMH study, their remarks were quite different in tone. Televised violence "may be related" to aggression, but the magnitude of the relationship is small and the meaning of aggression is unclear.[37]

In our judgment, there is only a small amount of systematic, carefully done research that lends strong support to the view that prolonged viewing of televised violence will, independently of individual characteristics, produce a significant and lasting increase in the incidence or prevalence of serious violence. Even giving to existing research the most generous interpretation, viewing televised violence cannot explain more than a very small proportion of the variation in aggressive acts among young persons. The clearest effect of the media on violent behavior appears to come from the tendency of some people to imitate recent, specific, newsworthy incidents, such as the suicide of a celebrity or a championship prizefight. There is little evidence that these imitative effects are lasting or that televised accounts of the incidents have a greater effect than newspaper accounts. The Rip Van Winkle Study (and perhaps, when they are fully analyzed, the Chicago and European field studies) is consistent with the claim that watching televised violence leads to greater personal violence, but the methodological issues involved in reaching this conclusion have not been resolved to everyone's satisfaction.

We know only a little about the characteristics of persons more or less susceptible to the influence of pictorial violence. Apart from being a male and having a prior disposition toward aggressiveness, few of the other individual differences have been studied with sufficient care to establish their connection with response to pictorial violence. Aggressive boys tend to watch more television than nonaggressive ones, but what other temperamental factors may influence how individuals react to what they see are largely unknown. There is some evidence linking response and intelligence. It seems clear that persons with lower IQs spend more time watching television, and more time watching televised violence, than persons with high IQs.[38] Underaroused personalities may be more attracted to the immediate stimulus of televised adventures than normal personalities.[39] It may also be the case that "pro-social" films—that is, ones emphasizing cooperation and delay of gratification—have more of an effect on higher-IQ than on lower-IQ children.[40] These IQ effects persist after controlling for the families' socio-economic status.

Perhaps the greatest shortcoming of the research on the effects of pictorial violence, and of television in particular, is that, as we stated earlier in this chapter, we know virtually nothing about the effects of prolonged television viewing on attitudes and behavior other than those described as "aggressive." We can only conjecture about the effects of television on the sense of equity, a tendency toward impulsiveness, or an accurate estimate of the likely costs and benefits of alternative courses of action. Were all the facts known, it might be the case that merely being addicted to television, regardless of its contents, so poaches the brain or predisposes viewers to immediate gratification that they become unable to work for distant goals or to engage in disciplined activity. It might then make engaging in crime (not necessarily violent crime) somewhat more likely, other things being equal.

The extent to which television inculcates values, beliefs, and dispositions that affect behavior is hinted at in studies that suggest that certain kinds of programs reduce a viewer's tolerance for delay,[41] increase the extent to which viewers become more ambitious about the jobs they want and more materialistic about how they define success,[42] and increase the viewers' belief that while most criminals get caught every criminal has and can invoke a large array of civil rights.[43] But these are only hints or, at best, fragmentary and heavily qualified findings. As Edgar concludes, the proposition most in need of investigation—though how it could be investigated is far from clear—is that television affects behavior by selling a life-style that is beyond the limits of most people.[44]

Nor do we know much about the potential of the media to produce desirable or undesirable effects. The findings about the effect of pictorial violence on human aggression may be weak and equivocal in part because the magnitude of televised violence is much less than it would be in a market wholly unconstrained by public sentiment, the threat of government regulation, and the beliefs of the producers. If *every* program were equivalent to *A Clockwork Orange,* we might be a very different nation than if such films appeared only occasionally. By the same token, if *every* program were the *Gospel Hour,* we might also behave very differently.[45] Such speculations are, of course, entirely idle, since we would have to change so much as a society before our viewing fare were of one extreme or the other as to obscure the independent effect, if any, of what we watched.

14

ALCOHOL AND HEROIN

The use of drugs—by which we mean any substances that are "psychoactive," or tending to affect the mental and emotional state of the user—might be related to criminality either directly or indirectly. A drug might make its consumer more impulsive and thus less concerned with the delayed costs and more attracted to the immediate benefits of an act. As a result, the user might do things—break a window, grab a purse, race a car, or assault a person—that he would not ordinarily do. Some drugs are thought to make persons more aggressive, by which is meant that they derive more satisfaction from, and thus are more strongly reinforced by, the act of inflicting injury on a target, such as another fellow's jaw. But it is also possible that some drugs may reduce the satisfaction users derive from aggressive acts and thus make persons who ordinarily would receive pleasure from using violence more subdued.

If a user becomes dependent on a psychoactive drug, he may commit crimes to obtain the funds necessary to purchase it. This indirect effect on criminality is especially likely if the price of the drug is very high (as it will be if its sale is illegal).

Though there are many drugs that may have either a direct or an indirect effect on crime, we will discuss only two, alcohol and heroin, in part because their effects are best understood and in part because their usage, and thus their effects, are so widespread.

The Direct Effect of Drugs: Alcohol

The most commonly used drug that is thought to have a direct effect on crime and aggression is alcohol. There are many other drugs that might have such an effect, but the evidence is fragmentary. Ellinwood, for example, recounted the histories of thirteen men who committed homicides while under the influence of amphetamines, a central-nervous-system stimulant. Heavy use induced in the men feelings of being persecuted, coupled with impulsiveness and emotional excitability.[1] But there have been few systematic studies of the effect on crime of amphetamines or other stimulants, of sedatives such as barbiturates, or of hallucinogens such as LSD. There is no evidence that opiates, such as heroin, have any *direct* effect on criminality or aggression; on the contrary, heroin, being a narcotic, tends to produce among its users drowsiness, a reduction in tension, and lessened sexual activity.[2]

Alcohol is another matter. The statistical association between alcohol use and crime is overwhelming. In one study of 588 homicides in Philadelphia, Wolfgang found that alcohol had been used by assailant, victim, or both in nearly two-thirds of the cases.[3] There have, in fact, been at least twenty-eight separate studies of alcohol involvement in murder; fourteen of these found alcohol present in at least 60 percent of the cases, and the great majority found it present in a third or more of the cases.[4] There have been at least nine studies of the relationship between alcohol use and sexual offenses, primarily rape; most of these studies found alcohol had been used in at least 40 percent of the cases.[5] About one-fourth of the prison inmates who were interviewed in California said that during the three years preceding their incarceration, they had "got drunk and hurt someone" at least once.[6] Nationally, prison inmates are three times as likely as males of the same age who are not in prison to say that they drink two ounces or more of liquor per day.[7]

We are frequently told that a large fraction—about one-half—of all fatal auto accidents are "alcohol related," implying that if the driver had not been drunk, the death (which under the circumstances is probably a crime) would not have occurred. In fact, this is in some respects a misleading statement. There are no reliable national figures on the blood alcohol content (BAC) of all drivers involved in accidents. Some drivers in these accidents may have been drunk; others may have had only one drink. Moreover, "alcohol related" includes passengers and pedestrians who may have been drinking, as well as drivers.[8] Finally, these claims tell us nothing about the proportion of all drivers who are drinking—perhaps as many drivers not in accidents had been drinking as those who were involved.

A better way to find out what effect drinking has on auto accidents is to compare drivers with various levels of alcohol in their blood (precisely measured, and not guessed at by a police officer or ambulance driver) who are and are not involved in accidents on similar roads at comparable times of the day. A few such studies have been done. A careful review of them suggests that the risk of having an accident leading to property damage, an injury, or a fatality is between six and thirteen times greater for drivers with a BAC of 0.15 percent or higher (drivers, that is, who would be classified as legally drunk in every state of the union) than it is for drivers who have a zero BAC.[9] Since drivers who drink are only a small fraction of all drivers, the reduction in deaths and injuries that might occur if none drove while drunk is smaller than sometimes believed, though still significant. One scholar estimated that there would be 16 percent fewer injurious accidents and 24 percent fewer fatal accidents if all drivers had a zero BAC.[10] This reduction might be even greater if, as may well be the case, drivers who are likely to get drunk drive more frequently than sober ones. On the other hand, this estimate might be lower if, as also seems to be the case, persons who frequently get drunk are also, even when sober, likely to have more accidents because of their aggressive or impulsive personalities.[11]

This evidence of an association between alcohol use and crime will come as no surprise to the reader. The statistics merely confirm, or so it would seem, our own experience with ordinary people who became mean, abusive, or careless when drunk. What may come as a surprise is the fact that many scholars who study the association between alcohol and crime are by no means convinced that the former causes the latter. As far as the statistics go, they tend to show only an association between drinking and criminality, not a causal connection. And as far as everyday experiences go, for every drunk who is abusive or violent there is another who is morose, quiet, or sleepy.

There are four possible relationships between alcohol (or any drug) and crime (or any behavior). The relationship may be *spurious*—that is, there may be no real causal connection at all. The relationship may be *directly causal*—that is, swallowing the alcohol alters behavior directly, without regard to the presence or absence of other factors. The relationship may be *conditionally causal*—that is, using alcohol will cause crime (or some other behavior) provided certain other conditions also exist. Finally, both alcohol abuse and crime may be the effects of some *common cause*—that is, some factor (such as one's personality) may lead some people both to drink a lot and to engage in violent or criminal acts.[12]

Despite all the research that has been done on alcohol, we do not yet know enough to choose with any certainty among these four possibilities.

However, the possibility that the relationship between alcohol and crime is entirely spurious—a mere statistical accident, so to speak—can almost surely be ruled out. The studies cited earlier suggest that alcohol contributes directly to some serious automobile accidents involving the crime of drunk driving. Even the most cautious interpreters of the data concede that there would be about 12,000 fewer fatalities and 200,000 fewer injuries on the highways if no one drove an automobile with any alcohol in his or her bloodstream.[13] This view is reinforced by studies to which we will refer in Chapter 15 showing that the number of fatal motor accidents in a state is apparently affected by the minimum legal drinking age. Moreover, a study of changes in the price of alcohol that result from changes in the level of state taxes imposed on liquor suggests that higher prices for alcoholic beverages lead to decreases in the consumption of liquor and a corresponding decrease in the auto fatality rate.[14]

Even if we accept the fact that alcohol can cause crime, we still want to know whether it does so directly or whether other factors must first be present. And we want to know whether alcohol use can affect individual differences in the commission of ordinary street crime as opposed to vehicular homicide. The latter crime, though surely serious, might be regarded as unintentional and even accidental, and thus quite different from a murder, rape, or robbery. The fact that drunks drive recklessly or too fast does not mean they will assault, stab, or shoot another person.

For a long time it was thought that people have in them a "drive" to be aggressive that is kept in check by various internal inhibitions, and that drinking alcohol weakened these inhibitions and thus released the aggression. An experiment in 1969 that measured the willingness of persons, having first drunk various amounts of alcohol, to give one another electrical shocks (or what they imagined were electrical shocks) failed to produce the expected correlation between drinking and aggression.[15] Subsequently, the experiment was modified in several ways. Subjects asked to work the electrical-shock device were now placed under varying degrees of provocation, by being asked to compete with another person or subjected to an annoyingly loud tone. In these cases, higher BACs seemed to lead to higher levels of "aggression."[16] Given the widespread knowledge among college students of the use of fake electric shocks in psychological experiments, one cannot be certain that these findings (almost all of which were based on the behavior of college men) are entirely valid or applicable to the real world.[17] Moreover, it is not clear whether it is the effects of alcohol or one's attitudes toward alcohol that are being assessed. In one revealing experiment, the subjects who had been told that they had drunk alcohol administered more severe shocks than did the subjects who had been told they had drunk a nonalcoholic beverage, even though both groups in fact had received alcohol, and in the same amounts.[18]

A more realistic set of experiments involved "parties," arranged by a psychologist in which men were brought together in a pleasant setting to drink while playing various games. Their level of aggressiveness was scored. In general, men who drank were more aggressive than those who did not, and those who drank distilled liquor were more aggressive than those who drank beer.[19] More important, the drinking men who became aggressive in these experimental parties revealed, in questionnaires, that they were more likely than the nonaggressive drinkers to have had a history of getting into arguments and fights.[20]

All this suggests that not only the setting in which drinking occurs but also the personality of the individuals may make a difference in how people behave. One of the difficulties in sorting out these personality factors arises from a confusion, in much of the literature on alcohol, among different kinds of drinkers. A great deal of research has been done on alcoholics, by which is meant, generally, persons who are unable to control their drinking habits—they will drink in the morning or on other occasions when it is inappropriate, and once drinking they will find it difficult to stop. But it is far from clear that alcoholics commit predatory crimes more commonly than nonalcoholics who may or may not have other kinds of drinking problems—for example, drinking occasionally to excess, but not frequently going on benders.

One effort to summarize the vast literature on the personality traits of true alcoholics concluded that they tended to be neurotic, anxious persons lacking in strong egos.[21] Bearing in mind what we said about criminal personalities in Chapter 7, this suggests that alcoholics may overlap with only one kind of criminal (the neurotic), that many alcoholics may not be criminal at all (except as causes of traffic accidents or as public nuisances), and that many serious criminals (the extroverted, aggressive type) may not be alcoholics (though they may drink frequently). In addition to the study of aggressive behavior at experimental parties,[22] another study found that heavy drinkers who are hostile, irritable, or rebellious are those most likely to engage in violent behavior.[23] The aggressive drinker (as opposed to the compulsive drinker) is likely to reveal, in a personality test, that he feels himself directed by external forces, not by inner controls. What happens to such drinkers is "somebody else's fault," and this includes traffic accidents and episodes of violence.[24]

This is revealed most clearly in studies of persons arrested for drunk driving. One such inquiry divided those who had been arrested into five groups on the basis of a personality test. Though all had been involved in a traffic accident and convicted of a traffic violation, there were sharp differences among their total driving records. The group with the most accidents (over three times as many per year as the drunk drivers with the fewest accidents) ranked highest on measures of hostility, irritability, resentment, and sensation seeking. The group with the second-worst driving record was characterized by strong feelings of depression, resentment, moodiness, and being controlled by others. The amount of drinking reported by the five groups was about the same, but obviously the consequences were not.[25]

Since personality affects how people react to alcohol and how they behave after using it, we naturally look to the family backgrounds of drinkers for clues as to the sources of these effects. When we do, we are immediately struck by the fact that virtually every study of alcoholism and alcohol-related problems is in agreement that these difficulties run in families. A recent review of thirty-nine studies of alcoholics and nonalcoholics, totaling over ten thousand subjects, concluded that an alcoholic is much more likely than a nonalcoholic to have a mother, father, or other relative who is also an alcoholic. Averaging the findings of all these studies, it appears that one-third of all alcoholics have at least one alcoholic parent, and over 80 percent of all alcoholics have at least one alcoholic relative.[26] Moreover, these figures probably *under*estimate the true extent of familial alcoholism, since many people have an incentive to conceal the fact that they have relatives who drink compulsively.[27] Other reviews of the literature have come to essentially the same conclusions.[28] These studies also confirm that men are much more likely to become alcoholics than women, even after allowing for the fact that women may feel greater social pressure to conceal any drinking problems they have.[29]

For many years, it was assumed that drinking was entirely a result of social learning and that problem drinking was the result of bad learning. A study published in 1944 seemed to put an end to any speculation about a genetic factor being implicated in alcoholism. It claimed that the number of adopted children who later had drinking problems was not affected by whether their biological parents had such problems,[30] but the number of cases was small (only twenty-one men of "alcoholic" parentage) and the measure of alcoholism among parents and offspring was unclear.

Beginning in the early 1970s, however, a number of studies appeared that came to quite different conclusions on the basis of larger samples drawn primarily from Scandinavian countries that keep excellent records on both the drinking problems and the criminality of their citizenry. Donald W.

Goodwin and his colleagues compared fifty-five Danish men separated shortly after birth from their parents, at least one of whom had been hospitalized for alcoholism, with a matched control group of adopted men whose biological parents had no known record of alcoholism. The men whose biological parents had an alcoholism problem were almost four times as likely as the men with nonalcoholic biological parents to become alcoholic, despite the fact that they had been separated from the natural parents within the first six weeks of life and subsequently had had no contact with them.[31] Goodwin then examined the medical records of the blood brothers of the adopted men whose parents (usually the father) had been alcoholics. The brothers had not been put up for adoption; they had been raised with their natural parents. Despite this, the rates of alcoholism for both of the sets of brothers were about the same. Put another way, the "sons of alcoholics were no more likely to become alcoholic if they were reared by their alcoholic parent than if they were separated from their alcoholic parent soon after birth and reared by nonrelatives."[32]

A few years later, Michael Bohman published the results of his study of over two thousand adoptees in Sweden, and came to much the same conclusion. Adopted males whose biological fathers were known to be alcoholic were three times as likely as adopted males without alcoholic biological fathers to abuse alcohol, and this remained true after controlling for the age (and age at placement) of the adoptees and the occupational status of the adoptive parents.[33]

Consistent as these and other studies were, one result of them was puzzling. The studies by Goodwin, Bohman, and others did not reveal any tendency for persons with alcoholic biological fathers to become more criminal than those without. Since we have already seen, in Chapter 3, that constitutional factors can have some effect on who becomes criminal and who does not, the absence of a connection between the heritability of alcoholism and the heritability of crime may seem strange.

Once we remember that alcoholism and aggression are not the same thing, much of the mystery disappears. Alcoholics tend to be neurotic personalities; overtly aggressive men tend to be impulsive ones. Both alcoholism and aggressiveness may have some genetic component, but, if it is a different component, there would be no reason to assume that a predisposition to alcoholism and a predisposition to criminality would appear in the same person more frequently than by chance. In 1982, C. Robert Cloninger, Michael Bohman, Soren Sigvardsson, and Anne-Liis von Knorring published a re-analysis of the data about adopted Swedish men that is consistent with this explanation of the divergent bases of alcoholism and aggression. They examined the heritability of alcoholism and criminality among 862 Swedish men who constituted virtually all of the males born out of wedlock in Stockholm and adopted, before the age of three, between 1930 and 1949. Whereas Mednick et al. had been unable to say anything about alcoholism among Danish adopted men, Cloninger et al. had excellent data on drinking among Swedes because in that country each community has a Temperance Board charged with maintaining sobriety and authorized to impose fines on, and supervise the treatment of, intemperate persons. Elaborate records are kept. Based on these, Cloninger et al. were able to describe their subjects as well as their biological and adoptive parents as having no known alcohol problem, a mild problem, a moderate problem, or a severe problem.

Cloninger et al. found that, as we saw in Chapter 3, the sons whose biological parents had a criminal record were themselves four times as likely to have a serious criminal record as were the sons of biological parents who had no convictions for crime.[34] At the same time, the sons of biological parents who had a record of alcohol abuse were themselves much more likely to be alcohol abusers. But there seemed to be little overlap between the two groups. Biological parents who were criminals (but not alcoholics) or alcoholics (but not criminals) tended to produce children who, after adoption, displayed the same sorts of problems.[35] However, for those adopted men who were *both* alcohol abusers and criminals, the *form* of the criminality was distinctive—they tended to commit more crimes, and more violent ones, than did the adopted men who had a criminal record but no record of alcohol abuse. In short, different genetic mechanisms seem to account for the heritability of crime and of alcoholism, but when the two are found in conjunction, the criminal behavior of the men becomes much more serious.

There is some congenital influence in alcoholism, but we cannot say by what mechanisms this influence operates. There are several possibilities, none inherently implausible. After all, daily experience tells us that some people get drunk after one drink, while others can down several with no visible effect. Some people—Jews and Italians, for example—drink frequently but have low rates of alcoholism, while others drink frequently and have high rates of alcoholism—the Irish-Americans, some American Indian tribes, and Eskimos, for example.[36] Differences exist and are stable over time; there is no reason why genetic as well as cultural and social factors should not be responsible for them.

Among the factors that may have some biological basis are the following. First, persons may differ in their tolerance for alcohol, such that one person quickly experiences unpleasant sensations from a single drink while another person experiences either no sensation or pleasant ones from the same amount. As Goodwin put it, to become a heavy drinker, one must not be "allergic" to alcohol.[37] Several studies suggest that Orientals experience, more frequently than Caucasians, a flushed skin and an unpleasant reaction to even a small amount of alcohol.[38] The amount of pleasure one derives from drinking will depend on the extent to which such behavior is reinforced.

Second, persons may differ in the speed with which alcohol enters the blood and the length of time it remains there before being converted into other substances. One study found that blood alcohol levels dropped faster in whites than in Eskimos or American Indians who drank similar amounts,[39] but this finding has been disputed by others.[40]

Third, persons may differ in personality (impulsiveness, aggressiveness, extroversion), and some component of these personality differences may be affected by congenital factors. Alcohol may interact with these aspects of personality in ways that lead either to more aggressive behavior or to greater dependence on alcohol or both.[41]

These genetic factors may be related to other aspects of one's family background. Indeed, some of the factors that are loosely called "genetic" may have an environmental source. This would be the case, for example, if during pregnancy the mother drank heavily, thus producing important biochemical changes in the fetus. Thus far, the evidence suggests that this is not an important factor, as the adoption studies reviewed do not implicate the mother's drinking habits as much as the father's, but the matter cannot be regarded as settled.

A number of studies suggest that men with serious adult drinking problems have had absent, weak, emotionally distant, or deviant fathers.[42] A longitudinal study of black men born in St. Louis during 1930–1934 who were interviewed about thirty years later suggests that over half had been "heavy drinkers" at some time in their lives and that among the factors associated with heavy drinking was the absence of a father or the presence of a deviant one.[43] Whether an alcoholic heritage produced heavy drinking among both fathers and sons, or whether the behavior of the fathers affected the later drinking of the sons, or both, we cannot say.

Moreover, biological and familial factors may combine with broad cultural or subcultural norms that shape the circumstances under which drinking occurs and the rituals and ceremonies attached to it. A review of 110 societies studied by anthropologists revealed that alcohol was consumed in at least 90 percent of them, but these cultures differed sharply in the ways it was consumed and the consequences of its consumption for other kinds of behavior. In some, drinking had largely a ceremonial function, and took place under certain ritual guidelines that helped prevent drunkenness. In others, drunkenness was commonplace.[44] Though the authors of this review interpreted these differences entirely in terms of learned cultural values, it is likely, given the existence of some genetic component in susceptibility to alcohol, that these differences in fact represent a complex combination of genetic and cultural factors. For example, the low rates of alcoholism among Jews may be the result of a congenital distaste for the sensation of intoxication, the use of wine in moderation throughout the year for ritual purposes, a high level of achievement motivation, an absence of sexual repression, a fear of persecution from the majority society, or some combination of all of those factors.[45] Similarly, though many American Indians have much higher rates of alcoholism and alcohol-related crimes than do Anglo-Americans,[46] there are important differences in drinking and crimes among various tribes, and, within a single tribe, there have been important changes over time.[47]

The Indirect Effect of Drugs: Heroin

Though the sale of many drugs is illegal, the drug most often thought to have an indirect effect on individual rates of offending is heroin. This is in part because of its physiological properties. It is addictive, by which we mean that after continued use, the cessation of use can produce serious discomfort—"withdrawal symptoms." Moreover, the body's tolerance for the drug increases with increased use, so many users find that they must steadily increase the dosage in order to achieve a given level of euphoria. Since heroin is available only through illicit transactions, the purity of the drug is often undependable—it will be "cut" with varying and often unknown proportions of other, generally inert substances. This means that the user will sometimes experience a "high" and sometimes not. As a result, the user is confronting what psychologists call a variable-ratio reinforcement schedule, much the same as is a person putting coins into a slot machine hoping for a payoff.[48] Such a reinforcement schedule is likely to produce especially persistent behavior, which means that the user's addiction to heroin under circumstances of intermittent reinforcement is likely to be especially strong. It also means that a person dependent on the drug may be to some degree "addicted" not only to heroin but to the entire process of finding the drug and injecting it in a certain ritualized manner, in much the same way as a gambler becomes addicted to the rituals of gambling.

At one time, dependence on heroin was thought to lead inevitably to more and more frequent use, to higher and higher dosages, and thus to greater and greater expense, so that the great majority of addicts (all, except for a few physicians with direct access to opiates or wealthy persons who could afford to buy in the illegal market) would become criminals and steal large sums to support their habits. We now know that this is a quite exaggerated portrait of the relationship between heroin use and crime. After interviewing a number of male addicts in England, where heroin could be obtained legally from doctors who prescribed it to addict-patients enrolled in government-licensed clinics, Stimson concluded that there were four types of addicts: *stable addicts,* who managed to combine heroin use and a regular job and who avoided both crime and the drug culture; *loners,* who were not employed but managed to get enough money from friends and welfare programs so as to avoid crime and the drug culture; *two-worlders,* who were employed and could support their own habits but who also mingled frequently with the underworld and the drug culture; and *junkies,* who were unemployed, bought heroin illegally on the black market, and were heavily involved in crime and with other addicts. Stimson estimated that among his London cases, about 20 percent were junkies.[49]

It is worth noting that even in England, where addicts can obtain heroin legally, there is still a black market in illegal heroin and a large number of addicts who use that market and support their use with crime. The black market exists for several reasons. It is the only means whereby persons who want to become addicts can find the drugs—doctors are not supposed to prescribe heroin to persons who are not already dependent on it and who do not need it for other reasons, such as to kill pain after surgery. Moreover, British doctors are supposed to give only a "maintenance" dose to addicts, not one that will produce a "high" or increase the user's tolerance level. This means that doctors and addicts are in an adversary relationship—the former wants to give the smallest possible dose and the latter wants to get the largest possible one. Thus, some addicts who get legal heroin will supplement their supplies with black-market purchases. Finally, many addicts have an incentive to sell on the black market, at high prices, some of the heroin they obtain legally and at low (often zero) prices.

In a country such as the United States, where heroin is illegal under all circumstances, the proportion of all persons dependent on the drug who are "junkies" is probably higher than it is in Great Britain. Analyzing persons admitted to the District of Columbia jail, Bass and associates concluded that about two-thirds used heroin to some degree. Of the users who were arrested, about 70 percent were daily users ("junkies"), and the rest, about 30 percent, only used it occasionally ("chippers").[50] A Rand survey of prison inmates in California found that over 40 percent of the prisoners reported using "heavy drugs," mostly heroin, during the three years before their present incarceration, spending (at the median) $85 per day on their habit.[51] A subsequent study of inmates in California, Michigan, and Texas revealed that the most serious, high-rate offenders—whom the authors called "violent predators"—were also the inmates who had been using drugs (heroin alone or in combination with other drugs) for a long period of time.[52] One should bear in mind that heroin users who are in prison are probably not typical of all heroin users; in society at large, the proportion of all users who are junkies is probably smaller than is true of users who are in jail.

Because only a portion of all heroin users are junkies—that is, those who use it at least daily—the economic need of all users is much less than is sometimes supposed by persons who believe that all users are junkies obliged to steal. Also, there is great variability in the daily heroin consumption patterns even among the junkies. Mark Moore gives some estimates of this variability among users in New York,[53] and various observers who have developed close relations with users on the street confirm the general pattern if not the precise figures.[54] Moreover, even among junkies there are ways of obtaining heroin without stealing, including employment, welfare, donations from family and friends, and selling the drugs oneself.[55]

In short, no one, knowing only the total number of heroin users or even knowing their maximum or average drug habits, can calculate how much crime will be committed by addicts. In addition, it is a mistake to assume that all or even most addicts turn to crime for the first time as a result of becoming dependent on an illegal drug. Most studies of addicts reveal, on the contrary, that they started committing crimes before they started using heroin.[56] This could mean that crime and addiction have for some persons common causes or that the former causes the latter (by, for example, exposing criminals to deviant subcultures). Studies of addicts enrolled in treatment programs suggest that many who are no longer dependent on heroin continue to commit crimes.[57] Even addicts maintained at government expense on heroin, and thus relieved of the need to obtain it illegally, will often continue in crime. One group of English addicts, receiving heroin maintenance from a clinic in London, was followed for a year. Nearly half (43 percent) reported that they relied on crime as a source of income, and a third were arrested at least once during the year.[58] For all these reasons, one cannot assume that if addicts were not addicts, or if they were able to obtain their heroin legally, they would be crime-free.

We can, however, find out whether crimes committed by addicts increase during periods when they are on a "run"—that is, when they are using heroin heavily (at least daily and often much more frequently)—as compared to times when they are not using it at all or using it only occasionally (as "chippers"). The answer is that they do, often dramatically. The most vivid evidence of this comes from a study of 243 male addicts in Baltimore who were randomly selected from a list of all addicts in the city known to the police between 1952 and 1971. When interviewed, their average age was thirty-six and most had been using heroin, off and on, for ten years or more. During these years, the average addict had been making regular use of heroin about 60 percent of the time and had been using it lightly or not at all the remainder of the time. Each was asked about his criminal activities while free on the street. Over their careers (which averaged eleven years), these men claimed to have committed at least half a million crimes, mostly thefts, which would mean an average output of two thousand crimes per addict. The rate at which they committed these offenses was strongly influenced by whether or not they were on a "run." When they were regular users, their crime rate was, on the average, six times higher than when they were abstinent, and they were hardly law-abiding while abstinent.[59]

One cannot rely on the memories of addicts (or the memories of anyone) for a faithful account of their entire criminal career, and so the estimate of the number of crimes committed by this group may be seriously in error. However, the fact that the crime rate was substantially higher while regularly using heroin has been confirmed by other studies of other addicts. In Denver, two hundred addicts in the city jail were interviewed about their criminal careers. The crime rate of the users when addicted was more than five times greater than their crime rate before addiction. Much of that increase was due to becoming involved in the sale of drugs, but there were also very substantial increases in the rates of larceny, burglary, robbery, and assault.[60]

A high rate of crimes committed by active addicts—junkies—is also found in a study of Miami heroin users. A group of 239 males in that city admitted to interviewers committing an average of 337 crimes each during the preceding year, about half of which were drug sales. A group of 117 female addicts in that city reported committing an average of 320 offenses each during the year, about half of which involved prostitution.[61] A quite similar estimate of the criminality of addicts was obtained from studies in Philadelphia, Phoenix, Washington, D.C., and San Antonio—an average of 26 crimes per month, or 312 per year per addict, with most of these crimes involving drug sales or prostitution.[62]

The direct effect of heroin on the user is, in general, to sedate him, and thus to make him less active and less aggressive. The indirect effect of heroin use on the kinds of crime committed is more complicated. Addicts in need of money have a strong incentive to commit the easiest crimes—they need money quickly and frequently, and this leaves little time or energy for extensive planning. Studies of junkies on the street confirm that most of their crimes are highly opportunistic—snatching purses, taking things from unlocked cars or trucks, shoplifting, or stealing from a sleeping drunk. While most of the junkies in these studies stole, very few were skilled career criminals.[63] Being opportunistic means taking the easy and unplanned chances, and this in turn means avoiding, where possible, the need to confront a victim who is prepared to resist. Because of this, junkies tend to prefer nonviolent to violent crimes.

However, three factors partially offset this preference for nonviolent crimes. First, homes burglarized because the residents are not thought to be at home might in fact be occupied; victims robbed because they are thought to be passive might in fact offer resistance. In these circumstances, there is no reason to assume that an addict will shun violence more than any determined thief would. Second, heroin trafficking is illegal, and thus those dealing in the drug have only their own resources to protect them from thieves. When a great deal of illicit money is changing hands, many persons, including many addicts, will have an incentive to take some of that money by force. Finally, residents of high-crime-rate areas will increasingly take steps to protect themselves—buying guns, hiring guards—and as a neighborhood becomes increasingly well defended, addicts stealing in that neighborhood will have to become increasingly better armed and prepared to use more force.

Carl D. Chambers and his colleagues, in a study of the criminal activities of addicts in various cities, found that between a quarter and a half of the illicit income of the male addicts came from committing crimes against a person (i.e., crimes in which violence or the threat of violence was used). For the addicts it made sense—the average yield from a crime against property was only $59, whereas the average yield from a crime against a person was $187.[64] The survey of street addicts in Miami revealed a comparable pattern—though drug sales and other nonviolent crimes were by far the most common, nearly half the male addicts had committed at least one robbery, and this group committed, on the average, nearly thirty robberies a year.[65]

A large number of assaults and murders can be attributed to the effort by one person to steal drugs or money from a drug dealer (being "ripped off"), by the effort of one drug dealer to intimidate or eliminate a rival, or by an addict seeking vengeance on a dealer who sold him poor-quality drugs (who "burned" him). Because of this, murder is a leading cause of death among addicts. In one drug treatment program, homicide accounted for one-fourth of all deaths; in another, it accounted for two-thirds.[66] In Wayne County, Michigan, which includes Detroit, one study in 1975, when Detroit was among the most murderous cities in the nation, estimated that a majority of *all* the homicide victims were drug users or involved with drug dealing.[67]

Describing persons who are more likely to become heavy heroin users is much more difficult than describing those who become alcoholics, because heroin use, being illegal, occurs under circumstances not easily viewed and among people not easily identified. The characteristics of heroin users who are in jail or in treatment programs may well differ substantially from the characteristics of those free in the community. And while this latter group might be contacted by means of a household survey, it is not at all clear that they will answer honestly questions about their illegal drug habits; indeed, there is strong evidence, to be presented in a moment, that such surveys lead to large underestimates of heroin use.

What we can be most confident about, therefore, are only those traits of heroin users that appear in several different kinds of inquiries. All studies—of persons in jail, in treatment, and at large in the community—agree that the typical heroin addict is disproportionately a young male, black or Hispanic, living in a big city.[68] But there are many younger and older addicts, many who live in small- and medium-sized cities, and (perhaps) a growing number of female addicts.

It would be helpful—and even comforting—if we knew that persons most likely to become dependent on heroin had a distinctive personality or easily diagnosed psychological state, for then we could aim our prevention efforts at such persons and cease worrying about friends or children who did not display these recognized predispositions. Unfortunately, we know too little about who is more or less likely to become an addict, and what we do know is biased to some unknown degree by the fact that studies of addicts are typically studies of addicts in treatment programs, who may be unrepresentative of all users.

For example, one study compared the personality characteristics of hospitalized opiate addicts with a control group of persons of similar age, ethnicity, and exposure to illicit drugs. The addicts had more severe personality disorders, with almost half being classified as schizophrenic.[69] But these hospitalized addicts (in Lexington, Kentucky) may have been very different from ordinary street addicts; moreover, the study was done in 1955, a decade or more before the major heroin epidemic of the late 1960s. Drug abusers often use many different drugs, sometimes simultaneously (e.g., heroin and cocaine on the same day) and sometimes sequentially (e.g., substituting barbiturates for heroin when the latter becomes hard to find), so it is difficult to speak of the traits of a heroin-only user.

Perhaps the most detailed and useful study of American addicts was that done by Isidor Chein and colleagues in New York City. They compared the personal backgrounds of males (median age: nineteen) drawn from neighborhoods that had similar levels of drug usage and delinquency. One group consisted of hospitalized heroin users, some delinquents and some not. The second group consisted of males from similar neighborhoods who had avoided heroin use, some delinquents and some not. The authors concluded that the male addict in treatment tends to be a person with little ego strength, inadequate masculine identification, an unrealistic orientation toward the future, and a distrust of major social institutions.[70] The users were not aggressive, confident persons; they were not active gang members or good students. They were neither "tough" nor "square," but rather loners and losers who drifted into association with other drug users.

Almost all the addicts came from families in which relations between the parents had been broken by separation or divorce (about half the cases) or by hostility and bickering (most of the rest of the cases). In the great majority of the male addicts' families, the mother was the most important figure (this was much less true among the nonaddicts), because the father was absent, unstable, hostile, or emotionally distant.[71]

There has been no research as yet showing that genetic factors account for individual differences in susceptibility to heroin addiction, as there has for alcohol abuse. It is possible such research may appear, especially in light of recent findings as to the biochemical processes by which brain cells receive (or are blocked from receiving) the stimulus provided by heroin and other drugs in the bloodstream.[72] Individuals may differ constitutionally in the extent to which heroin produces pleasurable sensations via these mechanisms.

To the extent social processes are the cause of addiction, these processes are similar to those that contribute to criminality generally. This helps us to understand why criminality and addiction are so often found in the same person and why it is futile to try to decide whether the first use of drugs "causes" crime or criminality "causes" drug use. Both are the result of common factors operating on and through the personality. But not the personality alone—one cannot explain the spread of heroin use simply by reference to individual differences. Heroin, after all, has been a problem in this country at least since the 1930s, but during most of the 1940s and 1950s there was nothing approaching the heroin epidemic of the sort that erupted in the late 1960s. It would be farfetched to assume that heroin use suddenly increased exponentially because there had been an equally sudden exponential increase in the number of men from unhappy homes or lacking in ego strength.

The other major factor in the use of heroin is sheer availability: a large supply, the cash with which to make the first purchases, and the information necessary to locate a source of supply. Studies of these processes here and abroad can be summarized this way: "Heroin use—like marijuana, alcohol, cigarettes, slang, clothing fads and popular music—spreads within groups of closely associated youths by a process of peer emulation and influence."[73] Or to put the matter a bit differently, drug use spreads like an infectious disease. In Crawley, England, Grosse Pointe, Michigan, and Chicago, Illinois, scholars have been able to trace in detail how one heroin user, during the brief period (perhaps a year) in which he is an enthusiastic user and not a withdrawn and solitary addict, persuades a few friends to try the drug.[74] Some fraction of these respond enthusiastically, and they in turn recruit some of their friends.

Since only a fraction of all persons who come into contact with a single user will want to try heroin or, if they try it, will like it, heroin use will not spread very far—unless there are many initiators at work in the same community and unless supplies are readily available with which newly formed habits can be sustained. Personality characteristics of the sort we described above help determine who in a peer group is at risk; the amount of disposable income and the availability of the drug help determine which of those at risk will continue using heroin; and the number of initiators and the patterns of their contacts will determine how far the epidemic spreads. Hunt and Chambers have shown that by knowing only the friendship pattern of peer groups, one can derive a mathematical model of the predicted spread of heroin use in a community that conforms quite closely to the observed spread.[75]

During the heroin epidemic of the late 1960s, surveys of random samples of men living in those neighborhoods of Manhattan (New York City) known to be areas of high drug use reveal that the prevalence of heroin among these men reached very high levels between 1967 and 1971. By 1970, about one-fifth of all the men in the samples had used heroin sometime during their lives; most had begun using it during the years after 1965.[76] And even this may be an underestimate, as may be surmised from an independent, and perhaps more reliable, bit of evidence. The New York Telephone Company administers physical examinations to persons applying for employment; part of that exam is a urinalysis. In 1970, 4 percent of the whites and 15 percent of the blacks who applied for a job had traces in their urine of either heroin or the substance (quinine) typically used to dilute heroin.[77] Since heroin disappears from the urine in one day and quinine in about five days, this means that a large fraction of ordinary persons (almost all were high school graduates) applying for work in New York had probably used heroin within the last five days. Because the survey reported earlier asked only whether persons had *ever* used heroin and asked it of persons specially selected from areas where drug use was common, there is good reason to believe that the survey was actually undercounting the number of users by a substantial amount.

The reason for the sudden increase in the prevalence of heroin use is not well understood. Supplies of heroin from overseas became more abundant and incomes of users were adequate to at least begin a habit. Both nationally and in Manhattan, a larger proportion of black males with fathers in *higher*-ranking occupations used heroin than was true of those with fathers in low-ranking occupations.[78] The general affluence of the 1960s may have enabled persons at risk to purchase more of everything, including more drugs. And there were changes in cultural norms and social attitudes (which we discuss in Chapter 16) that probably played a role as well. As more and more persons tried heroin, more and more became daily users, and a significant fraction of these, in turn, increased dramatically their rates of criminality in order to support their habits. By the mid-1970s, there was some evidence that the rate at which new users were being recruited had dropped significantly, owing, perhaps, to a growing awareness of the dangers in using the drug.[79]

Conclusion

Alcohol affects crime directly, by the changes it works in the aggressiveness, impulsiveness, and time horizon of some of the persons who consume it; heroin affects crime indirectly by increasing the incentive to steal among many of those persons using it on a daily basis. The differences among persons in their tendency to abuse alcohol can be attributed to congenital susceptibilities as well as to social circumstances; differences among persons in their susceptibility to heroin dependence can (at present) be attributed to some combination of personality and opportunity. For many persons (but not all), both drugs act as powerful reinforcers. The effect of that reinforcement for users of alcohol varies greatly among individuals, but for certain persons it intensifies their aggressiveness and impulsiveness. On personality tests, such persons tend to deny that they are, or ought to be, controlled by internal restraints and find it easy to blame the external world for the problems they face. The effect of heroin as a reinforcer is ordinarily quite different—it seems especially appealing to persons who are neither "tough" nor "square," who are sexually inadequate, or who are in physical or psychological pain; for all of these, the drug provides escape, a generally pleasurable sensation, and a rationale for not coping with the affairs of the world.

15

ALTERING THE SOCIAL CONTEXT

The central argument of this book is that behavior, including criminal behavior, is controlled by its consequences. If that is the case, then behavior ought to change if some institution is able to alter those consequences. The purpose of this chapter is to review what we know about attempts to alter, by plan, the likelihood of criminal activity by changing the reinforcements for it. Note that we say "by plan." The probability of an individual's committing a crime may change dramatically from one moment or one year to the next. We already know, for example, that most young men who commit one or two offenses cease committing any offenses as they grow older. In this and countless other ways, an individual's offense rate changes. But many of these changes take place in response to naturally occurring circumstances, such as age, that society cannot change or does not wish to change.

Moreover, it may not be easy for an institution, such as the government, to observe the results of its efforts to alter reinforcements. A given individual—for reasons of temperament, lack of conscience, or a short time horizon—may be so predisposed to crime that no feasible change in institutionally controlled reinforcers (such as altering his job prospects or the risk of imprisonment) may make any difference. Another individual may be so easily conscience-stricken or so preoccupied with distant and unlikely consequences as to respond quickly to the merest hint (or perhaps just an imagined hint) that the government is altering its policy. In the first case, we may observe no results from our efforts; in the second, we may not be aware we

374

have made any efforts and hence fail to look for the results. But most people are not at either extreme but somewhere in between, so that if a change in reinforcements has any effect at all, it should be noticed at the margin when we look systematically at the behavior of large numbers of persons.

Some of the most important reinforcers, such as those employed by families in socializing their children, may change so slowly that, though their effect is great, the change is never noticed. Behaviors frequently and consistently rewarded in the past tend to be repeated. If there is a gradual increase, for whatever reason, in the proportion of families that reward aggressive acts (by letting children have their way or failing to make consistent use of rewards and punishments), the children are more likely to act aggressively when they grow up. Not having noticed that families have changed, observers may wrongly suppose that the resistance of the aggressive adults to short-term alterations in the probability of punishment means that they are acting "irrationally" or that changes in the risk of arrest have no effects. In Chapter 16 we shall try to assess the significance of long-term, hard-to-measure changes in the social context of behavior.

Of course, many of the most important reinforcers governing behavior are beyond the ready control of governments or any institutions. For example, when a person has a choice of helping or not helping a stranger who has been victimized in a public place (by being hit by a car, for example, or attacked by a mugger), the probability of his getting involved will be greater the fewer the number of bystanders.[1] The reason is that when fewer bystanders are present, it is harder for any given bystander to think that "other people" are responsible and thus harder for him to avoid experiencing a pang of conscience for not helping. The consequences of action (or inaction) control an individual's behavior more when he has difficulty denying personal responsibility for acting or not acting. We take note of these facts, but otherwise confine ourselves to evidence about the effects, if any, of efforts to change, by plan, the consequences of criminal action.

Deterrence, Opportunities, and Rehabilitation

It is customary to think of efforts to change crime rates by modifying behavior as involving three different policies. If society tries to increase the swiftness, certainty, or severity of punishment for a crime, we say it is practicing deterrence. If it seeks to increase the value of attractive alternatives to crime (such as good jobs), we say that it is enlarging opportunities. And if it tries to reduce the willingness of an individual to commit a crime, we say it is attempting to rehabilitate him. Advocates of one kind of policy are often at loggerheads with advocates of another, with one group frequently accusing the other of being "too punitive" or "hopelessly softheaded."

We think that these distinctions are misleading if not altogether wrong, and that the passionate arguments among the defenders of these alternative policies are somewhat misplaced. If we try to change the likelihood of an individual's committing a crime by increasing the risk of imprisonment, psychologically we are not doing anything very different from trying to lower the crime rate by increasing the attractiveness of legitimate work; in both cases, we are trying to increase the expected value of noncrime relative to crime.* The knowledge we obtain about human nature from observing the effect of giving jobs to law-obeyers is the same as that which we get from giving prison terms to law-breakers. In both instances we learn that an individual responds rationally to the choices confronting him and that future consequences shape present behavior. For political or ideological reasons, we may prefer jobs to prison, or vice versa, but the use of both reinforcers is based on the same theory of behavior.

When we try to change an individual's offense rate by placing him in a halfway house where he obtains privileges for obeying the rules, we may call it rehabilitation, but it is not obvious that this embodies any different a view of human nature than is implicit in the policy of placing him in a prison where he loses privileges if he breaks the rules. Persons who run halfway houses (and practitioners of rehabilitation generally) often dislike prisons and in particular dislike efforts to change behavior by using penalties rather than rewards, but there is no good reason in theory why the proper use of penalties should affect behavior any differently from the proper use of rewards. Moreover, to say that rehabilitation relies on positive reinforcers and deterrence relies on punishments is simply incorrect. If the offender is required to participate in a rehabilitative program, he may find it as penalizing (in terms of lost freedom) as paying a fine or even going to jail. Joining, even voluntarily, an encounter group that tries by verbal attacks to strip away the defenses of a drug addict can be as punishing to the addict as being committed to a hospital or jail cell where he is left alone to dry out.

We think it more useful to distinguish not between rewards and penalties, or between coercive and voluntary programs, but between efforts to change the subjective state of a person and attempts to alter the contingen-

---

* There is one qualification to this that we shall discuss in a later chapter. Rewarding a person who does not commit a crime may have different consequences than punishing one who does if these two kinds of reinforcers have different effects on the sense of equity of either the individual or society.

cies attached to his behavior. When we attempt to alter someone's subjective state, we are endeavoring to recondition him—that is, to replace the behaviors and feelings learned by association with past reinforcers with new behaviors and attitudes learned by their association with new reinforcers, so as to enlarge his conscience, extend his time horizon, or increase the value he attaches to the rewards of noncrime. When we attempt to change the contingencies attached to his behavior, we are leaving the way a person values consequences unchanged while trying to alter his behavior by altering the speed, the certainty, or the magnitude of those consequences.

In practice, of course, we often try to do both and may even do both without trying. For example, to convince an offender that in the future he ought to expect good consequences to occur more speedily and certainly from abstaining from crime, we may have to make such consequences actually occur so often that in the process we alter his time horizon or the value he assigns to these consequences. For analytical purposes, however, the distinction is worth preserving.

Strategies to alter the subjective state of an offender include most forms of verbal therapy such as psychoanalysis, mood-altering techniques such as meditation or drug therapy, and classical conditioning that involves associating criminal acts with unpleasant mental images. Strategies to alter the contingencies facing an offender include changes in the expected value of criminal justice penalties ("deterrence"), improvements in the expected value of alternatives to crime (such as jobs), and behavior modification employing altered contingencies (such as "token economies").

Changing Subjective States

Given all that we have said in this book about the relationship between temperamental disposition and early familial and school experiences, the reader should be prepared for the fact that it is very hard for society to change, by plan, the subjective state of large numbers of persons. And it is a fact.

In a well-known review of all the evaluations of criminal rehabilitation efforts between 1945 and 1967 that met certain minimal methodological criteria, Douglas Lipton, Robert Martinson, and Judith Wilks were able to find thirty-one accounts of attempts to use individual or group psychotherapy to reduce the recidivism rates of delinquents and criminals.[2] The actual techniques employed in these therapies differed widely; some used Freudian analysis and others involved providing suggestions for solving practical problems. Thus, we cannot be certain that these programs solely entailed efforts to alter the subjective states of the offenders.

In any event, the reviewers found little consistent evidence that such programs had a beneficial effect. Group therapies in particular seemed to be of small value: There were "few reliable and valid findings concerning their effectiveness."[3] There were some examples of improvement resulting from individual psychotherapy, but these gains accrued chiefly to persons who were judged to be "amenable" to treatment, and were sometimes offset by the losses (i.e., by an *increase* in subsequent criminality) occurring among subjects found not amenable to treatment.[4] But one should be cautious about assuming that psychotherapy will work if we just target it on amenable subjects, for the very meaning of "amenable" is far from clear, and how we determine in advance of treatment who is likely to be amenable is even more uncertain. Claims have been made that offenders can be screened for amenability, but a committee of the National Research Council, a part of the National Academy of Sciences, convened to review the evidence on rehabilitation, concluded that it "does not believe that one could with any confidence classify offenders in any way with the expectation that treatment effects could be maximized by matching of treatments and offenders."[5]

There have been criticisms of the conclusions of Lipton, Martinson, and Wilks, but when these rejoinders were taken up by the National Research Council committee, it found them to be unsupported. Lipton et al. were "reasonably accurate and fair" and their conclusions were "essentially correct."[6] Studies published since the Lipton et al. review have not changed matters, at least insofar as psychotherapy is concerned. Some persons have claimed, however, that techniques of behavior modification, not generally in use when Lipton et al. wrote, have shown promise;[7] this is a matter to which we shall return later in this chapter.

These reviews should not persuade us that verbal therapy never works, only that its value for offenders has yet to be established *and* that there are good reasons for supposing that its value will prove difficult to establish, at least for offenders strongly predisposed, by temperament and socialization, to commit crimes. Changing the subjective state of criminals is no different in principle from changing that of persons generally, and so psychotherapy should not be expected to produce any better results when directed at offenders than when it is directed at neurotics. In fact, there are reasons for believing that it is harder to help offenders than neurotics.

A controversy has raged for many years among psychologists over whether or not psychotherapy has any value. In a famous pair of articles, H. J. Eysenck reviewed studies of the outcomes of therapy and decided that there was little evidence it did anybody much good—many people got better after a period of therapy, but they were about equal in proportion to those who got better simply as a result of the passage of time.[8] Other psychologists have disputed Eysenck's claim. Mary Lee Smith and Gene V Glass examined some four hundred evaluations of psychotherapy and decided that the client was often better off being treated than not.[9] However, they noted that the improvements were generally in such matters as fear and self-esteem and less often in such areas as "adjustment," under which heading, of course, one finds most criminal behavior. Moreover, Smith and Glass found that certain kinds of offenders were more likely to benefit than others: those who had a higher than average IQ and those who dealt with a therapist much like the clients themselves.

There are other bits of evidence that certain kinds of persons, including those convicted of crimes, can benefit to a degree from therapeutic programs. Palmer showed that the monthly arrest rates of neurotic (what he called "conflicted") delinquents were lower after treatment in an intensive probation program than were the rates of the "power-oriented" delinquents; indeed, the latter had *higher* arrest rates as a consequence of treatment, probably because they found that they could manipulate to their own advantage the therapeutic setting in which they had been placed.[10] A similar conclusion was reached by Adams, who found the delinquents who seemed most amenable to treatment were "bright, verbal, and anxious."[11] Glaser has summarized this line of argument by suggesting that the offenders whose subjective states are most amenable to planned change are those who can easily communicate and who have not found their prior criminal career to be especially rewarding.[12]

This is what one would have predicted on the basis of the theory advanced in this book. More intelligent persons are probably more likely than less intelligent ones to have a longer time horizon and to take into account a wider array of likely consequences of both crime and noncrime; moreover, if their higher IQ chiefly reflects superior performance on the verbal tests, they will more easily be engaged by psychotherapists who, by definition, rely on verbal therapies. A person who in the past has found crime relatively unrewarding—who has been, in short, an unsuccessful crook—will be easier to resocialize by associating crime with unpleasant consequences and noncrime with pleasant ones. And an offender who is similar to his therapist is more likely, by that fact, to be attractive to him and thus to elicit from the therapist greater interest and enthusiasm, and thus a higher level of reinforcement, than is an offender who is so dissimilar to the therapist as to be unappealing. Imagine, for example, how differently a young, college-educated, middle-class therapist would react to an anxious but bright young shoplifter as opposed to an assertive, defiant, strong-armed robber. We caution the reader, however, that these findings are sparse and tentative and admit of many exceptions. There are plenty of hardened offenders who are verbally skillful and many neurotic offenders who, lacking any strength of character, drift steadily into criminal habits.

Changing Contingencies

There is no question that the behavior of most would-be offenders can be altered by changing the reinforcements attached to alternative courses of action. Burglars do not break into stores while police officers are watching, and muggers are less likely to attack an armed soldier carrying no money than a defenseless woman who has just cashed her Social Security check. The problem is not to establish that behavior can be changed by altering its rewards but to show that it can be changed for large numbers of persons, many of them temperamentally impulsive, by marginally altering delayed and uncertain rewards, and doing so within existing moral and political constraints.

Most of us are accustomed to deferring immediate pleasures for delayed rewards. The authors of this book, to pick an especially poignant example, must forgo many days at the beach or playing tennis in order to write something that may or may not be purchased and read several years in the future. And if the book is read, it will be by persons who think, rightly or wrongly, that they will obtain some intellectual or educational benefit from doing so, and not by persons who think that reading it is more fun than going to the movies.

Criminals, as we have seen, are much more likely to be impulsive, which is to say they are much more likely than authors and students to assign a very low value to distant rewards, especially if those rewards are (like the ones that come from writing or reading books) of uncertain value. Yet most of the reinforcements at the disposal of society that might be used to change individual rates of offending—the prospect of a job, entry into respectable society, the risk of arrest or imprisonment—will be available after a considerable delay and then only for a small, and hard to estimate, fraction of all potential offenders. Because of this, some people think that the government can have little or no effect on individual crime rates. More accurately, some persons think it can have no effect if it changes the probability of arrest and punishment but can have a substantial effect if it changes the probability of getting a job, while others think that the government can have little effect by changing the availability of jobs but much effect by changing the risk of imprisonment. Of course, each of these positions is internally inconsistent, given what we know about human nature—if an individual is so present-oriented as to be indifferent to changes in the probability of future rewards (such as jobs), then he will also be indifferent to changes in the probability of future penalties (such as imprisonment), and vice versa. Let us ignore the inconsistency, which is a political, not scientific, issue. It is clearly possible that offenders are too impulsive to take into account any feasible changes in the delayed and uncertain reinforcements and punishments at the disposal of society. The remainder of this chapter will assess this possibility.

Changing Contingencies at the Individual Level

There have been countless demonstrations of the effect of changed reinforcements on the deviant behavior of individuals in schools, prisons, and clinics.[13] Virtually all of these demonstrations have involved various forms of behavior modification, which is nothing more than the application of the principles of behavioral psychology to human disorders. Scarcely any of these applications were made before 1967, so none was included in the well-known review done by Lipton, Martinson, and Wilks.[14] For present purposes, the main limitations of these efforts at behavior modification are two: First, most have been directed at changing behavior other than criminality (e.g., getting students to study harder, children to throw fewer tantrums, and prisoners to obey institutional rules). Second, the successful application of these methods generally has occurred in institutional settings rather than in the community.

These methods involve a variety of techniques—token economies, contingency management, behavioral contracting, and programmed learning—all of which have in common making rewards (and occasionally punishments) contingent on displaying desirable (or undesirable) behavior and ignoring, for the most part, the subjective state of the offender and his past history.

Between 1965 and 1975, at least twenty-four such programs were described in publications reviewed by Ross and McKay.[15] Most were aimed at getting delinquent youth to behave themselves in the institution to which they were confined; some also sought to induce better performance on educational tests. Virtually all were successful while the youth was in the institution.

However, only four of the projects followed their subjects after they had returned to the community. Three of the four reported no significant, lasting effect on crime reduction. The fourth, by Jesness and colleagues, did report such a reduction.[16]

Jesness et al. randomly assigned delinquent boys in California to an institution employing either behavior modification or transactional analysis (a kind of group discussion leading to each boy's setting behavioral goals for himself). The behavior-modification program had several components, but chiefly involved the use of a token economy whereby the boys who complied with institutional rules, made progress in their studies, and stopped behaving in ways thought likely to increase the risk of parole failure were rewarded with tokens that could be exchanged for various privileges. Moreover, the boys had to earn a certain number of points before they could apply for parole. The transactional program at the other institution did not involve the use of contingent reinforcers. One year after they had returned to the community, the boys who had been in the token-economy program had a lower rate of parole violations than those released from conventional juvenile institutions but no lower than those sent to the other experimental school where no token economy operated. This is interesting but not persuasive: There was no effort to match carefully boys in the experimental and conventional institutions, and the follow-up period (one year) was too brief to permit judgments about lasting effects.

There have been many other token economies in correctional institutions (indeed, left to their own devices, the inmates themselves will organize one based on the exchange of contraband for favors). All seem to have an effect on inmate behavior, but so far we cannot demonstrate that this effect endures after release.[17] Nevertheless, these token economies (as well as other, similar behavior-modification techniques) show that however impulsive offenders may be, they will alter their behavior if the consequences are altered, even if those consequences are somewhat delayed (there is always a lapse of time between the behavior and the receipt of the token, and a further delay before it can be cashed in for something of intrinsic value). Still, the controlled environment of an institution must affect the inmates' perceptions of the certainty of reward; if they believe a reward will certainly follow, then they apparently will allow it to affect their behavior even if its receipt is delayed.

We want to know, then, whether changed contingencies will change behavior in settings less controlled than a prison or a school. Schwitzgebel and Kolb recruited about forty delinquents off the street by walking up to them and offering them small cash payments in exchange for talking about themselves into a tape recorder in an office.[18] By manipulating the size of the rewards (which in time came to include food and companionship, as well as money, and which were offered in varying amounts and at varying times), the experimenters were able to induce almost all these young men, who began solely with an interest in making a "fast buck" and who were erratic in their habits, to attend the sessions dependably and punctually. Three years later, the arrest records of the boys who completed this program were compared to a matched (in nationality, residence, prison experience, and type of criminal record) group of boys selected from the records of the state correctional agencies. The experimental group had accumulated only half as many arrests as the control group during the three-year follow-up. Both groups were equally likely to be returned to prison, however, though the experimental group served shorter terms. The authors explain these results as a consequence of reconditioning the boys so as to reinforce noncriminal behaviors (such as being dependable and keeping track of time), though the results could also have been the result of an inadvertent bias in the selection of the original sample.

A less successful outcome was reported for what has been perhaps the best-known and most widely copied system of behavior modification in a community setting. Achievement Place, in Lawrence, Kansas, is a foster home, led by two professionally trained foster parents, in which six to eight delinquent adolescents live. By use of instruction reinforced by a token economy, the leaders of Achievement Place hope to teach the delinquents to take care of their living quarters, study hard in school, improve their social skills, become punctual, and otherwise display self-control and conformity to rules. The token economy uses both reinforcements and punishments—that is, not only can youths earn points for obeying the rules, they can lose them for violations. Since its inception, the Achievement Place strategy, now called the Teaching-Family Model, has been followed in many parts of the country; by 1982, there were about 170 such group homes in operation, staffed by parents trained at six regional centers. Moreover, the system has been used not only for delinquents but also for autistic or emotionally disturbed youth, mentally retarded persons, schizophrenic adults, and even the aged. By 1980, just the bibliography of books, articles, and dissertations written about the Teaching-Family Model ran to nearly fifty single-spaced pages.[19]

There seems to be little doubt that the Teaching-Family system alters the behavior, including the delinquency, of those in the group homes.[20] But there is no evidence that it alters the rate at which the youth commit offenses one year after their release from treatment,[21] or that it has any greater effect on delinquency than do other community-based programs.[22]

The evidence from the Teaching-Family program and from behavior-modification programs in prisons and reformatories shows that behavior can be modified, but that the modification usually does not last. This failure of rule-abiding behavior to persist can be explained by the fact that, absent a change in the offender's subjective state (the strength of internal inhibitions or the value assigned to time), the reinforcers present in the natural environment to which the offender returns will once again make crime seem more attractive than noncrime. A boy who leaves a discordant home in a high-crime neighborhood dominated by street gangs that profitably buy and sell narcotics and who enters a foster home may well behave decently when, for the first time, the rewards he can get are consistently made contingent on his decent behavior. But when he leaves the home and returns to his discordant family and the criminal street life, most of the rewards he encounters will once again reinforce impulsive or criminal activity.

There are two ways to cope with this re-entry problem. The first is to alter the reinforcements available in the community; the second is to change the value the person assigns to the reinforcements that are naturally available.

Changing the Rewards of Familial and Community Life

The first method has been followed by those who have sought to increase the availability of jobs, alter the pattern of street life, raise the risk of punishment, or improve the quality of familial relationships. Because of its pre-eminent importance as a source of rewards, we will begin with the family and the efforts that have been made to change the extent to which it fails to make rewards consistently contingent on proper behavior (see Chapter 8).

Various programs have been established to teach the parents of troublesome youth to be better parents. Among the first was one carried out in Tucson, Arizona, by Roland Tharp and Ralph Wetzel.[23] Believing that the parents of delinquents often failed to reinforce good behavior and instead denigrated or nagged their offspring, Tharp and Wetzel tried to persuade parents and children to manage their conflicts more constructively. To help do this, Tharp and Wetzel designed a "behavioral contract" that set forth the rights and obligations of parents and children in a particular family. For example, instead of arguing over whether he could use the family car, a boy would enter into a contract with his parents whereby he would get the car at stated intervals in exchange for performing certain chores and being home at a specified time. These and other efforts at family contracting, or, as it is sometimes called, contingency management, were based on the assumption that rewards should be stably linked to desired behavior on the basis of an agreement that seems fair to both sides.[24] The youths whose families followed a behavioral contract experienced a reduction in offenses, an increase in grades, and an improvement in behavior, but the significance of these changes is hard to assess inasmuch as there was no control group to which the youths in the experimental program could be compared.

A variation of this approach to altering family life was tried in Salt Lake City by James F. Alexander and Bruce V. Parsons, then of the University of Utah. Several dozen boys and girls who had been involved with the juvenile court for various minor delinquencies—truancy, shoplifting, drinking, and running away from home—were referred to a clinic at the university. There, the youths and their families were randomly assigned to one of four groups: a behavior-modification program, a conventional group-discussion counseling program, a church-sponsored family counseling program, and a no-treatment group. The behavior-modification program involved inducing family members to talk more constructively with one another, to tolerate interruptions, and to agree on certain standards of conduct and the consequences of conforming to those standards ("contingency contracting"). Over the ensuing year and a half, the youths who had been in the behavior-modification program were only half as likely to reappear in juvenile court as were those who got no treatment or who were in the conventional counseling programs;[25] moreover, the brothers and sisters of the youths in the treatment program were also less likely to get in trouble with the law than were the siblings of the youths in the control groups.[26] The number of persons involved was so small and the kinds of delinquencies averted so minor that the Utah project cannot be regarded as settling the question of whether family life can be altered in ways that will reduce serious criminality, but it has provided a promising lead.

That lead has been most thoroughly explored by Gerald R. Patterson and his colleagues at the Oregon Social Learning Center, whose work we described in Chapter 8. Unlike many other therapists, they have concentrated on reducing deviant behavior among preadolescents rather than rehabilitating teen-age delinquents; in fact, much of their research suggests that beyond a certain age, changes in the family environment will have little, if any, effect on young persons because they will now be more responsive to peer than to parental reinforcers. And unlike some programs, theirs is not based on the assumption that families need to communicate more (or less); what is crucial is the way in which parents define, monitor, and control the behavior of their children in routine settings. Finally, Patterson and his associates do not underestimate the difficulty of getting families to change.

Some projects quickly discovered that the parents did not always share the therapists' enthusiasm for the principles of behavior modification. To these mothers and fathers, "reinforcing socially desirable behavior" sounded too much like bribing kids to do what they were supposed to do anyway, and relying on positive reinforcers rather than punishments seemed to them to be spoiling the child by sparing the rod.[27] Moreover, parents do not socialize their offspring into deviant ways in a fit of absentmindedness or because of errors in judgment they are eager to correct; rather, their defective parental styles are often the result of their own deep-seated temperamental problems that lead them to act impulsively, inconsistently, or aggressively and, some-times, to lack much desire to change their children's behavior.

Since the mid-1970s, the Oregon center has treated over 250 families whose children ranged in age from five to thirteen.[28] Most had been referred to the clinic because they had set fires, stolen property, picked fights, or up-set their teachers or parents; some also were victims of child abuse. At the clinic or in the home, the therapists precisely measured the pattern of family interactions, coding in great detail (using a twenty-nine-item Family Inter-action Coding System) all that transpired between a child and his parents every six seconds for nearly an hour. Fourteen of the twenty-nine possible ways of behaving were termed "aversive," meaning unpleasant; these in-cluded whining, yelling, teasing, and hitting.

As we saw in Chapter 8, the Patterson group concluded that the fami-lies of problem children differed from those of normal children in not know-ing *how* to punish. The former were more likely than the latter to use more punishment and to punish erratically and inconsistently; as a result, the child had difficulty learning that what happened to him would depend on how he behaved. Since his behavior had no predictable consequences, that behavior itself became unpredictable.

To improve matters it was necessary to teach these families how to set clear rules, monitor behavior, and make rewards contingent on good be-havior and punishment contingent on bad behavior. By rewards the thera-pists did not only mean giving presents or privileges in exchange for some major instance of good conduct but also routinely responding in pleasant and supportive ways to pleasant and constructive language and gestures. And by punishment they meant not only assessing major penalties for major misdemeanors but also consistently penalizing unpleasant and destructive language and conduct. An especially favored penalty, the value of which was established by repeated trials, was "time out"—that is, being sent briefly, usually for five or ten minutes, into seclusion in another room.[29] (The effi-cacy of time out as opposed to verbal reprimands had earlier been demonstrated by Tyler and Brown.)[30] Teaching these commonsense methods was difficult, but not nearly as difficult as motivating the parents to put them to use. Both instruction and motivation required extraordinary clinical skills and patience, neither of which was easy to sustain.

When nineteen families of excessively aggressive children were randomly assigned to either the parent-training program or to some conventional form of therapy available in the local community, the children in the parent-training program displayed a sharp drop in the frequency of aversive behavior, while those in the conventional programs showed, on the average, no change.[31]

One finding at the Oregon center is especially interesting because it illuminates the dynamic effects of reinforcements. It turned out that it was much easier for Patterson and his colleagues to reduce the rate of aggression (tantrums, fighting, hitting) among children than to reduce the rate of theft. At first this seems contrary to common sense. Aggression, it is popularly believed, is the supreme example of irrational, impulsive, hard-to-control behavior, whereas theft is the result of calculation and greed and thus more easily controlled by changing the circumstances of the thief. Not so, at least in families. The reason is that parental behavior that reduces aggression even slightly among children is, for the parent, reinforcing in its own right. The reduction in tantrums, yelling, and punching induce the parent to do more controlling. But parents who act in ways that reduce their offspring's tendency to steal often go unrewarded, since they do not know if the thievery has been reduced (it is, after all, stealthy behavior), and if they do know about any stealing they may choose to believe that it was a misunderstanding or that the child was wrongly accused. Or the parents may simply not attach much importance to theft because it does not inconvenience them personally. Without any natural reinforcement for controlling behavior aimed at theft, those controls are less likely to continue and, thus, theft is more likely to continue.[32]

The family is the most important locus of reinforcements, but it is not the only one. Efforts have been made to change the reinforcements available in the neighborhood and the local job market, but as we move farther away from the individual in the family, the strength of the reinforcers declines. As a result, though evidence of individuals changing their behavior as a result of planned changes in family practices is not yet as strong as one might like, the evidence of offenders changing their behavior owing to planned changes in the neighborhood or the labor market is even weaker.

For example, during the 1950s, many attempts were made to reduce crime by altering the behavior of street gangs by the use of such techniques as assigning social workers (called "detached workers") to the gangs. The workers' job was to induce the gangs to redirect their energies toward more constructive ends. There is no evidence that they succeeded.[33] The detached workers could form good relationships with the gangs, but they could not affect the reinforcements operating on gang members and thus could not affect their behavior, except marginally.

More recently, there has been an effort to pair a delinquent boy or girl with a "buddy" who, by virtue of his one-on-one relationship with the youngster, would be able to alter the latter's behavior by altering the reinforcement he received from his adult companion. The buddy system was tested in Honolulu by randomly assigning some troublesome youths to adults who would meet with them in the community and attempt, through the use of either social approval or small monetary rewards or both, to get the young persons to attend school regularly and stay out of trouble and by assigning others to a control group that had no buddies. An interesting feature of the project was that the buddies were told to treat some of their charges in a warm and supportive way regardless of how they acted and to treat others warmly only if they behaved themselves. The contingent reinforcements were effective in reducing truancy[34] and, over three years, in reducing the rates of delinquency among boys who had already been delinquents;[35] the noncontingent reinforcement had no effect. Unfortunately, there was also an *increase* in delinquency among boys who had not been delinquent before acquiring a buddy, perhaps because the program brought them into association with confirmed delinquents.

In Chapter 12 we reviewed the efforts to measure the connection between criminality and economic conditions and to alter criminality directly by supplying money, jobs, or job training to school dropouts and convicted offenders. The reader will recall that we concluded that the statistical evidence for any association at all is relatively weak and probably reflects the operation of partially offsetting factors—a need effect, an affluence effect, a common-cause relationship, and an envy effect. And we noted the discouraging results of efforts to alter criminal behavior by placing convicts in work-release programs, giving money to ex-convicts (the TARP program), or supplying intensive training in job-related and personal skills to ex-convicts and delinquent school dropouts (the MDRC program). The failures of these programs to reduce crime does not show that persons inclined to crime are indifferent to the value of employment alternatives to crime. But they do suggest that by the time an individual has become eligible for such programs—by dropping out of school, committing crimes, or being sent to prison—he has already learned to value crime and leisure, in some combination, over the kinds of jobs that society might feasibly make available to him, and that he has failed to learn those skills and habits that would make him an attractive candidate for an employer. There have so far been very few evaluated efforts to discover whether increasing the availability of jobs to individuals not yet socialized into criminal habits will make a difference in the likelihood of later criminal behavior.

Changing the Penalties of Community Life

Like the prospects of getting a job that might serve as an alternative to crime, the chances of being caught and punished for having committed a crime are delayed and uncertain. Just as a teen-ager may be badly informed about the kinds of jobs to which he might aspire and about the relationship between his present conduct and future employability, he also may be ignorant of the true risks of crime and of the connection between youthful misdeeds and adult satisfactions. If the person has a low IQ, he may have a special difficulty in grasping these connections; if as a result of his low verbal skills (or for any other reason) he has found schooling and its routines unrewarding, he may assign a low value even to those future consequences he does grasp. If he is impulsive (if he has, that is, steep delay-of-reinforcement curves), then any distant consequences, however well understood or valued, may exert little influence on present conduct.

For all these reasons, we would expect that scholars would have a difficult time measuring the connection, if any, between the risk of punishment and the commission of crime. And they have. Hardly any scholars have denied that a crime is less likely to take place when a police officer is watching, but many have denied that feasible (and thus small) changes in the delayed (often greatly delayed) risk of conviction and punishment will cause any measurable change in the crime rate.

The difficulty in showing a connection between the risk of sanction and the rate of crime is compounded by the poor quality of the data on which we must rely and by the need, in most cases, to look for this connection in the behavior of large numbers of persons (entire cities, counties, or states), only a few of whom are likely to commit a crime at all. The effort to find out whether changing the penalties attached to criminal activity will change the crime rate has typically involved finding out whether there is a correlation between naturally occurring variations in the rate of some offense (say, robbery) among American states and naturally occurring variations in the probability of an offender's going to prison in those states (in this case, the ratio between the number of robberies reported and the number of robbers imprisoned). In doing this, of course, the researchers attempt to hold constant the effect of other factors, such as density, employment levels, and the age composition of the population, that are also likely to affect the crime rate.[36]

In general, the evidence is consistent with the view that states (or other jurisdictions) in which the probability of going to prison is high have, other things being equal, lower crime rates than states in which that probability is low.[37] Moreover, for reasons we do not entirely understand, the evidence showing a link between sanctions and crime is somewhat stronger than that showing a connection between economic conditions and crime.[38] But there are various methodological problems that make it hard to be entirely confident that this connection is a causal one—that is, that it is the higher risk of punishment that is keeping down the crime rate.[39]

Among these problems, two stand out. First, errors in measuring the key variables in our studies, especially errors in measuring the number of crimes, may bias our results if those errors are not random. For example, if some states are more accurate than others in recording the number of crimes that have been committed, then an observed negative correlation between crime rates (i.e., the number of crimes reported divided by the population of a state) and imprisonment rates (i.e., the number of persons going to prison divided by the number of crimes reported) may to some degree be a spurious correlation because of nonrandom errors in measuring something (the number of crimes) that is both the numerator of one variable (the crime rate) and the denominator of another (the imprisonment rate). Thus, a state whose crime rate is overestimated will automatically be one whose imprisonment rate is underestimated.

Second, if states with a high robbery rate are also states that send a low proportion of robbers to prison, this could mean either that the high robbery rates are caused by the low imprisonment rates (i.e., the states have failed to deter robbers) or that the low imprisonment rates are caused by the high robbery rates. The latter possibility might occur if states experiencing, for some reason, a rapidly rising robbery rate find themselves unable to arrest, convict, and imprison the same proportion of robbers as they once did. The robberies are increasing so fast that they swamp the criminal justice system. Prosecutors and judges, in order to keep the system from becoming hopelessly clogged, let off without a prison sentence robbers they might once have imprisoned. As a result, the proportion of arrested robbers sent to prison decreases while the robbery rate goes up. In this case, we should conclude not that prison deters robbers but that high robbery rates "deter" prosecutors and judges.

There are ways of coping with these methodological problems and some studies that manage to overcome them. The errors in police reports of crime can be addressed by using other measures of crime—in particular, by using victimization reports gathered by the Census Bureau directly from citizens. While these surveys have errors of their own, they are not the same errors as the ones that afflict police reports. Thus, if we find by using victimization data the same negative correlation between the rate of robbery and the chances of a robbery resulting in punishment, our confidence that this is not a spurious correlation is strengthened. Precisely such results have been obtained by Goldberg[40] and Wilson and Boland.[41] However one measures crime, it is less common in places where sanctions are more likely.

The problem of a swamped system, though statistically difficult to resolve, is likely to be a real problem only for the more common but less serious offenses. One can imagine prosecutors and judges deciding, because of their rising work loads, not to imprison shoplifters, drug users, or petty thieves, with the effect of making it hard, if not impossible, for observers to decide whether the lessened penalties were causing increases in these offenses or the increases in these offenses were causing lessened penalties. But one cannot easily imagine judges letting convicted murderers and armed robbers off with no prison sentences, partly because such offenses are so serious and partly because the total number of such crimes is not great enough to overwhelm the resources of the criminal justice system. There is no evidence that convicted murderers are any less likely to go to prison today than they were twenty years ago; moreover, the apparent deterrent effect of prison on serious crimes, such as murder and robbery, was as great in 1940 and 1950, when they were much less common, as it is today.[42] Thus, the swamping argument probably does not invalidate the statistical showing of a deterrent effect of prison, at least for major crimes.

Moreover, there are studies that manage to avoid the swamping problem entirely. During the Vietnam War, draft evasion was lowest in those states where the chances of being punished for evasion were the highest, even after controlling for other characteristics of those states, including public opinion about the war.[43] Draft evaders were accurately identified, so there was not likely to be any bias resulting from measurement errors, and the crime was sufficiently uncommon—only 7 percent of the case load of federal courts—so there was not likely to be a swamping effect.

One can also minimize the swamping problem by looking at the effect on crime rates of changes over time in the risk of punishment (provided certain other methodological conditions are met).[44] American criminal statistics are so poor that it is almost impossible to do this kind of longitudinal research. In England, however, the statistics are much better. A longitudinal study of crime rates in England between 1894 and 1967 showed that decreases in the risk of a penalty were associated with increases in the rate of crime, other things being equal, and suggested reasons for believing that this association was a causal one.[45]

Though we think the weight of the evidence supports the view that changes in the risk of punishment in society affect, at the margin, the behavior of would-be offenders, we are aware that the evidence so far presented, relying, as it does, on cross-sectional or longitudinal studies of large aggregations of people, is not overpowering. It is especially not likely to be persuasive to persons who find it hard to believe that individual offenders are aware of what risks they run in a given community.

There are two ways to approach this issue. The first is to find out whether offenders are in fact aware of the costs (more accurately, the expected disutility) of crime; the second is to see whether their behavior changes when they actually experience changes in those costs.

Given all the attention paid to making communities safer by increasing either the costs of crime or the benefits of noncrime, it is somewhat surprising to discover that very little systematic research has been done on how would-be offenders perceive either source of reinforcements. Law-abiding persons, such as (we hope) the readers of this book, largely get their information about the costs and benefits of crime from the mass media and thus may be quite unaware of what the actual costs and benefits are. But persons who offend, or who know offenders, are much better informed. We saw in Chapter 11 that the youthful criminals in an urban neighborhood intensively studied by Sally Engle Merry were quite sophisticated about the immediate circumstances defining their criminal opportunities.[46] They distinguished carefully between more and less affluent targets, between persons more and less likely to call the police, and between the kinds of offenses more and less likely to lead to arrest and prosecution.[47] The street youths knew the names and reputations of many of the detectives assigned to the area and had formed a judgment about what kinds of stories the judge would and would not believe.

Experienced criminals seem to be aware of the risk of crime in their states. Over two thousand inmates of jails and prisons in California, Michigan, and Texas were interviewed about their criminal careers and attitudes. Based on the inmates' self-reported crimes, the analysts, Jan and Marcia Chaiken, concluded that the rate at which Texas convicts committed robberies was significantly lower and the chances of going to prison for a crime in Texas significantly higher than they were in either California or Michigan.

The reason became apparent from the inmates' answer to the following question: "Do you think you could do the same crime(s) again without getting caught?" Even though the California inmates had committed more serious crimes than those in Texas, they were over twice as likely to believe that if they continued they could get away with it. The Texas inmates committed the fewest serious crimes and were least likely to believe they could get away with it. There was, in short, a close correspondence between the actual and perceived risk of imprisonment in the two states.[48] Among convicts within California, however, it appears that self-reported rates of offending are related more to the convicts' perception of the benefits than to the costs of crime.[49]

It is not clear whether the perceptions that a law-abiding person has of the risks of crime affect the likelihood that he will commit one. Surveys among college students,[50] high school students,[51] and the adult population at large[52] suggest that persons who think the risk of punishment is high are more likely than those who think it low to say that they would not commit a crime. While these results are consistent with the theory of deterrence, they are hard to interpret; both a person's claim that he would not commit a crime and his belief that he would surely be caught if he did commit one may reflect an underlying concern for the moral opprobrium with which he and others view crime. Tittle, for example, concludes that among the population at large it is the fear of informal sanctions—that is, the loss of reputation—more than the fear of formal ones that is the most powerful deterrent to crime, a finding that strikes us as quite plausible.[53] If only the risk of arrest and punishment was keeping the average citizen from crime, we would be up to our ears in criminality. But surveys of (primarily) law-abiding persons, most of whom are inhibited from committing crimes by the bite of conscience reinforced by the possible loss of reputation, cannot tell us much about how persons lacking that conscience or that regard for conventional opinion will act in the face of small differences in the risk of apprehension. To illuminate this matter, we think the observations of Merry[54] and of the Chaikens[55] are more helpful.

In any event, the crucial question is whether changes in the risk of formal sanctions will in fact alter behavior among persons at risk. No simple answer can be given to that question for reasons that can be anticipated by a reader who has studied the theory presented in Chapter 2. One must first hold roughly constant the gains of crime before one can see changes in behavior associated with changes in the costs of crime. Ideally, one would want also to hold constant the subjective state of the would-be offenders by, for example, randomly exposing them to either sanctions or no sanctions and then following their subsequent behavior.

Happily, something approaching such an experiment in deterrence has been carried out, and with a form of behavior—spouse assault—that is often thought to be the product of emotions so powerful as to be insensitive to the consequences of action. Violence in the family is quite common; police officers frequently respond to calls from the victims of domestic attacks. For many years, the conventional wisdom was that such incidents were best handled informally—by police mediation—or by referring the parties to a social-work agency for counseling, and not by making an arrest. To test these ideas, the police in Minneapolis began randomly assigning misdemeanor spouse-assault cases to one of three dispositions: arresting the assaulter, giving him informal, on-the-spot advice, or sending him out of the house to cool off. Over 250 cases were handled in this experimental manner; the subsequent behavior of the assaulters was followed up for six months. The assaulters who were arrested were less likely to be reported to the police for a subsequent assault than were those who were counseled and much less likely than those who were sent out of the house. And arrests had this effect even though the arrested person, in the vast majority of cases, spent no more than a night or two in jail. [56]

There have been very few true experiments of the sort done in Minneapolis, but there is some confirming evidence from quasi experiments. In Cook County (Chicago), the juvenile-justice authorities wanted to know what effect their programs were having on delinquents. There already had been many efforts to answer that question, usually with the negative results found by Lipton, Martinson, and Wilks.[57] But the researchers involved in this study, Charles A. Murray and Louis A. Cox, Jr., redefined the measure of success in a way that seems to make a striking difference.[58] Previously, almost all students of criminal recidivism had measured the outcome of a program by the percentage of the participants who failed because they were re-arrested or reconvicted after they left the program. Failure was an either-or proposition: If you got into trouble again, *even once,* you were a failure. The proportion who failed was called the "recidivism rate," but in fact it was not a rate at all; rather it was the percentage who got in trouble again. A true rate would show *frequency* of misconduct, not simply whether it ever occurred. In the Cook County study, Murray and Cox supplied a true recidivism rate by calculating how many times per month a group of delinquents were arrested before and after being in one of several programs.

They first made this calculation for 317 serious, repeat offenders who had been arrested an average of thirteen times apiece before being sent, for the first time, to the Department of Corrections, in whose institutions they spent an average of ten months. Murray and Cox followed them for (on the average) seventeen months after release. By the conventional measure of recidivism, the results were, as usual, discouraging—82 percent were rearrested. But the frequency with which they were rearrested fell dramatically—the monthly arrest rate per hundred boys declined by about two-thirds. To be exact, the monthly arrest rate was 6.3 per month per hundred boys before incarceration and 2.9 per month per hundred boys after release.

Murray and Cox also looked at the police records of 266 delinquents who, though eligible to go to the state reformatory, were sent instead to one of several less custodial, more community-based programs such as foster homes, halfway houses, wilderness camps, and the like. Despite the fact that these boys, all serious offenders, had been judged to be more amenable to the presumably rehabilitative effects of community-based programs, the reduction in their monthly arrest rates was less than it had been for the boys sent to the reformatories. Even more interesting, Murray and Cox found that the more restrictive the supervision in these more benign programs, the greater the reduction in recidivism.

A number of criticisms have been made of these findings,[59] and the issue cannot be regarded as settled. But so far none of the criticisms appears to be fatal. One is that the decline in arrest rates may simply reflect the reduction in criminality that is the result of aging. This argument, however, cannot explain why the boys in the least restrictive program experienced less of a reduction in criminality than those in the most restrictive one, since they were, naturally, aging at the same rate. As an additional check on this, Murray and Cox looked at the arrest records of nearly fifteen hundred youths born in Chicago and arrested at least once before their seventeenth birthday. Since this was a random sample of all arrested youths, their criminal records were, of course, less serious than those of the boys sent to institutions. Yet the monthly arrest rates of these boys showed a more or less steady increase throughout their teen-age years, with no evidence of a reduction owing to maturation. Being arrested or being placed on probation, unlike being put into some kind of institution for even a brief period, apparently had no effect on subsequent delinquency.

We cannot be certain whether the reduction in arrest rates corresponds to an equivalent reduction in actual crime rates. It is possible that boys who spent some time in an institution learned there how to commit crimes without being detected. It is impossible to disprove this since the true crime rate of an individual is unknown. But there are reasons for doubting that juvenile institutions could be such effective schools for crime. Ten months in a reformatory would have to be much more "educational" than ten years on the street if those months were to produce sufficient new skills to account for a two-thirds decline in arrest frequency. Moreover, the boys when interviewed made it clear that in their minds institutionalization had reduced, not increased, their commitment to a criminal career.

Comparable results have been obtained in an experimental project that involved randomly assigning delinquent boys in Provo, Utah, either to a community-based program involving close supervision or to a conventional institution.[60] Failure to participate in the community program was penalized by sending the boy to a reformatory. Though the project ended prematurely, data covering four years suggested that there was a reduction in the frequency of arrests that could not be explained by maturation for both the boys incarcerated and those in the intensive community program.

There is, in sum, good though not yet entirely conclusive evidence that the behavior of offenders can be altered by altering the consequences attached to their behavior (children of families that undergo training in how to manage discipline, husbands arrested on spouse-assault charges, delinquents sent to an institution, as well as among those subject to behavior-control programs in an institutional setting). Some of the observed change in behavior may also result from a change in the value offenders attach to a reinforcement. That is, a person may become less likely to commit an offense either because he has learned (by experiencing punishment) that certain consequences of that offense are more likely than he had once supposed or because he has come to take more seriously the consequences (again, by having experienced them) that he knew were attached to that behavior. There is no way, using available studies, that we can establish whether the positive results were due to changes in perceived probabilities or changes in perceived magnitudes.

If criminal behavior is reduced because the probability of it being punished has increased, then that reduction is not likely to persist unless the individual continues to experience punishment at some reasonably great frequency whenever he misbehaves in the future, and not just while he is in the experimental program. It is common for the effects of any one-shot intervention to decay over time. The Minneapolis police followed the spouse assaulters for only six months; Murray and Cox followed the delinquent boys for only seventeen months. It is possible that after more time has passed, the observed effects of being arrested or placed in a program will diminish or vanish altogether. To avoid this, society must try to alter permanently and for large numbers of people the expected disutility of crime. To see if such lasting and widespread changes can alter the crime rate, we must examine the effect on crime of differences in the risk of punishment that one encounters as one moves from state to state, or over time in one state.

Changing Contingencies in Society

To increase the expected disutility of crime for people in general, society must increase either the speed, the certainty, or the severity of punishment, or some combination of all three. We saw earlier in this chapter that when scholars have compared variations among states in the probability of imprisonment, they have found that states where the chances of imprisonment are high have lower crime rates than states where it is low, other things being equal. But we also saw that there are important methodological problems in inferring from that association that it is the higher risk of imprisonment that is keeping the crime rate down. (The reader should bear in mind that these problems bedevil the effort to measure the effect on aggregate crime rates of natural variations in *any* kind of reinforcement or punishment, whether it be the availability of jobs, the extent of poverty, or the level of education.) Though we think that these studies of naturally occurring variations do support the view that criminal behavior is sensitive to the level of punishment available in a community—even punishments whose effect is delayed and uncertain—we shall here confine our attention only to studies of efforts to change crime rates by changing the speed, certainty, or severity of penalties.

We know of no study that estimates the effect of changes in the speed of punishment on the probability of crime. We intuitively know that a burglary is less likely to occur when a police officer is watching than when his back is turned, and we plausibly guess that a burglary would be less likely if the offender were punished one day rather than one year later, but we have no evidence with which we can test our guess. As H. Laurence Ross has put it, "Celerity is an orphan variable in deterrence research."[61]

There are several studies of the effect on aggregate crime rates of changes in the certainty and severity of punishment. Unfortunately, almost all of these deal with only one kind of punishment, imprisonment, and not with the full range of sanctions that are available and that, in fact, are much more commonly used than imprisonment. These include fines, short jail terms, suspended sentences, assignment to community service, and restitution payments to victims.

The largest number of these inquiries have to do with attempts to reduce traffic accidents and especially to reduce drunk driving. Many of these attempts, patterned on laws initially enacted in Sweden and Norway, have sought to discourage drunk driving by increasing the penalties attached to it, by increasing the risk of apprehension, or both. Ross has summarized those studies that have been done in ten countries.[62]

In general, efforts to change driving habits by merely announcing an increase in the severity of the penalty have had little effect. In 1950, Finland doubled the prison sentence for drunk driving (from two to four years) and in 1957 increased it again, to a maximum of eight years (actual sentences handed out were on the order of three to six months in jail). In 1970, a judge in Chicago announced that henceforth he was imposing seven-day jail sentences for drunk driving. A judge in an Australian city did much the same thing. In none of the three places was there a decline in traffic accidents that could be attributed to the increased severity of the penalty.[63]

Most efforts have involved changing both the certainty and the severity of punishment for drunk driving, usually by allowing the police to arrest motorists whose blood alcohol content exceeded a certain level and by equipping police with the devices necessary to detect this level. Places that do this ordinarily experience a decline in various indicators of drunk driving, such as accidents, injuries, and fatalities. The effect seemed to be greater in those cases where the new policy was highly publicized, but unless the policy was accompanied by a determined effort actually to increase the risk of apprehension, its effect was short-lived.[64] Where that determined effort was made, as it was in several countries, the reduction in indicators of drunk driving was even sharper and more lasting. For example, the police in Cheshire, England, used breathalyzers to catch drunk motorists. There was a two-thirds reduction in traffic casualties during weekend evenings when drunk driving is likely to be most common. The police, it turned out, did not like to enforce the law in this way since it could lead to the mandatory revocation of the offender's driver's license. As the police eased up, traffic casualties mounted. When they were persuaded to crack down again, casualties dropped again.[65] Ross summarizes his findings this way: Increasing the severity of a penalty without also increasing its certainty has little effect on behavior.[66] Increasing the certainty of punishment does have an effect, especially if it is well publicized and reinforced by special police efforts. In the long run, there is a tendency for behavior to return to the preenforcement level, in part because the chances of being caught and punished while driving under the influence of alcohol are so small—one authority estimates it to be about four chances in ten thousand[67]—that even very large increases in the chance of arrest (say, by tripling it) would still leave very high odds in favor of a drunk driver on any given trip. By contrast, the odds that a given armed robbery will result in an arrest are estimated (for California prison inmates) to be about one in five and that a given burglary will lead to apprehension about one in fourteen.[68]

Even when there are no reported changes in police activity, there are some grounds for believing that altering penalties will alter behavior. Between 1970 and 1973, twenty-five states lowered the legal drinking age, thereby removing penalties for drinking once faced by some youths. Research suggested that this produced an increase in highway accidents owing to the greater number of teen-agers who were driving after drinking.[69] Learning this, many states raised the legal drinking age back to twenty or twenty-one. Studies in these states suggest that this change in the law produced a reduction in the number of persons ages eighteen to twenty who were involved in traffic accidents.[70]

The extent to which changed sanctions will change behavior will be affected by the benefits of crime and by the array of background reinforcements operating on the individual. Doubling the risk of apprehension, or increasing the severity of the penalty after apprehension, may affect the frequency with which a person drives after drinking even though the chances of detection on any given trip are very small. The reason, of course, is that for many persons drinking heavily is behavior from which they can readily refrain because its benefits are not that great and because, having a long time horizon, they can plan on passing up that extra drink if they know they must drive home from the party. And there are other sources of gratification available to a person—provided he is not a chronic alcoholic—that might readily substitute for a drink. By contrast, the perceived benefit to a woman of an abortion may be so high she will seek one out even if it is illegal. This benefit, along with the fact that an illegal abortion is a consensual act and thus hard to detect, may explain why legalizing abortions in Hawaii did not appear to have much of an effect on the number performed.[71] And reducing burglaries by increasing the certainty or severity of penalties may produce only small changes in the burglary rate if the gains from burglary are very great and those from legitimate jobs are very poor, even though, as we have seen, the chances of a burglar's being arrested are already vastly greater than are the chances of a drunk driver's being detected. None of this means that some crimes can be deterred and others cannot; all behavior is affected, at the margin, by its consequences. But the degree to which changed sanctions change criminal behavior—in the technical language of the economist, the price elasticity of crime—will vary depending on the value of the reinforcements operating on an individual.

Two quasi experiments that illustrate the differing effects of sanctions are found in studies of the Bartley-Fox gun law in Massachusetts and the Rockefeller drug laws in New York. The Bartley-Fox law, passed in 1974, stipulated that persons carrying a handgun without a license, already a crime, would now face, if caught and convicted, a mandatory one-year prison sentence that could not be reduced or evaded by parole or probation. The new law was heavily publicized, but there was no evidence that the police made any special effort to enforce it. If citizen behavior changed, the change would have to be the result of perceived increases in the severity of the penalty rather than in the probability of apprehension. Several studies have been done of the effect of the law, and all find evidence that there was a reduction in the kinds of crime that involve the unplanned use of firearms. To be precise,[72] after the law went into effect there was a reduction in the proportion of assaults, robberies, and homicides in which a handgun was used, even though the total number of such crimes was either constant or increasing. The theory offered in this book supplies an interpretation of these findings. A person determined to rob a liquor store or murder his wife would plan the offense in advance, arrange to have a gun available at the crucial moment, and take steps to avoid apprehension. The new law might have some effect on this behavior, but probably not much—if caught, the robber or murderer will go to prison in any event, and the one-year sentence for carrying the gun will be the least of his worries. But persons who plan no definite crime but like to carry a gun "just in case" may well take the new law into account. Knowing ahead of time that carrying a gun is more risky than it was, and having no offsetting benefit that would make the risk worthwhile, many of these casual gun carriers will leave the gun at home. Those who carry one anyway may find themselves in certain situations—a barroom argument, a sudden chance to take some loot—when a gun would be handy and, since they have one, they use it. Their own delay-of-reinforcement curves make a gun of great value to them only when they are very close to a criminal opportunity. The deterrent effect of the Bartley-Fox law, it seems, operated on casual gun carriers when they were well to the left of their crossover points (see Chapter 2), and thus reduced the frequency of certain kinds of unplanned gun crimes. This is an example of a proposition that, without a suitable theory, might otherwise seem inexplicable: The gun law changed the behavior of impulsive more than that of calculating offenders.

By contrast, the Rockefeller drug laws were aimed chiefly at the deliberate, calculating, professional offender—in this case, persons who dealt in heroin in amounts of one ounce or more. In 1973, New York State revised its laws against drug dealing by making major dealers in heroin liable to a minimum prison term of fifteen years and a maximum of life. Some plea bargaining was allowed, but in no event could a convicted ounce-or-more dealer escape a term of at least one year in prison (unless he was a police informant or a juvenile). After the law went into effect, the police and prosecutors continued to behave pretty much as before—there was no change in the number of arrests or indictments, and thus in the risk of apprehension or prosecution. Nor was there a change in the proportion of accused offenders going to prison—the chance of incarceration was about one in nine before and after the new law. What did change was the severity of penalty if convicted. Before the law, only 3 percent of the persons imprisoned for drug offenses had terms of three years or more; after the law, 22 percent received such sentences. But according to a major evaluation of the effect of the law, there was no observable change in heroin trafficking despite the more severe penalties: There were no marked decreases in drug overdose deaths, in admissions to drug treatment programs, or in the incidence of serum hepatitis (a disease frequently contracted by junkies who use dirty needles), nor was there a change in the street price of heroin (as inferred from undercover buys made by narcotics agents).[73] One interpretation of these results, based on the theoretical perspective of this book, is that the increase in the severity of the penalties, with no accompanying increase in their certainty, was not enough to alter measurably the behavior of persons who stood to gain a great deal by selling large amounts of heroin and who planned their sales, including their likely yield, carefully and well in advance. As severe as it was, the new sanction still left the crime more reinforcing than noncrime, at least for the major dealers. There is no doubt that some level of severity would have made heroin trafficking no longer worth the cost to such persons, but that level apparently was not reached in New York. One wonders what the effect of this law would have been were it applied to small-scale, casual drug dealers for whom the increase in penalty might have seemed very large, especially when their illegal activities, being opportunistic, were not seriously contemplated until they were to the right of a crossover point, close to the opportunity itself. Up to a point, severe sanctions imposed on very profitable behavior may have their greatest effect on offenders with short time horizons, and their least effect on those with long ones, *if* the offenders must take preparatory steps (carrying a gun or a packet of heroin) in order to commit the crime.

Conclusions

So far we have discussed changing the subjective state of a person and altering the consequences of his behavior as if they were two entirely separate enterprises. Obviously, that is not the case. One of the ways our subjective state is formed—or re-formed—is by experiencing the consequences of our behavior. And what consequences our behavior will have is shaped by our preferences and our time horizon; in short, by our subjective state.

At a minimum, this means that a rigid distinction between planned changes in reinforcements and punishments (increases in the speed, certainty, or magnitude of criminal justice sanctions or employment opportunities) and deliberate efforts to modify a person's conscience or values is rather artificial. Moreover, the intimate connection between how we think and what we experience may suggest that the most efficacious ways of altering behavior are those that link programs designed to alter subjective states with those designed to alter contingencies.

For example, the apparent reduction in criminality that was a consequence of exposing Chicago delinquents to higher levels of restrictive supervision[74] may have occurred because the boys acquired a greater appreciation of the risks of being caught ("I never thought I would wind up in a reformatory! I hadn't realized you were serious about crime!") or because the value they attached to the benefits of noncrime was increased ("I had no idea the reformatory was so miserable a place to be! Maybe being a law-abiding citizen isn't so dumb an idea after all!"). Probably both processes were at work, at least in some boys. Similarly, it is possible that the crime-reduction effect of the intensive group discussion sessions in the community-based treatment program in Provo would have been much less if whatever changes in subjective state occurred in that setting were not reinforced by the knowledge that if the delinquent caused trouble in or failed to attend the sessions he would be shipped off to the reformatory.[75]

Differing combinations of constraint and re-education probably are effective for differing kinds of offenders; our present knowledge only hints at what some of those connections may be. In general, it may be easier to change the subjective states of offenders who have not found crime particularly rewarding, in whom a conscience exists with sufficient strength to make them feel somewhat uneasy about committing crimes, and whose temperament and intelligence make them amenable to therapeutic efforts. It may be hardest to change the subjective states of offenders who have found crime rewarding, who can commit crimes without experiencing the bite of conscience, and whose temperament and intelligence make them regard therapy as irrelevant, incomprehensible, or an opportunity for manipulation.[76]

These practical possibilities are worth exploring, but it has not been our intention in this chapter to recommend methods of changing criminals or reducing crime. Rather, our object has been to assess the extent to which evidence drawn from studies of what are conventionally called deterrence, rehabilitation, and the enlargement of opportunities does or does not support the theory of human nature set forth in this book. By and large, we find that it does.

If behavior were not controlled by its consequences but instead were primarily shaped by the subjective state of the offender, and if that state were amenable to change, then we surely would have found stronger evidence than we now possess that treatments relying on verbal persuasion rather than the manipulation of consequences have a significant effect on criminality. Instead, we find that the effects of verbal therapies are weak and limited, whereas the effects of altered contingencies, as in behavior-modification programs, are strong and immediate, at least when administered in an institutional setting.

The fact that it is very hard to sustain the new patterns of behavior outside the institutional setting means only, we think, that the reinforcements operating in the world at large do not reward the behavior desired by the institution. There is some evidence, however, that these desirable patterns can be sustained in the community when the therapist's contact with the offender is close and frequent[77] or when the processes of familial discipline can be altered in a constructive direction.[78]

Attempting to create and sustain law-abiding behavior solely by manipulating society-wide, as opposed to intimate, reinforcements is the most difficult task of all, and its effects are the hardest to measure. The rewards of noncrime can be increased through employment programs, but so far the evidence suggests that this has little effect on repeat offenders (Chapter 12). The costs of crime can also be increased, and the evidence is consistent with the hypothesis that this will affect the rate of criminal activity—not, perhaps, by changing the behavior of many serious, repeat offenders (any more than job programs change their behavior), but at least by changing the dispositions of marginal or would-be offenders.

Methodological problems make it difficult to be certain that these changes occur when one can observe naturally occurring differences only among large aggregates of people, but the evidence from experiments and quasi experiments in the real world provides strong support for the findings of cross-sectional statistical studies. Behavior changed when assaultive spouses were arrested instead of merely counseled, when Chicago delinquents were placed in more rather than less restrictive institutions, and when the penalties for carrying guns or driving while drunk were made either more certain or more severe. Not all forms of criminal behavior change with changes in sanctions, however. If the crime is sufficiently rewarding or its detection sufficiently unlikely, then little observable change in behavior will result from any feasible change in sanctions, a conclusion we inferred from studies of the effect of changing the penalties for large-scale heroin trafficking.

V

HISTORY AND CULTURE

16

HISTORICAL TRENDS IN CRIME

Many readers are probably more interested in knowing why crime rates go up than why individuals differ in their propensity to commit crimes. That is understandable; most people are more worried about the increased risk that their property will be stolen than they are about who may do the stealing. In our view, however, explanations of changes in crime rates are likely to be partial and misleading if they are not firmly based on an understanding of individual differences in criminality. Just as people have their pet theories for why some persons are criminal and others are not, so also do they have favored—and inevitably incomplete—theories of why crime rates change. Any explanation of historical trends in crime rates should take into account the operation of all those factors—personal predispositions, the socializing forces of family, peers, and school, and the reinforcements supplied by community circumstances and institutional arrangements—that affect the choice between crime and its alternatives.

An explanation should meet other tests as well. Though we experienced more or less steady increases in crime during the 1960s and 1970s, we experienced long periods of declining or stable crime rates in the 1940s and 1950s; our theories should help us understand why crime rates sometimes go down as well as why they go up. These long-term increases and decreases are not peculiar to American society but tend to occur simultaneously in most industrial nations; thus, any explanation of historical trends should give principal attention to those forces operating in all societies rather than to those unique to one or a few nations.

The Trends

The trends we wish to explain can be generally though not precisely described. In very few nations do we have any systematic data on crimes known to the police (much less on all crimes that occurred) during any period much earlier than about a half a century ago, and even the facts for the modern period are fraught with all the errors and uncertainties described in Chapter 1. The lack of systematic national data for the nineteenth and early twentieth centuries can be partially overcome by piecing together information from those cities and counties that happened to keep records, and the well-known deficiencies in these statistics need not be crippling if all we wish to discern are the broad, long-term trends in crime rates. Of course, if the information from all these sources reveals no broad trends, or if the trend in one place is confounded by an opposite trend in another, then we would be wise to abandon the effort and ascribe our contradictory findings to the vagaries of reporting systems.

Fortunately, there is a large, even striking, congruence among the results of various inquiries, here and abroad, into long-term trends in crime rates. It seems unlikely that these patterns could all be the result of the same reporting biases occurring everywhere at the same time; moreover, given the large swings in the crime statistics, it seems plausible that they bear some relationship to what was actually happening on the streets. Within limits, people may think they are more crime-ridden when they are not, or safer when in fact they are more threatened, but not, we believe, to the extent of imagining a threefold increase or a fourfold decrease in the rates of serious crime. Finally, the statistical data tend to be consistent with contemporary accounts and with the generalizations of later historians.

In general, the level of crime and disorder in large cities and industrializing nations of the Western world was very high in the early decades of the nineteenth century, decreased substantially during the latter part of that century, and then worsened again in the mid-twentieth century. Ted Robert Gurr found that in London, Stockholm, and Sydney, "the numbers of murders, assaults, and thefts of almost all kinds which came to police attention declined irregularly, but consistently, for half a century or more," as did the "numbers of persons arrested and convicted for such offenses."[1] The common feature of several measures of serious criminal behavior in England and Wales from 1805 to 1890 was "their long-term increase until mid-century, and their subsequent long-term decline."[2] Public order continued to improve in London until the 1920s, and in Stockholm and Sydney through the 1930s, but by the 1950s a sharp increase in crime began that continued at an accelerating rate in all three cities during the 1960s and 1970s.[3]

Crime in American cities seems to have followed the same pattern. Crime rates went up in Boston, Philadelphia, Rochester, Muncie, and New York City during the early decades of the nineteenth century and then began, around the middle of that century, a long, uneven, but steady decline.[4] Eric H. Monkkonen reviewed all the American studies available by 1979 and found that all but two showed a general decline in crime rates during the latter part of the nineteenth and early part of the twentieth centuries.[5]

Despite the agreement among all these studies, one might still be skeptical that the drop in crime rates was real, given the many changes that occurred during this period in the organization of the police and the behavior of the courts. But the general pattern is confirmed by Roger Lane's detailed analysis of death records in the city of Philadelphia.[6] Since death is a less ambiguous event than assault or theft, it is probably our most reliable measure of crime trends. In the middle of the nineteenth century, there were 3.3 murder indictments per hundred thousand persons in that city; by the end of the century, that rate had dropped to 2.1, a decline of 36 percent. An even greater decline occurred in Boston.[7]

Nationwide figures on the rate of death from homicide did not become available until 1933.[8] For about three decades, it fell more or less steadily, from 9.7 per hundred thousand population in 1933 to 4.7 per hundred thousand in 1961.[9] Thereafter it moved sharply upward, reaching a peak of 10.2 in 1974.[10]

Almost all other measures of crime in this country reveal the same general pattern of a flat or declining rate of serious crime during the 1930s and 1940s, followed by a sharp and lasting upturn starting in the early 1960s.[11] Between 1960 and 1978, reported robberies more than tripled, auto thefts more than doubled, and burglaries nearly tripled. This trend has been duplicated in most other industrial nations for which statistics are available (Soviet-bloc nations do not publish reliable figures), though in some places the turn upward began even earlier than it did in the United States. In London, murder was trending upward in the 1950s,[12] and in England as a whole, most serious crimes ("indictable offenses") began increasing at an average rate of about 10 percent a year beginning in 1955.[13] Murder rates rose during the 1960s in, among other cities, Amsterdam, Belfast, Colombo, Dublin, Glasgow, and Helsinki,[14] and crimes generally rose in this same period in Denmark, Finland, Norway, and Sweden.[15]

In sum, there seems to be a U-shaped curve in the crime rates of many industrial nations, especially in their larger cities, with very high rates of crime and disorder in the early decades of the nineteenth century, declining crime rates (with some intermittent ups and downs) during the latter half of the nineteenth century and the early part of the twentieth, and another large increase beginning in the middle part of this century and continuing through the 1970s. There is some preliminary evidence that crime rates in the 1980s, at least in the United States and Great Britain, have flattened out and even begun to decline.[16]

Variables Affecting Crime Trends

The theory of criminality given in Chapter 2 provides a comprehensive list of the variables that affect individual differences at one moment in time and thus also of those factors that may cause individuals to change over time. These latter changes can be of three kinds: in the prevalence of crime (increases or decreases in the proportion of the population that commits crimes), in the incidence of crime (increases or decreases in the number of offenses a given criminal commits per year), and in the length of the criminal career (increases or decreases in the number of years an offender is criminally active).

It is difficult to disentangle these three factors using the best available contemporary data; it is next to impossible using historical data. Thus, we cannot be certain how much of a given increase (or decrease) in the crime rate of a city or nation is the result of changes in prevalence, incidence, or criminal career, or some combination of all three. As we work our way through the variables that can affect historical patterns of criminality, we shall indicate, where possible, our best guess, based on the fragmentary evidence we have.

Opportunity

An individual encounters opportunities to commit crimes at varying rates as he goes about his daily business. Crime rates may go up or down because of changes in the density of such opportunities or their accessibility to criminal penetration or both, all without any change in the dispositions of the individual. In our model, opportunities are measured by the time delay between the present moment and the occurrence of a criminal opportunity. A person willing to steal a car may have to spend an hour or two getting to one if he lives in the country but only two minutes if he lives in a busy city. And if the car is locked with an alarm ready to go off, stealing it involves more time and even more risks than if it is unlocked and unguarded. Considering the rate at which the strength of reinforcements decays (rapidly for most "impulsive" offenders), these time delays, created by the distribution and security of opportunities, will importantly affect the observed crime rate.

Given these facts, one need make no assumptions about the supposed effect of urban living on the attitudes and habits of persons to understand why there is more robbery and burglary, in proportion to the population, in big cities than in small ones or in rural areas. Murder rates, though highest in the big cities, are much less affected by city size than are property crimes,[17] and for a simple reason. Most murder victims are the relatives or acquaintances of their assailants. There is no need to spend time searching for a target for this kind of crime; he or she is right there in the front room or on the next stool in the tavern.

It is not surprising, therefore, that one cause of an increase in criminality is the increased urbanization of the population. The spurt of crime in the United States and England in the 1820s and 1830s occurred during, and was in part stimulated by, the initial rapid growth of city populations (though, as we shall see, continued city growth did not necessarily mean continued growth in crime rates). Developing nations are experiencing rapid growths in crime owing in part to the sudden growth of their principal cities.[18] When we add to urbanization the fact that during the last two or three decades there has been, at least in the more advanced nations, a heavy emphasis on making access to commercial establishments more convenient—branch banking, self-service stores, easy access to and from superhighways—it is easy to understand why crime rates may have risen as opportunities become both denser and more accessible.

What may be surprising, however, is the fact that though crime rates are always higher in large cities, those rates do not always increase or decrease as the cities gain or lose population. In New York City, Istanbul, Manila, and Calcutta, among other major cities, increases in the homicide rate were positively correlated with changes in the population during the last half century or so, but in Bombay, Helsinki, Tokyo, Madrid, Belfast, and Nairobi, among other places, there was a negative correlation between murder rates and population—as these cities got larger, their murder rate got smaller.[19] During the 1960s and 1970s, New York, Chicago, Philadelphia, and Detroit—indeed, most old, large American cities—lost population rather steadily but their rate of violent crime has either gone up or stayed constant. Though these cities began to experience crime decreases in the 1980s, they still were the site of a disproportionate share of many kinds of violent crime. In 1980, for example, one-third of all the robberies committed in the

United States occurred in the six largest cities; one-sixth occurred in New York City alone.[20] Clearly, factors in addition to the density or accessibility of opportunities are at work.

The Value of Crime

The rewards of crime have three components: the material value of the loot, the psychic gain that accrues from committing the crime, and the extent to which either gain is reduced by the bite of conscience.

If there are more material things worth stealing, then, other things being equal, more will be stolen. Auto theft was impossible before automobiles were invented and mass-marketed. Today, auto theft is common, but we measure the rate at which it occurs incorrectly—we divide the number of cars stolen by the population. What we should do, obviously, is divide the number of cars stolen by the number on the road. Leroy C. Gould has recalculated the auto theft rate in this way (autos stolen per hundred thousand registered) and shown that since 1933 this rate has followed a curvilinear path.[21] In the 1930s, the rate was declining steeply from a very high initial level; during the war years (1941–1945) it rose sharply; during the immediate postwar years (the late 1940s and early 1950s) it fell sharply; and during the 1960s it rose again. (By our calculations, it declined during the latter half of the 1970s.)

Gould suggests that when cars were very scarce (the early 1930s and the war years), the rate at which they were stolen was high. When they became more abundant, after World War II, they were less frequently stolen. But then, beginning in the 1960s, the rate went up even though cars were becoming still more abundant. (In the early 1980s, the auto theft rate seemed to be dropping even though cars continued to become more numerous.) As we noted in Chapter 11, Gould explains the changing relationship between abundance and theft by observing that, in the 1940s, when cars were scarce but were stolen at high rates, the average age of arrested auto thieves was much higher than it was during the 1960s, when cars were abundant but were still stolen at a high rate.[22] When autos are scarce, their theft is dominated by professionals who resell them to eager buyers; when most adults have cars of their own, their theft is dominated by juveniles who want the cars for impulsive joyrides. Of course, matters are more complicated than this—there were joyriders stealing cars in the 1940s, and there are professionals stealing them today (especially if the car is a luxury or sports model). But in general, Gould's findings fit the theoretical perspective of this book. The availability of things worth stealing seems to affect somewhat the rate at which they are stolen. When the value of loot is very high, as it is when scarce stolen cars have a ready resale market, persons with a long time horizon (i.e., shallow reward-decay curves) will often find stealing worthwhile and spend some time planning the theft; when the value of the loot is lower, as it is when the average car is so abundant that selling a stolen one is not very profitable, theft will be attractive chiefly to impulsive (i.e., younger) persons. One can make a similar analysis of the relationship between rising crime and the introduction of other attractive products, such as stereo recorders, color television sets, citizen-band radios, and ten-speed bicycles.[23]

Not only have all manner of attractive, portable consumer goods entered the market since World War II, but they are not as securely guarded in their homes as they once were, owing to the increased proportion of houses that are not occupied during the day. This abundant stock of valuable merchandise has become more accessible to thieves, despite the growing use of locks and alarms, because women have entered the job market in growing numbers, and an increased number of families can afford to take lengthy vacations away from home.[24]

The aggregate material rewards of crime have undoubtedly increased in all prosperous societies, though the rewards per thief may or may not have increased, depending on whether the more abundant and valuable loot has attracted new thieves whose activities have depressed the yield per crime. This would be a consequence of an increase in the prevalence of crime. Between 1962 and 1978, the average reported value of things stolen increased by 95 percent (from $223 to $434) for robberies and by 174 percent (from $192 to $526) for burglaries.[25] During this same period, the consumer price index increased by 116 percent. In short, the average take per robbery lagged slightly behind inflation, while the average take from burglary substantially exceeded it. This is consistent with what one might expect. Robberies typically involve the theft of cash in a personal confrontation; the amount of cash persons or businesses have on hand is likely to grow more slowly than per capita personal income as people rely more on checks and credit cards as ways of paying bills and carry less money as a way of avoiding robbery losses. But durable consumer goods, such as television sets, cannot be converted into theftproof forms, and the supply of these has grown rapidly. From 1962 to 1978, the dollar value of purchases of furniture and household equipment more than tripled,[26] and thus the supply of things to be burgled went up sharply.

The value of crime may also have changed owing to changes in the psychic rewards of crime. There are several intangible components of these rewards; an important one is the sense of equity or inequity. As we explained in Chapter 2, a sense of inequity arises whenever a person believes that the ratio of his outputs (income, status, power) to his inputs (skill, effort, time) is less than the ratio of the outputs to inputs of a person or group with whom he compares himself. The first person believes he is getting less than he deserves from what he is and does. This inequity can be handled in several ways: He can devalue his own inputs ("I guess I'm not as skilled or worthy as I thought"), revalue the other party's inputs ("after all, he is older, has worked harder, or knows more than I"), or take the other's outputs ("the rascal doesn't deserve what he is getting and so there is nothing wrong with my having it"). As we have observed, certain personality types are more likely than others to adopt the last course—that is, to externalize their sense of inequity—and accordingly are more likely to commit crimes.

It is possible that important changes in society have altered the way we value the inputs of ourselves and others. The more that people accept a status hierarchy (based on education, wealth, birth, ancient lineage, or whatever), the more likely they will be to accept claimed differences in the value of inputs. If the rich, the wellborn, or the highly educated get a large share of the income, many persons in a hierarchical or status-conscious society will conclude that these disproportionate gains have been earned by virtue of the skills, worth, or efforts of those who receive them. But as a society becomes more egalitarian in its outlook, it becomes skeptical of claims that the inputs of some persons are intrinsically superior to those of others, and thus its members become more disposed to describe others' outputs as unjustly earned. There can be little doubt, we think, that the trend of thought in modern nations has been toward more egalitarian views, buttressed in some instances by the rising belief among disadvantaged racial, ethnic, and religious minorities that the deference they once paid need be paid no longer; on the contrary, now the majority group owes them something as reparations for past injustices. Of course, persons can acquire more egalitarian or even more reparations-seeking views without becoming more criminal. But at the margin, some individuals—perhaps those impulsive ones who value the products of an affluent society—find that value suddenly enhanced when they allow themselves to be persuaded that the current owner of a car has no greater (i.e., no more just) claim to it than do they.

We know of few data that bear directly on changes that have occurred in how people evaluate the inputs of others and on how those changes in evaluation affect individual differences in criminal behavior. But we think the hypothesis that such changes have taken place with some effect on the crime rate is a plausible one and, in principle, capable of being tested.

Finally, the value of crime will be affected by the degree to which a person committing one is likely to experience the bite of conscience. Data on changes in internalized inhibitions against crime are virtually nonexistent. Moreover, even if such data existed, it would be hard to distinguish between those internal inhibitions that depend on the fear of being caught and those that arise immediately out of a sense of guilt whether or not one is caught. One tantalizing but isolated fact may suggest that internal inhibitions have in fact changed, at least in some societies. Wolpin finds that in England the ratio of murderers who committed suicide before being arrested to all convicted murderers fell more or less steadily from about three out of four in 1929 to about one in four in 1967.[27] This decline in murderer-suicides preceded by many years the abolition of capital punishment in 1965, so it cannot be explained by the murderer's realization that there was no longer any need to take one's own life to avoid the pain of a trial and a state execution. It is more plausible to assume—though we stress it is only an assumption—that for some reason murderers in England became less likely to feel such intense guilt that they would take their own lives.

The pang of conscience is a classically conditioned response. Its strength may change with changes in the proportion of persons who are hard to condition or of families that practice child-rearing techniques that induce a conditioned response, or with changes in the effectiveness of other social institutions in inducing that conditioning.

There is some evidence that impulsive, mesomorphic, low-verbal-intelligence persons may be harder to condition than persons with the opposite traits (see Chapters 3, 6, and 7). Even if the evidence on this were conclusive, it is not clear that changes in the individual traits of at-risk (e.g., young male) members of the population can change fast enough to account for even a small part of the changes in crime rates in a society. But over the long run, some change may occur, a matter to which we shall return when, in the next section, we consider possible explanations for an increase in impulsiveness among young persons.

Similarly, if family practices have changed (as many persons, without citing much evidence, assume they have), then the effect of those changes may be to alter the extent to which young persons are either classically conditioned (to feel guilty about violating a rule) or instrumentally conditioned (to worry about the consequences of breaking a rule) or both. Since we know of no way of disentangling these separate effects, we shall later treat changes in family practices in a way that unavoidably lumps these effects together.

Other institutions besides the family may influence the development of conscience, though we suspect that few, if any, do so except in association with, or as auxiliaries to, the family. There is some evidence that differences

in church membership among metropolitan areas are associated with differences in crime rates, even after controlling for demographic factors that influence crime, and that in metropolitan areas where there is rapid population
turnover, church membership is depressed.[28] A more mobile society is a less
religious one, and this may affect—the evidence so far is only suggestive—
trends in crime rates.

Time Horizon

Crime rates may change if an individual comes to value time differently. If,
to him, the strengths of the reinforcements and punishments associated with
crime and noncrime decay more quickly, he will commit more crimes; if they
decay less quickly, he will commit fewer. If such changes in time horizon occur, they could affect either the prevalence of criminality (because a larger
or smaller fraction of the whole population is highly present-oriented) or
the incidence of crime (because offenders come to discount the future more
or less heavily).

Many, if not most, readers probably believe that much if not all of the
increase in crime rates during the 1960s and 1970s can be explained by the
increase in the proportion of young persons in the population—an increase,
that is, in the proportion of impulsive young males who will get in trouble.
There is no doubt that the changing age structure of our society accounted
for a significant part of the crime increase, but considerable doubt that age
effects explained most of it. Less than half—in several estimates, much less
than half—of the increase can be attributed to the greater proportion of
young persons in the population (see Chapter 5).[29] The clear implication of
these studies is that the average male committed more crimes during the
1960s and 1970s.*

This conclusion is borne out by a close analysis of the ages of persons

---

* One study, however, argues that nearly all of the increase in crime in Pittsburgh
between 1967 and 1972 was caused by demographic changes; thus, the average male
did not become more criminal during this period.[30] This conclusion rests on a complex
statistical analysis that attempts to take into account changes in police arrest practices
as well as in reported crimes. We are skeptical of its conclusions, in part because a
significant portion of the reported increase in crime is attributed by the authors to
changes in police behavior that are (in our judgment) poorly modeled. Blumstein and
Nagin assume that the probability of being arrested is determined by the ratio of
police to the population in a given precinct; we believe, on the basis of other studies,[31]
that arrest probabilities are poorly predicted by the number of officers assigned to an
area. Arrest activity will be chiefly determined by the ratio of crimes to the number
of patrol units actually on the street (and not just assigned to the city or precinct) and
by the aggressiveness of the patrol officers. Moreover, the authors' findings are inconsistent with the conclusions of studies of actual cohorts of young males.[32]

arrested for homicide, our most accurately known offense. Between 1960 and 1973, the arrest rate for homicide of persons in the age group fifteen to twenty-four increased by 69 percent; in the age group twenty-five to thirty-four, it increased by almost as much.[33] Since most homicides are solved, the arrest rates are probably a relatively unbiased measure of the true age-specific offense rate. Thus, the homicide rate was going up because young persons were becoming more homicidal and not simply because there were more young persons.

By following the criminal careers of youths born during, just after, and a decade after World War II (and thus reaching age eighteen just before, during, and toward the end of the crime wave of the 1960s and 1970s), various scholars have been able to observe changes in the rate at which young males come into contact with the police, and so, presumably, the rate at which they commit crimes. Males born in Racine, Wisconsin, in 1949 were more likely to be charged with theft, assault, and burglary by the time they were seventeen than were males who had been born in that city in 1942.[34] This increase in the prevalence of crime remained after one controlled for race and ethnicity: Both blacks and whites showed a sharp increase in these offenses. Only auto theft, among the major, common offenses, became less prevalent.

A somewhat different change seems to have occurred in Philadelphia between boys born in 1945 and those born in 1958. The prevalence of crime—that is, the proportion of all boys who got in trouble with the police—did not change (about a third of both groups had a police contact), but the incidence changed dramatically. Among the boys in the 1958 cohort (those who turned eighteen in 1976, at the peak of the crime wave) who committed at least one offense, the proportion who went on to commit more crimes was much higher than among the boys born in 1945 who ever committed a crime. Those in the more recent cohort, if they became criminal at all, would, in comparison with the earlier cohort, start their criminal careers at an earlier age, commit more crimes before reaching the age of eighteen, and commit more violent crimes during their juvenile careers.[35] The boys who grew up in the 1960s were twice as likely to commit a burglary, three times as likely to commit a homicide, and five times as likely to commit a robbery as the boys who grew up in the 1950s.[36]

We do not know why the Racine cohorts showed a growth in the prevalence of crime and the Philadelphia ones did not, but both indicate an increase in the incidence of criminality. How can this increased incidence be explained?

One possibility is that young persons growing up in the 1960s became more present-oriented and thus more impulsive than those who grew up earlier. There is some evidence that this is true. In 1959, Davids, Kidder, and Reich administered to a group of institutionalized male and female delinquents in Rhode Island various tests (completing a story, telling the interviewer whether they would save or spend various sums of money if given to them) designed to measure their time orientation.[37] The results showed them to be markedly more present-oriented than were comparable nondelinquents.[38] Fifteen years later, essentially the same tests were given to a new group of institutionalized delinquents in the same state and of the same age.[39] This group was much more present-oriented and thus much less willing to delay gratification (by, for example, saving rather than spending the money) than the earlier group of delinquents. Moreover, the more recent group frequently mentioned spending the gift money on drugs (nobody suggested that in 1959) and never mentioned giving it to someone else (several had said they would do that in 1959). We can infer from this that the strength of future reinforcements decayed much more rapidly for delinquents of the 1960s than for those of the 1950s, but lacking data on the number of offenses committed by the two groups, we cannot be confident that the shorter time horizon was associated with a higher incidence of crime. Moreover, since the authors did not measure changes (if any) in the time horizon of nondelinquent youths, we do not know whether the delinquents of the 1960s had become disproportionately more present-oriented than other youths of the same age (in which case the incidence of the former's criminality would have increased) or had only become more present-oriented to the same degree as other youths (in which case it is likely that delinquency may have become more prevalent).

There are many possible explanations for why young offenders are more present-oriented today than formerly. One may be that young males are, perhaps, constitutionally different. The genetic basis of a society changes, if at all, very slowly, but short-run changes in human constitutions, owing to differences in prenatal and perinatal circumstances, may occur in no more than a generation or two. Suppose that there is an increase in the proportion of infants with low birth weight or certain learning disabilities who survive into adolescence or adulthood. If, as some evidence suggests (see Chapters 8 and 9), such infants are likely to display those temperamental qualities, endure those family experiences (such as rejection or abuse), and experience those schooling difficulties that predispose them to criminality, then the longer life expectancy of these children may increase the number of adolescents at risk for delinquency. We know that about one-fourth of all low-birth-weight babies will have some major handicap, such as low IQ;[40] we also know that the proportion of low-birth-weight babies who survive has grown appreciably.[41] This enhanced survivability of at-risk children may have increased the proportion of hard-to-condition adolescents and thus the supply of potential delinquents. Though the baby boom has now been replaced with the baby bust, the decline in the number of births may have been partially offset by an increase in the proportion of births that involve handicaps. The number of babies born with physical and mental defects, including low birth weight and learning disabilities, seems to have increased markedly since the late 1950s.[42] This may be the result of an increase in prenatal hazards confronting the infant (e.g., a greater use by pregnant women of tobacco, liquor, or drugs, or their greater exposure to environmental toxins), an improvement in medical procedures that permit such infants to come to term, or the increased ability of persons with such defects to survive into adulthood and pass their disabilities along to the next generation.

Indeed, the poorer life chances of at-risk persons in the past may have contributed to the suppression of the rates of certain kinds of crimes. If young males predisposed, constitutionally or by family experiences, to commit violent acts once ran the risk of an early death as a consequence of those acts, then any increase in the murder rate may have been self-limiting. As emergency medical services improved—owing to the increased availability of telephones, radios, motorized ambulances, antibiotics, blood transfusions, and skilled physicians—the likelihood of a violent encounter's having a fatal result would be reduced, thereby enabling any violent perpetrator who sustained an injury to live and attack again. We know that the ratio of (reported) aggravated assaults to homicides increased from about nine to one in 1935 to over twenty-eight to one in 1980. This suggests that the risk of a felonious attack's having a fatal outcome may have declined by a factor of three. If so, assaults are less risky today than once was the case. Since assaults and homicides are often victim-precipitated[43]—that is, the loser is as much an instigator as the victor—anything that makes an assault less risky increases the life expectancy of violent persons as well as of innocent ones.

A second explanation is more easily grasped, though no less difficult to prove. Children may become more impulsive owing to changes in family experiences. Families that do not consistently and effectively make the consequences of a child's behavior contingent on that behavior are more likely, other things being equal, to produce offspring who do not carefully take into account future consequences in choosing present behaviors—offspring who are, in a word, impulsive. Everyone seems to have a firm view as to whether families have changed in this way as a result of (take your pick) greater permissiveness, absent fathers, working mothers, geographical mobility, or the

distractions of television. There are, unhappily, scarcely any careful studies
of actual changes in child-rearing practices over the last few generations.
One of the few longitudinal surveys of directly observed (as opposed to
parent-reported) child-rearing practices was carried out at the Fels Institute
in Ohio. Beginning in 1937, trained observers made semiannual visits to the
homes participating in the program. The behavior of three groups of socially
similar mothers was compared: those mothers raising children aged three to
five around 1940, those raising them around 1950, and those raising them
around 1960.[44] There was a consistent decline over the two decades in the
degree of coerciveness employed by the mothers: "The mothers studied have
become less prone to make coercive suggestions requiring mandatory compliance from their children, employ less restrictive regulations of their children's activities, and are less severe in the way they punish misbehaviors."[45]

Whether these changes in maternal behavior produced corresponding
changes in the children, the authors of the study do not—and probably cannot—say. Moreover, we need information on changes over a much longer
period of time if we wish to use family socialization factors as a way of
explaining long-term trends in crime rates. The best we can say with what
we now know is that over the last half century or so there have been important changes in how parents were *advised* to raise their children and,
since the advice was given in popular magazines that had to sell their advice
to survive, there may well be a relationship between what was advised and
what was done.

In the mid-nineteenth century, child-rearing advice emphasized the importance of inculcating moral and religious principles so as to make the
child "at an early age a self-maintaining moral being."[46] This view persisted
into the early part of the twentieth century, but beginning in the 1920s it was
partially replaced by a different one. Whereas the child was once thought to
be endowed by nature with dangerous impulses that had to be curbed, he
was now seen as equipped with harmless instincts that ought to be developed. Previously it was thought to be a mistake to play with the child too
much; now play was urged on mothers. Earlier, the popular advice had
stressed the child's moral development; now, the literature began to emphasize his capacity for enjoyment.[47] In 1890, 1900, and 1910, one-third of the
child-rearing topics discussed in a sample of articles from *Ladies' Home
Journal, Woman's Home Companion,* and *Good Housekeeping* were about
character development; in 1920, only 3 percent were. By 1930, articles on
character development had by and large been replaced with ones on personality development. And whereas the magazines in 1890 had said that
character was best developed by providing a good home influence, by 1920

the route to a well-adjusted personality was thought chiefly to involve proper feeding.[48] As we shall suggest later in this chapter, this change in child-rearing advice—and perhaps also in child-rearing practices—was part of a more fundamental change in the popular view of human nature and society's responsibility, if any, for its formation.

Would-be offenders might also behave more impulsively for reasons having little to do with any lasting change in their time horizon. This would be the case, for example, if they came to have regular and easy access to substances that, when ingested, reduced the significance of future events and made them intensely preoccupied with the present. The increase in the availability of heroin and alcohol, noted in Chapter 14, would have this effect. The annual per capita consumption of alcohol increased by only 0.11 liter between 1950 and 1960, a period of relatively flat crime rates, but by 2.34 liters between 1960 and 1973, a period of rapidly rising crime rates.[49] There are no reliable data on the increase in the use of other psychoactive substances during this latter period, but obviously it was very great. It is difficult to disentangle the causal linkages here. Ordinary young men with reasonably flat delay-of-reinforcement curves might act impulsively and criminally after using a psychoactive substance (the belief that this happens gives rise to the "demon rum" or "dope fiend" theory of behavior). More likely, many of the young men who use alcohol or drugs to excess are predisposed to aggressive or impulsive behavior, and so the effect of the psychoactive substance is only to increase, at least in some cases, the already high probability of deviant behavior. Thus, the increase in consumption of alcohol and drugs must be seen as both a symptom and a cause of a shift toward more present-oriented conduct.

Not only what we consume but what we see might affect our orientation toward the future. Though scholars who have studied the effects of television and the mass media on young persons have been chiefly interested in determining whether these media "teach" aggression by modeling it in favorable ways, in our view a larger possible effect may have been on the public's willingness to postpone gratification. As we saw in Chapter 13, there seems to be no evidence bearing directly on this possibility.

Among the things that we "see" are wars and political upheavals. Throughout this century, scholars and statesmen have suggested that nations at war will sooner or later experience an upsurge in murder and violent crime.[50] During a major war, a combatant nation that is not itself the scene of combat—for example, the United States during World War I, World War II, and the Vietnam War—will probably experience a decrease in certain forms of crime owing to the removal into the military of so many at-risk young males. By one estimate, 82 percent of American men between the ages of twenty and twenty-five enlisted or were drafted into the armed services during World War II; New York City alone lost three-quarters of a million people, mostly young males.[51] Between 1940 and 1944, the homicide rate in this country fell by 21 percent. But after a war, so the theory goes, violent crime will increase.

Dane Archer and Rosemary Gartner examined the changes in reported homicides in forty-four nations during the five years before and after World Wars I and II.[52] The nations that were not combatants were about evenly divided between those that did and did not experience a sharp postwar increase in homicide, but among nations that were combatants, three times as many had an increase as had a decrease. (The homicide rate in the United States went up after World War I but down after World War II.) This general increase was not, apparently, the result of violence-prone returning veterans but of other social changes, possibly including social disorganization, the legitimation of violence, and the growth in personal freedom.

In sum, there is good reason to believe that rising crime rates are accompanied by, and perhaps partially caused by, a shortening of the time horizons of at-risk young persons as well as by an increase in the numbers of such persons. We can only speculate on the reasons for the shift in time horizons.

The Value of Noncrime

Crime rates may change because the expected value of alternatives to crime, in particular the expected value of avoiding punishment or of obtaining a legitimate income, have changed. In Chapter 15, we presented evidence that changes in the value of certain consequences of behavior, especially the probability of punishment, seemed to be associated with and may well cause changes in crime rates. For the United States, most such evidence is based on cross-sectional studies, relatively short-term longitudinal studies, or one-shot social experiments, so we cannot be certain that changes in the likelihood of punishment can account for trends in crime rates extending over many decades. The evidence on the effect on crime of employment opportunities is even more equivocal.

The data necessary to examine the relationship between crime and the value of noncrime over a long period of time are not available for the United States, except, perhaps, for homicide. For the best studies of this matter, we must turn to other nations. Over half a century ago, Dorothy Swaine Thomas sought to discover what correlation, if any, existed between the business cycle and the crime rate in England between 1857 and 1913.[53] She concluded that there was no general correlation, but that the rates of certain offenses, chiefly burglary and robbery, seemed to go up when the economy turned down. She did not, however, take into account other factors that might have been operating concurrently with the business cycle, such as the changing age distribution of the population or the effectiveness of the criminal justice system. A more comprehensive effort was mounted by Wolpin, who sought to explain changes in English crime rates between 1894 and 1967 in a way that took into account the effects of changes in both the risk of punishment and the availability of legitimate earnings (as measured by the unemployment rate, real wage levels, and the gross domestic product per capita), as well as in demographic factors such as age.[54] He found that, other things being equal, the rates of most crimes went up when the probability of being punished went down. However, while the burglary rate went up when unemployment went up, the robbery rate went up when the level of real wages rose. Changes in sanctions seemed to make a consistent difference in crime, but changes in economic conditions seemed to have inconsistent effects.

Though a precise understanding of how the value of alternatives to crime affects the crime rate has so far eluded us, one must be struck by the fact that the broad, lasting trends in crime rates in this country and this century have moved in directions quite unrelated to the business cycle. Crime rates, insofar as we can tell, drifted more or less steadily downward between 1933 and the 1950s, despite the fact that the first part of this period (1933–1941) was characterized by a severe economic depression and the latter part (1941–1960) by reasonable prosperity; crime rates then rose during the 1960s, a period of unparalleled prosperity, and continued high during the 1970s, a period of alternating booms and modest recessions. Short-term movements in economic conditions may affect short-term changes in property crime rates, as suggested by Cook and Zarkin, but they concede that "the major movements in crime rates during the last half century cannot be attributed to the business cycle."[55]

It is also possible that the relationship between crime rates and economic conditions has changed over time. Gatrell and Hadden[56] found evidence in British data, as did Thomas,[57] that during the nineteenth century property crimes went up in times of recession and down in times of prosperity. But according to Wolpin, that connection was no longer evident in the twentieth century.[58] It may be that, owing to social and cultural changes to be discussed later in this chapter, the influence of economic factors on crime has been altered, so that during a period when traditional values were very strong, crime increased only out of necessity, but in times when those values were weaker, crime increased out of mere opportunity.

One reason why the business cycle of late has, at best, only a short-term and modest effect on crime rates may be that the cycle sometimes has different effects on different population groups. During the 1960s, for example, the economy generally was booming, and adult unemployment rates were very low, but the teen-age unemployment rate was high, and the rate at which young persons were participating in the labor market was declining. There is some evidence that these labor-market experiences were associated with increased youthful crime,[59] though the nature of the association is not well understood. As we remarked in Chapter 12, we lack studies that examine the effect of employment on persons who may be most strongly affected by it—urban young males who are at that point in their lives when they are choosing among schooling, leisure, employment, and crime.

Moreover, the value young persons assign to work may change along with the availability of work. Throughout this century, there has been a steady decline in the proportion of young persons working. Much of the decline in employed youth has been made up for by an increase in the proportion of youth in school, suggesting that a major function of schooling may not only be to train young persons for better jobs but to occupy the time of young persons who prefer schooling to work (but may well prefer leisure to either). Between 1870 and 1970, the average number of days of school attendance per year more than doubled, from 78 to 163.[60] In 1900, fewer than one-tenth of all eighteen-year-olds were high school graduates; today, about eight-tenths are. If learning difficulties and school frustrations contribute to delinquency, the long-term increase in the age-specific crime rate for young persons may have something to do with the fact that an increased proportion of the at-risk youth have been induced to spend time doing things (sitting still in classrooms) that they find less rewarding than things they once did (earning money at a job). And to the extent that being out of work is no longer as costly as it once was (owing to the growth in the coverage and value of unemployment benefits, welfare payments, and food stamps), leisure—occasionally interrupted by opportunistic criminality—may have become a feasible alternative to both school and work.

Whether changing crime rates can be attributed in part to changes in the risk of punishment is a matter hotly contested among scholars (Chapter 15). The weight of the evidence suggests that they can be, but the matter cannot be regarded as settled. In evaluating this argument, it is important to bear in mind that there have been very great changes in the risk of punishment. Between 1962 and 1979, the probability that a reported Index crime (as defined by the FBI) would result in an arrest fell from .32 to .18, the probability that an arrest for an Index crime would result in imprisonment fell from .32 to .14, and thus the probability that an Index crime would result in imprisonment fell fivefold, from .10 to .02. These national averages conceal a good deal of local variation, of course. But in some places where the matter has been closely studied, the changes in the risk of punishment were very great. Between 1966 and 1976, the number of juvenile offenders institutionalized in Cook County (Chicago) fell from more than fourteen hundred to fewer than four hundred.[61] The decline in the use of at least one form of punishment, both nationally and in places such as Cook County, occurred during the midst of a sharply rising crime rate. When one examines how individual offenders reacted to such changes, there is evidence, albeit only from the few careful studies that have been done, that the number of crimes committed per month free on the street was higher for offenders not punished.[62]

Explaining Change

It is not difficult to think of reasons why crime rates change; on the contrary, it is too easy. While the theory we have presented helps us resist the natural tendency to favor a partial explanation to the exclusion of other possibilities, it does not enable us to choose among these possibilities. Almost every factor we consider seems to point us in the same direction: It seems plausible that when crime rates go up it is because criminal opportunities are denser, more valuable, and more accessible, because youthful would-be offenders are more numerous, less inhibited by conscience, more impulsive, and less persuaded that the distribution of wealth is equitable, and because the benefits of avoiding crime have become more delayed, less certain, or less substantial. In the language of social science, the explanation of increasing crime rates is overdetermined.

Lacking the data with which to put our theory to a rigorous test in ways that lead to careful estimations of the relative contribution of each of the variables, there are only a few ways by which this plausible list of factors can be narrowed down. One is to ask whether any of the variables that can be measured account for so large a part of any change in crime that we can assume that even if other variables could be measured they would not account for more of the change. From the evidence we have, we judge that the combined effects of age and urbanization may be such factors. A presidential commission estimated that the combined effect of the growth in population, the increase in the proportion of young persons in that population, and the movement of the population into metropolitan areas jointly accounted for 46 percent of the increase in the absolute number of reported crimes between 1960 and 1965.[63] We estimate that changes in age alone probably accounted for at least one-sixth of the increase in violent crime between 1960 and 1980. A more elaborate analysis by James Fox enabled him to predict year-to-year changes in the rate of violent crime between 1972 and 1978 knowing only three variables—the proportion of the population that is nonwhite and between the ages of fourteen and seventeen, the proportion that is nonwhite and between the ages of eighteen and twenty-one, and the consumer price index.[64] (The Fox model has been criticized, especially for its use of the price index.)[65]

Though these analyses covered periods of only a few years, there are good grounds for assuming that much longer trends in crime rates are similarly affected by age changes. Figure 1 shows the ratio of young persons (aged fifteen to twenty-four) to young adults (aged twenty-five to thirty-four) in the American population between 1860 and 1980. The years in which the ratio was at its highest (the late 1920s, the 1960s) were also the years of high or rising crime rates as judged from the historical evidence we have; the periods in which the ratio was declining (1880–1920, 1930–1955) were also the periods in which crime rates were stable or declining.

Changes in the age distribution of the population do not merely have direct effects on the crime rate by increasing the supply of at-risk (impulsive) persons; they probably also have second-order effects owing to the impact of the glut of young persons on family behavior, schooling, economic activity, and peer-group formation. Increases in the number of children per family increase the burdens on parents of socializing children. Even after controlling for family income and the education of the parents, children in large families receive less education (and, we suspect, less parental care generally) than do children in smaller ones.[66] Moreover, a child born into a large family is (obviously) less likely to be the firstborn than one born into a small family. There is substantial evidence that firstborn children enjoy advantages—in intelligence, school achievement, and career success—over their later-born siblings,[67] and we have shown (Chapters 6 and 10) that young persons with higher IQs and good school records are significantly less likely to commit crimes.

Not only does a large influx of children burden parents and reduce the time each parent can spend with any given child, it reduces each young person's share of the economic pie when he enters the labor market. During the 1950s, a decade before the baby boom came of age, young men in their

FIGURE 1

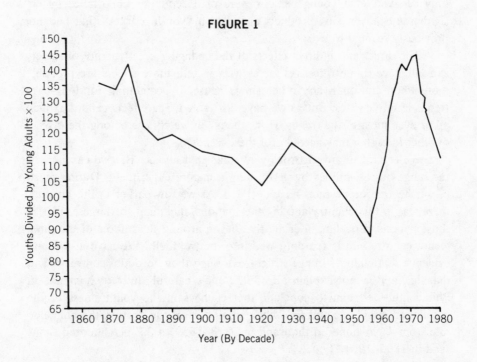

Ratio of young persons (aged 15–24) to young adults (aged 25–34) in the United States, expressed as a percentage.

twenties earned a larger relative income (relative, that is, to the average income of all men) than did young men during the 1970s, when they were competing with their baby-boom colleagues.[68] Economists have found that the unemployment rate of young persons is affected not only by prevailing economic conditions but also by the size of the young person's cohort.[69] The more young persons with whom any given youth is competing, the worse his chances of finding a job.

When there is an abnormally large number of young persons reaching the adolescent years, it is probably easier for these youth to form peer cultures that are not easily susceptible to adult control. As the baby boom comes of age, it may well form a "critical mass," such that young persons outnumber or overpower their would-be controllers. We have no direct evi-

dence on this score other than to note that in the 1960s and 1970s the economy behaved as if young persons were of exceptional importance by de-
signing and advertising products aimed at a "youth market" that had not
previously seemed to exist.

The direct and indirect effects of the changing age structure of society
can influence crime rates. As far as we can tell, these effects are probably
more important than any other single cause in accounting for long-term
trends in crime rates. But as we have also noted, age effects cannot explain
all or even most of the trends. How, then, can we choose among the myriad
of other facts that may account for these trends?

We cannot in any rigorous way make that choice. But we can narrow
the range of possibilities by performing a mental experiment. During much
of our history, crime rates have declined. As we saw earlier in this chapter,
there was in this country and in other nations, including the largest cities in
those nations, a decline in crime that began around the middle of the nineteenth century and lasted until well into the twentieth. We have also found
evidence that changes in age structure, though they no doubt contributed to
that decline, cannot explain all of it. Lane's careful study of homicide in
Philadelphia led him to conclude that changes in the youthfulness of the
population could account for only a small part of the drop in the homicide
rate from 4 per hundred thousand in 1853–1859 to 2.7 per hundred thousand in 1895–1901.[70]

These worldwide trends surely cast serious doubt on the importance of
some factors. Crime was decreasing during a period of rapid urbanization
(making criminal opportunities denser), massive industrialization (causing
class cleavages to widen), wholesale immigration (bringing persons to this
country who may not have shared the values of the older residents), and
increased ownership of handguns (making targets more vulnerable). Each
of these factors may have had some effect then and may have some effect
now, but since crime rates declined when these things were occurring, it is
clear that such factors alone could not cause crime rates to go up.

If age structure can explain only part of these downward trends and if
changes in accessible opportunities, population composition, and economic
conditions cannot explain much of what remains, our attention must inevitably be drawn toward those factors that, independent (to some degree) of
urbanization and economic circumstances, lowered the age-specific crime
rate. And if those factors were able to lower the age-specific crime rate
eighty or a hundred years ago, we must at least entertain the possibility that
they could have helped increase that rate during the last twenty or thirty
years. Apart from any unknown and probably unknowable changes in con-

stitutional factors, what remains are two possibilities—a change in the risks of crime and a change in the capacity for self-control of would-be offenders.

The risks of crime probably did increase in the latter part of the nineteenth century owing to the creation and spread of urban police forces and (possibly) to the increased use of prisons. Volunteer citizen watchmen were replaced by hired police officers beginning in the third decade of the nineteenth century. The first uniformed police force in America was created in New York City in 1853, and other cities quickly followed suit. Monkkonen estimated that by 1860–1870 there were about 1.5 police officers per thousand residents in a sample of twenty large American cities.[71] Gurr,[72] among others, believes that the advent of modern policing is among the major factors that account for the apparent reduction in crime in industrializing cities during the second half of the nineteenth century; indeed, Gatrell and Hadden conclude their review of English crime statistics by remarking that Britain by 1890 had succeeded in becoming a "policed society."[73]

It is hard to evaluate any claims about the effectiveness of the police, especially claims about effects that occurred more than a century ago. But the history of the police contains a puzzle: If city police were so effective in curbing crime when there were 1.5 officers per thousand population, when they lacked any specialized training or equipment, and when they spent much of their time providing welfare services for the poor, how is it that the police can be so ineffective today when there are twice as many officers per thousand population,[74] when they have been given motorcars, radios, and laboratories, and when they no longer perform many nonpolice functions? Almost certainly the police made some difference, but we are struck by the fact that at the turn of the century our cities (whose population densities were much greater then than they are today) were very lightly policed compared to modern practice.

There is also evidence that greater use was made of prisons toward the end than at the middle of the nineteenth century.[75] We do not know exactly what relationship existed between crime and the risk of punishment, though if prison populations were rising when crime rates were stable or declining, then on the average the risk of punishment must have been increasing. This long-term rise in imprisonment rates ended in the late 1950s and early 1960s, just as the crime wave of the 1960s was beginning, and stayed abnormally low throughout the 1960s.[76] The combined effect of uniformed policing and greater use of prisons probably means that the costs of crime were greater by the end of the nineteenth century than at the beginning.

Since we lack the necessary longitudinal data, we cannot estimate the extent to which changes in the risk of punishment explain long-term changes in the American crime rate. Moreover, another change was occurring simultaneously with the rise of uniformed policing, a change involving a much broader array of institutions than merely the police and a much deeper set of attitudes than merely the fear of punishment. This was the rise and then the decline of social arrangements designed to foster self-control.

The Changing Investment in Impulse Control

The rising rates of crime and disorder during the first two or three decades of the nineteenth century prompted Americans and Englishmen (and possibly Europeans generally) to develop an array of voluntary associations and public institutions designed to instill character and teach self-control. This effort was dependent on and gave expression to a set of essentially Victorian values that began to take hold simultaneously with the advent of industrialization and that by the end of the century had acquired a remarkable degree of hegemony in America and England.[77] Though these values were not the property of any single church and were not expressed only by churchgoing persons, they rested firmly on a religious foundation. Though many different and seemingly unrelated activities were animated by these values—the abolition of slavery, the spread of temperance, the development of public schools, the drive to eliminate corporal and capital punishment, the creation of urban police forces, the elaboration of rules for the conduct of warfare—these activities had in common a desire to teach the principles of right conduct. Though these principles were often violated in practice, especially those pretending at familial virtue and personal self-improvement while tolerating a libertine subculture and a growing class cleavage, there was general agreement that when conduct departed from the proper standards it was a matter of common concern requiring strenuous efforts at correction.

It is not possible, except in a few cases and then indirectly, to measure the extent to which nineteenth-century Americans and Englishmen acquired a common morality that produced in them internalized inhibitions against immediate self-gratification. But there can be no mistaking the extent of the effort to propagate such a morality or the reasons why persons believed its propagation important.

In the 1820s and 1830s, Americans were appalled at the disorder of their growing cities. For centuries, young men had been leaving the farms in order to find new opportunities in villages and towns, but the urban migration of the 1820s and 1830s had a new and more threatening dimension. In the past, a young person who had gone off to seek his fortune had not only

worked but lived with his patron family—a large landholder, a village crafts-
man, a town merchant. In the early nineteenth century, however, cities were
growing so rapidly and the productive processes were changing so radically
that young men (and later, young women) who left home now went off to
live in boardinghouses with other young persons.[78] As a result, adult supervision of young men was weakened, not because the family had weakened
but because the necessary alternative to family life was no longer under
adult control.[79]

Young male workers living in cities suddenly acquired an autonomous
social life. The opportunities of the cities, magnified by the mutual urgings
of peers and the absence of restraints once supplied by family admonitions,
became irresistible. Americans had always drunk intoxicating beverages, but
before, it was done in a family setting and subject to familial control; now it
was done in saloons in the company of other young men. Just as this market
for alcohol was growing, the price of the beverage was falling. New distilla-
tion methods and abundant grain harvests were increasing the supply and
lowering the cost of alcohol. The result was a sudden, dramatic spurt in consumption—from an estimated 2.5 gallons per capita in 1790 to 7 gallons per
capita in 1810 and then to 10 gallons per capita by 1829.[80] By 1829, there
was in Rochester, New York, one establishment selling liquor for every
twenty-eight adult males;[81] the situation in other cities was much the same.
To respectable Americans, the effect of this change could be seen in the
rowdy, brawling life of city streets.

The responses of these horrified citizens were various—religious revivals, temperance movements, Sunday-school instruction, YMCA buildings,
the foster-home movement, the creation of public schools—but all had in
common a desire to instill "decision of character," by which was meant a
"strenuous will" aimed at "inner control" and "self-restraint."[82] Since young
men no longer lived and worked under around-the-clock adult supervision,
there was little hope that their behavior could be regulated by external rewards; instead, internalized inhibitions, reinforced by social sanctions, would
have to be created.

The first few decades of the nineteenth century witnessed a series of
religious revivals that have since become known as the Second Great Awakening. Most of the converts were young persons, and many revival preachers
aimed their efforts especially at them. Though the initial appeal was often to
the middle class, particular efforts were made to reach the workers. The success of the revivals depended on a combination of spontaneous conversion
and social compulsion: Many employers, for example, insisted on evidence
of church membership as a prerequisite for employment and advancement.[83]

The reach of the religious movement was impressive. In 1820, fewer than 5 percent of the adult males in New York City were on the lay boards of the various Protestant organizations located there; by 1860, that fraction had increased to 20 percent. In the latter year, nearly *half* of all adult Protestant males in the city were members of at least one church-related voluntary association.[84]

An important offspring of the religious movement was the creation of Sunday schools. Such schools supplied not merely a brief lesson from the Bible but a daylong exercise in "decorum and restraint" that emphasized, through the minute application of rules and procedures, the duties of the pupils toward work, family, and community.[85] The participation in this effort was very large. In 1825, the American Sunday School Union claimed to enroll one-third of all the children in Philadelphia between the ages of six and fifteen; in 1829, over 40 percent of the children in New York City between the ages of four and fourteen were said to attend Sunday schools.[86] In England, Sunday-school enrollment tripled between 1821 and 1851; by the latter year, it accounted for over half of all children ages five to fifteen and three-fourths of all the working-class children of those ages.[87]

Though originally stimulated by churches, the Sunday schools soon became a more or less autonomous, self-sustaining activity staffed and financed by working-class parents who sought to inculcate in their children not only literacy and religion but respectability as well. Every detail of the schools' regimen stressed order, punctuality, and effort. Laqueur concluded that through these means "the bourgeois world view triumphed in the late nineteenth century largely through consent, not through force."[88]

The Sunday schools did not reach the young men employed in factories, stores, and offices. For them, the Young Men's Christian Association provided facilities intended to serve as a functional alternative to the village and farm life the men had left behind. Within a decade after being introduced into the United States in 1851, there were over two hundred residential YMCAs with more than twenty-five thousand members.[89] For younger street urchins lacking family or work, various foster-home programs were developed, such as the Children's Aid Society, designed to relocate urban children to western farms.

Perhaps the most far-reaching reform effort, and almost the only one whose impact can be estimated, was the temperance movement. In the decades leading up to the tumultuous 1830s, the consumption of alcoholic beverages, as we have seen, had been increasing rapidly. Reducing that consumption was the object of a century-long, broadly based social movement that may have been the single most effective effort in American history to change human behavior by plan. Temperance advocates differed both as to their goals (some seeking total abstinence, others only moderation) and as to their means (some emphasizing moral suasion, others relying on legal compulsion). Among their ranks were to be found urban as well as rural leaders, intellectuals as well as revival preachers, members of the social elites as well as representatives of the workers. By the tens of thousands, individuals were induced to sign temperance pledges. In 1851, Maine became the first state to prohibit the manufacture and sale of intoxicating beverages; within four years, thirteen states, including New York and Massachusetts, had enacted comparable laws. The desire to enforce these laws was one of the chief reasons for the growth in urban police forces and for the creation of some state police agencies.

The effect of all this activity seems to have been profound. Beginning around 1830, per capita alcohol consumption began to decline—between 1829 and 1850, it fell from 10 to 2.1 gallons per year.[90] The Civil War caused a setback to the temperance movement, as did the perfection of large-scale production methods for beer, but despite these difficulties alcohol consumption never again reached the levels attained in 1830. We have no way of measuring the connection between reduced consumption and reduced crime and disorder except to note that most contemporary observers believed there was such a connection and, given the evidence presented in Chapter 14, there are good grounds for taking such beliefs seriously.

The origins and aspirations of the public school movement were thoroughly entwined with these moralistic reform movements. From the beginning, the purpose of the tax-supported public school was character formation more than intellectual development. Training pupils for occupations was subordinate to "the goal of character building," even in programs that emphasized manual arts.[91] Public schools were originally not the secular institutions they have since become but rather privately managed, nondenominational Protestant schools that received government funds. Special efforts were made to recruit the children of poor families because the school leaders believed that if such children could be brought into the schools and kept there, crime would decrease.[92]

This was a tall order, since the proportion of poor families in the cities was growing rapidly; by 1847, one-fourth of the families in New York City received some form of charity. The children of workers' families frequently dropped out of school, and the question therefore arose as to what should be done with them when they misbehaved. At its peak, the Children's Aid Society was able to place about three thousand street urchins a year in farm homes,[93] but this was not enough. School leaders pressed for compulsory school attendance laws and at the same time supported efforts to create "houses of refuge," or reform schools, in which derelict or "stubborn" children could be placed.

The majority of youngsters in these houses were not there because they had committed a serious crime but because they were homeless, vagrants, or otherwise unfortunate, or "stubborn."[94] Stubbornness included idling in the streets in bad company, being profane or untruthful, using liquor or tobacco, or treating one's mother shamefully. Many decades were to pass before the reform school became in effect a juvenile prison devoted almost entirely to youth who had a serious criminal record. The early enthusiasts of these schools even tried to calculate their success rate. One person estimated in 1859 that only 17 percent of 1,653 former inmates of Massachusetts reform schools "turned out badly."[95]

In myriad ways but with extraordinary singleness of purpose, Americans (and Englishmen) in the mid-nineteenth century invested heavily in programs designed to inculcate self-control and thereby enhance character. These efforts were directed at what reformers took to be the causes of crime and disorder—impulsiveness and a lack of conscience. There is no way to assess their total impact. But their sponsors can be pardoned for believing that they were making a difference. During the second half of the nineteenth century, despite industrialization, urbanization, immigration, and a widening gulf between the social classes, crime seems to have gone down, aided (but, we think, not wholly caused) by a declining birth rate and possibly also by the rise of professional police forces.

The most striking difference in outlook between those days and the contemporary period is that the broadly based effort at moral uplift, and the religious convictions of those elites who led and sustained it, have been weakened or abandoned. Religious revivals, once led by liberal college students such as Theodore Weld, the mid-nineteenth-century abolitionist, are now scorned by college-educated persons as being the province of narrow-minded preachers, political opportunists, and exotic cultists. Revivalism became synonymous with fundamentalist Protestantism, and that was discredited among intellectuals by the defense of creationism by William Jennings Bryan at the Scopes trial and by his modern successors in the Bible-belt counties of the South. Daylong Sunday schools were made unnecessary, or so it was thought, by secular public schools that no longer saw themselves as having primarily a moral mission. The YMCA movement continued, but now largely because it offered gymnasiums rather than moral uplift.

Temperance was destroyed by Prohibition, perhaps for the wrong reasons. Though not a peculiarly American phenomenon (national laws restricting the use of alcohol were passed at about the same time in Finland,

Norway, and Sweden), and though it had never been simply a rural effort, Prohibition in the 1920s came to be seen by sophisticated Americans as an expression of bluenosed American farmers. There is not much evidence that crime went up to any large extent during Prohibition, but many persons came to believe that it had caused a crime wave.[96] While Prohibition succeeded in reducing alcohol consumption in the United States by between one-third and one-half, in the eyes of its critics the effort was a failure.[97]

The very idea of "Victorian morality" itself fell into disrepute; the phrase now stands for a narrow priggishness and arrant hypocrisy. The importance of teaching self-control has been to some extent supplanted by the value of stimulating self-expression. The notion that social institutions dealing with the young were chiefly intended to convert young persons into conforming adults has been partially replaced by the view that such institutions primarily exist to protect the young from adults.

This change, part of a much larger (and, we stress, worldwide) transformation of values, began roughly at the time that the concept of adolescence—a period between childhood and adulthood, characterized by special stresses and creating special needs—had been discovered.[98] In the early nineteenth century, children became adults as soon as they began to work, and that was at a very early age, indeed. Around the turn of the century, the movement from childhood to adulthood was seen to be interrupted by adolescence. In the nineteenth century scarcely anyone dissented from the view that character formation required teaching people to restrain self-indulgent impulses. By the 1920s, popular versions of the theories of Sigmund Freud had led many persons to believe that adult problems arose *because* children and adolescents had been taught to repress their instincts.

It was this argument between more traditional and more modern spokesmen that made the reception accorded Margaret Mead's *Coming of Age in Samoa* and the more recent challenge to the accuracy of its findings so important. Mead had said, in effect, that Samoans were happier than Americans because they were raised in less repressive families that accorded greater freedom to sexual expression, a conclusion we now know to be somewhat overdrawn.

The change can be traced in the contents of children's stories. In the first half of the nineteenth century, these stories portrayed a world in which there was no conflict between moral correctness and worldly success; a "Christian citizen" would prosper in this world and the next. In the second half of the century, this literature became less moralistic, though it still emphasized success. By the 1920s, it had begun to emphasize happiness over success.[99]

We have earlier seen how child-rearing advice to parents changed between the 1920s and the 1940s. That change was part of the larger transformation by which the value of self-expression was enhanced and that of
self-control diminished. The effect on behavior of whatever change in child-
rearing practice accompanied this change in advice was not immediately noticed, in part because the change may initially have affected only the attentive elites, in part because a decade or more would elapse before adolescent
behavior would have reflected childhood experiences, and in part because of
the advent of the Depression and World War II.

The fragmentary crime statistics we have suggest that property crime
may have increased during the early years of the Depression, but there was
no lasting increase; on the contrary, crime rates seemed to drop from at
least 1933 onwards. Studies done at the time in various cities and counties
found little evidence of a crime wave,[100] and one of the few cohort studies
done at the time showed no increase in the incidence of crime among children born in the 1920s and reaching maturity in the 1930s.[101] The reason
seems to be that the Depression tightened, rather than loosened, social controls on crime by accelerating the movement of young males into adult responsibilities.[102] Poverty drove children quickly into the labor market in
order to help families survive. World War II not only continued to tighten
social bonds, it exported millions of men during their crime-prone years to
foreign lands and provided a military outlet for such aggressive impulses as
they had.

The decade of the 1960s brought with it a coming-of-age baby boom, a
protracted period of great prosperity, a lessened use of sanctions for crime,
and a shift in the dominant values from self-control to self-expression. It is
hopeless to try to disentangle these social forces or to assign exact numerical
weights to each. Indeed, each of these forces helped create the other—the
baby boom helped fuel a youth market and a youth culture that in turn gave
support to the ethos of self-expression; a belief in the malleability and perfectibility of human nature both sustained that ethos and encouraged the authorities to prefer rehabilitating criminals to deterring crime; prosperity made
the youth market profitable and equipped a rising fraction of the population
with the material means to take advantage of newfound freedoms and, in the
process, to press for more of them; and the prosperity and freedom that
liberated some persons frustrated others by sharpening their sense of inequity. Behavior that once was thought to require social intervention, including custodial care, was now thought to be purely a matter of personal
choice. Stubborn or vagrant children were no longer sent to reform schools;
these behaviors were regarded as "status offenses" and hence not as offenses

at all. Public drunkenness was decriminalized by law, and private use of certain drugs was decriminalized by common agreement. Behavior among consenting adults that was once thought to be criminal was no longer regarded in this way. In these and countless other ways, law lost its tutelary function and retained only its function of protecting specific individuals from identifiable and palpable harms.[103]

The reader should not misunderstand the argument we are making. We are not saying that it would have been a good thing for society to have refrained from encouraging college education, making child labor illegal, entertaining the theories of Darwin and Freud, and repealing Prohibition, because if it had not done these things we would be enjoying a golden age of low crime rates and general contentment. We are only observing that broad, long-term social changes have at their root a changing theory of human nature and of society's responsibility for it, and that all social changes, especially those that entail a new definition of human nature and its nurture, bring both gains and losses.

Conclusions

We suggest that long-term trends in crime rates can be accounted for primarily by three factors. First, shifts in the age structure of the population will increase or decrease the proportion of persons—young males—in the population who are likely to be temperamentally aggressive and to have short time horizons. Second, changes in the benefits of crime (the accessibility, density, and value of criminal opportunities) and in the costs of crime (the risk of punishment and the cost of being both out of school and out of work) will change the rate at which crimes occur, especially property crimes. The evidence on this score for the United States is quite limited, but studies done using English data are consistent with the hypothesis. Third, broad social and cultural changes in the level and intensity of society's investment (via families, schools, churches, and the mass media) in inculcating an internalized commitment to self-control will affect the extent to which individuals at risk are willing to postpone gratification, accept as equitable the outcomes of others, and conform to rules.

These three factors taken together imply that certain simpler assumptions about the causes of crime waves are too simple. Depending on other factors, both recessions *and* prosperity can cause increases in crime—the former owing to the reduction in economically attractive alternatives to crime, the latter owing to its effect on the availability of criminal opportunities, the equity equation of young persons, and society's tendency to substitute increased consumption for investments in impulse control. Crime rates can rise faster than the proportion of young persons in the population if there is a lowered per capita investment in socializing those persons, if an increase in family size reduces the proportion of firstborn children or decreases the level of parental attention to any given child, or if improvements in health care facilitate the survival into adolescence of an increased proportion of infants with constitutional defects that affect their ability to learn. Crime rates can go up with the growth of large cities as a result of the greater availability of criminal opportunities and the psychic reinforcements supplied by street-corner peer groups, but they can also go up with a movement *out* of large cities if that out-migration is selective, so that low-crime-rate families who participate in communal efforts to protect public spaces and instill character development move out first, and if the out-migration creates hard-to-defend targets (e.g., abandoned buildings).

The evidence presented in this chapter is not enough to provide convincing support of the dominant effect of some of the key factors we have discussed, especially familial and cultural factors. The case for the importance of such factors can be substantially strengthened, however, in two ways. First, we note that there was during the 1960s and 1970s an increase not only in crime but also in other social pathologies, the rising prevalence of which is not consistent with some of the popular explanations of rising crime but is consistent with the explanation offered here. Suicide, divorce, illegitimate births, alcohol and drug abuse, and riotous conduct in public places (e.g., football matches) all increased during this period.[104] It is hard to imagine that each of these changes could have been caused by economic problems (indeed, some of them, such as drug use, divorce, and spectator riots, require a certain degree of prosperity for them to occur at all). It is not hard to imagine that each was influenced by familial and cultural factors.

Second, by comparing societies that have high crime rates with those that have low ones, we can further test the explanatory power of various theories that purport to account for increases in crime. Many of these theories depend heavily or fully on factors unique to the United States (e.g., the high level of private ownership of handguns or the extent of female-headed households), or on factors that appear to be associated with rising crime rates in this country but are not associated with it in other nations (e.g., the violent content of television). In the next chapter, we shall assess the extent to which familial and cultural factors, among others, can account for national differences in crime rates.

17

CRIME ACROSS CULTURES

The comparative approach—comparing nations or cultures—is one way social scientists compensate for not often being able to do genuine experiments. If they cannot control the variables that govern social life, they can at least make the best of the accidents of time and place to gain information about those variables. Emile Durkheim, the French trailblazer in sociology, left his followers a famous dictum: "Comparative sociology is not a particular branch of sociology; it is sociology itself."[1] If we want to know about human—rather than specifically French or English or Chinese—society, we should look at it in more than one place and time. To the extent that there is such a thing as human nature, the universals of culture and of social institutions ought to reveal it, comparative sociologists would say. This principle applies to how social institutions break down, as with crime, no less than to how they evolve and survive.

On the other hand, the (Polish-born) English anthropologist Bronislaw Malinowski warned that comparative social science was a "perilous undertaking."[2] His concern was that the Western social scientist may misread what he or she sees in the lives of alien people, not to mention that he or she might, while a guest in someone else's home, simply be unable to gather data. Social science is itself an institution with strong cultural coloration; it may or may not travel well.

The two views—Durkheim's and Malinowski's—are not so much opposed as complementary. We would like to know about crime at other times and in other places to broaden our understanding of it here and now, but our expectations for the data should be modest. Beyond the obvious difficulties of gathering cross-cultural data and the variations in the quality of the data that can be collected is the variation in the categories of crimes themselves.[3] Income tax evasion is a crime, for example, only where there is a legal obligation to pay income tax. Political crimes identified as such are a risk mainly in authoritarian or totalitarian states. Under communism, making a personal profit or "speculation" may be crimes.[4] Even the universal categories vary in their detailed definitions. For example, murder, as Leslie Wilkins points out, is the charge against the survivor of a suicide pact or the victor in a duel to the death in some parts of the world, but not in others.[5] With such difficulties, it is not surprising that an international commission concluded, in 1946, that "a material comparison of national criminal statistics [has] been judged impossible from the beginning because of the diversity of penal law and of the statistical-technical methods of the various countries."[6] The presence of this chapter proves we do not agree that comparisons are impossible, but we grant that they can only be qualitative for most categories of crime. The numbers cited below are meant to indicate rough relationships among nations, not firm quantitative differences.

An International Perspective

In 1972, the General Assembly of the United Nations asked each member state (plus several nonmember states) for official police statistics and other information about its crime and prevention. The survey garnered answers from sixty-four nations spread widely, if not uniformly, over the world,* with great diversity in culture, religion, political organization, and traditions of criminal law.[7] Information was gathered for 1970–1975 on numbers of offenders by sex and age, numbers of offenses in the broad categories of major crimes (see Table 1 for more specific categories), particular changes in criminal patterns, and crime control and prevention.

* The governments providing information represented Algeria, Argentina, Australia, Austria, Bahamas, Bahrain, Barbados, Belgium, Canada, Chile, Colombia, Costa Rica, Cyprus, Czechoslovakia, Denmark, Ecuador, Egypt, El Salvador, Ethiopia, Federal Republic of Germany, Finland, France, Gabon, German Democratic Republic, Greece, Guatemala, Guyana, Iceland, Indonesia, Iran, Iraq, Ireland, Italy, Jamaica, Japan, Kuwait, Libya, Luxembourg, Malaysia, Maldives, Mauritius, Morocco, Netherlands, New Zealand, Norway, Oman, Pakistan, Peru, Philippines, Poland, Qatar, San Marino, Saudi Arabia, Seychelles, Singapore, Spain, Sweden, Switzerland, Syrian Arab Republic, Trinidad and Tobago, Turkey, United Kingdom, United States of America, and Yugoslavia.

TABLE 1

World Rates (per 100,000 Population) of Reported Offenses, 1970–1975

Intentional homicide	3.9
Assault	184.1
Sex crimes	24.2
Kidnapping	0.7
Robbery	46.1
Theft	862.4
Fraud	83.3
Illegal drug traffic	9.8
Drug abuse	28.9
Alcohol abuse	67.8
Total offense rate	1,311.2

Source: From *Report of the Secretary-General on Crime Prevention and Control*, U.N. Report A/32/199, September 22, 1977, p. 9.

As in the United States, so in the world—property crimes outnumber crimes against persons, which outnumber drug offenses, as the pie chart in Figure 1 illustrates for the U.N. survey data. The more detailed summary in Table 1 also shows the actual annual rates of reported offenses per 100,000 population during the six years surveyed. Intentional homicide and kidnapping may command the attention of the world public, but they are negligible and minuscule categories, respectively, compared to the high-volume offenses of theft and assault. Indeed, crimes like murder and kidnapping may be newsworthy just because they are both serious and scarce.

A trained eye might have noted in Figure 1 that the world's ratio of property to personal crime was about 3.5 to 1, rather than the 5 to 1 and more extreme ratios we often see in American official statistics. The discrepancy is related to differences in crime patterns for countries at different stages of industrialization and urbanization. The world as a whole is at an earlier stage of development than is the United States. Subdividing the U.N. survey's sample into the two broad categories of developing and developed nations shows the difference plainly.

Figure 2 shows property and personal crimes about equally divided for developing nations, but in developed nations, property crime exceeded personal crime eightfold. Drug offenses were the same fraction of each pie, but note that the pie for developing nations is less than half the size of that for developed nations. Because the total per capita offense rates are about 800

FIGURE 1

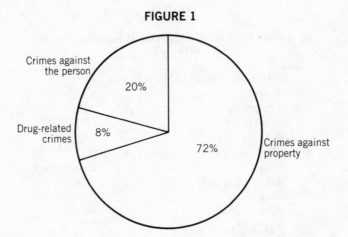

Source: From *Report of the Secretary-General on Crime Prevention and Control,* U.N. Report A/32/199, September 22, 1977, p. 10.

Proportions of crime in three major categories for sixty-four nations during 1970–1975.

and 1,800 (per 100,000), respectively, the 8 percent on the left represents less than half the rate of drug offenses as the 8 percent on the right. Crimes against persons were not only relatively but absolutely more common in developing countries (43 percent of 800 is larger than 10 percent of 1,800). The per capita rate of property crime in developed countries was more than three times as great as that of developing countries. During the six years surveyed, world crime was rising, but at about twice the growth rate (in numbers of offenses) in developing countries as in developed, presumably as the developing world was evolving toward the developed.

Besides the higher overall rates and disproportionate number of property offenses, developed countries had relatively more female and juvenile crime. A country-by-country analysis showed that per capita productivity (or gross national product) was usually accompanied by more property offenses, fewer murders, and a net increase in crime overall. Experts in the various countries did not generally blame the rising crime rates directly on economic progress. They were more likely to point to a breakdown of family bonds, or a weakening of religious belief or other value systems, as the corroding forces in development. These are matters to which we alluded in Chapter 16 and to which we will return later in this chapter.

The major empirical results of the U.N. report are substantiated by numerous other international surveys of crime. Using statistics from Interpol

FIGURE 2

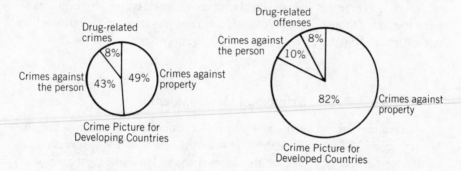

Crime Picture for
Developing Countries

Crime Picture for
Developed Countries

Source: Adapted from A. D. Viccica, World crime trends, *International Journal of Offender Therapy and Comparative Criminology* (1980), 24:272.

The data from Figure 1 separated for developing and developed countries.

(International Police Organization) and the FBI's Uniform Crime Reports (UCR), the Danish criminologist Preben Wolf examined overall crime rates, murder rates, and larceny rates in over two dozen countries between 1958 and 1964.[8] He also used a number of standard objective measures of each country's stage of development, such as literacy rate, per capita numbers of newspapers and telephones, degree of urbanization, infant survival rates, and so on. He concluded that more developed countries have higher overall crime rates and smaller ratios of murder rates to larceny rates. From another international study covering approximately the same period of time,[9] it seems that not only does murder decline relative to property crime as a country develops but suicide rises.

Even in Marxist totalitarian states, according to the fragmentary data available to Western scholars, the basic pattern is that of crime shifting toward property (and other economic) offenses as a country becomes industrialized and urbanized. Louise Shelley has pointed out that in the Soviet Union, the regions around the Baltic Sea, including the old Baltic states, are relatively developed, and the crimes are accordingly less violent and more directed against property, as compared to crime in the preindustrial, rural regions of Soviet Georgia in the south.[10] The more developed communist states, like Hungary and East Germany, and the less developed ones, like Bulgaria and much of the Soviet Union, each seem to have the general features of developed and developing nations outside the communist bloc, at least in regard to the split between violent and property crime. Police states, where the government can be highly intrusive, may enjoy less crime than freer societies (though, in the Soviet Union, not less murder[11]), but they do not escape it altogether. They, too, feel the strains of modernization.

Crime and Development

Given the link between crime and socioeconomic development, the differences in crime among the nations of the world must reflect different stages of development at the time of the comparisons. The world geography of crime, in other words, is to some extent a snapshot of each country's history of crime. If, for example, the United States has more crime than Yugoslavia, or property crime is a larger fraction of Sweden's total crime than it is Yemen's, at least part of the reason may be the more advanced stage of development of Sweden and the United States. Nations need not (and surely do not) follow precisely the same path of modernization for that modernization to have common effects on the pattern and level of offending.

Theories purporting to explain why development fosters and changes the character of crime are in good supply. Most of them concentrate on how social life changes when people move from the countryside and the small towns to the cities, a migration that seems to be an essential feature of development. The importance of this shift gets indirect support from evidence that even within countries, cities have more crime than the towns and countryside, especially more property crime.[12] On the average, the rural-urban differential is greater in less developed countries, a fact that sheds further light on the effects of modern development. Among other things, a modern society has greater internal mobility and greater dissemination of culture. In a developed nation, there is less of a rural-urban difference in life-style than in an undeveloped one, where people in the countryside and the small towns live, in some sense, in a different epoch from those in the cities.

By cities, it should be understood, we mean *modern* cities, large areas of which may be unlike the cities that stretch back for hundreds, if not thousands, of years. Rather than being clusters of villages with enduring extended families and stable local customs, modern cities are populated more by transient individuals and small nuclear families—that is, one or two parents and their children, often with only superficial contacts among neighbors. Evidence suggests that it is not so much the absolute size of the modern city that gives it its criminogenic characteristics but its size relative to other communities in the nation.[13] The urban way of life, opportunity among the densely packed targets for theft, may be a magnet for those in the countryside for whom rural life is too structured, personal, and hard.

In the typical modern city of almost any size, anonymity is the rule rather than the exception (but see Chapter 11 for our reservations about urban anonymity). A migrant from the countryside with any preexisting tendency to commit crime will find the tendency strengthened when the risk of recognition is slight, and where he finds property owned by people he does not know.[14] The owners of the goods in an urban shop or of a bicycle on a city street are unknown and remote, abstractions that may have little impact on the thinking of a potential criminal. In the countryside, likely targets of theft probably belong to people one knows and to whom one's feelings of attachment—or, if not that, about whom one's fears of retaliation—may be strong enough to keep the criminal impulse in check. The city provides opportunities for crime and it diminishes the internal prohibitions against it.

The anonymity of urban life also means being surrounded by strangers rather than, as in traditional rural society, by family members who are eager and willing to impose standards of conduct. If the city is a school for crime, as some say it is, the countryside may be the reverse, a school for noncrime. Among American blacks, for example, evidence suggests that migrants coming from the countryside to the cities are less likely to break the law than comparable people who grew up in cities.[15] The contrast is most likely to be apparent in youth and early adulthood, the period of maximum learning, and that too fits the data. As a society modernizes, juvenile crime increases even more sharply than adult crime.[16]

As Jackson Toby pointed out,[17] in cities, where the family has often been reduced to its smallest dimensions, the most common pattern is to be part of two nuclear families in the course of life, the one the city child is born into and the one he or she founds in adulthood. In between, the urban adolescent may be adrift, in comparison with the adolescents of extended rural families. To bridge the gap, an identifiable teen-age urban culture has arisen, usually distinguished by its own jargon and its own tastes in music, dress, food, and entertainment, which often includes drugs. The Teddy boys of Great Britain, *vitelloni* of Italy, *stilyagi* of the Soviet Union, *halbstarke* of West Germany, and punk rockers of the United States are some of the recent tags given to adolescents displaying the more extreme manifestations of teen-age culture in modern cities. Defiance of adult standards of conduct is often a further part of self-definition. A taste for flashy clothes and cars, for music and other forms of entertainment that can be costly, and an alienation from adult society may be explanation enough for the disproportionate rise in juvenile crime as a country modernizes and urbanizes.

The transition to a modern industrial society is driven by the economic benefits of development. People crave the affluence of an industrialized nation, with its goods, services, creature comforts, and personal opportunities. Ironically, the cost of this economic success is an increase in property crime. Using Interpol crime data for 1967–1968 for seventy-five nations and data on national economies and demography from the "Dimensions of Nations" project, Charles Wellford showed that wealthier countries, as measured by gross national product, had somewhat higher overall crime rates and that the relationship was even stronger if only property crimes were used in the analysis.[18] According to Wellford, gross national product, population size, and the political orientation of the government are, singly or in combination, the major independent variables for a large number of sociological characteristics of a nation. For the criminal statistics he was using, only affluence mattered; differences in population size or in political system had little if any impact.

What is it about affluence that fosters crime? An obvious answer is the rise in opportunities. In the individualistic environment of the cities that grow along with a nation's economic development, there are targets for theft in some rough proportion to the general level of affluence. Where the streets are full of cars, the shops and homes full of goods, and the wallets and handbags full of cash and credit cards, the liberated impulse to steal finds opportunities aplenty.

But this may not be the whole story. The suggestion has also been made (see Chapter 12) that it is not only affluence that fosters crime, it is relative deprivation, or, in terms of our theory, inequity. Wealth tends to be accumulated unequally, and to those not possessing it, it may seem (and may, in some sense, be) inequitable as well as unequal. The contrast between the haves and have-nots becomes more, not less, palpable, the theory says, as affluence grows, if people are separated by wider gaps in wealth, especially if they live side by side in cities. This is even more so if the family and community ties of traditional society have been dissolved in the impersonal exchanges of commercial society, and wealth has become the measure of individual worth.

The theory is plausible, and, in the extreme case, is almost self-evidently true. If there were no inequalities in wealth, then crime would probably not be much increased by rising affluence. However, confirmation of the theory with the data available has been elusive. The role of inequality as such has been examined by John and Valerie Braithwaite,[19] using Interpol homicide statistics for thirty-one nations over twenty years (1955–1974). Inequality was measured in various ways—the wage gap between high or low incomes and the average, the wage differential between various occupational categories, the smallest proportion of the population that receives half the total annual income, and so on. The Braithwaites also examined indices of land inequality—the range of farm sizes and the degrees of concentration of ownership of total farm acreage.

However it was measured, inequality in monetary wealth, but not in land ownership, was correlated with homicide rates. The relationship between income inequality and homicide had also been found in international statistics by Henry Hansmann and John Quigley.[20] They discovered that, besides income differences, ethnic diversity in a community raised the homicide rate, a relationship confirmed within the United States by Steven Messner.[21] In the Braithwaites' study, affluence per se, in contrast with inequality, was not associated with homicide, while in the Hansmann and Quigley study, it was. Other than the inevitable differences from sample to sample, no explanation can be offered for the discrepancy.

Interesting as these studies are, they are of limited value here because all of them used as their measure of crime the homicide rate. The choice was dictated by methodological considerations. Homicide rates are statistically more trustworthy and consistent from nation to nation than rates of various property crimes. Unfortunately for our purposes, homicide is not a crime that rises consistently with modern development, as property crimes do. To answer the question before us—whether inequality has much to do with increases in crime when a nation develops—it would be better to look at other categories, or at crime as a whole.

One such study again used Interpol statistics and examined, in addition to homicide, overall crime rates and property crime rates.[22] Inequality was again associated with homicide, but, against expectation, not with property crime and not with the overall crime rate. If anything, countries with greater income inequality had less property crime than countries with less inequality. The hypothesis was disconfirmed, but the reason was clear. In this particular sample, inequality happened to be inversely related to affluence. The wealthier countries had more property crime, less homicide, less income inequality, and less unemployment. At this point we must reject the hypothesis that inequality is *the* essential criminogenic feature of modernization. That it is one of the significant features remains plausible but unproved.

Cross-cultural Surveys

Crime rates may be the bottom line for criminology, but sometimes it helps to look at other measures of criminal behavior, where the vagaries of law enforcement and the inaccuracies of national crime data sources have not taken their toll. A popular technique is the cross-cultural survey, asking people to describe how they feel about crime and its control. Properly measured, such attitudes, like crime rates, can be the basis of comparative analysis. To what extent are these attitudes toward crime and its control universal, and to what extent do they depend on a local or national culture? How do attitudes relate to a population's stage of development and to other sociological characteristics?

One cross-cultural study is Graeme Newman's survey of people in India, Indonesia, Iran, Italy (Sardinia), U.S.A., and Yugoslavia.[23] Since each country encompasses numerous ethnic groups, religions, languages, and cultures, no realistically manageable sample could be considered broadly representative. Instead, Newman sampled several hundred people in each country, divided into rural and urban populations (except for Sardinia, where all two hundred respondents were rural). The other major individual variables were age, sex, education, and strength of religious sentiment. People were questioned about nine activities that are considered criminal in at least some cultures: incest, robbery, appropriation of public funds, abortion, homosexuality, taking drugs, environmental pollution by a factory, not helping a person in danger, and protesting publicly against the government. Among other matters, the survey asked people if they felt these acts should be prohibited by law, how seriously illegal they considered the acts to be, and what legal sanctions they favored.

Of the nine acts, robbery was most universally regarded as deserving legal prohibition: An average of 98.8 percent across the countries sampled said that it should be illegal. The act least regarded as criminal was public protest, for which the average was 44.9 percent. Between robbery and public protest, the other acts were judged criminal in the following decreasing order (see Table 2): appropriation of public funds, pollution, incest, taking drugs, homosexuality, not helping, and abortion. For the acts at the top of the list, there was considerable cross-national and within-country agreement. Acts, like abortion, that split agreement across countries also divided opinion within countries.

Another way to summarize responses is to average across acts, as a rough measure of a country's permissiveness. For the United States, the nine acts earned an average judgment of illegality of 58.1 percent. This was by a good measure the lowest average. The highest was Indonesia's, for which the nine acts averaged almost 90 percent. The more developed countries had more differentiated attitudes toward the acts; the less developed ones disapproved more, and more uniformly. Table 2 lists the averages for the six countries, and also gives the averages for the acts pooled across countries.

TABLE 2

**Percent Answering "Yes" to "Do you think this act
should be prohibited by law?"**

Countries: Averaged Across Acts		Acts: Averaged Across Countries	
Indonesia	89.6	Robbery	98.8
Iran	87.6	Appropriation	97.3
Italy	84.7	Factory pollution	96.1
Yugoslavia	77.0	Incest	92.3
India	72.7	Taking drugs	88.1
U.S.	58.1	Homosexuality	71.1
		Not helping	58.8
		Abortion	57.2
		Public protest	44.9

Adapted from G. Newman, *Comparative Deviance: Perception and Law in Six Cultures* (New York: Elsevier, 1976), Table 4.

Newman constructed a "deviance control scale" based on answers to questions about how seriously illegal each act was and how punitive a reaction seemed appropriate to the respondent. The samples from Iran, Yugoslavia, and Indonesia tilted toward stricter "deviance control," while the Indians and the Americans tilted toward leniency. Italy was at about the average over all samples.

Looking at individuals, rather than at countries as a whole, uncovers the individual factors associated with attitudes. Except in Yugoslavia, strength of religious feeling was the single most powerful correlate of a person's desire for strict governmental control of criminal behavior. The Yugoslavian exception is interesting, for in that country, the only authoritarian socialist state in the sample, religiosity is antigovernment and thus opposed to the instruments of government, including the legal system. In several of the countries, less educated people favored strict control, as compared to more educated people. Rural respondents were also stricter than urban, especially in their attitudes toward homosexuality, abortion, and public protest. The rising crime rates of the modern urban environment seem to be reflected here in the lenient attitudes of urban, educated respondents. Social class, age, or sex failed to show any clear relationship to the desire for strict sanctions.

In another cross-national survey of perceptions of crime and punishment, Joseph Scott and Fahad Al-Thakeb and a staff of interviewers asked a few hundred people in eight countries to pick fitting penalties for each of twenty-two offenses.[24] The countries were Denmark, Finland, Great Britain,

Kuwait, the Netherlands, Norway, Sweden, and the U.S.A. The offenses could be classified as violent, property, economic, drug, and sexual.* The punishments recommended by the respondents were grouped into ten categories of terms of imprisonment, from zero to life, plus an eleventh category for execution. For purposes of analysis, life imprisonment was treated as a term of twenty years and execution as twenty-five years, equivalences that seem to us to underestimate the subjective if not actual severities of those two punishments.

The main result was the uniformity of responses from the eight countries. Figure 3 groups the offenses under the main headings. At this general level of description, perceptions of crime seem to be transnational. For the narrower categories listed in the footnote, some secondary national differences emerge—for example, income tax evasion is not a meaningful category in Kuwait, where there is no such tax, nor is oil price fixing meaningful there. For the broad categories in Figure 3, the respondents in all the countries except Kuwait recommended the severest penalty for violent crime, followed in decreasing order by drug, economic, property, and sexual offenses. The Kuwaitis recommended more severe penalties than the other nationalities across the board, and they gave the sexual category the third most, rather than the least, severe penalties. In this study, which surveyed attitudes toward more conventional serious crimes than Newman's, the American recommendations were also generally more punitive, especially for violent crime, perhaps reflecting America's troubled preoccupation with the rise in violence in recent decades.[25]

Despite the differences in crimes, countries, and procedures, the two cross-cultural surveys convey a sense of universality in people's concepts of, and attitudes toward, crime, particularly toward the more severe and enduring offenses, like murder and theft. The modern democratic states are generally more tolerant of lesser offenses and, with the possible exception of the United States, less inclined to favor punitive legal sanctions than the more traditional, more authoritarian, or more religious nations.

The responses people give to questions about their attitudes toward crime round out the picture in cross-national official statistics. Rather than being an indivisible attribute, a country's stage of development refers to a shifting set of influences on crime, present in varying degrees in a nation's

---

* The offenses surveyed were: *violent:* murder, rape, robbery, assault; *property:* burglary, larceny, auto theft; *economic:* negligent drug manufacturing, oil price fixing, bribery, illegal land acquisition, income tax evasion, false advertising of product quality, false advertising of price reduction, auto repair fraud; *drug:* heroin sale, marijuana sale, heroin use, marijuana use; *sexual:* prostitution, homosexuality, illegal abortion.

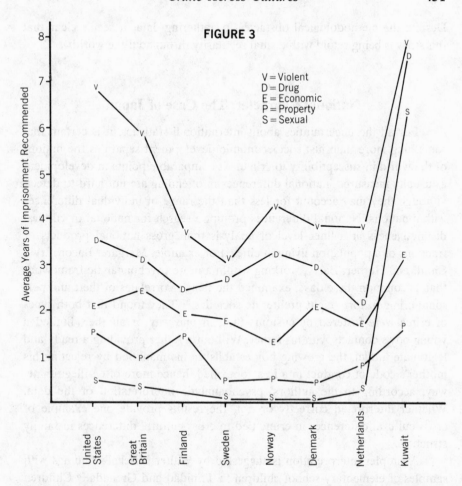

FIGURE 3

V = Violent
D = Drug
E = Economic
P = Property
S = Sexual

Source: Adapted from J. E. Scott and F. Al-Thakeb, Perceptions of deviance cross-culturally. In G. R. Newman (ed.), *Crime and Deviance: A Comparative Perspective* (Beverly Hills: Sage, 1980), p. 64.

Respondents in eight countries were asked their opinions about appropriate penalties for twenty-two offenses, which are here grouped into five larger categories of crime.

history. Some theorists[26] challenge the very idea of development itself, but dropping it would not much change our account of crime internationally. Increasing opportunities for theft; inequality; the rise of modern cities, with their anonymity, their weakening of traditional family, community, and religious bonds, their mixing of mutually alien populations, and their concentration of unattached young males and others at risk for offending—these are among the penalties societies pay for making the transition to modernity.

Despite the methodological obstacles to gathering data, it seems clear that this story is being retold with dismal regularity throughout the world.

National Character: The Case of Japan

For all the uncertainties about international statistics, it is certain that something more than just socioeconomic development separates the nations of the world in susceptibility to crime. At comparable points in development as usually measured, national differences in offending are not hard to detect, although they may account for less than the range of individual differences within nations. National differences prompt a search for national or cultural distinctiveness at a finer level of analysis than gross national products or fractions of a population living in cities. For example, Margaret Bacon, Irvin Child, and Herbert Barry, working within a more psychoanalytic framework than is common these days, examined the family correlates of theft and personal crime in forty-eight preliterate societies.[27] They found that both types of crime were fostered by customs that, in one way or another, limited a young boy's contacts with his father. Without a father providing a ready and legitimate model, the growing boy establishes his manhood by rejecting his mother's code of conduct in a less controlled, hence more often illegitimate, way, according to the authors' psychoanalytic interpretation of the data. Whether interpreted correctly or not, the results provide one example of cross-cultural differences in crime tied to cross-cultural differences in family structure.

A simpler interpretation is suggested by Walter Mischel's findings with samples of elementary-school children in Trinidad and Grenada.[28] Children growing up in homes lacking fathers were less disposed to defer gratification than those with fathers at home, in a choice between a small piece of candy immediately versus a large piece of candy a week later. Mischel interpreted the difference as showing that fatherless children fail to be taught forbearance (especially in relation to male social agents), hence tend to be more impulsive.

Despite these suggestive but isolated findings, differences between nations that transcend differences in the stage of development have not yet been systematically associated with child rearing, or any other influence on individual characteristics related to criminal behavior, such as impulsiveness. That there are cross-cultural individual differences is beyond question; where they originate and how they relate to differences in crime, we can, in most instances, only surmise.

We know a little more than that about crime in Japan. The Japanese have been particularly interesting to criminologists, for these people have not only bucked the tide of development; as far as crime is concerned, they have somehow managed to swim against it.[29] Between 1962 and 1972, a period of rapid industrialization, total crime (excluding traffic violations) fell 20 percent in Japan. Leaving out simple theft, so as to focus on more serious crime, the drop was 40 percent. In New York City during that decade, per capita reports of nontraffic offenses almost tripled; in West Berlin, they more than doubled; in London, Los Angeles, and Hamburg, they rose by more than 50 percent. In Tokyo and Osaka, per capita reported crime fell.[30]

In 1974, the United States had four times as much *serious* (i.e., UCR Index categories) crime per capita as Japan had crime of *any* sort, excluding only traffic offenses.[31] These figures are for reported crime. The true differences between the two nations are probably larger, for the American proportion of unreported crime is by all odds bigger than the Japanese. David Bayley in 1976 estimated that the risk of being robbed was 208 times greater in the United States than it was in Japan. A newspaper article recently[32] reported concern among Japanese authorities over a rise in senseless street murders, which had brought the total for their entire nation for the year of 1982 up to thirteen. The American newspaperman observed that a single bad weekend in New York City could result in thirteen street murders. Other indications suggest that Japan is in fact experiencing some increase in crime, but still at levels far below the American. The same newspaper article noted that the robbery rates for the two countries had narrowed to a ratio of 125 to 1.

Japan is an industrialized and urbanized nation. Its cities are more than three times as densely packed with people as cities in the United States. About 70 percent of each country's population is urban.[33] In the 1970s, Japan showed some of the strains of modern city life in its crime statistics—a growing volume of serious traffic offenses and of crime by fourteen- and fifteen-year-olds. Minor theft also rose with increased affluence, relative to total crime. Yet, so far, Japan has been spared the more disastrous effects of development on criminal behavior. The challenge is to find what it is in this society or these people that so diminishes the criminogenic consequences of modernization.

Japan has fewer police officers per capita[34] than the United States, which is hardly surprising considering its much lower crime rate. This fact is sometimes mentioned as evidence against the value of law enforcement, but the inference is unfounded. A more relevant statistic is that there are many more police per criminal offense in Japan than in the United States.

A practical result of the greater investment per crime may be the higher success rate of Japanese law enforcement, discussed below. In addition, the ratio of police to crime per capita is a way of measuring the importance a society attaches to crime, and, by this measure, Japan attaches more than the United States. Other, related interpretations of the ratio come to mind. Presumably, there are always political, economic, and social forces pushing for and against investment in law enforcement. In Japan, the balance of forces tips more toward investment in police than it does in the United States, for a given level of crime. Or, to put it simply, the Japanese seem to feel better about their police than the Americans do.[35]

American commentators are often struck by the prestige of the Japanese police officer, as well as by his professionalism, his dedication to public service, and his role as counselor and arbiter to his neighborhood. "In all of Japan there were 123 complaints made [against the police] during an entire year," wrote Ezra Vogel in his book *Japan as Number One*.[36] The public reciprocates its police's performance, not only by granting high status, but by reporting a large proportion of crimes, compared to the American public.

Statutory penalties for given crimes are less severe in Japan than in the United States. But, if what counts is not the statutory but the actual risk of experiencing the penalties, this is greater in Japan. Clearance rates for serious crime are about three times higher in Japan—60 percent or more versus 20 to 22 percent in the United States as of the early 1970s.[37] For homicide, crimes involving bodily injury, and rape, the Japanese clearance rates were each above 90 percent. These official statistics, as we noted, contain a larger fraction of the total crimes in those categories than the corresponding clearance rates for the United States, yet the American clearance rates are significantly lower.

Once indicted and prosecuted, an alleged offender faces a 90 percent chance of conviction in Japan, higher, on the average, than in the United States. Confession and public apology are common for Japanese defendants. American observers are impressed that in Japan a person accused of a crime will readily respond to questions put by authorities, rather than maintain silence under anything like the American constitutional protection against self-incrimination. Legal proceedings in Japan are not so sharply separated from the pretrial fact-finding efforts of police and prosecutors. Japanese trials are less adversarial, less formalized, and less constrained by legal "technicalities." The per capita number of lawyers in Japan is about one-seventeenth what it is in the United States.[38]

These differences between criminal justice systems may be important in determining crime rates, but they rest on more fundamental differences between the two cultures. The Japanese are not law-abiding because of un-common strictness in standards of conduct or because of a gentle disposi-tion, two hypotheses that may spring to the mind of someone living in the United States, where the excessive crime is blamed, by one commentator or another, on moral laxity or ingrained violence. The Japanese have proved themselves capable of considerable ferocity in wartime, and even in peace-time, their political radicals—most recently in the various factions of the "Red Army"—have not shunned terrorism. Nor do Japanese personal or family relationships strike observers from other modern cultures as particu-larly strict or disciplined.[39] On the contrary, to Westerners, the Japanese seem overindulgent of their children and, in their attitudes toward adults, surprisingly tolerant of public drunkenness, prostitution, and other social or moral lapses within a broad range of established forms of unconventionality.

If not strictness or gentleness, what is it that distinguishes Japanese cul-ture and protects it from crime? Western observers mention several con-trasts between Japan and other modern countries. We will describe four of them here, and attempt to show how they may bear on crime and also to show their interrelations. The Japanese population, it is observed, contains a larger core of racial, ethnic, and cultural uniformity than the mixed popula-tions found in, for example, the United States. Even the major Japanese cit-ies are homogeneous compared to large cities found elsewhere. More homo-geneous populations, such as Japan's and Sweden's, live together more tranquilly than mixed populations, such as America's and Chile's.

Whether the tranquillity is purely cultural, or, as Thomas Moore sug-gests,[40] partly the expression of a biologically inherited disposition that was selected for over centuries of shared communal life, the homogeneity of the population may have some bearing on the second contrast. The Japanese are said to have somehow preserved village life in the neighborhoods of their cities. Perhaps this is why they can tolerate population densities greater than in most crowded Western cities. The Japanese city dweller has avoided at least some of the anonymity of modern urban life in other countries. Not only do neighbors know each other, but the local policeman is likely to know the people on his beat, and they, to know him.

Another familiar contrast is between the Japanese emphasis on group solidarity and group achievement, compared to Western (especially Ameri-can) individualism. Thinking about commercial or scientific creativity, West-erners may cherish the individualism their societies foster. Thinking about crime, they may wish it were different. The strength of the group bond in Japan may preclude the extreme anonymity of most modern society else-where, and may have other anticriminogenic results.

Finally, compared to other contemporary populations, the Japanese seem to Western observers to be less preoccupied with their rights and more concerned with their obligations. The emphasis placed in Western philosophical traditions on protection from the state is distinctly non-Japanese. The Japanese heritage instead gives its people a sense of collective responsibility. In this respect, Japanese morality resembles the Confucian principle according to which "the individual is expected to subordinate his own identity to the interest of the group."[41]

These four contrasts describe much the same notion at four levels. Looking at the homogeneous demography of its population, the villagelike sociology of its cities, the group-centered psychology of its people, or a philosophical heritage that places duties above rights, we think we can discern how Japan has so far withstood the criminogenic forces of modernization. The rewards for crime are so diminished by the internalized penalties for violating community prohibitions that the Japanese are relatively immune to the abundant and growing opportunities for crime in their cities. A corollary effect is the strengthened reward for noncrime, owing to high probabilities of arrest and conviction in a population that habitually reports offenses and whose offenders habitually confess to them.

We would like to be able to probe even more deeply into these features of Japanese life. Where do they originate and what sustains them in the face of the pressures of modern development? A complete answer, reaching back into history to unearth the sources of a culture, is well beyond the scope of this discussion, let alone the abilities of its authors. Let us instead consider a narrower question. What is there about Japanese psychology that lends itself to such powerful internalized ties to the community? Sure answers are again not available, but we have some guesses.

The average Japanese IQ score is about 110, well above that for any country for which data are available.[42] It is certainly above the American average, which is set at 100 for the tests on which the Japanese score 110. Japan therefore has a smaller fraction of its population in the range of scores between 60 and 100, the range at highest risk for criminal behavior. Chapter 6 has discussed the reasons that people with low scores are at risk, which include some disability for internalizing standards of conduct. The difference in the proportions of high-risk individuals would not by itself account fully for the large difference in crime rates between Japan and the United States, but it is possible that a society's willingness to rely on internalized values depends, inversely, on how large a segment of the population will fail to learn them. The segment in Japan is much smaller than that in America.

It could be argued, as some have done,[43] that the high Japanese scores are themselves mainly a result of Japanese culture, rather than vice versa. If so, the high scores would presumably be expressing much the same cultural features as the lower crime rates do, namely a willingness to adhere to group standards, whether in regard to learning the kinds of things that intelligence tests test or the kinds of things that inhibit criminal behavior. If, on the other hand, we accept the evidence that test scores reflect inherited factors, then it would follow that there may be reasons beyond the accidents of a nation's history and culture that affect its crime rate. We will not press the case here (see Chapter 3), but we think it is important to take note of the principle that cultural differences may grow out of biological differences.

Similar issues arise around the evidence[44] that the average Japanese personality is atypical in just such a way as to reduce the risk of crime. On personality inventories, and from other kinds of data, it seems that Japanese people are, on the average, more introverted, more anxious, and less impulsive than the norms established in international samples. The American population is even farther toward the extroverted end of the scale than the Japanese is toward the introverted. Extremes along the dimension of impulsiveness would help explain both the strength of internalized prohibitions among the Japanese and the high-volume street crime that plagues American cities (see Chapter 7). If personality has any biological basis, as evidence suggests it has,[45] then Japan's recent resistance to crime resides to some extent in what could be called its national character interacting with the historical and political forces of the time.

Conclusion

Although Japan, as a highly developed country with a low crime rate, is an irresistible case to consider at length, it is likely that, given adequate knowledge, any country would teach lessons of its own. Reviews of international crime statistics[46] demonstrate that deviating from the global averages is the rule rather than the exception. On the average, national differences in crime can be attributed to differences in countries' stages of development, but few if any countries are "on the average." Each one has features of its own that makes its patterns of criminal behavior distinctive. We would like, for example, to be able to explain such potentially illuminating phenomena as the remarkably low rate of juvenile delinquency in Switzerland, the rising rate of crimes of public disorder and the declining rate of sexual offenses in the Netherlands, the 400 percent increase in armed robbery in Austria in a seven-year period (1971–1977), the frighteningly high rate of murder in

South Africa, where, according to Holyst, the number in a single year in the 1970s exceeded the total English plus Welsh murders for the fifty years beginning in 1900.[47] None of these facts follow from the generalities of crime and development; to explain any of them would require some further information and insight into the sources of individual behavior. Each country, perhaps even each locality, places its own stamp on crime as history, culture, and current circumstances act on the individual differences that bear on criminal behavior.

18

RACE AND CRIME

In virtually every society, there are differences in crime rates among some racial and ethnic groups. Americans of Chinese and Japanese origin have significantly lower crime rates than other Americans, and this is true both when the Orientals are in the minority, as they are in California, or in the plurality, as they are in Hawaii.[1] Hungarian and Yugoslav immigrants to Sweden have higher crime rates than do native Swedes; similarly, Irish immigrants to England have higher rates than do the native English.[2] But it is not simply being an immigrant that causes the higher crime rates—German, Dutch, and Scandinavian immigrants to the United States have been much less likely to get into trouble with the police than old-stock Americans.[3] And crime rates among Israelis differ according to their immigrant origins, with those from Africa and Asia having higher rates than those from Europe and America.[4]

In one sense, these group differences are not very interesting. For almost any behavior—whether intelligence, temperament, school achievement, economic success, or criminal activity—there is more variation among individuals within a given ethnic or racial group than there is between the members of two groups. Among Orientals, Jews, blacks, Swedes, Hungarians, or whatever, we will find the full range of traits, from mental retardation to creative genius, from desperate poverty to immense wealth, from complete law-abidingness to vicious criminality. The individual differences with which this book has been chiefly concerned are far greater in magnitude than the differences between the average traits of any two groups.

But in another sense, group differences are of great significance. When we observe the distribution of crime rates across society, we tend to see those rates in the context of the most visible features of the settings in which crime is highest or lowest. Big cities are less safe than small towns, young men are more threatening than older women, a black neighborhood seems more dangerous than Chinatown. Sometimes we make mistakes in our judgment of group differences—at one time, Americans thought that all immigrants were disproportionately criminal, perhaps because the oddities of language and manner of immigrants, combined with their poverty, gave to them a faintly sinister cast. Thinking this, some Americans pressed all the harder for restrictions on immigration, a pressure that was not entirely abated even by the 1931 report of the Wickersham Commission which held that, taken as a whole, immigrants were no more criminal than old-stock Americans. Though individual differences are always greater than group differences, we tend to perceive social reality largely in terms of the groups within which that reality seems embedded; the more distant or unfamiliar the reality, the greater the apparent significance of its group characteristics. It is important, therefore, to assess the facts that lie behind these perceptions and to offer, insofar as we can, an explanation of those facts that is consistent with our general theory. We have already seen (Chapters 4 and 5) that two perceived group differences are indeed correct: men are, on the average, five to fifty times as likely to commit crimes as women, and young persons are, on the average, two to four times as likely to commit crimes as older ones.

Discussing racial and ethnic differences is a more difficult matter. For one thing, the racial or ethnic identity of a person is far less certain than is his sex or age. The ancestors of many blacks and Orientals include some, perhaps many, Caucasians, and vice versa; when parentage is mixed, a decision that someone is "really" black, Oriental, or Caucasian is a bit arbitrary. At times it is even ludicrous, as when custom sometimes dictates that a person who has only one black grandparent is a black, whereas a person who has three white grandparents may not be white. And ethnic identity is often based on linguistic, cultural, and historical affiliations that are hard to define and may exist largely in the preferences of the person. A person born in Ireland is Irish, but if his children are born in America, are they Irish? Are his grandchildren? His great-grandchildren? Is a person born in a small village in what is now Yugoslavia a Yugoslav, or a Serb, or a Serbo-Croat?

If these definitional problems were all that stood in the way of analyzing racial and ethnic differences in crime rates, the matter would be manageable. But of course what makes any discussion of these differences so difficult is that some groups that have higher crime rates than others have been the objects of exploitation and repression. In the United States, the higher average crime rates of blacks have been used to support claims that blacks were morally inferior. The presumption that because an individual was black he must be guilty or be deserving of especially severe punishment has been used to justify discriminatory arrest and sentencing decisions. Today, many persons, white and black, remembering the sorry history of racism in this country, prefer not to discuss race differences in crime rates at all, for fear of either giving offense to a group that has been persecuted enough or giving encouragement to those who would continue the persecution. A few persons deny that there are any real differences in crime rates between the races; many more are inclined to attribute such differences as may exist to differences in economic advantage. As we shall see, the denial of differences is false, and the attribution of differences to economic factors is only one of several possible explanations, each with some supporting evidence.

Black-White Differences in Crime Rates

Even allowing for the existence of discrimination in the criminal justice system, the higher rates of crime among black Americans cannot be denied. As we saw in Chapter 1, every study of crime using official data shows blacks to be overrepresented among persons arrested, convicted, and imprisoned for street crimes. Blacks are about one-eighth of the population but accounted in 1980 for about one-half of all those arrested for murder, rape, and robbery, and for between one-fourth and one-third of all those arrested for burglary, larceny, auto theft, and aggravated assault.[5] Since blacks are, on the average, younger than whites (in 1980, the median age of black males was seven years less than that of white males), some of this increased risk of arrest may be the result of there being relatively more young males among blacks than among whites. But if we look only at arrestees under the age of eighteen, we still find blacks greatly overrepresented—among young persons, they account for about half of those arrested for murder and rape, and for nearly two-thirds of those arrested for robbery.[6] Blacks are somewhat more likely than whites to live in cities where criminal opportunities are more numerous and, perhaps, the chances of arrest greater, but among city arrests, blacks are also overrepresented, and to about the same degree as they are nationally. No matter how one adjusts for other demographic factors, blacks tend to be overrepresented by a factor of four to one among persons arrested for violent crimes, and by a factor of nearly three to one among those arrested for property crimes. Stated another way, if blacks were arrested for robbery at the same rate as are whites, there would be half as many robbers arrested in the United States.

The overrepresentation of blacks among arrested persons persists throughout the criminal justice system. Though prosecutors and judges may well make discriminatory judgments, such decisions do not account for more than a small fraction of the overrepresentation of blacks in prison. Alfred Blumstein has calculated that about 80 percent of the disproportionality between black and white incarceration rates is accounted for by the initial black-white disproportionality in arrest rates.[7]

Thus, if blacks get in trouble with the law because the system is biased, the bias must appear right at the start. It is possible that some of the overrepresentation of blacks among arrestees may be the result of police procedures, including, perhaps, a tendency to patrol black areas more heavily than white ones, a disposition to take street crimes involving blacks more seriously than off-the-street ("white collar") crimes involving whites, and discriminatory arrest decisions. But these factors cannot account for all or even most of the overrepresentation. With respect to so-called "white collar" or "off-the-street" crimes, it is often forgotten that blacks are overrepresented among persons arrested for most of these offenses to about the same degree that they are overrepresented among persons arrested for burglary, larceny, and auto theft. For example, in 1980 blacks made up about one-third of those arrested for fraud, forgery, counterfeiting, and receiving stolen property, and about one-fourth of those arrested for embezzlement.[8] Blacks are underrepresented among those white-collar offenses (tax fraud, securities violations) that ordinarily require, for their commission, access to high-status occupations.

We can check on the extent of bias in police arrest records by using three other sources of data—self-reports, victim testimony, and the racial patterns evident in homicide. Self-reports generally show less racial disproportionality than do arrest data, but as we have observed (Chapter 1), self-report studies ordinarily emphasize lesser—even trivial—offenses that are so common, at least among males, that we would expect to find lessened racial differences. And self-reports suffer from underreporting by high-rate offenders. One of the largest and most recent self-report studies, involving a national sample of 1,726 youth aged eleven to seventeen, initially found a clear racial difference in total self-reported delinquency, particularly in predatory crimes, with the difference most apparent among high-rate offenders.[9] In subsequent analyses of their data, however, the authors discovered the racial difference to be much reduced.[10] Though this study, unlike most earlier ones, included a comprehensive list of offenses, major and minor, it did not—and could not—address the question of whether high-rate offenders underreport their offenses. There is some evidence that black youth tend to underreport their delinquencies more than white juveniles.[11] Moreover, a recent study of the self-reported crimes of the inmates of three state prison systems finds no difference between white and black inmates in the probability that, having committed a crime, they would be arrested.[12] In view of all the uncertainties, however, it seems safest to judge the evidence from self-report studies on race differences in offending as inconclusive.

Victim surveys provide clearer evidence. As we have seen, these surveys tell us something about the persons and households that are the victims of crime and about the offenders who are seen by their victims. Repeatedly, the National Crime Survey (NCS) has shown that blacks are the victims of robbery and burglary at a higher rate than whites. (By contrast, whites are more likely to be the victims of auto theft.) The average American black has a 40 percent greater risk of being burgled and twice as great a risk of being robbed as the average white.[13] To believe that blacks do not commit such offenses at greater rates than whites, one would have to believe that these higher rates of victimization are caused by whites entering black neighborhoods in order to break into homes and hold up citizens. While that is possible, it seems most unlikely.

These surveys also record what the victim saw when he or she was raped, assaulted, or robbed. The results generally confirm what we learn from arrest data. In 1974, 62 percent of the persons arrested for robbery were black, and 62 percent of the robbers who could be described by their victims were black.[14] In a later study, Hindelang calculated, using victim surveys, that the ratio of the black proportion of arrested robbers to the black proportion of victim-identified robbers was about 1.03 to 1, too small to make more than a trivial difference in any conclusions we might draw from arrest figures. For rape and assault, however, blacks were somewhat overrepresented among arrestees, though not by enough (about ten percentage points) to account for the very large black-white differential in arrest data.[15]

Finally, we know that the great majority—in 1980, 72 percent—of all homicides are cleared by arresting the offender.[16] We also know that the great majority of those arrested for homicide are of the same race as their victims. Therefore, the racial identity of homicide victims provides a reasonably good guide to the racial identity of murderers. In 1980, there were 24,278 homicides; of these victims, 10,283, or 35 percent, were black.[17] This means that the overall rate at which black men were the victims of homicide was more than six times greater than the rate at which white men

FIGURE 1

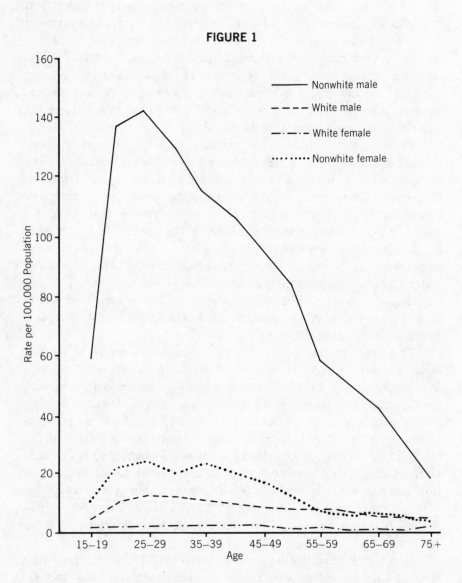

Source: From R. E. Dennis, The role of homicide in decreasing life expectancy. In H. M. Rose (ed.), *Lethal Aspects of Urban Violence* (Lexington, Mass.: D. C. Heath & Co., 1979), p. 20.

Homicide victimization rates per 100,000 population by age, sex, and race, for 1970.

FIGURE 2

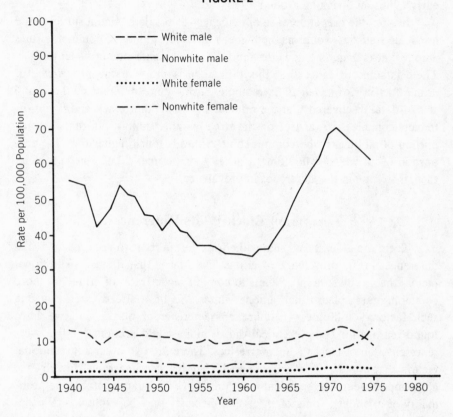

Source: From R. E. Dennis, The role of homicide in decreasing life expectancy. In H. M. Rose (ed.), *Lethal Aspects of Urban Violence* (Lexington, Mass.: D. C. Heath & Co., 1979), p. 22.

Homicide victimization rates by sex and race for 1940–1975.

were killed. Figure 1 shows the age- and sex-specific homicide rates for black and white victims in 1970. As is evident, young black males are overwhelmingly the most likely victims of homicide; their rate, at ages twenty-five to twenty-nine, is well over seven times greater than that for white males of the same age. Figure 2 shows the changes over time (1940–1975) in the homicide rates for black and white men and women. After a long period during which white homicide rates were fairly constant and black rates were declining, we see a sharp upward turn in black male rates beginning in the early 1960s and peaking around 1975.

In sum, the preponderance of evidence—arrest data, victim surveys, and homicide statistics—confirms the higher rate of most kinds of common crimes among blacks than among whites, and the much higher rate of violent crime. There is some evidence that this difference is more in the *prevalence* of crime than in its *incidence*. Two studies, using quite different methods and sets of data, discovered that the number of crimes that black and white offenders commit per year free on the street is quite similar, but that the proportion of all blacks who commit some crimes is much higher than the proportion of all whites who commit at least one crime.[18] The chief problem, then, is to explain this difference in prevalence.

Theories of Black-White Differences

There are at least four major theories that purport to account for racial differences in the prevalence of crime. The first is that those constitutional factors that predispose individuals to commit higher rates of crime are more common among blacks than among whites. We have already seen that one such factor—youthfulness—is more characteristic of blacks, but we have found reasons for being skeptical that it alone could account for the over-representation of blacks among arrestees. There are two other constitutional factors that could also contribute to higher black crime rates, intelligence and temperament. To the extent these differences exist and increase the probability of offending, some of the racial disparity may be explained. We describe these two factors as "constitutional" in the sense suggested in Chapter 3—they are, to some degree, present at or soon after birth and their behavioral consequences appear gradually during the child's development. Constitutional factors may or may not be genetic. If blacks are more likely to have an impulsive temperament or a somewhat lower measured IQ, these traits may be the result of patterns of prenatal care as well as of inheritance. For example, if successive generations of black children received, on the average, poorer prenatal and obstetrical care than white children, this could contribute to differences in average IQ or temperament. The poorer care could, in turn, be caused by a variety of factors, including maternal attitudes, economic opportunity, and the availability of adequate medical services. Obviously, any initial difference in intelligence or temperament might, to some degree (in the case of temperament, to a large degree) be magnified or reduced by the subsequent operation of familial and social factors, so this theory, like each of the others, is likely to provide, at best, only a partial explanation of group differences in crime rates.

The second theory is better known, usually under a name like economic deprivation. Criminologists, as we saw in Chapter 2, often call it strain theory. In this view, blacks, more than whites, have faced an acute shortage of economic opportunities as the result of the inequitable distribution of services and wealth; being thereby frustrated in their efforts to achieve legitimate goals by legitimate means, they have turned, in relatively greater numbers than whites, to crime. As we argued in Chapter 15, the psychological theory underlying strain or deprivation theory is incomplete, for it directs attention only to the positive rewards (jobs and status) associated with not committing a crime and neglects the avoidance of the penalties that are connected, however imperfectly, with noncrime. If a person is sufficiently rational and forward-looking to take into account deferred reinforcements, he will presumably take into account deferred punishments as well. Accordingly, we suggest that this explanation of black crime rates be renamed the theory of net advantage, thereby bringing together both strain and deterrence theories.

The third view is that, for whatever reason, black family life does not induce in children either a sufficiently strong regard for the good opinion of others or a sufficiently long time horizon to make them value conventional norms or defer instant pleasures for delayed rewards. In some variants, this is referred to as the "culture of poverty," implying both that it may be protracted poverty that causes such socialization and that such socialization keeps its objects in a life of poverty. Obviously, this view is akin to control theory, as described in Chapter 2, and that is the way we shall refer to it. In another variant, the inadequacies in self-control that result from imperfect socialization are said to be compounded in families that are headed by a single, usually female, parent.

The final theory suggests that blacks are more likely to commit crimes than whites not as a result of rational economic choice or inadequate family socialization but because many of them have acquired through experience a hostile view of the larger society and its values. Sometimes this is referred to as the "subculture of violence," though in fact most black crime is not violent; at other times the explanation is called the "subcultural deviance" theory; and at still other times it is described, by certain psychologists, as the result of a "reaction formation." What all these variants have in common is that those whose behavior is being explained do not (as in the net advantage theory) value legitimate goals and do not (as in the control theory) suffer from an inability to take into account distant rewards; rather, they have acquired a culture that supplies distinctive modes of dress, speech, and conduct designed to display qualities ("soul," "cool") that are at odds with, and possibly defiant of, the manners of white society. If the criminal laws reflect the norms of white society, then, to a degree, those laws will be broken in the process of flouting those norms.

Since each of these theories of black crime directs attention to only a part of the general model of criminal behavior that we have set forth, the reader is by now no doubt quite prepared for our conclusion that none is likely to be entirely satisfactory.

Constitutional Factors

There is no way to discuss the evidence, such as it is, on constitutional factors underlying the association between race and crime without giving offense. Even to allude to the possibility that races may differ in the distribution of those constitutional factors that are associated with criminality will strike some persons as factually, ethically, or prudentially wrong. We disagree. One cannot dismiss such possible connections as factually wrong without first investigating them. Honest, open scientific inquiry that results in carefully stated findings cannot be ethically wrong, unless one believes that truth itself is wrong. But it still might be thought imprudent to discuss such matters because of the uses to which mean-spirited persons will put even the most careful scientific assertions.

That concern is not easily answered, since we know that both good science and pseudoscience have at times been put to mistaken or even wicked uses. But any knowledge, even about seemingly noncontroversial matters, can be placed in the service of bad purposes; everything depends on the motives of the users. Some persons assert that certain aspects of racial differences should not be investigated at all,[19] because evidence that there is a constitutional basis for these differences implies that nothing can or should be done to remedy whatever disadvantage may afflict the group in question. In fact, the opposite is more nearly the case. It is wrong to suppose that because one has uncovered a constitutional, even a genetic, basis for some behavior that "nothing can be done" about that behavior.

First of all, a constitutional factor merely makes a person somewhat more likely to display a certain behavior; it does not make it inevitable. There is no evidence for the existence of a "crime gene" in the same sense that we may know there is a gene that produces red hair. Second, helping a person who is constitutionally more at risk is only possible if we look for those predisposing factors early in life. For example, if we refused to study the constitutional basis for certain learning difficulties, we would never know about dyslexia and thus we would treat slow learners as if they were generally retarded or lazy, thereby making them worse off. Finally, even genetic problems can sometimes be corrected. Phenylketonuria, for instance, is a heritable enzyme deficiency that, undetected, can cause brain damage and severe mental retardation; once detected, however, it can be treated by altering the person's diet. By the same token, there is a genetic susceptibility to alcoholism (see Chapter 14) and to high blood pressure that, if recognized and investigated, may also be liable to medical control or even reversal. And these susceptibilities seem to differ among racial and ethnic groups.

In any event, the evidence that black-white differences in crime rates have a constitutional basis is limited, and the explanatory power of such constitutional factors as have been identified is largely unknown. Further research is as likely to reduce as to increase the significance of those factors.

Among whites, being a mesomorph is an indicator of a predisposition to crime. Young black males are more mesomorphic (5.14 on Sheldon's scale) than are young white males (4.29), though the measuring techniques are sometimes not exactly the same as those used by Sheldon.[20] Whether mesomorphy is associated with offending among blacks in the same way that it is among whites is not clear. One of the few studies of this question found that among institutionalized male delinquents, blacks were more likely to be mesomorphic than whites but that somatotype scores bore no relationship to either official or self-reported rates of offending.[21]

Blacks often have different scores than whites on standardized personality tests. On the best-known such test, the MMPI, black males tend to have higher scores (that is, to be less "normal") than white males on all scales except the one measuring femininity, and these differences persist after controlling for socioeconomic status.[22] It is quite possible, however, that the MMPI, which was developed to detect pathology in a white population, may not accurately predict black behavior. If this is true, then many MMPI questions may be answered by blacks in ways that reflect not psychopathology but simply differences in cultural values. Victor H. Elion and Edwin I. Megargee have attempted to deal with this problem by comparing the MMPI scores, especially on the Psychopathic deviate (Pd) scale, of young black offenders with those of both black nonoffenders and white offenders and nonoffenders.[23] They found that blacks in a federal prison had significantly higher scores on the Pd scale than either whites in prison or black college students (who themselves tended to come from deprived backgrounds); that among the prisoners, recidivists had higher scores than first offenders; and that among the black college students, the Pd scale discriminated between those who on a self-report questionnaire showed themselves to have committed the most and the fewest delinquent acts. The authors concluded that the Pd scale on the MMPI was "as valid for blacks as for whites," but before the matter can be regarded as settled, much more research would have to be done on blacks of different ages and both sexes and drawn from a variety of institutional and occupational backgrounds.

If these personality differences are to be taken as indicative of a constitutional predisposition, one would have to show that for blacks as well as for whites personality is to a significant degree heritable. Though there is substantial evidence from twin studies of the heritability of some aspects of personality,[24] adequate research using black subjects—in particular black twins—has only begun to appear. The most important of these involved 123 school-age black twins, 62 percent of whom were identical twins, who were given two personality tests (not the MMPI). Perhaps because of defects in the tests, perhaps for other reasons, the authors were unable to isolate a significant genetic component.[25]

The one factor that both seems clearly associated with offending and appears disproportionately among blacks is a low intelligence score. Virtually every careful review of the evidence on racial differences in measured IQ comes to essentially the same conclusion—namely, that black IQ scores are, on the average, about twelve to fifteen points lower than those of whites.[26] These differences are usually not manifest until the age of three or four but then remain reasonably constant during the school years. Some of the differences in measured IQ reflect social class differences, but controlling for class does not eliminate the difference. Among the lowest-status persons, for example, the black-white difference is about eleven points. The most careful reviews of the testing procedures and results, carried out by the most dispassionate and qualified outside observers, such as the National Academy of Sciences, have concluded that the test results cannot be dismissed on the grounds that the tests are culturally biased.[27] In Chapter 6 we discussed this question at length and concluded, as did the National Academy committee, that the "tests predict about as well for one group as for another."[28] In fact, many of the differences in IQ scores emerge from tests that rely mainly on nonverbal questions or otherwise call for knowledge that is not likely to have a large cultural component.

We cannot emphasize too much that we speak of average differences. There is, of course, much more variation in measured intelligence within any racial group than there is between two such groups. The range in IQ among blacks is at least ten times greater than the average difference between blacks and whites. Indeed, the fact that IQ tests distinguish among individuals so much better than they do between groups of individuals is in itself evidence that the tests are to a large degree measuring something other than culture or social class.[29]

Though the evidence strongly supports the existence of racial differences in measured intelligence, it does not allow us to say much about the degree, if any, to which those differences are heritable. The variation among *individuals* in IQ is to a large degree (probably on the order of .6) the result of inheritance, but this says little or nothing about the extent to which differences between *groups* are heritable. The social conditions in which two racial groups find themselves may differ so greatly and so persistently that the average difference between the two groups will be caused almost entirely by these conditions, while differences among individuals within one racial group will reflect a large genetic component. To the extent that the economic, cultural, and geographic position of blacks imposes long-term disadvantages on them, average IQ scores may differ between whites and blacks for reasons having little to do with heritability. We have already noted, for example, that black infants are twice as likely as white ones to have abnormally low birth weights,[30] and that low birth weight is associated with slower intellectual development. The majority of students of intelligence testing, to judge from what they have published, do not believe that there is yet strong evidence for the inheritability of group differences.[31]

In their review of sixteen studies measuring the IQ-crime linkage in which some or all of the subjects were black, Osborne and McGurk concluded that offenders have lower scores than nonoffenders, that there is (as we observed in Chapter 6) a tendency for the verbal scores of offenders to be lower than their performance scores, and that the lower scores of incarcerated offenders were not the result of their lacking an incentive to follow the test instructions.[32] In their analysis of the achievement scores and social status of delinquents and nondelinquents growing up in Philadelphia, Wolfgang, Figlio, and Sellin found that at every socioeconomic level and among blacks as well as whites, delinquents had lower IQ scores than nondelinquents.[33]

If lower measured intelligence is associated with crime independently of socioeconomic status, and if blacks, on the average, have lower such scores, than these facts may help explain some of the black-white differences in crime rates. Of course, we still must be able to say *why* a lowered IQ score is associated with offending; in Chapter 6 we offered some speculations, and that is about the best we can do.

Yet constitutional factors cannot alone account for black-white differences in crime rates because those differences have changed in ways that are not likely to be associated with the slow changes—if any changes at all—in constitutional factors. For example, the homicide fatality rate among black males nearly doubled between the early 1960s and 1973, increasing from 34.3 to 65.8 per 100,000; the change among whites was much smaller.[34] The youthfulness of the urban black population cannot explain that change— Barnett, Kleitman, and Larson estimate that only 10 percent of the increase in the homicide rate in fifty large cities over an eight-year period can be attributed to changes in the age structure of the population.[35] Roger Lane estimates that in Philadelphia the black homicide rate was about three times greater than that of whites during the nineteenth century but had become about twelve times larger by the middle of the twentieth century and nearly twenty times larger by the 1970s.[36] It is inconceivable that these changes in rate could be wholly or even largely explained by changes in purely genetic factors. Of course, such factors may have made the average black male more vulnerable to changing circumstances, such as the greater availability of handguns, alterations in economic opportunities, or the pressures of racial animosity, so that adversities and opportunities that would have merely angered one person drove another to a homicidal attack. And that is exactly the point: Whatever the interaction between constitution and circumstance, changes in rates can only be explained by taking into account changes in those circumstances.

Net Advantage

Among the circumstances that may have changed are the economic opportunities available to blacks. There is little doubt that people, black or white, who have low incomes and poor employment records are more likely than better-off people to break the law. But as we saw in Chapter 12, there are several possible—and not entirely consistent—explanations for this fact, and it is by no means clear which is correct.

It would be surprising if poverty or the absence of employment opportunities had no effect on the crime rates of blacks or any other distinctive group, but there are good grounds for supposing that economic disadvantage alone cannot explain all or possibly even most of the black-white disparity in crime rates. The higher arrest rates among blacks persist after controlling (no doubt imperfectly*) for socioeconomic status. Moreover, high-rate of-

* It is difficult to match exactly blacks and whites for socioeconomic status. In the Philadelphia cohort study,[37] the youths were assigned to a social class based on the median family income of the census tract in which they lived. Obviously, some youths could have come from higher-status families living in lower-status neighborhoods, and vice versa. As long as blacks and whites were equally likely to be misclassified, this error would not bias the results, but we cannot be certain this was the case.

fenders, black or white, begin to manifest delinquent behavior quite early in life, often in the elementary-school grades, long before they would have had any direct experience with the labor market and become discouraged with a futile search for jobs. Among the Philadelphia boys whose criminal careers were tracked by Wolfgang and his associates, lower-status blacks had an official delinquency rate that was more than twice as great as that for lower-status whites.[38] The disparity was even larger for the chronic offenders—that is, those who had been arrested five times or more. Lower-status black males were over three times as likely to be chronic offenders than were lower-status whites.[39] Black boys had their first contact with the police at an earlier age than white boys,[40] and this earlier age of onset persisted after controlling for socioeconomic status. A preliminary analysis of a second cohort of Philadelphia youths—all born in 1958—suggests much the same conclusion: Among lower-socioeconomic-status offenders, blacks committed more offenses than whites, with the differences particularly striking among the chronic recidivists.[41]

It is possible, however, that the greater prevalence of early delinquency among blacks is due to their having learned to anticipate bleaker economic prospects than whites—that long before they encounter the labor market, they sense that crime will pay more. This theory is plausible, but we know of no evidence directly bearing on it. And there is some evidence to suggest that the mere fact of racial isolation and the prospect of encountering racist barriers to legitimate employment cannot be the whole story.

During the 1960s, one neighborhood in San Francisco had the lowest income, the highest unemployment rate, the highest proportion of families with incomes under $4,000 per year, the least educational attainment, the highest tuberculosis rate, and the highest proportion of substandard housing of any area of the city. That neighborhood was called Chinatown. Yet in 1965, there were only five persons of Chinese ancestry committed to prison in the entire state of California.[42]

The low rates of crime among Orientals living in the United States was once a frequent topic of social science investigation.[43] The theme of many of the reports that emerged was that crime rates were low not in spite of ghetto life but because of it. Though Orientals were the object of racist opinion and legislation, they were thought to have low crime rates because they lived in cohesive, isolated communities. The Chinese were for many years denied access to the public schools of California, not allowed to testify against whites in trials, and made the object of discriminatory taxation. The Japanese faced not only these barriers but in addition were "relocated" from their homes during World War II and sent to camps in the desert on the suspicion that some of them might have become spies or saboteurs.

There was crime enough in the nineteenth- and early-twentieth-century Oriental communities of California, but not in proportion to the Oriental fraction of the whole population. The arrest rate of Chinese and Japanese was higher in San Francisco than in any other California city during the 1920s, but even so Orientals were underrepresented by a factor of two, the Japanese more so than the Chinese.[44] Such crime as occurred tended to involve narcotics, commercialized vice, or public disorder and rarely crimes against persons or property.

When crime rates did rise among Orientals, the rise was typically explained as the result of the failure of the familial and cultural heritage of the group combined with "disorganizing contacts with Americans."[45] (The claimed virtues of solidarity and of avoiding contacts with Americans were not limited to Orientals; such advice was also thought to be good for Hungarians living in Detroit.)[46] Of late, some inquiry has been made into the psychological characteristics of those Orientals who do become offenders, and the same conclusion—a failure to identify with the native group—has been reached.[47] Whether these conclusions are justified is another matter; what is striking is that the argument used by social scientists to explain *low* crime rates among Orientals—namely, being separate from the larger society—has been the same as the argument used to explain *high* rates among blacks.

The experience of the Chinese and Japanese suggests that social isolation, substandard living conditions, and general poverty are not invariably associated with high rates of crime among racially distinct groups. Of course, the origins and nature of the separation that blacks have endured have been somewhat different from that encountered by Orientals, a matter to which we shall shortly turn. But even among blacks, the experience of ghetto life is not the sole determinant of crime rates. West Indian blacks are indistinguishable, physically, from native American blacks, at least to whites inclined to discriminate. West Indian immigrants have lived in the same inner-city areas as native blacks, sometimes much to the irritation of the latter.[48] We have found only one study that compares crime rates among immigrant and native blacks, and that was carried out in the 1930s by the black scholar Ira Reid.[49] During this period, West Indians made up a much smaller percentage of the inmates of New York state prisons than one would predict knowing their share of the state's population, while native blacks were overrepresented by a factor of three to seven.

That economic factors cannot be the whole story is further suggested by changes over time in crime rates. The black male homicide rate, as we saw in Figure 2, rose sharply during the 1960s and early 1970s, despite generally rising incomes. Between 1960 and 1976, there was a sizable increase in real (i.e., inflation-adjusted) per capita income and a considerable reduction in the proportion of households below the poverty line.[50] Another study, covering a longer period and including in-kind income (cash transfers by the government) found much the same improvement,[51] though blacks, both as individuals and as households, continue to have incomes significantly below that of whites, especially in the case of female-headed households, a matter to which we shall give greater attention later in this chapter. Offsetting the gains in income was the rise in the 1960s and the persistence in the ensuing decade of high rates of unemployment among black youth.[52] It is possible that the effects of economic factors on black crime rates differ among segments of the black community, with those young persons who lived in female-headed households (where they experienced small or no gains in economic well-being) and who faced chronic unemployment turning disproportionately to crime.

Thus far we have been discussing the possible impact of net economic advantage (or disadvantage) on crime rates as if that advantage consisted entirely of income from legitimate work. Naturally, one must deduct from that income the expected losses from punishments meted out by the courts and the opprobrium of others. If incomes of both blacks and whites were rising during the 1960s and 1970s but the costs of crime were declining for blacks but not for whites, we would not be surprised to find that black-white differences in crime rates were increasing. Unfortunately, we are not aware of any evidence bearing on the question of whether blacks, compared to whites, were becoming more or less likely to be penalized for crimes. In general, the evidence reviewed at the beginning of this chapter suggests that whatever systematic biases may exist in the criminal justice system, they are not sufficient to explain the black overrepresentation among arrestees and prison inmates, and so we are skeptical that adding the behavior of the police and courts into the net advantage equation would increase its explanatory power. But the question remains open.

If we take a longer view of the matter, however, it is possible that differences in sanctions have had an impact on the extent to which members of different races are inclined to handle aggression by resort to assaults and homicide. Suppose that over the generations, law enforcement officials ignored or treated leniently the most common forms of serious black crime (dangerous or fatal assaults on blacks by blacks), reserving the full force of their sanctions for the much rarer cases of assaults by blacks on whites. In 1937 John Dollard wrote of the harmful effects of the double standard of justice then evident in a small southern town and which probably persisted for many decades throughout the South and in some parts of the North: "Negro crime" was less serious than "white crime," a view sometimes defended on grounds of a high-minded indulgence of "Negro ways." As Dollard wrote:

> The formal machinery of the law takes care of the Negroes' grievances much less adequately than that of the whites, and to a much higher degree the Negro is compelled to make and enforce his own law with other Negroes. . . . The result is that the individual Negro is, to a considerable degree, outside the protection of the white law, and must shift for himself. This leads to the frontier psychology. . . . [This] condoning of Negro violence . . . may be indulgent in the case of any given Negro, but its effect on the Negro group as a whole is dangerous and destructive.[53]

Though the double standard may be much less in evidence today, it has not disappeared, owing in part to the fact that the most common form of black assaultive crime is communal—that is, a person attacking or killing a relative or acquaintance. In Houston, communal homicides are punished less severely than stranger-to-stranger ones,[54] and the same pattern probably would be found in many other cities. If a group that already has a high rate of violent offending discovers that the most common form of that violence— attacking a friend or relative—is dealt with leniently, then the rate at which that crime occurs, other things being equal, will increase. Whether this has in fact occurred, we cannot say, but the possibility cannot be dismissed.[55]

Inadequate Socialization

A variety of familial and community experiences could affect the extent to which a black youth assigns a high value to future events or gives a positive value to legitimate employment or the good opinion of respectable adults.

It is inadequate socialization that lies at the heart of many theories of "cultural pathology" or the "culture of poverty." The view that inadequate socialization can help explain black-white differences in crime rates depends on showing that, other things being equal, black families on the average do a poorer job of socializing their children than do white families, or that certain kinds of families (e.g., single-parent ones) that are especially common among blacks do an especially poor job of it. Even if these propositions can be supported, there remains the question of *why* this problem exists, and the answers to that may include forces as various as the legacy of slavery, the impact of urbanization, the lack of economic opportunity, or the persistence of racism. In short, the root causes of inadequate socialization may well include factors over which blacks have had only limited control. Thus, it is something of a misnomer to call these theories "cultural," except in the important sense that one generation's pattern of child rearing tends to become that of the next.

The passions that surround any discussion of constitutional differences do not markedly abate when one shifts the topic to family processes. Since the publication of the famous Moynihan Report[56] on the problems of the black family—a report that, at its root, said little more than what black sociologists, such as E. Franklin Frazier,[57] had said a quarter of a century earlier—there has appeared a flood of books and articles claiming that the black family, even though headed by an unmarried woman, has adaptive inner strengths or is embedded in a supportive network of kith and kin such that it can as readily socialize its offspring as can a conventional two-parent white family.[58] In this view, if socialization fails, it has nothing to do with culture and everything to do with blocked economic opportunities.[59]

This controversy between those observers who emphasize the pathological and those who emphasize the adaptive features of black family life should not blind us to certain elemental facts: Only a small fraction of families, black or white, produce high-rate offenders; there is a greater range of differences among families of a single race than between the average families of two races; and the family itself has survived from the beginning of time in the face of threats at least as formidable as anything offered by contemporary circumstances.

Having made clear that we are, at best, trying to identify differences at the margin, we must also confess that much of the scholarship on this interesting issue is so infused with ideology, *ad hominem* argumentation, and generalizations drawn from observations of but one or two families that the more we read the less we know.

But even the most dispassionate studies that investigate the connection among blacks between mother-only families and delinquency tend, for the most part, to be as inconclusive as those discussed in Chapter 9 that report on this connection among families of all races. Monahan,[60] Anderson,[61] Mosher,[62] Chilton and Markle,[63] and Clarke and Koch[64] find that living in a single-parent family is associated with a higher prevalence of black delinquency; Robins and Hill,[65] Rosen,[66] and Drayton[67] find no such connection. Most of these studies were cross-sectional—they compared children in broken homes with those in intact ones—and so could not in principle say much about causality; the few that were longitudinal, such as that by Robins and Hill,[68] were retrospective and hence subject to the normal problems of bad memories, incomplete records, and uncertainty about timing.

One can also investigate the connection between family structure and delinquency indirectly by asking whether female-headed black households are more likely to produce children whose intellectual or personality traits are associated with high rates of delinquency. A review of this research by Marybeth Shinn found fifty-four studies of the effects of absent fathers on intelligence or school achievement; fourteen of these studies involved blacks.[69] In only six of the fourteen was the absence of the father associated with detrimental consequences. Perhaps the most impressive of these, because it involved over twenty-six thousand children followed from before birth to age four, found that families similar in race and socioeconomic status had children whose early IQ scores were somewhat higher if the father was present, but that this difference was not large and was greater for whites than for blacks.[70]

The only kind of research that can settle the question of the effect of single-parent homes on behavior is that which identifies a group of black children at or near birth and follows them as they grow up, measuring, over many years, the joint effects of family structure, personal traits, economic status, and community experiences on crime. At least one study that approximates this ideal was described in Chapter 9. That research, directed by Sheppard Kellam, followed for over ten years more than one thousand black children growing up in the Woodlawn section of Chicago.[71] By the time they were in the third grade, it was clear that the children from mother-only families were much more likely to be judged by their teachers as "maladapting" than were those from other kinds of families, especially mother-father ones. By the time they were in high school, boys who had lived in mother-only families while very young were more likely than those from other family backgrounds to say that they had committed various delinquent acts.[72] Family circumstance, as we saw in Chapter 9, was not the whole story, however. Temperamentally aggressive boys tended to get into trouble even if they were raised in mother-father families, but if the boys were not temperamentally aggressive, then growing up in a mother-father family was associated with lower rates of self-reported delinquency than was the case for such boys in mother-only families.

We cannot be certain that this study proves that family structure is an important cause of delinquency, because other possible explanations cannot be ruled out. For example, if the men most likely to abandon their families had a greater predisposition to criminality (owing, perhaps, to being temperamentally aggressive or impulsive), and if those traits are, to some degree, heritable, then the association between absent fathers and delinquency might have occurred for reasons that had little to do with the problems of a lone mother raising a boy. In our judgment, however, the interaction between constitutional traits and family socialization, described in Chapters 8 and 9, is sufficiently great as to suggest that the father's biological makeup probably does not by itself account for the findings of Kellam and his colleagues.

Black families, like any families, may increase the chances of a child's becoming delinquent even when they are composed of a mother-father pair. If black families contribute disproportionately to delinquency, it could be because their socialization practices, apart from their structure, contribute to that result. If so, then the socialization practices of black families should differ from those of whites, holding social class constant. Do they?

We are not certain. Generalizing about child-rearing practices from the reports of parents or children is risky (see Chapters 8 and 9), and very few observational studies have been made. When Hess and Shipman watched black mothers and their children solving problems together in a laboratory, they found that the lower-status mothers spoke to their children less frequently than the higher-status mothers, were much more likely to define adult-child relations in terms of authority rather than personality, and gave poorer directions.[73] Some of these differences that were attributable to social class (though they also may have been the result of class-linked differences in verbal aptitude) reappeared when black and white mothers of the same class were compared.[74] The black mothers were less likely than the white ones to make supportive comments to the child or to offer helpful suggestions. We also have Arthur Hippler's more impressionistic record of his observations of low-income black families in the Hunter's Point section of San Francisco.[75] As we saw in Chapter 8, the mothers played affectionately with their infants but then, as the child began to walk and explore, shifted to a colder, less consistent pattern of care, including occasionally locking the child out of the apartment, even when he was still very young.

Given the tendency of many persons to explain behavior chiefly by reference to family processes, it is astonishing how little we know about the consequences of being raised in a black family, intact or broken. There can be little question that black families are, on the average, different in structure and income from white ones. In 1965, when Moynihan issued his report to the government on the black family, 25 percent of all such families were female-headed; by 1980, 40 percent were. During this same period, the proportion of white families that were female-headed also rose, but to a much smaller degree—from 9 to about 12 percent.[76] In 1978, more than *half* of all black children under the age of eighteen were living in households headed by only one parent (or other adult). Of these female-headed households, about half were living below the poverty line.[77]

This "feminization of poverty," as it is sometimes called, is widespread, has been growing rapidly, and is disproportionately a black phenomenon. Of the 6.9 million families below the poverty line in 1981, 30 percent were black; of these, 70 percent were female-headed.[78] In 1980, the median income of the 40 percent or so of black families that were female-headed was $7,425, less than half that of black husband-wife families, and less than a third that of white husband-wife families.[79] In short, roughly a half of all black children were growing up in poverty and about a half were growing up with less than half the family income of intact black families.

To some, poverty explains the rise of female-headed black families, but that does not seem to be the case. Within the low-income group, female-headed families are still twice as common among blacks as they are among whites: Two-thirds of all black families earning less than $5,000 a year but only one-third of all white families earning that amount were female-headed in 1977.[80]

To others, female-headed families are a legacy of slavery, but that does not seem to be the case, either. Herbert G. Gutman has shown that black families were not disproportionately headed by women in the South after slavery or even in New York City as late as the first two decades of this century.[81] In 1925, for example, 84 percent of all native black families and 86 percent of West Indian black families living in central Harlem were headed by males, and in most of the few female-headed households, the woman was not a teen-ager but over the age of thirty. Similar conclusions have been reached by other scholars.[82]

And to still others, female-headed families are the result of the availability of welfare benefits that encourage fathers to desert their children and make it easier for women who do not wish to marry the fathers of their children to live apart from men at state expense. The relationship between the prevalence and growth of female-headed households and the welfare system is complex and controversial. The best evidence we have on this matter comes from a major social experiment conducted by the federal government to assess the effects of giving to lower-income families a cash subsidy—the so-called negative income tax. The results seem quite clear. John Bishop summarized them as follows: The families in the experimental group receiving the cash subsidy were much more likely to break up than similar families in the control group not receiving it.[83] The subsidized families were 36 percent more likely to dissolve their marriages in the case of whites and 42 percent more likely among blacks. Whether welfare payments in their present form have the same effect on families is less clear.[84]

Whatever the cause of female-headed families, and however uncertain the evidence as to their effects on youthful behavior, black leaders increasingly deplore them and urge that steps be taken to reverse the trend. A conference of black scholars at Tarrytown, New York, produced a statement entitled *A Policy Framework for Racial Justice,* which said that the black family today faces a "crisis" manifested chiefly in the rise of female-headed households. It described the results of that rise as follows: "The consequences are predictable. Children grow up with few consistent male role models. In many cases, the young mothers of these children are themselves hardly removed from childhood—their education is incomplete, their preparation for parenthood underdeveloped, and their own personal potential unfulfilled. . . . these women and their children are at considerable risk."[85]

Given the confused and uncertain state of the evidence, we can neither add to nor detract from this assessment.

Subcultural Deviance

Some blacks may break the law not because their families have failed to teach them self-control or because their experience with the labor market has convinced them that crime pays but because they distrust or reject some of the values and interests of the larger, governing society. They have become part of a subculture that values crime and noncrime differently than the larger one.

In a book that received much attention, Charles E. Silberman restated one major explanation for why blacks should assign so different a meaning to the world in which they find themselves.[86] Unlike other ethnic or immigrant groups, blacks were subjected to slavery, racism, and oppression in ways that led to the festering growth of anger directed at those who oppressed them, but it was an anger that could not safely be expressed and so had to be hidden for many decades behind a mask of docility.

This rage was especially intense among black men because of the unwillingness of white society to allow them to exhibit their manhood in conventional ways—by marrying, owning property, earning a living, and defending themselves physically against attacks and insults. They were treated, and even referred to, as "boys," they were severely punished when they assaulted white men but ignored or treated leniently when they assaulted one another, and their access to women was strictly limited to members of their own race. It has even been suggested by some[87] that the psychological emasculation of black males by slavery contributed to the rise of female-headed households, but we now know that this rise is of such recent origin that the cause must be more complex than this.[88]

Because it was so risky to do otherwise, blacks, especially men, concealed their anger or turned it inward on themselves or one another. When they concealed it, however, the disguise was imperfect, and so glimpses of it can be found stated subtly or indirectly in poems, songs, and folk tales wherein a wily black man—or sometimes, as in the Br'er Rabbit stories of Uncle Remus, a wily animal that is an obvious proxy for a black person—outwits or destroys his nominally more powerful opponents.

The sexual and physical activities of the black man that could find only guarded expression in the real world of white power were expressed in larger than life form in a vast oral tradition of folk tales. Roger D. Abrahams[89] and Bruce Jackson[90] have recorded and compiled much of this tradition, including the "toasts" and the "signifying" that are at its heart. A toast is a narrative poem, recited with many improvised variations, celebrating the legendary and often obscene exploits of either an especially violent and virile black man or some animal, such as the "Signifying Monkey," that by cunning defeats a stronger rival. ("Signifying" means a boastful claim that one possesses exceptional sexual or physical capacities.) Often the anger was turned directly against other blacks, as in such verbal contests as "playing the dozens," an exchange of taunts typically reflecting adversely on the morality of the rival's mother.

Every ethnic and racial group has its distinctive folklore and virtually every child grows up in a world in which taunts and ribald stories are commonplace, but such an oral tradition does not signify for every group a deep resentment at the larger society or provide a latent rationale for violence. What makes the tradition of blacks distinctive, in the opinion of some observers, is that so many of its forms—jokes, toasts, and boasts—have in common an effort to convert the negative stereotypes about blacks into positive ones.[91] White beliefs and fears about the impulsiveness, sexual prowess, and physical strength of black men are transformed in these black legends into desirable attributes. Traits that to others are bad become good; even the meaning of the adjectives change, so that a "bad" black is, to other blacks, a good one, and the "baddest" man becomes the best one. The humor associated with legends serves to "deaden the pain."[92]

In this view, crime began to increase markedly when blacks no longer needed to fear whites, and so some of them—young black males, primarily—could express directly and physically a rage and a desire to prove one's manhood that formerly could be expressed only indirectly and verbally. Crime further increased as forces maintaining residential segregation moderated somewhat, thereby allowing middle-class blacks to move out from the old ghettos, taking with them the informal social control they once exercised.

This theory of black crime can be recast into the terms employed in the model of criminal choice set forth in Chapter 2. Accumulated resentment and the preoccupation with sublimating normal desires to establish one's manhood and express one's physical capacities lead to a reduction in the internalization of rules against crime, so that the value of a crime is increased by the (relative) lack of a conscience decrement. Its value also rises to the extent one's peers find in one another's crimes a covert but laudable expression of forbidden manliness. To the extent the values of the larger white society are thought to be hypocritical or even wrong, the value of not committing a crime is lessened. All that restrains crime, in this circumstance, is the prospect of swift, certain, and harsh punishment. Crime rates rise when that prospect changes because of a reduction in the brutality of repression or an increase in the observance of legal rules that temper the force, reduce the certainty, or delay the imposition of punishment.

Such, at least, is the theory. But is it true? Neither Silberman nor anyone else cites much direct evidence of a link between subcultural norms and criminal activities, though, to be fair, it is always hard to prove any cultural explanation of behavior inasmuch as culture is, by definition, so pervasive and subtle in its effects as to leave few visible traces. There is some suggestive evidence, such as that gathered by two scholars who studied youthful inmates in a New Jersey correctional institution. They measured the expected value of crime to each inmate and the extent to which each one identified with leading a life of crime. Even though the black and white inmates were of about the same age and economic background and had comparable criminal careers, they differed greatly in the relationship between their own sense of worth and their criminal prospects. As the expected value of crime increased, the self-esteem of the black inmates also increased, but that of the white inmates decreased. The more that white inmates identified with the criminal class, the less self-esteem they had, but this was not the case for blacks. Harris and Lewis concluded that whites who choose criminality "must traverse a greater moral and psychological distance than blacks making the same choice," perhaps because blacks come from a world in which crime is regarded as less illegitimate.[93]

There are, in addition, several volumes of research done among blacks in the South, notably those sponsored by the American Council on Education during the 1930s, that vividly portray the extent to which black boys and girls felt the stigma of the subordinate racial caste to which they had been assigned. Allison Davis and John Dollard give detailed personality profiles of several black youths, among whom were a number who reacted to racism with "a hatred which is held in check by fear."[94] The authors concluded, however, that important as racial status may be in the lives of these children, class differences were more important than racial ones: "In the formation of personality, caste is important as an added burden which Negroes must bear, rather than as the single most important factor about Negro life; it is easily outranked by general cultural and class factors."[95] Much the same conclusion was reached by Charles S. Johnson, the author of another volume in this series. "Segregation does not seem to generate active resentment" among the several hundred rural black youths Johnson studied,[96] and the racial antagonism that did exist seemed to vary with the age, intelligence, and social class of the child.[97]

These studies suggest what the theory of subcultural deviance neglects, namely, that there are important individual differences among blacks in how they react to oppression and segregation. All blacks suffer from racism, yet relatively few blacks become high-rate offenders. Oppression unquestionably generates resentment and hostility among some, but the connection between that hostility and later criminality, and the intervening effects of familial experiences, have yet to be demonstrated by any systematic research of which we are aware.

Contemporary anthropological accounts of street-corner life among black males confirm the existence of important differences in attitudes toward conventional and deviant life-styles, differences too great and too apparent to be ignored by any theory claiming that rage produces or tolerates crime. Elijah Anderson has recorded the daily comings and goings of black men in and around Jelly's bar on the south side of Chicago, among whom were some petty criminals. But most were men who called themselves "regulars," by which they meant they had or wanted jobs and desired to distance themselves from the "hoodlums." While some hoodlums felt wronged by the larger society and thus did not treat its rules as legitimate,[98] most did not talk so much about their anger or resentment as about their desire for "big money" and "being tough."[99] The objects of their conversation were rarely powerful whites whom they disliked, but rather successful black criminals whom they admired because they were getting "big money" or were ready to display their toughness.[100]

Moreover, if black crime has its roots partly in long-suppressed antiwhite sentiment, why is so much black crime—especially crimes of violence—directed not at whites but at other blacks? One can invent a psychological process by which rage-induced crime might be displaced against blacks, but it would be, to say the least, a complex process that would require a good deal of fancy theoretical footwork.

By the same token, if some blacks have been forced for so long to internalize, or even turn against themselves, the anger they felt, one must wonder why, when violence appears, blacks do not more often direct it at themselves. Overall, blacks have always had much lower suicide rates than whites; in 1978, for example, blacks were less than half as likely to kill themselves as were whites.[101] For reasons that are not entirely clear, black males in the age group twenty-five to thirty-four have about the same suicide rate as whites of that age, but both younger and older black males have significantly lower rates.[102]

None of these objections is fatal to the theory that some part of the higher black crime rates can be attributed to the release of pent-up anger, but they do suggest that the process is more complex, more constrained by other factors, and more sensitive to individual differences than Silberman and others imply.

Conclusions

There are facts and arguments that support each of the four major theories of black crime, but there is not enough systematic evidence to evaluate their claims carefully. What is wanted is a prospective, longitudinal study of black and white children growing up in a big city, a study that attends closely to constitutional factors; early familial and school experiences; the ways in which young people come into contact with peers, the labor market, and the criminal justice system; and the development of a set of values and an orientation toward the larger society. No such research has ever been done.

It is tempting—and probably true—to say that each theory is partially correct. William Julius Wilson has argued that it is the complex interaction between the economic and social position of blacks on the one hand and their personal and familial modes of adaptation on the other that has produced such social problems as high crime rates.[103] These are caused, in his view, not by the current level of discrimination but by the long history of it, not by short-term changes in the unemployment rates of blacks but by their long-term adverse position in the labor market coupled with a flooding of the cities by millions of young migrants seeking such jobs as existed. A family system that could survive the strains of urban life under normal conditions broke down under these extraordinary conditions and contributed, in Wilson's judgment, to a continuing tangle of pathology.

This eclectic view may be correct, but no one has yet unraveled in any detail the causal processes that underlie it. And given the sensitivity of any discussion of black crime and the very different policy implications that some persons draw from competing explanations of that crime rate, no theory will be saved from controversy merely because it is eclectic.

To the extent there are important constitutional factors at work, then programs would have to be tailored to individuals rather than to groups, a difficult and painstaking task. To the degree that net economic disadvantage is a cause, then widening opportunities and improving the criminal justice system will have, in time, the same effect on blacks that similar efforts had for other ethnic groups that, like Irish-Americans, once had unusually high crime rates. If there is a pattern of cultural pathology rooted in familial experiences, then change will be far more difficult and will require self-help efforts by blacks as well as resources from whites. And if black rage at accumulated injustice is the cause of black crime, then it is difficult to imagine any solution short of a long and painful reconstruction of deeply held human beliefs. The passionate certainty with which these competing views are held belies the tenuous and incomplete evidence that underlies them.

VI

CRIME,
HUMAN NATURE,
AND SOCIETY

19

PUNISHMENT AND
PERSONAL RESPONSIBILITY

To the extent that scientists can explain why people commit crimes, the case for punishment may appear weak. If a man breaks the law because he was abused as a child, is addicted to heroin, or is genetically inclined to drink alcohol without restraint and as a result unleash antisocial aggression, then putting him in jail for having broken the law may seem as pointless and cruel as jailing him for having developed hay fever or being schizophrenic. Society will still want to protect other people from his criminal tendencies, but it may seem obvious that it should do this in ways little different from how it goes about protecting others from a person carrying smallpox.

Just such a view was expressed by the eminent psychiatrist Karl Menninger in his book *The Crime of Punishment,* in which he argued against legal punishment altogether.[1] A convicted offender should be required to make good any losses of his victims, he suggested, and to bear the costs of his conviction, but beyond such "penalties," no additional pain should be inflicted, no "moral surcharge," as Menninger put it.[2] The moral surcharge, he believed, arises in a spirit of vengeance that is inappropriate in a civilized society:

> And just so long as the spirit of vengeance has the slightest vestige of re-spectability, so long as it pervades the public mind and infuses its evil upon the statute books of the law, we will make no headway toward the control of crime. We cannot assess the most appropriate and effective penalties so long as we seek to inflict retaliation.[3]

The retributive aspect of punishment repelled Menninger because, in our legal tradition, it presupposes that the offender acted freely, while modern psychiatry teaches "psychic determinism," the idea that every action is caused by the actor's circumstances, as they have impressed themselves on the psyche. The circumstances may be obscure, hidden from conscious awareness, or lost in a forgotten past, but according to the theory they, rather than the actor's free will, are in control. To hold the offender responsible, and thereupon to punish him for his evil intention, seemed to Menninger a barbarism, a throwback to a time before psychiatry had unearthed the buried stream that sweeps our behavior along. Rather than punishing offenders, Menninger argued, the criminal justice system should be rehabilitating them if possible, or, if not, isolating them in the most humane way possible from the potential targets of their disabilities.

Even if one does not accept psychiatric explanations of crime, the reader who is convinced that we can—or in time will be able to—explain individual differences in criminality may wonder whether punishment has any purpose. What is the point of punishing an offender for crimes that he was doomed to commit? One possible answer to that question has been given by some behavioral psychologists and economists.[4] They would argue that since behavior is determined by its consequences, punishment should be used only to alter the consequences in ways that, at the least cost to society, will reduce the probability of a crime, or crimes generally, being committed. For example, society might wish to alter the expected value of a robbery by either increasing its costs (by making more certain, more swift, or more severe the punishment for robbery) or increasing the benefits of alternatives to robbery (by making legitimate jobs more abundant or lucrative). A strict utilitarian—that is, a person who judges a policy solely by its consequences for the happiness or material well-being of specific persons—might well think it odd that we even want to call a policy of altering, by plan, the costs and benefits of alternative courses of action "punishment." It would be better, in this view, to call that policy one of "social control" and simply to experiment with various combinations of fines, penal sanctions, and job programs that provide the most cost-effective way of reducing crime.

We are of a different view. In our opinion, progress made toward explaining criminality does not reduce the need for punishment; it only enables us to think more clearly about how punishment might work on people who commit, or might commit, crimes. Moreover, the behavioral perspective on crime that we have set forth does not require us to limit our discussion of punishment to how the purely objective costs and benefits of crime and its alternatives might be altered. Rather, it requires us to explore the implications for punishment of the existence of conscience (and how it is formed) and of the sense of justice (and how it is satisfied). Conscience and justice (or equity) are not philosophical abstractions that clutter up the straightforward business of finding a scientific explanation for criminality; they are a necessary part of the explanation itself, and as such they (along with an individual's time horizon and sensitivity to the reinforcements associated with a course of action) can help us understand criminal behavior and the social structures that deal with it.

All these considerations come to the fore in the account given by Willard Gaylin, a psychiatrist much concerned about the criminal law, of a famous and deeply troubling case of homicide in *The Killing of Bonnie Garland*.[5]

In July 1977, twenty-three-year-old Richard Herrin hammered to death twenty-year-old Bonnie Garland, a girl with whom he was at that moment sharing a bed and with whom he had had an intimate relationship for three years, ever since they met when she was a freshman at Yale University and he a junior. But the relationship was foundering, evidently on the verge of collapsing altogether, and the threat of loss so deranged Herrin that he killed Garland while she lay sleeping next to him. Several hours later, he turned himself in to the authorities and confessed his crime, claiming that he had intended to commit suicide after the killing but had been unable to do so.

What made the case so famous and troubling were not merely the facts of the crime itself—a graduate of an elite college brutally killing his sweetheart—but the reaction of people who knew the principals and, also, the outcome of the trial. Protecting Richard Herrin from the full force of the law became a cause for many of his fellow students and for dedicated supporters in the official Catholic community, which included the Catholic Chaplaincy at Yale, the Catholic priest he went to first while still covered with blood, and members of the Christian Brothers in Albany, who took him in while he was on bail awaiting trial. What these people hoped and agitated for was compassion and forgiveness for Herrin. They were, it seems, moved not just by the facts of the case, but by Herrin himself, a former scholarship student who had come to Yale from an underprivileged Mexican-American family after having grown up in a Mexican-American barrio of Los Angeles.

At the trial, what had happened in the homicide was hardly in dispute; instead, the question was the extent to which Herrin's unhappy, perhaps pathological, state of mind should have been considered an extenuating factor in defining the crime of which he was to be found guilty. In New York State, where the killing took place, the law allows a charge of murder to be reduced to one of manslaughter if "extreme emotional disturbance" at the time of the act could be demonstrated. Evidently, the jury was convinced by the defense. The prosecution asked for a conviction for murder, but it received only a conviction for manslaughter. Instead of fifteen years to life, Herrin was sentenced to eight and one-third to twenty-five years. By the time he was interviewed by Gaylin, after serving more than two years in prison, Herrin was feeling that even the punishment for manslaughter was excessively severe, and so were some of his supporters.

The psychiatrist Gaylin recognized the power of psychic determinism no less than the psychiatrist Menninger. It was Gaylin who wrote, "Psychiatrically speaking, nothing is wrong—only sick. If an act is not a choice but merely the inevitable product of a series of past experiences, a man can be no more guilty of a crime than he is guilty of an abscess."[6] Yet Gaylin disapproved of the desire to spare Herrin the legal consequences of his act though he understood the desire well. For Gaylin, the law should exact retribution even for an act that he, as a psychiatrist, could see as the inevitable expression of psychopathology:

> The new psychological definition of human beings that had each of us operating in a reality different from those around us destroyed the actual world. But it is the actual world that the law must operate in [in] order to preserve equity. In our search for individual justice we must not destroy the sense that we are living in a fair and just state. . . . A just society traditionally does some disservice to its individual members. The common good demands sacrifice of the individual. That is the lesson in the most moral of doctrines. The community under Jehovah is a community of law and justice, and yet the prophets may demand the ultimate sacrifices, even unto death, for the preservation of the law and the people of the law.[7]

The issues in this case pose in dramatic form the relationship between the criminal law and human nature properly understood. In this chapter, we take up those issues in order to address the following questions: How can punishment be justified? What purpose does punishment serve in light of what we have learned about the causes of crime? Who should decide on the kind and amount of punishment, and on what grounds? Should those decisions depend on the offender's state of mind (what if he is "insane" or "not responsible" for his behavior?) or only on his actions? If crime can be explained, what becomes of our belief in free will?

The Uses of Punishment

The retributive function of punishment is just one of a set of uses that can be found in textbook discussions of legal punishment.[8] It is the one that arouses the most enduring, the deepest, the most divisive, and in some sense the most interesting questions, but it may not be the most important in practice, at least in the short run, if there are other reasons for using punishment about which people do not disagree so passionately, as there are and as we discuss below. Because of this, our system of legal punishment has continued to operate even while there have been profound disagreements about punishment as retribution. The disagreements have not incapacitated the legal system, but they have shaken public confidence in its morality and its fairness. They may also contribute to lawlessness by undermining the respect in which the law is held. In the long run, then, answers to the philosophical questions that surround punishment are not just academic.

What are the reasons for punishment, retributive and otherwise? It should be understood that the question refers to punishment in the sense of the legal sanction for a criminal act; whether the sanction should also be punishing in the psychological sense of causing pain or discomfort depends on the use being intended. We are not here considering the rehabilitation of offenders per se, although that may be a by-product or, in some people's eyes, a justification of legal punishment (see Chapter 15 for a discussion of rehabilitation), for rehabilitation is not necessarily a penalty set by due process. The list given below does not correspond precisely to any other list we have seen of the uses of punishment, but it approximates many of them.

Incapacitation

As long as legal punishment physically separates the convicted offender from the public, it may protect the public, though perhaps not fellow offenders. Prisons and jails serve this function, and so does execution. In an earlier era, so also did exile and transportation. Such punishments as fines, losses of license, or other privileges may not. In its pure form, incapacitation works, if it works at all, simply by removing opportunities for crime, but few if any actual legal punishments are pure in this sense. Prisons, exile, and surely execution have other qualities besides separating the convicted offender from potential victims. They are, in addition, disagreeable to say the least and may also be shameful. Inflicting suffering and guilt are, in and of themselves, characteristics of legal punishment that a society may or may not want to forgo, but the answer depends on whether incapacitation is viewed as its sole function. Making prisons more pleasant than they are now may seem right to someone who favors pure incapacitation, but not to someone who expects it to serve other uses as well.

Deterrence

This is the function served by the suffering associated with legal punishment. Like a child who learns to avoid hot stoves either by being burned for touching one or by observing someone else's expression of pain when touching one, so may a criminal learn not to break the law if it results in consequences sufficiently aversive to outweigh future occurrences of that, and other comparable, crime. In terms of the theory described in Chapter 2, this use of punishment corresponds to that part of the reward for noncrime that depends on avoidance of legal punishment. Without repeating the details of this relationship, we should note that there is no guarantee that a particular punishment will be strong enough to counteract the rewards of a particular crime for a particular offender—given the offender's time-discounting rates, drives for the gains of crime, sensitivities to the punishments used by the criminal justice system, etc. Punishment may sometimes fail to deter, and may even exacerbate a given offender's criminal activities, by reducing legitimate options for employment, leaving the offender embittered about society and its conventions, or exposing him to the bad company he may encounter in prison. In principle, however, punishment works; that is to say, if a connection has been established between action and aversive consequence, and if the aversive consequence is adequately intense, then, barring confounding influences such as those just mentioned, the action will be prevented or reduced in frequency.[9]

This effect of punishment on an offender is usually called *particular* (or *special*) deterrence. It is usually contrasted with *general* deterrence, which is the effect of the punishment on others besides the offender himself. Others, learning that an offender has suffered for his crimes, are deterred if this knowledge strengthens their own rewards for noncrime. Indeed, others may be more susceptible to deterrence than the offender is, for the offender is someone who has already betrayed an insensitivity to legal punishment. An argument can be made for using punishment for general deterrence even when special deterrence is likely to fail.

Moral Education

As Chapter 2 pointed out, punishment acts not only on the rewards for noncrime but on the rewards for crime. If deterrence deals with punishment on the basis of "rational calculation," as that notion was used by traditional utilitarian theorists (see next chapter), moral education deals with it as the basis for conscience. A punished action is not only reduced in frequency so as to avoid further punishment, a change that depends on the process of instrumental conditioning, it is also likely, through classical conditioning, to take on a quality of disapproval. Crime is held in check not only by the objective risk of punishment but by the subjective sense of wrongdoing. If such a sense of wrongdoing develops, it would be contemporaneous with the punished act, hence not subject to the diluting effects of delays and uncertainties of legal punishment. Because it has become part of the illegal act itself, this effect of punishment ceases being dependent on the accidents of law enforcement. For those reasons, punishment as moral education almost certainly reduces more crime than punishment as deterrence. An internalized prohibition against offending is like an additional cost of crime, possibly strong enough to prevent its occurrence even when there is no risk of being caught and punished by society.

Once established, conscience operates without external agents to enforce it, yet it arises to begin with in society's abhorrence of certain acts, encountered either in the informal disapproval that the law institutionalizes or in formal legal punishments. Many automobile drivers stop for red lights even when they are on the road late at night with neither police nor other drivers to witness a transgression. For them, the reward for running the light does not overcome the internalized prohibitions against it.

Like deterrence, the educational use of punishment depends on the aversiveness of the legal sanction. A punishment that causes no psychic pain, either because it is not enforced or because it is too mild, will not support the classical conditioning whose effects we ordinarily identify as conscience. Similarly, individuals vary in their susceptibility to this form of conditioning, as several of the earlier chapters have suggested (see Chapters 6–9 for the evidence that cognitive, temperamental, and family-rearing differences are involved). It is not just varying risks of arrest and varying reasons for speed that allow some people to run the light while others stop.

Also like deterrence, moral education can be either "particular" or "general." Punishment may classically condition not just the person who suffers the punishment, but others also, assuming they have some exposure to it. Legal punishment as public spectacle strengthens noncrime by publicizing the risks of apprehension and conviction, and it weakens crime by inculcating disapproval. It has been said that "a community which is too ready to forgive the wrongdoer may end by condoning the crime."[10] If punishment tells the members of a community what it considers wrong, the absence of punishment must tell them what it does not consider wrong. Pickpockets may well have found the crowds at public executions good to work, as some who have denigrated punishment point out, but that may have had something to do with how engrossed the crowd was as it absorbed the lesson of the law while enjoying the spectacle.

Retribution

According to the ancient idea of an eye for an eye or a tooth for a tooth— the *lex talionis,* as the Biblical version (Exodus 21) is called—punishment should exact from the offender a degree of suffering that matches the offense. Old as the idea is, it has lately been much in question. About punishment as retribution or retaliation for wrongdoing, a distinguished textbook on criminal law says: "This is the oldest theory of punishment, and the one which is least accepted today by theorists (although it still commands considerable respect from the general public)."[11] One should be curious, if not suspicious, about a claim that an idea that has endured for thousands of years and through all the cultural changes of those millennia, has suddenly, in our time, fallen into disrepute. In fact, the textbook's comment, published in 1972, seemed a fair characterization of the prevailing (though hardly unanimous) legal opinion on the matter at that time and for at least a generation before it. Punishment as retaliation had for some time seemed to express a lesser degree of humaneness than many theorists demanded of modern civilization. If the *lex talionis* was the harsh spirit of the Old Testament, then forgiveness of the offender's offenses, as in the reaction of some clerics to the case of Richard Herrin that started this chapter, was the more benign spirit of the New Testament.

But within just a few years, it was clear that the tide had already been shifting. Legal thinking had been moving back toward the retributive inclinations of the "general public" even as textbooks were disapproving of them. For example, Herbert L. Packer and Norval Morris, both highly regarded professors of law, published books suggesting that retribution sets limits on the severity of punishment imposed for utilitarian purposes.[12] This does not take us all the way back to the *lex talionis,* but it certainly makes retribution more than a minor reason for punishment. The practical purpose of punishment may be to reduce crime by offenders and others, the argument went, but the state was not free to punish without restraint; it could only inflict suffering to the extent that the conduct was blameworthy and therefore warranted retaliation, a view that we share and will discuss below.

Similar arguments turn up in court rulings (about which more later) and in the recommendations of various institutions. A Committee for the Study of Incarceration, supported by private foundations and legal agencies, staffed by prominent legal and correctional scholars and public administrators, and chaired by a former U.S. Senator, Charles E. Goodell, known for his liberal views on social policy, issued a report (written by its executive secretary, Andrew von Hirsch) arguing that retribution is an essential—indeed, the dominant—function of legal punishment: "The principle of commensurate deserts, in our opinion, is a requirement of justice."[13] The report acknowledged, and approved of, the practical benefits of punishment—namely, incapacitation, deterrence, and moral education—but considered retribution (though preferring the term "deserts") to be more important, for reasons of equity: "The social benefits of punishing do not alone justify depriving the convicted offender of his rights; it is also necessary that the deprivation be deserved."[14]

It may seem that we need to explain why retribution has returned to favor, after seeming to be eclipsed by the other uses of punishment. Actually, it would be more appropriate to invert the question, to ask why retribution, the most ancient of all uses, temporarily fell into disfavor with philosophers and social theorists, if not with the general public. We will not try to prove our answer to the latter question, but we guess that it had something to do with the modern belief in the perfectibility of mankind and the responsibility of the state to strive for that perfection. The claim that psychiatry and the other behavioral sciences can, or soon will be able to, change human behavior encouraged those who rejected retribution. A crime then becomes, in this modern view, an occasion when society should try to change behavior rather than to retaliate. Punishment as retribution looks backward, at what the offender did; by contrast, punishment as incapacitation, deterrence, or moral education looks ahead at what offenders will do.

Retribution, unlike incapacitation, deterrence, and moral education, does not presuppose that an offender, or anyone else, will be reformed or restrained by punishment. The punishment is, rather, often justified simply on the grounds that it is just, not on the grounds that it is effective. Immanuel Kant, the eighteenth-century German philosopher, expressed this conviction in a memorable passage:

> Even if a civil society were to dissolve itself by common agreement of all its members (for example, if the people inhabiting an island decided to separate and disperse themselves around the world), the last murderer remaining in prison must be executed, so that everyone will duly receive what his actions are worth and so that the bloodguilt thereof will not be fixed on the people because they failed to insist on carrying out the punishment; for if they fail to do so, they may be regarded as accomplices in this public violation of legal justice.[15]

For Kant, retribution was a *sufficient* justification for punishment; for modern commentators who accept the validity of retribution, it is usually only *necessary*, not sufficient.* Most modern theorists also require that there be some basis for believing that the punishment will reduce criminal behavior, if not the offender's then the general public's. A punishment inflicted in total secrecy on an offender who is known to be already cured of his criminal tendencies may satisfy a pure retributionist, but it will not satisfy many modern writers on the subject. Packer, for example, said that retribution and prevention are each necessary but not sufficient reasons for punishment; together they are sufficient.[18]

Defenses of retribution center on the notion of equity. An offender has violated an implicit social contract that ties the members of a community together. The contract gives the members rights to goods obtained only in legal ways. Goods gained illegally violate the equity principle, as it was defined in Chapter 2, because an illegal act is by definition not an acceptable input. Breaking the law gives an offender an unfair advantage in the pursuit of reward. Hence the criminal's ratio of gains to inputs will seem to other parties to the social contract to be unacceptably high. The criminal is therefore said to "owe a debt" to society. Punishment as retribution balances the books. Crimes of violence also earn "goods" in a metaphoric sense—they are, at least at the moment they occur, rewards exceeding what has been earned by legitimate inputs—and are similarly reckoned as a debt requiring repayment.

The equity argument may take different forms. It may be said that the state must exact retribution so that the victims or their allies do not feel they have to do it. Or perhaps the state restores equity so that the injured parties do not exact more suffering from the offender than the community as a whole considers just. When the individual restores equity, it is revenge; when the legal system does it, it is justice. James Fitzjames Stephen, the Victorian legal historian, said that the criminal law stands in the same relation to the urge for revenge as marriage does to sexual passion.[19] In both cases, society's institutions are responding to and channeling innate drives. Alternatively, one might argue that the debt is paid not so much to satisfy the community's desire for equity as to relieve the offender's own presumed sense of guilt at having unjustly gained rewards to which he or she was not entitled, especially if obtained at the cost of the suffering of others.

---

* There are modern Kantians too. For example, Jeffrie Murphy writes that "a retributive theory of punishment . . . is the only morally acceptable theory of punishment."[16] He adds that the "twentieth century's faddish movement toward a 'scientific' or therapeutic response to crime runs grave risks of undermining the foundations of justice."[17]

How Much Punishment?

The first three uses of punishment described above mesh in obvious ways with our theory of criminal behavior. Incapacitation reduces crime by reducing the opportunities for crime; deterrence, by increasing the rewards for noncrime; and moral education, by decreasing the rewards for crime. These three can be characterized as the utilitarian aspects of punishment, which naturally find places in a theory that views behavior as guided by its consequences. But retribution fits into the theoretical framework too, although the connection is more subtle. Calculations of equity unavoidably involve collective comparisons, and are therefore unavoidably communal. Depending as it does on equity, retribution takes into account the relation of all the members of a society to a social institution rather than merely the relationship between individual offenders and their potential victims.

If only incapacitation or *special* deterrence or moral education were at issue, there would be no natural limits on punishment besides those depending on the state of the offender. A reformed offender, if that could be established without doubt, would be released, no matter how heinous a crime he or she had committed. An unreformed offender could be kept in prison indefinitely, no matter how trivial the crime. *General* deterrence or moral education would allow the criminal justice system to punish the wholly innocent for the sake of impressing the public at large with the power of the law. Only retribution saves the system from such absurdities as murderers released in haste or jaywalkers detained for life. The special role of retribution is to govern the magnitude of punishment that a society can exact for given offenses and still seem just.

It has mainly fallen to legislators to decide how much punishment a given crime deserves, often in the form of a range of sentences. Presumably, the legislature represents public sentiment when it chooses a range for the crime. The particular circumstances of each case, as established in a legal proceeding, then determine where within the range an offender should fall. The legislative mandate is not absolute, for it may be measured against various legal precedents that are based in part on the Eighth Amendment to the U.S. Constitution (and beyond that to English common law and the Magna Carta) which prohibits "excessive bail," "excessive fines," and "cruel and unusual punishments." A recent case may help clarify how the system attempts to find the "right" punishment.

In 1979, a state court in South Dakota sentenced Jerry Buckley Helm to life imprisonment with no possibility of parole.[20] His crime had been to pass a bad check for $100. Ordinarily, passing bad checks carried a maximum punishment in South Dakota of five years in prison and a fine of $5,000, but Helm's record of six prior felony convictions (three burglaries and one each of obtaining money under false pretenses, grand larceny, and drunk driving) raised the ceiling to life in prison, according to state law.

The sentence was upheld on appeal by the South Dakota Supreme Court and by the federal district court, but then, in the federal court of appeals, it was reversed. Finally, in an unusual 5–4 decision, the reversal was affirmed in the U.S. Supreme Court. The reversal was based on a judgment that the original sentence, though in keeping with state law, was nevertheless "disproportionate," a violation of the Eighth Amendment. Writing for the slim majority, Justice Lewis Powell said:

> We hold as a matter of principle that a criminal sentence must be proportionate to the crime for which the defendant has been convicted. Reviewing courts . . . should grant substantial deference to the broad authority that legislatures necessarily possess in determining the types and limits of punishments for crimes, as well as to the discretion that trial courts possess in sentencing convicted criminals. But no penalty is *per se* constitutional. . . . A single day in prison may be unconstitutional in some circumstances.[21]

This is an argument based on punishment limited by considerations of equity (i.e., "proportionality") rather than anything else, such as incapacitation, deterrence, or moral education. The dissenting minority accepted the principle but objected to having the U.S. Supreme Court, rather than the legislature and courts of South Dakota, apply it. Chief Justice Warren Burger, for the minority, wrote:

> The Court's traditional abstention from reviewing sentences of imprisonment to ensure that punishment is "proportionate" to the crime is well founded in history. . . . Today's conclusion by five Justices that they are able to say that one offense has less "gravity" than another is nothing other than a bald substitution of individual subjective moral values for those of the legislature.[22]

In the transcript of the trial, it is plain that the sentencing judge was thinking of other uses of punishment in addition to equitable retribution—incapacitation, for one thing, and possibly also general deterrence and moral education—when he said:

> I think you certainly earned this sentence and certainly proved that you're an habitual criminal and the record would indicate that you're beyond rehabilitation and that the only prudent thing to do is to lock you up for the rest of your natural life, so you won't have further victims of your crimes. . . . You'll have plenty of time to think this one over.[23]

A "proportionate" punishment is usually justified in terms of both the harm done by the offender and his or her culpability. These are the negative "inputs" that the legal punishment should offset, just as reward is measured against the magnitude of the legitimate inputs that a person invests in gaining the rewards. A greater harm or a greater culpability calls for a greater punishment, according to the principle of just deserts, just as a greater legitimate input calls for a greater reward. Such quantities are admittedly subjective, but that is as it must be to satisfy the equally subjective sense of justice that the criminal law strives to achieve. Society has attempted to deal with the issue of subjectivity by dispersing the judgment broadly, by having, for example, a representative legislature establishing a range of punishments within which the courts must operate. Subjective as these quantities are, they are inescapable for any system of justice. It may, for example, be likely that a poor man who commits theft and who has little to lose needs a greater punishment to be deterred than a rich man who has much to lose. Yet our instincts rebel at this utilitarian argument if the poor man seems less culpable. If he is less culpable, he deserves less punishment. When utility is pitted against equity, utility often loses. And when it does, it is because we instinctively measure punishment more against a standard of retribution than of utility. Retribution is not only important to a scientific account of criminal behavior and criminal justice, but, as an expression of the human concern for equity, it is central to any understanding of social institutions that govern the relations among people.

Personal Responsibility

Barely two months after his inauguration in January 1981, President Ronald Reagan was shot and seriously wounded on a Washington, D.C., street as he and his party were leaving a hotel, in full view of an American television audience. Besides the President, three other men were hit, including one left permanently damaged by a bullet in the brain. The assailant, also in full view on television, was John W. Hinckley, Jr., a young man in the grip of an obsessive romantic fantasy about a movie actress. The shooting, Hinckley apparently thought, would demonstrate the depth of his devotion to the actress, and would also prove to his educated and well-to-do family how much he needed their solicitude.

The public's reaction to the shooting was scarcely greater than its reaction, fifteen months later, to the jury's verdict that Hinckley was innocent on the grounds of insanity of each of the charges brought against him.[24] The verdict did not free Hinckley, but it sent him to a mental hospital, rather than a prison, and it gave him a chance to petition the attending physicians for release at six-month intervals, rather than to have to endure a term of punishment for attempted murder.

The trial had lasted eight weeks, with most of the time consumed by arguments over Hinckley's state of mind and whether it justified acquittal. In Washington, the burden of proof fell on the prosecution to show that Hinckley was not so impaired in mental capacity that he could not be held responsible for his actions. Its case evidently failed to persuade the jury, much to the dismay of almost everyone who expressed a reaction publicly. The U.S. Attorney General proposed a drastic curtailment of the insanity defense. The United States Congress passed a law that shifted the burden of proof, so that now the defense must prove that an accused person is insane. The American Psychiatric Association called for a clear limitation on what a psychiatrist on the witness stand as an expert should be allowed to testify to.[25] Numerous politicians, editorialists, psychiatrists, lawyers, and legal scholars criticized the trial—the judge for the excessive complexity of his instructions to the jury, the statute for placing the burden of proof on the prosecution, the jury for its lack of wisdom or understanding, the expert psychiatric witnesses for prosecution and defense for their unprofessionalism, the legal system as a whole for not exacting retribution for a terrible crime, and so on—but no consensus has yet to emerge about how the outcome could properly have been averted or about how the laws should be changed.

Many people were reminded of another famous case involving an attack on a public official, in which it also seemed that a desire for fairness to an offender had undermined the broader purposes of the criminal law. On a London street in January 1843, a young Scotsman named Daniel M'Naghten shot Edward Drummond, private secretary to Sir Robert Peel, the British Prime Minister. A few days later, Drummond died of his injury. The shooting had taken place in broad daylight, within sight and hearing of a policeman who heard M'Naghten say immediately afterward, "He shall not disturb my mind any longer."[26] Investigation soon revealed that M'Naghten thought he was shooting the Prime Minister himself, whom he had for some time delusionally blamed for tormenting him. He had, for example, told his landlady in Glasgow two years before that "there were devils in human shape seeking his life."[27] The devils, it seems, were Tories, the party led by Peel.

At M'Naghten's trial there was no great enthusiasm for punishing him with the hanging that was usual for capital crimes. English common law had a long tradition of taking into account an offender's mental state. A person could be held responsible, hence punished, only for acts committed under certain conditions. Actions judged criminal at the hands of a normal adult would traditionally be acquitted, or not tried, or their punishments suspended, if committed by children or the profoundly mentally retarded or the insane. Since M'Naghten certainly seemed insane, the legal point at issue in the trial was to establish a connection between his abnormality and his offense. Without much ado the connection was established and he was acquitted on the grounds of insanity, which must have been small comfort to M'Naghten, who spent the remaining twenty-two years of his life in insane asylums.

But that was hardly the end of the M'Naghten case, for the acquittal displeased Queen Victoria, the reigning monarch, as well as the Lord Chancellor and many other spokesmen at the time, for reasons that are reminiscent of the objections to the acquittal of John Hinckley—the concern that judgments of insanity were hard to substantiate, that the failure to convict and punish undermined the criminal law, and that injury to a public figure was not redressed. At the Queen's request, the House of Lords called upon the fifteen judges of the English common-law courts to consider and to codify the notion of acquittal on the grounds of insanity. The results of those deliberations have since been referred to as the M'Naghten rules, or the M'Naghten test, and are the point of departure for most modern discussions of the role of insanity in questions of personal responsibility for criminal behavior.

To pass the M'Naghten test, a defense on the grounds of insanity must prove that the accused, at the time of the offense, was suffering from a mental disease resulting in a defect of understanding such that he (or she) did not know what he was doing, *or,* if he knew what he was doing, did not know that it was wrong. The M'Naghten test would, for example, excuse a homicide committed under a delusion that it was self-defense, but not one that was revenge for an unpaid debt. Although delusions provoked both killings, only the former hid the wrongfulness of the act. While the test clarified certain features of an insanity defense, a moment's reflection should show that it uncovered even more unanswered questions: What counts as a mental disease or a defect of understanding? Are mental diseases that cause defects of emotion or volition, rather than of "understanding," ineligible for an insanity defense? What does it mean to "know" what one is doing? How incomplete must the self-knowledge be before it passes the test? Must the accused know that the act was morally, or only legally, wrong? In addition, the M'Naghten rules dealt with such other questions as the role of expert testimony and of judge and jury in cases invoking an insanity defense, and these too left unresolved difficulties.[28]

Within a year of the publication of the M'Naghten rules, legal jurisdictions in the United States were already beginning to modify them presumably to improve them, and they are at it still. For example, in a murder case in Massachusetts in 1844, the judge instructed the jury in the M'Naghten test, then added that the accused could be acquitted if it had been proved that in committing the homicide, he had "acted from an irresistible and uncontrollable impulse."[29] The "irresistible impulse" defense was a way of broadening the range of mental disease that could excuse an offender, adding a defect in volition to the purely cognitive defects allowed by the M'Naghten test. Many other changes in, and alternatives to, the M'Naghten test have been proposed and tried in the United States and elsewhere,[30] but the continuing controversies, as illustrated in the Hinckley case, prove that the solution remains out of reach.

What is this concept of "personal responsibility" that our legal institutions have so exhaustively, and as yet unsuccessfully, tried to define with the provisions for insanity? In the literature of legal philosophy, one can find countless discussions of the insanity defense, but it is sufficient for our purposes to consider a standard explanation: Since the only moral justification for inflicting suffering on an offender is as just deserts, and since deserts can only be just if the offense was freely committed, a just society should punish only freely committed acts. In the words of a newspaper editorial supporting some sort of insanity defense on the occasion of the Hinckley case, "Our criminal code is founded on the idea of rational choices made by individuals free to do good or evil."[31] Insanity, the argument goes, may deprive one of the freedom to commit a justly punishable act. In legal writings, the critical phrase is *mens rea,* the guilty mind that freely intended the malicious act and that insanity may preclude. In almost all criminal cases, the prosecution must prove that the accused committed, intended to commit, and could have refrained from committing, the criminal act.* The recurrent theme for the concept of personal responsibility, hence for the appropriateness of punishment, is behavior freely and intentionally engaged in.

The difficulty is that this conception places the legal sanction against offensive behavior in direct confrontation with the science of human behavior. If society should not punish acts that science has shown to have been caused by antecedent conditions, then every advance in knowledge about why people behave as they do may shrink the scope of criminal law. If, for example, it is shown that sex offenders suffer from abnormal hormones combined with certain atypical relations with their parents, then, by the existing

---

* The exceptions to these usual requirements of due process are laws that specifically exclude demonstrations of guilty intent—for example, curfew laws—or laws that establish strict liability for certain acts—for example, selling contaminated milk.

standards of responsibility, why should their attorneys not demand acquittal on grounds of bad hormones combined with a particular family history? Likewise, a mugger should be excused if science proves that nonectomorphic mesomorphs such as he, who are from indigent families and who do poorly in school, are impelled to break the law. The actual explanations are no doubt more complex, but the principle should be clear.

Knowledge of human behavior has, in fact, not advanced on many fronts to the point where such challenges to the legitimacy of punishment have become irresistible. But, here and there, it is apparent that the challenges are well begun. Samuel Butler, in his Utopian novel, *Erewhon,* had the criminals being sent to doctors for the afflictions that drove them to crime and the sick people punished for not taking care of themselves.[32] At least with the first half of that, Karl Menninger, the psychiatrist whose views we discussed at the beginning of this chapter, would agree. Lady Barbara Wootton, the British criminologist, suggested replacing the concept of legal responsibility with a determination by experts of the offender's prognosis for future criminal behavior,[33] and, if necessary, a prescription for whatever therapy was called for by the criminogenic condition. The modern liberal position on criminal justice is rehabilitative, not retributive, because the offender is believed to have been driven to his crimes, rather than to have committed them freely and intentionally, as *mens rea* requires.

Scientific explanations of criminal behavior do, in fact, undermine a view of criminal responsibility based on freedom of action. And it is also correct that this book has taken pains to show that much, if not all, criminal behavior can be traced to antecedent conditions. Yet we view legal punishment as essential, a virtual corollary of the theory of criminal behavior upon which the book is built. The British legal philosopher H. L. A. Hart has formulated an account of criminal responsibility that seems to us to resolve the apparent paradox of holding people responsible for actions that they could not help committing,[34] and to do so in a way that fits naturally with the theory of criminal behavior proposed in this book. An act deserves punishment, according to the principle of equity, if it was committed without certain explicit *excusing conditions.* In Hart's scheme, free will is a negative, rather than a positive, attribute of behavior: For the purposes of the law, behavior is considered as "free" if not subject to these excusing conditions. One such condition is insanity, but there are others, such as duress, provocation, entrapment, mistake, and accident. It is not that the behavior is *actually* free in the absence of the excusing conditions, but that, without them, society directs its disapproval, when it punishes, at the very sources of the behavior it abhors—malice, lust, treachery, greed, envy, cruelty, hatred, and the other precipitating impulses toward crime. By proving that excusing conditions are absent and then punishing, the criminal justice system sharply outlines for its citizens the choice between crime and noncrime and then makes sure that the appropriate consequences are attached to each alternative. To the extent that excusing conditions can be demonstrated, punishment should be mitigated or totally suspended.

A comparable set of excusing conditions exempts people from rights to positive reward. Society protects legitimate work with laws against copyright and patent infringements, plagiarism, and violations of civil contracts. In general, it tries to assure that people earn their rewards in approved ways. It may place extra taxes on windfall profits, inheritances, and winnings from lotteries, but not on the merited rewards of the Nobel Prize or of inventing and selling a successful product. The principle of equity, which governs both just reward and just punishment, has nothing to do with freedom of action but everything to do with the relationships among people and between them and society as a whole.

Conclusion

We started this chapter by asking some questions—about the appropriateness of punishment in a theory that treats criminal behavior as the outcome of social and biological influences—which now we attempt to answer. Punishment incapacitates, deters, and educates morally, but those justifications alone would seem insufficient to many members of a civilized society. From the vantage point of our theory, it seems insufficient to us too. In addition to those utilitarian purposes, punishment must also restore the equity that the criminal offense violated, which is to say, punishment must seem to people to be just. A society's calculation of just punishment obeys the same underlying principle that governs the fair distribution of rewards, a principle that is often implemented only with difficulty and uncertainty, but without which a society would seem, and be, unjust.

Legislatures and courts are the formal instruments for setting just penalties, but they must conform to the prevailing consensus on what is fair or the legal system loses legitimacy. Deviating from the consensus in either direction damages society. An excessively cruel system of law may control the behavior of its citizens even more strictly than a just one, but people will surely hate it, may resist submitting to it, and, if the occasion ever arises, may try to overthrow it. Too lax a system of law will fail to satisfy the public desire for justice and thereby risk vigilantism. It will fail to deter and to educate morally. And it will impair the public's sense of respect for the law. Inconsistent enforcement of laws will also seem unjust and fail to serve the purposes of the law, from incapacitation to retribution.

The legal concept of personal responsibility, usually couched in the vocabulary of free will, is part of our idea of a proper system too, even though we do not believe that behavior is literally and wholly "free" in any scientific sense of the term. As the sciences of behavior evolve, it will become more and more apparent how tied human actions are to the circumstances in which they occur, but the legal system will continue to need to determine whether an offense deserves punishment. The confrontation between science and the criterion of free action has already distorted and inhibited the operation of the criminal justice system, as this chapter has illustrated. As scientific knowledge grows, the distortions and inhibitions will worsen, unless the criterion is dropped, replaced by a conception that preserves personal responsibility without denying, perhaps even making practical use of, the growing knowledge about the sources of criminal behavior.

The punishments of the legal system are an essential part of the story of why criminal behavior may or may not take place. Avoiding punishment provides a major incentive for noncrime, and, as internalized prohibitions arise in conditioning, it exacts costs for crime that are not easily vitiated by occasional failures in law enforcement. If the legal system stopped punishing offenders, and no other institution took over its functions, criminal behavior would rise because it was no longer deterred and no longer disapproved. This is no different, at least in principle, from what would happen if the labor market ceased paying more for industrious, skilled workers than for sluggish, incompetent ones. Other things being equal, we would expect the quality of labor to decline and the value placed on good work to decline too. When equity constrains punishment, in the case of crime, and reward, in the case of labor, people intuitively accept the principle (if not the concrete results in every instance) as just. So long as legal punishments are no more or less severe than dictated by the principle of equity, they will simultaneously control the actions of people and satisfy their desire for justice.

20

HUMAN NATURE AND THE POLITICAL ORDER

The argument of this book is that there *is* a human nature that develops in intimate settings out of a complex interaction of constitutional and social factors, and that this nature affects how people choose between the consequences of crime and its alternatives. Young men are everywhere more likely than females or older persons to commit common street crimes, because of the way nature and nurture combine to make male children more impulsive and aggressive and less concerned with the well-being of others than are females or adults. Most male children outgrow such behavior, but whenever the socializing processes of family and community are insufficient to extend the time horizon or enlarge the sympathies of young boys, the incidence of crime among them will tend to remain high. Even when the conditions of family and community life are favorable, a few young persons (especially those displaying psychopathic personalities) may persist in criminality. Among the many who experiment with crime and the few who persist in it, the contingencies of reinforcements and punishments will have an effect on the rate at which they offend, but it may often be less than the effect obtained by the presence or absence of internalized restraints on crime, notably conscience and a desire for the good opinion of others. Society, by the institutions it designs and the values it sustains, affects the extent to which families and communities are able and willing to lengthen the time horizon, inculcate a conscience, and instill a concern for others among the young in ways that make an orderly society possible.

Though there is much we have yet to learn and though controversies abound over how best to interpret what we do know, the facts summarized in the preceding chapters rivet our attention on the earliest stages of the life cycle. There are high-rate offenders who are late bloomers, there are mass murderers who first kill in middle age, there are serious delinquents who enter the path of righteousness when they reach their early twenties. But these cases account for the minority of all those persons who frequently commit serious crimes. We have seen that what happens in school has some effect on criminality, that television and the mass media *may* have a small impact, and that experiences in the community and the labor market no doubt make some difference; but after all is said and done, the most serious offenders are those boys who begin their delinquent careers at a very early age. The correlation between early age of onset and a high rate of offending is one of the best-established generalizations in all of criminology. As the twig is bent . . .

That is not a counsel of despair or an argument for the inevitability of crime among certain kinds of persons. Society's discovery that some young persons enter school with a serious learning disability was not greeted with a sense of hopelessness or scornfully rejected as the misguided conclusion of social Darwinism; instead, it was hailed as a good reason for abandoning educational methods that punished slow learners and as a new opportunity for finding better ways to identify and help those youngsters most at risk.

We are aware that criminality is not quite the same as a learning disability, though we remind our readers that until recently many people thought they were the same ("he won't learn because he's a rotten kid"). When we explain such a disability, or when we give an account of many other forms of behavior—for example, anxiety, extroversion, athletic prowess, or school achievement—there is rarely much dispute about the conclusion that both constitutional factors and social circumstances, especially those occurring at an early age, are properly part of the explanation. But explaining criminality arouses our moral and political sensibilities, and as a result many persons are more inclined to accept one set of explanations for crime over another almost without regard to the facts.

To some extent, that is understandable. Crime brings a person into conflict with society; having violated its rules, he risks shame and punishment. It is the mark of a decent and compassionate instinct for people to fear any explanation of crime that could be interpreted as suggesting that some individuals are destined, beyond hope, to experience those penalties.

We offer no such theory of predestination. If one asks whether criminals are born or made, the answer, in one sense, is that they are both and, in a more important sense, that the question is badly phrased. The words "born or made" imply that some part of criminality may be assigned, categorically and permanently, to constitutional (including genetic) factors and the other part, categorically and permanently, to social factors. Such an effort at partitioning variations in criminality between two types of causes neglects, obviously, the complex interactions that exist between those causes.

This partitioning, properly done, may make sense when the trait to be explained is relatively stable and easily measured. For example, it may make perfectly good sense to say that differences among persons in their allergy to ragweed is "largely" (or 80 percent, or whatever) attributable to their genetic makeup. An allergic reaction can be reliably, repeatedly, and measurably induced in a subject by means of a double-blind patch test. Though some people may be allergic to ragweed for psychological reasons having nothing to do with constitutional factors, such persons can be identified and sorted out. It also may make some sense to speak of the degree to which schizophrenia is heritable. Schizophrenia is a mental condition that can often (but not always) be diagnosed by independent observers, that is much more common (i.e., concordant), especially in its more severe forms, among identical than among fraternal twins, and that is better treated with drugs than with verbal therapy. But how much of the variation among persons in their tendency (and it is only a tendency) to display schizophrenic symptoms is genetic is hard to say, because the chemicals in the blood that are associated with the condition may be produced, to unknown degrees, by both genetic factors and environmental stress. Among the sources of that stress is the behavior of other family members, some of whom may themselves be constitutionally predisposed to schizophrenia.

Criminality is an even more difficult problem because it is harder to measure its incidence and prevalence (schizophrenics do not usually conceal their aberrant behavior; criminals usually do), because we do not have any good clues as to what biochemical agents may be responsible for putting individuals at risk, and because we know of no drugs that constitute an effective treatment for it.

Nevertheless, the evidence from Part II of this book leaves little doubt, we think, that constitutional factors are implicated, to an unknown but not trivial degree, in the prevalence of high-rate offending. The problem is to acquire a better understanding of how those factors interact with familial and other social experiences.

The Interaction Problem

The lay reader will probably think it so obvious that constitutional and social factors interact in producing human behavior as to wonder why it is necessary to explore the matter. There are two reasons: First, many of our professional colleagues either deny the importance of constitutional factors altogether or argue that they are, at best, only trivially implicated in criminality. Second, even the lay reader willing to consider constitutional factors often uses, unthinkingly, the language of pure social causation in explaining behavior. Some examples drawn from the previous chapters will illustrate this tendency.

It is widely accepted that discordant families produce troublesome children. We have already shown that this is not necessarily the case; one can identify youth who are, in the title of an important book on this subject, "vulnerable but invincible."[1] But we can also show that some families are more likely to *become* discordant if they must deal with a troublesome child.[2] An impulsive, hyperactive young boy may lead his parents to argue about how best to cope with his behavior, and these arguments may in turn reinforce the tendency of the boy to make unreasonable demands and exploit parental discord for his own advantage. Constitutional factors are implicated in the boy's behavior, but they interact with familial factors that are in part a response to behavior of (to the parents) unknown origin and in part the result of one or both parents themselves being impulsive or aggressive owing to some combination of constitutional and social factors.

We know that parents treat little boys differently from little girls. That difference in treatment explains some of the differences in behavior of boys and girls. But parents also treat boys differently from girls in part because boys tend, from earliest infancy, to behave differently from girls. Recall the study of pseudohermaphrodites in the Dominican Republic which we discussed in Chapter 4. Note also those experiments in which infants dressed in such a way as to conceal their gender were presented to adults for play. The adults were told which infants were boys and which girls, but in fact those identities had been randomly assigned. The way in which the adults played with the babies reflected *both* their own beliefs about how to play with boys and with girls *and* the sex-specific behavior of the infants themselves.[3]

Children from large families are, other things being equal, more likely to become delinquent than children from small ones. Unless we have a comprehensive theoretical perspective on delinquency, how we interpret that fact will depend on our beliefs about what *ought* to be the explanation. If we worry about economic disadvantage, we may assume that large families produce more delinquents because the per capita incomes of such families will be lower (and thus the financial stress will be higher) than similar families with fewer children. If we worry about the psychological environment, we may suppose that each child in a large family gets less parental attention than each child in a smaller one. We should also consider a third possibility: namely, that parents who have many children may themselves differ importantly from parents who have but a few, and these differences—in temperament, intelligence, or competence—may not be associated with any of the obvious socioeconomic factors taken into account in our analyses.

Everyone knows that criminals tend to have poorer employment records than noncriminals. That fact may reflect a necessary choice of available criminal opportunities over nonexistent legitimate ones, a rational preference for more lucrative criminal enterprises over less lucrative jobs, or the existence of certain traits that make offenders unattractive to employers even when jobs are abundantly available. Those traits, in turn, may be the result of social learning (growing up in a slum in which regular employment seems either hopeless or stupid), school experiences (failing to acquire the skills necessary for employment), family life (learning the advantages of seeing what you can get away with), or constitutional factors (being of low intelligence, having an impulsive temperament, or lacking the ready capacity for classical conditioning).

Michael Rutter has brought together a number of studies that bear on the ways in which individual traits and social setting interact to affect human behavior. A given trait may magnify or reduce the effect of some social adversity; the magnification or reduction may be additive (one problem piled up on top of another) or multiplicative (the trait may make the circumstance two or three times as harmful as it would otherwise be); and so on.[4] For example, when a mother is especially responsive to a child, it will increase the exploratory behavior of that child if it is a boy but decrease it if it is a girl.[5] An injury sustained during birth may impede the intellectual development of a child living in a weak family but have no effect on the development of one in a strong family.[6] Marital turmoil seems to have a greater effect on boys than on girls.[7] As we saw in Chapter 15, delinquents who are anxious, intelligent, and neurotic may be helped by certain kinds of rehabilitative programs while those who are "power-oriented" and extroverted may become worse as a result of the same treatment.

At present, we do not know enough to be able to explain all these complex interactions. Some people think we never will know enough. We are not so certain. We are struck, instead, with how incomplete have been the efforts so far made to understand these processes. The best way to sort them out is by means of a comprehensive, prospective, longitudinal study of persons from birth into adolescence. There have been a few such studies, but none that gathers data on all the factors, constitutional and social, that need to be taken into account in explaining criminality. Some have been based on theories that explicitly ruled out certain factors. Some have been based on no theory at all. This book has no specific policy recommendations to make, save one: We are about at the limit of what can be learned from available or easily gathered data. If we wish to learn more about the links between traits and circumstances—whether to understand the causes of crime or to cope with them—we must mount a more wide-ranging, sophisticated effort to learn how children grow up.

Human Nature and Political Ideology

The view set forth here implies that there is a substantial constancy in human nature. We do not assert that this is the case with respect to all forms of behavior; we do assert that the best evidence suggests that this continuity exists with respect to antisocial aggression among males.

This conclusion should not lead the reader to embrace any particular political view. We are aware that liberals and conservatives differ in how they propose to deal with crime, and they may suppose that their differences are wholly the result of differing views of human nature. Liberals, we are told, think human nature is sufficiently malleable that society, by putting in place the right arrangements, can improve it so as either to prevent crime or rehabilitate criminals. And if these arrangements do not succeed, then society should use the least intrusive means available for dealing with offenders, and do so with a high regard for equity. Conservatives, we are told, think human nature is fixed, and so improving mankind by changing its nature is futile. Instead, society can best control crime by using punishment to deter would-be offenders and incapacitate active ones. And if these methods fail, then society should not flinch from using punishment for reasons of retribution.

We think this dichotomy is largely false. Though people disagree in just the way we have described them, they are wrong to think that their differences over policy flow necessarily, or even very clearly, from their different assessments of human nature. Liberals may believe human nature can be changed and be willing to try to change it by altering schools, communities, labor markets, or the mass media, but they are often quite reluctant to change it by intervening in the family or by intensified religious instruction. Conservatives may be skeptical of plans to reduce crime by hiring the unemployed or enlarging social welfare programs, but they often are sympathetic to the possibility of changing it by restoring traditional familial virtues and rekindling religious faith. And when the two camps meet to do battle over the one institution about which they share a common optimism, the schools, they differ greatly in their prescriptions. Liberals want instruction that will more fully emancipate the individual, sharpen his desire to participate in social action, and endow him with a surer sense of his rights; conservatives want instruction that will better shape the character of the individual, improve his command of basic skills, and endow him with a greater awareness of his duties.

Though present-day liberals and conservatives may have different views of human nature, their policy recommendations do not depend centrally or wholly on such differences, but reflect as well differences in beliefs about what constitutes virtue, how large or intrusive the state should be, and the proper balance between liberty and order. The argument of this book, thus, is not one that can give unmixed comfort to either ideology, or any ideology. Nor is it an argument from which many (possibly any) clear policy recommendations can be deduced. It is an argument, however, about a larger philosophical issue: What is man?

Three Views of Human Nature

Modern criminology has by and large taken one of two views of human nature. The first is that man is a self-seeking rational calculator who responds to the rewards and punishments he encounters in his dealings with others. The second is that man is naturally good; his goodness will be realized if social arrangements are decent, corrupted if they are defective. The facts in this book permit us to assess those theories.

Man the Calculator

The first view was systematically applied to crime by Jeremy Bentham[8] but originally derives from the thought of Thomas Hobbes. In *Leviathan,* published in 1651, Hobbes described men as neither good nor bad, but as creatures of their senses who desire certain things and who quarrel when their desires are in conflict. "If any two men desire the same thing, which nevertheless they cannot both enjoy, they become enemies."[9] The three principal things that men desire in ways that lead to quarrels are material gain, personal safety, and social reputation. Men are substantially equal in their faculties of body and (especially) prudence, so that their pursuit of gain, safety, and reputation brings them, absent a proper government, into a state of war of all against all in which life, in Hobbes's memorable phrase, is "solitary, poor, nasty, brutish, and short."[10] To avert such an unhappy state, men enter into society to whose governing authority they cede their right to self-preservation in exchange for the ruler's pledge to protect them all from one another, and from foreign enemies. Government, thus, exists because it confers a net advantage on its subjects. Crime may nonetheless occur even after governments are formed; among the reasons for crime is that some men (from a "defect in reasoning") will believe that they are entitled to whatever they can get away with.[11] To prevent this, the punishment for the crime must exceed the benefit that derives from committing it: "when men compare the benefit of their injustice [i.e., crime], with the harm of their punishment," they will "choose that which appeareth best for themselves."[12]

This view of man as a self-interested rational calculator pervades the first great modern treatise on crime and punishment, *Dei Delitti e delle Pene,* by the Italian Cesare Beccaria, published in 1764. Beccaria was not a systematic philosopher but a pamphleteer and so, though he had read Hobbes, he did not follow the Englishman in trying to set forth a clear understanding of human psychology. Instead, he absorbed from Hobbes and from the many currents of the eighteenth-century Enlightenment the view that laws should be judged by their tendency to provide the "greatest happiness shared by the greatest number."[13] Beccaria may not have been the first to use this phrase, but there is little doubt that Jeremy Bentham, who was later to make it famous, first encountered it in Beccaria. Since men are rationally self-interested, they will not commit crimes if the costs outweigh the benefits. Since the sole purpose of punishment is to prevent crime, punishment need only just exceed in pain the value to be obtained from the crime. Thus, for Beccaria, swift and certain punishment will reduce crime; any punishment more than that is arbitrary, unnecessary, and despotic.

It was Bentham who converted this insight into an elaborate system of thought. In his *Introduction to the Principles of Morals and Legislation,* published in 1789, he announced his famous principle of utility: "Nature has placed mankind under the governance of two sovereign masters, *pain* and *pleasure.*"[14] The object of law is to enlarge the happiness of the community by increasing the pleasure and decreasing the pain of those persons who compose it. Since punishment confers pain, it can be justified only insofar as it promises to prevent some greater pain. That greater pain arises from the crimes committed by persons who stand to benefit from them. Punishment is awarded so as to outweigh the profit from the crime, thereby inducing the would-be offender to refrain from committing any crime at all, or at least to commit lesser rather than graver crimes. Punishment in excess of what is necessary to induce people to obey the law is unjustified.[15]

Today, we say that the policies based on this utilitarian* calculus emphasize deterrence, and we sometimes refer to them as "conservative" or "hard line." Such a label misrepresents their origin, for in its day, and for many decades thereafter, the utilitarian school of criminology was a reform movement aimed at making the criminal justice system, and the government generally, less vengeful. As developed by Beccaria and Bentham, utilitarianism provided a philosophical foundation for opposing cruel, arbitrary, or excessive punishment, including torture, executions, and long prison terms. Such measures were wrong because they were wasteful and inefficient.[16]

The view of human nature developed by Hobbes accords with much of what we have learned about the causes of crime. It is clear that families socialize their children in part by manipulating rewards and penalties; without that manipulation, the struggle for gain, safety, and reputation would be bitter (it is bad enough in families that make skillful use of such socialization methods!). There is strong evidence that techniques of behavior modification can alter behavior, quite in keeping with Hobbesian predictions, at least while persons are in an institutional setting. There is some evidence that manipulating the probability (and possibly the severity) of punishment in society changes the frequency with which crimes are committed.

The theory that men, substantially equal in faculties, act in rational response to the pains and pleasures of the alternatives before them obviously neglects the fact that behavior often seems irrational. It was in recognition of this that the insanity defense was developed in the early nineteenth century. But the defenders of a purely utilitarian (or hedonistic) psychology might grant this exception to their theory on the reasonable grounds that only a very small fraction of all behavior (and of all crime) is attributable to people acting in the grip of some delusion that is manifestly at odds with reality.

A more important problem for the utilitarian view is that people differ in their faculties. John takes into account distant prospects, but Tom only immediate ones; John can quickly infer the likely consequences of a given act, but Tom can do so only with great difficulty; John fears unknown or uncertain outcomes, but Tom relishes the thrill of a risky adventure; John enters imaginatively and sympathetically into the feelings of another person, but Tom is indifferent to those feelings. To some degree, these differences are present at birth; to a large degree, they manifest themselves early in life. Economists, concerned chiefly with estimating the marginal effects of employment opportunities or judicial sanctions on criminal behavior, concede that people differ in these ways, but dismiss such differences as "tastes" that

* Criminologists often call the utilitarian school of crime and punishment the "classical" doctrine.

lie outside econometric models of how behavior changes in response to changes in the net value of alternative courses of action. If one is interested only in discovering how behavior changes with changes in readily available policy instruments, that dismissal is often quite appropriate. But if one is interested in explaining individual differences in behavior, that dismissal is tantamount to discarding the most important set of explanatory variables.

And even if one is interested only in predicting changes in behavior, one must be puzzled by certain anomalies. Economists typically include race in their predictive equations, but what is the theoretical significance of this variable? Why include race? Do blacks and whites have different "tastes"? What can be meant by "taste" in this regard? Unexamined, race has no obvious behavioral meaning at all. And even when examined (see Chapter 18), race can mean several things, each of which has (at present) only thin empirical support.

Consider also the significance of gender in any explanation of crime. A strict utilitarian might justifiably assume that men and women differ in, say, their taste for risk, and so be prepared to discover that the proportion of males in a population will have an influence on the prevalence of crime. But beyond this difference in taste, men and women presumably respond identically to changes in the relative advantage of crime and noncrime. How, then, do we account for the fact that the rate at which women commit certain kinds of crimes has apparently increased in this country (see Chapter 4) at the same time that there has been an increase in the proportion of women in the labor force and their per capita earnings in legitimate jobs?

We can only conclude that man is governed by something more than mere calculation. Among other things, he is governed by conscience, sympathy, and a sense of justice. By conscience (see Chapters 2 and 8) we mean an internal anxiety experienced in contemplation of even a riskless action that violates some rule (say, lying to a polygraph operator).

By sympathy we mean, as did Adam Smith in *The Theory of Moral Sentiments,* feeling sorrow for the sorrow of others and happiness for the happiness of others, based on imagining how we would feel were we in the others' place.[17] A strict utilitarian might argue that we manifest sympathy for others in hope of that sympathy being reciprocated; sympathy, in this view, is a form of self-interest based on an exchange of mutual aid. But it must be something more than this, for we feel sympathy for strangers of whom we hear but whom we never meet and even (especially?) for animals that can do little for us.*

---

* We grant that sympathy extended to a dog or horse may be reciprocated with affection and service, but few would claim that sympathy given a cat elicits much more than mere tolerance.

By justice we mean a belief that what one receives should be proportionate to what one deserves. As between two persons, justice requires equity—that is, that the ratio of one person's inputs to his outputs should equal the ratio of the other person's inputs to his outputs (see Chapters 2 and 19). Again, a strict utilitarian might suggest that maintaining equity is to each person's mutual advantage because it supplies a rule for allocating valuable things between them in a way that minimizes conflict. But why should inequity, above and beyond the ordinary clash of interests, ever cause conflict? Moreover, we often feel inequitably treated, and act on that feeling, in circumstances in which the advantage to be gained by enforcing the rule is far outweighed by the costs, in time, effort, and physical risk, of asserting it. If one person ostentatiously crowds ahead of us in a line at a movie theater where we have been waiting for an hour, it has a negligible effect on how long we will have to wait to enter the theater, or even on our chances of finding a seat. But we react strongly at the sight of the interloper; the timid among us fume and mutter, risking an ulcer, and the bold among us remonstrate or even shove, risking retaliation.

Criminality—and human behavior generally—cannot be understood except by reference to those sentiments, such as conscience, sympathy, and justice, that determine what value we will assign to the rewards and penalties associated with alternative courses of action.

Man the Naturally Good

Jean Jacques Rousseau, the eighteenth-century French philosopher, had read Hobbes and described his views as "pernicious,"[18] especially insofar as Hobbes viewed man as naturally wicked (or naturally scheming, which to Rousseau was much the same thing). Rousseau seized on the failure of Hobbes to consider compassion or sympathy as a natural sentiment.[19] Man is naturally good, by which Rousseau meant, among other things, that he does not wantonly attack others (unless he is taught to do so), and he is naturally capable of pity, by which Rousseau meant that it is painful for him to see suffering in others (again, unless he is taught to be callous). Though man loves himself, it is not the kind of love that inevitably makes him wish to raise himself above his fellow or practice the small arts of enhancing one's honor and reputation.[20]

In the state of nature, before the advent of society and its conventions, man is "natural," that is, solitary and unaffected, a creature of sentiments rather than calculation; he is premoral and prerational, a wanderer who is connected to others by neither attachments nor hostility. Sexual contact between man and woman has no lasting consequences; a child might be conceived, but no family emerges.

The corruption of man began with the formation of society. Rousseau vividly describes the decisive event: "The first man, who having enclosed a piece of ground, bethought himself of saying, 'This is mine,' and found people simple enough to believe him, was the real founder of civil society."[21] With property came laws, crimes, armies, wars, and social inequality. One man seeks to dominate another. The desire for glory and gain, which to Hobbes was natural, was for Rousseau the result of social conventions; the desire for self-preservation, which was natural for both Hobbes and Rousseau, takes on an exaggerated importance only, according to Rousseau, when society sets one man against another.

Man can be rescued from this unhappy and immoral state only by a "healing education which returns him to himself."[22] Through self-discovery, man will rediscover nature and his natural sentiments.[23] The most important of those sentiments is compassion. In a just society, governed by the principles of the general will, those natural sentiments can to some extent be preserved.

Much of modern criminology, directly or indirectly, draws on Rousseau. It is indebted to him when it favors preventing crime through proper education and constructive social arrangements as well as when it prefers helping offenders by rehabilitation instead of preventing offenses by deterrence. This view, naturally, assigns great importance to motives in judging an offender, and so is sympathetic to the insanity defense, to excuses based on human need and social stress, and to applying the doctrine of diminished responsibility to the behavior of juvenile delinquents. Indeed, the very concept of a juvenile (or an adolescent) owes much to Rousseau and his belief in the importance of avoiding measures (such as laws and penalties) that might warp the unformed youthful mind.

Some modern criminologists have re-examined these views; there is, for example, less support today for the feasibility of rehabilitation or the principle underlying the insanity defense than once was the case. And for almost all of modern criminology, there is less optimism than there used to be about the perfectibility of human nature. But the view that crime is caused by social forces (a view that criminologists often called "positivist") and that the individual is not fully to blame for his behavior is still widespread.

We have found evidence that is consistent with this theory of human nature. Families and, to a lesser extent, schools socialize children. There are ways in which economic need may affect crime rates. Community forces—

gangs, peers, ethnic cleavages, patterns of migration and anonymity—seem to affect the prevalence of crime. Rousseau, unlike Hobbes, was a moralist who saw man as evolving toward a greater or lesser degree of morality depending on the circumstances in which he found himself. One can, and should, quarrel with Rousseau's view as to the nature of that morality, both his belief that man is naturally innocent and his claim that good social arrangements are necessarily those that preserve (by force if necessary!) this original simplicity. But his view of childhood development was closer to the modern evidence than were the views of the English environmentalists. To Rousseau, unlike Hobbes, the child's mind is not a blank slate on which society can write at will; it contains its own innate sentiments and tendencies.

But Rousseau's view of man, especially of man-as-child, was hopelessly romantic. The innate structures of the mind were all good; self-interest existed, but only in its most benign forms. The child matures through an interaction between his nature and his environment, but the interaction should stress the development of imagination, not calculation, and should leave intact the child's original innocence and simplicity. One wonders what Rousseau would have done with willful children, or hyperactive ones, or those that rarely repay parental attention with spontaneous smiles and quiet nights. (He sent his own children to a foundling home.) Rousseau offers no guidance to the problem of getting children to foresee and act on the consequences of their own actions in ways that allow for a decent and civilized social life. Parents (as we saw in Chapters 8, 9, and 15) can make two kinds of errors, not just one—they can deprive the child of affection, thus impeding the formation of the vital parental bond, and they can be inconsistent in the way in which they reward and punish particular actions. Rousseau, and many later theorists of the family, understood the first failing but not the second.

In his great treatise on education, *Emile,* Rousseau set forth a mode of self-discovery that emphasized the development of a rich inner life and of such personal qualities as sincerity and self-sufficiency. He did not set forth a way of learning that equips man for a life of competition, law-abidingness, and acceptance of responsibility. He did not set forth such a way because he rejected such a life. It was the life of the bourgeoisie, and he detested it.[24] As a consequence, Rousseau and many students of crime who have followed (knowingly or not) in his footsteps have been blind to the need to harness self-interest to social purposes.

Purely sociological theories of crime owe a debt to Rousseau that they may or may not acknowledge. Any effort to locate the causes of crime in family practices, school failings, and economic disadvantage imply that these experiences are the decisive ones. But much of the modern attention given to those institutions is defective in two respects.

First, those who emphasize such institutions often neglect the extent to which individual differences among children, students, and workers profoundly affect how parents, teachers, and employers behave. In principle, Rousseau cannot be blamed for this shortsightedness, for he was by no means of the view that men and women are created equal in their endowments. He passionately advocated political equality while recognizing natural differences. But in practice, he was at fault. He did not fully consider the extent to which constitutional differences in intelligence and temperament shape the ease with which people can be socialized. Every child has tendencies toward sociability and toward self-regard; the balance differs from child to child, often radically, and to the extent this balance is heritable, the parents who must deal with the difficult child will be somewhat more likely themselves to lack the aptitude and temperament for dealing constructively with difficulties.

Second, contemporary advocates of the supremacy of social factors in causing crime are reluctant to think through the implications of that view for the internal life of the family. Society, in this view, should radically alter its schools and fundamentally reshape its economy, but it should merely provide "support" or "aid" or "services" for families. We suspect there are at least two reasons for this caution. One is that families occupy a privileged position in a free society; to suggest ways whereby the state should intervene directly in family life is to challenge head on a powerful moral, political, and legal tradition. (Of course, it can be challenged indirectly by making use of the accepted instruments of our legal order, as happens when proposals are made to enlarge "children's rights.") The other is that the family is the locus and nursery of traditional values, and some students of crime may worry that any proposal (difficult as it may be to conceive) that might strengthen the family for the purpose of reducing crime will at the same time strengthen those traditional values of which these students are personally somewhat skeptical. To help the family is to foster middle-class life and middle-class thought, an unhappy prospect for those who think that the evils of our society stem from its excessively middle-class nature. In this respect, such scholars can find little comfort in Rousseau, who argued that the father ought to command the wife as well as the children.[25]

The watered-down Rousseauism of some modern students of the social origins of crime leaves them with few tools that they can employ. They can strive to improve schools in furtherance of the reasonable, but only partially supported, view that school experiences make a difference in delinquency.

But the difference schools do make has not yet been fully explored and in any case is not likely to be great (see Chapter 10). They can strive to improve employment opportunities and the training necessary to take advantage of them, but the evidence so far suggests that reducing crime by altering either opportunities or training is not very promising (see Chapter 12). They can cope with city gangs, but so far the gangs have done a better job of coping with the social workers sent to help them (see Chapter 11). They may advocate less violence in television entertainment, but they cannot in good faith point to a substantial body of valid evidence that strongly implicates pictorial violence in actual violence (see Chapter 13). They can make heroin easier to obtain; this will almost surely reduce the incidence of crime among heroin addicts but probably at the cost of increasing the number of such addicts (see Chapter 14). They can continue to search for better ways of rehabilitating offenders—and there are some promising leads worth exploring—but they must do so against the background of countless dashed hopes and failed experiments (see Chapter 15). They can manipulate the certainty or the severity of sanctions for crime and probably expect some reduction in crime, but it will neither be large nor easy to verify. A moderate Rousseauism is not a prescription for social transformation; Rousseau, of course, knew this, which is why, politically, he was not moderate.

Man the Social Animal

There is a third view of human nature, one less commonly represented in contemporary criminology. It finds its first expression in Aristotle, who gives us an account of human nature that asserts that man has a nature that reflects, to a degree, heritable traits (thus he is an "animal") but that requires for its development communal living (and thus he is "social"). "Man is a being meant for political"—that is, communal—"association."[26]

He is meant for social living because he alone, of all the animals, is equipped with verbal language. Language enables him to communicate his experiences, but it also enables him to declare what is just and unjust. "Man alone possesses a perception of good and evil"; it is his perception of these things that both requires and makes possible the family and the community.[27]

To Aristotle, it is impossible to speak of man in a presocial state of nature; man exists only in association with others. The primary association is the family. Natural impulses lead men and women to unite; the family is naturally and necessarily instituted for the satisfaction of the daily, recurrent needs that arise out of this union. But some needs cannot be satisfied by the family, and for that reason villages are formed, which may begin as a kind of extended family but which then grow well beyond the borders of kinship. Villages, in turn, are brought together into larger political communities. Each of these associations—family, village, *polis*—tends toward some purpose or good; the *polis* tends toward the highest good.

Those larger associations that Rousseau described as unnatural and destructive are described by Aristotle as natural and desirable. The most important purpose of the family, and of all associations, is to develop the character of its members, that is, to inculcate virtue. This is done by the force of habit: ". . . we become just by the practice of just actions, self-controlled by exercising self-control, and courageous by performing acts of courage."[28] Virtue arises from the routine repetition of right actions, so that we come to "feel pleasure and pain at the proper things."[29]

Since the end or purpose of the political community is to aid the family, and since the end or purpose of the family is to develop the virtue of its members, then political or communal life is ultimately about virtue. Rousseau understood that politics was about virtue, but he thought that the ordinary forms of communal life would corrupt the natural innocence of man. To Aristotle, by contrast, communal life is essential if man is to have a good character. The task is not to oppose anyone who first builds a fence or claims a piece of land, but to distinguish between good and bad ways of doing these natural things.

Aristotle's understanding of how constitutional factors shape human nature is difficult for modern readers to understand and accept, for it principally occurs in the course of his discussion of slavery. One need not accept all the implications of his view to understand that it rested essentially on an observation that is difficult to contest—namely, that there are natural distinctions among persons with respect to their capacity to rule others. The term "rule" is introduced not in the discussion of politics but in the discussion of the family. A child is a "natural slave" (we wince, understandably, at this formulation of the matter) in that he cannot judge what is best for himself. At one stage of life, differences in age create masters and "slaves." A natural slave is one who cannot be allowed to rely on feelings of pleasure and pain to judge how he must behave. For example, some persons (such as the very young) will shun bad-tasting medicine or a surgeon's knife and eagerly play with glittering but dangerous knives or readily swallow pleasant-tasting but harmful fluids.* Some persons who are not so young will continue to do these things.

---

* There is more to Aristotle's discussion of slavery; in omitting the rest we should not be assumed to be embracing it. He was opposed to any form of slavery not based on nature—that is, on the real as opposed to the conventional differences among people. But he supplied no easily applicable principle by which to make this distinction, inviting some readers to think they had found ancient support for hideous practices.

The body is under the influence of the principles of pleasure and pain, but unlike in Hobbes and Bentham, matters cannot be left there. The mind must be taught to rule the body so as to shun immediate pleasures that lead to deferred pain and accept present pains that lead in time to greater pleasures. Little in Hobbes or Bentham prepares us for how the mind gradually acquires sovereignty over the body by coming to understand the circumstances in which pain ought to be preferred to pleasure. That philosophy should have difficulty with this problem is easily understood, since men so often fail to achieve the mind's sovereignty over the body's preferences. But to fail to note that mature humans differ from animals in part precisely because they need *not* be governed wholly by immediate pleasures and pains is to ignore the psychological process that is central to learning not to offend.

We have found ample evidence that there is a human nature that sets limits to, and supplies inclinations toward, social development. We have already noted the universality of age and sex differences in crime and the heritability, to some degree, of differences in intelligence and temperament. It is pointless to say whether this nature is good or bad; it is better to say that it is incomplete, but contains within itself the capacity for completion. An infant cries when hungry, thus signaling its greedy, egoistic nature, but it also smiles, signaling its readiness to enter into the feelings of others. Those smiles are not wholly learned; even blind infants smile.

Aristotle did not develop a full-scale human psychology,* but his political and moral philosophy, grounded in his understanding of human history, creates for us an integrated view of the problem of human development that much of modern thought was at pains to break apart into partial and incomplete views.

The family is the centerpiece of his analysis. He said it was a natural—and thus perhaps inevitable—association, but we now know that it did not arise automatically with the first appearance of human males and females. Instead, it is the most important social achievement of mankind, evolving in ways still imperfectly understood. Consider what was accomplished, as set forth in the vivid language of Werner Stark: "To develop, from a fleeting instant of physical lust, a lifelong community encompassing the whole of the conjoint lives—that has been and is one of the greatest triumphs of sociality in the struggle against the persistent animality of our species."[30]

---

* He wrote a book explicitly about psychology, *De Anima* (*On the Soul*), in which he discussed the senses and the "affections" or temperaments of the soul—anger, courage, appetite, and the like. But his treatment tended toward the classification rather than the explanation of phenomena and he supplied no single principle of action.

Little in utilitarian psychology quite prepares us for this. If mankind is governed by pleasure and pain, how is it that some men and women undertake, in return for immediate emotional pleasures, lifetime responsibility for helping to care for each other and their children, while others do not? And why care for them in ways that confer immediate costs (crying children) in return for deferred pleasures (successful children)? Only with great difficulty can a theory of behavior resting wholly on the principle of exchange account for this.*

No theory of behavior that neglects the formation and maintenance of family life in favor of the "natural" development of virtue seems satisfactory. The problem is especially puzzling in the case of males, since they seem far more inclined than females to desert mates and offspring. And it is the socialization of the male that we must chiefly explain if we are to understand why not everyone commits crimes whenever it is advantageous to do so. Aristotle's answer, it appears, is that men and women are law-abiding and faithful in part because they have learned it is the right and just way to behave and in part because the larger political community reinforces that belief.

Human Nature and the Political Order

The family is a remarkably durable institution, existing in every society and persisting over millennia of change. The clearest measure of its strength is the fact that most people in most places do not live under a pervasive fear of criminal victimization. The family rarely teaches its members to avoid all occasions of crime (a majority of American males commit at least one relatively serious crime), but it does succeed in preventing more than a small percentage of males from becoming chronic offenders.

Though under great stress today, by and large the structure of the

---

* One such theory is that of Gary S. Becker, whose *A Treatise on the Family*[31] is an imaginative effort to apply the traditional assumptions of economists—that individuals try to maximize the realization of certain fixed preferences—so as to answer such questions as: Who will marry? How many children will they have? How will they allocate duties and income among family members? The answers he gives to these and other questions are ingenious and help explain certain facts about criminality, such as its tendency to run in families, a predictable result of assortative mating whereby likes attract likes. But he has little to say about many aspects of family life central to understanding the prevalence of criminality. It is not clear why wealth-maximizing spouses should want to have any children at all (especially if the parents do not live on farms, where children can help produce income) or why, having given birth to them, they should seek to inculcate in their offspring a conscience (as opposed

family has proved strong. Even in modern industrial nations such as the United States, where rates of divorce have been rising and the proportion of children raised in single-parent families is high, 97 percent of all children under the age of eighteen live with at least one parent and 80 percent live with two. (Fewer than half of all black children live in two-parent families.) When only one parent cares for the child, that parent, in the overwhelming majority of cases (93 percent of the time in the United States), is the mother.[32]

As we have seen (Chapter 9), the evidence that one-parent families are more likely to produce delinquents than two-parent ones is ambiguous. (By contrast, the evidence that discordant families tend to produce delinquents is very strong.) We suspect that the ambiguity of the evidence results from a failure to take simultaneously into account the temperament of the child and its parent and the economic and social circumstances of the family, as well as the presence or absence of a second parent. The interaction effects between constitutional traits and familial circumstances are likely to be especially pronounced in one-person families, but in only a few studies have such interactions been examined.

The largest changes in crime rates over time, and the greatest differences in crime rates across cultures, are closely associated with changes in family processes. The most obvious of these are changes in the birth rate: Crime rates rise when a baby boom comes of age and declines when a baby bust matures. But there are also some less obvious, and perhaps equally important, family effects. Crime rates in the United States during the latter half of the nineteenth century declined faster than can be explained by dropping birth rates, owing, we think, to intense efforts to inculcate an ethic of self-control ("Victorian morality"), and rose faster in the twentieth century than can be explained by higher birth rates, owing to a shift from that ethic to one emphasizing self-expression (see Chapter 16). Crime rates are un-

---

to skill at calculating the net benefits of alternative courses of action). Once married and enjoying their joint incomes, why should the couple insist on sexual fidelity, or quarrel over the unjustness of one spouse's peccadilloes? Nor is it clear why such persons should form lifelong marriages. Becker assumes that persons in the marriage market have perfect information about the productive value of potential spouses, but he argues that they turn to divorce when they discover that they have made a mistake—that is, they had imperfect information. Becker's explanation for the most obvious fact about marriages—that they are almost always monogamous—requires us to believe that neither law nor religion has much of an effect on the practice; rather, it results from rationally self-interested men and women surveying the marriage market, calculating their likely incomes from every available partner, estimating how much the husband and wife separately contribute to total family income, and then entering into monogamous marriages because they cannot do better in polygamous ones.

usually low in nations such as Japan where the norms inculcated by the family (and the general culture) emphasize obligations as much or more than rights and where families transmit a sense of collective responsibility for behavior (see Chapter 17). Some of these cross-cultural differences may reflect, to a degree, differences in constitutional factors, such as temperament, that facilitate conditioning and allow the Japanese family to be remarkably permissive and still inculcate a lengthened time horizon, a degree of conscience, or a concern for the well-being of others.

It is natural to think that religion may play some role in how families train children. Of all the gaps in our knowledge of the causes of crime, the one that has struck us most forcefully is the lack of systematic studies of the relationship between religiosity and criminality. In theory, religiosity ought to make a great difference in criminality. To the extent a person believes in an afterlife, and especially the prospect of eternal bliss or damnation, then the rewards and punishments associated with crime and noncrime become very great (in fact, unimaginably great), albeit long deferred. Of course, a person may be deeply religious but wholly impulsive, such that even divine rewards are heavily discounted if much delayed, or his religion may teach him of the eternal delights awaiting the man who slays a thousand infidels.

Religion is not as pervasive a part of family life in Japan as it is in many Latin-American nations; despite this, crime rates are much lower in Japan than in the Latin countries. Fundamentalist religions that attempt to transform their adherents into "born again" Christians are more common in the American South than in the North, yet the rates of violent crime have traditionally been higher in the South than in the North. Obviously, Japan and Latin America, and the American North and South, differ in many other ways as well; the research task, and it is a formidable one, is to estimate the effect, if any, of religiosity independently of other traits and circumstances.

There have been some case studies of the impact on blacks of the Black Muslim (or Nation of Islam) movement, a religion that seeks to transform the personalities of lower-class blacks by instilling in them a sense of pride and requiring of them a strict conformity to rules of right conduct. *The Autobiography of Malcolm X* is a vivid account of one such transformation,[33] but the evidence is unclear as to whether equivalent changes are characteristic of adherents generally or whether most adherents have come from a background of crime similar to that of Malcolm.[34]

The uncertainty we face in attempting to assess the influence of religion on family life is but a special case of the general problem of understanding the relationship among personal traits, family processes, cultural values, and the development of human character. That relationship is peculiarly equivocal in the United States, a society whose national government was founded on the understanding that it would take human nature pretty much as it was, relying in large measure on the competitive pursuit of self-interest and individual rights to protect freedom and forswearing the traditional role of government which was, beginning with the ancients, to develop virtue in its citizens.

That arrangement has worked surprisingly well, but not as well as many would like. It leaves to the family and the local community the task of cultivating character, and in doing so, it sometimes is less attentive than it ought to be to how fragile and besieged some families are. Families (and communities) require resources, competence, and moral authority. For some families, poverty and single-parent households have reduced the resources and strained the competence necessary for the awesome task they face. To this is sometimes added attacks on the moral authority of the family in the name of radical individualism, the supremacy of rights over obligations, and the dangers of "stigmatizing" persons by holding them accountable for bad conduct or identifying those who at an early age need help.

The most important consequences of public policy toward crime may be their tutelary, not their direct, effects. How we spend money on schools, job training, or welfare programs may be less important than the message accompanying such expenditures: Do we appear to be rewarding the acceptance or the rejection of personal responsibility? When we punish offenders, we hope to prevent them from offending again and to deter like-minded persons from committing similar offenses. But we are also reaffirming the moral order of society and reminding people of what constitutes right conduct, in hopes that this reaffirmation and reminder will help people, especially in families, teach each other about virtue.

A society made up of persons who are purely hedonic calculators is no society at all. In endorsing the tutelary functions of private associations and public institutions, we endorse a delicate balance. We know that people differ from birth and require, therefore, differences in treatment, but we cannot let this knowledge lead us to treat anybody as if he or she were inevitably decent or corrupt or in ways that are incompatible with political and legal equality. We want our collective institutions to uphold standards of right conduct, even when wrong conduct seems to do no physical harm, but without those institutions becoming busybodies. We know that crime, like all human behavior, has causes, and that science has made progress—and will make more progress—in identifying them, but the very process by which we learn to avoid crime requires that the courts act as if crime were wholly the result of free choice. Contemplating the complexity and mystery of human behavior, whether we study its criminal or noncriminal forms, should make us determined to keep that balance—of causes, and of social responses—firmly in mind.

APPENDIX

It is well known that there is an inverse relationship between behavior and the delay in its reinforcement—the more delayed the reward, the less of a strengthening effect it has on the behavior that earns it. From laboratory research, and from certain theoretical considerations,[1] it appears that this inverse relationship is reasonably well approximated by the following equation:

$$B = \frac{R}{R + R_e + Di} \qquad (1)$$

where: B = strength of a given class of behavior expressed as a fraction of total behavior.

   R = net reinforcement conditional on B.

   R_e = total reinforcements being obtained, exclusive of those conditional on B.

   D = time interval between B and R, hence the delay of reinforcement.

   i = a parameter—the "impulsiveness" parameter—whose value determines how steeply discounted the value of a delayed reinforcement is.

For the choice between crime (B_c) and the avoidance of it, noncrime (B_n), two versions of Equation 1 need to be taken into account:

$$B_c = \frac{p_c R}{p_c R + R_e + Di} \qquad (2)$$

531

$$B_n = \frac{p_n m R}{p_n m R + R_e + (D + \Delta)i} \tag{3}$$

where: R = net reinforcement for the criminal behavior—the tangible and intangible gains less the tangible and intangible contemporaneous costs.

m = ratio of the reinforcement for the noncrime (i.e., the legal and other penalties forgone by resisting the crime) to that for the crime.

p_c = probability of successfully executing the crime.

p_n = probability of receiving the legal and other penalties of the crime, if it is committed.

Δ = average delay between the reinforcers for the crime per se (i.e., R) and the penalties issuing, directly or indirectly, from apprehension, conviction, imprisonment, etc. Besides the legal penalties are the losses of prestige, earnings ability, association with family and friends, and so on.

D = time interval between B_c and R (i.e., the delay of the criminal act's reinforcer).

i = impulsiveness parameter, taken to be the same for B_c and B_n, the crime and the noncrime.

It should be apparent that crime tends to become stronger than noncrime (and, therefore, is more likely to occur, given the opportunity) as m or p_n gets smaller, or p_c or Δ gets larger. If the connection between present behavior and future consequences is *clearer* (as distinguished from merely nearer or more certain) for crime than noncrime, then i would be smaller for crime than noncrime. By itself, such a difference would favor crime by elevating the values of B_c relative to B_n, when all other terms are held constant. In the discussion that follows, however, we assume, for the sake of theoretical parsimony, that i is the same for crime and noncrime.

The effects of all the terms can be seen by solving for D at the moment that $B_c = B_n$, which is the crossover point in Figure 1, Case 2 (page 51). At all shorter delays of the criminal reinforcement, crime becomes irresistible (like the chocolate cake at the end of dinner), and at all longer delays, noncrime predominates.

Setting Equations 2 and 3 equal and solving for D:

$$D = \frac{\Delta}{\dfrac{p_n}{p_c} m - 1} - \frac{R_e}{i} \tag{4}$$

The larger the value of D (positive values only), the greater the likelihood that the crime will occur. If D is zero or negative, the crime will not occur. Indeed, if D is less than the time it takes to execute the crime, shown as a in Figure 1 (page 51), the crime will not occur. The likelihood of finding an opportunity to break the law must depend on how long or how often the individual is disposed to seek one, and this state is quantified by positive values of D in Equation 4. Equation 4 tells us that crime is fostered by delays in the criminal justice system (large values of Δ) or by feeble or improbable penalties (small values of m and p_n, respectively). Likewise, a large potential gain (reciprocal of m) or a high probability of success (p_c) fosters crime by increasing D. Finally, characteristics of the criminal, rather than of the particular crime or of the criminal justice system, are expressed by the second term on the right side of Equation 4. A large general context of reinforcement, R_e, reduces D, hence the likelihood of the crime, while steep discounting of future consequences (large values of i) increases it.

The balance of opposing forces in Equation 4 can be stated by the following Inequality, which follows from it:

$$\frac{\dfrac{p_n}{p_c} m - 1}{i} < \frac{\Delta}{R_e} \tag{5}$$

Since Inequality 5 holds only when $D > 0$ in Equation 4, this Inequality defines the preconditions for crime. Figures 1–3 in the text (pages 51, 55, and 60) and Figure A1 (next page) illustrate some of the implications of the Inequality. The three cases in Figure 1 (page 51) show the effects of increasing values of i (impulsiveness), while all other quantities are held constant. Changes in impulsiveness can produce a swing from a compulsive offender to a total nonoffender, within certain ranges of values for the other variables in the Inequality.

Figure 2 (page 55) shows what happens when $\dfrac{p_n}{p_c} m \leqq 1$. The expression at the upper left in Inequality 5 then goes to zero or below, to negative values, either because the probability of a successful crime (p_c) has gotten so large, or that of the penalty (p_n) so low, or the ratio of the criminal penalty to the criminal gain (m) has gotten so small. At this point, the crime will occur (given the opportunity) no matter what the other variables are. This is a "rational" crime from the criminal's point of view.

Figure 3 (page 60) illustrates the effect of an increased value of R_e, the context of reinforcement. An increase in R_e may result in a violation of Inequality 5, hence may tip the balance toward noncrime, even with every-

FIGURE A1

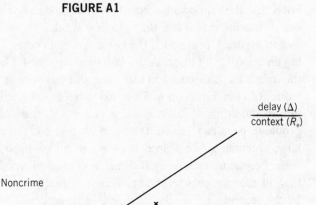

From Inequality 5.

The diagonal line is a frontier between crime and noncrime. For each degree of impulsiveness, the relative advantage or certainty of the reward for noncrime must be above the diagonal or the crime will be committed, given the opportunity. The *X*, for example, represents a combination of circumstances that will result in criminal behavior. The slope of the diagonal line equals the ratio of the delays in the criminal justice system to the overall context of reward. The lower the slope, the greater the resistance to criminal behavior.

thing else held constant. When other things improve, a crime that looked attractive may suddenly look inconceivable.

Figure A1 puts the separate pieces together, and is a representation of Inequality 5. The line is a frontier between noncrime and crime. If $\frac{p_n}{p_c} m$ is above the line, the crime will not occur; if below, it will occur. That the frontier is a rising line when plotted against impulsiveness (i.e., i) means that the more impulsive someone is, the stronger or more certain the penalty must be (in relation to the criminal reward) in order to prevent the crime.

There are, however, many such frontiers, not just one, depending on the two remaining variables. The slope of the frontier line rises directly with the delays in the criminal justice system, and inversely with the individual's general context of reinforcement. The steeper the frontier, the stronger the deterrent must be in order to work, for any given degree of impulsiveness. Increasing the total array of reinforcements or decreasing the delay produces a line of lower slope. A line of lower slope means that, for any time-discounting rate, noncrime need have a smaller relative advantage over crime in order to prevent crime. The theory asserts, in other words, that generalized social reinforcements (e.g., other interests, a larger network of friends, a wider array of activities) can compensate to a degree for such individual factors as impulsiveness or a strong desire for the fruits of crime.

Consider the point labeled x. In the circumstances portrayed, this represents a criminal occasion. The person, with his or her degree of impulsiveness, will engage in a criminal act whose benefits are sufficiently large or certain to hold the relative advantage of noncrime below some value (given by the line). The slope of this line declines as delays in the criminal justice system are reduced, or as the person's general context of reinforcement is increased. To convert this criminal occasion into a nonoccasion, one or more of four things must happen: the relative benefits or certainty of the consequences of noncrime must increase, impulsiveness must decrease, delays in the criminal justice system must be shortened, or the person's context of reinforcement must be enlarged.

NOTES

CHAPTER 1

1. Wolfgang, 1973.
2. Farrington, 1979c, 1981.
3. Newman, G., 1976.
4. Hoebel, 1954.
5. Sellin and Wolfgang, 1964; Figlio, 1972.
6. Akman and Normandeau, 1968.
7. Valez-Diaz and Megargee, 1971.
8. Hsu, cited in Wellford, 1975.
9. DeBoeck and Houschou, cited in Wellford, 1975.
10. Hirschi and Gottfredson, 1984.
11. Durkheim, 1964, p. 102.
12. Bordua, 1962.
13. Radzinowicz and King, 1977; Archer, Gartner, Akert, and Lockwood, 1978.
14. Braithwaite, 1981.
15. Tittle, Villemez, and Smith, 1978.
16. Elliott and Ageton, 1980; Elliott and Huizinga, 1983.
17. Hindelang, Hirschi, and Weis, 1979, 1981.
18. For example, Kleck, 1982.
19. Johnson, R. E., 1979.
20. Braithwaite, 1981.
21. For example, Wolfgang, Figlio, and Sellin, 1972.
22. Hindelang, Hirschi, and Weis, 1979, 1981; Berger and Simon, 1974; Elliott and Ageton, 1980; Shannon, 1982.
23. Hindelang, Hirschi, and Weis, 1979, p. 1002; Hindelang, 1978.
24. Blumstein, 1982; Petersilia, 1983.
25. Blumstein and Nagin, 1978.
26. Chaiken and Chaiken, 1983.
27. Task Force on Assessment, 1967, pp. 22–24.
28. Bureau of Justice Statistics, 1981.
29. Skogan, 1981.
30. Turner, 1981.
31. Eck and Riccio, 1979.
32. Weiss, 1976; Holinger, 1979.
33. Wolfgang, 1958; McClintock, 1963; Mulvihill, Tumin, and Curtis, 1969.
34. Wilson, J. Q., 1968a.
35. Hindelang, 1978; Hindelang, Hirschi, and Weis, 1979, 1981.
36. Black and Reiss, 1967, 1970.
37. Dunford and Elliott, 1984.
38. For example, Erickson and Empey, 1963.
39. For example, Gold and Reimer, 1975; Hirschi, 1969.
40. Reiss, 1972; Hindelang, Hirschi, and Weis, 1981.
41. Reiss and Rhodes, 1961.

42. Hirschi, 1969, pp. 41–46.
43. *Ibid.*, pp. 44–45.
44. Clark, J. P., and Tifft, L. L., 1966.
45. Gold, 1970.
46. Reiss and Rhodes, 1959.
47. Hirschi, 1969, p. 77.
48. Clark, J. P., and Tifft, L. L., 1966.
49. Elliott and Ageton, 1980.
50. Miller, 1967.
51. Blumstein and Graddy, 1981–1982.
52. Tinbergen, 1951.
53. Burgess, 1980.

CHAPTER 2

1. Eysenck, H. J., 1977.
2. As reported in Ainslie, 1975; Ainslie
   and Herrnstein, 1981; Chung and
   Herrnstein, 1967; de Villiers and
   Herrnstein, 1976; Herrnstein, 1970,
   1981; and Rachlin, H., 1974.
3. Ainslie, 1974; Chung and Herrnstein, 1967; Rachlin, H., and
   Green, L., 1972.
4. Adams, J. S., 1965; Blau, P. M.,
   1964; Greenberg, J., and Cohen,
   R. L., 1982a; Homans, 1961.
5. Aristotle, *Nichomachean Ethics*, v,
   iii, 1131b.
6. Hook, J. G., and Cook, T. D., 1979.
7. Damon, W., 1975.
8. Greenberg, J., and Cohen, R. L.,
   1982b.
9. Blau, P. M., 1964; Sampson, E. E.,
   1975.
10. Krebs, 1982.
11. Newman, R. A., 1973.
12. Walster, Walster, and Berschied,
    1978.
13. Donnerstein and Hatfield, 1982.
14. *Ibid.*
15. Lerner, 1982.
16. Catania, 1973; de Villiers, 1977;
    Donahoe, 1977; Herrnstein, 1970,
    1974, 1979; Premack, 1965, 1971.
17. For example, Bradshaw, Szabadi,
    and Lowe, 1981; Commons, Herrn-
    stein, and Rachlin, 1982.
18. Hirschi, 1969, p. 3.
19. Cloward and Ohlin, 1960.
20. Cohen, A. K., 1955.
21. Matza, 1964; Hirschi, 1969.

22. Hirschi, 1969, p. 120.
23. Mischel, 1961b.
24. Sutherland and Cressey, 1966.
25. Miller, 1958.
26. Hirschi, 1969, Chapter 8.

CHAPTER 3

1. *Encyclopaedia Britannica,* 1885,
   Vol. 19, p. 3ff.
2. See Ellis, H., 1914, for this and
   many other examples.
3. Quoted by Parmelee, 1912, p. xiv.
4. Stevenson, R. L., 1886.
5. Ellis, H., 1914, p. 43.
6. Goring, 1913.
7. *Ibid.*, p. 370.
8. Hooton, 1939a, 1939b.
9. Hooton, 1939b.
10. Hooton, 1939a, p. 75.
11. Hooton, 1939b, p. 308.
12. Reuter, 1939.
13. Hooton, 1939a, p. 3ff.
14. For example, Levin and Lindesmith,
    1937; Shaw and McKay, 1942;
    Sutherland, 1947; Tannenbaum,
    1938; Wootton, 1959; Whyte, 1943.
15. Thornton, 1939.
16. Kozeny, 1962.
17. Bull and Green, 1980.
18. Hooton, 1939a.
19. Sheldon, 1940, 1942, 1949.
20. Hartl, Monnelly, and Elderkin,
    1982.
21. Sheldon, 1949.
22. Hartl, Monnelly, and Elderkin,
    1982, p. 549.
23. For example, Sutherland, 1951.
24. Epps and Parnell, 1952.
25. Glueck, S., and Glueck, E. T., 1956.
26. Gibbens, 1963.
27. Shasby and Kingsley, 1978.
28. Cortes and Gatti, 1972.
29. *Ibid.*
30. Glueck, S., and Glueck, E. T., 1956;
    Cortes and Gatti, 1972; Sheldon,
    1942.
31. For which see Rosenthal, D., 1970;
    Plomin, DeFries, and McClearn,
    1980.
32. As illustrated in Plomin, DeFries,
    and McClearn, 1980.

33. Drawn mainly from Christiansen, 1977b.
34. Lange, 1929.
35. Kranz, 1936.
36. Dalgard and Kringlen, 1976.
37. Christiansen, 1977a.
38. Harvald and Hauge, 1965.
39. Rowe, D. C., 1983; Rowe, D. C., and Osgood, D. W., 1984.
40. Rowe, D. C., and Osgood, D. W., 1984.
41. Rowe, D. C., 1983.
42. See Christiansen, 1977b.
43. Mednick, Gabrielli, and Hutchings, 1984.
44. Roth and Visher, 1984.
45. Van Dusen, Mednick, and Gabrielli, 1983.
46. Bohman, Cloninger, Sigvardsson, and von Knorring, 1982; Sigvardsson, Cloninger, Bohman, and von Knorring, 1982.
47. Crowe, 1975.
48. Cadoret, Cain, and Crowe, 1983.
49. Jacobs, P. A., Brunton, M., Melville, M. M., Brittain, R. P., and McClemont, W., 1965.
50. Hook, E. B., 1973.
51. Jacobs, P. A., Brunton, M., Melville, M. M., Brittain, R. P., and McClemont, W., 1965; Jacobs, P. A., Price, W. H., Richmond, S., and Ratcliff, R. A. W., 1971.
52. Hook, E. B., 1973; Kessler, 1975; Shah, 1970.
53. Witkin, Mednick, Schulsinger, Bakkestrom, Christiansen, Goodenough, Hirschhorn, Lundsteen, Owen, Philip, Rubin, and Stocking, 1976.

CHAPTER 4

1. Quetelet, 1842, cited in Hindelang, 1979.
2. Heidensohn, 1968.
3. Hindelang, Hirschi, and Weis, 1981.
4. Steffensmeier and Cobb, 1981.
5. Steffensmeier, 1980.
6. As well as other factors; see Pollak, 1950; Nagel, I. H., and Hagen, J., 1983.
7. Hindelang, 1979.
8. Moulds, 1980; Nagel, I. H., and Hagen, J., 1983.
9. Hindelang, Hirschi, and Weis, 1981.
10. Summarized by Datesman and Scarpitti, 1980a; Bowker, 1977.
11. Datesman and Scarpitti, 1980a.
12. Ward, Jackson, and Ward, 1969.
13. Smith, D. A., and Visher, C. A., 1980.
14. Hindelang, Hirschi, and Weis, 1981.
15. See also Canter, 1982.
16. Glueck, S., and Glueck, E. T., 1934.
17. Glueck, S., and Glueck, E. T., 1930.
18. Glueck, S., and Glueck, E. T., 1934, p. 299.
19. For example, Cowie, Cowie, and Slater, 1968; Konopka, 1966; Vedder and Sommerville, 1970.
20. Cloninger and Guze, 1970.
21. Capwell, 1945; Panton, 1974; Widom, 1978.
22. Eysenck, S. B. G., and Eysenck, H. J., 1973.
23. Calculated from Glueck, S., and Glueck, E. T., 1934; Cowie, Cowie, and Slater, 1968.
24. See Caplan, 1965, for counterevidence.
25. Cowie, Cowie, and Slater, 1968.
26. West and Farrington, 1977.
27. Maccoby and Jacklin, 1974, pp. 242–243.
28. Tieger, 1980, challenges all four.
29. Goldberg, S., 1973.
30. Whiting, B., and Edwards, C. P., 1973.
31. Maccoby and Jacklin, 1974.
32. Maccoby and Jacklin, 1980.
33. Martin, M. K., and Voorhies, B., 1975.
34. Tieger, 1980.
35. *Ibid.*
36. Birch and Clark, 1950; Michael, 1968.
37. For example, Quadagno, Briscoe, and Quadagno, 1977.
38. Dixson, 1980; Goldman, 1977.
39. Elias, 1981.
40. Imperato-McGinley, Peterson, Gautier, and Sturla, 1979.
41. Kreuz and Rose, 1972.

42. Ehrenkrantz, Bliss, and Sheard, 1974.
43. Chatz, 1972; Field and Williams, 1970.
44. Dalton, 1961, 1964; Wallach and Rubin, 1971–1972.
45. Ivey and Bardwick, 1968; Moos, Kopell, Melges, Yalom, Lunde, Clayton, and Hamburg, 1969.
46. Parlee, 1973.
47. Pollak, 1950.
48. Morton, J., Addison, H., Addison, R., Hunt, L., and Sullivan, J., 1953.
49. Dalton, 1961.
50. Ellis, D. P., and Austin, P., 1971.
51. Dalton, 1960.
52. Lombroso and Ferrero, 1897.
53. Adler, 1975.
54. Adler, 1977, p. 152, in Datesman and Scarpitti, 1980b.
55. Cochrane, 1971.
56. Ward, Jackson, and Ward, 1969.
57. Widom, 1979.
58. Norland, Wessel, and Shover, 1981.
59. Simon, 1975.
60. Adler and Simon, 1979, p. 113, from Simon, 1975, pp. 34–38.
61. Datesman and Scarpitti, 1980b; Renzetti and Curran, 1981.
62. Renzetti and Curran, 1981.
63. *Ibid.*
64. *Ibid.,* p. 15.
65. Crites, 1976.
66. Widom, 1978.
67. Canter, 1982.

CHAPTER 5

1. Earlier data are similar: e.g., Keller and Vedder, 1968.
2. Adams, M. E., and Vedder, C. B., 1961; Moberg, 1953; Schroeder, 1936; Teller and Howell, 1981.
3. Schroeder, 1936; Teller and Howell, 1981.
4. Pollak, 1941.
5. Hindelang, 1981; Hindelang and McDermott, 1981; McDermott, 1979; McDermott and Hindelang, 1981.

6. Rowe, A. R., and Tittle, C. R., 1977.
7. Hirschi and Gottfredson, 1983.
8. Shannon, 1982.
9. Wolfgang, Figlio, and Sellin, 1972; Wolfgang, 1977.
10. Farrington, 1979c; Hirschi and Gottfredson, 1983.
11. Blumstein and Cohen, 1979.
12. *Ibid.,* p. 573.
13. Chaiken and Chaiken, 1983; Ferdinand, 1970; Fox, J. A., 1978; Sagi and Wellford, 1968; Wellford, 1973.
14. Wellford, 1973.
15. Gold and Reimer, 1975.
16. But see Zimring, 1979.
17. d'Orban, 1971; Daniel, Harris, and Husain, 1981.
18. Williams, J. R., and Gold, M., 1972.
19. Boland and Wilson, 1978.
20. Wolfgang, 1977.
21. See Moberg, 1953, for fourteen of them.
22. Wootton, 1959; Hirschi and Gottfredson, 1983.
23. Hirschi and Gottfredson, 1983.
24. Flanagan, 1979, reproduced in Hirschi and Gottfredson, 1983.
25. McKissack, 1967, 1973a, b.
26. See Greenberg, D. F., 1984, for some examples of varying age distributions.
27. Kohlberg, 1976.

CHAPTER 6

1. Peterson, J., 1925; Sattler, 1982; Tuddenham, 1962.
2. Galton, 1869, 1883; Herrnstein and Boring, 1965.
3. Binet and Henri, 1895.
4. Stern, 1912.
5. Merrill, M. A., 1947.
6. Goddard, 1912.
7. See Goddard, 1914, pp. 6–10.
8. Goddard, 1921.
9. Zeleny, 1933.
10. For example, Tulchin, 1939.
11. Sutherland, 1931.
12. Haskell and Yablonsky, 1978, p. 268.
13. Reid, S. T., 1979, p. 156.

14. Bartol, 1980, p. 125.
15. Hirschi and Hindelang, 1977.
16. Caplan, 1965; Woodward, 1955; Hirschi and Hindelang, 1977; Gordon, 1975.
17. Gordon, 1975; Hirschi and Hindelang, 1977; Short and Strodtbeck, 1965.
18. Ferguson, in Gordon, 1975; Hirschi and Hindelang, 1977; Reckless and Smith, 1932.
19. Hirschi, 1969; Hirschi and Hindelang, 1977.
20. Caplan, 1965, p. 104.
21. *Ibid.*
22. *Ibid.*, p. 106.
23. Healy and Bronner, 1936; Ackerly, 1933; Shulman, 1929.
24. Reiss and Rhodes, 1961.
25. Hirschi and Hindelang, 1977.
26. Wolfgang, Figlio, and Sellin, 1972.
27. West and Farrington, 1973.
28. Woodward, 1955; Wootton, 1959.
29. Glueck, S., and Glueck, E. T., 1950.
30. Jensen, A. R., 1980.
31. Wigdor and Garner, 1982, Part I, p. 3; Linn's chapter in Part II of the report provides additional data.
32. See Jensen, A. R., 1980, for an extensive review and analysis of the data.
33. Darlington, 1971; Hunter and Schmidt, 1976; Jensen, A. R., 1980; Miele, 1979; Petersen, N. S., and Novick, M. R., 1976.
34. Taken from Hirschi and Hindelang's review, 1977, which samples the views of leading criminological theorists.
35. Jensen, A. R., 1981.
36. Shulman, 1951; McCord, W., and McCord, J., 1959.
37. Gordon, 1975; Short and Strodtbeck, 1965.
38. Wechsler, D., 1944.
39. Caplan, 1965.
40. Glueck, S., and Glueck, E. T., 1950.
41. Prentice and Kelly, 1963.
42. Graham and Kamano, 1959.
43. Kaufman, A. S., 1976.
44. Manne, Kandel, and Rosenthal, 1962.
45. Black, W. A., and Hornblow, A. R., 1973; Kahn, 1968.
46. Warren, 1971.
47. Andrew, 1974, 1977, 1980.
48. Freedman, B. J., Rosenthal, L., Donahoe, C. P., Jr., Schlundt, D. G., and McFall, R. M., 1978.
49. *Ibid.*
50. *Ibid.*
51. For example, Camp, 1977.
52. Cattell, 1971.
53. For example, Gould, S. J., 1981; Herrnstein, 1973; Jensen, A. R., 1981; Cattell, 1971; Guilford, 1967.
54. Hirschi and Hindelang, 1977.
55. Hirschi, 1969.
56. Williams, J. R., and Gold, M., 1972; Hindelang, Hirschi, and Weis, 1981; Hirschi, 1969.
57. Hirschi and Hindelang, 1977.
58. Manne, Kandel, and Rosenthal, 1962.
59. West and Farrington, 1973.
60. Wolfgang, Figlio, and Sellin, 1972.
61. Ganzer and Sarason, 1973.
62. For example, Mann and Mann, 1939; Glueck, E. T., 1935.
63. Merrill, M. A., 1947.
64. Hartman, 1940.
65. For example, Caplan, 1965; Marcus, 1955; Shulman, 1951.
66. Sutherland, 1931.
67. For example, Caplan and Gligor, 1964; Fox, V., 1946; Merrill, M. A., 1947; Tulchin, 1939.
68. Fox, V., 1946.
69. Merrill, M. A., 1947.
70. Caplan and Gligor, 1964.
71. Megargee and Bohn, 1979.
72. Prentice and Kelly, 1963.
73. Sutherland, 1931, p. 373.
74. Heilbrun, 1979.
75. Gath, D., Tennent, G., and Pidduck, R., 1971.
76. Hirschi and Hindelang, 1977.
77. For example, Wolfgang, Figlio, and Sellin, 1972; Hirschi, 1969.
78. West and Farrington, 1973.
79. Hirschi, 1969, p. 111.
80. Hirschi, 1969.
81. Gordon, 1975, p. 34.
82. Jencks, 1979.

CHAPTER 7

1. Porteus, 1933.
2. See Riddle and Roberts, 1977, for a review of the data.
3. Porteus, 1942.
4. Porteus, 1945, 1954.
5. Riddle and Roberts, 1977, p. 423.
6. Riddle and Roberts, 1977.
7. See, for example, contemporary textbooks like Kleinmuntz, 1982, or Hall and Lindzey, 1978.
8. Mischel, 1968, 1969.
9. For example, Rushton, Brainerd, and Pressley, 1983.
10. For example, Allport, 1937.
11. *Webster's Third New International Dictionary,* 1961.
12. See Farrington, 1979c, for a useful survey.
13. Glueck, S., and Glueck, E. T., 1950, 1968.
14. Rorschach, 1921; Exner, 1978.
15. Glueck, S., and Glueck, E. T., 1968.
16. For example, Reiss, 1951; Rubin, 1951.
17. Conger, J. J., and Miller, W. C., 1966.
18. *Ibid.,* p. 185.
19. Taylor, T., and Watt, D. C., 1977.
20. *Ibid.,* p. 164.
21. Robins, 1966.
22. Robins, 1978, p. 256.
23. Robins, Murphy, Woodruff, and King, 1971.
24. Robins, 1978, p. 262.
25. For example, West and Farrington, 1973, 1977; Farrington, 1982; Farrington and West, 1981.
26. West and Farrington, 1977, p. 1.
27. *Ibid.,* p. 158.
28. See Loeber, 1982, and Loeber and Dishion, 1983, for surveys of intercorrelations in antisocial behavior over the life cycle; and Mednick and Baert, 1981, for psychological deviance more generally. Monahan, 1981, deals with the clinical procedures in predicting violent behavior.
29. Schuessler and Cressey, 1950, p. 476.
30. Passingham, 1972, p. 355.
31. Waldo and Dinitz, 1967.
32. Tennenbaum, 1977.
33. *Ibid.,* Table 1.
34. Hathaway and McKinley, 1942, 1951; also, Dahlstrom, Welsh, and Dahlstrom, 1972, 1975.
35. See Gearing, 1979, for review.
36. Hathaway and Monachesi, 1953, and Monachesi and Hathaway, 1969.
37. Megargee and Bohn, 1979.
38. Gearing, 1979.
39. For example, Edinger, Reuterfors, and Logue, 1982.
40. For evidence of practical usefulness of the system, see Megargee, 1984.
41. Megargee, 1972.
42. Gough, 1957; Megargee, 1972.
43. Gough, 1968.
44. Megargee, 1966a.
45. Gough, 1948, p. 362.
46. Gough, 1965.
47. See review in Megargee, 1972.
48. Hogan, Mankin, Conway, and Fox, 1970.
49. Hetherington and Feldman, 1964.
50. Vincent, 1961.
51. Megargee, 1972.
52. Gough, 1965.
53. See Gearing, 1979, for a review focusing on MMPI data.
54. Farrington, 1982.
55. Panton, 1958.
56. *Ibid.,* p. 307ff.; see also Christensen and LeUnes, 1974.
57. Gough, Wenk, and Rozynko, 1965.
58. Gough and Heilbrun, 1965.
59. See Gearing, 1979.
60. Megargee, 1966b, 1973.
61. Megargee, 1966b.
62. For example, Blackburn, 1968.
63. Megargee, Cook, and Mendelsohn, 1967; Megargee and Cook, 1975.
64. Megargee, Cook, and Mendelsohn, 1967.
65. Laufer, Johnson, and Hogan, 1981.
66. Davis, K. R., and Sines, J., 1971; Persons and Marks, 1971.
67. Quoted by Pichot, 1978, p. 57.
68. Cleckley, 1964, p. 419.
69. *Ibid.,* p. 406.
70. *Ibid.,* p. 426.

71. Quay, 1965.
72. See especially Zuckerman's work, for example, 1978.
73. Blackburn, 1969, 1978.
74. See reviews in Hare, 1978; Mawson and Mawson, 1977; Siddle and Trasler, 1981.
75. Hare, 1965, 1978; House and Milligan, 1976; Lippert and Senter, 1966; Sutker, 1970; Syndulko, Parker, Jens, Maltzman, and Ziskind, 1975.
76. Waid, Orne, and Wilson, 1979.
77. Mawson and Mawson, 1977; Syndulko, 1978.
78. Syndulko, 1978, p. 149.
79. Forssman and Frey, 1953, cited by Mawson and Mawson, 1977.
80. Petersen, K. G. I., Matousek, M., Mednick, S. A., Volavka, J., and Pollock, V., 1982.
81. See also Hill, D., and Watterson, D., 1942.
82. Mednick, Volavka, Gabrielli, and Itil, 1981.
83. Reviewed by Satterfield, 1978; Willerman, 1979.
84. Firestone and Peters, 1983; Firestone and Prabhu, 1983.
85. Cleckley, 1964, p. 363.
86. Ziskind, 1978, p. 49; Ziskind, Syndulko, and Maltzman, 1978.
87. Hare and Quinn, 1971.
88. Hare, 1975; Ziskind, Syndulko, and Maltzman, 1978.
89. Moffitt, 1983; Trasler, 1978.
90. Ax, Lloyd, Gorham, Lootens, and Robinson, 1978.
91. Ax and Bamford, 1968.
92. Johns and Quay, 1962; Quay and Hunt, 1965.
93. Sarbin, Allen, and Rutherford, 1965.
94. As in the study of Schalling and Rosen, 1968.
95. Davids and Falkof, 1975.
96. Barndt and Johnson, 1955; Black, W. A., and Gregson, R. A., 1973; Mischel, 1961b; Stein, K. B., Sarbin, T. R., and Kulik, J. A., 1968.
97. Kelly, F. J., and Veldman, D. J., 1964.
98. Camp, 1977; Meichenbaum, 1975.

99. Mark and Ervin, 1970; Spellacy, 1978.
100. Hardyck and Petrinovich, 1977.
101. Ornstein, 1972.
102. Fitzhugh, 1973; Gabrielli and Mednick, 1980.
103. Hare, 1979.
104. Lykken, 1957.
105. Karpman, 1941, 1947.
106. Spielberger, Kling, and O'Hagan, 1978.
107. McGurk, McEwan, and Graham, 1981.
108. Eysenck, H. J., 1977.
109. Eysenck, H. J., and Eysenck, S. B. G., 1978.
110. Eaves and Eysenck, 1975; Eysenck, S. B. G., and Eysenck, H. J., 1970.
111. For example, West and Farrington, 1977.
112. Bouchard and McGue, 1981; Cattell, 1982; Eaves and Young, 1981; Eysenck, H. J., 1977; Eysenck, H. J., and Eysenck, S. B. G., 1978; Satterfield, 1978; Vernon, 1979; Willerman, 1979.

CHAPTER 8

1. Glueck, S., and Glueck, E. T., 1950, pp. 281–282.
2. Sutherland and Cressey, 1966, p. 30.
3. Cohen, A. K., 1955; Miller, 1958.
4. Merton, 1957.
5. Cloward and Ohlin, 1960.
6. For example, Lemert, 1951.
7. Hirschi, 1969.
8. Merton, 1957, p. 146.
9. Baumrind, 1967.
10. Baumrind, 1971.
11. Aronfreed, 1968, p. 2.
12. Eysenck, H. J., 1977.
13. Milgram, 1974.
14. Thomas, A., Chess, S., and Birch, H. G., 1968, 1970; Thomas, A., and Chess, S., 1976, 1984.
15. Freedman, D. G., 1974.
16. Plomin and Rowe, 1979.
17. Freedman, D. G., 1974.
18. Kagan, Kearsley, and Zelazo, 1978.
19. *Ibid.*, p. 272.
20. Sameroff and Chandler, 1975.

21. McCall, 1979.
22. Kopp and Parmelee, 1979.
23. Korner, 1973, 1974.
24. Kagan, 1978, p. 130.
25. Bell, R. Q., and Costello, N., 1964.
26. Bell, R. Q., and Darling, J. F., 1965.
27. Smith, C., and Lloyd, B., 1978;
    Bell, N. J., and Carver, W., 1980;
    Rossi, A. S., 1977; Kagan, 1978.
28. Bowlby, 1951, 1958, 1969.
29. Feldman, 1977, pp. 38–40.
30. Summarized in Rutter, 1972.
31. Ainsworth, Blehar, Walters, and
    Wall, 1978, p. 302.
32. Ainsworth, 1973; Goldfarb, 1943;
    Provence and Lipton, 1962.
33. Schaffer and Emerson, 1964.
34. Yarrow, L. J., 1963; Ainsworth,
    1973.
35. Rutter, 1972.
36. *Ibid.*, p. 103.
37. Ainsworth, 1973, p. 53.
38. Pringle and Bossio, 1960.
39. Goldfarb, 1955.
40. Matas, Arendt, and Sroufe, 1978.
41. Arendt, Gove, and Sroufe, 1979;
    Sroufe, 1979; Ainsworth, 1982;
    Sroufe, 1984.
42. Harlow and Harlow, 1969, 1970.
43. See the summaries in Mussen, Con-
    ger, and Kagan, 1979, pp. 187–189.
44. Novak and Harlow, 1975; Suomi
    and Harlow, 1972; Cummins and
    Suomi, 1976.
45. Rutter, 1972.
46. Hirschi, 1969.
47. Hindelang, 1973.
48. Wiatrowski, Griswold, and Roberts,
    1981.
49. Conger, R. D., 1976.
50. Mussen, Conger, and Kagan, 1979,
    p. 328.
51. Gardner, 1978, pp. 197–209, 484–
    493.
52. Kurtines and Grief, 1974.
53. For example, Bandura, 1973, 1977;
    Bandura and Walters, 1959.
54. Berkowitz, 1973, pp. 114–115.
55. Sears, Maccoby, and Levin, 1957,
    p. 259.
56. Martin, B., 1975.
57. *Ibid.*

58. Patterson, 1982, p. 108.
59. *Ibid.*, p. 123.
60. *Ibid.*, pp. 67–82.
61. *Ibid.*, p. 304.
62. *Ibid.*, p. 68.
63. Seligman, 1975.
64. Patterson, 1982, pp. 87–94.
65. Baumrind, 1978, p. 253.
66. Baumrind, 1967, 1971; Baumrind
    and Black, 1967.
67. Baumrind, 1978, p. 256.
68. McCord, W., and McCord, J., 1959.
69. *Ibid.*, pp. 77–84.
70. McCord, W., McCord, J., and
    Howard, A., 1961.
71. West, 1982, p. 16.
72. West and Farrington, 1973.
73. Farrington, 1978, pp. 83, 88, 90.
74. West and Farrington, 1977, pp.
    114–121.
75. West, 1982, pp. 29–30.
76. *Ibid.*, p. 37.
77. *Ibid.*, p. 50.
78. *Ibid.*, p. 57.
79. Patterson, 1982.
80. Hirschi, 1969.
81. *Ibid.*, pp. 88–94.
82. *Ibid.*, pp. 89–91.
83. Conger, R. D., 1976.
84. Cf. Miller, 1958.
85. Hirschi, 1969, p. 97.
86. West and Farrington, 1973, p. 116.
87. West, 1982, p. 49.
88. Orr and Cochran, 1969.
89. Patterson, 1982, p. 282.
90. Goodstein, L. D., and Rowley,
    V. N., 1961.
91. Loeber and Dishion, 1983.
92. Glueck, S., and Glueck, E. T., 1950.
93. Baumrind, 1967, 1971, 1978.
94. Hirschi, 1969.
95. West and Farrington, 1973, 1977.
96. Patterson, 1982.
97. Pulkkinen, 1980, 1982.
98. Olweus, 1980.
99. Schaefer, 1959.
100. Becker, W. C., 1964, pp. 174–175.
101. Martin, B., 1975, p. 466. See also
     Maccoby and Martin, 1983.
102. Cf. Becker, W. C., 1964; Martin, B.,
     1975.
103. Hogan, Johnson, and Emler, 1978.

104. Becker, W. C., 1964.
105. Blum, 1972.
106. Hippler, 1974.
107. *Ibid.*, pp. 24–25.
108. Parke, 1975; Martin, B., 1975.
109. Brim and Kagan, 1980.
110. Farrington, 1978; West and Farrington, 1977; West, 1982, p. 72.
111. Mitchell, S., and Rosa, P., 1981.
112. Pulkkinen, 1980, 1982.
113. Robins, 1966; Robins and Wish, 1977.
114. Glueck, S., and Glueck, E. T., 1968.
115. Kagan and Moss, 1962.
116. Olweus, 1979; Loeber, 1982.
117. Olweus, 1979.
118. Davids, Kidder, and Reich, 1962; Mischel, 1961a, b; Bixenstine and Buterbaugh, 1967; Rosenquist and Megargee, 1969; Landau, 1975.
119. Roberts, Erikson, Riddle, and Bacon, 1974.
120. Messer, 1976.
121. Rutter and Giller, 1984, pp. 173–175.
122. Mischel, 1974, p. 250.
123. Collins, 1977.
124. Wolfgang, Figlio, and Sellin, 1972, chap. 8.

CHAPTER 9

1. Glueck, S., and Glueck, E. T., 1950.
2. Monahan, T. P., 1957.
3. Wadsworth, 1979.
4. Hamparian, Schuster, Dinitz, and Conrad, 1978.
5. Wilkinson, 1980.
6. Rosenquist and Megargee, 1969.
7. Horne, 1980.
8. Elliott, Knowles, and Canter, 1981.
9. Bacon, Child, and Barry, 1963.
10. McCord, W., and McCord, J., 1959, p. 164; McCord, J., McCord, W., and Thurber, E., 1962; McCord, J., 1979.
11. Robins, 1966, pp. 79, 111, 172.
12. Montare and Boone, 1980.
13. Belson, 1975.
14. Sterne, 1964.
15. Tennyson, 1967.
16. Hirschi, 1969.
17. Ahlstrom and Havighurst, 1971; Dentler and Moore, 1961; Nye, 1958.
18. Herzog and Sudia, 1973.
19. For example, Monahan, T. P., 1957; Wadsworth, 1979; Hamparian, Schuster, Dinitz, and Conrad, 1978.
20. Cicourel, 1968; Emerson, 1969; Nye, 1958; Monahan, T. P., 1957, p. 257.
21. Wadsworth, 1976.
22. For example, Wilkinson, 1980.
23. McCord, W., and McCord, J., 1959, p. 164.
24. McCord, J., McCord, W., and Thurber, E., 1962, p. 367.
25. Nye, 1958.
26. Robins, 1966, p. 172.
27. Hirschi, 1969.
28. West and Farrington, 1973. See also the literature review in Rutter, 1971, 1980, and in Rutter and Giller, 1984.
29. Winch, 1977, p. 195.
30. Eisenberg, Langer, and Gersten, 1975.
31. Kellam, Ensminger, and Turner, 1977; Kellam, Adams, Brown, and Ensminger, 1982.
32. Ensminger, Kellam, and Rubin, 1983.
33. Patterson, 1982; see also Chapter 8, supra.
34. Shinn, 1978.
35. Broman, Nichols, and Kennedy, 1975. See also Lessing, Zagorin, and Nelson, 1970; Ilardi, 1966.
36. Parker and Kleiner, 1966.
37. Biller, 1968.
38. Anderson, R. E., 1968.
39. Hartnagel, 1970.
40. Nobers, 1968. See also Jackson, J. J., 1973.
41. Whiting, B. B., and Whiting, J. W. M., 1975; Whiting, J. W. M., and Whiting, B. B., 1975.
42. Tiller, 1957, 1958; Ancona, Cesa-Bianchi, and Bocquet, 1963.
43. Mischel, 1958, 1961a, b.
44. Herzog and Sudia, 1973, p. 184.

45. Belsky, 1981, p. 8.
46. Russell, C., 1974.
47. Gath, A., 1978.
48. Cain, Kelly, and Shannon, 1980.
49. For example, Spinetta and Rigler, 1972; Kempe, C. H., Silverman, F. N., Steele, B. F., Droegmueller, W., and Silver, H. K., 1962.
50. For example, Straus, Gelles, and Steinmetz, 1980.
51. For example, Clegg and Megson, 1968.
52. George and Main, 1979, 1980.
53. Reidy, 1977.
54. Kinard, 1980.
55. Elmer, 1967, 1977.
56. Egeland and Sroufe, 1981.
57. Rosen, K. S., and Cicchetti, D., 1984.
58. Egeland and Sroufe, 1981; Gersten, Coster, Weiss, and Cicchetti, 1983.
59. Burgess and Conger, 1978.
60. Spinetta and Rigler, 1972, p. 298.
61. Allan, 1978.
62. *Ibid.*, p. 59.
63. Yarrow, M., Campbell, J., and Burton, R., 1968.
64. Belsky, 1980.
65. Straus, M. A., Gelles, R. J., and Steinmetz, S. K., 1980.
66. For example, Duncan, G. M., Frazier, S. H., Litin, E. M., Johnson, A. M., and Barron, A. J., 1958; Satten, Menninger, and Rosen, 1960; Duncan, J. W., and Duncan, G. M., 1971; King, 1975.
67. Duncan, J. W., and Duncan, G. M., 1971.
68. Climent and Ervin, 1972.
69. New York State Assembly, Select Committee on Child Abuse, 1978.
70. Merrill, E. J., 1962.
71. Megargee, 1966a; Lane, P., 1978.
72. Rolston, 1971.
73. See the summary in Aber and Cicchetti, 1983.
74. Belsky, 1978, 1980; Herrenkohl and Herrenkohl, 1981.
75. Herrenkohl and Herrenkohl, 1981.
76. Belsky, 1980.
77. Gil, 1970.
78. Burgess, 1980.
79. Elmer, 1967.
80. Gil, 1970.
81. Straus, M. A., Gelles, R. J., and Steinmetz, S. K., 1980.
82. Pelton, 1978.
83. Merrill, E. J., 1962.
84. Rutter and Giller, 1984, pp. 127–129.
85. Hetherington, Cox, and Cox, 1978, 1979a, b.
86. Eme, 1979.
87. Block, J. H., Block, J., and Morrison, A., 1981.
88. Werner and Smith, 1977, 1982.

CHAPTER 10

1. Gottfredson, 1981, p. 436.
2. Bachman, Green, and Wirtanen, 1971; Gottfredson, 1981, pp. 441–442.
3. Elliott and Ageton, 1980; Hindelang, Hirschi, and Weis, 1979; Braithwaite, 1981; Gottfredson, 1981, p. 434.
4. Kelly, D. H., 1975.
5. For example, Johnson, R. E., 1979.
6. Glueck, S., and Glueck, E. T., 1950.
7. *Ibid.*, p. 140.
8. *Ibid.*, pp. 146–147.
9. Glueck, S., and Glueck, E. T., 1968, pp. 29–32, 73–78.
10. Glueck, S., and Glueck, E. T., 1950, p. 106.
11. *Ibid.*, p. 144.
12. Powers and Witmer, 1951, pp. 264–269.
13. West, 1982.
14. Polk and Schafer, 1972; Schafer and Polk, 1967.
15. Polk and Schafer, 1972.
16. Bachman, Green, and Wirtanen, 1971. See also the reanalysis in Wiatrowski, Hansell, Massey, and Wilson, 1982.
17. Rosenthal, R., and Jacobson, L., 1968.
18. Thorndike, 1968.
19. Rosenthal, R., and Jacobson, L., 1968, p. 75.
20. Elashoff and Snow, 1971.
21. Fleming and Anttonen, 1971a, b.
22. Jencks, 1979, p. 153; Murphy, J., 1974.

23. Pilling and Pringle, 1978, pp. 20, 245.
24. Reckless and Dinitz, 1972.
25. Ahlstrom and Havighurst, 1971.
26. Cf. Jeffery and Jeffery, 1969.
27. Stinchcombe, 1964.
28. Hirschi, 1969.
29. Hirschi and Hindelang, 1977.
30. Hirschi, 1969, p. 121.
31. *Ibid.*, pp. 129–130.
32. Bachman, Green, and Wirtanen, 1971.
33. Elliott and Voss, 1974.
34. Wilkins, 1965; McKissack, 1973b.
35. McMichael, 1979; Richman, Stevenson, and Graham, 1982; Rutter and Giller, 1984, pp. 165–168.
36. Murray, 1976. But cf. Sturge, 1982.
37. Zimmerman, Rich, Keilitz, and Broder, 1981; Broder, Dunivant, Smith, and Sutton, 1981.
38. Hirschi, 1969, p. 220.
39. Bachman et al., 1971.
40. Cf. Lefkowitz, 1968.
41. Coleman, Campbell, Hobson, McPartland, Mood, Weinfeld, and York, 1966; Jencks, 1972.
42. Rutter, Maughan, Mortimore, and Ouston, 1979.
43. *Ibid.*, pp. 77–78.
44. *Ibid.*, p. 80.
45. *Ibid.*, p. 156.
46. *Ibid.*, pp. 159–160.
47. *Ibid.*, pp. 173–175.
48. Nagel, T. W., 1982.
49. Purkey and Smith, 1983. Cf. also Rutter, 1983b.
50. National Institute of Education, 1978; Gottfredson and Gottfredson, 1982.
51. Gottfredson, 1983.
52. Coleman, Hoffer, and Kilgore, 1982.
53. *Ibid.*
54. Schweinhart and Weikart, 1980, 1983; Berrueta-Clement, Schweinhart, Barnett, and Weikart, n.d.

CHAPTER 11

1. Shaw, 1929; Shaw and McKay, 1931, 1942.
2. Cf. Baldwin, 1979; Bursik and Webb, 1982.
3. For example, Lander, 1954; Schmid, 1960; Bordua, 1958; Chilton, 1964.
4. Taft, 1933; Baldwin, 1979.
5. Maule and Martin, 1956; Baldwin and Bottoms, 1976; Baldwin, 1979.
6. Bursik and Webb, 1982.
7. Wolfgang, Figlio, and Sellin, 1972; Collins, 1977; West and Farrington, 1977; West, 1982; McCord, W., and McCord, J., 1959.
8. Shaw and McKay, 1931.
9. Eynon, cited in Reckless, 1955.
10. Vera Institute, 1980.
11. Erickson, 1971.
12. Erickson and Jensen, 1977.
13. Hindelang, 1976.
14. Greenwood, Petersilia, and Zimring, 1980.
15. McDermott and Hindelang, 1981.
16. Lerman, 1967; Hindelang, 1971.
17. Sutherland and Cressey, 1978.
18. Miller, 1958.
19. Bloch and Niederhofer, 1958.
20. Yablonsky, 1962.
21. Cloward and Ohlin, 1960.
22. Cohen, A. K., 1955.
23. *Ibid.;* Cloward and Ohlin, 1960; Sutherland and Cressey, 1978.
24. Short, 1957.
25. Erickson and Empey, 1965.
26. Hirschi, 1969.
27. *Ibid.*, p. 99.
28. *Ibid.*, ch. 8.
29. *Ibid.*, pp. 146–147.
30. Short, 1957.
31. Short and Strodtbeck, 1965.
32. Glueck, S., and Glueck, E. T., 1950.
33. Cartwright, Howard, and Reuterman, 1970.
34. Verlade, 1978.
35. Matza, 1964.
36. Hepburn, 1977.
37. Gould, L. C., 1969.
38. Short and Strodtbeck, 1965, p. 238.
39. Hirschi, 1969, p. 161.
40. Johnson, R. E., 1979.
41. Stanfield, 1966; Poole and Regoli, 1979.
42. Jensen, G. F., 1972.
43. Sherif, Harvey, White, Hood, and Sherif, 1961.
44. See also Sherif and Sherif, 1964.

45. Hindelang, 1976; Erickson and Jensen, 1977.
46. Kandel, 1978.
47. Knight and West, 1975; Richards, Berk, and Forster, 1979.
48. Hoffman, 1980.
49. Miller, 1976.
50. Friedman, Mann, and Friedman, 1975.
51. Yablonsky, 1962.
52. Thrasher, 1927.
53. Whyte, 1943.
54. Short and Strodtbeck, 1965; Drake and Cayton, 1945.
55. Moore, J. W., 1978.
56. Jacobs, J. B., 1977.
57. Spergel, 1964. For another account of neighborhood and racial differences among gangs, see Sullivan, 1983.
58. Wirth, 1928.
59. Zorbaugh, 1929.
60. Whyte, 1943.
61. Cohen, A. K., 1955; Cloward and Ohlin, 1960.
62. Miller, 1958.
63. Wolfgang and Ferracuti, 1982, pp. 152–153, 273–284.
64. Pettigrew and Spier, 1962.
65. Clinard and Abbott, 1973.
66. Jones, H., 1981.
67. Rutter, 1978; Rutter and Quinton, 1977; Rutter, Quinton, Rowlands, Yule, and Berger, 1975.
68. Rutter, 1978.
69. Reiss and Rhodes, 1961.
70. Merton, 1949.
71. Whyte, 1943, p. 256.
72. Suttles, 1968, p. 232.
73. Hippler, 1974.
74. *Ibid.*, pp. 159, 219.
75. *Ibid.*, p. 145.
76. Suttles, 1968, p. 232.
77. Whyte, 1943, pp. 272–276.
78. Hippler, 1974, pp. 140, 170.
79. Jacobs, J., 1961.
80. Newman, O., 1972.
81. Wirth, 1938.
82. Sampson, R. J., Castellano, T. C., and Laub, J. H., 1981.
83. Decker, D. L., Shichor, D., and O'Brien, R. M., 1982; Wilson, J. Q., and Boland, B., 1978.
84. Beasley and Antunes, 1974; Kobrin and Schuerman, 1981. But cf. Choldin, 1978.
85. Sampson, R. J., Castellano, T. C., and Laub, J. H., 1981, pp. 38–40.
86. Newman, O., 1972.
87. Cf. Murray, 1983.
88. Cf. Wilson, J. Q., and Kelling, G., 1982.
89. Taylor, R. B., Gottfredson, S. D., and Brower, S., 1980; Rubenstein, Murray, Motoyama, and Rouse, 1980; Murray, 1983.
90. Angel, 1969; Brill Associates, 1977.
91. Kohn, Franck, and Fox, 1975, cited in Murray, 1983.
92. Tien, O'Donnell, Barnett, and Mirchandane, 1977.
93. Fowler and Mangione, 1982.
94. Murray, 1983; Taylor, R. B., Gottfredson, S. D., and Brower, S., 1980.
95. Merry, 1981.
96. *Ibid.*, p. 142.
97. *Ibid.*
98. *Ibid.*, chap. 6.
99. Murray, 1983.
100. Greenberg, S. W., Rohe, W. M., and Williams, J. R., 1982.
101. Richards, Berk, and Forster, 1979.

CHAPTER 12

1. Schmid, 1960.
2. Rossi, P. H., Berk, R. A., and Lenihan, K. J., 1980; Peterson, M. A., and Braiker, H. B., 1980; Chaiken and Chaiken, 1982.
3. Gillespie, 1975.
4. *Ibid.*, p. 4.
5. Orsagh and Witte, 1981.
6. Thompson, Sviridoff, and McElroy, 1981, p. 6.
7. Freeman, 1983.
8. Becker, G. S., 1968; Ehrlich, 1973.
9. Banfield, 1970, 1974.
10. For example, Lewis, 1959, 1961, 1966.
11. Miller, 1958.
12. Cf. McClintock and Avison, 1968.
13. Adams, A. V., and Mangum, G. L., 1978, p. 39.
14. Freeman, 1983.

15. *Ibid.*
16. Cook, P. J., and Zarkin, G. A., 1985.
17. Phillips, L., Votey, H. L., and Maxwell, D., 1972.
18. *Ibid.;* Phillips, L., and Votey, H. L., 1981.
19. Ehrlich, 1973.
20. Brenner, 1976, 1984.
21. Brenner, 1976, p. 53 and preface.
22. Greenwood, 1982.
23. Greenwood, Wildhorn, Poggio, Strumwasser, and De Leon, 1976.
24. Pruitt, 1982.
25. Wilson, J. Q., 1975, p. 173.
26. Catalano and Dooley, 1979.
27. Brenner, 1976, pp. 70–71, 76–77, 141–146.
28. Cook, P. J., and Zarkin, G. A., 1983.
29. Brenner, 1984, pp. 56, 67, 105.
30. Cook, P. J., and Zarkin, G. A., 1984.
31. Witte, 1980.
32. Myers, 1983; cf. also Witte, 1983.
33. Cook, P. J., 1975.
34. Berk, R. A., Lenihan, K. J., and Rossi, P. H., 1980; Rossi, P. H., Berk, R. A., and Lenihan, K. J., 1980, chap. 12.
35. Rossi, P. H., Berk, R. A., and Lenihan, K. J., 1980, p. 192.
36. Auletta, 1982.
37. Gueron, 1980; Piliavin and Gartner, 1981; Maynard, 1980.
38. Phillips, L., Votey, H. L., and Maxwell, D., 1972.
39. Bachman, O'Malley, and Johnston, 1978.
40. *Ibid.*, pp. 200–202, fn. 2, 6.
41. *Ibid.*, p. 205.
42. *Ibid.*, pp. 178–180.
43. *Ibid.*, p. 202, fn. 6.
44. *Ibid.*, p. 184.
45. West and Farrington, 1977.
46. *Ibid.*, p. 149.
47. *Ibid.*, pp. 63–67.
48. Cf. Jencks, 1979.
49. Wolpin, 1978a.
50. Ehrlich, 1973.
51. Fox, J. A., 1978.
52. Block, M., and Nold, F., 1978; Blumstein, Cohen, and Nagin, 1978;

Decker, S. H., and Kohfeld, C. W., 1982; Fox, J. A., 1982.
53. Gould, L. C., 1971.
54. Mansfield, Gould, and Namenwirth, 1974.
55. Cohen, L. E., Felson, M., and Land, K. C., 1980.
56. Tocqueville, 1955.
57. Easterlin, 1973.
58. Brickman and Campbell, 1971.
59. Danziger and Wheeler, 1975.
60. Eberts and Schwirian, 1968.
61. Blau, J. R., and Blau, P. M., 1982.
62. Piore, 1977; Bluestone, 1970; Doeringer and Piore, 1971, 1975.
63. Harrison, 1972.
64. Viscusi, 1983.
65. Offner, 1970.
66. Stevenson, W., 1978.
67. Levitan, Mangum, and Marshall, 1976.
68. Brown, 1982.
69. Clark, K. B., and Summers, L. H., 1982.
70. Stevenson, W., 1978.
71. Rosenberg and Silverstein, 1969.
72. Liebow, 1967; Hannerz, 1969.
73. Hippler, 1974, p. 160.
74. Cf. Thompson, Sviridoff, and McElroy, 1981, p. 68.

CHAPTER 13

1. Goethe, cited in Phillips, D. P., 1974.
2. Phillips, D. P., 1974, 1979.
3. Phillips, D. P., 1974.
4. Phillips, D. P., 1983.
5. Berkowitz and Macaulay, 1971.
6. Phillips, D. P., 1984.
7. Dominick and Greenberg, 1972; Greenberg, B. S., 1974; Belson, 1978.
8. Lefkowitz, Eron, Walder, and Huesmann, 1977; Eron, Lefkowitz, Huesmann, and Walder, 1972.
9. Huesmann, Eron, Lefkowitz, and Walder, 1984.
10. Lefkowitz, Eron, Walder, and Huesmann, 1977, chap. 4; Eron, Lefkowitz, Huesmann, and Walder, 1972.
11. Chaffee, 1972.

12. Singer and Singer, 1981.
13. Rogosa, 1980. See also Armor, 1975.
14. Huesmann, Lagerspetz, and Eron, 1984; Milavsky, Kessler, Stipp, and Rubens, 1982.
15. Cook, Kendzierski, and Thomas, 1983; Freedman, J. L., 1984.
16. See the summary in Eysenck, H. J., and Nias, D. K. B., 1978, chap. 7.
17. Walters, Thomas, and Acker, 1962; Walters and Thomas, 1963.
18. Berkowitz and Geen, 1966.
19. Kniveton and Stephenson, 1970; Hicks, 1965; Kniveton, 1973.
20. Himmelweit, Oppenheim, and Vince, 1958.
21. *Ibid.*, p. 20.
22. *Ibid.*, p. 417.
23. Feshbach and Singer, 1971.
24. Eysenck, H. J., and Nias, D. K. B., 1978, p. 216.
25. Stein, A. H., and Friedrich, L. K., 1972.
26. Parke, Berkowitz, Leyens, West, and Sebastian, 1977.
27. Leyens, Camino, Parke, and Berkowitz, 1975.
28. Milgram and Shotland, 1973.
29. Surgeon General's Scientific Advisory Committee on Television and Social Behavior, 1972, p. 10.
30. For a summary of the debate, see Cater and Strickland, 1975.
31. Andison, 1977.
32. Kaplan, R. M., and Singer, R. D., 1976.
33. Edgar, 1977, p. 13.
34. Eysenck, H. J., and Nias, D. K. B., 1978, p. 252.
35. National Institute of Mental Health, 1982, p. 38.
36. *Time*, 1982; *Newsweek*, 1982.
37. National Academy of Sciences/ National Research Council, 1983. Cf. also Cook, T. D., Kendzierski, D. A., and Thomas, S. V., 1983; Freedman, J. L., 1984.
38. Himmelweit, Oppenheim, and Vince, 1958, pp. 12–13; Chaffee, 1972, p. 9.
39. Himmelweit and Swift, 1976.

40. Stein, A. H., and Friedrich, L. K., 1972.
41. *Ibid.*
42. Himmelweit, Oppenheim, and Vince, 1958, pp. 235–236, 258.
43. Dominick, 1974; Janis, 1980, p. 166.
44. Edgar, 1977, pp. 210–211.
45. Cf. Berkowitz, 1984.

CHAPTER 14

1. Ellinwood, 1971.
2. Blaine, Bozzetti, and Ohlson, 1973.
3. Wolfgang, 1958.
4. Greenberg, S. W., 1981, p. 81.
5. *Ibid.*
6. Peterson, M. A., and Braiker, H. B., 1980, p. 19.
7. Bureau of Justice Statistics, 1983.
8. Reed, D. S., 1981.
9. *Ibid.*, p. 383.
10. *Ibid.*, p. 339.
11. *Ibid.*, p. 383.
12. Pernanen, 1981.
13. Gerstein, 1981, p. 215.
14. Cook, P. J., 1981.
15. Bennett, Buss, and Carpenter, 1969.
16. Taylor, S. P., Schmutte, G. T., Leonard, K. E., and Cranston, J. W., 1979; Zeichner and Pihl, 1980; Pihl, Zeichner, Niaura, Nagy, and Zacchia, 1981; Taylor, S. P., and Gammon, C. B., 1975; Shuntich and Taylor, 1972.
17. Evans, 1980.
18. Lang, Goeckner, Adesso, and Marlatt, 1975.
19. Boyatzis, 1974.
20. Boyatzis, 1975.
21. Barnes, 1979.
22. Boyatzis, 1975.
23. Renson, Adams, and Tinklenberg, 1978.
24. O'Leary, M. R., Donovan, D. M., Freeman, C. W., and Chaney, E. F., 1976.
25. Donovan and Marlatt, 1982; Selzer, Payne, Westervelt, and Quinn, 1967.
26. Cotton, 1979, pp. 103, 111.
27. *Ibid.*, p. 108.

28. Goodwin, 1976; Frances, Timm, and Bucky, 1980.
29. Cotton, 1979, p. 109.
30. Roe, 1944.
31. Goodwin, Schlusinger, Hermansen, Guze, and Winokur, 1973.
32. Goodwin, Schlusinger, Moller, Hermansen, Winokur, and Guze, 1974, p. 168; Goodwin, 1977.
33. Bohman, 1978; see also Vaillant, 1983.
34. Cloninger, Sigvardsson, Bohman, and von Knorring, 1982.
35. Bohman, Cloninger, Sigvardsson, and von Knorring, 1982.
36. Snyder, 1958; Pittman and Snyder, 1962; Bales, 1944; Stewart, 1964; Vaillant, 1983.
37. Goodwin, 1979.
38. Ewing, Rouse, and Pellizari, 1974; Wolff, 1972; Wolff, 1973.
39. Fenna, Mix, Schaefer, and Gilbert, 1971.
40. Lieber, 1972.
41. Schuckit, 1980.
42. Wechsler, H., and Thum, D., 1973; Zucker and Barron, 1971; O'Leary, D. E., and O'Leary, M. R., 1976.
43. Robins, Murphy, and Breckenridge, 1968.
44. Bacon, Barry, and Child, 1965.
45. Cf. Snyder, 1958.
46. Whittaker, 1982.
47. Levy and Kunitz, 1974; MacAndrew and Edgerton, 1969.
48. Kaplan, J., 1983; O'Brien, Testa, O'Brien, Brady, and Wells, 1977.
49. Stimson, 1973.
50. Bass, Brown, and Dupont, 1971.
51. Peterson, M. A., and Braiker, H. B., 1980, p. 148.
52. Chaiken and Chaiken, 1982, chap. 3.
53. Moore, M. H., 1977, p. 84.
54. Goldstein, P. J., 1981, p. 81.
55. *Ibid.*, pp. 70–81.
56. Kaplan, J., 1983; Robins and Murphy, 1967.
57. Lukoff, 1974.
58. Hartnoll, Mitcheson, Battersby, Brown, Ellis, Fleming, and Hedley, 1980.

59. Ball, Rosen, Flueck, and Nurco, 1981.
60. Weisman, Marr, and Katsampes, 1976.
61. Inciardi, 1979.
62. Chambers, Dean, and Pletcher, 1981.
63. Goldstein, 1981, pp. 69–70.
64. Chambers, Dean, and Pletcher, 1981, pp. 151–152.
65. Inciardi, 1979, p. 342.
66. McBride, 1981.
67. Monforte and Spitz, 1975.
68. Gandossy, Williams, Cohen, and Harwood, 1980, pp. 24–26, 30–32, 34; Hunt and Chambers, 1976, pp. 78–81; Gersick, 1981, pp. 43–45.
69. Gerard and Kornetsky, 1955.
70. Chein, 1964, p. 255.
71. *Ibid.*, pp. 272–274; see also Eldred and Brown, 1974, and Robins, Davis, and Wish, 1977.
72. Cohen, S., 1981.
73. Hunt and Chambers, 1976, p. 3.
74. Alarcón, 1969; Hughes, Crawford, and Jaffe, 1971; Levengood, Lowinger, and Schooff, 1973.
75. Hunt and Chambers, 1976, chap. 1.
76. Clayton and Voss, 1981, p. 39.
77. Hunt and Chambers, 1976, p. 98.
78. Clayton and Voss, 1981, pp. 15, 17.
79. Boyle and Brunswick, 1980.

CHAPTER 15

1. Latané and Darley, 1970.
2. Lipton, Martinson, and Wilks, 1975.
3. *Ibid.*, p. 228.
4. *Ibid.*, pp. 213–214; Adams, S., 1962.
5. Sechrest, White, and Brown, 1979, p. 46.
6. *Ibid.*, p. 31.
7. Gendreau and Ross, 1979.
8. Eysenck, H. J., 1952, 1965.
9. Smith, M. L., and Glass, G. V, 1977.
10. Palmer, 1978.
11. Adams, S., 1962.
12. Glaser, 1974.
13. See the reviews in Davidson and Seidman, 1974; Burchard and Harig, 1976; Emery and Marholin,

1977; Ross, R. R., and McKay, H. B., 1978; Nietzel, 1979; Gross and Brigham, 1980.

14. Lipton, Martinson, and Wilks, 1975.

15. Ross, R. R., and McKay, H. B., 1978.

16. Jesness, DeRisi, McCormick, and Wedge, 1972.

17. Johnson, V. S., 1977.

18. Schwitzgebel and Kolb, 1964.

19. Watson, Maloney, Brooks, Blase, and Collins, 1980.

20. Burchard and Harig, 1976; Kirigin, Braukmann, Atwater, and Wolf, 1982.

21. Kirigin, Braukmann, Atwater, and Wolf, 1982, pp. 8–9.

22. Jones, R. R., Weinrott, M. R., and Howard, J. R., 1981.

23. Tharp and Wetzel, 1969.

24. Cf. Burchard and Harig, 1976.

25. Alexander and Parsons, 1973.

26. Klein, N. C., Alexander, J. F., and Parsons, B. V., 1977.

27. Farrington, 1979a.

28. Patterson, 1982, p. 293.

29. Patterson, 1982, pp. 118–121.

30. Tyler and Brown, 1967.

31. Patterson, Chamberlain, and Reid, 1982.

32. Patterson, 1982, pp. 305–306.

33. Miller, 1962.

34. Fo and O'Donnell, 1974.

35. Fo and O'Donnell, 1975; O'Donnell, Lydgate, and Fo, 1979.

36. For example, Ehrlich, 1973.

37. Wilson, J. Q., 1983, chap. 7.

38. Freeman, 1983.

39. Nagin, 1978; Blumstein, Cohen, and Nagin, 1978.

40. Goldberg, I., 1978.

41. Wilson, J. Q., and Boland, B., 1978.

42. Ehrlich and Mark, 1977.

43. Blumstein and Nagin, 1977.

44. Blumstein, Cohen, and Nagin, 1978, p. 49.

45. Wolpin, 1978a.

46. Merry, 1981.

47. *Ibid.*, pp. 167–172.

48. Chaiken and Chaiken, 1982, pp. 172–173.

49. Peterson, M. A., and Braiker, H. B., 1980, chap. 6.

50. Silberman, M., 1976.

51. Erickson, Gibbs, and Jensen, 1977.

52. Tittle, 1980.

53. *Ibid.* See also Grasmick and Green, 1980, and Grasmick and Bryjak, 1980.

54. Merry, 1981.

55. Chaiken and Chaiken, 1982.

56. Sherman and Berk, 1984.

57. Lipton, Martinson, and Wilks, 1975.

58. Murray and Cox, 1979.

59. Maltz, Gordon, McDowall, and McCleary, 1980.

60. Empey and Erickson, 1972.

61. Ross, H. L., 1981, p. 105.

62. *Ibid.*

63. *Ibid.*, p. 96.

64. *Ibid.*, pp. 69–70.

65. *Ibid.*, 1973, 1977.

66. Ross, H. L., 1981.

67. Summers and Harris, 1978.

68. Peterson, M. A., and Braiker, H. B., 1980, p. 28.

69. Williams, A. F., Zador, P. L., Harris, S. S., and Karpf, R. S., 1983.

70. Wagenaar, 1981; Klein, T. M., 1981.

71. Zimring, 1972.

72. Beha, 1977; Deutsch and Alt, 1977; Pierce and Bowers, 1981.

73. Joint Committee on New York Drug Law Evaluation, 1977.

74. Murray and Cox, 1979.

75. Empey and Erickson, 1972.

76. Cf. Glaser, 1974, 1983.

77. Schwitzgebel and Kolb, 1964; Fo and O'Donnell, 1974, 1975; O'Donnell, Lydgate, and Fo, 1979.

78. Tharp and Wetzel, 1969; Alexander and Parsons, 1973; Patterson, 1982.

CHAPTER 16

1. Gurr, 1977, p. 118.

2. Gatrell and Hadden, 1972, p. 377.

3. Cf. also Gurr, Grabosky, and Hula, 1977.

4. Lane, R., 1979, 1980; Johnson, P. E., 1978; Richardson, 1970;

Gurr, 1981; Hewitt and Hoover, 1982.

5. Monkkonen, 1981a, 1982. See also McDonald, 1982.
6. Lane, R., 1979.
7. Ferdinand, 1967.
8. Bureau of the Census, 1975, Vol. I, p. 408.
9. *Ibid.,* p. 414. See also Holinger and Klemen, 1982.
10. Bureau of the Census, 1981, p. 177.
11. Hindelang, Gottfredson, and Flanagan, 1981, p. 290.
12. Gurr, 1977.
13. McClintock and Avison, 1968, p. 59.
14. Archer and Gartner, 1980.
15. Gurr, 1980; Davies, 1983.
16. Chaiken and Chaiken, 1983; Farrington and Dowds, 1984.
17. Loftin, 1980.
18. Clinard and Abbott, 1973, esp. p. 101.
19. Archer and Gartner, 1980.
20. Cook, P. J., 1983.
21. Gould, L. C., 1971.
22. *Ibid*.
23. Cohen, L. E., 1981.
24. *Ibid.;* Chaiken and Chaiken, 1983.
25. Federal Bureau of Investigation, 1962, 1978.
26. Bureau of the Census, 1981, p. 424.
27. Wolpin, 1978b.
28. Stark, R., Doyle, D. P., and Kent, L., 1980; Higgins and Albrecht, 1977.
29. Ferdinand, 1970; Task Force on Assessment, 1967; Sagi and Wellford, 1968; Mulvihill, Tumin, and Curtis, 1969; Wellford, 1973; Jones, E. T., 1976. See also Chapter 5 of this book.
30. Blumstein and Nagin, 1975.
31. Wilson, J. Q., and Boland, B., 1978.
32. Wolfgang, 1983; Shannon, 1976.
33. Archer and Gartner, 1976.
34. Shannon, 1976.
35. Wolfgang, 1981.
36. Wolfgang and Tracy, 1982.
37. Davids, Kidder, and Reich, 1962.
38. Cf. Barndt and Johnson, 1955.
39. Davids and Falkof, 1975.

40. Kumar, Anday, Sacks, Ting, and Delivoria-Papadopoulos, 1980.
41. Fuchs, 1983; Williams, R. L., and Chen, P. M., 1982.
42. Lyons, 1983.
43. Wolfgang, 1958.
44. Waters and Crandall, 1964.
45. *Ibid.,* p. 1032.
46. Sunley, 1955.
47. Wolfenstein, 1955.
48. Stendler, 1950.
49. Weiss, 1976.
50. Cf. Sellin, 1926.
51. Bennett, J. V., 1953; von Hentig, 1947, quoted in Archer and Gartner, 1976.
52. Archer and Gartner, 1976.
53. Thomas, D. S., 1925.
54. Wolpin, 1978a.
55. Cook, P. J., and Zarkin, G. A., 1983a.
56. Gatrell and Hadden, 1972.
57. Thomas, D. S., 1925.
58. Wolpin, 1978a.
59. Phillips, L., Votey, H. L., and Maxwell, D., 1972.
60. Gottfredson, 1981.
61. Murray, 1980.
62. Murray and Cox, 1979.
63. Task Force on Assessment, 1967, Appendix D; Sagi and Wellford, 1968.
64. Fox, J. A., 1978.
65. Decker, S. H., and Kohfeld, C. W., 1982. See also the reply by Fox, J. A., 1982.
66. De Tray, 1978; Fuchs, 1983.
67. Belmont and Marolla, 1973; Zajonc and Markus, 1975; Lindert, 1977.
68. Easterlin, 1980; Freeman, 1978.
69. Wachter, 1976; Russell, L. B., 1979.
70. Lane, R., 1979, pp. 60, 71, 153.
71. Monkkonen, 1982.
72. Gurr, 1977.
73. Gatrell and Hadden, 1972, p. 377.
74. Monkkonen, 1982.
75. Cahalan, 1979. But see the critique in Blumstein and Moitra, 1980.
76. Cf. Blumstein and Moitra, 1980.
77. Howe, 1976.
78. Johnson, P. E., 1978.

79. Kett, 1977.
80. Clark, N. H., 1976.
81. Johnson, P. E., 1978, p. 82.
82. Kett, 1977, pp. 29, 60; Johnson, P. E., 1978, pp. 38, 55–60.
83. Johnson, P. E., 1978, pp. 121–128.
84. Singleton, 1976.
85. Boyer, 1978, pp. 43–49.
86. *Ibid.*, p. 41.
87. Laqueur, 1976, p. 44.
88. *Ibid.*, pp. 219–227, 239, 241.
89. Boyer, 1978, p. 113.
90. Clark, N. H., 1976, p. 20; Rorabaugh, 1979, p. 233.
91. Kaestle, 1973, p. 112; Tyack and Hansot, 1982; Kaestle and Vinovskis, 1980; Schultz, 1973; Lazerson, 1971; Katz, 1971.
92. Kaestle, 1973, pp. 115–116.
93. *Ibid.*, p. 128.
94. *Ibid.;* Katz, 1968.
95. Quoted in Katz, 1968, p. 203.
96. Clark, N. H., 1976; Burnham, 1968.
97. Clark, N. H., 1976; Fisher, 1930; Gusfield, 1968.
98. Kett, 1977.
99. Wishy, 1968.
100. Jones, V., 1932; Kirkpatrick, 1934; Simpson, 1934.
101. Cavan and Ranck, 1969.
102. Elder, 1974.
103. Wilson, J. Q., and Kelling, G., 1982.
104. Holinger, 1979; Davies, 1983; Wynne, 1979; Davis, K., 1983.

CHAPTER 17

1. Durkheim, 1964 (1895).
2. Malinowski, 1926, p. 13.
3. Beirne, 1983.
4. Neznansky, 1979.
5. Wilkins, 1980.
6. Quoted in Wilkins, 1980, p. 23.
7. *Report of the Secretary-General,* 1977; Viccica, 1980.
8. Wolf, 1971.
9. Quinney, 1965.
10. Shelley, 1981.
11. See Neznansky, 1979.
12. Archer and Gartner, 1981a; Clinard and Abbott, 1973.

13. Archer and Gartner, 1981a.
14. Toby, 1979.
15. Kerner, 1968; Savitz, 1962.
16. *Report of the Secretary-General,* 1977.
17. Toby, 1979.
18. Wellford, 1974.
19. Braithwaite, J., and Braithwaite, V., 1980.
20. Hansmann and Quigley, 1979.
21. Messner, 1983.
22. Krohn, 1976.
23. Newman, G., 1976.
24. Scott and Al-Thakeb, 1980.
25. See Parkin, 1977, for a discussion of violence in America.
26. For example, Beirne, 1983.
27. Bacon, Child, and Barry, 1963.
28. Mischel, 1958, 1961a.
29. Clifford, 1976.
30. *Ibid.*
31. Bayley, 1976.
32. *New York Times,* 1983b.
33. Bayley, 1976.
34. *Ibid.*
35. *Ibid.;* Clifford, 1976; Vogel, 1979.
36. Vogel, 1979, p. 208.
37. Clifford, 1976; Vogel, 1979.
38. Vogel, 1979.
39. For example, the Australian William Clifford, 1976, or the American Ezra Vogel, 1979.
40. Moore, T. G., 1982.
41. Dien, 1982, p. 334, for a discussion of moral conceptions and legal practices in China, which makes some of the same observations as this discussion of Japan.
42. Lynn and Dziobon, 1980.
43. Lynn, 1982.
44. Reviewed in Lynn, 1981.
45. Eaves and Young, 1981.
46. Such as that in Holyst, 1979.
47. Holyst, 1979, p. 116.

CHAPTER 18

1. Nettler, 1974; Voss, 1963; Werner and Smith, 1977.
2. Sveri, 1960; Gibbens and Ahrenfeldt, 1966.
3. Reckless, 1955.

4. Shoham, 1966.
5. Federal Bureau of Investigation, 1981.
6. *Ibid.;* Bureau of the Census, 1981, p. 26.
7. Blumstein, 1982.
8. Federal Bureau of Investigation, 1981.
9. Elliott and Ageton, 1980.
10. Elliott, Knowles, and Canter, 1981, pp. 158–160.
11. Hackler and Lautt, 1969; Kleck, 1982.
12. Petersilia, 1983.
13. Bureau of Justice Statistics, 1982.
14. Hindelang, 1978.
15. Hindelang, 1981.
16. Federal Bureau of Investigation, 1981.
17. Bureau of the Census, 1984, p. 180. See also McGhee, 1984.
18. Blumstein and Graddy, 1981–1982; Petersilia, 1983.
19. Block, N. H., and Dworkin, G., 1974.
20. Damon, A., Bleibtreu, H. K., Elliot, O., and Giles, E., 1962; Damon, A., Stoudt, H. W., and McFarland, R. A., 1966; Malina, 1973; Malina and Rarick, 1973.
21. McCandless, Persons, and Roberts, 1972.
22. Gynther, 1972. But cf. Bertelson, Marks, and May, 1982, and Lanyon, 1984.
23. Elion and Megargee, 1975.
24. Osborne, 1980, chap. 4.
25. *Ibid.,* chap. 12.
26. Shuey, 1966; Osborne, 1980; Osborne and McGurk, 1982; Loehlin, Lindzey, and Spuhler, 1975. Snyderman, 1984.
27. Linn, 1982; Wigdor and Garner, 1982.
28. Wigdor and Garner, 1982, Part I, p. 3.
29. Snyderman, 1984.
30. Fuchs, 1983; Williams, R. L., and Chen, P. M., 1982; Malina, 1973.
31. Dreger, 1973b; Morton, N. E., 1972; Willerman, 1979.
32. Osborne and McGurk, 1982.

33. Wolfgang, Figlio, and Sellin, 1972.
34. Rose, 1981.
35. Barnett, Kleitman, and Larson, 1975.
36. Lane, R., 1979, p. 113.
37. Wolfgang, Figlio, and Sellin, 1972.
38. *Ibid.,* p. 118.
39. *Ibid.,* p. 91.
40. *Ibid.,* p. 135.
41. Wolfgang and Weiner, 1982.
42. Tagaki and Platt, 1978.
43. Beach, 1932; Hayner, 1933, 1938; Lind, 1930.
44. Beach, 1932, p. 49.
45. Hayner, 1938, p. 919.
46. Beynon, 1935.
47. Kitano, 1967.
48. Anderson, J., 1982, pp. 299–304.
49. Reid, I. D. A., 1939.
50. Bianchi, 1980; Levitan, Johnston, and Taggart, 1975.
51. Danziger and Plotnick, 1981.
52. Votey and Phillips, 1974.
53. Dollard, 1957, pp. 274, 279, 280–81.
54. Lundsgaarde, 1977.
55. Cf. Hawkins, 1983.
56. U.S. Department of Labor, 1965.
57. Frazier, 1939.
58. For example, Billingsley, 1969; Hill, R. D., 1972; Ladner, 1972; Stack, 1974; Shimkin, Shimkin, and Frate, 1978; Engram, 1982.
59. Scanzoni, 1971.
60. Monahan, T. P., 1957.
61. Anderson, R. E., 1968.
62. Mosher, 1969.
63. Chilton and Markle, 1972.
64. Clarke and Koch, 1975.
65. Robins and Hill, 1966.
66. Rosen, L., 1970.
67. Drayton, 1978.
68. Robins and Hill, 1966.
69. Shinn, 1978.
70. Broman, Nichols, and Kennedy, 1975.
71. Kellam, Ensminger, and Turner, 1977.
72. Kellam, Adams, Brown, and Ensminger, 1982.
73. Hess and Shipman, 1965; see also Brophy, 1970.

74. Bee, Van Egeren, Streissguth, Nyman, and Leckie, 1969.
75. Hippler, 1974.
76. Darity and Myers, 1983.
77. Spanier, 1980.
78. Bureau of the Census, 1981.
79. Green and Welniak, 1983.
80. Spanier, 1980.
81. Gutman, 1976.
82. Furstenberg, Hershberg, and Modell, 1975.
83. Bishop, 1980.
84. Cf. Darity and Myers, 1983.
85. Joint Center for Political Studies, 1983.
86. Silberman, 1978.
87. Grier and Cobbs, 1968.
88. Gutman, 1976.
89. Abrahams, 1970.
90. Jackson, B., 1974.
91. Silberman, 1978, p. 149.
92. *Ibid.*, p. 152.
93. Harris and Lewis, 1974.
94. Davis, A., and Dollard, J., 1940, p. 122.
95. *Ibid.*, p. 121.
96. Johnson, C. S., 1941, p. 288.
97. *Ibid.*, pp. 289–327.
98. Anderson, E., 1978, p. 130.
99. *Ibid.*, p. 129.
100. *Ibid.*, p. 155.
101. Bureau of the Census, 1981, p. 77.
102. *Ibid.*, p. 79.
103. Wilson, W. J., 1982.

CHAPTER 19

1. Menninger, 1968.
2. *Ibid.*, p. 203.
3. *Ibid.*, p. 218.
4. For example, Skinner, 1953; Posner, 1981.
5. Gaylin, 1982.
6. *Ibid.*, p. 253.
7. *Ibid.*, p. 341.
8. For example, LaFave and Scott, 1972; Reid, S. T., 1982.
9. de Villiers, 1982; Rachlin and Herrnstein, 1969.
10. Goodhart, 1953, quoted in Weinreb, 1975, p. 548.
11. LaFave and Scott, 1972, p. 24.
12. Morris, 1974; Packer, 1968.
13. von Hirsch, 1976, p. 69.
14. *Ibid.*, p. 70.
15. Kant, 1979 (1797), p. 333.
16. Murphy, J. G., 1979, p. xi.
17. *Ibid.*
18. Packer, 1968.
19. From Stephen, 1883, quoted in Weinreb, 1975, p. 549.
20. *Solem* v. *Helm*, 1983.
21. *Ibid.*, pp. 3009–3010.
22. *Ibid.*, p. 3022.
23. *Ibid.*, p. 3006.
24. Kaufman, I. R., 1982.
25. *New York Times,* 1983a.
26. London *Times* for January 21, 1843, quoted in Weinreb, 1975, p. 367.
27. London *Times* for January 26, 1843, quoted in Weinreb, 1975, p. 370.
28. For a review of the test and its problems, see Fingarette and Hasse, 1979; LaFave and Scott, 1972; Weinreb, 1975.
29. Weinreb, 1975, p. 393.
30. See Weinreb, 1975, for a review.
31. *New York Times,* 1982.
32. Butler, 1927 (1872).
33. Wootton, 1959.
34. Hart, 1978.

CHAPTER 20

1. Werner and Smith, 1982.
2. Patterson, 1982; Quinton and Rutter, 1983.
3. Bell, N. J., and Carver, W., 1980; Smith, C., and Lloyd, B., 1978.
4. Rutter, 1983a.
5. Martin, J. A., Maccoby, E. E., and Jacklin, C. N., 1981.
6. Sameroff and Chandler, 1975.
7. Emery, 1982; Rutter, 1970, 1971; Rutter and Giller, 1984.
8. Bentham, 1948 (1789).
9. Hobbes, *Leviathan,* 1957 (1651), chap. 13.
10. *Ibid.*
11. *Ibid.*, chap. 27.

12. *Ibid.*

13. Beccaria, *On Crimes and Punishments,* 1963 (1764), p. 8.

14. Bentham, *Introduction to the Principles of Morals and Legislation,* 1948 (1789), chap. 1.

15. *Ibid.,* chap. 14.

16. Beccaria, 1963.

17. Smith, A., 1976 (1759), chap. 1.

18. Rousseau, *Discourse on the Arts and Sciences,* 1973 (1750), p. 24.

19. Rousseau, *Discourse on Inequality,* 1973 (1755), pp. 65–66.

20. *Ibid.,* p. 66 fn.

21. *Ibid.,* p. 76.

22. Bloom, 1978, p. 135.

23. Rousseau, *Emile,* 1974 (1762).

24. Bloom, 1978, pp. 136–137.

25. Rousseau, *Discourse on Political Economy,* 1973 (1755), p. 118.

26. Aristotle, *Politics,* Bk. I, ch. i, sec. 10; *Nichomachean Ethics,* Bk. IX, ch. ix, sec. 3.

27. Aristotle, *Politics,* Bk. I, ch. i, sec. 10.

28. Aristotle, *Nichomachean Ethics,* Bk. II, sec. 1.

29. *Ibid.,* Bk. II, sec. 3.

30. Stark, W., 1980, Vol. III, p. 98.

31. Becker, G. S., 1981; see also Hannan, 1982.

32. Bureau of the Census, 1978, Tables 22 and 23 (pp. 26–27).

33. Malcolm X, 1964.

34. Essien-Udom, 1962, pp. 31–62.

APPENDIX

1. Ainslie, 1975; Herrnstein, 1981; Rachlin, 1974.

REFERENCES

Aber, J. L., and Cicchetti, D. 1983. The socio-emotional development of maltreated children: An empirical and theoretical analysis. In H. Fitzgerald, B. Lester, and M. Yongman (eds.), *Theory and Research in Behavioral Pediatrics,* Vol. 1. New York: Plenum Press.

Abrahams, R. D. 1970. *Deep Down in the Jungle,* rev. ed. Chicago: Aldine.

Ackerly, S. 1933. Rebellion and its relation to delinquency and neurosis in sixty adolescents. *American Journal of Orthopsychiatry* 3:146–160.

Adams, A. V., and Mangum, G. L. 1978. *The Lingering Crisis of Youth Unemployment.* Kalamazoo, Mich.: W. E. Upjohn Institute for Employment Research.

Adams, J. S. 1965. Inequity in social exchange. In L. Berkowitz (ed.), *Advances in Experimental Social Psychology,* Vol. 2. New York: Academic Press.

Adams, M. E., and Vedder, C. B. 1961. Age and crime: Medical and sociological characteristics of prisoners over 50. *Geriatrics* 16:177–181.

Adams, S. 1962. The PICO project. In N. Johnston, L. Savitz, and M. Wolfgang (eds.), *The Sociology of Punishment and Corrections.* New York: John Wiley.

Adler, F. 1975. *Sisters in Crime: The Rise of the New Female Criminal.* New York: McGraw-Hill.

————. 1977. The interaction between women's emancipation and female criminality: A cross-cultural perspective. *International Journal of Criminology and Penology* 5:101–112.

Adler, F., and Simon, R. J. (eds.). 1979. *The Criminology of Deviant Women.* Boston: Houghton Mifflin.

Ahlstrom, W. M., and Havighurst, R. J. 1971. *Four Hundred Losers: Delinquent Boys in High School.* San Francisco: Jossey-Bass.

Ainslie, G. 1974. Impulse control in pigeons. *Journal of the Experimental Analysis of Behavior* 21:485–489.

————. 1975. Specious reward: A behavioral theory of impulsiveness and impulse control. *Psychological Bulletin* 82:463–496.

Ainslie, G., and Herrnstein, R. J. 1981. Preference reversal and delayed reinforcement. *Animal Learning and Behavior* 9:476–482.

559

Ainsworth, M. D. S. 1973. The development of infant-mother attachment. In B. C. Caldwell and H. R. Ricciuti (eds.), *Review of Child Development and Research,* Vol. 3. Chicago: University of Chicago Press, pp. 1–94.

———. 1982. Attachment: Retrospect and prospect. In C. M. Parkes and J. Stevenson (eds.), *The Place of Attachment in Human Behavior.* London: Tavistock.

Ainsworth, M. D. S., Blehar, M. C., Walters, E., and Wall, S. 1978. *Patterns of Attachment.* Hillsdale, N.J.: Lawrence Erlbaum.

Akman, D., and Normandeau, A. 1968. Towards the measurement of criminality in Canada: A replication study. *Acta Criminologica* 1:135–260.

Alarcón, R. de. 1969. The spread of heroin abuse in a community. *United Nations Bulletin on Narcotics* 21:17–22.

Alexander, J. F., and Parsons, B. V. 1973. Short-term behavioral intervention with delinquent families: Impact on family process and recidivism. *Journal of Abnormal Psychology* 81:219–225.

Allan, L. J. 1978. Child abuse: A critical review of the research and the theory. In J. P. Martin (ed.), *Violence and the Family.* Chichester, England: John Wiley & Sons.

Allport, G. W. 1937. *Personality: A Psychological Interpretation.* New York: Holt.

Ancona, L., Cesa-Bianchi, M., and Bocquet, F. 1963. Identification with the father in the absence of a paternal model. *Archivo di Psicologia, Neurologia, e Psichiatrica* 24:339–361.

Anderson, E. 1978. *A Place on the Corner.* Chicago: University of Chicago Press.

Anderson, J. 1982. *This Was Harlem: A Cultural Portrait, 1900–1950.* New York: Farrar, Straus, Giroux.

Anderson, R. E. 1968. Where's dad? Paternal deprivation and delinquency. *Archives of General Psychiatry* 18:641–649.

Andison, F. S. 1977. TV violence and viewer aggression: A cumulation of study results, 1956–1976. *Public Opinion Quarterly* 41:314–331.

Andrew, J. M. 1974. Immaturity, delinquency, and the Wechsler P V sign. *Journal of Abnormal Child Psychology* 2:245–251.

———. 1977. Delinquency: Intellectual imbalance? *Criminal Justice and Behavior* 4: 99–104.

———. 1980. Verbal IQ and the I-level classification system for delinquents. *Criminal Justice and Behavior* 7:193–202.

Angel, S. 1969. *Discouraging Crime Through City Planning.* Berkeley, Calif.: University of California Press.

Archer, D., and Gartner, R. 1976. Violent acts and violent times: A comparative approach to post war homicide rates. *American Sociological Review* 41:937–963.

———. 1980. Homicide in 110 nations: The development of the comparative crime data file. In E. Bittner and S. L. Messinger (eds.), *Criminology Review Yearbook,* Vol. 2. Beverly Hills, Calif.: Sage Publications, pp. 433–463.

———. 1981a. Homicide in 110 nations. In L. I. Shelley (ed.), *Readings in Comparative Criminology.* Carbondale, Ill.: Southern Illinois University Press.

———. 1981b. Peacetime casualties: The effects of war on the violent behavior of noncombatants. In E. Aronson (ed.), *Readings About the Social Animal,* 3rd ed. San Francisco: W. H. Freeman, pp. 236–248.

Archer, D., Gartner, R., Akert, R., and Lockwood, T. 1978. Cities and homicide: A new look at an old paradox. *Comparative Studies in Sociology* 1:73–95.

Arendt, R., Gove, F. L., and Sroufe, L. A. 1979. Continuity of individual adaptation from infancy to kindergarten: A predictive study of ego resiliency and curiosity in pre-schoolers. *Child Development* 50:950–959.

Aristotle. 1941. *Nichomachean Ethics.* In Richard McKeon (ed.), *The Basic Works of Aristotle.* New York: Random House.

————. 1952. *Politics*. Trans. Ernest Barker. Oxford: Clarendon Press.

Armor, D. J. 1975. *Measuring the Effects of Television on Aggressive Behavior*. Unpublished study. Santa Monica, Calif.: Rand.

Aronfreed, J. 1968. *Conduct and Conscience: The Socialization of Internalized Control over Behavior*. New York: Academic Press.

Auletta, K. 1982. *The Underclass*. New York: Random House.

Ax, A. F., and Bamford, J. L. 1968. Validation of a psychophysiological test of aptitude for learning social motives. *Psychophysiology* 5:316–322.

Ax, A. F., Lloyd, R., Gorham, J. C., Lootens, A. M., and Robinson, R. 1978. Autonomic learning: A measure of motivation. *Motivation and Emotion* 2:213–242.

Bachman, J. G., Green, S., and Wirtanen, I. D. 1971. *Dropping Out—Problem or Symptom?* Vol. 3 of *Youth in Transition*. Ann Arbor, Mich.: University of Michigan Institute for Social Research.

Bachman, J. G., O'Malley, P. M., and Johnston, J. 1978. *Adolescence to Adulthood—Change and Stability in the Lives of Young Men*, Vol. 6 of *Youth in Transition*. Ann Arbor, Mich.: University of Michigan Institute for Social Research.

Bacon, M. K., Barry, H., and Child, I. L. 1965. A cross-cultural study of drinking. *Quarterly Journal of Studies on Alcohol*. Supplement No. 3, pp. 29–48.

Bacon, M. K., Child, I. L., and Barry, H. 1963. A cross-cultural study of correlates of crime. *Journal of Abnormal and Social Psychology* 66:291–300.

Baldwin, J. 1979. Ecological and areal studies in Great Britain and the United States. In N. Morris and M. Tonry (eds.), *Crime and Justice: An Annual Review of Research*, Vol. 1. Chicago: University of Chicago Press, pp. 29–66.

Baldwin, J., and Bottoms, A. E. 1976. *The Urban Criminal*. London: Tavistock.

Bales, R. F. 1944. The fixation factor in alcohol addiction: An hypothesis derived from a comparative study of Irish and Jewish social norms. Ph.D. dissertation, Harvard University.

Ball, J. C., Rosen, L., Flueck, J. A., and Nurco, D. N. 1981. The criminality of heroin addicts: When addicted and when off opiates. In J. A. Inciardi (ed.), *The Drugs-Crime Connection*. Beverly Hills, Calif.: Sage Publications, pp. 39–65.

Bandura, A. 1973. *Aggression: A Social Learning Analysis*. Englewood Cliffs, N.J.: Prentice-Hall.

————. 1977. *Social Learning Theory*. New York: General Learning Press.

Bandura, A., and Walters, R. H. 1959. *Adolescent Aggression*. New York: Ronald Press.

Banfield, E. C. 1970. *The Unheavenly City*. Boston, Mass.: Little, Brown & Co.

————. 1974. *The Unheavenly City Revisited*. Boston, Mass.: Little, Brown & Co.

Barndt, R. J., and Johnson, D. M. 1955. Time orientation in delinquents. *Journal of Abnormal and Social Psychology* 51:343–345.

Barnes, G. E. 1979. The alcoholic personality: A reanalysis of the literature. *Journal of Studies on Alcohol* 40:571–623.

Barnett, A., Kleitman, D. J., and Larson, R. C. 1975. On urban homicide: A statistical analysis. *Journal of Criminal Justice* 3:85–110.

Bartol, C. R. 1980. *Criminal Behavior: A Psychosocial Approach*. Englewood Cliffs, N.J.: Prentice-Hall.

Bass, U. F., Brown, B. S., and Dupont, R. L. 1971. *A Study of Narcotics Addicted Offenders at the D.C. Jail*. Washington, D.C.: Narcotics Treatment Administration.

Baumrind, D. 1967. Child care practices anteceding three patterns of preschool behavior. *Genetic Psychology Monographs* 75:43–88.

————. 1971. Current patterns of parental authority. *Developmental Psychology Monographs* 4:1–103.

————. 1978. Parental disciplinary patterns and social competence in children. *Youth and Society* 9:239–276.

Baumrind, D., and Black, A. E. 1967. Socialization practices associated with dimensions of competence in preschool boys and girls. *Child Development* 38:291–327.

Bayley, D. H. 1976. Learning about crime: The Japanese experience. *Public Interest* 44:55–68.

Beach, W. G. 1932. Oriental crime in California. *Stanford University Publications in History, Economics, and Political Science* 3:404–497.

Beasley, R. W., and Antunes, G. 1974. The etiology of urban crime: An ecological analysis. *Criminology* 11:439–461.

Beccaria, C. 1963 (1764). *On Crimes and Punishments.* Trans. Henry Paolucci. Indianapolis: Library of Liberal Arts/Bobbs-Merrill.

Becker, G. S. 1968. Crime and punishment: An economic approach. *Journal of Political Economy* 76:169–217.

———. 1981. *A Treatise on the Family.* Cambridge, Mass.: Harvard University Press.

Becker, W. C. 1964. Consequences of different kinds of parental discipline. In M. L. Hoffman and L. W. Hoffman (eds.), *Review of Child Development Research,* Vol. 1. New York: Russell Sage Foundation, pp. 169–208.

Bee, H. L., Van Egeren, L. F., Streissguth, A. P., Nyman, B. A., and Leckie, M. S. 1969. Social class differences in maternal teaching strategies. *Developmental Psychology* 1:726–734.

Beha, J. A. 1977. And nobody can get you out: The impact of a mandatory prison sentence for the illegal carrying of a firearm on the use of firearms and the administration of criminal justice in Boston. *Boston University Law Review* 57:98–146, 289–333.

Beirne, P. 1983. Generalization and its discontents: The comparative study of crime. In I. L. Barak-Glantz and E. H. Johnson (eds.), *Comparative Criminology.* Beverly Hills, Calif.: Sage.

Bell, N. J., and Carver, W. 1980. A re-evaluation of gender label effects: Expectant mothers' responses to infants. *Child Development* 51:925–927.

Bell, R. Q., and Costello, N. 1964. Three tests for sex differences in tactile sensitivity in the newborn. *Biologia Neonatorum* 7:335–347.

Bell, R. Q., and Darling, J. F. 1965. The prone head reaction in the human neonate. *Child Development* 36:943–949.

Belmont, L., and Marolla, F. A. 1973. Birth order, family size, and intelligence. *Science* 182:1096–1101.

Belsky, J. 1978. Three theoretical models of child abuse: A critical review. *Child Abuse and Neglect* 2:37–49.

———. 1980. Child maltreatment: An ecological integration. *American Psychologist* 35:320–335.

———. 1981. Early human experience: A family perspective. *Developmental Psychology* 17:3–23.

Belson, W. A. 1975. *Juvenile Theft: The Causal Factors.* London: Harper & Row.

———. 1978. *Television Violence and the Adolescent Boy.* Farnborough, England: Saxon House.

Bennett, J. V. 1953. The ex-GI in federal prisons. *Proceedings of the American Correctional Association,* pp. 131–136.

Bennett, R. M., Buss, A. H., and Carpenter, J. A. 1969. Alcohol and human physical aggression. *Quarterly Journal of Studies on Alcohol* 30:870–876.

Bentham, J. 1948 (1789). *An Introduction to the Principles of Morals and Legislation.* Ed. by W. Harrison. Oxford: Basil Blackwell.

Berger, A. S., and Simon, W. 1974. Black families and the Moynihan report: A research evaluation. *Social Problems* 22:146–161.

Berger, M., Yule, W., and Rutter, M. 1975. Attainment and adjustment in two geographic areas: II—The prevalence of specific reading retardation. *British Journal of Psychiatry* 126:510–519.

Berk, R. A., Lenihan, K. J., and Rossi, P. H. 1980. Crime and poverty: Some experimental evidence from ex-offenders. *American Sociological Review* 45:766–786.

Berk, S. F., and Loseke, D. R. 1980–1981. "Handling" family violence: Situational determinants of police arrest in domestic disturbances. *Law and Society Review* 15: 317–346.

Berkowitz, L. 1973. Control of aggression. In B. Caldwell and H. N. Ricciuti (eds.), *Review of Child Development Research*, Vol. 3. Chicago: University of Chicago Press, pp. 95–140.

———. 1984. Some effects of thoughts on anti- and prosocial influences of media events: A cognitive-neoassociation analysis. *Psychological Bulletin* 95:410–427.

Berkowitz, L., and Geen, R. G. 1966. Film violence and the cue properties of available targets. *Journal of Personality and Social Psychology* 3:525–530.

Berkowitz, L., and Macaulay, J. 1971. The contagion of criminal violence. *Sociometry* 34:238–260.

Berrueta-Clement, J. R., Schweinhart, L. J., Barnett, W. S., and Weikart, D. P. n.d. The effects of early educational intervention on crime and delinquency in adolescence and early adulthood. Center for the Study of Public Policies for Young Children, Ypsilanti, Mich.

Bertelson, A. D., Marks, P. A., and May, G. D. 1982. MMPI and race: a controlled study. *Journal of Consulting and Clinical Psychology* 50:316–318.

Beynon, E. D. 1935. Crime and custom of the Hungarians of Detroit. *Journal of Criminal Law and Criminology* 25:755–774.

Bianchi, S. M. 1980. Racial differences in per capita income, 1960–1976: The importance of household size, headship, and labor force participation. *Demography* 17: 129–143.

Biller, H. B. 1968. A note on father absence and masculine development in lower-class Negro and white boys. *Child Development* 39:1003–1006.

Billingsley, A. 1969. *Black Families in White America*. Englewood Cliffs, N.J.: Prentice-Hall.

Binet, A., and Henri, V. 1895. La psychologie individuelle. *L'Annee Psychologique* 2: 411–465.

Birch, H. G., and Clark, G. 1950. Hormonal modification of social behavior. IV. The mechanism of estrogen-induced dominance in chimpanzees. *Journal of Comparative and Physiological Psychology* 43:181–193.

Bishop, J. H. 1980. Jobs, cash transfers, and marital instability: A review and synthesis of the evidence. *Journal of Human Resources* 15:312–321.

Bixenstine, V. E., and Buterbaugh, R. L. 1967. Integrative behavior in adolescent boys as a function of delinquency and race. *Journal of Consulting Psychology* 31: 471–476.

Black, D. J., and Reiss, A. J. 1967. Patterns of behavior in police and citizen transactions. In *Studies of Crime and Law Enforcement in Major Metropolitan Areas*, Vol. 2. Washington, D.C.: President's Commission on Law Enforcement and Administration of Justice.

———. 1970. Police control of juveniles. *American Sociological Review* 35:63–77.

Black, W. A., and Gregson, R. A. 1973. Time perspective, purpose in life, extroversion and neuroticism in New Zealand prisoners. *British Journal of Social and Clinical Psychology* 12:50–60.

Black, W. A., and Hornblow, A. R. 1973. Intelligence and criminality. *Australia and New Zealand Journal of Criminology* 6:83–92.

Blackburn, R. 1968. Personality in relation to extreme aggression in psychiatric offenders. *British Journal of Psychiatry* 114:821–828.

———. 1969. Sensation seeking, impulsivity, and psychopathic personality. *Journal of Consulting and Clinical Psychology* 33:571–574.

———. 1978. Psychopathy, arousal, and the need for stimulation. In R. D. Hare and D. Schalling (eds.), *Psychopathic Behaviour: Approaches to Research.* Chichester, England: Wiley.

Blaine, J. D., Bozzetti, L. P., and Ohlson, K. E. 1973. The narcotic analgesics: The opiates. In National Commission on Marihuana and Drug Abuse, *Drug Use in America: Problem in Perspective.* Technical Papers (Appendix, Vol. 1). Washington, D.C.: Government Printing Office, pp. 60–83.

Blau, J. R., and Blau, P. M. 1982. The cost of inequality: Metropolitan structure and violent crime. *American Sociological Review* 47:114–129.

Blau, P. M. 1964. *Exchange and Power in Social Life.* New York: John Wiley.

Bloch, H. S., and Niederhofer, A. 1958. *The Gang.* New York: Philosophical Library.

Block, J. H. 1973. Conceptions of sex-role: Some cross-cultural and longitudinal perspectives. *American Psychologist* 28:512–526.

Block, J. H., Block, J., and Morrison, A. 1981. Parental agreement-disagreement on childrearing orientations and gender-related personality correlates in children. *Child Development* 52:965–974.

Block, M., and Nold, F. 1978. A review of some of the results in *Estimating the Social Costs of National Economic Policy: Implications for Mental and Physical Health, and Criminal Aggression.* Unpub. paper, Hoover Institution, Stanford University.

Block, N. H., and Dworkin, G. 1974. IQ, heritability, and inequality. *Philosophy and Public Affairs* 4:40–99.

Bloom, A. 1978. The education of democratic man: *Emile. Daedalus* 107:135–153.

Bluestone, B. 1970. The tripartite economy: Labor markets and the working poor. *Poverty and Human Resources* 4:15–35.

Blum, R. H. 1972. *Horatio Alger's Children: The Role of the Family in the Origin and Prevention of Drug Risk.* San Francisco: Jossey-Bass.

Blumstein, A. 1982. On the racial disproportionality of United States' prison populations. *Journal of Criminal Law and Criminology* 73:1259–1281.

Blumstein, A., and Cohen, J. 1979. Estimation of individual crime rates from arrest records. *Journal of Criminal Law and Criminology* 70:561–585.

Blumstein, A., Cohen, J., and Nagin, D. (eds.). 1978. *Deterrence and Incapacitation: Estimating the Effects of Criminal Sanctions on Crime Rates.* Washington, D.C.: National Academy of Sciences.

Blumstein, A., and Graddy, E. 1981–1982. Prevalence and recidivism in index arrests: A feedback model. *Law and Society Review* 16:265–290.

Blumstein, A., and Moitra, S. 1979. An analysis of the time series of the imprisonment rate in the states of the United States: A further test of the stability of punishment hypothesis. *Journal of Criminal Law and Criminology* 70:376–390.

———. 1980. Growing or stable incarceration rates: A comment on Cahalan's 'Trends in incarceration in the United States since 1880.' *Crime and Delinquency* 26:91–94.

Blumstein, A., and Nagin, D. 1975. Analysis of arrest rates for trends in criminality. *Socio-economic Planning Sciences* 9:221–227.

———. 1977. The deterrent effect of legal sanctions on draft evasion. *Stanford Law Review* 28:241–275.

———. 1978. On the optimum use of incarceration for crime control. *Operations Research* 26:381–405.

Bohman, M. 1978. Some genetic aspects of alcoholism and criminality. *Archives of General Psychiatry* 35:269–276.

Bohman, M., Cloninger, C. R., Sigvardsson, S., and von Knorring, A.-L. 1982. Predisposition to petty criminality in Swedish adoptees. I. Genetic and environmental heterogeneity. *Archives of General Psychiatry* 39:1233–1241.

Boland, B., and Wilson, J. Q. 1978. Age, crime, and punishment. *The Public Interest* 51:22–34.

Bordua, D. J. 1958. Juvenile delinquency and "anomie": An attempt at replication. *Social Problems* 6:230–238.

———. 1962. Some comments on theories of group delinquency. *Sociological Inquiry* 32:245–260.

Bouchard, T. J., Jr., and McGue, M. 1981. Familial studies of intelligence: A review. *Science* 212:1055–1059.

Bowker, L. 1977. The incidence of female crime and delinquency: A comparison of official and self-report statistics. *International Journal of Women's Studies* 1:178–192.

Bowlby, J. H. 1951. *Maternal Care and Mental Health*. Geneva: World Health Organization.

———. 1958. The nature of a child's tie to his mother. *International Journal of Psychoanalysis* 39:350–373.

———. 1969. *Attachment and Loss,* Vol. 1. New York: Basic Books.

Boyatzis, R. E. 1974. The effect of alcohol consumption on the aggressive behavior of men. *Quarterly Journal of Studies on Alcohol* 35:959–972.

———. 1975. The predisposition toward alcohol-related interpersonal aggression in men. *Journal of Studies on Alcohol* 36:1196–1207.

Boyer, P. 1978. *Urban Masses and Moral Order in America, 1820–1920*. Cambridge, Mass.: Harvard University Press.

Boyle, J. M., and Brunswick, A. F. 1980. What happened in Harlem? Analysis of a decline in heroin use among a generation unit of urban black youth. *Journal of Drug Issues* 3:109–130.

Bradshaw, C. M., Szabadi, E., and Lowe, C. F. (eds.). 1981. *Quantification of Steady-State Operant Behavior*. Amsterdam: Elsevier/North Holland Biomedical Press.

Braithwaite, J. 1979. *Inequality, Crime and Public Policy*. London: Routledge and Kegan Paul.

———. 1981. The myth of social class and criminality reconsidered. *American Sociological Review* 46:36–57.

Braithwaite, J., and Braithwaite, V. 1980. Effect of income inequality and social democracy on homicide. *British Journal of Criminology* 20:45–53.

Brenner, M. H. 1976. *Estimating the Social Costs of National Economic Policy: Implications for Mental and Physical Health, and Criminal Aggression*. Volume I, Paper No. 5 of *Achieving the Goals of the Employment Act of 1946—Thirtieth Anniversary Review*. Joint Economic Committee, United States Congress, 94th Cong., 2d Sess., October 26.

———. 1984. *Estimating the Effects of Economic Change on National Health and Social Well-Being*. A study prepared for the Joint Economic Committee, United States Congress, 98th Cong., 2d Sess., June 15.

Brickman, P., and Campbell, D. T. 1971. Hedonic relativism and planning the good society. In M. H. Appley (ed.), *Adaptation-Level Theory: A Symposium*. New York: Academic Press.

Brill Associates. 1977. *Comprehensive Security Planning: A Program for William Nickerson Gardens, Los Angeles, California*. Washington, D.C.: Department of Housing and Urban Development, Office of Policy Development and Research.

Brim, O. G., and Kagan, J. (eds.). 1980. *Constancy and Change in Human Development*. Cambridge, Mass.: Harvard University Press.

Broder, P. K., Dunivant, N., Smith, E. C., and Sutton, L. P. 1981. Further observations on the link between learning disabilities and juvenile delinquency. *Journal of Educational Psychology* 73:838–850.

Broman, S. H., Nichols, P. L., and Kennedy, W. A. 1975. *Preschool IQ: Prenatal and Early Developmental Correlates.* New York: John Wiley.

Brophy, J. E. 1970. Mothers as teachers of their own preschool children: The influence of socioeconomic status and task structure on teaching specificity. *Child Development* 41:79–94.

Brown, C. 1982. Dead-end jobs and youth unemployment. In R. B. Freeman and D. A. Wise, *The Youth Labor Market Problem: Its Nature, Causes, and Consequences.* Chicago: University of Chicago Press.

Bull, R. H., and Green, J. 1980. The relationship between physical appearance and criminality. *Medicine, Science and the Law* 20:79–83.

Burchard, J. D., and Harig, P. T. 1976. Behavior modification and juvenile delinquency. In H. Leitenberg (ed.). *Handbook of Behavior Modification and Behavior Therapy.* Englewood Cliffs, N.J.: Prentice-Hall.

Bureau of Justice Statistics. 1981. Measuring crime. *Bureau of Justice Statistics Bulletin.* Washington, D.C.: Department of Justice, February.

———. 1982. *Criminal Victimization in the United States, 1980.* National Crime Survey Report NCJ-84015. Washington, D.C.: U.S. Department of Justice, Bureau of Justice Statistics, November.

———. 1983. Prisoners and alcohol. *Bulletin,* January.

Bureau of the Census. 1975. *Historical Statistics of the United States,* Part 1. Washington, D.C.: Government Printing Office.

———. 1978. *Characteristics of American Children and Youth: 1976.* Current Population Reports, Special Studies Series P-23, No. 66. Washington, D.C.: Government Printing Office.

———. 1981. *Statistical Abstract of the United States.* Washington, D.C.: Government Printing Office.

———. 1984. *Statistical Abstract of the United States.* Washington, D.C.: Government Printing Office.

Burgess, R. L. 1980. Family violence: Implications from evolutionary biology. In T. Hirschi and M. Gottfredson (eds.), *Understanding Crime: Current Theory and Research.* Beverly Hills, Calif.: Sage Publications.

Burgess, R. L., and Conger, R. D. 1978. Family interaction in abusive, neglectful, and normal families. *Child Development* 49:1163–1173.

Burnham, J. 1968. New perspectives on the prohibition 'experiment' of the 1920s. *Journal of Social History* 2:51–68.

Bursik, R. J., and Webb, J. 1982. Community change and patterns of delinquency. *American Journal of Sociology* 88:24–42.

Burt, C. 1925. *The Young Delinquent.* London: University of London Press.

Butler, S. 1927 (1872). *Erewhon.* Reprinted by the Modern Library, New York: Random House.

Cadoret, R. J., Cain, C. A., and Crowe, R. R. 1983. Evidence for gene-environment interaction in the development of adolescent antisocial behavior. *Behavior Genetics* 13:301–310.

Cahalan, M. 1979. Trends in incarceration in the United States since 1880: A summary of reported rates and the distribution of offenses. *Crime and Delinquency* 25:9–41.

Cain, L. P., Kelly, D. H., and Shannon, D. C. 1980. Parents' perceptions of the psychological and social impact of home monitoring. *Pediatrics* 66:37–40.

Camp, B. W. 1977. Verbal mediation in young aggressive boys. *Journal of Abnormal Psychology* 86:145–153.

Canter, R. J. 1982. Family correlates of male and female delinquency. *Criminology* 20:149–167.

Caplan, N. S. 1965. Intellectual functioning. In H. C. Quay (ed.), *Juvenile Delinquency*. Princeton: Van Nostrand, pp. 100–138.

Caplan, N. S., and Gligor, A. M. 1964. A study of the relationship between intelligence and offense among juvenile delinquents. Unpublished paper. Cited in Caplan, 1965.

Capwell, D. F. 1945. Personality patterns of adolescent girls: II. Delinquents and non-delinquents. *Journal of Applied Psychology* 29:289–297.

Cartwright, D. C., Howard, K. I., and Reuterman, N. A. 1970. Multivariate analysis of gang delinquency. *Multivariate Behavioral Research* 5:303–323.

Catalano, R., and Dooley, D. 1979. Does economic change provoke or uncover behavioral disorder? In L. A. Freeman and J. P. Gordus (eds.), *Mental Health and the Economy*. Kalamazoo, Mich.: W. E. Upjohn Institute of Employment Research.

Catania, A. C. 1973. Self-inhibiting effects of reinforcement. *Journal of the Experimental Analysis of Behavior* 19:517–526.

Cater, D., and Strickland, S. 1975. *TV Violence and the Child*. New York: Russell Sage Foundation.

Cattell, R. B. 1971. *Abilities: Their Structure, Growth, and Action*. Boston: Houghton Mifflin.

———. 1982. *The Inheritance of Personality and Ability: Research Methods and Findings*. New York: Academic.

Cavan, R. S., and Ranck, K. H. 1969. *The Family and the Depression*. Freeport, N.Y.: Books for Libraries Press (first published in 1938).

Chaffee, S. H. 1972. Television and adolescent aggressiveness (overview). In G. A. Comstock and E. A. Rubinstein (eds.), *Television and Adolescent Aggressiveness*. A Technical Report to the Surgeon General's Scientific Advisory Committee on Television and Social Behavior (Vol. 3). Rockville, Md.: National Institute of Mental Health, pp. 1–34.

Chaiken, J. M., and Chaiken, M. R. 1982. *Varieties of Criminal Behavior*. Santa Monica, Calif.: Rand.

———. 1983. Crime rates and the active criminal. In J. Q. Wilson (ed.), *Crime and Public Policy*. San Francisco: Institute for Contemporary Studies.

Chambers, C. D., Dean, S. W., and Pletcher, M. F. 1981. Criminal involvements of minority group addicts. In J. A. Inciardi (ed.), *The Drugs-Crime Connection*. Beverly Hills, Calif.: Sage Publications, pp. 125–154.

Chatz, T. L. 1972. Management of male adolescent sex offenders. *International Journal of Offender Therapy* 2:109–115.

Chein, I. 1964. *The Road to H: Narcotics, Delinquency, and Social Policy*. New York: Basic Books.

Chilton, R. J. 1964. Continuity in delinquency area research: A comparison of studies of Baltimore, Detroit, and Indianapolis. *American Sociological Review* 29:71–83.

Chilton, R. J., and Markle, G. E. 1972. Family disruption, delinquent conduct, and the effect of subclassification. *American Sociological Review* 37:93–99.

Choldin, H. M. 1978. Urban density and pathology. *Annual Review of Sociology* 4:91–113.

Christensen, L., and LeUnes, A. 1974. Discriminating criminal types and recidivism by means of the MMPI. *Journal of Clinical Psychology* 30:192–193.

Christiansen, K. O. 1977a. A preliminary study of criminality among twins. In S. A. Mednick and K. O. Christiansen (eds.), *Biosocial Bases of Criminal Behavior*. New York: Wiley.

———. 1977b. A review of studies of criminality among twins. In S. A. Mednick and K. O. Christiansen (eds.), *Biosocial Bases of Criminal Behavior*. New York: Wiley.

Chung, S. H., and Herrnstein, R. J. 1967. Choice and delay of reinforcement. *Journal of the Experimental Analysis of Behavior* 10:67–74.

Cicchetti, D., and Rizley, R. 1981. Developmental perspectives on the etiology, inter-generational transmission, and sequelae of child maltreatment. In R. Rizley and D. Cicchetti (eds.), *Developmental Perspectives on Child Maltreatment*. San Francisco: Jossey-Bass.

Cicourel, A. V. 1968. *The Social Organization of Juvenile Justice*. New York: John Wiley & Sons.

Clark, J. P., and Tifft, L. L. 1966. Polygraph and interview validation of self-reported deviant behavior. *American Sociological Review* 31:516–523.

Clark, K. B., and Summers, L. H. 1982. The dynamics of youth unemployment. In R. B. Freeman and D. A. Wise, *The Youth Labor Market Problem: Its Nature, Causes, and Consequences*. Chicago: University of Chicago Press.

Clark, N. H. 1976. *Deliver Us From Evil: An Interpretation of American Prohibition*. New York: Norton.

Clarke, S. H., and Koch, G. G. 1975. A study of self-reported delinquency in Char-lotte/Mecklenburg. *Popular Government*, pp. 37–43.

Clayton, R. R., and Voss, H. L. 1981. *Young Men and Drugs in Manhattan: A Causal Analysis* (Research Mono. No. 39). Rockville, Md.: National Institute of Drug Abuse.

Cleckley, H. 1964. *The Mask of Sanity*, 4th ed. St. Louis: Mosby.

Clegg, A., and Megson, B. 1968. *Children in Distress*. London: Penguin Books.

Clifford, W. 1976. *Crime Control in Japan*. Lexington, Mass.: Lexington Books.

Climent, C. E., and Ervin, F. R. 1972. Historical data in the evaluation of violent sub-jects. *Archives of General Psychiatry* 27:621–624.

Clinard, M. B., and Abbott, J. S. 1973. *Crime in Developing Countries: A Comparative Perspective*. New York: John Wiley.

Cloninger, C. R., Bohman, M., and Sigvardsson, S. 1981. Inheritance of alcohol abuse. *Archives of General Psychiatry* 38:861–868.

Cloninger, C. R., and Guze, S. B. 1970. Female criminals: Their personal, familial and social backgrounds. *Archives of General Psychiatry* 23:554–558.

Cloninger, C. R., Reich, T., and Wetzel, R. 1979. Alcoholism and affective disorders: Familial associations and genetic models. In D. W. Goodwin and C. K. Erickson (eds.), *Alcoholism and Affective Disorders*. New York: Spectrum, pp. 57–86.

Cloninger, C. R., Sigvardsson, S., Bohman, M., and von Knorring, A.-L. 1982. Predis-position to petty criminality in Swedish adoptees. II. Cross-fostering analysis of gene-environment interaction. *Archives of General Psychiatry* 39:1242–1247.

Cloward, R. A., and Ohlin, L. E. 1960. *Delinquency and Opportunity*. New York: Free Press.

Cochrane, R. 1971. The structure of value systems in male and female prisoners. *British Journal of Criminology* 12:73–79.

Cohen, A. K. 1955. *Delinquent Boys*. New York: Free Press.

Cohen, L. E. 1981. Modeling crime trends: Criminal opportunity perspective. *Journal of Research in Crime and Delinquency* 18:138–164.

Cohen, L. E., Felson, M., and Land, K. C. 1980. Property crime rates in the United States: A macrodynamic analysis, 1947–1977, with ex-ante forecasts for the mid-1980s. *American Journal of Sociology* 86:90–118.

Cohen, S. 1981. Adolescents and drug abuse: Biomedical consequences. In D. J. Lettieri and J. P. Ludford (eds.), *Drug Abuse and the American Adolescent* (Re-search Mono. No. 38). Rockville, Md.: National Institute of Drug Abuse, pp. 104–112.

Coleman, J. S., Campbell, E. Q., Hobson, C. J., McPartland, J., Mood, A. M., Weinfeld, F. D., and York, R. L. 1966. *Equality of Educational Opportunity,* 2 vols. Washington, D.C.: Office of Education.

Coleman, J. S., Hoffer, T., and Kilgore, S. 1982. *High School Achievement: Public, Catholic, and Private Schools Compared.* New York: Basic Books.

Collins, J. J. 1977. Offender careers and restraint: Probabilities and policy implications. Final draft report to Law Enforcement Assistance Administration, Washington, D.C.

Commons, M. L., Herrnstein, R. J., and Rachlin, H. (eds.). 1982. *Quantitative Analyses of Behavior: Matching and Maximizing Accounts.* Cambridge, Mass.: Ballinger.

Comstock, G. A. 1980. New emphases in research on the effects of television and film violence. In E. L. Palmer and A. Dorr (eds.), *Children and the Faces of Television: Teaching, Violence, Selling.* New York: Academic Press, pp. 129–148.

Conger, J. J., and Miller, W. C. 1966. *Personality, Social Class, and Delinquency.* New York: Wiley.

Conger, R. D. 1976. Social control and social learning models of delinquent behavior: A synthesis. *Criminology* 14:17–40.

Consortium for Longitudinal Studies. 1983. *As the Twig Is Bent: The Lasting Effects of Preschool Programs.* Hillsdale, N.J.: Lawrence Erlbaum Associates.

Cook, P. J. 1975. The correctional carrot: Better jobs for parolees. *Policy Analysis* 1:11–54.

———. 1981. The effect of liquor taxes on drinking, cirrhosis, and auto accidents. In M. H. Moore and D. R. Gerstein (eds.), *Alcohol and Public Policy.* Washington, D.C.: National Academy of Sciences, pp. 255–285.

———. 1983. Robbery in the United States: An analysis of recent trends and patterns. Unpub. manuscript, Institute of Policy Sciences, Duke University, Durham, N.C.

———. 1983. Homicide and business conditions: A replication of H. Brenner's analysis. Unpub. paper, Institute of Policy Sciences and Public Affairs, Duke University.

———. 1984. Homicide and economic conditions: A replication and critique of M. Harvey Brenner's new report to the U.S. Congress. Unpub. paper, Institute of Policy Sciences and Public Affairs, Duke University.

Cook, P. J., and Zarkin, G. A. 1985. Crime and the business cycle. *Journal of Legal Studies* 14:115–128.

Cook, T. D., Kendzierski, D. A., and Thomas, S. V. 1983. The implicit assumptions of television research: An alien analysis of the 1982 NIMH Report on *Television and Behavior. Public Opinion Quarterly* 47:161–201.

Cortes, J. B., and Gatti, F. M. 1972. *Delinquency and Crime: A Biopsychological Approach.* New York: Seminar Press.

Cotton, N. S. 1979. The familial incidence of alcoholism: A review. *Journal of Studies on Alcohol* 40:89–112.

Cowie, J., Cowie, V., and Slater, E. 1968. *Delinquency in Girls.* London: Heinemann.

Crawford, G. A., Hughes, P. H., and Kohler, M. F. 1977. The dynamics of heroin spread in endemic neighborhoods. *Addictive Diseases* 3:141–150.

Crites, L. 1976. Women offenders: Myth vs. reality. In L. Crites (ed.), *The Female Offender.* Lexington, Mass.: Heath, pp. 33–44.

Crowe, R. R. 1975. An adoptive study of psychopathy: Preliminary results from arrest records and psychiatric hospital records. In R. R. Fieve, D. Rosenthal, and H. Brill (eds.), *Genetic Research in Psychiatry.* Baltimore: Johns Hopkins University Press.

Cummins, M. S., and Suomi, S. J. 1976. Long-term effects of social rehabilitation in rhesus monkeys. *Primates* 17:43–51.

Dahlstrom, W. G., Welsh, G. S., and Dahlstrom, L. E. 1972. *An MMPI Handbook:* Vol. I, *Clinical Interpretations.* Minneapolis: University of Minnesota Press.

———. 1975. *An MMPI Handbook:* Vol. II, *Research Applications.* Minneapolis: University of Minnesota Press.

Daley, M., and Wilson, M. I. 1981. Child maltreatment from a sociobiological perspective. In R. Rizley and D. Cicchetti (eds.), *Developmental Perspectives on Child Maltreatment.* San Francisco: Jossey-Bass.

Dalgard, O. S., and Kringlen, E. 1976. A Norwegian twin study of criminality. *British Journal of Criminology* 16:213–232.

Dalton, K. 1960. Effect of menstruation on schoolgirls' weekly work. *British Medical Journal* 1:326–328.

———. 1961. Menstruation and crime. *British Medical Journal* 2:1752–1753.

———. 1964. *The Premenstrual Syndrome.* Springfield, Ill.: Charles C. Thomas.

Damon, A., Bleibtreu, H. K., Elliot, O., and Giles, E. 1962. Predicting somatype from body measurements. *American Journal of Physical Anthropology* 20:461–474.

Damon, A., Stoudt, H. W., and McFarland, R. A. 1966. *The Human Body in Equipment Design.* Cambridge, Mass.: Harvard University Press.

Damon, W. 1975. Early conception of positive justice as related to the development of logical operations. *Child Development* 46:301–312.

Daniel, A. E., Harris, P. W., and Husain, S. A. 1981. Differences between midlife female offenders and those younger than 40. *American Journal of Psychiatry* 138: 1225–1228.

Danziger, S., and Plotnick, R. D. 1981. Has the war on poverty been won? Unpub. paper, Institute for Research on Poverty, University of Wisconsin.

Danziger, S., and Wheeler, D. 1975. The economics of crime: Punishment or income redistribution. *Review of Social Economy,* 33:113–131.

Darity, W., and Myers, S. L. 1983. Changes in black family structure: Implications for welfare dependency. *American Economic Review* 73:59–64.

Darlington, R. B. 1971. Another look at "culture fairness." *Journal of Educational Measurement* 8:71–82.

Datesman, S. K., and Scarpitti, F. R. 1980a. The extent and nature of female crime. In D. K. Datesman and F. R. Scarpitti (eds.), *Women, Crime, and Justice.* New York: Oxford, pp. 3–64.

———. 1980b. Women's crime and women's emancipation. In S. K. Datesman and F. R. Scarpitti (eds.), *Women, Crime, and Justice.* New York: Oxford, pp. 355–376.

Davids, A., and Falkof, B. B. 1975. Juvenile delinquents then and now: Comparison of findings from 1959 and 1974. *Journal of Abnormal Psychology* 84:161–164.

Davids, A., Kidder, C., and Reich, M. 1962. Time orientation in male and female juvenile delinquents. *Journal of Abnormal and Social Psychology* 64:239–240.

Davidson, W. S., and Seidman, E. 1974. Studies of behavior modification and juvenile delinquency. *Psychological Bulletin* 81:998–1011.

Davies, C. 1983. Crime, bureaucracy, and equality. *Policy Review* 23:89–105.

Davis, A., and Dollard, J. 1940. *Children of Bondage: The Personality Development of Negro Youth in the Urban South.* Washington, D.C.: American Council on Education.

Davis, K. 1983. The future of marriage. *Bulletin* of the American Academy of Arts and Sciences, May.

Davis, K. R., and Sines, J. An antisocial behavior pattern associated with a specific MMPI profile. *Journal of Consulting and Clinical Psychology* 36:229–234.

Decker, D. L., Shichor, D., and O'Brien, R. M. 1982. *Urban Structure and Victimization.* Lexington, Mass.: Lexington Books/D. C. Heath.

Decker, S. H., and Kohfeld, C. W. 1982. Fox reexamined: A research note examining the perils of quantification. *Journal of Research in Crime and Delinquency* 19: 111–121.

Dennis, R. E. 1979. The role of homicide in decreasing life expectancy. In Harold M. Rose (ed.), *Lethal Aspects of Urban Violence*. Lexington, Mass.: D. C. Heath & Co.

Dentler, R. A., and Moore, L. J. 1961. Social correlates of early adolescent theft. *American Sociological Review* 26:733–743.

De Tray, D. 1978. Child schooling and family size: An economic analysis. Paper No. R-2301-NICHD. Santa Monica, Calif.: Rand Corp.

Deutsch, S. J., and Alt, F. B. 1977. The effect of Massachusetts' gun control law on gun-related crimes in the city of Boston. *Evaluation Quarterly* 1:543–568.

de Villiers, P. A. 1977. Choice in concurrent schedules and a quantitative formulation of the law of effect. In W. K. Honig and J. E. R. Staddon (eds.), *Handbook of Operant Behavior*. Englewood Cliffs, N.J.: Prentice-Hall.

―――. 1982. Toward a quantitative theory of punishment. In M. L. Commons, R. J. Herrnstein, and H. Rachlin (eds.), *Quantitative Analyses of Behavior, II, Matching and Maximizing Accounts*. Cambridge, Mass.: Ballinger, pp. 327–344.

de Villiers, P. A., and Herrnstein, R. J. 1976. Toward a law of response strength. *Psychological Bulletin* 83:1131–1153.

Dien, D. S. 1982. A Chinese perspective on Kohlberg's theory of moral development. *Developmental Review* 2:331–341.

Dixson, A. F. 1980. Androgens and aggressive behavior in primates: A review. *Aggressive Behavior* 6:37–67.

Doeringer, P. B., and Piore, M. J. 1971. *Internal Labor Markets and Manpower Analysis*. Lexington, Mass.: D. C. Heath and Co.

―――. 1975. Unemployment and the dual labor market. *The Public Interest* 38: 67–79.

Dollard, J. 1957. *Caste and Class in a Southern Town*. Garden City, N.Y.: Doubleday Anchor Books. (Originally published in 1937.)

Dominick, J. R. 1974. Children's viewing of crime shows and attitudes on law enforcement. *Journalism Quarterly* 51:5–12.

Dominick, J. R., and Greenberg, B. S. 1972. Attitudes toward violence: The interaction of television exposure, family attitudes, and social class. In G. A. Comstock and E. A. Rubinstein (eds.), *Television and Adolescent Aggressiveness,* Report to the Surgeon General's Scientific Advisory Committee on Television and Social Behavior (Vol. 3). Rockville, Md.: National Institute of Mental Health, pp. 314–335.

Donahoe, J. W. 1977. Some implications of a relational principle of reinforcement. *Journal of the Experimental Analysis of Behavior* 27:341–350.

Donnerstein, E., and Hatfield, E. 1982. Aggression and inequity. In J. Greenberg and R. L. Cogen (eds.), *Equity and Justice in Social Behavior*. New York: Academic Press.

Donovan, D. M., and Marlatt, G. A. 1982. Personality subtypes among driving-while-intoxicated offenders: Relationship to drinking behavior and driving risk. *Journal of Consulting and Clinical Psychology* 50:241–249.

d'Orban, P. T. 1971. Social and psychiatric aspects of female crime. *Medicine, Science and the Law* 11:104–116.

Drake, S. C., and Cayton, H. R. 1945. *Black Metropolis*. New York: Harcourt, Brace and Co.

Drayton, E. L. 1978. The effect of father absence upon social adjustment of male and female institutionalized juvenile delinquents. Unpub. Ph.D. thesis, Fordham University.

Dreger, R. M. 1973a. Temperament. In K. S. Miller and R. M. Dreger (eds.), *Com-*

parative Studies of Blacks and Whites in the United States. New York: Seminar Press, pp. 231–248.

———. 1973b. Intellectual functioning. In K. S. Miller and R. M. Dreger (eds.), *Comparative Studies of Blacks and Whites in the United States.* New York: Seminar Press, pp. 185–229.

Dreger, R. M., and Miller, K. S. 1960. Comparative psychological studies of Negroes and whites in the United States. *Psychological Bulletin* 57:361–402.

———. 1968. Comparative psychological studies of Negroes and whites in the United States, 1959–1965. *Psychological Bulletin* 70:1–58.

Duncan, G. M., Frazier, S. H., Litin, E. M., Johnson, A. M., and Barron, A. J. 1958. Etiological factors in first-degree murder. *Journal of the American Medical Association* 168:1755–1758.

Duncan, J. W., and Duncan, G. M. 1971. Murder in the family: A study of some homicidal adolescents. *American Journal of Psychiatry* 127:74–78.

Dunford, F. W., and Elliott, D. S. 1984. Identifying career offenders using self-reported data. *Journal of Research in Crime and Delinquency* 21:57–86.

Durkheim, E. 1964. *The Rules of Sociological Method.* Trans. S. A. Solovay and J. H. Mueller; ed. G. E. G. Catlin. New York: Free Press. (First published in 1895.)

Easterlin, R. A. 1973. Does money buy happiness? *The Public Interest* 30:3–10.

———. 1980. *Birth and Fortune: The Impact on Numbers of Personal Welfare.* New York: Basic Books.

Eaves, L., and Eysenck, H. J. 1975. The nature of extraversion: A genetical analysis. *Journal of Personality and Social Psychology* 32:102–112.

Eaves, L., and Young, P. A. 1981. Genetical theory and personality differences. In R. Lynn (ed.), *Dimensions of Personality: Papers in Honour of H. J. Eysenck.* Oxford: Pergamon.

Eberts, P., and Schwirian, K. P. 1968. Metropolitan crime rates and relative deprivation. *Criminologica* 5:43–52.

Eck, J. E., and Riccio, L. J. 1979. Relationship between reported crime rates and victimization survey results: An empirical and analytical study. *Journal of Criminal Justice* 7:293–308.

Edgar, P. 1977. *Children and Screen Violence.* St. Lucia, Australia: University of Queensland Press.

Edinger, J. D., Reuterfors, D., and Logue, P. E. 1982. Cross-validation of the Megargee MMPI Typology: A study of specialized inmate populations. *Criminal Justice and Behavior* 9:177–184.

Edmonds, R. R. 1979. Some schools work and more can. *Social Policy* March–April: 28–32.

Egeland, B., and Sroufe, A. 1981. Developmental sequelae of maltreatment in infancy. In R. Rizley and D. Cicchetti (eds.), *Developmental Perspectives on Child Maltreatment.* San Francisco: Jossey-Bass.

Ehrenkrantz, J., Bliss, E., and Sheard, M. 1974. Plasma testosterone: Correlation with aggressive behavior and social dominance in man. *Psychosomatic Medicine* 36: 469–475.

Ehrlich, I. 1973. Participation in illegitimate activities: A theoretical and empirical investigation. *Journal of Political Economy* 81:521–565.

———. 1979. The economic approach to crime: A preliminary assessment. In S. E. Messinger and E. Bittner (eds.), *Criminology Review Yearbook,* Vol. 1. Beverly Hills, Calif.: Sage Publications, pp. 25–60.

Ehrlich, I., and Mark, R. 1977. Fear of deterrence: A critical evaluation of the "Report of the Panel on Research on Deterrent and Incapacitative Effects." *Journal of Legal Studies* 6:293–316.

Eisenberg, J., Langner, T. S., and Gersten, J. C. 1975. Differences in the behavior of welfare and non-welfare children in relation to parental characteristics. *Journal of Community Psychology* 3:311–340.

Elashoff, J. D., and Snow, R. E. 1971. *Pygmalion Reconsidered*. Worthington, Ohio: Charles A. Jones.

Elder, G. H. 1974. *Children of the Great Depression*. Chicago: University of Chicago Press.

Eldred, C. A., and Brown, B. S. 1974. Heroin addict clients' description of their families of origin. *International Journal of the Addictions* 9:315–320.

Elias, M. 1981. Serum cortisol, testosterone, and testosterone-binding globulin responses to competitive fighting in human males. *Aggressive Behavior* 1:215–244.

Elion, V. H., and Megargee, E. I. 1975. Validity of the MMPI *Pd* scale among black males. *Journal of Consulting and Clinical Psychology* 43:166–172.

Ellinwood, E. H. 1971. Assault and homicide associated with amphetamine abuse. *American Journal of Psychiatry* 127:1170–1175.

Elliott, D. S., and Ageton, S. S. 1980. Reconciling race and class differences in self-reported and official estimates of delinquency. *American Sociological Review* 45:95–110.

Elliott, D. S., and Huizinga, D. 1983. Social class and delinquent behavior in a national youth panel. *Criminology* 21:149–177.

Elliott, D. S., Knowles, B. A., and Canter, R. J. 1981. *The Epidemiology of Delinquent Behavior and Drug Use Among American Adolescents*. National Youth Survey Project Report No. 14. Boulder, Colo.: Behavioral Research Institute, June.

Elliott, D. S., and Voss, H. 1974. *Delinquency and Dropout*. Lexington, Mass.: D. C. Heath.

Ellis, D. P., and Austin, P. 1971. Menstruation and aggressive behavior in a correctional center for women. *Journal of Criminal Law, Criminology, and Police Science* 62:388–395.

Ellis, H. 1914. *The Criminal*, 5th ed. London: Scott.

Elmer, E. 1967. *Children in Jeopardy: A Study of Abused Minors and Their Families*. Pittsburgh: University of Pittsburgh Press.

———. 1977. *Fragile Families, Troubled Children*. Pittsburgh: University of Pittsburgh Press.

Eme, R. F. 1979. Sex differences in childhood psychopathology: A review. *Psychological Bulletin* 86:574–585.

Emerson, R. M. 1969. *Judging Delinquents: Context and Process in Juvenile Court*. Chicago: Aldine.

Emery, R. E. 1982. Interparental conflict and the children of discord and divorce. *Psychological Bulletin* 92:310–330.

Emery, R. E., and Marholin, D. 1977. An applied behavior analysis of delinquency: The irrelevancy of relevant behavior. *American Psychologist* 32:860–873.

Empey, L. T., and Erickson, M. L. 1972. *The Provo Experiment: Evaluating Community Control of Delinquency*. Lexington, Mass.: D. C. Heath.

Encyclopaedia Britannica, Vol. 19, 9th ed. 1885. New York: Scribner's.

Engram, E. 1982. *Science, Myth, and Reality: The Black Family in One-Half Century of Research*. Westport, Conn.: Greenwood Press.

Ensminger, M. E., Kellam, S. G., and Rubin, B. R. 1983. School and family origins of delinquency: Comparisons by sex. In K. T. Van Dusen and S. A. Mednick (eds.), *Prospective Studies of Crime and Delinquency*. Boston: Kluwer-Nijhoff Publishing Co.

Epps, P., and Parnell, R. W. 1952. Physique and temperament of women delinquents compared with women undergraduates. *British Journal of Medical Psychology* 25: 249–255.

Erickson, M. 1971. The group context of delinquent behavior. *Social Problems* 19: 114–129.

Erickson, M., and Empey, L. T. 1963. Court records, undetected delinquency and decision-making. *Journal of Criminal Law, Criminology, and Police Science* 54: 456–469.

———. 1965. Class position, peers, and delinquency. *Sociology and Social Research* 49:268–282.

Erickson, M., Gibbs, J. P., and Jensen, G. F. 1977. The deterrence doctrine and the perceived certainty of legal punishment. *American Sociological Review* 42:305–317.

Erickson, M., and Jensen, G. F. 1977. Delinquency is still group behavior! Toward revitalizing the group premise in the sociology of deviance. *Journal of Criminal Law and Criminology* 68:262–273.

Eron, L. D. 1982. Parent-child interaction, television violence, and aggression of children. *American Psychologist* 37:197–211.

Eron, L. D., Lefkowitz, M. M., Huesmann, L. R., and Walder, L. O. 1972. Does television violence cause aggression? *American Psychologist* 27:253–263.

Essien-Udom, E. U. 1962. *Black Nationalism.* Chicago: University of Chicago Press.

Evans, C. M. 1980. Alcohol, violence, and aggression. *British Journal on Alcohol and Alcoholism* 15:104–117.

Ewing, J. A., Rouse, B. A., and Pellizari, E. D. 1974. Alcohol sensitivity and ethnic background. *Journal of Psychiatry* 131:206–210.

Exner, J. E. 1978. *The Rorschach. A Comprehensive System: Current Research and Advanced Interpretation,* Vol. 2. New York: Wiley.

Eysenck, H. J. 1952. The effects of psychotherapy: An evaluation. *Journal of Consulting Psychology* 16:316–324.

———. 1965. The effects of psychotherapy. *International Journal of Psychiatry* 1:99–144.

———. 1977. *Crime and Personality,* rev. ed. London: Routledge and Kegan Paul.

———. 1979. *The Structure and Measurement of Intelligence.* Berlin: Springer.

Eysenck, H. J., and Eysenck, S. B. G. 1978. Psychopathy, personality, and genetics. In R. D. Hare and D. Schalling (eds.), *Psychopathic Behaviour: Approaches to Research.* Chichester, England: Wiley.

Eysenck, H. J., and Nias, D. K. B. 1978. *Sex, Violence and the Media.* New York: Harper Colophon Books.

Eysenck, S. B. G., and Eysenck, H. J. 1970. Crime and personality: An empirical study of the three-factor theory. *British Journal of Criminology* 10:225–239.

———. 1973. The personality of female prisoners. *British Journal of Psychiatry* 122: 693–698.

Farrington, D. P. 1978. The family backgrounds of aggressive youth. In L. A. Hersov and M. Berger (eds.), *Aggression and Anti-Social Behavior in Childhood and Adolescence.* Oxford: Pergamon Press, pp. 73–93.

———. 1979a. Delinquent behaviour modification in the natural environment. *British Journal of Criminology* 19:353–372.

———. 1979b. Experiments on deviance with special reference to dishonesty. *Advances in Experimental Psychology* 12:207–252.

———. 1979c. Longitudinal research on crime and delinquency. In N. Morris and M. Tonry (eds.), *Crime and Justice: An Annual Review of Research,* Vol. 1. Chicago: University of Chicago Press.

———. 1981. The prevalence of convictions. *British Journal of Criminology* 21:173–175.

———. 1982. Longitudinal analyses of criminal violence. In M. E. Wolfgang and N. A. Weiner (eds.), *Criminal Violence*. Beverly Hills, Calif.: Sage.

Farrington, D. P., and Dowds, E. A. 1984. Why does crime decrease? *Justice of the Peace* 148:506–508.

Farrington, D. P., and Knight, B. J. 1979. Two non-reactive field experiments on stealing from a "lost" letter. *British Journal of Social and Clinical Psychology* 18: 277–284.

Farrington, D. P., and West, D. J. 1981. The Cambridge study in delinquent development (United Kingdom). In S. A. Mednick and A. E. Baert (eds.), *Prospective Longitudinal Research: An Empirical Basis for the Primary Prevention of Psychosocial Disorders*. Oxford: Oxford University Press.

Federal Bureau of Investigation, *Uniform Crime Reports*. Washington, D.C.: Government Printing Office, various years.

Feldman, M. P. 1977. *Criminal Behaviour: A Psychological Analysis*. New York: John Wiley.

Fenna, D., Mix, L., Schaefer, O., and Gilbert, J. A. 1971. Ethanol metabolism in various racial groups. *Canadian Medical Association Journal* 105:472–475.

Ferdinand, T. N. 1967. The criminal patterns of Boston since 1846. *American Journal of Sociology* 73:84–99.

———. 1970. Demographic shifts and criminality: An inquiry. *British Journal of Criminology* 10:169–175.

Feshbach, S., and Singer, R. D. 1971. *Television and Aggression: An Experimental Field Study*. San Francisco: Jossey-Bass.

Field, L. H., and Williams, M. 1970. The hormonal treatment of sexual offenders. *Medicine, Science, and the Law* 10:27–34.

Figlio, R. 1972. The seriousness of offenses: An evaluation of offenders and non-offenders. Unpub. Ph.D. dissertation, Department of Sociology, University of Pennsylvania.

Fingarette, H., and Hasse, A. F. 1979. *Mental Disabilities and Criminal Responsibility*. Berkeley, Calif.: University of California Press.

Firestone, P., and Peters, S. 1983. Minor physical anomalies and behavior in children: A review. *Journal of Autism and Developmental Disorders* 13:411–425.

Firestone, P., and Prabhu, A. N. 1983. Minor physical anomalies and obstetrical complications. *Journal of Abnormal Child Psychology* 11:207–216.

Fisher, I. 1930. *The Noble Experiment*. New York: Alcohol Information Committee.

Fitzhugh, K. B. 1973. Some neuropsychological features of delinquent subjects. *Perceptual and Motor Skills* 36:494.

Flanagan, T. 1979. Long term prisoners. Unpublished doctoral dissertation. SUNY at Albany (N.Y.).

Fleming, E. S., and Anttonen, R. G. 1971a. Teacher expectancy, or my fair lady. *American Educational Research Journal* 8:241–252.

———. 1971b. Teacher-expectancy effect examined at different ability levels. *Journal of Special Education* 5:127–131.

Fo, W. S. O., and O'Donnell, C. R. 1974. The buddy system: Relationship and contingency conditions in a community intervention program for youth with non-professionals as behavior change agents. *Journal of Consulting and Clinical Psychology* 42:163–169.

———. 1975. The buddy system: Effect of community intervention on delinquent offenses. *Behavior Therapy* 6:522–524.

Forssman, H., and Frey, T. S. 1953. Electroencephalograms of boys with behavior disorders. *Acta Psychiatrica et Neurologica Scandinavia* 28:61–73.

Fowler, F. J., and Magione, T. W. 1982. *Neighborhood Crime, Fear and Social Con-*

trol: A Second Look at the Hartford Program. Washington, D.C.: National Institute of Justice.

Fox, J. A. 1978. *Forecasting Crime Data.* Lexington, Mass.: Lexington/D. C. Heath.

———. 1982. Reexamining some perils of quantification in the econometric study of crime: A reply to Decker and Kohfeld. *Journal of Research in Crime and Delinquency* 19:122–131.

Fox, V. 1946. Intelligence, race, and age as selective factors in crime. *Journal of Criminal Law and Criminology* 32:141–152.

Frances, R. J., Timm, S., and Bucky, S. 1980. Studies of familial and nonfamilial alcoholism. *Archives of General Psychiatry* 37:564–566.

Frazier, E. F. 1939. *The Negro Family in the United States.* Chicago: University of Chicago Press.

Freedman, B. J., Rosenthal, L., Donahoe, C. P., Jr., Schlundt, D. G., and McFall, R. M. 1978. A social-behavioral analysis of skill deficits in delinquent and nondelinquent adolescent boys. *Journal of Consulting and Clinical Psychology* 46: 1448–1462.

Freedman, D. G. 1974. *Human Infancy: An Evolutionary Perspective.* New York: John Wiley/Halstead Press.

Freedman, J. L. 1984. Effect of television violence on aggressiveness. *Psychological Bulletin* 96:227–246.

Freeman, R. B. 1978. The effect of the youth population on the wages of young workers. Testimony before the Select Committee on Population, United States House of Representatives, Washington, D.C.

———. 1983. Crime and unemployment. In J. Q. Wilson (ed.), *Crime and Public Policy.* San Francisco: Institute for Contemporary Studies, pp. 89–106.

Friedman, C. J., Mann, F., and Friedman, A. S. 1975. A profile of juvenile street gang members. *Adolescence* 40:563–607.

Fuchs, V. R. 1983. *How We Live: An Economic Perspective on Americans from Birth to Death.* New York: Basic Books.

Furstenberg, F. F., Hershberg, T., and Modell, J. 1975. The origins of the female-headed black family: The impact of the urban experience. *Journal of Interdisciplinary History* 6:211–233.

Gabrielli, W. F., Jr., and Mednick, S. A. 1980. Sinistrality and delinquency. *Journal of Abnormal Psychology* 89:654–661.

Galton, F. 1869. *Hereditary Genius: An Inquiry into Its Laws and Consequences.* London: Macmillan.

———. 1883. *Inquiries into Human Faculty and Its Development.* London.

Gandossy, R. P., Williams, J. R., Cohen, J., and Harwood, H. J. 1980. *Drugs and Crime: A Survey and Analysis of the Literature.* Washington, D.C.: National Institute of Justice.

Ganzer, V. J., and Sarason, I. G. 1973. Variables associated with recidivism among juvenile delinquents. *Journal of Consulting and Clinical Psychology* 41:1–5.

Gardner, H. 1978. *Developmental Psychology.* Boston: Little, Brown.

Gath, A. 1978. *Down's Syndrome and the Family: The Early Years.* New York: Academic Press.

Gath, D., Tennent, G., and Pidduck, R. 1971. Criminological characteristics of bright delinquents. *British Journal of Criminology* 11:275–279.

Gatrell, V. A. C., and Hadden, T. B. 1972. Criminal statistics and their interpretation. In E. A. Wrigley (ed.), *Nineteenth-Century Society: Essays in the Use of Quantitative Methods for the Study of Social Data.* Cambridge: Cambridge University Press, pp. 336–396.

Gaylin, W. 1982. *The Killing of Bonnie Garland.* New York: Simon and Schuster.

Gearing, M. L., II. 1979. The MMPI as a primary differentiator and predictor of behavior in prison: A methodological critique and review of the recent literature. *Psychological Bulletin* 86:929–963.

Gendreau, P., and Ross, B. 1979. Effective correctional treatment: Bibliotherapy for cynics. *Crime and Delinquency* 25:463–489.

George, C., and Main, M. 1979. Social interactions of young abused children: Approach, avoidance, and aggression. *Child Development* 50:306–318.

———. 1980. Abused children: Their rejection of peers and caregivers. In T. M. Field, S. Goldberg, D. Stern, and A. M. Sostek (eds.), *High Risk Infants and Children: Adult and Peer Interactions*. New York: Academic Press.

Gerard, D. L., and Kornetsky, C. 1955. Adolescent opiate addiction: A study of control and addict subjects. *Psychiatric Quarterly* 29:457–486.

Gersick, K. E. 1981. Personality and sociodemographic factors in adolescent drug use. In D. J. Lettieri and J. P. Ludford (eds.), *Drug Use and the American* (Research Mono. No. 38). Rockville, Md.: National Institute of Drug Abuse, pp. 39–56.

Gerstein, D. R. 1981. Alcohol use and consequences. In M. H. Moore and D. R. Gerstein (eds.), *Alcohol and Public Policy*. Washington, D.C.: National Academy of Sciences, pp. 182–224.

Gersten, M. S., Coster, W. J., Weiss, B. R., and Cicchetti, D. 1983. Communicative behavior and symbolic play in maltreated toddlers. Unpub. manuscript, Department of Psychology, Harvard University, Cambridge, Mass.

Gibbens, T. C. N. 1963. *Psychiatric Studies of Borstal Lads*. London: Oxford University Press.

Gibbens, T. C. N., and Ahrenfeldt, R. H. (eds.) 1966. *Cultural Factors in Delinquency*. London: Tavistock.

Gil, D. G. 1970. *Violence Against Children: Physical Child Abuse in the United States*. Cambridge, Mass.: Harvard University Press.

Gillespie, R. W. 1975. *Economic Factors in Crime and Delinquency: A Critical Review of the Empirical Evidence*. Washington, D.C.: National Institute of Law Enforcement and Criminal Justice.

Glaser, D. 1974. Remedies for the key deficiency in criminal justice evaluation research. *Journal of Research in Crime and Delinquency* 11:144–153.

———. 1983. Supervising offenders outside of prison. In J. Q. Wilson (ed.), *Crime and Public Policy*. San Francisco: Institute for Contemporary Studies, pp. 207–227.

Glueck, E. T. 1935. Mental retardation and juvenile delinquency. *Mental Hygiene* 19:549–573.

Glueck, S. 1960. Ten years of unraveling juvenile delinquency: An examination of criticisms. *Journal of Criminal Law, Criminology and Police Science* 51:283–308.

Glueck, S., and Glueck, E. T. 1930. *Five Hundred Criminal Careers*. New York: Knopf.

———. 1934. *Five Hundred Delinquent Women*. New York: Knopf.

———. 1950. *Unraveling Juvenile Delinquency*. Cambridge, Mass.: Harvard University Press.

———. 1956. *Physique and Delinquency*. New York: Harper.

———. 1968. *Delinquents and Nondelinquents in Perspective*. Cambridge, Mass.: Harvard University.

Goddard, H. H. 1912. *The Kallikak Family: A Study in the Heredity of Feeble-Mindedness*. New York: Macmillan.

———. 1914. *Feeble-Mindedness. Its Causes and Consequences*. New York: Macmillan.

———. 1921. *Juvenile Delinquency*. New York: Dodd, Mead.

Gold, M. 1970. *Deviant Behavior in an American City*. Belmont, Calif.: Brooks-Cole Publishing Co.

Gold, M., and Reimer, D. J. 1975. Changing patterns of delinquent behavior among Americans 13 through 16 years old: 1967–1972. *Crime and Delinquency Literature* 7:483–517.

Goldberg, I. 1978. A note on using victimization rates to test deterrence. Technical Report CERDCR-5-78, Center for Econometric Studies of the Justice System, Hoover Institution, Stanford University, Stanford, Calif.

Goldberg, S., and Lewis, M. 1969. Play behavior in the year-old infant: early sex differences. *Child Development* 40:21–31.

Goldberg, S. 1973. *The Inevitability of Patriarchy*. New York: Morrow.

Goldfarb, W. 1943. Effects of early institutional care on adolescent personality. *Journal of Experimental Education* 12:106–129.

———. 1955. Emotional and intellectual consequences of psychologic deprivation in infancy: A revaluation. In P. H. Hooch and J. Zubin (eds.), *Psychopathology of Childhood*. New York: Grune and Stratton.

Goldman, H. 1977. The limits of clockwork: The neurobiology of violent behavior. In J. P. Conrad and S. Dintz (eds.), *In Fear of Each Other*. Lexington, Mass.: Lexington Books, pp. 43–76.

Goldstein, P. J. 1981. Getting over: Economic alternatives to predatory crime among street drug users. In J. A. Inciardi (ed.), *The Drugs-Crime Connection*. Beverly Hills, Calif.: Sage Publications, pp. 67–84.

Goodstein, L. D., and Rowley, V. N. 1961. A further study of MMPI differences between parents of disturbed and nondisturbed children. *Journal of Consulting Psychology* 25:460–464.

Goodwin, D. W. 1976. *Is Alcoholism Hereditary?* New York: Oxford University Press.

———. 1977. Family and adoption studies of alcoholism. In S. A. Mednick and K. O. Christiansen (eds.), *Biosocial Bases of Criminal Behavior*. New York: Gardner Press, pp. 143–157.

———. 1979. Alcoholism and heredity: A review and hypothesis. *Archives of General Psychiatry* 36:57–61.

Goodwin, D. W., Schlusinger, F., Hermansen, L., Guze, S. B., and Winokur, G. 1973. Alcohol problems in adoptees raised apart from alcoholic biological parents. *Archives of General Psychiatry* 28:238–243.

Goodwin, D. W., Schlusinger, F., Moller, N., Hermansen, L., Winokur, G., and Guze, S. B. 1974. Drinking problems in adopted and nonadopted sons of alcoholics. *Archives of General Psychiatry* 31:164–169.

Gordon, R. A. 1975. Crime and cognition: An evolutionary perspective. *Proceedings of the II International Symposium on Criminology*. San Paulo, Brazil: International Center for Biological and Medico-forensic Criminology.

Goring, C. 1913. *The English Convict: A Statistical Study*. London: Darling and Son.

Gottfredson, G. D. 1981. Schooling and delinquency. In S. E. Martin, L. B. Sechrest, and R. Redner (eds.), *New Directions in the Rehabilitation of Criminal Offenders*. Report of the Panel on Research on Rehabilitative Techniques. Washington, D.C.: National Academy Press.

———. 1982. Role models, bonding, and delinquency: An examination of competing perspectives. Report No. 331, Center for Social Organization of Schools, Johns Hopkins University, November.

———. 1983. The school action effectiveness study: Interim summary of the alternative education evaluation. Paper distributed by the Center for Social Organization of Schools, Johns Hopkins University, May.

Gottfredson, G. D., and Gottfredson, D. C. 1982. *Victimization in Six Hundred Schools: An Analysis of the Roots of Disorder*. Baltimore, Md.: Center for Social Organization of Schools of Johns Hopkins University.

Gough, H. G. 1948. A sociological theory of psychopathy. *American Journal of Sociology* 53:359–366.

———. 1957. *Manual for the California Psychological Inventory*. Palo Alto, Calif.: Consulting Psychologists Press.

———. 1965. Cross-cultural validation of a measure of asocial behavior. *Psychological Reports* 17:379–387.

———. 1968. An interpreter's syllabus for the California Psychological Inventory. In P. McReynolds (ed.), *Advances in Psychological Assessment*, Vol. 1. Palo Alto, Calif.: Science and Behavior Books.

———. 1969. *Manual for the California Psychological Inventory*, rev. ed. Palo Alto, Calif.: Consulting Psychologists Press.

Gough, H. G., and Heilbrun, A. B., Jr. 1965. *The Adjective Check List Manual*. Palo Alto, Calif.: Consulting Psychologists Press.

Gough, H. G., Wenk, E. A., and Rozynko, V. V. 1965. Parole outcome as predicted from the CPI, the MMPI, and a base expectancy table. *Journal of Abnormal Psychology* 70:432–441.

Gould, L. C. 1969. Juvenile entrepreneurs. *American Journal of Sociology* 74:710–720.

———. 1971. Crime and its impact in an affluent society. In J. D. Douglas (ed.), *Crime and Justice in American Society*. Indianapolis, Ind.: Bobbs-Merrill, pp. 81–118.

Gould, S. J. 1981. *The Mismeasure of Man*. New York: W. W. Norton.

Graham, E. E., and Kamano, D. 1959. Reading failure as a factor in the WAIS subtest patterns of youthful offenders. *Journal of Clinical Psychology* 15:302–305.

Grasmick, H. G., and Bryjak, G. J. 1980. The deterrent effect of perceived severity of punishment. *Social Forces* 59:471–491.

Grasmick, H. G., and Green, D. E. 1980. Legal punishment, social disapproval and internalization as inhibitors of illegal behavior. *Journal of Criminal Law and Criminology* 71:325–335.

Green, G., and Welniak, E. 1983. Changing families, shifting incomes. *American Demographics* pp. 40–42.

Greenberg, B. S. 1974. British children and televised violence. *Public Opinion Quarterly* 38:531–547.

Greenberg, D. F. 1984. Age and crime: In search of sociology. Mimeo.

Greenberg, J., and Cohen, R. L. (eds.) 1982a. *Equity and Justice in Social Behavior*. New York: Academic Press.

———. 1982b. Why justice? Normative and instrumental interpretations. In J. Greenberg and R. L. Cohen (eds.), *Equity and Justice in Social Behavior*. New York: Academic Press.

Greenberg, S. W. 1981. Alcohol and crime: A methodological critique of the literature. In J. J. Collins, Jr. (ed.), *Drinking and Crime*. New York: Guilford Press, pp. 70–109.

Greenberg, S. W., Rohe, W. M., and Williams, J. R. 1982. *Informal Social Control and Crime Prevention at the Neighborhood Level*. Denver: Denver Research Institute.

Greenwood, P. W. 1982. *Selective Incapacitation*. Santa Monica, Calif.: Rand.

Greenwood, P. W., Petersilia, J., and Zimring, F. E. 1980. *Age, Crime, and Sanctions: The Transition from Juvenile to Adult Court*. Report R-2642-NIJ. Santa Monica, Calif.: Rand.

Greenwood, P. W., Wildhorn, S., Poggio, E. C., Strumwasser, M. J., and De Leon, P. 1976. *Prosecution of Adult Felony Defendants*. Lexington, Mass.: D. C. Heath/Lexington Books.

Grier, W. H., and Cobbs, P. M. 1968. *Black Rage*. New York: Basic Books.

Gross, A. M., and Brigham, T. A. 1980. Behavior modification and the treatment of juvenile delinquency: A review and proposal for further research. *Corrective and Social Psychiatry and Journal of Behavior Technology, Methods, and Theory* 26: 98–106.

Gueron, J. 1980. The supported-work experiment. In E. Ginzberg (ed.), *Employing the Unemployed*. New York: Basic Books, pp. 73–93.

Guilford, J. P. 1967. *The Nature of Human Intelligence*. New York: McGraw-Hill.

Gurr, T. R. 1977. Contemporary crime in historical perspective: A comparative study of London, Stockholm, and Sydney. *Annals* 434:114–136.

———. 1980. On the history of violent crime in Europe and America. In E. Bittner and S. L. Messinger (eds.), *Criminology Review Yearbook*, Vol. 2. Beverly Hills, Calif.: Sage Publications, pp. 411–432.

———. 1981. Historical trends in violent crime: A critical review of the evidence. In M. Tonry and N. Morris (eds.), *Crime and Justice: An Annual Review of Research*, Vol. 3. Chicago: University of Chicago Press, pp. 295–353.

Gurr, T. R., Grabosky, P. N., and Hula, R. C. 1977. *The Politics of Crime and Conflict: A Comparative History of Four Cities*. Beverly Hills, Calif.: Sage Publications.

Gusfield, J. R. 1968. Prohibition: the impact of political utopianism. In J. Braeman (ed.), *Change and Continuity in Twentieth Century America: The 1920s*. Columbus, Ohio: Ohio State University Press.

Gutman, H. G. 1976. *The Black Family in Slavery and Freedom, 1750–1925*. New York: Pantheon.

Gynther, M. D. 1972. White norms and black MMPIs: A prescription for discrimination? *Psychological Bulletin* 78:386–402.

Hackler, J. C., and Lautt, M. 1969. Systematic bias in measuring self-reported delinquency. *Canadian Review of Sociology and Anthropology* 6:92–106.

Hall, C. S., and Lindzey, G. 1978. *Theories of Personality*, 3rd ed. New York: Wiley.

Hamparian, D. M., Schuster, R., Dinitz, S., and Conrad, J. P. 1978. *The Violent Few*. Lexington, Mass.: Lexington/D. C. Heath.

Hannan, M. T. 1982. Families, markets, and social structures: An essay on Becker's *A Treatise on the Family*. *Journal of Economic Literature* 20:65–72.

Hannerz, U. 1969. *Soulside*. New York: Columbia University Press.

Hansmann, H. B., and Quigley, J. M. 1979. *Population Heterogeneity and the Sociogenesis of Homicide*. Institution for Social and Policy Studies. Yale University. Working paper No. 824, August.

Hardyck, C., and Petrinovich, L. F. 1977. Left-handedness. *Psychological Bulletin* 84: 385–404.

Hare, R. D. 1965. Temporal gradient of fear arousal in psychopaths. *Journal of Abnormal Psychology* 70:442–445.

———. 1975. Psychophysiological studies of psychopathy. In D. C. Fowles (ed.), *Clinical Application of Psychophysiology*. New York: Columbia University Press.

———. 1978. Electrodermal and cardiovascular correlates of psychopathy. In R. D. Hare and D. Schalling (eds.), *Psychopathic Behaviour*. New York: Wiley.

———. 1979. Psychopathy and laterality of cerebral function. *Journal of Abnormal Psychology* 88:605–610.

Hare, R. D., and Quinn, M. J. 1971. Psychopathy and autonomic conditioning. *Journal of Abnormal Psychology* 77:223–235.

Harlow, H. F., and Harlow, M. K. 1969. Effects of various infant-mother relationships on rhesus monkey behaviours. In B. M. Foss (ed.), *Determinants of Infant Behaviour*, Vol. 4. London: Methuen.

———. 1970. Developmental aspects of emotional behavior. In P. Black (ed.), *Physiological Correlates of Emotion*. New York: Academic Press.

Harris, A. R., and Lewis, M. 1974. Race and criminal deviance: A study of youthful offenders. Paper presented to the annual meeting of the American Sociological Association.

Harrison, B. 1972. *Education, Training, and the Urban Ghetto.* Baltimore, Md.: Johns Hopkins University Press.

Hart, H. L. A. 1978. *Punishment and Responsibility,* rev. ed. Oxford: Oxford University Press.

Hartl, E. M., Monnelly, E. P., and Elderkin, R. D. 1982. *Physique and Delinquent Behavior: A Thirty-Year Follow-Up of William H. Sheldon's Varieties of Delinquent Youth.* New York: Academic Press.

Hartman, A. A. 1940. Recidivism and intelligence. *Journal of Criminal Law and Criminology* 31:417–426.

Hartnagel, T. F. 1970. Father absence and self-conception among lower class white and Negro boys. *Social Problems* 18:152–163.

Hartnoll, R. L., Mitcheson, M. C., Battersby, A., Brown, G., Ellis, M., Fleming, P., and Hedley, N. 1980. Evaluation of heroin maintenance in controlled trial. *Archives of General Psychiatry* 37:877–884.

Harvald, B., and Hauge, M. 1965. *Genetics and the Epidemiology of Chronic Diseases.* Washington, D.C.: U.S. Public Health Service.

Haskell, M. R., and Yablonsky, L. 1978. *Criminology: Crime and Criminality,* 2nd ed. Chicago: Rand McNally.

Hathaway, S. R., and McKinley, J. C. 1942. *Minnesota Multiphasic Personality Inventory.* Minneapolis: University of Minnesota Press.

———. 1951. *Minnesota Multiphasic Personality Inventory,* rev. ed. New York: Psychological Corporation.

Hathaway, S. R., and Monachesi, E. D. 1953. *Analyzing and Predicting Juvenile Delinquency with the MMPI.* Minneapolis: University of Minnesota Press.

Hawkins, D. F. 1983. Black and white homicide differentials. *Criminal Justice and Behavior* 10:407–440.

Hayner, N. S. 1933. Delinquency areas in the Puget Sound region. *American Journal of Sociology* 39:314–328.

———. 1938. Social factors in oriental crime. *American Journal of Sociology* 43:908–919.

Healy, W., and Bronner, A. F. 1936. *New Light on Delinquency and Its Treatment.* New Haven, Conn.: Yale University Press.

Heidensohn, F. 1968. The deviance of women: A critique and an enquiry. *British Journal of Sociology* 19:160–175.

Heilbrun, A. B., Jr. 1979. Psychopathy and violent crime. *Journal of Consulting and Clinical Psychology* 47:509–516.

Hentig, H. von. 1947. *Crime: Causes and Conditions.* New York: McGraw-Hill.

Hepburn, J. R. 1977. Testing alternative models of delinquency causation. *Journal of Criminal Law and Criminology* 67:450–460.

Herrenkohl, R. C., and Herrenkohl, E. C. 1981. Some antedecents and developmental consequences of child maltreatment. In R. Rizley and D. Cicchetti (eds.), *Developmental Perspectives on Child Maltreatment.* San Francisco: Jossey-Bass.

Herrnstein, R. J. 1970. On the law of effect. *Journal of the Experimental Analysis of Behavior* 13:243–266.

———. 1973. *IQ in the Meritocracy.* Boston: Atlantic-Little, Brown.

———. 1974. Formal properties of the matching law. *Journal of the Experimental Analysis of Behavior* 21:159–164.

———. 1979. Derivatives of matching. *Psychological Review* 86:486–495.

———. 1981. Self control as response strength. In C. M. Bradshaw, E. Szabadi, and

C. F. Lowe (eds.), *Quantification of Steady-State Operant Behavior*. Amsterdam: Elsevier/North Holland Biomedical Press.

——. 1983. Some criminogenic traits of offenders. In J. Q. Wilson (ed.), *Crime and Public Policy*. San Francisco: ICS Press, pp. 31–49.

Herrnstein, R. J., and Boring, E. G. 1965. *A Sourcebook in the History of Psychology*. Cambridge, Mass.: Harvard University Press.

Herzog, E., and Sudia, C. E. 1973. Children in fatherless families. In B. M. Caldwell and H. N. Riccuti (eds.), *Review of Child Development Research,* Vol. 3. Chicago: University of Chicago Press, pp. 141–232.

Hess, R., and Shipman, V. 1965. Early experience and the socialization of cognitive modes in children. *Child Development* 36:869–886.

Hetherington, E. M., Cox, M., and Cox, R. 1978. The aftermath of divorce. In J. H. Stevens, Jr., and M. Mathews (eds.), *Mother-Child Father-Child Relations*. Washington, D.C.: The National Association for the Education of Young Children.

——. 1979a. Play and social interaction in children following divorce. *Journal of Social Issues* 35:26–49.

——. 1979b. Family interaction and the social, emotional and cognitive development of children following divorce. In V. Vaughan and T. Brazelton (eds.), *The Family: Setting Priorities*. New York: Science and Medicine.

Hetherington, E. M., and Feldman, S. E. 1964. College cheating as a function of subject and situational variables. *Journal of Educational Psychology* 55:212–218.

Hewitt, J. D., and Hoover, D. W. 1982. Local modernization and crime: The effects of modernization on crime in Middletown, 1845–1910. *Law and Human Behavior* 6:313–325.

Hicks, D. J. 1965. Imitation and retention of film-mediated aggressive peer and adult models. *Journal of Personality and Social Psychology* 2:97–100.

Higgins, P. C., and Albrecht, G. L. 1977. Hellfire and delinquency revisited. *Social Forces* 55:952–958.

Hill, D., and Watterson, D. 1942. Electro-encephalographic studies of psychopathic personalities. *Journal of Neurology and Psychiatry* 5:47–65.

Hill, R. D. 1972. *The Strengths of Black Families*. New York: Emerson Hall.

Himmelweit, H. T., Oppenheim, A. N., and Vince, P. 1958. *Television and the Child*. London: Oxford University Press.

Himmelweit, H. T., and Swift, B. 1976. Continuities and discontinuities in media usage and taste: A longitudinal study. *Journal of Social Issues* 32:133–156.

Hindelang, M. J. 1971. The social versus solitary nature of delinquent involvements. *British Journal of Criminology* 11:167–175.

——. 1973. Causes of delinquency: A partial replication and extension. *Social Problems* 20:471–487.

——. 1976. With a little help from their friends: Group participation in reported delinquent behaviour. *British Journal of Criminology* 16:109–125.

——. 1978. Race and involvement in common law personal crimes. *American Sociological Review* 43:93–109.

——. 1979. Sex differences in criminal activity. *Social Problems* 27:143–156.

——. 1981. Variations in sex-race-age-specific incidence rates of offending. *American Sociological Review* 46:461–474.

Hindelang, M. J., Gottfredson, M. R., and Flanagan, T. J. 1981. *Sourcebook of Criminal Justice Statistics, 1980*. Washington, D.C.: Bureau of Justice Statistics.

Hindelang, M. J., Hirschi, T., and Weis, J. G. 1979. Correlates of delinquency: The illusion of discrepancy between self-report and official measures. *American Sociological Review* 44:995–1014.

——. 1981. *Measuring Delinquency*. Beverly Hills, Calif.: Sage Publications.

Hindelang, M. J., and McDermott, M. J. 1981. *Juvenile Criminal Behavior: An Analysis of Rates and Victim Characteristics.* Washington, D.C.: Government Printing Office.

Hippler, A. E. 1974. *Hunter's Point: A Black Ghetto.* New York: Basic Books.

Hirschi, T. 1969. *Causes of Delinquency.* Berkeley, Calif.: University of California Press.

Hirschi, T., and Gottfredson, M. 1983. Age and the explanation of crime. *American Journal of Sociology* 89:552–584.

———. 1984. The distinction between crime and criminality. Unpub. paper, Department of Sociology, University of Arizona, April.

Hirschi, T., and Hindelang, M. J. 1977. Intelligence and delinquency: A revisionist view. *American Sociological Review* 42:571–587.

Hobbes, T. 1957 (1651). *Leviathan.* Ed. by Michael Oakeshott. Oxford: Basil Blackwell.

Hoebel, E. A. 1954. *The Law of Primitive Man.* Cambridge, Mass.: Harvard University Press.

Hoffman, M. L. 1980. Moral development in adolescence. In Joseph Adelson (ed.), *Handbook of Adolescent Psychology.* New York: John Wiley, pp. 295–343.

Hogan, R. 1973. Moral conduct and moral character: A psychological perspective. *Psychological Bulletin* 79:217–232.

Hogan, R., Johnson, J. A., and Emler, N. P. 1978. A socioanalytic theory of moral development. *New Directions for Child Development* 2:1–18.

Hogan, R., Mankin, D., Conway, J., and Fox, S. 1970. Personality correlates of undergraduate marijuana use. *Journal of Consulting and Clinical Psychology* 35:58–63.

Holinger, P. C. 1979. Violent deaths among the young: Recent trends in suicide, homicide, and accidents. *American Journal of Psychiatry* 136:1144–1147.

Holinger, P. C., and Klemen, E. H. 1982. Violent deaths in the United States, 1900–1975: Relationships between suicide, homicide, and accidental deaths. *Social Science and Medicine* 16:1919–1938.

Holyst, B. 1979. *Comparative Criminology.* Lexington, Mass.: Lexington Books.

Homans, G. C. 1961. *Social Behavior: Its Elementary Forms.* New York: Harcourt, Brace & World.

Hook, E. B. 1973. Behavior implications of the human XYY genotype. *Science* 179:139–150.

Hook, J. G., and Cook, T. D. 1979. Equity theory and the cognitive ability of children. *Psychological Bulletin* 86:429–445.

Hooton, E. A. 1939a. *Crime and the Man.* Cambridge, Mass.: Harvard University Press.

———. 1939b. *The American Criminal: An Anthropological Study.* Cambridge, Mass.: Harvard University Press.

Horne, A. M. 1980. Aggressive behavior in normal and deviant families of intact and mother-only families. Paper presented at the American Psychological Association annual meeting, September.

House, T. H., and Milligan, W. L. 1976. Autonomic responses to modeled distress in prison psychopaths. *Journal of Personality and Social Psychology* 34:556–560.

Howe, D. W. (ed.). 1976. *Victorian America.* Philadelphia: University of Pennsylvania Press.

Huesmann, L. R., Eron, L. D., Lefkowitz, M. M., and Walder, L. O. 1973. Television violence and aggression: The causal effect remains. *American Psychologist* 28:617–620.

———. 1984. The stability of aggression over time and generations. *Developmental Psychology* 20:1120–1134.

Huesmann, L. R., Lagerspetz, K., and Eron, L. D. 1984. Intervening variables in the TV violence-aggression relation: Evidence from two countries. *Developmental Psychology* 20:746–775.

Hughes, P. H., Crawford, G. A., and Jaffe, J. H. 1971. Heroin epidemic in Chicago. *Proceedings of the World Congress of Psychiatry.* (Mexico City.)

Hunt, L. G., and Chambers, C. D. 1976. *The Heroin Epidemics: A Study of Heroin Use in the United States, 1965–1975.* New York: Spectrum Publications.

Hunter, J. E., and Schmidt, F. L. 1976. A critical analysis of the statistical and ethical implications of various definitions of "test bias." *Psychological Bulletin* 83:1053–1071.

Ilardi, R. L. 1966. Family disorganization and intelligence in Negro preschool children. *Dissertation Abstracts* 27:2137B.

Imperato-McGinley, J., Peterson, R. E., Gautier, T., and Sturla, E. 1979. Androgens and the evolution of male-gender identity among pseudohermaphrodites with 5-reductase deficiency. *New England Journal of Medicine* 300:1233–1237.

Inciardi, J. A. 1979. Heroin use and street crime. *Crime and Delinquency* 25:335–348.

Ivey, M. E., and Bardwick, J. M. 1968. Patterns of affective fluctuation in the menstrual cycle. *Psychosomatic Medicine* 30:336–345.

Jackson, B. 1974. *"Get Your Ass in the Water and Swim Like Me."* Cambridge, Mass.: Harvard University Press.

Jackson, J. J. 1973. Family organization and ideology. In K. S. Miller and R. M. Dreger (eds.), *Comparative Studies of Blacks and Whites in the United States.* New York: Seminar Press, pp. 408–445.

Jacobs, J. 1961. *The Death and Life of Great American Cities.* New York: Vintage Books.

Jacobs, J. B. 1977. *Stateville: The Penitentiary in Mass Society.* Chicago: University of Chicago Press.

Jacobs, P. A., Brunton, M., Melville, M. M., Brittain, R. P., and McClemont, W. F. 1965. Aggressive behaviour, mental sub-normality, and the XYY male. *Nature* 208:1351–1352.

Jacobs, P. A., Price, W. H., Richmond, S., and Ratcliff, R. A. W. 1971. Chromosome surveys in penal institutions and approved schools. *Journal of Medical Genetics* 8:49–58.

Janis, I. 1980. The influence of television on personal decision-making. In S. B. Whithey and R. P. Abeles (eds.), *Television and Social Behavior: Beyond Violence and Children.* Hillsdale, N.J.: Lawrence Erlbaum Associates, pp. 161–189.

Jeffery, C. R., and Jeffery, I. A. 1969. Delinquents and dropouts: An experimental program in behavior change. *Education and Urban Society* 1:325–336.

Jencks, C. S. 1972. The Coleman report and the conventional wisdom. In F. Mosteller and D. P. Moynihan (eds.), *On Equality of Educational Opportunity.* New York: Random House.

——. 1979. *Who Gets Ahead? The Determinants of Economic Success in America.* New York: Basic Books.

Jensen, A. R. 1980. *Bias in Mental Testing.* New York: Macmillan.

——. 1981. *Straight Talk about Mental Tests.* New York: Macmillan.

Jensen, G. F. 1972. Parents, peers, and delinquent action: A test of the differential association perspective. *American Journal of Sociology* 78:562–575.

Jesness, C. F., DeRisi, W. J., McCormick, P. M., and Wedge, R. F. 1972. *The Youth Center Research Project.* Sacramento, Calif.: American Justice Institute.

Johns, J. H., and Quay, H. C. 1962. The effect of social reward on verbal conditioning in psychopathic and neurotic military offenders. *Journal of Consulting Psychology* 26:217–220.

Johnson, C. S. 1941. *Growing Up in the Black Belt: Negro Youth in the Rural South.* Washington, D.C.: American Council on Education.

Johnson, R. E. 1978. *A Shopkeeper's Millennium: Society and Revivals in Rochester, New York, 1815–1837.* New York: Hill and Wang.

Johnson, R. E. 1979. *Juvenile Delinquency and Its Origins.* Cambridge, England: Cambridge University Press.

Johnson, V. S. 1977. Behavior modification in the correctional setting. *Criminal Justice and Behavior* 4:397–428.

Joint Center for Political Studies. 1983. *A Policy Framework for Racial Justice.* Washington, D.C.: Joint Center for Political Studies.

Joint Committee on New York Drug Law Evaluation. 1977. *The Nation's Toughest Drug Law: Evaluating the New York Experience.* New York: Association of the Bar of the City of New York.

Jones, E. T. 1976. Crime change patterns in American cities. *Journal of Criminal Justice* 4:333–340.

Jones, H. 1981. *Crime, Race and Culture.* New York: John Wiley.

Jones, R. R., Weinrott, M. R., and Howard, J. R. 1981. The national evaluation of the teaching family model. Final Report to the Center for Studies of Crime and Delinquency, National Institute of Mental Health, Bethesda, Md.

Jones, V. 1932. Relation of economic depression to delinquency, crime, and drunkenness in Massachusetts. *Journal of Social Psychology* 3:259–282.

Kaestle, C. F. 1973. *The Evolution of an Urban School System: New York City, 1750–1850.* Cambridge, Mass.: Harvard University Press.

Kaestle, C. F., and Vinovskis, M. A. 1980. *Education and Social Change in Nineteenth-Century Massachusetts.* Cambridge, England: Cambridge University Press.

Kagan, J. 1978. *The Growth of the Child.* New York: W. W. Norton.

Kagan, J., Kearsley, R. B., and Zelazo, P. R. 1978. *Infancy: Its Place in Human Development.* Cambridge, Mass.: Harvard University Press.

Kagan, J., and Moss, H. A. 1962. *Birth to Maturity.* New York: John Wiley.

Kahn, M. W. 1968. Superior performance IQ of murderers as a function of overt act or diagnosis. *Journal of Social Psychology* 76:113–116.

Kandel, D. B. 1978. *Longitudinal Research on Drug Use.* Washington, D.C.: Hemisphere Publishing Corp.

Kant, I. 1979 (1797). *Metaphysiche Anfanggruende der Rechtslehre.* Quoted in J. G. Murphy, *Retribution, Justice, and Therapy.* Dordrecht, Holland: D. Reidel.

Kaplan, J. 1983. *The Hardest Drug: Heroin and Public Policy.* Chicago: University of Chicago Press.

Kaplan, R. M., and Singer, R. D. 1976. Television violence and viewer aggression: A reexamination of the evidence. *Journal of Social Issues* 32:35–70.

Karpman, B. 1941. On the need for separating psychopathy into two distinct types: The symptomatic and the idiopathic. *Journal of Criminal Psychopathology* 3:112–137.

————. 1947. Passive parasitic psychopathy: Toward the personality structure and psychogenesis of idiopathic psychopathy (antopathy). *Psychoanalysis Review* 34:102–118, 198–222.

Katz, M. 1968. *The Irony of Early School Reform: Educational Innovation in Mid-Nineteenth Century Massachusetts.* Cambridge, Mass.: Harvard University Press.

————. 1971. *Class, Bureaucracy, and Schools: The Illusion of Educational Change in America.* New York: Praeger.

Kaufman, A. S. 1976. Verbal-performance IQ discrepancies on the WISC-R. *Journal of Consulting and Clinical Psychology* 44:739–744.

Kaufman, I. R. 1982. The insanity plea on trial. *New York Times Magazine.* August 8.

Kellam, S. G., Adams, R. G., Brown, H. C., and Ensminger, M. E. 1982. The long-term evolution of the family structure of teenage and older mothers. *Journal of Marriage and the Family* 44:539–554.

Kellam, S. G., Ensminger, M. E., and Turner, J. 1977. Family structure and the mental health of children. *Archives of General Psychiatry* 34:1012–1022.

Keller, D. J., and Vedder, C. B. 1968. The crimes that old persons commit. *Gerontologist* 8:43–50.

Kelly, D. H. 1975. Status origins, track positions, and delinquent involvement: A self-report analysis. *Sociological Quarterly* 16:264–271.

Kelly, F. J., and Veldman, D. J. 1964. Delinquency and school dropout behavior as a function of impulsivity and nondominant values. *Journal of Abnormal and Social Psychology* 69:190–194.

Kempe, C. H., Silverman, F. N., Steele, B. F., Droegmueller, W., and Silver, H. K. 1962. The battered-child syndrome. *Journal of the American Medical Association* 181:17–24.

Kempe, R., and Kempe, C. H. 1978. *Child Abuse*. London: Fontana/Open Books.

Kerner, O. 1968. *Supplemental Studies for the National Advisory Commission on Civil Disorders*. Washington, D.C.: U.S. Government Printing Office.

Kessler, S. 1975. Extra chromosomes and criminality. In R. R. Fieve, D. Rosenthal, and H. Brill (eds.), *Genetic Research in Psychiatry*. Baltimore: The Johns Hopkins University Press.

Kett, J. F. 1977. *Rites of Passage: Adolescence in America, 1790 to the Present*. New York: Basic Books.

Kinard, E. M. 1980. Emotional development in physically abused children. *American Journal of Orthopsychiatry* 50:686–696.

King, C. H. 1975. The ego and the integration of violence in homicidal youth. *American Journal of Orthopsychiatry* 45:134–145.

Kirigin, K. A., Braukmann, C. J., Atwater, J. D., and Wolf, M. M. 1982. An evaluation of teaching-family (Achievement Place) group homes for juvenile offenders. *Journal of Applied Behavior Analysis* 15:1–16.

Kirkpatrick, M. E. 1934. Delinquency in Cleveland and Cuyahoga County during the Depression period. *American Journal of Orthopsychiatry* 4:383–386.

Kitano, H. H. L. 1967. Japanese-American crime and delinquency. *The Journal of Psychology* 66:253–263.

Kleck, G. 1982. On the use of self-report data to determine the class distribution of criminal and delinquent behavior. *American Sociological Review* 47:427–433.

Klein, N. C., Alexander, J. F., and Parsons, B. V. 1977. Impact of family systems intervention on recidivism and sibling delinquency: A model of primary prevention and program evaluation. *Journal of Consulting and Clinical Psychology* 45:469–474.

Klein, T. M. 1981. The effect of raising the minimum legal drinking age on traffic accidents in the state of Maine. Technical Report, National Highway Traffic Safety Administration, Washington, D.C.

Kleinmuntz, B. 1982. *Personality and Psychological Assessment*. New York: St. Martin's Press.

Knight, B. J., and West, D. J. 1975. Temporary and continuing delinquency. *British Journal of Criminology* 15:43–50.

Kniveton, B. H. 1973. The effect of rehearsed delay on long-term imitation of filmed aggression. *British Journal of Psychology* 64:259–265.

Kniveton, B. H., and Stephenson, G. M. 1970. The effect of pre-experience on imitation of an aggressive film model. *British Journal of Social and Clinical Psychology* 9:31–36.

Kobrin, S., and Schuerman, L. A. 1981. Interaction between neighborhood change and criminal activity. Interim Report to National Institute of Justice, Washington, D.C., September 22.

Kohlberg, L. 1976. Moral stages and moralization. In R. Lickona (ed.), *Moral Development and Behavior: Theory, Research and Social Issues.* New York: Holt, Rinehart & Winston.

Konopka, G. 1966. *The Adolescent Girl in Conflict.* Englewood Cliffs, N.J.: Prentice-Hall.

Kopp, C. B., and Parmelee, A. H. 1979. Prenatal and perinatal influences on infant behavior. In J. D. Osofsky (ed.), *Handbook of Infant Development.* New York: John Wiley, pp. 29–75.

Korner, A. F. 1973. Sex differences in newborns with special reference to differences in the organization of oral behavior. *Journal of Child Psychology* 14:19–29.

———. 1974. The effect of the infant's state, level of arousal, sex, and orthogenetic stage on the caregiver. In M. Lewis and L. A. Rosenblum (eds.), *The Effect of the Infant on the Caregiver.* New York: John Wiley, pp. 105–121.

Kozeny, E. 1962. Experimentelle Untersuchungen zur Ausdruckskundemittel photographisch-statistischer Methode. *Archiv fur die Gesamte Psychologie* 114:55–71.

Kranz, H. 1936. *Lebensschicksale Kriminellen Zwillinge.* Berlin: Springer.

Krebs, D. 1982. Prosocial behavior, equity, and justice. In J. Greenberg and R. L. Cohen (eds.), *Equity and Justice in Social Behavior.* New York: Academic Press.

Kreuz, L. E., and Rose, R. M. 1972. Assessment of aggressive behavior and plasma testosterone in a young criminal population. *Psychosomatic Medicine* 34:321–332.

Krohn, M. O. 1976. Inequality, unemployment and crime: A cross-national analysis. *Sociological Quarterly* 17:303–313.

Kumar, S. P., Anday, E. K., Sacks, L. M., Ting, R. Y., and Delivoria-Papadopoulos, M. 1980. Follow-up studies of very low birth weight infants treated within a perinatal center. *Pediatrics* 66:438–444.

Kurtines, W., and Grief, E. B. 1974. The development of moral thought. *Psychological Bulletin* 81:453–470.

Ladner, J. A. 1972. *Tomorrow's Tomorrow: The Black Woman.* New York: Doubleday Anchor.

LaFave, W. R., and Scott, A. W., Jr. 1972. *Handbook on Criminal Law.* St. Paul, Minn.: West.

Landau, S. F. 1975. Future time perspective of delinquents and non-delinquents. *Criminal Justice and Behavior* 2:22–36.

Lander, B. 1954. *Towards an Understanding of Juvenile Delinquency.* New York: Columbia University Press.

Lane, P. 1978. Bibliography of the overcontrolled-undercontrolled assaultive personality literature and the overcontrolled-hostility (O-H) scale of the MMPI. Journal Supplement Abstract Service of the American Psychological Association.

Lane, R. 1979. *Violent Death in the City: Suicide, Accident, and Murder in 19th Century Philadelphia.* Cambridge, Mass.: Harvard University Press.

———. 1980. Urban police and crime in nineteenth-century America. In N. Morris and M. Tonry (eds.), *Crime and Justice: An Annual Review of Research,* Vol. 2. Chicago: University of Chicago Press, pp. 1–43.

Lang, A. R., Goeckner, D. J., Adesso, O. S., and Marlatt, G. A. 1975. Effects of alcohol on aggression in male social drinkers. *Journal of Abnormal Psychology* 84:508–518.

Lange, J. 1929. *Verbrechen als Schicksal.* Leipzig: Thieme. (Translated as *Crime as Destiny.* London: Unwin, 1931.)

Lanyon, R. I. 1984. Personality assessment. *Annual Review of Psychology* 35:667–701.

Laqueur, T. W. 1976. *Religion and Respectability: Sunday Schools and Working Class Culture, 1780–1850.* New Haven: Yale University Press.

Latané, B., and Darley, J. M. 1970. *The Unresponsive Bystander: Why Doesn't He Help?* New York: Appleton.

Laufer, W. S., Johnson, J. A., and Hogan, R. 1981. Ego control and criminal behavior. *Journal of Personality and Social Psychology* 41:179–184.

Lazerson, M. 1971. *Origins of the Public School: Public Education in Massachusetts, 1870–1915.* Cambridge, Mass.: Harvard University Press.

Lefkowitz, M. M. 1968. Nonintellective components in the school performance of juvenile delinquents. *Perceptual and Motor Skills* 26:1185–1186.

Lefkowitz, M. M., Eron, L. D., Walder, L. O., and Huesmann, L. R. 1977. *Growing Up to Be Violent: A Longitudinal Study of the Development of Aggression.* New York: Pergamon.

Lemert, E. M. 1951. *Social Pathology.* New York: McGraw-Hill.

Lerman, P. 1967. Gangs, networks, and subcultural delinquency. *American Journal of Sociology* 73:63–72.

Lerner, M. J. 1982. The justice motive in human relations and the economic model of man: A radical analysis of facts and fictions. In V. Delega and J. Grzelak (eds.), *Cooperation and Helping Behavior: Theories and Research.* New York: Academic Press.

Lessing, E. E., Zagorin, S. W., and Nelson, D. 1970. WISC subtest and IQ score correlates of father absence. *Journal of General Psychiatry* 117:181–195.

Levengood, R., Lowinger, P., and Schooff, K. 1973. Heroin addiction in the suburbs— an epidemiologic study. *American Journal of Public Health* 63:209–214.

Levin, Y., and Lindesmith, A. 1937. English ecology and criminology of the past century. *Journal of Criminal Law, Criminology and Police Science* 27:801–816.

Levitan, S., Johnston, W. B., and Taggart, R. 1975. *Still a Dream.* Cambridge, Mass.: Harvard University Press.

Levitan, S., Mangum, G. L., and Marshall, R. 1976. *Human Resources and Labor Markets.* New York: Harper and Row.

Levy, J. E., and Kunitz, S. J. 1974. *Indian Drinking.* New York: Wiley.

Lewis, O. 1959. *Five Families: Mexican Case Studies in the Culture of Poverty.* New York: Basic Books.

———. 1961. *The Children of Sanchez.* New York: Random House.

———. 1966. *La Vida: A Puerto Rican Family in the Culture of Poverty.* New York: Random House.

Leyens, J. P., Camino, L., Parke, R. D., and Berkowitz, L. 1975. Effects of movie violence on aggression in a field setting as a function of group dominance and cohesion. *Journal of Personality and Social Psychology* 32:346–360.

Lieber, C. S. 1972. Metabolism of ethanol and alcoholism: Racial and acquired factors. *Annals of Internal Medicine* 76:326–327.

Liebow, E. 1967. *Tally's Corner: A Study of Negro Street Corner Men.* Boston: Little, Brown and Co.

Lind, A. W. 1930. Some ecological patterns of community disorganization in Honolulu. *American Journal of Sociology* 26:206–220.

Lindert, P. H. 1977. Sibling position and achievement. *Journal of Human Resources* 12:198–219.

Linn, R. 1982. Ability testing: Individual differences, prediction and differential prediction. In A. K. Wigdor and W. R. Garner (eds.), *Ability Testing: Uses, Consequences, and Controversies.* Washington, D.C.: National Academy Press.

Lippert, W. W., Jr., and Senter, R. J. 1966. Electrodermal responses in the sociopath. *Psychonomic Science* 4:25–26.

Lipton, D., Martinson, R., and Wilks, J. 1975. *The Effectiveness of Correctional Treatment: A Survey of Treatment Evaluation Studies.* New York: Praeger.

Loeber, R. 1982. The stability of antisocial and delinquent child behavior: A review. *Child Development* 53:1431–1446.

Loeber, R., and Dishion, T. 1983. Early predictors of male delinquency: A review. *Psychological Bulletin* 94:68–99.

Loehlin, J. C., Lindzey, G., and Spuhler, J. N. 1975. *Race Differences in Intelligence.* San Francisco: W. H. Freeman & Co.

Loftin, C. 1980. Population redistribution and the criminal justice system. In B. J. L. Berry and L. P. Silverman (eds.), *Population Redistribution and Public Policy.* Washington, D.C.: National Academy Press, pp. 287–331.

Lombroso, C., and Ferrero, W. 1897. *The Female Offender.* New York: Appleton.

Lombroso-Ferrero, G. 1972. *Criminal Man.* Montclair, N.J.: Patterson Smith. (Originally published in 1911.)

Lukoff, I. F. 1974. Issues in the evaluation of heroin treatment. In E. Josephson and E. E. Carroll (eds.), *Drug Use: Epidemiological and Sociological Approaches.* Washington, D.C.: Hemisphere, pp. 129–157.

Lundsgaarde, H. P. 1977. *Murder in Space City.* New York: Oxford University Press.

Lykken, D. T. 1957. A study of anxiety in the sociopathic personality. *Journal of Abnormal and Social Psychology* 55:6–10.

Lynn, R. 1981. Cross-cultural differences in neuroticism, extraversion and psychoticism. In R. Lynn (ed.), *Dimensions of Personality: Papers in Honour of H. J. Eysenck.* Oxford: Pergamon.

———. 1982. IQ in Japan and the United States shows a growing disparity. *Nature* 297:222–223.

Lynn, R., and Dziobon, J. 1980. On the intelligence of the Japanese and other Mongoloid peoples. *Personality and Individual Differences* 1:95–96.

Lyons, R. D. 1983. Physical and mental disabilities in newborns doubled in 25 years. *New York Times,* July 18, p. 1.

MacAndrew, C., and Edgerton, R. B. 1969. *Drunken Comportment.* Chicago: Aldine.

Maccoby, E. E., and Jacklin, C. N. 1974. *The Psychology of Sex Differences.* Stanford: Stanford University Press.

———. 1980. Sex differences in aggression: A rejoinder and reprise. *Child Development* 51:964–980.

Maccoby, E. E., and Martin, J. A. 1983. Socialization in the context of the family: Parent-child interaction. In P. H. Mussen (ed.), *Handbook of Child Psychology,* 4th ed. New York: John Wiley & Sons.

MacIver, R. M. 1940. *Social Causation.* Boston: Ginn.

Malcolm X. 1964. *The Autobiography of Malcolm X.* (With the assistance of Alex Haley.) New York: Grove Press.

Malina, R. M. 1973. Biological substrata. In K. S. Miller and R. M. Dreger (eds.), *Comparative Studies of Blacks and Whites in the United States.* New York: Seminar Press, pp. 53–123.

Malina, R. M., and Rarick, G. L. 1973. Growth, physique, and motor performance. In G. L. Rarick (ed.), *Physical Activity: Human Growth and Development.* New York: Academic Press, pp. 125–153.

Malinowski, B. 1926. *Crime and Custom in Savage Society.* New York: Harcourt, Brace.

Maltz, M. D., Gordon, A. C., McDowall, D., and McCleary, R. 1980. An artifact in pretest-posttest designs: How it can mistakenly make delinquency programs look effective. *Evaluation Review* 4:225–240.

Mann, C. W., and Mann, H. P. 1939. Age and intelligence of a group of juvenile delinquents. *Journal of Abnormal and Social Psychology* 34:351–360.

Manne, S. H., Kandel, A., and Rosenthal, D. 1962. Differences between performance

IQ and verbal IQ in a severely sociopathic population. *Journal of Clinical Psychology* 18:73–77.

Mansfield, R., Gould, L. C., and Namenwirth, J. Z. 1974. A socioeconomic model for the prediction of societal rates of property theft. *Social Forces* 52:462–472.

Marcus, B. 1955. Intelligence, criminality, and expectation of recidivism. *British Journal of Delinquency* 6:147–151.

Mark, V. H., and Ervin, F. R. 1970. *Violence and the Brain*. New York: Harper & Row.

Martin, B. 1975. Parent-child relations. In F. Horowitz (ed.), *Review of Child Development Research,* Vol. 4. Chicago: University of Chicago Press, pp. 463–540.

Martin, E. P., and Martin, J. M. 1978. *The Black Extended Family*. Chicago: University of Chicago Press.

Martin, J. A., Maccoby, E. E., and Jacklin, C. N. 1981. Mothers' responsiveness to interactive bidding and nonbidding in boys and girls. *Child Development* 52:1064–1067.

Martin, M. K., and Voorhies, B. 1975. *Female of the Species*. New York: Columbia University Press.

Matas, L., Arendt, R. A., and Sroufe, L. A. 1978. Continuity of adaptation in the second year: The relationship between quality of attachment and later competence. *Child Development* 49:547–556.

Matza, D. 1964. *Delinquency and Drift*. New York: John Wiley.

Maule, H. G., and Martin, F. M. 1956. Social and psychological aspects of rehousing. *Advancement of Science* 12:443–453.

Mawson, A. R., and Mawson, C. D. 1977. Psychopathy and arousal: A new interpretation of the psychophysiological literature. *Biological Psychiatry* 12:49–74.

Maynard, R. 1980. *The Impact of Supported Work on Young School Dropouts*. New York: Manpower Demonstration Research Corp.

McBride, D. C. 1981. Drugs and violence. In J. A. Inciardi (ed.), *The Drugs-Crime Connections*. Beverly Hills, Calif.: Sage Publications, pp. 105–123.

McCall, R. B. 1979. The development of intellectual functioning in infancy and the prediction of later IQ. In J. D. Osofsky (ed.), *Handbook of Infant Development*. New York: John Wiley, pp. 707–741.

McCandless, B. R., Persons, W. S., III, and Roberts, A. 1972. Perceived opportunity, delinquency, race, and body build among delinquent youth. *Journal of Consulting and Clinical Psychology* 38:281–287.

McClintock, F. H. 1963. *Crimes of Violence*. London: Macmillan.

McClintock, F. H., and Avison, N. H. 1968. *Crime in England and Wales*. London: Heinemann.

McCord, J. 1979. Consideration of the impact of parental behavior on subsequent criminality. Paper presented at the American Sociological Association annual meeting.

McCord, J., McCord, W., and Thurber, E. 1962. Some effects of parental absence on male children. *Journal of Abnormal and Social Psychology* 64:361–369.

McCord, J., McCord, W., and Verden, P. 1962. Familial and behavioral correlates of dependency in male children. *Child Development* 33:313–326.

McCord, W., and McCord, J. 1959. *Origins of Crime: A New Evaluation of the Cambridge-Somerville Study*. New York: Columbia University Press.

McCord, W., McCord, J., and Howard, A. 1961. Familial correlates of aggression in non-delinquent male children. *Journal of Abnormal and Social Psychology* 62:79–93.

McDermott, M. J. 1979. The criminal behavior of juveniles and adults: Comparisons within crime categories. Unpublished doctoral dissertation, SUNY at Albany (N.Y.).

McDermott, M. J., and Hindelang, M. J. 1981. *Juvenile Criminal Behavior in the United States: Its Trends and Implications.* Washington, D.C.: Office of Juvenile Justice and Delinquency Prevention.

McDonald, L. 1982. Theory and evidence of rising crime in the nineteenth century. *British Journal of Sociology* 33:404–420.

McGhee, J. D. 1984. *Running the Gauntlet: Black Men in America.* New York: National Urban League.

McGurk, B. J., McEwan, A. W., and Graham, F. 1981. Personality types and recidivism among young delinquents. *British Journal of Criminology* 21:159–165.

McKissack, J. J. 1967. The peak age of property crimes. *British Journal of Criminology* 7:184–194.

———. 1973a. The peak age of property crimes: Further data. *British Journal of Criminology* 13:253–261.

———. 1973b. Property offending and the school leaving age. *International Journal of Criminology and Penology* 1:353–362.

McMichael, P. 1979. The hen or the egg? Which comes first—antisocial emotional disorders or reading disability? *British Journal of Educational Psychology* 49:226–238.

Mednick, S. A., and Baert, A. E. (eds.). 1981. *Prospective Longitudinal Research: An Empirical Basis for the Primary Prevention of Psychosocial Disorders.* Oxford: Oxford University Press.

Mednick, S. A., Gabrielli, W. F., Jr., and Hutchings, B. 1984. Genetic influences in criminal convictions: Evidence from an adoption cohort. *Science* 224:891–894.

Mednick, S. A., Volavka, J., Gabrielli, W. F., Jr., and Itil, T. M. 1981. EEG as a predictor of antisocial behavior. *Criminology* 19:212–229.

Megargee, E. I. 1966a. Undercontrolled and overcontrolled personality types in extreme antisocial aggression. *Psychological Monographs* 80 (3, whole No. 611).

———. 1966b. Estimation of CPI scores from MMPI protocols. *Journal of Clinical Psychology* 22:456–458.

———. 1972. *The California Psychological Inventory Handbook.* San Francisco: Jossey-Bass.

———. 1973. Recent research on overcontrolled and undercontrolled personality patterns among violent offenders. *Sociological Symposium* 9:37–50.

———. 1984. Derivation, validation and application of an MMPI-based system for classifying criminal offenders. *Medicine and Law* 3:109–118.

Megargee, E. I., and Bohn, M. J., Jr. 1979. *Classifying Criminal Offenders: A New System Based on the MMPI.* Beverly Hills, Calif.: Sage.

Megargee, E. I., and Cook, P. E. 1975. Negative response bias and the MMPI *O-H* scale: A response to Deiker. *Journal of Consulting and Clinical Psychology* 43:725–729.

Megargee, E. I., Cook, P. R., and Mendelsohn, G. A. 1967. Development and validation of an MMPI scale of assaultiveness in overcontrolled individuals. *Journal of Abnormal Psychology* 72:519–528.

Meichenbaum, D. 1975. Theoretical and treatment implications of developmental research on verbal control of behavior. *Psychologic Canadienne/Canadian Psychological Review* 16:22–27.

Menninger, K. 1968. *The Crime of Punishment.* New York: Viking.

Merrill, E. J. 1962. Physical abuse of children: An agency study. In V. De Francis (ed.), *Protecting the Battered Child.* Denver, Colo.: American Humane Association.

Merrill, M. A. 1947. *Problems of Child Delinquency.* Boston: Houghton Mifflin.

Merry, S. E. 1981. *Urban Danger: Life in a Neighborhood of Strangers*. Philadelphia: Temple University Press.

Merton, R. K. 1949. Patterns of influence: Local and cosmopolitan influentials. In Merton, *Social Theory and Social Structure*. Glencoe, Ill.: Free Press.

———. 1957. Social structure and anomie. In Merton, *Social Theory and Social Structure*, rev. ed. New York: Free Press.

Messer, S. B. 1976. Reflection-impulsivity: A review. *Psychological Bulletin* 83:1026–1052.

Messner, S. F. 1983. Regional and racial effects on the urban homicide rate: The subculture of violence revisited. *American Journal of Sociology* 88:997–1007.

Michael, R. P. 1968. Gonadal hormones and the control of primate behavior. In P. P. Michael (ed.), *Endocrinology and Human Behavior*. Oxford: Oxford University Press.

Miele, F. 1979. Cultural bias in the WISC. *Intelligence* 3:149–164.

Milavsky, J. R., Stipp, H. H., Kessler, R. C., and Rubens, W. S. 1982. *Television and Aggression: A Panel Study*. New York: Academic Press.

Milgram, S. 1974. *Obedience to Authority*. New York: Harper & Row.

Milgram, S., and Shotland, R. L. 1973. *Television and Antisocial Behavior: Field Experiments*. New York: Academic Press.

Miller, W. B. 1958. Lower class culture as a generating milieu of gang delinquency. *Journal of Social Issues* 14:5–19.

———. 1962. The impact of a total community delinquency control project. *Social Problems* 10:169–191.

———. 1967. Theft behavior in city gangs. In M. W. Klein (ed.), *Juvenile Gangs in Context*. Englewood Cliffs, N.J.: Prentice-Hall.

———. 1976. *Violence by Youth Gangs and Youth Groups in Major American Cities*. Unpublished manuscript, Harvard Law School Center for Criminal Justice (National Criminal Justice Reference Service microfiche 034289).

Mischel, W. 1958. Preferences for delayed reinforcements: An experimental study of a cultural observation. *Journal of Abnormal and Social Psychology* 56:57–61.

———. 1961a. Father-absence and delay of gratification: Cross-cultural comparisons. *Journal of Abnormal and Social Psychology* 63:116–124.

———. 1961b. Preference for delayed reinforcement and social responsibility. *Journal of Abnormal and Social Psychology* 62:1–7.

———. 1968. *Personality and Assessment*. New York: Wiley.

———. 1969. Continuity and change in personality. *American Psychologist* 24:1012–1018.

———. 1974. Processes in delay of gratification. *Advances in Experimental Psychology* 7:249–292.

Mischel, W., and Metzner, R. 1962. Preference for delayed reward as a function of age, intelligence, and length of delay interval. *Journal of Abnormal and Social Psychology* 64:425–431.

Mitchell, G. D. 1968. Attachment differences in male and female infant monkeys. *Child Development* 39:611–620.

Mitchell, S., and Rosa, P. 1981. Boyhood behaviour problems as precursors of criminality: A fifteen-year follow-up study. *Journal of Child Psychology and Psychiatry* 22:19–33.

Moberg, D. O. 1953. Old age and crime. *Journal of Criminal Law and Criminology* 43:764–776.

Moffitt, T. E. 1983. The learning theory model of punishment: Implications for delinquency deterrence. *Criminal Justice and Behavior* 10:131–158.

Monachesi, E. D., and Hathaway, S. R. 1969. The personality of delinquents. In J. N.

Butcher (ed.), *MMPI: Research Developments and Clinical Applications.* New York: McGraw-Hill, pp. 207–219.

Monahan, J. 1981. *Predicting Violent Behavior: An Assessment of Clinical Techniques.* Beverly Hills, Calif.: Sage.

Monahan, T. P. 1957. Family status and the delinquent child: A reappraisal and some new findings. *Social Forces* 35:250–258.

Monforte, J. R., and Spitz, W. U. 1975. Narcotic abuse among homicides in Detroit. *Journal of Forensic Sciences* 20:186–190.

Monkkonen, E. H. 1981a. A disorderly people? Urban order in the nineteenth and twentieth centuries. *Journal of American History* 68:536–559.

———. 1981b. *Police in Urban America, 1860–1920.* Cambridge, England: Cambridge University Press.

———. 1982. From cop history to social history: The significance of the police in American history. *Journal of Social History* 15:575–591.

Montare, A., and Boone, S. L. 1980. Aggression and paternal absence: Racial-ethnic differences among inner-city boys. *Journal of Genetic Psychology* 137:223–232.

Moore, J. W. 1978. *Homeboys: Gangs, Drugs, and Prison in the Barrios of Los Angeles.* Philadelphia: Temple University Press.

Moore, M. H. 1977. *Buy and Bust.* Lexington, Mass.: Lexington Books/D. C. Heath.

Moore, T. G. 1982. The future of capitalism: A sociobiological approach. *Working Papers in Economics.* No. E-82-19. The Hoover Institution, Stanford University.

Moos, R. H., Kopell, B. S., Melges, F. T., Yalom, J. D., Lunde, D. T., Clayton, R. B. and Hamburg, D. A. 1969. Fluctuations in symptoms and moods during the menstrual cycle. *Journal of Psychosomatic Research* 13:37–44.

Morris, N. 1974. *The Future of Imprisonment.* Chicago: University of Chicago Press.

Morton, J., Addison, H., Addison, R., Hunt, L., and Sullivan, J. 1953. A clinical study of premenstrual tension. *American Journal of Obstetrics and Gynecology* 65: 1182–1191.

Morton, N. E. 1972. Human behavioral genetics. In L. Ehrman, G. S. Omenn, and E. Caspari (eds.), *Genetics, Environment, and Behavior.* New York: Academic Press.

Mosher, L. R. 1969. Father absence and antisocial behavior in Negro and white males. *Acta Paedopsychiatrica* 36:186–202.

Moss, H. A. 1967. Sex, age and state as determinants of mother-infant interactions. *Merrill-Palmer Quarterly* 13:19–36.

Moulds, E. F. 1980. Chivalry and paternalism: Disparities of treatment in the criminal justice system. In S. K. Datesman and F. R. Scarpitti (eds.), *Women, Crime & Justice.* New York: Oxford, pp. 277–299.

Mukherjee, S. K. 1971. A typological study of school status and delinquency. Unpub. Ph.D. dissertation, Department of Sociology, University of Pennsylvania.

Mulvihill, D. J., Tumin, M. M., and Curtis, L. A. 1969. *Crimes of Violence,* Vol. 11. A staff report to the National Commission on the Causes and Prevention of Violence. Washington, D.C.: Government Printing Office.

Murchison, C. 1926. *Criminal Intelligence.* Worcester, Mass.: Clark University.

Murphy, J. 1974. Teacher expectations and working-class under-achievement. *British Journal of Sociology* 25:326–344.

Murphy, J. G. 1979. *Retribution, Justice, and Therapy.* Dordrecht, Holland: D. Reidel.

Murray, C. A. 1976. *The Link Between Learning Disabilities and Juvenile Delinquency.* Washington, D.C.: National Institute for Juvenile Justice and Delinquency Prevention.

———. 1980. *Days in Court: Patterns of Juvenile Court Response and Their Impact on Arrest Rates.* Washington, D.C.: American Institutes for Research.

────. 1983. The physical environment and community control of crime. In J. Q. Wilson (ed.), *Crime and Public Policy*. San Francisco: Institute for Contemporary Studies.

Murray, C. A., and Cox, L. A. 1979. *Beyond Probation: Juvenile Corrections and the Chronic Delinquent*. Beverly Hills, Calif.: Sage Publications.

Mussen, P. H., Conger, J. J., and Kagan, J. 1979. *Child Development and Personality*, 5th ed. New York: Harper & Row.

Myers, S. L. 1979–1980. Black-white differentials in crime rates. *Review of Black Political Economy* 10:133–152.

────. 1983. Estimating the economic model of crime: Employment versus punishment effects. *Quarterly Journal of Economics* 98:157–166.

Nagel, I. H., and Hagen, J. 1983. Gender and crime: Offense patterns and criminal court sanctions. In M. Tonry and N. Morris (eds.), *Crime and Justice: An Annual Review of Research*, Vol. 4. Chicago: University of Chicago Press, pp. 91–144.

Nagel, T. W. 1982. Do schools affect delinquency? Review of *Fifteen Thousand Hours. University of Chicago Law Review* 49:1118–1136.

Nagin, D. 1978. General deterrence: A review of the empirical evidence. In A. Blumstein, J. Cohen, and D. Nagin (eds.), *Deterrence and Incapacitation: Estimating the Effects of Criminal Sanctions on Crime Rates*. Washington, D.C.: National Academy of Sciences, pp. 95–139.

National Academy of Sciences/National Research Council. 1983. *NewsReport*, March, pp. 7ff.

National Institute of Education. 1978. *Violent Schools, Safe Schools: The Safe School Study Report to Congress*. Washington, D.C.: Government Printing Office.

National Institute of Mental Health. 1982. *Television and Behavior: Ten Years of Scientific Progress and Implications for the Eighties*. Vol. 1, *Summary Report*. Rockville, Md.: National Institute of Mental Health.

Nettler, G. 1974. *Explaining Crime*. New York: McGraw-Hill.

Newman, G. 1976. *Comparative Deviance: Perception and Law in Six Cultures*. New York: Elsevier.

Newman, O. 1972. *Defensible Space: Crime Prevention Through Urban Design*. New York: Macmillan.

Newman, R. A. (ed.). 1973. *Equity in the World's Legal Systems*. Brussels: Establishments Emile Bruyant.

Newsweek. 1982. May 17, p. 112.

New York State Assembly, Select Committee on Child Abuse. 1978. *Summary Report on the Relationship Between Child Abuse and Neglect and Later Socially Deviant Behavior*. March.

New York Times. 1982. A Radical View on Insanity (Editorial). August 8, p. 18e.

────. 1983a. A Sane View of Insanity (Editorial). January 28, p. A26.

────. 1983b. "In Japan, a Crime Wave Is Measured in Drops," by C. Haberman. August 2, p. A2.

Neznansky, F. 1979. Soviet crime statistics: Reading the political message. *Freedom at Issue*. November–December, No. 53, 21–25.

Nietzel, M. T. 1979. *Crime and Its Modification: A Social Learning Perspective*. New York: Pergamon.

Nobers, D. R. 1968. The effect of father absence and mothers' characteristics on the identification of adolescent white and negro males. Unpub. Ph.D. dissertation, St. Louis University.

Norland, S., Wessel, R. C., and Shover, N. 1981. Masculinity and delinquency. *Criminology* 19:421–433.

Novak, M. A., and Harlow, H. F. 1975. Social recovery of monkeys isolated for the first year of life. *Developmental Psychology* 11:453–465.

Nye, F. I. 1958. *Family Relationships and Delinquent Behavior*. New York: John Wiley & Sons.

O'Brien, C. P., Testa, T., O'Brien, T. J., Brady, J. P., and Wells, B. 1977. Conditioned narcotic withdrawal in humans. *Science* 195:1000–1002.

O'Donnell, C. R., Lydgate, T., and Fo, W. S. O. 1979. The buddy system: Review and follow-up. *Child Behavior Therapy* 1:161–169.

Offner, P. 1970. Labor force participation in the ghetto: A study of New York City poverty areas. Unpub. Ph.D. thesis, Department of Economics, Princeton University.

O'Leary, D. E., and O'Leary, M. R. 1976. Social skill acquisition and psychosocial development of alcoholics: A review. *Addictive Behaviors* 1:111–210.

O'Leary, M. R., Donovan, D. M., Freeman, C. W., and Chaney, E. F. 1976. Relationship between psychopathology, experienced control and perceived locus of control: In search of alcoholic subtypes. *Journal of Clinical Psychology* 32:899–904.

Olweus, D. 1979. Stability of aggressive reaction patterns in males: A review. *Psychological Bulletin* 86:852–875.

————. 1980. Familial and temperamental determinants of aggressive behavior in adolescent boys: A causal analysis. *Developmental Psychology* 16:644–660.

Ornstein, R. E. 1972. *The Psychology of Consciousness*. San Francisco: Freeman.

Orr, P. L., and Cochran, S. W. 1969. Personality characteristics of parents of delinquent and nondelinquent adolescent boys as measured by the Minnesota Multiphasic Personality Inventory. Unpub. paper, Department of Psychology, University of Arkansas.

Orsagh, T., and Witte, A. D. 1981. Economic status and crime: Implications for offender rehabilitation. *Journal of Criminal Law and Criminology* 72:1055–1071.

Osborne, R. T. 1980. *Twins: Black and White*. Athens, Ga.: Foundation for Human Understanding.

Osborne, R. T., and McGurk, F. C. J. 1982. *The Testing of Negro Intelligence*, Vol. 2. Athens, Ga.: Foundation for Human Understanding.

Packer, H. L. 1968. *The Limits of the Criminal Sanction*. Stanford: Stanford University Press.

Palmer, T. 1978. *Correctional Intervention and Research*. Lexington, Mass.: Lexington Books/D. C. Heath.

Panton, J. H. 1958. MMPI profile configurations among crime classification groups. *Journal of Clinical Psychology* 14:305–308.

————. 1974. Personality differences between male and famale prison inmates measured by MMPI. *Criminal Justice and Behavior* 1:332–339.

Parke, R. D. 1975. Rules, roles, and resistance to deviation: Recent advances in punishment, discipline, and selfcontrol. In *Minnesota Symposia on Child Psychology*. Minneapolis, Minn.: University of Minnesota Press.

Parke, R. D., Berkowitz, L., Leyens, J. P., West, S. G., and Sebastian, R. J. 1977. Some effects of violent and nonviolent movies on the behavior of juvenile delinquents. In L. Berkowitz (ed.), *Advances in Experimental Social Psychology*, Vol. 10. New York: Academic Press, pp. 135–172.

Parker, S., and Kleiner, R. J. 1966. Characteristics of Negro mothers in single-headed households. *Journal of Marriage and the Family* 28:507–513.

Parkin, A. 1977. The homicidal nation: An investigation into violence in the United States. *Politics* 12:78–88.

Parlee, M. B. 1973. The premenstrual syndrome. *Psychological Bulletin* 80:454–465.

Parmelee, M. 1912. Introduction. C. Lombroso, *Crime: Its Causes and Remedies.* Translated by H. P. Horton. Boston: Little, Brown.

Passingham, R. E. 1972. Crime and personality: A review of Eysenck's theory. In V. D. Nebylitsyn and J. S. Grey (eds.), *Biological Bases of Individual Behaviour.* London: Academic Press.

Patterson, G. R. 1982. *Coercive Family Process.* Eugene, Ore.: Castalia Publishing Co.

Patterson, G. R., Chamberlain, P., and Reid, J. B. 1982. A comparative evaluation of a parent-training program. *Behavior Therapy* 13:638–650.

Pelton, L. H. 1978. Child abuse and neglect: The myth of classlessness. *American Journal of Orthopsychiatry* 48:608–617.

Pernanen, K. 1981. Theoretical aspects of the relationship between alcohol use and crime. In J. J. Collins, Jr. (ed.), *Drinking and Crime.* New York: Guilford Press, pp. 1–69.

Persons, R. W., and Marks, P. A. 1971. The violent 4-3 MMPI personality type. *Journal of Consulting and Clinical Psychology* 36:189–196.

Petersen, K. G. I., Matousek, M., Mednick, S. A., Volavka, J., and Pollock, V. 1982. EEG antecedents of thievery. *Acta Psychiatrica Scandinavica* 65:331–338.

Petersen, N. S., and Novick, M. R. 1976. An evaluation of some models of culture-fair selection. *Journal of Educational Measurement* 13:3–29.

Petersilia, J. 1983. *Racial Disparities in the Criminal Justice System.* Santa Monica, Calif.: Rand.

Peterson, J. 1925. *Early Conceptions and Tests of Intelligence.* Yonkers, N.Y.: World Book.

Peterson, M. A., and Braiker, H. B. 1980. *Doing Crime: A Survey of California Prison Inmates.* Santa Monica, Calif.: Rand.

Pettigrew, T. F., and Spier, R. B. 1962. The ecological structure of Negro homicide. *American Journal of Sociology* 67:621–629.

Phillips, D. P. 1974. The influence of suggestion on suicide: Substantive and theoretical implications of the Werther effect. *American Sociological Review* 39:340–354.

———. 1979. Suicide, motor vehicle fatalities, and the mass media: Evidence toward a theory of suggestion. *American Journal of Sociology* 84:1150–1174.

———. 1980. The deterrent effect of capital punishment: New evidence on an old controversy. *American Journal of Sociology* 86:139–148.

———. 1983. The impact of mass media violence on U.S. homicides. *American Sociological Review* 48:560–568.

Phillips, D. P., and Hensley, J. E. 1985. When violence is rewarded or punished: The impact of mass media stories on homicide. *Journal of Communication* 34:101–116.

Phillips, L., and Votey, H. L. 1981. *The Economics of Crime Control.* Beverly Hills, Calif.: Sage Publications.

Phillips, L., Votey, H. L., and Maxwell, D. 1972. Crime, youth, and the labor market. *Journal of Political Economy* 80:491–504.

Pichot, P. 1978. Psychopathic behaviour: A historical overview. In R. D. Hare and D. Schalling (eds.), *Psychopathic Behaviour: Approaches to Research.* Chichester, England: Wiley.

Pierce, G. I., and Bowers, W. J. 1981. The Bartley-Fox gun law's short-term impact on crime in Boston. *Annals* 455:120–137.

Pihl, R. O., Zeichner, A., Niaura, R., Nagy, K., and Zacchia, C. 1981. Attribution and alcohol-mediated aggression. *Journal of Abnormal Psychology* 90:468–475.

Piliavin, I., and Gartner, R. 1981. *The Impact of Supported Work on Ex-Offenders.* New York: Manpower Demonstration Research Corp.

Pilling, D., and Pringle, M. K. 1978. *Controversial Issues in Child Development.* New York: Schocken Books.

Piore, M. J. 1977. The dual labor market: Theory and implications. In D. M. Gordon (ed.), *Problems in Political Economy: An Urban Perspective*, 2nd ed. Lexington, Mass.: D. C. Heath and Co., pp. 93–97.

Pittman, D. J., and Snyder, C. R. (eds.). 1962. *Society, Culture, and Drinking Patterns*. New York: John Wiley & Sons.

Plomin, R., DeFries, J. C., and McClearn, G. E. 1980. *Behavioral Genetics: A Primer*. San Francisco: W. H. Freeman.

Plomin, R., and Rowe, D. C. 1979. Genetic and environmental etiology of social behavior in infancy. *Developmental Psychology* 15:62–72.

Polk, K., and Schafer, W. E. 1972. *Schools and Delinquency*. Englewood Cliffs, N.J.: Prentice-Hall.

Pollak, O. 1941. The criminality of old age. *Journal of Criminal Psychopathology* 3: 213–235.

———. 1950. *The Criminality of Women*. Westport, Conn.: Greenwood.

Poole, E. D., and Regoli, R. M. 1979. Parental support, delinquent friends, and delinquency: A test of interaction effects. *Journal of Criminal Law and Criminology* 70:188–193.

Porteus, S. D. 1933. *The Maze Test and Mental Differences*. Vineland, N.J.: Smith.

———. 1942. *Qualitative Performance in the Maze Test*. Vineland, N.J.: Smith.

———. 1945. Q scores, temperament, and delinquency. *Journal of Social Psychology* 21:81–103.

———. 1954. Maze test qualitative aspects. *British Journal of Medical Psychology* 27:72–79.

Posner, R. A. 1981. *The Economics of Justice*. Cambridge, Mass.: Harvard University Press.

Powers, E., and Witmer, H. 1951. *An Experiment in the Prevention of Delinquency: The Cambridge-Somerville Youth Study*. New York: Columbia University Press.

Premack, D. 1965. Reinforcement theory. In D. Levine (ed.), *Nebraska Symposium on Motivation*. Lincoln, Neb.: University of Nebraska Press.

———. 1971. Catching up with common sense, or two sides of a generalization: Reinforcement and punishment. In D. Glaser (ed.), *The Nature of Reinforcement*. New York: Academic Press.

Prentice, N. M., and Kelly, F. J. 1963. Intelligence and delinquency: A reconsideration. *Journal of Social Psychology* 60:327–337.

Pringle, M. L. K., and Bossio, V. 1960. Early prolonged separations and emotional adjustment. *Journal of Child Psychology and Psychiatry* 1:37–48.

Provence, S., and Lipton, R. C. 1962. *Infants in Institutions*. New York: International Universities Press.

Pruitt, C. R. 1982. Crime and punishment: A longitudinal study of change in the criminal courts. Unpub. Ph.D. dissertation, Department of Government, Harvard University.

Pulkkinen, L. 1980. The child in the family. *Nordisk Psykologi* 32:147–157.

———. 1982. Self-control and continuity from childhood to late adolescence. In P. B. Baltes and O. G. Brim, Jr. (eds.), *Life-Span Development and Behavior*, Vol. 4. New York: Academic Press.

Purkey, S. C., and Smith, M. S. 1983. Effective schools: A review. *Elementary School Journal* 83:427–452.

Quadagno, D. M., Briscoe, R., and Quadagno, J. S. 1977. Effect of perinatal gonadal hormones on selected nonsexual behavior patterns: A critical assessment of the nonhuman and human literature. *Psychological Bulletin* 84:62–80.

Quay, H. C. 1965. Psychopathic personality as pathological stimulation seeking. *American Journal of Psychiatry* 122:180–183.

Quay, H. C., and Hunt, W. A. 1965. Psychopathy, neuroticism, and verbal condition-ing: A replication and extension. *Journal of Consulting Psychology* 29:283.

Quinney, R. 1965. Suicide, homicide and economic development. *Social Forces* 43: 401–406.

Quinton, D., and Rutter, M. 1983. Family pathology and child disorder: A four-year prospective study. In A. R. Nichol (ed.), *Practical Lessons from Longitudinal Studies*. Chichester, England: Wiley.

Quinton, D., Rutter, M., and Liddle, C. 1984. Institutional rearing, parenting diffi-culties, and marital support. *Psychological Medicine* 14:107–124.

Rachlin, H. 1974. Self-control. *Behaviorism* 2:94–107.

Rachlin, H., and Green, L. 1972. Commitment, choice, and self-control. *Journal of the Experimental Analysis of Behavior* 17:15–22.

Rachlin, H. C., and Herrnstein, R. J. 1969. Hedonism revisited: On the negative law of effect. In B. Campbell and R. M. Church (eds.), *Punishment and Aversive Behavior*. New York: Appleton-Century-Crofts, pp. 83–110.

Radzinowicz, L., and King, J. 1977. *The Growth of Crime: The International Expe-rience*. New York: Basic Books.

Reckless, W. C. 1955. *The Crime Problem*. New York: Appleton-Century-Crofts.

Reckless, W. C., and Dinitz, S. 1972. *The Prevention of Juvenile Delinquency: An Experiment*. Columbus, Ohio: Ohio State University Press.

Reckless, W. C., and Smith, M. 1932. *Juvenile Delinquency*. New York: McGraw-Hill.

Reed, D. S. 1981. Reducing the costs of drinking and driving. In M. H. Moore and D. R. Gerstein (eds.), *Alcohol and Public Policy*. Washington, D.C.: National Academy of Sciences, pp. 336–387.

Reid, I. D. A. 1939. *The Negro Immigrant: His Background, Characteristics and Social Adjustment, 1899–1937*. New York: Columbia University Press.

Reid, S. T. 1979. *Crime and Criminology*, 2nd ed. New York: Holt, Rinehart and Winston.

———. 1982. *Crime and Criminology*, 3rd ed. New York: Holt, Rinehart and Winston.

Reidy, T. J. 1977. The aggressive characteristics of abused and neglected children. *Journal of Clinical Psychology* 33:1140–1145.

Reiss, A. J. 1951. *Unraveling juvenile delinquency. II*. An appraisal of the research methods. *American Journal of Sociology* 57:115–120.

———. 1972. Surveys of self-reported delicts. Unpub. paper, Department of Sociology, Yale University.

Reiss, A. J., and Rhodes, A. L. 1959. A socio-psychological study of adolescent con-formity and deviation. Report to the United States Office of Education.

———. 1961. The distribution of juvenile delinquency in the social class structure. *American Sociological Review* 26:720–732.

Renson, G. J., Adams, J. E., and Tinklenberg, J. R. 1978. Russ-Durkee assessment and validation with violent versus nonviolent chronic alcohol abusers. *Journal of Con-sulting and Clinical Psychology* 46:360–361.

Renzetti, C. M., and Curran, P. J. 1981. Women, crime, and gender roles: A critical reappraisal. Paper presented at the Annual Meeting of the American Society of Criminology, Washington, D.C., November.

Report of the Secretary-General on Crime Prevention and Control. 1977. U.N. Report A/32/199, September 22.

Reuter, E. B. 1939. Review of E. A. Hooton, *Crime and the Man. American Journal of Sociology* 45:123–126.

Richards, P., Berk, R. A., and Forster, B. 1979. *Crime as Play: Delinquency in a Middle Class Suburb*. Cambridge, Mass.: Ballinger.

Richardson, J. F. 1970. *The New York Police, Colonial Times to 1901*. New York: Oxford University Press.

Richman, N., Stevenson, J., and Graham, P. J. 1982. *Pre-School to School: A Behavioural Study*. London: Academic Press.

Riddle, M., and Roberts, A. H. 1977. Delinquency, delay of gratification, recidivism, and the Porteus maze tests. *Psychological Bulletin* 84:417–425.

Roberts, A. H., Erikson, R. V., Riddle, M., and Bacon, J. G. 1974. Demographic variables, base rates, and personality characteristics associated with recidivism in male delinquents. *Journal of Consulting and Clinical Psychology* 42:833–841.

Robins, L. N. 1966. *Deviant Children Grown Up: A Sociological and Psychiatric Study of Sociopathic Personality*. Baltimore: Williams & Wilkins.

———. 1978. Aetiological implications in studies of childhood histories relating to antisocial personality. In R. D. Hare and D. Schalling (eds.), *Psychopathic Behaviour: Approaches to Research*. Chichester, England: Wiley.

Robins, L. N., Davis, D. H., and Wish, E. 1977. Detecting predictors of rare events: Demographic, family and personal deviance as predictors of stages in the progression toward narcotic addiction. In J. S. Strauss and H. M. Babigian (eds.). *The Origins and Course of Psychopathology*. New York: Plenum, pp. 379–406.

Robins, L. N., and Hill, S. Y. 1966. Assessing the contributions of family structure, class and peer groups to juvenile delinquency. *Journal of Criminal Law, Criminology, and Police Science* 57:325–334.

Robins, L. N., and Murphy, G. E. 1967. Drug use in a normal population of young Negro men. *American Journal of Public Health* 57:1580–1596.

Robins, L. N., Murphy, G., and Breckenridge, M. 1968. Drinking behavior of young urban Negro men. *Quarterly Journal of Studies on Alcohol* 29:657–683.

Robins, L. N., Murphy, G., Woodruff, R. A., Jr., and King, L. J. 1971. The adult psychiatric status of black schoolboys. *Archives of General Psychiatry* 24:338–345.

Robins, L. N., and O'Neal, P. 1958. Mortality, mobility, and crime: Problem children thirty years later. *American Sociological Review* 23:162–171.

Robins, L. N., and Wish, E. 1977. Childhood deviance as a developmental process: A study of 223 urban black men from birth to 18. *Social Forces* 56:448–473.

Roe, A. 1944. The adult adjustment of children of alcoholic parents raised in foster-homes. *Quarterly Journal of Studies of Alcohol* 5:378–394.

Rogosa, D. 1980. A critique of cross-lagged correlation. *Psychological Bulletin* 88:245–258.

Rolston, R. H. 1971. The effect of prior physical abuse on the expression of overt and fantasy aggressive behavior in children. Unpub. Ph.D. dissertation, Louisiana State University.

Rorabaugh, W. J. 1979. *The Alcoholic Republic*. New York: Oxford University Press.

Rorschach, H. 1921. *Psychodiagnostik*. Leipzig: Bircher.

Rose, H. M. 1981. Black homicide and the urban environment. Final Report to the Center for Minority Group Mental Health Programs, National Institute of Mental Health, U.S. Department of Health and Human Services, January.

Rosen, K. S., and Cicchetti, D. 1984. The relationship between affect and cognition in maltreated infants: Quality of attachment and the development of visual self-recognition. *Child Development* 55:648–658.

Rosen, L. 1970. Matriarchy and lower class negro male delinquency. *Social Problems* 17:175–189.

Rosenberg, B., and Silverstein, H. 1969. *The Varieties of Delinquent Experience*. Waltham, Mass.: Blaisdell Publishing Co.

Rosenquist, C. M., and Megargee, E. I. 1969. *Delinquency in Three Cultures*. Austin, Tex.: University of Texas Press.

Rosenthal, D. 1970. *Genetic Theory and Abnormal Behavior*. New York: McGraw-Hill.

Rosenthal, R., and Jacobson, L. 1968. *Pygmalion in the Classroom*. New York: Holt, Rinehart and Winston.

Rosenthal, R., and Rubin, D. B. 1971. Pygmalion reaffirmed. In J. D. Elashoff and R. E. Snow (eds.), *Pygmalion Reconsidered*. Worthington, Ohio: Charles A. Jones Publishing Co.

Ross, H. L. 1973. Law, science, and accidents: The British Road Safety Act of 1967. *Journal of Legal Studies* 2:1–78.

———. 1977. Deterrence regained: The Cheshire constabulary's "breathalyzer blitz." *Journal of Legal Studies* 6:241–249.

———. 1981. *Deterring the Drinking Driver: Legal Policy and Social Control*. Lexington, Mass.: Lexington Books/D. C. Heath.

Ross, R. R., and McKay, H. B. 1978. Behavioural approaches to treatment in corrections: Requiem for a panacea. *Canadian Journal of Criminology* 20:279–298.

Rossi, A. S. 1977. A biosocial perspective on parenting. *Daedalus* 106:1–31.

Rossi, P. H., Berk, R. A., and Lenihan, K. J. 1980. *Money, Work, and Crime*. New York: Academic Press.

Roth, J. A., and Visher, C. A. 1984. "Characterizing the Individual Offending Sequence—Prevalence, Duration, and Desistance." National Research Council Panel on Criminal Careers. July.

Rousseau, J. J. 1973. *Discourse on Inequality*. In Rousseau, *The Social Contract and Discourses*. Trans. G. D. H. Cole. London: J. M. Dent.

———. 1973. *Discourse on Political Economy*. In Rousseau, *op. cit.*

———. 1973. *Discourse on the Arts and Sciences*. In Rousseau, *op. cit.*

———. 1974. *Emile*. Trans. by B. Foxley. London: Dent/Everyman's Library.

Rowe, A. R., and Tittle, C. R. 1977. Life cycle changes and criminal propensity. *The Sociological Quarterly* 18:223–236.

Rowe, D. C. 1983. Biometrical genetic models of self-reported delinquent behavior: A twin study. *Behavior Genetics* 13:473–489.

Rowe, D. C., and Osgood, D. W. 1984. Heredity and sociological theories of delinquency: A reconsideration. *American Sociological Review* 49:526–540.

Rubenstein, H., Murray, C., Motoyama, T., and Rouse, W. V. 1980. *The Link Between Crime and the Built Environment*. Washington, D.C.: National Institute of Justice.

Rubin, S. 1951. Unraveling juvenile delinquency. I. Illusions in a research project using matched pairs. *American Journal of Sociology* 57:107–114.

Rushton, J. P., Brainerd, C. J., and Pressley, M. 1983. Behavioral development and construct validity: The principle of aggregation. *Psychological Bulletin* 94:18–38.

Russell, C. 1974. Transition to parenthood: Problems and gratifications. *Journal of Marriage and the Family* 36:294–301.

Russell, L. B. 1979. The macroeconomic effects of changes in the age structure of the population. In M. B. Ballabon (ed.), *Economic Perspectives: An Annual Survey of Economics*, Vol. 1. Amsterdam: OPA.

Rutter, M. 1970. Sex differences in children's response to family stress. In E. J. Anthony and C. Koupernik (eds.), *The Child in His Family*. New York: John Wiley.

———. 1971. Parent-child separation: Psychological effects on the children. *Journal of Child Psychology and Psychiatry* 12:233–260.

———. 1972. *Maternal Deprivation Reassessed*. New York: Penguin Books.

———. 1978. Family, area and school influences in the genesis of conduct disorders. In L. A. Hersov and M. Berger (eds.), *Aggression and Anti-Social Behaviour in Childhood and Adolescence*. Oxford: Pergamon Press, pp. 95–113.

———. 1980. *Changing Youth in a Changing Society*. Cambridge, Mass.: Harvard University Press.

————. 1983a. Statistical and personal interactions: Facets and perspectives. In D. Magnusson and V. Allen (eds.), *Human Development: An Interactionist Perspective.* New York: Academic Press, pp. 295–319.

————. 1983b. School effects on pupil progress: Research findings and policy implications. *Child Development* 54:1–29.

Rutter, M., and Giller, H. 1984. *Juvenile Delinquency: Trends and Perspectives.* New York: Guilford Press.

Rutter, M., Maughan, B., Mortimore, P., and Ouston, J. 1979. *Fifteen Thousand Hours: Secondary Schools and Their Effects on Children.* Cambridge, Mass.: Harvard University Press.

Rutter, M., and Quinton, D. 1977. Psychiatric disorder—ecological factors and concepts of causation. In McGurk, H. (ed.), *Ecological Factors in Human Development.* Amsterdam: North Holland.

Rutter, M., Yule, B., Quinton, D., Rowlands, O., Yule, W., and Berger, M. 1975. Attainment and adjustment in two geographical areas: Some factors accounting for area differences. *British Journal of Psychiatry* 126:520–533.

Sagi, P. C., and Wellford, C. F. 1968. Age composition and patterns of change in criminal statistics. *Journal of Criminal Law, Criminology, and Police Science* 59: 29–36.

Sameroff, A. J., and Chandler, M. J. 1975. Reproductive risk and the continuum of caretaking causality. In F. Horowitz (ed.), *Review of Child Development Research,* Vol. 4. Chicago: University of Chicago Press, pp. 187–244.

Sampson, E. E. 1975. On justice as equality. *Journal of Social Issues* 31:45–64.

Sampson, R. J., Castellano, T. C., and Laub, J. H. 1981. *Juvenile Criminal Behavior and Its Relation to Neighborhood Characteristics.* Washington, D.C.: Office of Juvenile Justice and Delinquency Prevention.

Sarbin, T. R., Allen, V. L., and Rutherford, E. E. 1965. Social reinforcement, socialization, and chronic delinquency. *British Journal of Social and Clinical Psychology* 4:179–184.

Satten, J., Menninger, K., and Rosen, I. 1960. Murder without apparent motive. *American Journal of Psychiatry* 117:48–53.

Satterfield, J. H. 1978. The hyperactive child syndrome: A precursor of adult psychopathy? In R. D. Hare and D. Schalling (eds.), *Psychopathic Behaviour: Approaches to Research.* Chichester, England: Wiley.

Sattler, J. M. 1982. *Assessment of Children's Intelligence and Special Abilities,* 2nd ed. Boston: Allyn and Bacon.

Savitz, L. 1962. Delinquency and migration. In M. E. Wolfgang, L. Savitz, and N. Johnson (eds.), *The Sociology of Crime and Delinquency.* New York: Wiley.

Scanzoni, J. H. 1971. *The Black Family in Modern Society.* Boston: Allyn and Bacon.

Schaefer, E. S. 1959. A circumplex model for maternal behavior. *Journal of Abnormal and Social Psychology* 59:226–235.

Schafer, W. E., and Polk, K. 1967. Delinquency and the schools. In *Juvenile Delinquency and Youth Crime:* Report of a task force to the President's Commission on Law Enforcement and Administration of Justice. Washington, D.C.: Government Printing Office.

Schaffer, H. R., and Emerson, P. E. 1964. The development of social attachments in infancy. *Monographs of the Society for Research in Child Development* 29:1–61.

Schalling, D., and Rosen, A.-S. 1968. Porteus Maze differences between psychopathic and non-psychopathic criminals. *British Journal of Social and Clinical Psychology* 7:224–228.

Schmid, C. F. 1960. Urban crime areas. *American Sociological Review* 25:527–554, 655–678.

Schroeder, P. L. 1936. Criminal behavior in the later period of life. *American Journal of Psychiatry* 92:915–924.

Schuckit, M. A. 1980. Alcoholism and genetics: Possible biological mediators. *Biological Psychiatry* 15:437–447.

Schuessler, K. F., and Cressey, D. F. 1950. Personality characteristics of criminals. *American Journal of Sociology* 55:476–484.

Schultz, S. K. 1973. *The Culture Factory: Boston Public Schools, 1789–1860.* New York: Oxford University Press.

Schweinhart, L. J., and Weikart, D. P. 1980. *Young Children Grow Up: The Effects of the Perry Preschool Program on Youths Through Age 15.* Monographs of the High/Scope Educational Research Foundation, No. 7. Ypsilanti, Mich.: High/Scope Educational Research Foundation.

———. 1983. The effect of the Perry Preschool Program on youths through age 15— a summary. In Consortium for Longitudinal Studies, *As the Twig Is Bent: The Lasting Effects of Preschool Programs.* Hillsdale, N.J.: Lawrence Erlbaum Associates, pp. 71–101.

Schwitzgebel, R., and Kolb, D. A. 1964. Inducing behaviour change in adolescent delinquents. *Behaviour Research and Therapy* 1:297–304.

Scott, J. E., and Al-Thakeb, F. 1980. Perceptions of deviance cross-culturally. In G. R. Newman (ed.), *Crime and Deviance: A Comparative Perspective.* Beverly Hills: Sage.

Sears, R. R., Macoby, E. E., and Levin, H. 1957. *Patterns of Child Rearing.* Evanston, Ill.: Row, Peterson & Co.

Sechrest, L., White, S. O., and Brown, E. D. (eds.). 1979. *The Rehabilitation of Criminal Offenders: Problems and Prospects.* Washington, D.C.: National Academy of Sciences.

Seligman, M. E. 1975. *Helplessness: On Depression, Development, and Death.* San Francisco: W. H. Freeman.

Sellin, T. 1926. Is murder increasing in Europe? *Annals* 126:29–34.

Sellin, T., and Wolfgang, M. E. 1964. *The Measurement of Delinquency.* New York: John Wiley.

Selzer, M. L., Payne, C. E., Westervelt, F. H., and Quinn, J. 1967. Automobile accidents as an expression of psychopathology in an alcoholic population. *Quarterly Journal of Studies on Alcohol* 28:505–516.

Shah, S. A. 1970. *Report on the XYY Chromosomal Abnormality.* U.S. Public Health Service pub. no. 2103. Washington, D.C.: U.S. Government Printing Office.

Shakespeare, W. 1942. The Tragedy of Julius Caesar. In W. A. Neilson and C. J. Hill (eds.), *The Complete Plays and Poems of William Shakespeare.* Cambridge, Mass.: Houghton Mifflin.

Shannon, L. W. 1976. Predicting adult criminal careers from juvenile careers. Unpub. paper, Department of Sociology, University of Iowa.

———. 1982. *Assessing the Relationship of Adult Criminal Careers to Juvenile Careers: A Summary.* Washington, D.C.: Office of Juvenile Justice and Delinquency Prevention.

Shasby, G., and Kingsley, R. F. 1978. A study of behavior and body type in troubled youth. *Journal of School Health* 48:103–107.

Shaw, C. R. 1929. *Delinquency Areas.* Chicago: University of Chicago Press.

Shaw, C. R., and McKay, H. D. 1931. *Social Factors in Juvenile Delinquency.* Washington, D.C.: Government Printing Office.

———. 1942. *Juvenile Delinquency and Urban Areas.* Chicago: University of Chicago Press.

Sheldon, W. H. (with the collaboration of S. S. Stevens and W. B. Tucker). 1940. *The Varieties of Human Physique.* New York: Harper.

Sheldon, W. H. (with the collaboration of S. S. Stevens). 1942. *The Varieties of Temperament.* New York: Harper.

Sheldon, W. H. (with the collaboration of E. M. Hartl and E. McDermott). 1949. *Varieties of Delinquent Youth.* New York: Harper.

Sheldon, W. H. (with the collaboration of C. W. Dupertius and E. McDermott). 1954. *Atlas of Men: A Guide for Somatotyping the Adult Male at All Ages.* New York: Harper.

Shelley, L. E. 1981. *Crime and Modernization: The Impact of Industrialization and Urbanization on Crime.* Carbondale, Ill.: SIU Press.

Sherif, M., Harvey, D. J., White, B. J., Hood, W. R., and Sherif, C. W. 1961. *Intergroup Conflict and Cooperation: The Robbers Cave Experiment.* Norman, Okla.: University of Oklahoma Book Exchange.

Sherif, M., and Sherif, C. 1964. *Reference Groups: Exploration into Conformity and Deviation of Adolescents.* New York: Harper and Row.

Sherman, L. W., and Berk, R. A. 1984. The specific deterrent effects of arrest for domestic assault. *American Sociological Review* 49:261–272.

Sherman, L. W., and Glick, B. D. 1984. The quality of police arrest statistics. *Police Foundation Reports,* No. 2, August.

Shimkin, D. B., Shimkin, E. M., and Frate, D. A. 1978. *The Extended Family in Black Societies.* The Hague: Mouton.

Shinn, M. 1978. Father absence and children's cognitive development. *Psychological Bulletin* 85:295–324.

Shoham, S. 1966. *Crime and Social Deviation.* Chicago: Henry Regnery.

Short, J. F. 1957. Differential association and delinquency. *Social Problems* 4:233–239.

Short, J. F., and Strodtbeck, F. L. 1965. *Group Process and Gang Delinquency.* Chicago: University of Chicago Press.

Shuey, A. M. 1966. *The Testing of Negro Intelligence.* New York: Social Science Press.

Shulman, H. M. 1929. *A Study of Problem Boys and Their Brothers.* Albany, N.Y.: New York State Crime Commission.

———. 1951. Intelligence and delinquency. *Journal of Criminal Law and Criminology* 41:763–781.

Shuntich, R. J., and Taylor, S. P. 1972. The effects of alcohol on human physical aggression. *Journal of Experimental Research in Personality* 6:34–38.

Siddle, D. A. T., and Trasler, G. B. 1981. The psychophysiology of psychopathic behaviour. In M. J. Christie and P. G. Mellet (eds.), *Foundations of Psychosomatics.* Chichester, England: Wiley.

Sigvardsson, S., Cloninger, C. R., Bohman, M., and von Knorring, A.-L. 1982. Predisposition to petty criminality in Swedish adoptees. III. Sex differences and validation of the male typology. *Archives of General Psychiatry* 39:1248–1253.

Silberman, C. E. 1978. *Criminal Violence, Criminal Justice.* New York: Random House.

Silberman, M. 1976. Toward a theory of criminal deterrence. *American Sociological Review* 41:442–461.

Simon, R. J. 1975. *Women and Crime.* Lexington, Mass.: Lexington Books/D. C. Heath.

Simon, R. J., and Sharma, N. 1979. Women and crime: Does the American experience generalize? In F. Adler and R. J. Simon (eds.), *Criminology of Deviant Women.* Boston: Houghton Mifflin, pp. 391–400.

Simpson, R. M. 1934. The employment index, arrests, court actions, and commitments in Illinois. *Journal of Criminal Law and Criminology* 24:914–922.

Singer, J. L., and Singer, D. G. 1981. *Television, Imagination, and Aggression: A Study of Preschoolers.* Hillsdale, N.J.: Lawrence Erlbaum Associates.

Singleton, G. H. 1976. Protestant voluntary organizations and the shaping of Victorian

America. In D. W. Howe (ed.), *Victorian America*. Philadelphia: University of Pennsylvania Press.

Skinner, B. F. 1953. *Science and Human Behavior*. New York: Macmillan.

Skogan, W. G. 1981. *Issues in the Measurement of Victimization*. Washington, D.C.: Bureau of Justice Statistics.

Smith, A. 1976 (1759). *The Theory of Moral Sentiments*. Indianapolis, Ind.: Liberty Classics.

Smith, C., and Lloyd, B. 1978. Maternal behavior and perceived sex of infant: Revisited. *Child Development* 49:1263–1265.

Smith, D. A., and Visher, C. A. 1980. Sex and involvement in deviance/crime: A quantitative review of the empirical literature. *American Sociological Review* 45: 691–701.

Smith, M. L., and Glass, G. V. 1977. Meta-analysis of psychotherapy outcome studies. *American Psychologist* 32:752–760.

Snyder, C. R. 1958. *Alcohol and the Jews*. New York: Free Press.

Snyderman, M. 1984. An overview of the IQ controversy. Unpub. paper, Department of Psychology and Social Relations, Harvard University. February.

Solem v. *Helm*. 1983. 103 Supreme Court Reporter. Pp. 3001–3024.

Spanier, G. B. 1980. Outsiders looking in. *The Wilson Quarterly* 4:122–135.

Spellacy, F. 1978. Neuropsychological discrimination between violent and nonviolent men. *Journal of Clinical Psychology* 34:49–52.

Spergel, I. 1964. *Racketville, Slumtown, Haulburg*. Chicago: University of Chicago Press.

Spielberger, C. D., Kling, J. K., O'Hagan, S. E. J. 1978. Dimensions of psychopathic personality: Antisocial behaviour and anxiety. In R. D. Hare and D. Schalling (eds.), *Psychopathic Behaviour: Approaches to Research*. Chichester, England: Wiley.

Spinetta, J. J., and Rigler, D. 1972. The child-abusing parent: A psychological review. *Psychological Bulletin* 77:296–304.

Sroufe, L. A. 1979. The coherence of individual development: Early care, attachment, and subsequent developmental issues. *American Psychologist* 34:834–841.

——. Infant-caregiver attachment and patterns of adaptation in preschool: The roots of maladaptation and competence. M. Perlmutter (ed.), *Minnesota Symposium in Child Psychology* (in press).

Stack, C. B. 1974. *All Our Kin: Strategies for Survival in a Black Community*. New York: Harper and Row.

Stanfield, R. E. 1966. The interaction of family variables and gang variables in the etiology of delinquency. *Social Problems* 13:411–417.

Stark, R., Doyle, D. P., and Kent, L. 1980. Rediscovering moral communities: Church membership and crime. In T. Hirschi and M. Gottfredson (eds.), *Understanding Crime*. Beverly Hills, Calif.: Sage Publications, pp. 43–52.

Stark, W. 1976–1980. *The Social Bond*, 3 vols. New York: Fordham University Press.

Steffensmeier, D. J. 1980. Sex differences in patterns of adult crime, 1965–1977: A review and assessment. *Social Forces* 58:1080–1108.

Steffensmeier, D. J., and Cobb, M. J. 1981. Sex differences in urban arrest patterns, 1934–79. *Social Problems* 29:37–49.

Stein, A. H., and Friedrich, L. K. 1972. Television content and young children's behavior. In J. P. Murray, E. A. Rubinstein, and G. A. Comstock (eds.), *Television and Social Learning*. A Technical Report to the Surgeon General's Scientific Advisory Committee on Television and Social Behavior (Vol. 2). Rockville, Md.: National Institute of Mental Health, pp. 202–317.

Stein, K. B., Sarbin, T. R., and Kulik, J. A. 1968. Future time perspective: Its relation to the socialization process and the delinquent role. *Journal of Consulting and Clinical Psychology* 32:257–264.

Stendler, C. B. 1950. Sixty years of child training practices. *Journal of Pediatrics* 36: 122–134.

Stephen, J. F. 1893. *A History of the Criminal Law of England.* London: Macmillan & Company.

Stern, W. 1912. *Die psychologische Methoden der Intelligenzprufung.* Leipzig: Barth.

Sterne, R. S. 1964. *Delinquent Conduct and Broken Homes.* New Haven, Conn.: College and University Press Services.

Stevenson, R. L. 1886. *The Strange Case of Dr. Jekyll and Mr. Hyde.* London: Longmans, Green.

Stevenson, W. 1978. The transition from school to work. In A. V. Adams and G. L. Mangum (eds.), *The Lingering Crisis of Youth Unemployment.* Kalamazoo, Mich.: W. E. Upjohn Institute for Employment Research.

Stewart, O. 1964. Questions regarding American Indian criminality. *Human Organization* 23:61–66.

Stimson, G. V. 1973. *Heroin and Behaviour.* New York: John Wiley & Sons.

Stinchcombe, A. 1963. Institutions of privacy in the determination of police administrative practice. *American Journal of Sociology* 69:150–160.

———. 1964. *Rebellion in a High School.* Chicago: Quadrangle Books.

Straus, M. A., Gelles, R. J., and Steinmetz, S. K. 1980. *Behind Closed Doors: Violence in the American Family.* Garden City, N.Y.: Anchor/Doubleday.

Sturge, C. 1982. Reading retardation and antisocial behavior. *Journal of Child Psychology and Psychiatry,* 23:21–31.

Sullivan, M. L. 1983. Youth crime: New York's two varieties. *New York Affairs* 8: 31–48.

Summers, L., and Harris, D. 1978. The general deterrence of driving while intoxicated. Technical Report DOT HS 803 582. Washington, D.C.: National Highway Traffic Safety Administration.

Sunley, R. 1955. Early nineteenth-century American literature on child rearing. In M. Mead and M. Wolfenstein (eds.), *Childhood in Contemporary Cultures.* Chicago: University of Chicago Press.

Suomi, S. J., and Harlow, H. F. 1972. Social rehabilitation of isolate reared monkeys. *Developmental Psychology* 6:487–496.

Surgeon General's Scientific Advisory Committee on Television and Social Behavior. 1972. *Television and Growing Up: The Impact of Televised Violence.* Washington, D.C.: Government Printing Office.

Sutherland, E. H. 1931. Mental deficiency and crime. In K. Young (ed.), *Social Attitudes.* New York: Holt.

———. 1947. *Principles of Criminology,* 4th ed. Philadelphia: Lippincott.

———. 1951. Critique of Sheldon's "Varieties of Delinquent Youth." *American Sociological Review* 16:10–13.

Sutherland, E. H., and Cressey, D. R. 1966. *Principles of Criminology,* 7th ed. Philadelphia: Lippincott.

———. 1978. *Principles of Criminology,* 10th ed. New York: Harper and Row.

Sutker, P. B. 1970. Vicarious conditioning and sociopathy. *Journal of Abnormal Psychology* 76:380–386.

Suttles, G. D. 1968. *The Social Order of the Slum.* Chicago: University of Chicago Press.

Sveri, K. 1960. *Kriminalitet og Older.* Stockholm: Almquist and Wiksell.

Syndulko, K. 1978. Electrocortical investigations of sociopathy. In R. D. Hare and

D. Schalling (eds.), *Psychopathic Behaviour: Approaches to Research.* Chichester, England: Wiley.

Syndulko, K., Parker, D. A., Jens, R., Maltzman, I., and Ziskind, E. 1975. Psychophysiology of sociopathy: Electrocortical measures. *Biological Psychology* 3:185–200.

Taft, D. R. 1933. Testing the selective influence of areas of delinquency. *American Journal of Sociology* 38:699–712.

Tagaki, P., and Platt, T. 1978. Behind the gilded ghetto: An analysis of race, class and crime in Chinatown. *Crime and Social Justice* 9:2–25.

Tannenbaum, F. 1938. *Crime and the Community.* Boston: Ginn.

Task Force on Assessment. 1967. *Crime and Its Impact: An Assessment.* Report to the President's Commission on Law Enforcement and Administration of Justice. Washington, D.C.: Government Printing Office.

Taylor, R. B., Gottfredson, S. D., and Brower, S. 1980. The defensibility of defensible space: A critical review and a synthetic framework for future research. In Travis Hirschi and Michael Gottfredson (eds.), *Understanding Crime: Current Theory and Research.* Beverly Hills, Calif.: Sage Publications, pp. 53–71.

Taylor, S. P., and Gammon, C. B. 1975. Effects of type and dose of alcohol on human physical aggression. *Journal of Personality and Social Psychology* 32:169–175.

Taylor, S. P., Schmutte, G. T., Leonard, K. E., and Cranston, J. W. 1979. The effects of alcohol and extreme provocation on the use of a highly noxious electric shock. *Motivation and Emotion* 3:73–81.

Taylor, T., and Watt, D. C. 1977. The relation of deviant symptoms and behaviour in a normal population to subsequent delinquency and maladjustment. *Psychological Medicine* 7:163–169.

Teller, F. E., and Howell, R. J. 1981. Older prisoner-criminal and psychological characteristics. *Criminology* 18:549–555.

Tennenbaum, D. J. 1977. Personality and criminality: A summary and implications of the literature. *Journal of Criminal Justice* 5:225–235.

Tennyson, R. A. 1967. Family structure and delinquent behavior. In M. W. Klein (ed.), *Juvenile Gangs in Context.* Englewood Cliffs, N.J.: Prentice-Hall, pp. 57–69.

Tharp, R. G., and Wetzel, R. J. 1969. *Behavior Modification in the Natural Environment.* New York: Academic Press.

Thomas, A., and Chess, S. 1976. Evolution of behavior disorders into adolescence. *American Journal of Psychiatry* 133:539–542.

———. 1984. Genesis and evolution of behavioral disorders: From infancy to early adult life. *American Journal of Psychiatry* 141:1–9.

Thomas, A., Chess, S., and Birch, H. G. 1968. *Temperament and Behavior Disorders in Children.* New York: New York University Press.

———. 1970. The origin of personality. *Scientific American* 223:2–9.

Thomas, D. S. 1925. *Social Aspects of the Business Cycle.* London: George Routledge and Sons.

Thompson, J. W., Sviridoff, M., and McElroy, J. E. 1981. *Employment and Crime: A Review of Theories and Research.* Washington, D.C.: National Institute of Justice.

Thornberry, T. P., and Farnsworth, M. 1982. Social correlates of criminal involvement: Further evidence on the relationship between social status and criminal behavior. *American Sociological Review* 47:505–518.

Thorndike, R. L. 1968. Review of Rosenthal and Jacobson, "Pygmalion in the Classroom." *American Educational Research Journal* 5:708–711.

Thornton, G. 1939. The ability to judge crimes from photographs of criminals. *Journal of Abnormal and Social Psychology* 34:378–383.

Thrasher, F. M. 1927. *The Gang*. Chicago: University of Chicago Press.

Tieger, T. 1980. On the biological basis of sex differences in aggression. *Child Development* 51:943–963.

Tien, J. M., O'Donnell, V. R., Barnett, A. K., and Mirchandane, P. B. 1977. *Street Lighting Projects: National Evaluation Report*. Cambridge, Mass.: Public Systems Evaluation, Inc.

Tiller, P. O. 1957. Father absence and personality development in children of sailor families. In N. Anderson (ed.), *Studies of the Family*, Vol. 2. Gottingen: Vandenhoeck and Ruprecht.

————. 1958. Father absence and personality development in children of sailor families. *Nordisk Psykologi Monographs* 9.

Time. 1982. May 17, p. 77.

Tinbergen, N. 1951. *The Study of Instinct*. London: Oxford University Press.

Tittle, C. R. 1980. *Sanctions and Social Deviance: The Question of Deterrence*. New York: Praeger.

Tittle, C. R., Villemez, W. J., and Smith, D. A. 1978. The myth of social class and criminality: An empirical assessment of the empirical evidence. *American Sociological Review* 43:643–656.

Toby, J. 1979. Delinquency in cross-cultural perspective. In L. T. Empey (ed.), *Juvenile Justice: The Progressive Legacy and Current Reforms*. Charlottesville, Va.: University Press of Virginia.

Tocqueville, A. 1955. *The Old Regime and the French Revolution*. Trans. S. Gilbert. Garden City, N.Y.: Doubleday Anchor Books. (First published in 1856.)

Trasler, G. 1978. Relations between psychopathy and persistent criminality—methodological and theoretical issues. In R. D. Hare and D. Schalling (eds.), *Psychopathic Behaviour: Approaches to Research*. Chichester, England: Wiley.

Tuddenham, R. D. 1962. The nature and measurement of intelligence. In L. J. Postman (ed.), *Psychology in the Making*. New York: Knopf.

Tulchin, S. H. 1939. *Intelligence and Crime: A Study of Penitentiary and Reformatory Offenders*. Chicago: University of Chicago Press.

Turner, A. G. 1981. The San Jose recall study. In R. G. Lehnen and W. G. Skogan (eds.), *The National Crime Survey: Working Papers*, Vol. I: *Current and Historical Perspectives*. Washington, D.C.: Bureau of Justice Statistics.

Tyack, D., and Hansot, E. 1982. *Managers of Virtue: Public School Leadership in America, 1820–1980*. New York: Basic Books.

Tyler, V. O., and Brown, G. D. 1967. The use of swift, brief isolation as a group control device for institutionalized delinquents. *Behaviour Research and Therapy* 5: 1–9.

United States Department of Labor (Office of Policy Planning and Research). 1965. *The Negro Family: The Case for National Action*. Washington, D.C.: Government Printing Office, March.

Vaillant, G. E. 1983. *The Natural History of Alcoholism*. Cambridge, Mass.: Harvard University Press.

Valez-Diaz, A., and Megargee, E. 1971. An investigation of differences in value judgments between youthful offenders and nonoffenders in Puerto Rico. *Journal of Criminal Law, Criminology, and Police Science* 61:549–556.

Van Dusen, K. T., Mednick, S. A., and Gabrielli, W. F., Jr. 1983. Social class and crime in an adoption cohort. In K. T. Van Dusen and S. A. Mednick (eds.), *Prospective Studies of Crime and Delinquency*. Hingham, Mass.: Kluwer Nijhoff.

Vedder, C., and Sommerville, D. 1970. *The Delinquent Girl*. Springfield, Ill.: Charles C. Thomas.

Vera Institute of Justice. 1980. *Family Court Disposition Study.* Unpublished draft. New York: Vera Institute of Justice.

Verlade, A. J. 1978. Do delinquents really drift? *British Journal of Criminology* 18: 23–39.

Vernon, P. E. 1979. *Intelligence: Heredity and Environment.* San Francisco: Freeman.

Viccica, A. D. 1980. World crime trends. *International Journal of Offender Therapy and Comparative Criminology* 24:270–277.

Vincent, C. 1961. *Unmarried Mothers.* New York: Free Press.

Viscusi, W. K. 1983. Market incentives for criminal behavior. Unpub. paper, National Bureau of Economic Research, July.

Vogel, E. G. 1979. *Japan as Number One: Lessons for America.* Cambridge, Mass.: Harvard University Press.

von Hirsch, A. 1976. *Doing Justice: The Choice of Punishments.* New York: Hill and Wang.

Voss, H. L. 1963. Ethnic differentials in delinquency in Honolulu. *Journal of Criminal Law, Criminology, and Police Science* 54:322–327.

Votey, H. L., and Phillips, L. 1974. The control of criminal activity: An economic analysis. In D. Glaser (ed.), *Handbook of Criminology.* Chicago: Rand McNally, pp. 1055–1093.

Wachter, M. L. 1976. The demographic impact on unemployment: Past experience and the outlook for the future. In *Demographic Trends and Full Employment.* Washington, D.C.: National Commission for Manpower Policy.

Wadsworth, M. E. J. 1976. Delinquency, pulse rates and early emotional deprivation. *British Journal of Criminology* 16:245–256.

———. 1979. *Roots of Delinquency.* New York: Barnes and Noble/Harper & Row.

Wagenaar, A. C. 1981. Effects of the raised legal drinking age on motor vehicle accidents in Michigan. *HSRI Research Review,* 1–8.

Waid, W. M., Orne, M. T., and Wilson, S. K. 1979. Socialization, awareness, and the electrodermal response to deception and self-disclosure. *Journal of Abnormal Psychology* 88:663–666.

Waldo, G. P., and Dinitz, S. 1967. Personality attributes of the criminal: An analysis of research studies, 1950–65. *Journal of Research in Crime and Delinquency* 4: 185–202.

Wallach, A., and Rubin, C. 1971–1972. The premenstrual syndrome and criminal responsibility. *UCLA Law Review* 19:209–312.

Walster, E., Walster, G. W., and Berschied, E. 1978. *Equity: Theory and Research.* Boston: Allyn and Bacon.

Walters, R. H., and Thomas, E. L. 1963. Enhancement of punitiveness by visual and audio-visual displays. *Canadian Journal of Psychology* 17:244–255.

Walters, R. H., Thomas, E. L., and Acker, C. W. 1962. Enhancement of punitive behavior by audio-visual displays. *Science* 136:872–873.

Ward, D. A., Jackson, M., and Ward, R. E. 1969. Crimes of violence by women. In D. J. Mulvihill and M. M. Tumin (eds.), *Crimes of Violence.* Washington, D.C.: Government Printing Office, pp. 843–909.

Warren, M. Q. 1971. Classification of offenders as an aid to efficient management and effective treatment. *Journal of Criminal Law, Criminology, and Police Science* 62:239–258.

Waters, E., and Crandall, V. J. 1964. Social class and observed maternal behavior from 1940 to 1960. *Child Development* 35:1021–1032.

Watson, E. W., Maloney, D. M., Brooks, L. E., Blase, K. B., and Collins, L. B. 1980. *Teaching-Family Bibliography.* Boys Town, Nebr.: Father Flanagan's Boys' Home.

Webster's Third New International Dictionary. 1961. Springfield, Mass.: Merriam.

Wechsler, D. 1944. *The Measurement of Adult Intelligence,* 3rd ed. Baltimore: Williams and Wilkins.

Wechsler, H., and Thum, D. 1973. Teenage drinking, drug use, and social correlates. *Quarterly Journal of Studies on Alcohol* 34:1220–1227.

Weinreb, L. L. 1975. *Criminal Law: Cases, Comments, Questions,* 2nd ed. Mineola, N.Y.: Foundation Press.

Weisman, J. C., Marr, S. W., and Katsampes, P. L. 1976. Addiction and criminal behavior: A continuing examination of criminal addicts. *Journal of Drug Issues* 6:153–165.

Weiss, N. S. 1976. Recent trends in violent deaths among young adults in the United States. *American Journal of Epidemiology* 103:416–422.

Wellford, C. F. 1973. Age composition and the increase in recorded crime. *Criminology* 2:61–70.

———. 1974. Crime and the dimensions of nations. *International Journal of Criminology and Penology* 2:1–10.

———. 1975. Labelling theory and criminology: An assessment. *Social Problems* 22: 332–345.

Werner, E. E., and Smith, R. S. 1977. *Kauai's Children Come of Age.* Honolulu: University of Hawaii Press.

———. 1982. *Vulnerable but Invincible: A Study of Resilient Children.* New York: McGraw-Hill.

West, D. J. 1982. *Delinquency: Its Roots, Careers, and Prospects.* Cambridge, Mass.: Harvard University Press.

West, D. J., and Farrington, D. P. 1973. *Who Becomes Delinquent?* London: Heinemann Educational Books.

———. 1977. *The Delinquent Way of Life.* New York: Crane Russak.

Whiting, B., and Edwards, C. P. 1973. A cross-cultural analysis of sex differences in the behavior of children aged 3 through 11. *Journal of Social Psychology* 91: 171–188.

Whiting, B. B., and Whiting, J. W. M. 1975. *Children of Six Cultures.* Cambridge, Mass.: Harvard University Press.

Whiting, J. W. M., and Whiting, B. B. 1975. Aloofness and intimacy of husbands and wives. *Ethos* 3:183–207.

Whittaker, J. O. 1982. Alcohol and the Standing Rock Sioux tribe. *Journal of Studies on Alcohol* 43:191–200.

Whyte, W. F. 1943. *Street Corner Society.* Chicago: University of Chicago Press.

Wiatrowski, M. D., Hansell, S., Massey, C. R., and Wilson, D. L. 1982. Curriculum tracking and delinquency. *American Sociological Review* 47:151–160.

Wiatrowski, M. D., Griswold, D. B., and Roberts, M. K. 1981. Social control theory and delinquency. *American Sociological Review* 46:525–541.

Widom, C. S. 1978. Toward an understanding of female criminality. In B. A. Maher (ed.), *Progress in Experimental Personality Research,* Vol. 8. New York: Academic Press, pp. 248–308.

———. 1979. Female offenders—three assumptions about self-esteem, sex-role identity and feminism. *Criminal Justice and Behavior* 6:365–382.

Wigdor, A. K., and Garner, W. R. (eds.). 1982. *Ability Testing: Uses, Consequences, and Controversies.* Washington, D.C.: National Academy Press.

Wilkins, L. T. 1965. *Social Deviance: Social Policy, Action, and Research.* Englewood Cliffs, N.J.: Prentice-Hall.

———. 1980. World crime. To measure or not to measure? In G. R. Newman (ed.), *Crime and Deviance: A Comparative Perspective.* Beverly Hills, Calif.: Sage.

Wilkinson, K. 1980. The broken home and delinquent behavior: An alternative interpretation of contradictory findings. In T. Hirschi and M. Gottfredson (eds.), *Understanding Crime: Current Theory and Research.* Beverly Hills, Calif.: Sage Publications.

Willerman, L. 1979. *The Psychology of Individual and Group Differences.* San Francisco: W. H. Freeman & Co.

Williams, A. F., Zador, P. L., Harris, S. S., and Karpf, R. S. 1983. The effect of raising the legal minimum drinking age on involvement in fatal crashes. *Journal of Legal Studies* 12:169–179.

Williams, J. R., and Gold, M. 1972. From delinquent behavior to official delinquency. *Social Problems* 20:209–229.

Williams, R. L., and Chen, P. M. 1982. Identifying the sources in the recent decline in perinatal mortality rates in California. *New England Journal of Medicine* 306: 207–214.

Williams, T., and Kornblum, W. 1983. *Teenagers and Hard Times.* Unpub. manuscript, Department of Sociology, City University of New York Graduate Center.

Wilson, J. Q. 1968a. The police and the delinquent in two cities. In S. Wheeler (ed.), *Controlling Delinquents.* New York: John Wiley, pp. 9–30.

———. 1968b. *Varieties of Police Behavior.* Cambridge, Mass.: Harvard University Press.

———. 1975. *Thinking About Crime.* New York: Basic Books.

———. 1983. *Thinking About Crime,* rev. ed. New York: Basic Books.

Wilson, J. Q., and Boland, B. 1978. The effect of the police on crime. *Law and Society Review* 12:367–390.

Wilson, J. Q., and Kelling, G. 1982. Broken windows: The police and neighborhood safety. *Atlantic Monthly,* March, pp. 29–38.

Wilson, W. J. 1982. Urban poverty, social dislocations, and public policy. Unpub. paper, Department of Sociology, University of Chicago, June.

Winch, R. F. 1977. *Familial Organization: A Quest for Determinants.* New York: Free Press.

Wirth, L. 1928. *The Ghetto.* Chicago: University of Chicago Press.

———. 1938. Urbanism as a way of life. *American Journal of Sociology* 44:1–24.

Wishy, B. 1968. *The Child and the Republic: The Dawn of Modern American Child Nurture.* Philadelphia: University of Pennsylvania Press.

Witkin, H. A., Mednick, S. A., Schulsinger, F., Bakkestrom, E., Christiansen, K. O., Goodenough, D. R., Hirschhorn, K., Lundsteen C., Owen, D. R., Philip, J., Rubin, D. B., and Stocking, M. 1976. XYY and XXY men: Criminality and aggression. *Science* 193:547–555.

Witte, A. D. 1980. Estimating the economic model of crime with individual data. *Quarterly Journal of Economics* 94:57–84.

———. 1983. Estimating the economic model of crime: Reply. *Quarterly Journal of Economics* 98:167–175.

Wolf, P. 1971. Crime and development: An international analysis of crime rates. *Scandinavian Studies in Criminology* 3:107–120.

Wolfenstein, M. 1955. Fun morality: An analysis of recent American child-training literature. In M. Mead and M. Wolfenstein (eds.), *Childhood in Contemporary Cultures.* Chicago: University of Chicago Press.

Wolff, P. H. 1972. Ethnic differences in alcohol sensitivity. *Science* 175:449–450.

———. 1973. Vasomotor sensitivity to alcohol in diverse mongoloid populations. *American Journal of Human Genetics* 25:193–199.

Wolfgang, M. 1958. *Patterns in Criminal Homicide.* Philadelphia: University of Pennsylvania Press.

————. 1973 Crime in a birth cohort. *Proceedings of the American Philosophical Society* 117:404–411.

————. 1977. From boy to man—From delinquency to crime. Paper presented at the National Symposium on the Serious Juvenile Offender, Department of Corrections, State of Minnesota, Minneapolis, Minn.

————. 1981. Delinquency in a birth cohort II: Some preliminary results. Paper presented to the Attorney General's Task Force on Violent Crime.

————. 1983. Delinquency in two birth cohorts. *American Behavioral Scientist* 27: 75–86.

Wolfgang, M., and Ferracuti, F. 1982. *The Subculture of Violence*. Beverly Hills, Calif.: Sage Publications. (First published in 1967.)

Wolfgang, M., Figlio, R. F., and Sellin, T. 1972. *Delinquency in a Birth Cohort*. Chicago: University of Chicago Press.

Wolfgang, M., and Tracy, P. E. 1982. The 1945 and 1958 birth cohorts: A comparison of the prevalence, incidence, and severity of delinquent behavior. Paper presented to the Conference on Public Danger, Dangerous Offenders, and the Criminal Justice System, Kennedy School of Government, Harvard University.

Wolfgang, M., and Weiner, N. A. 1982. Patterns in injurious and violent delinquency in a birth cohort: A preliminary analysis. Unpub. paper, Center for Studies in Criminology and Criminal Law, University of Pennsylvania.

Wolpin, K. I. 1978a. An economic analysis of crime and punishment in England and Wales, 1894–1967. *Journal of Political Economy* 86:815–840.

————. 1978b. Capital punishment and homicide in England. *American Economic Review: Proceedings and Papers* 68:422–427.

Woodward, M. 1955. The role of low intelligence in delinquency. *British Journal of Delinquency* 5:281–303.

Wootton, B. 1959. *Social Science and Social Pathology*. New York: Macmillan.

Wynne, E. A. 1979. Facts about the character of young Americans. *Character* 1:1–8.

Yablonsky, L. 1962. *The Violent Gang*. New York: Macmillan.

Yarrow, L. J. 1963. Research in dimensions of early maternal care. *Merrill-Palmer Quarterly* 9:101–114.

Yarrow, M., Campbell, J., and Burton, R. 1968. *Child Rearing*. San Francisco: Jossey-Bass.

Zajonc, R. B., and Markus, G. B. 1975. Birth order and intellectual development. *Psychological Review* 82:74–88.

Zeichner, A., and Pihl, R. O. 1980. Effects of alcohol and instigator intent on human aggression. *Journal of Studies of Alcohol* 41:265–276.

Zeleny, L. D. 1933. Feeble-mindedness and criminal conduct. *American Journal of Sociology* 38:564–578.

Zimmerman, J., Rich, W. D., Keilitz, I., and Broder, P. K. 1981. Some observations on the link between learning disabilities and juvenile delinquency. *Journal of Criminal Justice* 9:1–17.

Zimring, F. E. 1972. Of doctors, deterrence, and the dark figure of crime—a note on abortion in Hawaii. *University of Chicago Law Review* 39:699–721.

————. 1979. American youth violence: Issues and trends. In N. Morris and M. Tonry (eds.), *Crime and Justice: An Annual Review of Research*, Vol. 1. Chicago: University of Chicago Press.

Ziskind, E. 1978. The diagnosis of sociopathy. In R. D. Hare and D. Schalling (eds.), *Psychopathic Behaviour: Approaches to Research*. Chichester, England: Wiley.

Ziskind, E., Syndulko, K., and Maltzman, I. 1978. Aversive conditioning in the sociopath. *Pavlovian Journal of Biological Science* 13:199–205.

Zorbaugh, H. W. 1929. *The Gold Coast and the Slum*. Chicago: University of Chicago Press.

Zucker, R. A., and Barron, F. H. 1971. Parental behaviors associated with problem drinking and antisocial behavior among adolescent males. *Proceedings of the First Annual Alcoholism Conference*. Washington, D.C.: National Institute of Alcohol Abuse and Alcoholism, pp. 276–296.

Zuckerman, M. 1978. Sensation seeking and psychopathy. In R. D. Hare and D. Schalling (eds.), *Psychopathic Behaviour: Approaches to Research*. Chichester, England: Wiley.

INDEX

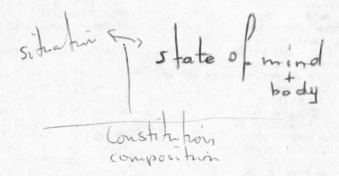

situation ⇄ state of mind + body
_____
constitution
composition

JAMES Q. WILSON teaches at Harvard University, where he is Henry Lee Shattuck Professor of Government, and at the University of California at Los Angeles, where he is Collins Professor of Management. He is the author of a number of books, including *Thinking About Crime*.

RICHARD J. HERRNSTEIN is Edgar Pierce Professor of Psychology at Harvard University, where he has primarily done research on human and animal motivational and learning processes. His books include *Psychology* and *I.Q. in the Meritocracy*.